Pahlavi Iran and the Politics of Occidentalism

Pahlavi Iran and the Politics of Occidentalism

The Shah and the Rastakhiz Party

Zhand Shakibi

I.B. TAURIS
LONDON • NEW YORK • OXFORD • NEW DELHI • SYDNEY

I.B. TAURIS
Bloomsbury Publishing Plc
50 Bedford Square, London, WC1B 3DP, UK
1385 Broadway, New York, NY 10018, USA
29 Earlsfort Terrace, Dublin 2, Ireland

BLOOMSBURY, I.B. TAURIS and the I.B. Tauris logo are trademarks of Bloomsbury Publishing Plc

First published in Great Britain 2020
Paperback edition published 2021

Copyright © Zhand Shakibi, 2020

Zhand Shakibi has asserted her right under the Copyright, Designs and Patents Act, 1988, to be identified as Author of this work.

Cover design: Adriana Brioso
Cover images © Patrick Hypscher & Fabian Krause / EyeEm / Getty Images

All rights reserved. No part of this publication may be reproduced or transmitted in any form or by any means, electronic or mechanical, including photocopying, recording, or any information storage or retrieval system, without prior permission in writing from the publishers.

Bloomsbury Publishing Plc does not have any control over, or responsibility for, any third-party websites referred to or in this book. All internet addresses given in this book were correct at the time of going to press. The author and publisher regret any inconvenience caused if addresses have changed or sites have ceased to exist, but can accept no responsibility for any such changes.

A catalogue record for this book is available from the British Library.

A catalog record for this book is available from the Library of Congress.

ISBN: HB: 978-1-7883-1736-8
PB: 978-0-7556-4506-0
ePDF: 978-1-7867-3630-7
eBook: 978-1-7867-2624-7

Typeset by Deanta Global Publishing Services, Chennai, India

To find out more about our authors and books visit www.bloomsbury.com and sign up for our newsletters.

Contents

List of illustrations	vi
Preface	vii

1	Introduction	1
2	Romanov Occidentalism	39
3	The apogee of Romanov Occidentalism	75
4	Pahlavi Occidentalism: The period of Reza Shah	103
5	Pahlavism	127
6	The shah and the imagery of the Occident	153
7	The Rastakhiz Party: Ideology and structure	189
8	Rastakhiz Occidentalism: Identity crisis and preservation of authenticity	221
9	Occidentosis: Culture and the arts	245
10	Occidentosis and the Shiraz Arts Festival	283
11	Occidentosis and the challenge of imperialism	301
12	The curing and preventing of Occidentosis	311
13	The apogee of Pahlavi Occidentalism	335

Epilogue	365
Notes	389
Select bibliography	432
Index	446

Illustrations

1. Amir Abbas Hoveyda. *Rastakhiz*, author's collection. — 136
2. The shah with members of the Supreme Council of Culture and Art. Mehrdad Pahlbod, far right. *Ferdowsi*, author's collection. — 171
3. Empress Farah and her cousin Reza Ghotbi, head of National Iranian Radio and Television, author's collection. — 178
4. Opening ceremony of the Party's Central Committee. Conducting the inaugural prayer is Majles deputy and cleric Gholamhossein Daneshi. He was executed after the Revolution. — 206
5. Mohammad Baheri, centre, Hushang Nahavandi, right. Rastakhiz, author's collection. — 212
6. Hushang Kavusi, author's collection. — 252
7. Top: Scenes from the film *Eivallah* starring Nematollah Aqassi. The headline reads: 'Eivallah has gone sexy!' Bottom left headline reads: 'The market of sex remains hot!'. *In Hafte*, author's collection. — 256
8. Scene from film *Sunday's Woman (Zan-e yekshanbe)*. *In Hafte*, author's collection. — 257
9. 'What is the difference between a sexy woman and an Azmaesh refrigerator?', author's collection. — 258
10. Snapshot from sexy *filmfarsi* 'Three-person Bed' (Takht-e Khab-e Senafare) published in *Ferdowsi* with condemning article 'The Naked Women of *filmfarsi*'. *Ferdowsi*, author's collection. — 260
11. Cover of *The Youth of Rastakhiz* providing illustrations of the condemned themes of *filmfarsi* that are cancelled by a big 'X'. *Javanan-e Rastakhiz*, author's collection. — 262
12. *The Youth of Rastakhiz*: 'The disseminators of cultural obscenity and culturelessness'. Included on the cover are pictures of Sattar, Mahasti, Dariush, Gugush and Hayedeh. *Javanan-e Rastakhiz*, author's collection. — 275
13. Arby Ovanessian, centre, author's collection. — 286
14. Jamshid Amuzegar. *Rastakhiz*, author's collection. — 339
15. Opening ceremony of III Party Congress dedicated to the struggle against imperialism, January 1978. *Javanan-e Rastakhiz*, author's collection. — 352

Preface

Rica, one of the two Iranian travellers to Louis XV's France in Montesquieu's *Persian Letters*, is famously asked by a Parisian enchanted with this exotic other, 'Ah! ah! Monsieur is Persian? That is extraordinary? How can one be Persian?'[1] Rica does not tell us in his XXX letter how he responded to this question. However, in a later letter discussing encounters and experiences in the West, Rica remarks to his fellow traveller Usbek: 'It seems to be Usbek that we never judge anything without secretly considering it in relation to our own self.'[2] This observation provides some insight when following the debates and course of Occidentalism.

The Pahlavi dynasty (1925–79) and its successor, the Islamic Republic of Iran (IRI), placed their answer to this question at the centre of their ruling ideologies. The 1979 Islamic Revolution brought a revolution in state discourses on the elements of Iranian identity. The Pahlavi emphasis on Aryanism and the grandeur of pre-Islamic Iranian empires was replaced by emphasis on Islamism and the greatness of Islamic civilization. Khomeini's Islamic jurisconsult (*Vali Faqi*) took the place of the King of Kings and Light of the Aryans (*Shahanshah Aryamehr*) as the supreme pillar of the political system.

Crowning understandings of the Revolution is the idea that it brought a fundamental break in state discourses on the place and imagery of the West within conceptions of the authenticity of Iranian culture and national identity. The binary of an IRI propagating a virulent anti-West nativism and a monarchical regime implementing intensive Westernization wrapped in a superficial skin of the pre-Islamic Iranian Empire continues to exercise a dominant influence on the historiography of modern Iran. This study targets this axiomatic binary. It shows that during the last quarter of the shah's reign the state initiated and intensified discourses of anti-West Occidentalism and provides reasons for this discursive and political change. Importantly, this study does not seek or present a new interpretation of the Revolution's causes. The focus is on the evolution of the Pahlavi state's discourses on the place and imagery of the West in its conceptions of the authenticity of Iranian culture and identity.

This work also offers a limited comparative aspect that focuses on Romanov Russia. The justification and dynamics of this comparison are detailed in the first chapter. Here however some points need to be made. The evolution of the Romanov state's discourses in regard to the place and imagery of the West in its conceptions of authenticity of Russian culture and identity and its influence on the country's domestic political trajectory and foreign policy have been frequent topics in the study of Russia. Thus, what is presented here does not claim to offer a fundamentally new interpretation of this issue. Nor is it a comprehensive study of the many varied intellectual debates and schools on this issue that emerged during the Romanov era. Rather, it presents a highly focused analytical interpretation of Romanov discourses on Occidentalism as defined by this study and in the mirror of the Iranian experience in order to temper the influence of essentialism and cultural relativism in examining not only Iran's but also Russia's state discourses on native authenticity, national identity and the West.

Given the great politicization of the historiography of the late Pahlavi period as a result of the victory of the 1979 Revolution and of comparisons between this period and that of the IRI, it is important to distinguish the two forms of primary sources used in this study: contemporaneous and retrospective. Retrospective sources, valuable and vital as they are, are frequently framed by attempts to explain the Revolution's causes and, in the case of memoirs, to allocate blame, settle old scores, justify previous actions and positions, and thus influence the narrative of the Revolution. They must be used alongside, and at times subordinated to, contemporaneous sources.

This book makes wide use of quotes from contemporaneous sources that include statements and remarks made by the shah, the empress and leading Pahlavi-era political figures, primary sources, and articles and commentaries in mass media and, importantly, official publications of the Rastakhiz Party. I chose this method with two issues in mind. First, given this axiomatic binary and the unorthodoxy of this study's argument I sought to demonstrate the full evolution of these discourses on the authenticity of Iranian culture and national identity while showing that the discourses of anti-West Occidentalism were not piecemeal and politically and ideologically insignificant but rather representative of a significant institutionalized and systematic transformation. Second, by allowing contemporaneous sources to speak for themselves, the reader is able to feel and comprehend the period's political, ideological and sociocultural dynamics. This also strengthens understandings of what replaced the Pahlavi system. One note of caution: this singular focus on anti-West Occidentalism in party discourses and publications might give the impression that they overshadowed other themes and subjects. Such discourses important as they were existed among a myriad of other cultural, social, domestic political and international issues.

Main themes running through this book – debates about the elements of the authenticity of culture and native identity, the intensity of such debates during periods of rapid change that create anxiety, disorientation and feelings of nostalgia and ultimately the politicization of such debates – are now dominant political and intellectual topics in Western countries, whose elites, or at least a majority of them, assumed that these issues had been pushed to the periphery of political life. While reading this work, keeping in mind the current state of the West would help place the Iranian and Russian responses to the challenge of the West, and of change in general, in a new context. Additionally, the reader will find that the vast majority of concerns expressed in intellectual and state narratives about manifestations attributed to Occidentosis, in spheres from music and film to morality and architecture, have been and remain all-too common themes in Western as well as non-Western societies.

Lastly, what this study shows with the help of its comparative aspects is that Iran and Iranians have responded not in an oddly unique and culturally essentialized way to the challenge posed by the power of the West, to the myriad problems and consequences flowing from that multidimensional response and to rapid change. Several generations of Iranians of the Pahlavi and IRI periods have debated and discussed and continue to do so in vivid terms the influence on them of Iran's political, geopolitical and/or economic trajectories during these two periods. Separating one's personal and/or familial experience, especially if that experience was painful and negative, from the study of the history of one's country is a complex process. However, a solid understanding of the history and contemporary conditions of countries constituting today's West and dispassionate study of the ways in which other non-Western countries have responded to the challenge of the West contextualize on a global scale the Iranian experience and thus relatively normalize it. Such a step is vital for avoiding a jingoistic form of nationalism based on the nostalgic imagery of a glorious and ancient imperial past as well as a pessimistically negative and overly cynical understanding of Iran's contemporary history that can influence views of national identity and the country's future.

This book evolved into a long project, eventually taking nine years to research and write. During this period varied academic and non-academic projects took much time and attention away from it. Many people and institutions have provided direct and indirect help in the research and writing of this book. The London School of Economics where I taught comparative politics, as well as the politics of Russia and Iran, for eleven years provided the resources, environment and research leave to begin this project. New York University provided me the opportunity to focus on this research while not having to be consistently in New York during the academic year. The Institute for Iran-Eurasian Studies in Tehran, under the management of Dr Davood Kiani, offered me the opportunity to conduct research and publish a Persian-language monograph, *Russia and Occidentalism* (*Rusie va Qarbangari*), on the historical and contemporary political and geopolitical relationship between Russia and the West. Writing it proved invaluable in the preparation of this book's chapters on Russia. A special thank you goes to Dr Mahmoud Shuri who read its manuscript and provided useful comments. Heartfelt thanks goes to the Department of World Studies of Tehran University and Dr Jahangir Karami. For the last twelve years they have provided me with the opportunity to be a visiting professor and teach postgraduate Iranian students specializing in Russian area studies and to offer among my courses one dedicated to the issue of Russia and the West. This course's seminars were useful in trying out some of the themes included in this book and in augmenting my understanding of current trends among the educated youth about Iranian identity and history.

One of the most difficult aspects in researching this topic was locating primary sources in Iran. In this respect I am deeply thankful to Mohsen Meshgini, a well-connected book dealer with whom I became acquainted at Tehran's Friday Bazaar some thirteen years ago. Over the years he found for me complete collections of Rastakhiz's popular and internal publications and other Pahlavi-era publications from the time of Reza Shah's reign as well as books I suspected were important to this study. Vitally, knowing my broad research interests, he frequently brought to my attention books and publications he came across in the sprawling Tehran market of second-hand books that enriched this study. I would also like to thank Baktash Goodarzi, a graduate student in World History at Shahid Beheshti University, for help in handling and classifying the vast amount of books, newspapers and magazines I was obtaining for this study and with filling gaps in my primary sources from his own archive.

A number of people have taken the time to read parts of this long book when in manuscript form and provide insight and advice in regard to the points I sought to address. In this regard I would like to thank Professor Sumantra Bose of LSE's Government Department, Professor Christopher Coker of LSE's Department of International Relations and Professor Dominic Lieven of Cambridge University. I greatly appreciated the opportunity provided by Professor Coker to read the manuscript of his recently published book, *The Rise of the Civilizational State*, which enabled me to question and fine-tune aspects of the arguments I tried to make in this work. The numerous long discussions I had with Dr Ali Qolipour, whose book recently published in Iran *Parvaresh-e zogh-e aame dar asr-e Pahlavi* (*The Cultivation of Mass Taste in the Pahlavi Era*) shares some themes with this work, were thought-provoking and provided the opportunity to try out some of the arguments I tried to make here.

I am deeply indebted to my editor Joanna Godfrey for accepting this long and slightly unorthodox work and then agreeing to raise the word limit so that its comparative aspects could be included. I also thank Olivia Dellow, editorial assistant at Bloomsbury, for her role in the stewardship of this work during the production process.

This book would not have been possible without the support of friends, a good number of whom have had to endure conversations and my whinging about this book: Irina, Raoul, Lucy, Tolik, Navid, Sergei, Makan, Ali, Bill, Josh, Simin, Sasha, Scott, Lewis, Farshad, Arash, Fardin and Sadjad.

In this regard I would also like to mention my two 'Cheers', hookah/shishe/ghalyun cafes that have served for a long time both as a place to write and as a refuge from the grind of everyday life and politics: Sahara East in the East Village in Manhattan and *Fanus-e Abi* (The Blue Lantern) off of Tajrish Square, my hangout in Tehran for the last nineteen years. Over that period Iran has experienced and changed much, while *Fanus*, its environment and core clientele have surprisingly changed little.

Last, but certainly not least, I would like to thank the American and Iranian sides of my family for their love and support and particularly my parents, Mohammad and Kathryn Shakibi, to whom this book is dedicated.

1

Introduction

To the whole world and to those who bear official responsibility it is clear that the consolidation and survival of the Islamic Republic of Iran depends on a policy that rejects both the [communist] East and the [liberal capitalist democratic] West. ... We wish to bring about the withering of the wicked roots of ... capitalism and communism across the globe.[1]

So proclaimed Ayatollah Ruhollah Khomeini, the Shi'i cleric who in 1979 overthrew Mohammad Reza Shah Pahlavi, Light of the Aryans. Only eight years prior, the shah, publicly hubristic and brimming with optimism about the country's future, had invited world leaders to join him and Empress Farah at Persepolis in celebrating the 2500th anniversary of the founding of the Iranian Empire by Cyrus the Great. Khomeini, standing on the ruins of this ancient monarchy, laid the ideological and institutional foundations of its successor, the Islamic Republic of Iran (IRI).

Michel Foucault believed that the Revolution was 'evidence that it is possible to transcend (Western) modernity and the spiritless world it has instituted'. What he discerned in the Revolution's ideology could be defined 'as an idiosyncratic convergence of political and religious views that formed a revolutionary ideology without a definite association to Western conceptual commitments to History'.[2] The IRI, indeed rejecting the West's modernities and meta-narratives, liberal democratic capitalism and communism, vowed to eradicate all Western cultural, moral and political influences. Even casual observers are familiar with IRI lexicon on the imagery of the West within its conceptions of the authenticity of Iranian culture and national identity: 'Occidentosis' (*qarbzadegi*) – the state of being infected with a blinding passion and infatuation with the Occident – 'Western Imperialism', 'Global [Western] Arrogance', 'Global hegemony', 'Cultural Invasion' and, until the collapse of the USSR, 'neither East nor West'. The IRI vowed to create a *homo Islamicus*, the antithesis of the Occidentosis-ridden *homo Pahlavicus*, the new person the imperial system strove to construct. *Homo Islamicus* was simultaneously the builder and result of the millenarian project of an IRI modernity superior to those the West offered. This goal entailed an unwavering crusade against the West's geopolitical and cultural imperialism.

This revolutionary ideological anti-West Occidentalism is frequently contrasted with the claimed pro-West Occidentalism of the Pahlavi state, and the Islamist, anti-West ayatollah with the Westernized and Westernizing shah. After all, the last Iranian monarch in his first book proclaimed, 'Westernization (is) our welcome ordeal', while emphasizing that Iranians and West Europeans were Aryan racial relations.³ In other words:

> In Pahlavi Iran (1925-1979) two worlds, two ways of life had parallel existences. Ignoring each other, one moved forward, while the other remained retrenched in tradition. These two trends continued to separate from each other until the rupture came. February 1979 witnessed the breakup and explosion of a cultural personality, of the project of Occidentalism, of a particular society that could no longer continue. One can speak of Occidentosis … in society and as an individual psychosis. The fever seized the entire society and affected two bodies, the body of those who were the masters of the project of Occidentalisation and provoked the disease and the body of those who always combatted it.⁴

This axiomatic binary of an IRI propagating a virulent anti-West Islamic nativism and a monarchical regime implementing an intense all-encompassing Westernization continues to exercise an influence on the historiography of modern Iran and popular conceptions of the Pahlavi period. This study shows that during the last quarter of the shah's reign the state initiated and intensified discourses of anti-West Occidentalism, which the IRI subsequently reformulated and expanded. Thus, IRI anti-West Occidentalism did not constitute a complete break with the discursive dynamics of the late Pahlavi state.

A main cause for this binary's resilience is that the historiography of the Pahlavi era and in particular of the post-Mossadegh period (1953–79) has been influenced by 'a methodological statist' axiom based on the assumption of a 'total division between state and society', and 'the glorification of the state'.⁵ According to it the absolutist Pahlavi monarchy dominated society, as it implemented radical sociocultural and economic Westernization. Society's role was passive and reactive; it did not exercise substantial influence on policymaking. Consequently, a gap between state and society emerged and in 1979 Khomeini toppled the monarchy.

The contradiction between the Pahlavi-generated, popularly accepted and eventually axiomatic image of a 'state omnipotent enough to be the ultimate reference point for all developments be they social, cultural, or economic'⁶ and the relatively quick collapse of that state meant that changing societal dynamics, and not state responses to them, would receive primary attention in the search for the Revolution's causes. At the top of this list was the intellectual and popular backlash to Westernization that emerged in the early 1960s and, gaining momentum, played an important role in Khomeini's victory. For example, one of the new works on this topic argues:

> The Pahlavi state's vision of social change neglected critical elements of modernity dealing with culture and politics: that is, the very complex process dealing with the accommodation of social change in the context of the Iranian cultural and historical experience.⁷

Strengthening this binary's influence is official IRI historiography according to which the political and cultural policies of the Pahlavi state constituted a malevolent crusade for cultural Occidentalization that ultimately brought the Revolution's victory and a return to Islamic authenticity.[8] While debates about the primary causes of the 1979 Revolution and the direction it assumed have continued without agreement, in regard to this binary of an Occidentalizing Pahlavi state and a nativist anti-West IRI, a broad agreement exists.

However, the Pahlavi state's reaction to this backlash and increasing concerns about the spread of cultural and political Occidentosis in the decade before its implosion have received some, but not comprehensive, research attention.[9] This study shows that these two axioms need revision because of the inadequate attention given to the changes in the shah's and the empress's rhetoric on the position and imagery of the West within their conceptions of the authenticity of Iranian culture and national identity. It demonstrates that by the late 1960s they and state intellectuals did recognize these 'critical elements' and implemented significant changes in state rhetoric and policies in regard to this multifaceted issue. These changes dealt with the definitional and ideological relationship between the terms 'Westernization' and 'modernization' and the place of Iran within the global civilizational order and the West as a civilizational and geopolitical concept. They were more substantive and impactful on state discourses and policy than has been assumed by the literature. Ultimately, these changes were part of the shah's attempts, initiated in the late 1960s, to create a modern ideology for the monarchy – a process culminating in the creation of a single party the Resurgence Party of the People of Iran (*Rastakhiz-e Mellat-e Iran*) in 1975 and the announcement of his millenarian goal – a superior Iranian modernity coined 'The Great Civilization'.[10] Central to this process were new discourses of anti-West Occidentalism that expanded and intensified during the Rastakhiz period (1975–late 1978).

The focus on the Revolution's causes, by depriving the latter period of the shah's reign of full analytical and research independence from the revolutionary events, has in an additional way distorted to an extent approaches to the study of these issues. This period simply became part of the grand narrative of the Revolution. What is needed is a strengthened normalization of the study of this period that provides the opportunity to examine it without the classification of the Revolution's causes as a goal. Therefore, this work with its focus on the changing rhetoric of the Pahlavi state in regard to Iranian authenticity and the issue of Occidentosis drags the analysis of approximately the last decade of Pahlavi rule from under the long shadow of the Revolution and its historiography.

This normalization is necessary since the Revolution and its trajectory have made the historiography of the Pahlavi period, and in particular, the last quarter of the shah's reign, highly susceptible to politicization. In this respect Iran's historiography is not unique. The historiographies of the French and Russian Revolutions, the two other great non-derivative revolutions of what is called the modern age, faced similar challenges. In many ways the historiography of the late Bourbon state and the French Revolution became normalized only in the twentieth century with the establishment and stabilization of the Fifth Republic.[11] In contemporary Russia the historiographies of the late tsarist and Soviet states, and especially the Bolshevik Revolution, remain discursive battlegrounds as political groups and the Putinist state propagate interpretations of these historical periods to advance political agendas and prove their individual credentials as bearers of the authenticity of Russian culture and national identity.[12]

One of the greatest consequences of a revolution in a country's history, above and beyond its addressed political, social and geopolitical consequences, is the great exacerbation of debates about the authenticity of national culture and identity and their expression in intellectual and political polarization. Revolution proclaims either a new authenticity of national culture and identity, as in the case of the French and Russian Revolutions, or the return to some form of national authenticity, as in the case of the propagandists of the Glorious Revolution of 1688 and the Islamic Revolution. Consequently, debates and discussions about forms of change, and in particular political and cultural reforms, were subsumed by intensified intellectual and political conflicts over the essence and constitutive elements of authenticity of national culture and identity.

The evolution and extent of the influence of politicized historiography of revolutions are, broadly speaking, dependent on both the producers of historiography and its audience. In the early 1970s François Furet in his seminal work *Interpreting the French Revolution* described the problems faced by any scholar writing on the French Revolution and, in reality, on any revolution.

> Historians engaged in the study of the Merovingian Kings or the Hundred Years War are not asked at every turn to present their research permits. So long as they can give proof of having learned the techniques of the trade, society and the profession assume that they possess the virtues of patience and objectivity. The discussion of their findings is a matter for scholars and scholarship only.
>
> The historian of the French Revolution, on the other hand, must produce more than proof of competence. He must show his colors. He must state from the outset where he comes from, what he thinks and what he is looking for; what he writes about the French Revolution is assigned a meaning and label even before he starts working; the writing is taken as his opinion, a form of judgement that is not required when dealing with the Merovingians but indispensable when it comes to treating 1789 or 1793. As soon as a historian states that opinion, the matter is settled; he is labelled a royalist, a liberal or a Jacobin.[13]

The historiography of revolutions, with politicization hanging over it, is significantly influenced by an unstable, fluctuating relationship between interpretations of the past, the conditions and circumstances of the present and debates about paths to the future. Moreover, the producer of historiography, who is not immune to intellectual and political sympathies and trends, too plays a role in the evolution and extent of politicization of historiography. Here differences in background, experience and education of various generations of researchers and scholars exercise a strong influence. For example, an academic who experienced life, participated in political action or held strong political beliefs during the Pahlavi regime, Revolution and/or IRI in all probability has a different take on these eras than one of a subsequent generation who did not. This is not to say the views and conclusions of one are superior and more objective than the other. Nonetheless, such factors influence one's approach, consciously or not.

By basing this study on the idea of the normalization of the history of modern Iran it is hoped that the challenges of politicization and its influence on the historiography of the Revolution and the late Pahlavi period can be minimized. Thus, this study's singular interest is how the Pahlavi state reformulated discourses and policies in regard to the imagery of the West within its conceptions of the authenticity of culture and national identity. This normalization not only enables a coherent understanding of the political dynamics of the Pahlavi state free from the shadow of the Revolution but also opens paths to viewing the extent to which continuity exists between the imperial and IRI periods in state and societal responses to the challenges posed by the West and Westernization that do not recognize changes in regimes and governing ideologies.

The lack of access to primary resource material after 1979 to those outside of Iran has also exercised a negative influence on the historiography of the late Pahlavi period and strengthened the binary of pro-West shah and anti-West ayatollah. Little scholarly work using primary contemporaneous sources chronicling the shah's and the empress's evolving views on identity and determining the extent to which these views exercised an impact on state policies has been completed. This binary and lack of access to such sources have also exercised a deleterious influence on research of the Rastakhiz Party. Literature dealing with the Party's role in the period leading to the Revolution has placed attention on two topics, to the detriment of all others: the claimed negative influence of its establishment on educated public opinion and the adverse impact of the Party's war against profiteering on the regime's reputation.[14] These topics have been examined as part of the search for the causes of the Revolution while the Party's intensifying anti-West Occidentalism has been neglected.

The issue of forms of continuity between the Pahlavi and IRI states also faces the problem of politicization. Again, Iranian historiography is not unique in this respect. The intellectual supporters of the French Revolution bristled at the contention of Alexis de Tocqueville in *The Old Regime and the Revolution* that the revolution, rather than representing a rupture with the centralized Bourbon state, had in fact taken its power and centralization to new heights and effectively completed the building of the administrative state. Therefore, 'what it [the French Revolution] magnified as a new dawn, was but the acceleration of a prior political and social trend'.[15] This study argues that IRI discourses of anti-West Occidentalism were in fact a 'prior political and social trend' seen in late Pahlavi discourses.

The same dynamic is seen in the historiography of the Bolshevik Revolution and the USSR. The Bolshevik Revolution, the horrors of the Civil War and the Stalinist terror strengthened the view in the West that Communist 'Red' Russia was as 'Oriental', a part of the uncivilized barbaric East, as had been the tsarist state. Leon Trotsky shot back: 'In reality ... the revolution means the final break with the Asiatic, Holy Rus, with its icons and cockroaches ... it is not a return to the pre-Petrine period but rather the opposite.'[16] The Cold War only deepened this belief. Many in the West, not satisfied with basing this classification of the barbaric 'Oriental' only on Bolshevism, sought the origins of Soviet otherness in uniquely Russian institutions and culture. In other words, continuity, and not rupture, characterized the relationship between the tsarist and Soviet states.[17] Taking this approach a step further, some argued that the Byzantine Empire, the bastard polity of the Roman Empire that failed to absorb the best in Roman legal and political traditions, was the main cause for Russia's problems and continued backwardness in comparison with the West. 'Surely, the argument went, the Byzantine ideal of Caesaro-papism was the prototype of that fusion of absolute state power, ideological orthodoxy, and messianic zeal, which, in secular guise, was the essence of Soviet totalitarianism.'[18]

These approaches contributed to the debates that emerged after the USSR's collapse about the meaning of the Soviet period in Russian history and its dynamic with the West. Post-Soviet liberal historiographical schools stressed that Russia, since the time of Peter I, was moving, however haphazardly, in the direction of the West, as it was defined in the nineteenth century. After all, in 1905 the country experienced a constitutional revolution. Certainly, Nicholas II weakened the constitution's provisions, but the overall movement of political culture and institutions was in the direction of constitutionalism. Moreover, its foreign policy was based on realism. Russia was only one of many players within Europe's international politics, aligning itself with other European great powers in order to maintain a balance of power on the continent. It did not lead an ideologically charged geopolitical struggle against a clearly defined 'West'.

This view was also propagated by some Russian émigré groups in the West. Marxism-Leninism and the USSR, according to this school of thought, symbolized Russia's greatest divergence from the West and an aberration in Russia's own developmental trajectory leading to a return or entrance to the West. This was the dominant view in the early 1990s, supported by Russian liberals clustered around the country's first post-Soviet president, Boris Yeltsin. Ultimately, this liberal nationalist perspective argues that Russia during the Soviet period was the least Russian and thus found itself in a geopolitical and ideological Cold War with the West. Therefore, in the post-Soviet period convergence would be possible. However, radical nationalists, some conservative groups and communists have argued that cultural, political and geopolitical convergence with the West and becoming part of it is in fact a betrayal of the authenticity of Russian culture and national identity. In the West strong misgivings existed about the true nature of Russia's historical and contemporary relationship with the West and whether the USSR was a rupture or continuation of the dynamics of the tsarist period.

Yet, other Russian émigré groups subscribed to Eurasianism which had obtained a limited following among the Russian intelligentsia from the end of the nineteenth century. It was a radical school of thought that reacted to sensed Western/European disrespect and unwillingness to accept Russia as part of its civilizational club. What distinguished this school from others was its celebration of Russia's semi-Asian civilizational roots, the Tatar heritage that the West Orientalized and used to disqualify Russia from that club. 'In the context of 1917 and Bolshevik power ... Eurasian ideas could also merge with belief in the new Russia's revolutionary energy and its potential to destroy Europe's bourgeois civilization.'[19] These trends are useful in understanding those of Iran.

Studies on modern Iran have given some attention to the issue of relative political continuity between the Pahlavi state and the IRI. For the most part, they have focused on similarities in the way they exercised power, a theme they situate within Iran's struggle for constitutionalism and democratization since the 1906 Constitutional

Revolution.²⁰ Recently, attention has been given within a longer time frame dating from Safavid rule (1501–1736) to the use of superstition in ideology and its political and cultural dynamics.²¹

Yet, the idea that parallels and continuity between the late Pahlavi state and the IRI exist in the meaning and thrust of their respective discourses on the West remains unexamined. Its exploration can shed new light on understandings of the direction in which both state and society had set off in the last quarter of the shah's reign. While this study does not debate the Revolution's causes, by focusing on the evolution and intensification of state anti-West Occidentalism during the Rastakhiz period, it not only places the late Pahlavi era in a new context but also indirectly contributes to understandings of the Revolution and state and societal responses to the twin challenges posed by the West's power and by implementing reforms needed to counter that power over a time period that does not recognize the events of 1979.

Within popular historiography of the Iranian Revolution a trend exists, similar to that of the Russian Revolution, that situates the debate about Iran's historical developmental trajectory within state discourses on identity. This approach is based on the idea that state concepts of the authenticity of national culture and identity that establish the framework of its civilizational relationship with the West play a determinative role in that country's political evolution. A state that sees itself as part of the West will move, however haphazardly, in the direction of democratic forms of governance, while those situating themselves in cultural and geopolitical competition with it tend to maintain authoritarianism wrapped in the rhetoric of nativism and protection of authenticity of national culture and identity. This approach can be called 'cultural Darwinism', that is

> a philosophy which taps into an idealised existential version of civilization in the often openly declared hope of giving a country a competitive edge in the zero-sum struggle for life. … It offers people a collective identity that is both inclusive and exclusive at the same time. It helps solidify the in-group while helping it to identify an out-group, which is to be defended against, not ignored in the discourse between the two.²²

In this vein, a recent work on the last years of the shah's reign, designed for an educated popular audience, posed a well-known 'what if' of the Revolution that tends to appear in the popular genre on this topic and in some quarters in opposition to the IRI.

> At a time when a new generation of authoritarian rulers in the Middle East and elsewhere will soon face internal and external pressure to democratize, the Shah's fall raises troubling questions. Did he move too slowly or not fast enough? Would a crackdown have prevented the revolution? If the Shah had not democratized when he did [sic], if he had waited another year, would Iran today be a multiparty democracy with Western-style rule of law?²³

The implicit assumption of this viewpoint, exaggerated in the quote above, is that the Westernized and Westernizing shah, despite his authoritarianism, would have eventually completed a transition to genuine constitutionalism but due to his bad timing and the Revolution, he failed. In other words, the 1979 Revolution, similar to the 1917 Bolshevik Revolution, in one way or another represented another unfortunate contingency that threw Iran from its path of development leading to Western forms of governance. This assumption too is addressed here.

These axiomatic binaries and assumptions introduced here are undermined by three dynamics brought into relief by this study's examination of Pahlavi discourses of anti-West Occidentalism and its crusade against Occidentosis. First, the shah and leading members of the elite recognized that from the mid-1960s cultural and geopolitical anti-West Occidentalism was spreading among the intellectual class and in society, as was the term 'Occidentosis' which was an increasingly popular catch-all phrase for negative tendencies emerging as a result of sociocultural and economic changes. The historiography of the Revolution focuses on this backlash: 'In fact, one of Ayatollah Khomeini's cleverest and most effective strategies for inciting the population was to blame Westernization and modernization for everything that the people found unfamiliar, hard to learn, unaffordable, elitist, or otherwise objectionable.'[24]

The study shows that the Pahlavi state, recognizing this popular backlash, attempted to limit its threat to state legitimacy by co-opting and reformulating intellectual discourses of anti-West Occidentalism and making them a pillar of Rastakhiz ideology. By doing this, from the early 1970s and especially during the Rastakhiz period it gave discourses of anti-West Occidentalism an official national platform in the press and media where Occidentosis was propagated as an existential threat to the authenticity of culture and national identity. In other words, the Pahlavi state adapted the main tenets of a strategy expanded by Ayatollah Khomeini to generate mass mobilization in support of the shah's overthrow. In light of this, the conclusion that 'cultural uprooting was also important in the late 1970s [as a cause of the Revolution], when Westernization was challenged by radical new interpretations of Shi'ism, associated with Ali Shariati' and Ayatollah Khomeini needs to be placed in a new context.[25] This work shows that the state through its discourses of anti-West Occidentalism and Occidentosis played a vital role in making intellectual and public opinion progressively more aware of the threats posed by Occidentosis and sympathetic to condemnations of it and calls for a return to authenticity made by revolutionary thinkers such as Shariati and Khomeini. The extent to which the Pahlavi state was able to shed its popular image as the leading agent of Occidentosis is a separate issue.

Second, Pahlavi discourses of anti-West Occidentalism were not solely politically instrumentalized. Certainly, Occidentalism is a discourse of domestic power politics based on the idea of culture as a means for elite domination underpinned and legitimized by the state's self-appointed role as the bearer of enlightenment and progress and/or defender of national authenticity of culture and identity in the face of the spread of Western concepts of enlightenment and progress and forms of governance. Marx's comments in *The Eighteenth Brumaire of Louis Bonaparte* about the use of historiography by elites to protect their own political and economic interests and Gramsci's work on the function and role of elite cultural hegemony are two of the best examples of the approach that would see Occidentalism in pure instrumental terms, deprived of true substantial beliefs on the part of elites. In this regard, Dariush

Ashrui, the well-known linguist, writer, translator and leftist of the Pahlavi period, a quarter century after the Revolution, argued that the Pahlavi state became 'obsessed with fantasies of preserving "authentic national culture"', one of whose pillars was 'the discourse of spirituality' because the state feared Leftist ideologies.[26]

The work argues, however, that discourses of Occidentalism should not be cynically viewed solely through the lens of power politics as an instrumentalized ideology used to protect state power in the face of competing ideologies, including those of the Left. It holds that the evolution and changes in Pahlavi Occidentalism were also a result of the cognitive beliefs and emotions of the monarch and many within the elite. Mehrdad Pahlbod, minister of culture and art (1964–78) and the shah's brother-in-law, in a post-revolution interview about art and cultural policy, provides a glimpse into the thinking within the elite in this period and counters the rational choice opinion offered by Ashuri. 'The world uses spirituality for inner psychological equilibrium, for the creation of inner growth and pleasure. Of course, one cannot touch it – it is not similar to bread and a building – but nonetheless it cannot be ignored [in state policy].'[27]

Without entering the perennial debate on the issue of personal versus political interests and sincerity and insincerity, it needs to be recognized that in most beliefs held by people elements of truth exist. Of course, one would rush to add a truth as experienced and understood by the individual. Although finding the border between personal beliefs and political interests and thus between sincerity and insincerity is notoriously difficult, if not impossible, the biographical context and human agency are equally, and at times more, important to the political, international and social contexts when discussing Occidentalism's emergence and evolution. Therefore, what is of interest is how Pahlavi monarchs articulated and re-articulated state discourses on the Occident to fit both personal views in regard to the dynamic between the West and national identity and cultural authenticity, on the one hand, and ideological and political goals, on the other.

The shah, the empress and groups within the elite had grown increasingly concerned about some of the sociocultural consequences of Westernization and specifically of rapid economic growth, industrialization and rural–urban migration. They came to believe to varying extents that manifestations attributed to cultural and moral Occidentosis, such as the spread of materialism and consumerism, the cult of celebrity, the commercialization of art and culture and decline in morals did indeed threaten Iranian authenticity. These concerns were both cause and consequence of the changes in the view of that authenticity held by the shah and reflected in state discourses.

This evolution from pro-West Occidentalism to anti-West Occidentalism represented 'a transvaluation of values'. In such a process 'those values and culture that were once envied are denigrated and replaced by other elements, usually, but not always, claiming to be superior to, and opposite of, those values and culture once envied'. Liah Greenfeld in her discussion of the emergence and evolution of Russian national identity argues that this transvaluation of values occurs due to the emergence of feelings of *ressentiment*.[28] According to her, *ressentiment* is a psychological condition emerging from suppressed feelings of envy and hatred (existential envy) and from the seeming impossibility of satisfying these feelings. Two factors constitute the base for this condition. The first factor, 'the structural condition of envy itself' is 'the fundamental comparability between the subject and the object of envy, or rather the belief on the part of the subject in the fundamental equality between them, which makes them in principle interchangeable'. The second factor is actual inequality whose seeming dimension 'rules out practical achievement of the theoretically existing equality'. These factors create conditions in which an individual or a society become susceptible to feelings of *ressentiment* that result in this transvaluation.

The way in which she defined *ressentiment* offers interesting albeit limited insight into the elements feeding into this transvaluation of values that was the basis of Pahlavi anti-West Occidentalism. In Greenfeld's account, the expectation is that feelings of *ressentiment* would become dominant at some point when the gap between Iran and the West in the minds of the intellectual and political elite was at its greatest or when cycles of reform had failed to achieve 'the theoretically existing equality'. Yet, subsequent chapters show that in Pahlavi Iran these feelings did not emerge in such conditions. Rather, they arose after Iran had experienced a decade of strong economic growth, social change and geopolitical ascendancy that led to the country becoming the Persian Gulf's gendarme backed by the superpower of the liberal West, the United States, while enjoying good relations with the superpower of the communist world, the USSR. At the same time, the West was experiencing a series of cultural, moral and economic challenges and crises that undermined in Iran the West's soft power and the assumption of the universality of the West's modernities. In sum, a growing sense of confidence, despite continuing awareness of native backwardness in regard to the West in some fields, perceived negative transformations in the West and greater links and thus understandings of the West and Westerners helped create the conditions for the push towards the transvaluation of values and anti-West Occidentalism.

Third, the evolved discourses propagating the idea of an existential threat of Occidentosis to Iranian authenticity played a key role in the justification of the monarchy's power. If from the time of Reza Shah's reign the Crown's power was justified by the need to push through a radical form of Westernization backed by pro-West Occidentalism, by the 1970s the Crown was propagated as the source and defender of the authenticity of culture and national identity in the face of the threats posed by Occidentosis and its sponsor, Western imperialism.

The Rastakhiz Party had two primary goals: the limited opening of the political space for intellectual and popular criticism of government performance and socio-economic and cultural conditions within a legal framework and the simultaneous creation of conditions for the strengthening of national unity and popular mobilization around the shah. Discourses of anti-West Occidentalism and attacks on manifestations of Occidentosis that warned of domestic and international enemies targeting Iran were one of the most effective ways of deflecting criticism from the monarchy and creating this unity and mobilization. Simply put, the limited and gradual popularization of politics implemented by the Rastakhiz Party was accompanied by the securitization of state conceptions of authenticity threatened by the West's cultural and geopolitical imperialism. The monarchy, the proclaimed source and defender of that authenticity, would lead this struggle. Moreover, an examination of the articles, editorials, news reports and analysis pieces shows that alongside these political motivations behind the discourses of anti-West Occidentalism existed genuine concerns among state and non-state intellectuals and publicists about the spread of the many manifestations of Occidentosis and the future of the authenticity of Iranian culture and national identity, although understandings of that authenticity that existed on an official or intellectual levels lacked a degree of clarity.

Book structure

This book consists of thirteen chapters. Following this introductory chapter are two chapters that analyse imperial Russia and Romanov Occidentalism and provide the basis for the limited comparative aspect of this work which is explained later in detail. Chapters 4–6 provide the essential context for understanding the discursive and ideological–political changes in Pahlavi discourses during the Rastakhiz period on the intertwined issues of authenticity of Iranian culture and national identity and the narrative and imagery of the West within it. Chapter 4 is a summary of particular elements in the state's discourses on these intertwined issues from the establishment of the Pahlavi dynasty in 1924 to the abdication of Reza Shah in 1941. These elements were not part of a systematic ideologization of monarchy. Rather, they played a vital role in the state's construction of national identity and nationalism. They were designed to create domestic unity and reformulate the legitimating cosmology of the Iranian monarchy as it sought to implement Westernizing reforms. The various historical and political narratives that emerged during this period constituted the fount from which the Pahlavi system, starting in the early 1960s, crafted its discourses for the ideologization of the monarchy and ideological framework of the Rastakhiz Party.

Chapter 5 examines how these elements making up early Pahlavi conceptions of state identity and nationalism evolved and became essential parts of the first piecemeal, and perhaps incoherent, attempts to ideologize the monarchy in the late 1960s. The primary source used in this chapter is the four-volume series *Pahlavism* published in the run-up to the shah's coronation in 1967 and was one of the first official works for those celebrations marking the 2,500th anniversary of the founding of the ancient Iranian Empire. This series has not been fully utilized previously in examining the evolution of the Pahlavi state's legitimating discourses.[29]

The attempts by Mohammad Reza Shah to defend his rule in the face of competing modern ideologies, namely liberal democracy/constitutionalism, socialism/communism and various forms of nationalism that integrated varied elements of the first two have been the subject of scholarly attention as part of the search for the causes of the monarchy's implosion.[30] This work aims to expand understandings of this issue. By analysing the evolution of attempts to provide a complete ideology to the monarchy, it shows that the Pahlavi state went beyond its initial ideological and discursive attempts to prevent a 'red revolution' and increasingly paid ideological and discursive attention from the late 1960s to the threat of nationalist constitutional and democratic forces that took inspiration from Western liberal political theory and forms of governance.

This work also shows that focusing on the political tensions between the monarchy and the clergy, and thus considering the primary ideological thrust of the Pahlavi state during this period to have been 'the upgrading of the Iranic aspect of political legitimacy at the expense of the Islamic' in order to struggle 'with ideological alternatives that were actively challenging the monarchy', provides limited insight into the ideological evolution of the Pahlavi monarchy.[31] The argument here is that this attempted ideologization, while certainly propagating a historiography that emphasized the monarchy, strove to construct a modern ideology that looked equally to the past and the future, claimed superiority to the West's modernities while adapting elements from them, and to establish some modern criteria for popular political legitimation.

Chapter 6 provides an overview of the shah's and the empress's rhetorical changes in regard to imagery and place of the West in the authenticity of Iranian culture and national identity in the context of economic, social and political changes wrought by Westernization. It also examines the institutional changes resulting from this new politics of culture and identity. Although these rhetorical changes, on the one hand, and the first attempts at the ideologization of the monarchy and the emergence of Pahlavism, on the other hand, are analysed in two different chapters, they emerged in the same time period; they were part of the same ideological evolution. It needs to be stressed that despite this narrative, the emergence of these institutional, ideological and discursive changes in the period leading to the establishment of the Rastakhiz Party was slow and often in less than coherent ways, as often happens in politics. Nonetheless, together they provide the backdrop to the Party's ideology and discourses.

Chapter 7 examines the varied interpretations of the reasons behind the shah's decision to establish a one-party state. It also addresses fundamental issues about the Party that deal directly with this book's main themes, such as party structure and ideology, the political and power relationship between the government and the Party, and internal party political and personal dynamics. Of particular importance are the shah's approach to the Party and his views in regard to the role it should play in combatting Occidentosis. This chapter does not provide a comprehensive history of the Party or an evaluation of its role in the coming of the Revolution. These issues are beyond the framework of this study.

Chapters 8 and 9 examine the ways by which the Rastakhiz Party through its main publications disseminated, re-articulated and expanded the shah's and the empress's evolved views on the authenticity of Iranian culture and national identity and announced policies for addressing them. They underscore the fundamental change in the state's approach to these issues. At the centre of this analysis are two-party publications. One is the Party's daily newspaper and mouthpiece, *Rastakhiz*.[32] The second publication is the periodical, *The Youth of Rastakhiz* (*Javanan-e Rastakhiz*, *JR*). According to party documents it was to be the leading popular intellectual publication.

Chapter 8 examines the first theme running through these publications, the official recognition of a crisis of identity resulting from Occidentosis and the threats it posed to relatively redefined authenticity of Iranian culture and national identity that was increasingly securitized and sacralized. This official recognition represented a fundamental change from the pro-West Occidentalism initiated by Reza Shah and the first decades of the reign of Mohammad Reza Shah.

In the 1960s and 1970s Iranian intellectuals were increasingly captivated by the idea of nativism set in opposition to the West. This nativism can be defined as

> the doctrine that calls for the resurgence, reinstatement or continuance of native or indigenous cultural customs, beliefs, and values. Nativism is grounded on such deeply held beliefs as resisting acculturation, privileging one's own 'authentic' ethnic identity, and longing for a return to an 'unsullied indigenous cultural tradition'.[33]

Chapters 9 examines how the Pahlavi state attempted to co-opt the discourses of this increasingly popular intellectual and cultural nativism within its emergent discourses of anti-West Occidentalism that focused on the cultural, moral and social manifestations of Occidentosis. Chapter 10 finishes the discussion of the issues addressed in the previous chapter by examining the politics of the Shiraz Arts Festival and the Party approach to it. Chapter 11 looks at those Rastakhiz discourses that cultivated the idea that cultural, social and moral Occidentosis was an instrument of the West's imperialism as it sought to achieve and maintain indirect hegemony over an Iran that was rapidly becoming strong, independent and a model for other countries seeking relief from the yoke of Western imperialism. These discourses aimed to transform the popular image of the Pahlavi state as an agent of Occidentosis and portray it as the source and defender of redefined and sacralized Iranian authenticity in the face of the threat of Occidentosis.

Chapter 12 focuses on those discourses and policies that aimed at the curing and preventing of Occidentosis: (1) the Revolution in Education; (2) the Party's programme of Political Education; and (3) the rhetorical revolution against the idea that the '–isms' and corresponding modernities of the West were superior and universally applicable. Chapter 13 examines the apogee of Pahlavi anti-West Occidentalism, in other words, the topical expansion and intensification of these discourses in the face of increased domestic and international criticism and pressure. It also sums up particular elements of the Pahlavi millenarian project of modernity, the Iranian 'Third Way' named 'The Great Civilization' and major tendencies that fed into the conceptions behind it.

Pahlavi and Romanov Occidentalism

Apollon Zimmerman (1825–84), aristocrat and general, who commanded Russian forces in Chechnya, Dagestan and Central Asia and in the crushing of revolutionary forces in Hungary threatening the Habsburg throne in 1848–9, noted: 'Generally we in Russia are normally much closer to Constantinople and Tehran than to Paris or London. The very understanding of the Russian people about good and evil, about rights, about law, and justice comes closest to that of the Eastern peoples.'[34] Building on this observation, this study argues that a basis exists for a comparison of the approaches of the Romanov and Pahlavi states in regard to the evolving position of the West in their conceptions of authenticity of native culture and national identity which constituted a vital element of their respective responses to the challenge posed by the West's power.

This comparative aspect is limited given this study's primal focus on Pahlavi discourses of Occidentalism and considerations of space. Chapters 2 and 3 provide a tightly focused interpretation within the framework of Occidentalism of the place of the West in imperial Russian state conceptions of authenticity of native culture and identity. This limited comparative aspect while providing additional context and the opportunity to view Pahlavi Occidentalism through the prism of the Romanov approach also tempers cultural determinism and essentialization that can emerge in singular focus on the Pahlavi state's political–ideological response to the challenges posed by the West's power and Westernization. A potential danger with area specialization or singular focus on one country in dealing with a global topic, such as responses to the challenge of the West, is a slip into inflexible research that propagates a sociocultural and/or political uniqueness which can distort understandings of a country's history, produce a spurious teleology and/or fail to address or challenge assumptions that have become axiomatic in national historiography. Moreover, this comparison argues against approaches that stress individual Iranian (or Russian) uniqueness or 'shortcomings' set against the historical experience of certain countries of the West. These approaches have a limited capacity to provide insight into the political and historical dynamics of either Iran or Russia and specifically into their positive and/or negative discourses on the West.

Peter I (r.1689–1725) initiated radical reforms with the goal to generate domestically the type of power already enjoyed by countries to the west of Russia. Vasilii Kluchevskii, the great late-nineteenth-century Russian historian, offered a characterization of the historical significance of Peter's controversial changes without making a value judgement on them; it is equally applicable to those of Reza Shah: 'The question of the meaning of Peter's reforms is to a great extent the question of the movement of our historical consciousness. … Peter's reforms are the central point of our history, containing the sum of our past and an indication of our future.'[35] This book holds that a reason the changes initiated by these men and modified by their successors transformed the 'movement of historical consciousness' and become 'a central point' of Iranian and Russian history, and continue to exercise an influence on Russian and Iranian politics and political discourses, is the ideological–political discursive framework, coined here state 'Occidentalism'.

The emergence and evolution of state Occidentalism constituted the answer of Iranian and Russian monarchs to the challenge of politically and historically rationalizing state-imposed transformations and the continuance of absolutism in the face of socio-economic consequences of these changes. The argument is that the discursive responses constituting Pahlavi and Romanov Occidentalisms examined comparatively show that they shared a number of trends and characteristics distinct enough to comprise an independent, political–ideological response to the challenge of the West among uncolonized monarchical states. Before outlining the elements of this limited comparative aspect that make the Romanov and Pahlavi response to the challenge of the West distinct, explaining and justifying the choice of the term Occidentalism over Westernism is necessary.

Occidentalism

Over the past two decades the term 'Occidentalism' has experienced an increase in its usage in academic and popular discourses as well as an evolution of its generally accepted meaning. It nonetheless remains a contested concept. In the wake of the attacks of 11 September 2001 and the consequent 'War on Terror' it came to signify primordial and essentialist anti-Westernism. This approach argues that the various forms of Occidentalism that have emerged across the globe share

> a chain of hostility-hostility to the City, with its image of the rootless, arrogant, greedy, decadent, frivolous cosmopolitanism; to the mind of the West, manifested in science and reason; to the settled bourgeois, whose existence is the antithesis of the self-sacrificing hero; to the infidel, who must be crushed to make a way for a world of pure faith.[36]

The authors jump across time and space in their examination of 'anti-West' intellectual and political movements, from German Romantics and Russian Salvophiles to Nazis, Japanese nativists and Islamic movements, all of which are lumped under the rubric of 'Occidentalist'. The underlying theme is that Occidentalism is a derivative but parallel discourse of Edward Said's Orientalism. Orientalism with its negative essentialization by the West of the East now faces Occidentalism, the negative essentialization by the East of the West. In this definitional framework, both have the goal of dominating and even destroying the other.[37]

However, before these events the idea of a pro-West Occidentalism existed. For example, Xiaomei Cheng argues that the government of post-Mao China practices 'official Occidentalism' in which it 'uses the essentialization of the West as a means for supporting a nationalism that effects the internal suppression of its own people'. In contrast with the dominant post-September 11 understanding of Occidentalism 'the Western Other is construed by a Chinese imagination, not for the purpose of dominating the West, but in order to discipline, and ultimately to dominate, the Chinese self at home'. In the more recent and direct words of Christopher Coker:

> The attack on liberal civilization should be seen for what it is, of course. Less an attack on the ideology of globalism or western exceptionalism than a cynical ploy by the state to reinforce its own cultural credentials in the eyes of its citizens. What is being secured against the West is not civilization as such, but the interests of a particular regime.[38]

According to Cheng, this official anti-West Occidentalism is countered by an 'anti-official Occidentalism' that is the domain of intellectuals, who, despite their differing ideological and political views, use their imaging of the West 'as a powerful anti-official discourse using the Western Other as a metaphor for political liberation against ideological oppression'.[39]

A third approach sees Occidentalism as 'a notion that contributed to the definition of post-Renaissance Europe' that symbolized the 'overreaching metaphor of the modern/colonial world'. It defines Occidentalism as the West's self-articulation as a powerful geopolitical entity and superior civilization rooted in conceptions of historical progress that overshadows and dominates the rest of the world. It became the measuring stick against which other cultures and civilizations were to be compared and judged. By the nineteenth century this conception, solidified by the expanding global power of the West's maritime empires to the four corners of the globe, provided a general inclusive identity of the countries of Europe constructed in the mirror of out-group non-white 'backward' peoples and nations of these four corners. It was an identity for the international arena that placed European and white peoples at the top of the global civilizational order and existed alongside debates and divisions in Europe over the civilizational and power ranking among the continent's countries. Importantly, this Occidentalist self-definition and expansion of colonial empires gave birth to Orientalism: 'Without Occidentalism there is no Orientalism'.[40] This form of Occidentalism obtained a dominant position in historiography in the West and the East where states and intellectuals, searching for the reasons for the decline of their countries in relation to those of the West, began to rewrite history as an unsuccessful form of the West's progressive historical trajectory while conflating that trajectory with the idea of universal history.

This racial 'white' definition of Occidentalism provided a possible justification for Russia's claim to be part of Europe/the West, despite its economic and political backwardness that, in the eyes of the West's main powers, denied Russia entrance to their club, and a sense of superiority in regard to the East. Dostoevsky summed up Russia's situation: 'In Europe we are hangers-on and slaves, but in Asia we are masters. In Europe we are Tatars, but in Asia we too are Europeans'.[41] Rudyard Kipling, in agreement with the great Russian author, in *The Man Who Was*, summed up an opinion common in the West about Russia's racial and cultural exclusion from the West:

> Let it be clearly understood that the Russian is a delightful person till he tucks in his shirt. As an Oriental he is charming. It is only when he insists upon being treated as the most easterly of western peoples instead of the most westerly of easterns that he becomes a racial anomaly extremely difficult to handle.

Broadly speaking, therefore, the main literature on Occidentalism offers three definitions: (1) primordial, essentialist anti-West Occidentalism; (2) anti-West Occidentalism as an authoritarian ideology utilized by a non-Western power to dominate its own people that engenders an unofficial pro-West Occidentalism symbolizing liberation from oppression; and (3) the West's self-identification as a powerful geopolitical entity based on a vastly superior civilization eclipsing and dominating the world. Some argue that this definitional ambiguity and the use of Occidentalism as both Westernism and anti-Westernism 'in different theoretical and political perspectives can be interpreted as a sign that testifies to the power of the concept rather than its inadequacy'.[42] Accepting to a point this position, this book argues that to understand the Iranian and Russian experience in dealing with the challenge of the West during the monarchical periods drawing definitional boundaries between the concepts 'Westernism' and 'Occidentalism' is useful. At the same time, the Iran-Russia comparative aspect also makes a contribution to the expansion of understandings of the causality, spectrum and dynamics of the various discursive responses of uncolonized non-Western monarchical states to the multilayered challenges posed by the spread of the West's power and the need to undertake Westernizing reforms.

Occidentalism in this study is constituted by state discourses initially justifying the practical process of Westernization and subsequently managing this process's socio-economic, cultural and political consequences. This practical process of Westernization is the appropriation by non-Western states to varying degrees of west-European and, by the twentieth century, United States, of various practices and norms in order to achieve Western forms of economic, military and technological power. This process includes (a) industrialization; (b) urbanization; (c) the centralization and institutionalization of power; (d) the valorization of the state as the most appropriate agent of 'enlightened' change in answering the challenge of the West; and (e) the transformation of old social elites or their supplanting by individuals and large professional groups with specialized education and/or capital. Included in it are attempts to stimulate personal economic and intellectual initiative, to create conditions for the withering away of old superstitions and the emergence of a rational mentality and individualism, all of which it was assumed was the cause of the West's rise and continuing development.[43] Both Pahlavi shahs saw Westernization in these terms. Yet, Mohammad Reza Shah implied that the term Westernization was a misnomer, suggesting it was a term that in reality described a global process of change, exercising a transformational, and potentially destabilizing, influence on Western societies just as it did on non-Western ones.

> Now in order to understand the Western impact upon Persia, one must remember that 'Westernization' in its present-day sense is new to the Western nations themselves. For example, life in America has been radically transformed over the past fifty years, and it even shows big changes over the past ten years. I visited America in 1949, 1955, and 1958, and on each of these last two trips I noticed major developments and innovations that were not seen when I first went. The explosive stimulus for such rapid change is not far to seek: American expenditures on scientific research and development have multiplied many times just before the Second World War, with commensurate returns. So you might say that America's own 'Westernization' programme is proceeding at an unprecedented rate. To greater or less degrees I have observed the same phenomenon on my visits to Britain, Germany, Russia, and other countries.[44]

This was true but the challenges facing Westernizing regimes, specifically monarchical ones, were more difficult. The question facing them was how and to what extent to integrate the process of Westernization and the socio-economic consequences of this process within a nativist cultural–religious identity and political framework. An answer to this can perhaps be found in the discursive dynamics of Pahlavi and Romanov Occidentalism.

Three interdependent conceptions collectively shape the parameters of the discourses on Occidentalism used in this work. They are (1) Occidentalism can be either the negative or positive essentialization by a state of the West as a civilizational zone; (2) Occidentalism is shaped by both cognitive beliefs and emotions, specifically here those of autocratic monarchs, as well as power politics; and (3) Occidentalism's dynamics are linked to geopolitics. The first and third conceptions need some explanation.

The first conception stresses the existence of state pro-West Occidentalism in addition to the more common and generally accepted anti-West Occidentalism. The central argument is that the ideological–political and historiographical discourses of the Pahlavi and Romanov polities in response to the challenge of the West differ from the various forms of pro- and anti-Westernism of other states and regimes given Iranian and Russian evolving claims, implicit and explicit, of a fluctuating mixture of racial and cultural links, however discursively ambiguous and haphazard at times, with Western Europe. This work shows that Pahlavi and Romanov discourses of pro and anti-West Occidentalism propagated these claims of a unique racial–cultural link with Europe/the West. Thus, they should be coined state Occidentalism. In other words, these claims of racial–cultural links with the West draw a boundary between Westernism and Occidentalism. This Occidentalism produced historically important political consequences, namely justifications for autocracy and path-dependent processes in regard to Iran's and Russia's ideological–political relationship with the West and intense Russian and Iranian intellectual and political debates on national identity which remain today and overshadow parallel debates on political change, geopolitics and even economic policies.

A vital point is that this study's principal focus is on the place of the West in *state* discourses on the authenticity of native culture and national identity and not on myriad nativist intellectual debates popular at the time that have been well covered in the literature. This is not to gainsay the influence of such debates on educated public opinion and consequently on the state's reactive discourses. The influence of such intellectual reactions to Occidentosis on the discourses of the Pahlavi state is one of this work's pillars. Moreover, the question of the veracity or falsity of the discursive elements of Pahlavi and Romanov Occidentalisms and the extent to which the cultural reforms of Reza Shah and Peter I and their successors were successful in distancing Iranians and Russians from their immediate past are not of direct importance to the argument here.

The third conception deals with the influence of geopolitics on the dynamics of Occidentalism. First, geopolitical challenges posed by the West's power combined with the belief of Iranian and Russian elites in their empires' historical destiny to be great powers were catalysts for state-imposed radical changes. Second, major domestic events in the West's leading powers with international ramifications, such as the French and 1848 Revolutions and the election in 1976 of Jimmy Carter to the US presidency, and developments in international politics, such as the expansion of the British and Russian empires into Iran, the Crimean War and the Cold War, influenced to varying degrees state discourses of Occidentalism. Third, geopolitics encapsulates the mental mapping of geography that situates a country and its people in space and within the global order of civilizations, ranging from the most civilized, progressive and powerful, to the least civilized, and thus barbaric and weak, serving as prey for powerful 'civilized' nations.

This mental mapping produces a state nationalized and nationalizing geography and historiography that is ultimately subjective, reflecting not only the world view of the monarch and the elite, but also its political–ideological use.

Occidentalism, thus, should also be seen as a vital element in the structure and politics of the production and evolution of state conceptions of national identity. Conceptions of national identity stem primarily from membership within a specific community (a people) that defines itself in the mirror of foreign societies and by its own national, religious, cultural, ethnic, historical, and/or imperial distinctiveness, endowing constituents with a sense of belonging to a superior or elite group.[45] Given this reality no mono-casual explanation of state or national identity exists, leaving it open to political and ideological contestation by competing political groups and factions.[46]

Politicized historical memory that produces state historiography is a vital part of the production of state conceptions of national identity. As the following chapters show, the various forms of state Occidentalisms, as well as intellectual-political discourses on authenticity, must articulate and propagate a particular historical memory and historiography in order to make prescriptions for the present and future. This politicized historical memory and historiography is used by both state elites and competing political groups to prove their individual cultural and national authenticity and allegiance to protecting that authenticity in the face of international as well as domestic enemies and threats. This claim to cultural and national authenticity and to its defence justifies their respective attempts to establish and/or maintain political and ideological hegemony. Once again, it is difficult to find the border between personal viewpoints and opinions and political interest and sincerity and insincerity in the propagation of these discourses.

The case for comparison

At first glance this limited comparative analysis of Russia and Iran seems misplaced given certain differences despite their shared claims of unique links to the West. But differences do not preclude an illuminating comparison. Similarities and differences between these two polities and in the dynamics of their Occidentalisms methodically compared can point to characteristics of their responses to the challenge of the West that might otherwise be less evident. They can enrich our understanding of the monarchical periods and their influence on contemporary Iranian and Russian state discourses on the place of the West within state conceptions of authenticity of culture and national identity. In particular, this comparative aspect enables a deeper and more objective understanding of the changes in the discourses of the Pahlavi state on these intertwined issues in the Rastakhiz period.

Romanov Russia was the world's largest land-based empire and a major player in European power politics since the Seven Years' War (1756–63). Pahlavi Iran, inheriting and using in its ideology and discourses an ancient imperial heritage, namely that of the Achaemenid (550–330 BCE) and Sasanian (224–651) empires, struggled against British and Soviet imperialism and relied on the United States during the Cold War.

The Romanov dynasty was an old established ruling house while the Pahlavis were monarchical newcomers. Yet, the institution of monarchy in Iran with its long history of the rise and fall of dynasties was much older than that in Russia which, unlike Iran, lacked an ancient imperial heritage and, until the sixteenth century, a strong secular high culture. Both were multi-ethnic and multi-confessional imperial polities with universalist religious cosmologies and, in the Iranian case the heritage of ancient empire, that, having become nationalized, had instilled elites with the belief in their cultural superiority and historical fate to be major international players.

Romanov Russia was Christian while Pahlavi Iran was Muslim, whose respective religious ideas and clerical structures constitute a difference between them. However, an examination of Romanov and Pahlavi discursive responses to the challenge of the West shows the great extent to which these religious differences are overshadowed by striking similarities, including their respective positions in the West's ordering of civilizations and peoples. Iran occupied the key position in the essentialized ancient Greek image of the cultural and political character of 'the East' that established the long-standing binary of the civilized West and the barbaric East. This essentialized Greek image would much later 'be drawn on by western Europeans to underpin the sharp dichotomization of East and West that would eventually be applied to Islam'.[47] Yet, Iran, as the sole Shi'i power, was confronted by neighbouring Sunni polities. In sum, Iran found itself Orientalized by the Greeks and then the West and in the periphery of the Muslim world, charged with heresy.

Russia found itself in a similar position in the West's evolving conceptions of itself. Although adapting in the late-tenth century Christianity via the Byzantine Empire, Russia, nonetheless, found itself outside the geographical and cultural boundaries the West came to establish for itself. In a parallel development, the schism of 1054 in the universal Christian Church between Constantinople and Rome and the sacking of Constantinople by Western Crusaders in 1204 helped create the conditions in which, subsequently, the Russian elite and public considered their polity to have a unique identity encapsulated within specific cultural and geopolitical borders that had to be defended in the face of the religious-cultural threat from the West's Catholicism. Byzantium's collapse at the hands of the Ottomans in 1453 and the subsequent declaration that Moscow was the Third Rome solidified this dynamic. Orthodox Russia now had a religious and historical responsibility to defend true Christianity in the face of Latin Catholicism and then Protestantism.[48] Briefly put, Christianity played a vital role in uniting Russia with Europe and dividing the country from it. Thus, even if at times in the West Orthodox Russia, given its membership in the Christian world, was preferable to Muslim Iran, it was nonetheless subjected to the same Orientalizing processes that the West used in regard to Iran.

This cultural–religious tension was manifested in the geopolitical arena. Since the thirteenth century Russia faced periodically geopolitical pressure from countries to its West, including crusades, some papal-sanctioned, in the twelfth and thirteenth centuries, that sought to bring Russian lands into the correct religious fold. However, despite this ideological-rhetorical dynamic, Russia and various countries of the West did find common geopolitical cause against either other Western countries or in fighting off non-Christian powers, such as the Ottoman Empire. One of the best examples of this is the geopolitical partnership between imperial Russia and the Catholic Holy Roman Empire beginning in the early eighteenth century.

In sum, Russia's and Iran's elites, even before the West's ascendancy, had faced a west-European discourse that situated them in the 'uncivilized', 'barbaric' and 'backward' East. When the West's economic and military power began to develop, Iran and Russia found themselves on the semi-periphery of this emerging global economic system and under geopolitical pressure from it although Iran was more peripheral and weak than Russia. The recognition of the superiority of the West's power created a loss of confidence among the Russian and Iranian elites in regard to their identities and histories and prompted intellectual and political debates on interpretations of Russia's and Iran's past that sought to determine the causes of 'backwardness', the path to achieving the power attained by the West and a place for their countries in universal history the West now seemingly symbolized.

Temporal differences between the periods of initiation of Occidentalism in Russia and Iran can present some methodological challenges to this comparative aspect. Peter I launched his changes at the beginning of the eighteenth century, during the era of 'enlightened absolutism', while Reza Shah established his dynasty in 1924, seven years after the overthrow of the Romanovs and during the era of competing modern ideologies that had threatened monarchies since the French Revolution. However, this book argues that the similarities of Romanov and Pahlavi Occidentalisms are interesting and worthy of comparison because of this temporal difference. They weaken explanations rooted in essentialism and cultural relativism by showing that this particular reaction to the challenge of the West, coined here Occidentalism, is not limited to a specific period, country or ideological spectrum. Moreover, the spectrum of modern ideologies facing the Pahlavi dynasty was also faced by Peter I's successors from the beginning of the nineteenth century until the crash of the Russian Empire in 1917.

Temporal differences are most pronounced in regard to the concept of race. As will become apparent in the following chapters, understandings of race in Russia in the seventeenth and eighteenth centuries were primitive and fluid, although conceptions of a Slavic race within Europe were emerging. These understandings differed from modern concepts and classifications of race, such as Aryanism and ideas of white racial superiority explaining the West's global ascendancy, which began to take hold in the nineteenth and twentieth centuries in Europe and the United States. Therefore, this study does not claim that the conceptions of race held by Russian monarchs and their elites from the Petrine period to at least the first quarter of the nineteenth century were the same as those held by the Pahlavi shahs and their elite. Nonetheless, during the early Romanov period, broadly speaking, Christianity and emerging ideas of a white people overlapped and provided an important basis for Europeans, including Russians, to distinguish themselves from lesser peoples, such as Muslims, Africans and Asians. Occidentalism's claims of Russia's racial and therefore cultural links with the polities to the country's west, however primitive they were relative to modern conceptions of race, were predicated on three elements: (a) geography that placed parts of the Russian Empire in Europe; (b) Christianity, albeit in its Orthodox form; and (c) this understanding of 'whiteness'. The Pahlavi state, in contrast, based its claims to such links with the West on Aryanism and its pre-Islamic imperial periods.

Imagining the West

While Pahlavi Iran and, to a lesser extent, Romanov Russia occupy centre stage in this study, the West is their backdrop. The discourses of both polities, as well as statements by their monarchs, praised or condemned a collective called 'the West'. For example, Nicholas I (r.1825–55), in the wake of the Decembrist Revolt launched by young aristocratic officers on the day in December he was to become emperor, privately thundered: 'Everything that took place there was the result of foreign [Western] influences. We must seek revenge for Russia and her honor'.[49] One hundred and fifty years later Mohammad Reza Shah was exhorting the youth: 'We must not become ridden with Occidentosis'.[50] But what was this West?

Within the European context over time the narratives on the spatial definition of civilized and powerful Europe changed. During the Classical and Renaissance periods the dominant discourse divided the continent between a civilized powerful south epitomized by Rome, Florence, Venice and Madrid, and a barbaric backward north. A sub-narrative rooted in religion emerged with the division of the Roman Empire into eastern and western parts that provided a subsequent dominant framework for Europe's self-identification, and in particular in relation to its immediate neighbours to the East. The disintegrating Western Empire gradually came to be packaged as 'Western Christendom', constituted by multifaceted groups of polities initially centred on Rome and the Papacy. The schism with the Eastern Church provided additional momentum to the idea of an identity of Western Christendom while the sacking of Constantinople by crusaders from the West solidified this sense and created a deep cleavage between the two Christian traditions, Roman and Orthodox. However, Islam's rise and expansion played a vital role in consolidating in the international area the conception of a unified Christendom defending itself against the antagonistic Muslim other.

While the early history of Western Christendom provided a vague geographical understanding of the West, it contained few indicators of the emergence of the wider political, civilizational and geopolitical understandings of the West that emerged during the Enlightenment and obtained greater definitional forms during the nineteenth and twentieth centuries. In other words, the perception of a barbaric north-civilized south divide in the region to the west of Russia and the Balkans remained dominant until the end of the Renaissance. Meanwhile, the emergence of Protestantism created cracks in this vague idea of the West.

During the Enlightenment the philosophes, helped by geopolitical changes within Europe and the rise of the Dutch, French, Spanish and English colonial empires, redefined the civilizational map of Europe along the lines of a civilized, rational, progressive Western Europe epitomized by the new cultural and financial centres of London, Paris and Amsterdam and backward 'demi-orientalized' Eastern Europe.[51] During the nineteenth century, the United States, given its shared intellectual and political heritage with the leaders of the Enlightenment, France, England and Scotland and its emergence as a world power, had a secure place in this concept of the West. This concept was based on elements developed during the Enlightenment: a scientific and rational world view, progressive linear history and universal civilization. This ideology of rationality and multifaceted progress became subsumed by the idea of the West given domestic and geopolitical transformations in specific west-European countries.

Underpinning this ideology were developing political and intellectual concepts, such as republican and constitutional forms of governance, civil liberties, human rights and an enlarging state role in social welfare, that came to define Western civilization. Their initial political expression came in 1789 at the beginning of the French Revolution. In 1848 the French thinker Auguste Comte published *The Republic of the West* 'which probably was the very first work to conceive of Western Europe as a single political community' founded on these concepts that became the basis for the West's claims not only to superiority but also exclusivity.[52] The ideas behind this concept of universal linear historical progress differed fundamentally from the historiography and meaning of history in classical Rome, Greece, ancient Iran and China and challenged the ideas not only of Orthodox and Shi'i universalisms and cosmologies but of Roman Catholicism and traditional monarchies.[53]

As subsequent chapters show, while Comte published his book and Europe experienced the Revolutions of 1848, in Russia during the reign of Nicholas I state discourses emerged portraying this 'West' as a fake Europe that threatened the political and cultural authenticity of true Europe represented by the Holy Alliance, founded after the defeat of Napoleon, whose membership included Protestant Prussia, the Catholic Austrian Empire and Orthodox tsarist Russia. They constituted a united front against godless Jacobinism, the threat of revolutionary contagion and the spread of liberal Western political ideals, the type of which Comte outlined. The 'gateway event' providing decisive momentum to this gradual political and intellectual consolidation of the West's identity and conception of itself as a superior political civilization in Europe and beyond was Napoleon III's humiliating defeat in the Franco-Prussian War (1870–1) and the consequent unification of Germany (1871) which was proclaimed by Otto von Bismarck, the Prussian chancellor, in the Hall of Mirrors at Louis XIV's palace at Versailles.

The establishment of the German Empire posed to the German state and society two fundamental and related questions: (1) What is the authenticity of German culture and national identity? and (2) What is the relationship of this unified German Empire with the idea of Europe and the concept of the West? Many German thinkers and intellectuals debated these questions but no consensus was achieved. The imperial state and its conservative supporters, however, provided a clear answer: to be German was 'to be everything that the French and English were not'.[54] In this context imperial Germany, unlike the kingdom of a united Italy established in 1861, rejected the liberal constitutionalist order on the grounds that it was incompatible with German authenticity of culture and national identity. With the racialization of the Franco-German antagonism by the end of the nineteenth century race was added to these justifications for German rejection of Western liberal constitutionalism. This rejection by Germany, a country located in the heart of Europe, despite the great contribution of German thinkers to the Enlightenment, could not but play a key role in crystallizing and consolidating the idea of an exclusive Western political and cultural civilization.

The political and ideological approach of the imperial German state to the concept of the West, which was determined by German conservatives and traditionalists dominating the political and economic elite and the bureaucracy, reflected a mixture of German Romantic thought and the French Counter-Enlightenment. Briefly put, by attacking the liberal foundations of the Enlightenment, they 'sought to prove the mistaken character of this rational-systematic method of thinking' that constituted the West.[55] This German political and ideological approach insisted that Germany represented another side of Europe and a different form of European development that did not belong to that geographical part of Europe that had been infected with those Enlightenment ideas forming the basis of this concept of Western civilization.

This rejection was also rooted in German social and moral criticism that from the mid-nineteenth century focused on the consequences of liberal capitalism in France and Britain, such as excessive materialism and consumerism, poor living conditions of the working class, an uncontrolled urbanization that brought moral corruption, all of which created serious and dangerous fractures in conceived organic social unity. It was determined that a German modernity, founded on a true authentic Germanness, could spare Germany these horrors. In other words, in political and intellectual circles, the liberal capitalism of France, Britain and the United States too was alien to German culture.

> At the end of the nineteenth century, from about 1880, technological progress and industrialization had reached such a pace in Central Europe that contemporaries felt increasingly uneasy in the face of constant change. Nervosität (anxiety or nervousness) was the first slogan to express unease at the impact of progress, from 1890. Added to this was criticism of the lifestyles of the middle classes from 1900 onwards, whether in Wilhelmine Germany or Edwardian Britain. Before the First World War, liberal thinking on progress, the bourgeoisie as its agents, and the constantly accelerating pace of everyday life as a result of industrialization and urbanization had become the focus of increasing criticism.[56]

Parallel to these developments in imperial Germany was the ongoing consolidation of the concept of the West that began to include the idea of human rights and freedom in the West's approach to foreign policy. This process began with William Gladstone's condemnations of Ottoman atrocities in Bulgaria (1876–8), a position that helped him electorally to become once again the prime minister of the United Kingdom. From the 1880s in Britain the concept of the West began to overshadow the idea of Europe in political and imperialist discourses while across the Atlantic from the 1890s the concept of Western civilization became increasingly prominent in US political and intellectual discourses.

These trends in both Germany and 'the West' came to a head during the First World War. According to German discourses, France, Britain and the United States constituted this West against which Germany was waging a civilizational war. It was a war between authentic German culture and alien Western civilization, between Germany's conception of organic unity and community united with the state and the West's liberal and corrupt democracy that gave preference to personal and party interests over those of the people and the state and promised the eternal social and national divisiveness of parliamentary politics. In the countries of the West the war was similarly portrayed in civilizational terms. It was a war of the liberal, civilized West whose liberal democratic capitalist modernity represented the end of history and German barbarism and irrationality.

The West defeated Germany. But in the 1920s and 1930s this West faced growing threats as economic and political turmoil spread across Europe. The establishment of the USSR, the emergence of fascism in Italy followed by the rise of Hitler in Germany and of Franco in Spain showed that the battles over the definition of true Europe did not end with the victory of the West in the First World War. Even France and Britain faced to varying degrees fascist and radical right movements that threatened these conceptions of this West.

In 1937 Winston Churchill, as war clouds emerged over Europe, in a major speech underlined that as a child he had been taught that a continent named Europe existed. This Europe, he stressed, still existed. However, to his chagrin, geographers were now arguing that Europe in reality was not a continent but only a peninsula of the Asian landmass. He rejected outright his argument. The real demarcation line between Europe and this Asian landmass was not a chain of mountains or a national frontier but 'a system of beliefs and ideas which we call Western civilisation'.[57] He said this as the greatest threat to this Western Civilization came from the heart of geographical Europe, Italy and Germany. Subsequent chapters point to instances in which the trajectory of state and intellectual discourses in imperial and Nazi Germany on the relationship between Germanness, on the one hand, and the concept of Europe and/or the West, on the other, have exercised an influence on Romanov Russia and Pahlavi Iran. In more practical terms, the example of imperial and Nazi Germany showed that economic and technological development could be achieved without succumbing to Western political and cultural values lumped under the rubric 'liberalism' and losing one's authenticity of culture and national identity.

With the end of the Second World War and the emergence of the Cold War the United States with its junior partner, Britain, came to play the key role in determining the concept of the West. The demarcation line was drawn more clearly around forms of capitalism and liberal democratic governance and assumed definite ideological and institutional shape with NATO, the evolution of European integration into the European Union, and the fundamentals of the United Nations, including the UN Commission on Human Rights (from 2006 the UN Human Rights Council). These forms became the criteria for membership in the West.

These changes in the European discourses on civilization and the spatial definition of the West in the context of Eastern and Western Europe were of little consequence for Russia, which Europeans since the Renaissance considered barbaric and backward, especially given the existence of the autocracy.[58] From the point of view of non-Christian peoples, such as Iranians, these changes in intra-European discourses did not alter the reality of the expansion of European maritime empires and power that threatened their country. Yet, the Enlightenment mapping of European civilization and power along the West–East divide exercised a determinative impact on the discourses of reform in polities that, feeling the European geopolitical threat, began to speak of 'Europeanization and Westernization' as the path to achieving these new forms of power. However, even here, as subsequent chapters show, the meaning of Europeanization and/or Westernization can be somewhat ambiguous as both Iran and Russia sought to find and define the 'real' West and determine the specific countries that constituted this West from which they should take example.[59]

This Enlightenment-defined West, proclaiming its civilization universal, did not initially close to non-Western peoples the doors of civilization and development leading to the power it enjoyed, although it held that this power was the result of elements in west-European civilization and could not be acquired without adopting them. Importantly, while this West, as the standard bearer of universal civilization and progress, contrasted and created itself in the mirror of the uncivilized peoples bordering it, whom, to use Said's term, it Orientalized, it also Orientalized the masses of their own countries. In other words, the Enlightenment ideas of progress, rationality and civilization propagated the idea of a universal civilizational ideology, 'modernism', that divided people into two broad categories, one rational, civilized and modern and the other irrational, uncivilized and backward, both within the societies of countries of the West and between the West and the East. The masses of the West as well as non-Westerners had to be inculcated with this civilization. For example, in England the emerging Occidentalist discourse at the end of the eighteenth century was initially directed against internal rather than primarily external groups of people, 'against *internal* non-Western, or more precisely, Orientalized, populations and spaces that were seen to be undesirably out of synch with the temporal requirements of modernity'.

> The 'us/them' that began to emerge in the late eighteenth and early nineteenth century did not operate simply along native/foreigner or native/immigrant axes; it cut across and among native indigenous English people as well, some of whom came to be seen from a certain privileged standpoint as culturally and racially separate and inferior, as not fit members of the race or nation, as alien and other (savage, Arab – a term used to describe homeless street urchins –, both unsettled and unsettling) compared to an emergent notion of those of 'us' who were seen to be more appropriately at home in England.[60]

From the second-quarter of the nineteenth century and with the expansion of the empire, a new cultural and civilizational notion of the Occident emerged and developed according to which England and its entire people could claim to belong to this Occident in opposition to an Orient in the geographical East. 'An internal Occidentalism and an internal Occidentalization were the necessary correlates of an Orientalism and Orientalization that would eventually be exclusively directed to the outside'.[61]

In France, this bifurcation of native populations was central to the cultural policies in the nineteenth and early twentieth centuries, as the secular republican state set out to create a new French people inculcated with the ideals of the Enlightenment and 'transform peasants into Frenchmen'.[62] The source and propagator of this 'civilized' culture were the great urban areas and specifically Paris, which targeted peasant religiosity, superstitions and barbarism. 'These peasants were the French citizens routinely described by their educated, urban compatriots in the nineteenth century as belonging to an alien, animalistic world.' In 1851 Adolphe Blanqui, the great French economist who supported the idea of liberal trade and was one of the first figures to use the term 'industrial revolution', in the midst of this long process noted that in reality 'two different peoples living on the same land a life so different that they seem foreign to each other'.[63] Of course, this attitude of elites towards the masses goes back to early history.

The Enlightenment belief that Western Europe and specifically its elite-educated groups, having accepted Enlightenment modernist thought stood at the pinnacle of universal history, a position that granted Europeans the knowledge and moral authority to impose progress on less-advanced societies, and therefore the justification for colonialism, was initially underpinned in the late seventeenth and most of the eighteenth centuries by a conviction in 'physical and moral homogeneity of man despite superficial differences'. Given the correct conditions 'backward' traditional societies could become a member of universal (i.e. Western) history. In other words, to be a member of the Occident meant acceptance of Enlightenment ideas of progress, and specifically its political and legal thought. Early Ottoman and Japanese reformist politicians and intellectuals seized on this initial Western interpretation, formulating

> a more inclusive notion of global civilization and international order, believing that they should encounter no religious, cultural, or racial obstacle to being as civilized as Europeans. They insisted that upon achieving a certain set of 'civilized' reforms, their societies could attain not only prosperity and might but also security and equality in the emerging world order.[64]

Emerging in the late eighteenth century and solidifying by the middle of the nineteenth century was a new understanding of the West's self-definition and of the causes of its claimed superiority-race.[65] This development in turn changed the approach to the internal 'Oriental' in the West who, despite his civilizational wretchedness, came, nonetheless, to be seen as racially superior to Eastern peoples. The assumption that human groups are characterized by deep differences in temperament and ability due to race became dominant and played a decisive role in the intellectual and political underpinnings of Orientalism and imperialism. Importantly, this turn to emphasis on racial superiority and external Orientalism in European state and intellectual discourses helped to consolidate metropolitan society's unity and elite legitimacy at a time of spreading mass literacy, urbanization and societal pressure for political change and democratization.

This emphasis on race exercised a strong impact on how non-Western countries reacted to the challenge of the West. The Ottomans and the Japanese responded 'to the perceived rejection by the European centre of its own claims to the universality of modern civilization and inclusiveness of the world order' by turning to Pan-Islamic and Pan-Asian thought.[66] On the contrary, the Romanov and Pahlavi polities accepted this racial argument while claiming to enjoy unique racial–cultural links with West Europeans.

Russian and Iranian elite understandings of what constituted the West not only at times differed from each other but also evolved as geopolitical and domestic political circumstances changed. What remained constant throughout the eras covered here was the belief that the construct of the West, regardless of debates in Europe over where the West began and ended, was generating new forms of power that threatened the Romanov and Pahlavi states. These countries' elites had to rise to this challenge or risk losing dynasty, empire and their political and social positions. The West meant economic, military and technological power that had to be replicated at home. Pro-West Occidentalism became their initial answer to this challenge.

Yet, parallel to these ideas of the West's power and Iranian and Russian unique links with the West existed Pahlavi and Romanov conceptions of a cultural and political West that evolved in order to maintain the claims to these links. This study shows how Romanov and Pahlavi Occidentalisms ultimately came to propagate the idea of a false West and/or Europe that had abandoned its political and/or cultural authenticity and a true West and/or Europe epitomized by Russia and Iran that had preserved this authenticity and therefore offered paths of salvation to a culturally and morally corrupt West once portrayed as an example to follow.

Change and the imagery of the self and other

The issues running through this study – questions of authenticity of native culture and identity, the fear of losing it in the face of foreign influences and the conundrum of balancing this fear with the imposed need to change as global conditions change – are not in principle new in world history. Certainly, the intensity of the West's power and its global reach raised the sense of urgency and sensitivity with which states and societies approached these issues. Moreover, the great extent of the West's power, the speed of its development and the attractiveness of its living conditions and technology were proof enough for many that the West had reached the future and did indeed represent 'the end of history'. This belief led to the spread of Occidentosis. We again turn to Kluchevskii's insight regarding the historical uniqueness of the dynamics of the challenge of the West:

> On the issue of the beginning of Western influence in Russia, it is necessary to determine a specific definition of the term influence. Before, in the fifteenth and sixteenth centuries Russia was acquainted with Western Europe and enjoyed diplomatic and trade relations with it. It even borrowed the fruits of Western education and recruited its artists, craftsmen, doctors, and military specialists. This can be called various forms of links and contact, but not influence. Influence comes when the society that accepts these links and contacts begins to recognize the superiority of the social environment and culture of the society from which they radiate, and the necessity to study from it, morally to submit to it, while borrowing not only its worldly conveniences, but also the very basis of its worldly cosmology, views, understandings, customs, and social relations. ... The state first

advanced the spread of Western influence in order to strengthen itself and satisfy its own material requirements. However, that influence did not remain within that limited sphere. ... Western influence took over the entire individual (of certain classes) while failing to take over the entire society (as did religion).[67]

Yet, the general fear of losing one's authenticity of culture that emerged in response to the challenge of the West is not a new phenomenon. The historical contexts cited below, whose themes appear in one way or another throughout this work, give a sense of both the longue durée and, as Jean-Baptiste Alphonse Karr famously put it, 'the more things change, the more they stay the same' to the issues that underpin the framework in which the Pahlavi shahs, Romanov emperors and their elites operated when faced with varied and changing domestic and geopolitical challenges posed by the West.

In the middle of the 1980s Anthony Smith in his first major work on national identity critically summed up the opinion of Westerners in regard to the concerns of non-Westerners about authenticity of national culture and identity and its possible loss:

> It is fashionable for Western observers, securely ensconced in their own national identities forged in toil and blood several centuries ago, to pour scorn on the rhetorical excesses and misguided scholarship of nationalist intellectuals in nineteenth-century Europe or twentieth-century Africa and Asia. Those whose identities are rarely questioned and who have never known exile or subjugation of land and culture, have little need to trace their 'roots' in order to establish a unique and recognizable identity.[68]

It needs to be added that responding to the challenge of Western power and the political and cultural challenges associated with Westernization also engenders vital questions for a society about the reasons for its backwardness in relation to the collective known as the West and how to achieve the elements of that power in domestic cultural and political contexts. The search for answers results in the undermining of the imagined elements of authenticity of native culture and national identity and the emergence of discourses proclaiming a crisis of identity.

Beginning at least in 2016 Smith's observation seemed increasingly out of date as the political life of nations in the West was increasingly dominated by debates over the constitutive elements of the authenticity of culture and national identity and the need to protect it in the face of globalizing economic, technological and cultural changes and immigration that created economic and cultural anxiety and disorientation. Brexit, the election of Donald Trump in the United States, and the rise of ethnic nationalism and nativism within countries of the European Union symbolized the popularity of these debates. For those who have worked on non-Western countries, such as Iran and Russia, these current discourses in the West are variations of an all-too common and long-standing theme; one only needs to replace the term Westernization with Globalization or even the European Union.

Smith argued that 'to regard the nation as a given of social existence, a "primordial" and natural unity of human association outside of time' is not possible, while to accept 'that it is a wholly modern phenomenon, be it the "nervous tie of capitalism", or the necessary form and culture of an industrial society' is also not historically correct. In reality, national and cultural identities are made up of 'myths, memories, symbols and values ... [that] can often be adapted to new circumstances by being accorded new meanings and new functions'.[69] Expanding on this definition, this work holds that the importance of the conceptions of the authenticity of culture and identity, along with the feelings attached to them, is also historical, reaching far back into time to the era of ancient empires. It needs to be recognized that a people's worries and concerns over the possible loss of its authenticity of culture and identity, however conceived and imagined in any historical period, in the face of cultural and/or geopolitical threats, however defined, is not particular to the modern era and to countries facing the challenge of the power of the collective eventually labelled the 'West'. Thus, it should not be assumed that state discourses emphasizing the defence of native authenticity and identity are solely politically instrumentalized.

The French Counter-Enlightenment that emerged during the reigns of Louis XV and Louis XVI was backed by clerics, leading members of the elite known as the Catholic *parti devot*, who supported domestic policies against Protestants and a strong alliance with the Hapsburg Holy Roman Empire, a large number of aristocrats, conservative members of the French parliaments, and many leading publicists, among others. These groups opposed the claims of the philosophers of the French Enlightenment that they had 'a new calling-the power to form and reflect public opinion' and inculcate the population with their radical new thoughts and philosophy. These opponents of French Enlightenment thinkers warned that their new thoughts and philosophy would result in anti-monarchism, cultural and political anarchy and the destruction of a base of French identity, Catholicism.

> What were the elements of this emergent right-wing vision? The fundamental importance of religion in maintaining political order, a preoccupation with the perils of intellectuals and social license, the valorization of the family and history, the critique of abstract rights, the dangers of dividing sovereignty, and the need for a strategic alliance between throne and altar – these all featured centrally in the new ideology.[70]

Describing the cultural costs and loss that would inevitably result from the spread of Enlightenment thought, the counter-Enlightenment intellectuals dwelled 'on the dark side of modern rationalism, individualism, and materialism'.[71] The well-known publicist and orator abbé Cambacérès 'warned in a celebrated sermon preached at the court of Louis XV' that the thought of French Enlightenment thinkers was producing a 'revolution' in 'the morals and character of the nation' that threatened not only religion but also the authenticity of French culture and national identity.[72]

Suffering from increasing feelings of nostalgia in the face of changes resulting from the Enlightenment, the proponents of the French Counter-Enlightenment glorified the past, specifically Louis XIV's reign. The sense that France had entered a period of decline after him intensified these sentiments. Rigoley de Juvigny, another well-known and respected orator, expressed this group's opinion that the rule of the Sun King was the lost golden age in which 'men were devout', motivated by 'valor, patriotism, and a deep traditional sense of self-sacrifice that had consolidated and preserved the unity of the French state and people'. Speaking during the reign of Louis XVI he lamented that 'all these grand sentiments' were now gone. As we shall see in the following chapters, the deep yearning for a perceived cultural wholeness and social unity underpinned by self-sacrifice, love of monarch, sense of duty, and traditional cultural and moral values constituted the bases of anti-West Occidentalism in the late Romanov and Pahlavi periods.

The main products of the Enlightenment, the conceptions of universal civilization and progressive linear history and the philosophical bases behind them that prompted the struggle between the *philosophes* and the supporters of the French Counter-Enlightenment, created the same division in German-speaking lands at the end of the eighteenth and beginning of the nineteenth centuries. Those German thinkers critical of these products argued that they did not constitute a universalist paradigm but rather a French cultural threat to emerging notions of the authenticity of German culture and identity. The writings of German Romanticists, such as Johann Hamann, his student Joseph Herder, and Friedrich Jacobi, broadly speaking called for a cultural nativism that rejected the claimed rationalism, universalism and struggle against religion propagated by French thought. They exercised an influence on German political thought until the middle of the twentieth century. In Russia in the first half of the nineteenth century, Slavophiles, taking inspiration from this German Romanticism, protested Romanov pro-West Occidentalism and called for the protection of the authenticity of Russian culture and national identity rooted in Orthodoxy, seeing in it the path to Russia's future. Slavophile thought, however, while echoing the concerns of figures of the French Counter-Enlightenment and German Romanticists, described this threat as a cultural invasion of the West. Thus, the debates about the authenticity of national culture and identity prompted by Enlightenment thinking had, already by the mid-nineteenth century, been framed in three geographically determined discursive forms. In France it was an internal debate between groups about the issue and character of change. After the French Revolution this internal debate over what it meant to be French greatly intensified and revolved around one's evaluation of the events of 1789 and 1793. In German-speaking lands before the establishment of imperial Germany the issue was defence of a German authenticity in the face of the invasion of French civilization in the context of debates over forms of change. In Russia, this intellectual debate crystallized in the first half of the nineteenth century in the confrontation between the Slavophiles, who condemned Occidentosis, and the Westernizers (*Zapadniki*), as they were known at the time. This dichotomy is hegemonic in contemporary Russia where the Putinist state claims to be leading a crusade against cultural, moral and political Occidentosis.

However, concerns about authenticity predate the Enlightenment and debates about the influence of Westernization and Western culture, however defined since the long eighteenth century, on the authenticity of culture and national identity of non-Western nations. For example, three elements that were vital to conceptions of ancient Roman identity, namely native dress, language and literature, and the fear of the influence of Hellenization on them, were equally important in the debates about Occidentalism in Pahlavi Iran and Romanov Russia, as we shall see. Suetonius (69–129), writing during Rome's imperial period, in discussing this fear and the tension between Roman and Greek identity stated: 'Roman identity has not elided with Greek identity. The very game played by swapping cloths, languages and thus identities, underlines how distinct they remain'.[73] Cicero (106–43 BCE), writing during the dying decades of the Roman Republic and translating Greek philosophy in order make it accessible to the Latin-reading Roman population, had to confront concerns about the possible loss of authenticity resulting from Hellenization. The issue was that the Romans felt to a significant extent cultural inferiority in regard to the Greeks given their contributions to philosophy and literature that indeed influenced strongly Roman forms. The well-known British classicist Michael Grant noted:

> Philosophy was Greek, and Cicero, however much he might look down on some of the more feeble manifestations of Hellenism in his own day, repeatedly shows his enormous admiration for classical Greek culture, which it was his proud purpose to transmit, in popularized form, to Rome. He was known as a phil-Hellene, and not always to his credit. A lot of Romans thought badly of statesmen who also went in for a literary career and studied Greek literature. Cicero knew this, and was therefore at pains, first, to emphasize his patriotic motives, secondly, to deplore Romans who hellenized themselves too completely, and thirdly, to explain reassuringly that their own ancestors would have done just as well as the Greeks if they had not been engaged in other occupations.[74]

Cicero in the initial pages of his major work *On Ends* (*De Finius Bonorum et Malorum*) was clear in his denunciation of those Romans who, to use this study's term, suffered from Hellenosis: 'I can never sufficiently express my wonder whence this arrogant disdain of everything national (*domesticarum*) arose amongst us'.[75] Condemning those who shunned Latin literature and preferred Greek literature, philosophy and language he noted: 'But given a noble theme, and a refined, dignified, and graceful style, who would not read a Latin book? Unless it be some one ambitious to be styled a Greek out-and-out…'.[76]

A little more than one thousand years after Cicero and some six to seven hundred years before the Enlightenment lived Abolqasim Ferdowsi Tusi (940–1020), the great Iranian poet, who wrote Iran's national epic poem, the *Shahnameh*. This work came to be seen as a reflection of long-standing concerns over the loss of authenticity of Iranian culture and identity that first emerged in light of the Arab-Islamic conquest of the Sassanian Empire (651). Written some 300 hundred years after this conquest, it is not only an expression of these concerns but also Iran's national epic poem. Its broad goals were (a) preservation of Iranian identity and culture; (b) definition and preservation of Iranian morality and spirituality; (c) preservation of the Persian language; and (d) preservation and/or creation of the national mission that focuses on the greatness of the Iranian Empire and Iran's rightful claim to world leadership by virtue of its morality, spirituality and culture.[77]

The *Shahnameh* describes the war between supreme good, symbolized by Iran, and evil, symbolized by non-Iranian enemies, usually Turks and Arabs. This work was patronized and propagated by dynasties searching for legitimation by linking themselves with pre-Islamic Iranian Empire. Over time it became

> the one indisputably great surviving cultural artifact that attempts to assert a continuity of collective memory across the moment of the conquest; at the least it salvaged the pre-conquest legendary history of Iran and made it available to the Iranian people as a memorial of a great and distinctive civilization.[78]

Not surprisingly, a cult of Ferdowsi was integral to Pahlavi discourses on national unity. Ferdowsi's famous quote 'If Iran does not exist, my being is no longer' was frequently used by Mohammad Reza Shah and leading Pahlavi-era political and cultural figures and became standard teaching fare in official primary- and secondary-school textbooks.[79]

Some five hundred years after Ferdowsi lived a Muscovite noble Ivan Nikitich Beklemishev, nicknamed Bersen, who was a state and diplomatic figure during the reigns of Ivan III (r.1462–1505) and Vasili III (r. 1505–33). He succinctly articulated the fundamental problem facing those advocating change in Muscovy at the beginning of the sixteenth century. His opposition to the slow but consistent flow of foreign cultural influence, in particular Italian and Greek, led to his arrest. What has come down to us is a record of his conversation with Maxim Grek (1475–1556), a Greek Orthodox monk and thinker who had arrived in Moscow in 1518. The conversation between the two men, quoted extensively below, is informative and illuminating. Of particular importance is Bersen's call for the protection of authenticity of native culture and identity in the face of the spread of cultural influences from countries to the west of Muscovy before the period of the Enlightenment and debates between Slavophiles and Westernizers in the early nineteenth century.

Bersen began by expressing concerns that God was no longer in the Muscovite polity given Vasilii's policies:

> The old Muscovite traditions and customs are beginning to shake. The person doing the shaking is the tsar. You yourself know, and we have heard it from wise men, that any land that abandons its customs and ways will not long stand. And now here with us the current grand prince has changed our traditions and ways. What kind of good could possibly await us?

Maxim replied: 'God punishes only those who do not obey the commandments. Rituals, traditions and customs of this world, whatever they are, are changed by rulers in accordance with circumstances and state interests.' He was articulating the rationale used by Romanov tsars and Pahlavi shahs when they launched their programmes of Westernization.

Bersen was not satisfied with this answer: 'That is true. However, in any case it is better to preserve them, to respect older wiser people, and to respect the people (and their customs) as a whole.' Maxim responded that the changes implemented by Vasilii, including the hiring of foreign specialists and allowing the activities of foreign merchants, were due to international pressures and internal disorder. Bersen rejected this interpretation, arguing for the role of human agency. He considered Vasilii's mother and Ivan III's wife, Sofia Paleologue (1455–1503), niece of the last Byzantine emperor, Constantine XI, as one of the main catalysts for these negative changes. 'As soon as these Greeks came our land became confused and mixed up. Until that time Russia lived in peace and quiet. As soon as the grand prince's mother, Sofia, arrived here with her Greeks (and the consequent spread of foreign ways), all these great disorders began.'[80]

Around the same time, in Iran the Safavids established a new dynasty and proclaimed a return to Iranian Empire whose guardianship would be in their hands. From the beginning of the Safavid period, pre-Islamic Iranian Empire, including its universalism, mixed with Shi'i Islam to provide a new imperial discourse legitimating and justifying Safavid power. Ismail based his image on Islamic and Shi'i writings, such as the Quran, and Iranian texts, such as the *Shahnameh*. Under his successor, Tahamsab (r.1524–76), the Safavids intensified their emphasis on the political aspect of the pre-Islamic Iranian title, shah, and pre-Islamic Iranian kingship. By the time of Abbas I (r.1588–1629), the Safavids regarded themselves as universal monarchs in the tradition of pre-Islamic Iranian shahs while Shi'ism played a supportive role legitimating and rationalizing the power of the monarchy and distinguishing it and Iran from the Sunni Ottoman Caliphate and Empire that claimed to be the leader of the Muslim world.

During Safavid rule two other narratives existed alongside state ones on the authenticity of Iranian culture and heritage. They help illustrate the potential tension in Iranian Islamic identity and the attempts to fuse these two elements and create a new authenticity. Dating from the Safavid period, and even before, they add to the context in which Pahlavi Occidentalism emerged. One group of discourses, epitomized by the popular saga, *Abu Moslemnameh*, sought an accommodation of the competing pre-Islamic Iranian and Arab Muslim narratives on conceptions of Iranian identity.[81] According to it, Shahrbano, the daughter of Yazdgerd III (r.632–51) the last Sassanian emperor, married Imam Hossein, the third Shi'i Imam, the grandson of the prophet Mohammad and the son of Ali, the first Shi'i Imam. Their son was Ali, the fourth Shi'i Imam. In this way, pre-Islamic Iranian historical narratives blended with those of Islam while Iranian cultural and historical independence from Arab Islam was also stressed.

The other discourse emphasized the superiority of Iranian culture and heritage to that of the Arabs. Mahmoud Pasikhani (d.1427), the founder of the Nuqtavi movement, propagated the idea that world history, made up of four periods of 16,000 years, would run 64,000 years. Alternating between periods of Iranian and Arab rule, world history would end with Iranian rule during which all of humanity would attain supreme truth. 'The cycle of the Ajam (Iranians) will prevail ... the religion of Mohammad is abrogated; now the religion is the religion of Mahmud. ... That with which the Arabs taunted the Iranians has passed.' For the Nuqtavis supreme truth was linked to a restoration of Iranian universal sovereignty.[82]

Back in Russia, in the 1660s a Croat, Urii Krizhanich (1617–83) came to Moscow to promote unity of the Slavic peoples. He articulated the dual challenges to be faced by Iranian and Russian monarchs of the possible loss of authenticity in the face of importation of Western ways and the need for their adaptation in order to prevent the weakening of these countries.

> Two peoples are trying to seduce Russia with their own allurements of opposing characters, taking her into two opposite directions. They are the Germans [the West] and the Greeks [Orthodoxy]. Despite their differences they are united by their ultimate goal. The Germans recommend all of their innovations. They want us to abandon all of our laudable ancient institutions and customs and to adapt their rights and laws. The Greeks, on the contrary, without reservation denounce all forms of newness. ... They declare that anything new is evil. But logic says that something new cannot automatically be bad or good because of its newness. That which is old today was once new. But it is not good to accept without debate everything that is new as mistakes can be made. But it is also not good to reject the new just because it is new. That too can be a mistake. Whether we accept or reject something new must be decided after serious contemplation. ... All human conditions are not constant and unchangeable. But a people cannot immediately, but over time, learn logic and wisdom ... [and attain positive change which] is needed for societal life and the state. ... Certain peoples in ancient times were well-known for their sciences, but now are ignorant, such as the Egyptians, Greeks, and the Jews. And other peoples in ancient times were crude and wild, but now in regard to handicrafts and other forms of wisdom and intelligence are extraordinary renown, for example the Germans, the French.[83]

Unwittingly following in his footsteps was Malkom Khan (1833–1908), an Iranian-Armenian Christian who converted to Islam. He was a well-known and controversial supporter of reforms as Iran during the rule of the Qajar dynasty (1796–1924) entered a period of decline and became a target of British and Russian imperialism. His writings and newspaper *Qanun* published outside of Iran, but read by the Iranian elite, including the monarch himself, were highly critical of the Qajar government's inability to respond to the challenge of the West and of reactionary elements within both the autocratic state and clergy. When not the target of the shah's anger he also occupied several high posts, including assistant to Chief Minister Mirza Hussein Sepahsalar and ambassador to London and Rome. In his work *The Sheikh and the Minister*, he articulated the dilemma facing the Iranian state, namely overcoming clerical resistance to Westernization and the powerful hold clerical interpretations of religion had over the people. He also offered a path to deal with it.

The sheikh wonders, 'How is adopting the principles of these infidels possible?' The minister replies, 'I do not deny that they are infidels. My only claim is that Europe's power comes from their unique mechanisms. If we wish to obtain the same power, we must adopt in full their mechanisms and instruments. If we do not take this step, we must not deceive ourselves – we will never equal them. ... The clergy must allow us to imitate the bases of European strength. If not, the clerics must bring squadrons of angels down from Heaven to defend us from European rule'.[84]

The threats to Iranian sovereignty and independence were indeed real. During the nineteenth and early twentieth centuries as the loss of territory and expansion of Russian and British influence over the country's economic and political life increasingly drove home the realization of Iran's weakness, debates emerged that touched on the reasons for the West's success, Iran's decline and appropriate paths to answer the challenge of the West and protect the country's sovereignty. The overall challenge of the West came to be recognized as consisting of individual but interrelated military, economic and administrative challenges. By the end of the nineteenth century, these debates concluded that the answer was culture.

In this vein, Malkom argued that a strong centralized state was needed to change people's values, culture and behaviour. But changing culture in the face of clerical obscurantism and the popular belief in religious superstitions were formidable obstacles. Therefore, the teaching of the West's ways to the East and 'the logic of change in Iran [are] a vain struggle if implemented in a European Western way. I therefore propose dressing [Western] thought of progress in the clothes of religion so that my compatriots recognize their wearing [of this thought and movement] as good and worthwhile.'[85] He argued that the progress he had witnessed in the Ottoman Empire (during the reign of Abdul Hamid II) was the result of telling the people, 'We have nothing to do with Europeans; these [reforms] are the true principles of our own religion [and indeed that is quite true] which have been *taken by the Europeans!*'[86] As we shall see Pahlavi Occidentalism rejected this path given conditions and context in Iran that differed from those of the Ottomans.

These varied historical contexts briefly discussed in this chapter provide a thematic backdrop to the eras of Pahlavi and Romanov Occidentalism. At their centre are concepts of identity and fears over the possible of loss of its authenticity that have occupied the minds of generations throughout history and expressed in politics. Centuries before facing the challenge of the West, various Iranian and Russian political and intellectual figures initially defined to a significant extent authenticity in opposition to those peoples, namely the Arabs and the Greeks, from whom Russia and Iran had obtained their respective religions, Islam and Orthodoxy, while nationalizing these religions to produce an Iranian Shi'i and a Russian Orthodox identity. However, eventually Russia and Iran on the battlefield realized the need for Westernization, even if for some time before military defeat both polities had some form of political, cultural and economic interaction with the collective known as the West. Thus, the tension between calls and structural demands for change and exhortations for the protection of imagined authenticity became more acute and intense. However, as Malkom Khan pointed out, failure to change would lead to succumbing to Western economic, geopolitical and political hegemony. The feelings and viewpoints voiced by Bersen eventually constituted a leading obstacle to the implementation of change in Russia and came to be expressed in the Occidentalism of the reigns of Alexander III (r.1881–94) and Nicholas II (r.1894–1917).

Maxim Grek's response to Bersen's opposition to changes epitomizes one of the main justifications of Reza Shah, Peter I and their successors for their pursuance of Westernizing reforms. Similar to Maxim, they stressed that the state had to change with the times and quickly in order to maintain its strength in the face of domestic and international threats. In this regard, Mohammad Reza Shah described the thinking held by both Romanov and Pahlavi monarchs:

> In order to enter the ranks of the developed world it was necessary that we, who unfortunately due to myriad factors had become backward, in one stage eliminate all traces of weakness and social, moral, and spiritual decline. Conditions did not allow that we one day take some reforming steps and gradually absorb them and then one or two years later take some more reforming steps and in such a way perhaps in twenty-five or thirty years we could to an extent be similar to [developed] nations. The trajectory of development of the wheel of civilization does not give that opportunity to anyone, especially to our country given its geographical position. Therefore, it was necessary in one stage to rid ourselves of the traces of our weakness and decline. Any step that was necessary to place the country within the ranks of the developed world we took. This action had a completely revolutionary character.[87]

This quote shows why these monarchs ultimately rejected Malkom's and Krizhanich's recommendations which reflected an interesting but perhaps politically unrealistic approach to the drafting and implementation of reforms. Krizhanich was correct that the discourses about reform and the character of policies tend to polarize eventually along the lines against which he warns. His approach to the debates about what is new and old supported the case for change and implicitly condemned reactionary and even conservative discourses. However, his suggestion that reforms be carried out slowly and after careful study went against the sense held by the Iranian and Russian elites that geopolitical threats were too great to allow such a course of action. Change had to come quickly and from above. In this opinion national self-dignity and self-respect demanded it. The following chapter, the beginning of the story of Romanov Occidentalism, shows why Krizhanich's and Malkom's proposed method for dressing up reforms in religious garb was not chosen by the Romanov state.

Concluding point

The discourses of Romanov and Pahlavi Occidentalisms, in other words, the place of the West in state conceptions of authenticity of native culture and identity, is a multifaceted and fluid set of ideological and political discourses that aimed (a) to justify state-imposed radical changes in response to the challenge posed by the West's power; (b) to rebuild national self-confidence damaged by the realization of backwardness vis-à-vis the West's power and the West's ultimately essentialized binaries of civilized-barbaric, progressive-backward and enlightened-unenlightened; (c) to rationalize monarchical power during the implementation of these changes and subsequently in face of the socio-economic and political consequences of these changes; and (d) to respond to changes in the international arena. Together they constituted over the long-term partially haphazard and partially preconceived attempts to construct a Pahlavi Iranian and Romanov Russian modernity that mixed Western forms of economic, military and technological power with conceptions of native culture and national identity, however defined by the state at any point in time, while maintaining claims to unique racial–cultural links with the West. Therefore, in this study modernity is not defined solely by the West's understanding of this term that emerged during the Enlightenment which is rooted in liberal democracy and capitalism, known otherwise as the End of History, or communism. Rather the term 'modernity' has a broader meaning here, sharing elements from Charles Taylor's idea of social imaginaries.

> From the beginning, the number one problem of modern social science has been modernity itself: that historically unprecedented amalgam of new practices and institutional forms (science, technology, industrial production, urbanization), of new ways of living (individualism, secularization, instrumental rationality); and of new forms of malaise (alienation, meaninglessness, a sense of impending social dissolution).

He argues that this problem must be addressed with a new approach: 'Is there a single phenomenon here, or do we need to speak of "multiple modernities" and thus accept that "non-Western cultures have modernized in their own way?"' Therefore, to study them within a framework 'designed originally with the Western case in mind' is not a fruitful exercise. Arguing that the West's modernity 'is inseparable from a certain kind of social imaginary' he thus stresses that 'today's modernities need to be understood in terms of the divergent social imaginaries involved'.[88] This is an issue vital to the narrative of Romanov and Pahlavi Occidentalisms.

2

Romanov Occidentalism

Given Russia's close geographical proximity to Europe in the era ending with Peter I's reign, the geopolitical, religious and ideological relationship between Russia and the West had been more intense than that between Iran and the West from the emergence of the Safavid state to Iran's defeats at the hands of the Russians in the early 1800s. The first major military confrontation between Russia and polities of the West in the post-Mongol period was the Livonian War (1557–82) which Ivan IV (r.1533–84) lost. This major defeat strengthened the emerging belief in the West's superiority in military and technological fields. Sergei Solovyov, the famous nineteenth-century Russian historian, described the dilemma. Ivan

> suffered a catastrophic failure. From that reign the idea of approaching the West ... became a leading thought and plan of the government and many Russians. ... But new challenges emerged. Under whom to study? Under foreigners and more importantly, under those of a different faith? To allow foreigners, those of a different faith, into the country and give them the high title of teacher? Thus, openly recognizing their superiority? Openly subordinating oneself to them? Would those people [the clergy] in whose hands [up to that point] resided the exclusive right to teach take such a step?[1]

Solovyov was underlining the challenges posed by the troubled relationship between Orthodox Russia and the Catholic and then Protestant countries to the West of her.

Almost two decades after Ivan's reign Russia descended into civil war and faced an invasion in 1610 led by King Sigismund III, who sat on the thrones of Poland and Lithuania. Known as the Time of Troubles, this period played an important role in the construction of state identity during the early Romanov period. Writing to Pope Paul V, Sigismund III stated that the war's goal was the 'spread of the Catholic faith' and proclaimed that 'Russians are not Christians. They belong to Asia and, with Eastern peoples, seek to destroy the Christian world'.[2] The Pontiff declared Sigismund's war a Crusade. This was not the first time. Previous crusades were launched against the 'heathens' of the Russian lands, especially during the papacies of Gregory IX (1227–41) and Alexander IV (r.1254–61).[3] A leading Catholic bishop stated that their goal was 'to exterminate their godless customs ... uncivilized barbarity and temper inhuman peoples'.[4] In the dynamic between this conception of Catholic West and Russia, Alexander, the Grand Prince of Kiev, Vladimir and Novgorod (r.1228–63) has exercised an enduring influence. He chose to side with the occupying Mongols against invading Catholic Swedes and Teutonic Knights. The Mongols were not considered threats to Orthodoxy, in other words, Russian authenticity, and to the domestic power of the grand princes, while Catholics from the West were seen to threaten both. He defeated them in 1240 at the Battle of the Neva. He thus became known as Alexander Nevskii. He fought off another offensive in 1256. In 1547 Macarius, the metropolitan of Russia, canonized him.

In the discourses of the conservative Orthodoxy clergy, and then early anti-West Occidentalism, Nevskii was a symbol of true Russianness – a leader who recognized the genuine elements of Russian authenticity and the source of the threat to it – the West. 'Beginning from the middle of the thirteenth century Russians have always viewed the West as a more dangerous opponent. The choice of Alexander Nevskii was based on the belief that the East is satisfied with external forms of subordination while not touching on the internal structure [of power and governance] and spiritual identity'.[5] This side of the Nevskii cult made a strong comeback during the Stalinist period and then Putinist Russia when relations between it and the West began to deteriorate. In 2016 Sergei Lavrov, Putin's long-serving foreign minister, in his summary of Russian foreign policy noted that Nevskii 'chose a temporary submission to the religiously tolerant [Mongol] rulers of the Golden Horde in order to protect the right of Russians to have and determine their own fate in the face of the European West that sought to subdue completely Russian lands and deprive them of their identity'.[6]

From the end of the fifteenth century emerged a state ideology and concept of nativist identity founded on the idea that the strength of Russia was tied to its religious superiority, having been chosen by God to be the site of the Third Rome. Integral to these discourses was the clerical view that Russia's strength and survival was tied to this religious superiority, unsullied by cultural infection by the forms of Christianity in the West. Given these conceptions of the country's cultural borders, tension existed over the kind of relations the state should have with the West. This tension can be seen in competing understandings of the causes of the collapse of the Byzantine Empire at the hands of the Muslim Ottomans. The clerical position was clear. Metropolitan Fillip in 1471 explained that the Ottomans conquered Byzantium because 'the Greeks ruled, the Greeks found glory in submissiveness, they united with Rome and now they are serving the Turks'.[7] He, among others, argued that Constantinople, by signing the Act of Union with the Papacy in 1439 and thereby accepting Rome's superiority in ecclesiastical matters in the hope of obtaining Western help in its struggle with the Ottomans, had betrayed the principles of authentic Christian doctrines. God punished it by allowing its defeat at the hands of Muslims. Russia, having rejected the union, was rewarded for its adherence to Orthodoxy by God who made Moscow the Third Rome.[8] The Byzantine Empire had turned to the West and thus collapsed. Russia had to avoid such a fate by shunning it.

Other pre-Petrine narratives had a more nuanced approach towards the place of the West in Russia's historical cosmology. They also sought to provide Russia a place in imperial antiquity in light of Russia's lack of an ancient imperial civilization. These narratives, multidimensional and at times contradictory, claimed a unique link with the West, sought the West's recognition of Russia's status as a great power equal to that of the West's other great powers while underlining Russia's religious, cultural and moral superiority to the West. An important early attempt in this regard was *The Tale of the Princes of Vladimir* and the supposed familial link between Prus, the brother of the Roman emperor, Augustus, and Russian monarchs. It was also claimed that the Byzantine emperor Constantine IX Monomakh (r.1042–55) had given his coronation regalia to his distant descendant, Grand Prince Vladimir Monomakh (r.1113–25), which was subsequently used by all Russian monarchs. In this way, this work asserted that Muscovite and then all-Russian monarchs were religious and political successors to the Byzantine Empire and thus a link existed between Russia and Rome.[9] Subsequently, Ivan IV at his coronation claimed for himself and his polity the heritage and prestige of the Byzantine Empire, along with that of Kievan Rus and the right to unify all Russian lands that had been split apart by the Mongol-Tatar invasion and occupation. He also introduced a genealogical table that linked his lineage with Roman Caesars through Rurik (r.862–79) the founder of the first dynasty to rule Novogorod and Kieven Rus at a time when many Russian princes claimed descendancy from Rurik.[10] These narratives remained parts of state narratives and works, such as *Gosudarev Rodoslovets* (1555) and *Steppenaia Kniga* (1547) until the end of the reign of Aleksei I (1645–76).

During this same period, Russia also tried to debunk the idea that she had obtained Christianity second-handedly via Rome and Byzantium. Ivan IV cited this historiographical approach in his debates with the counter-reformationist Jesuit Antonio Possivino, a papal envoy in Moscow seeking the re-unification of Orthodoxy with Catholicism under papal leadership and Catholic-Orthodox unity to struggle against the Ottoman Empire. Possivino urged the tsar to follow the lead of Greek-Byzantine Orthodoxy which had accepted this leadership in 1439 at the Council of Florence. Responding to this argument, Ivan rejected both the example of Greek-Byzantine Orthodoxy and its concessions to the pope.

> We don't believe in those Greeks. We received the Christian faith at the beginning of Christianity when Andrew, the apostle Peter's brother, came to this area on his way to Rome. Thus, we in Moscow obtained the Christian faith at the same time you did in Italy and since then we have faultlessly followed it.[11]

At the same time, the conception of Moscow as the Third Rome, protecting Christian authenticity, claimed ultimate Russian superiority to the West given religious and moral standards. Feodisi Pecherskii, a prolific Orthodox monk, summing up early opinions of Catholics wrote to Prince Iziaslavii that they 'are mistaken in faith and lead morally impure lives'.[12] During the eleventh to fifteenth centuries a majority of ecclesiastical pieces in Russia stressed that paradise was in the Russian East and hell was situated in the West.[13] These narratives played an important role in setting the intellectual and ideational conditions for the discourses of Romanov Occidentalism, both pro-West and anti-West.

In the Time of Troubles, Sigismund, entertaining geopolitical aspirations that corresponded with the idea of the spread of Catholicism, in reality sought the Russian throne for himself. In 1610 Polish and Lithuanian forces occupied Moscow. The possibility of a Catholic monarch sitting on the Russian throne unified Russia's forces under the leadership of Patriarch Hergomen. By 1612 Moscow was in Russian hands. The following year *Zemskii Sobor*, a consultative council made up of landowning nobles, elected Mikhail Romanov (r.1613–45) tsar. An official promise was proclaimed: 'In the future the great state of Russia will never be without a government and Orthodoxy will never be threatened and destroyed by Catholics and Lutherans'.[14] Henceforth official historiography portrayed the dynasty's establishment as the triumphant final chapter in Russia's struggle against Western threats to the country's religious, cultural and geopolitical borders.

During Mikhail's reign, contacts between Russians and Westerners were controlled while the number of foreign cultural and religious symbols decreased. The patriarch Filaret (r.1619–34), who was Mikhail's father, aggressively pursued protection of Orthodox authenticity. In 1610 the Poles had thrown him in prison where he remained for eight years. Returning to Moscow in 1619 after the signing of a peace treaty between Russia and Poland he became patriarch. In 1633 he set up a *nemetskaiia sloboda*, an enclosed area in Moscow in which all foreigners residing in the capital had to live while Mikhail ordered the destruction of Lutheran churches, forbade Russians from wearing Western clothes and foreigners from employing Russians. Mikhail expelled foreign merchants, except those living in the far-off port Archangelsk where they played a vital role in trade. In 1634 he banned the use of tobacco which the clergy viewed as a symbol of Western cultural influence and decadence. Lastly, non-Orthodox individuals, Russian subjects as well as foreigners, were forbidden from entering state service. Simultaneously, urban upper classes were increasingly curious about Western mores and material culture.[15]

During the reign of Tsar Aleksei (r.1645–76) the state's approach to the West was contradictory and inconsistent, reflecting the varied pressures it faced, as well as Aleksei's character. On the one hand, it increasingly hired Western artisans, merchants and specialists while Aleksei allowed Western music and theatre to be performed and had his agents abroad obtain for him items, such as scientific instruments and music boxes, which 'were difficult to link with the ideal of Orthodox piety'.[16] He also arranged for the delivery of Western newspapers to the capital and established a regular postal service with the West via Riga. On the other hand, came protests about Westerners. 'The clergy bombarded the state with complaints about the activities of Protestant churches in the center of the capital where they could be found next to Orthodox places of worship'.[17] The merchant middle class complained about the difficulties they had in competing with wealthy Western merchants while the middle and upper classes grumbled that Westerners were using their wealth to buy the best property in Moscow and thus driving native Russians from these areas. From the army came complaints about foreign specialists while nobles refused to serve under the command of Westerners on government hire. Even Aleksei himself reaffirmed the importance of protecting the country's cultural borders.

The state acted. In central Moscow it destroyed Protestant churches (they were rebuilt in the suburbs) and, after a great fire in 1652, banned foreigners from buying land and homes. They were again forced to live in *nemetskaiia sloboda*. Westerners were also banned from engaging in retail trade. A 1675 decree again forbade Russians 'to imitate the clothes of Westerners and to wear short hair' as they did.[18] Clerics called those 'who wear the heretical clothes of these foreign unbelievers from head to toe' sinners. Western clothing was considered an attack on Orthodox ideas of modesty and propriety. In 1672 the government banned books in 'Catholic' languages, Polish and Latin.[19] Moreover, 'travel abroad required the permission of the tsar and patriarch, who issued warnings of the dangers of corruption'.[20] Nonetheless, signs of creeping Occidentosis continued to emerge, provoking discontent and concern. Simon Medvedev (1641–91), a well-known publicist, criticizing the spread of aspects of Western culture warned: 'The cause of popular revolts and rebellions is the borrowing of foreign customs, norms, ranks and titles'.[21]

This negative reaction was not a new phenomenon. Already by the sixteenth century during Vasilii III's reign the increasing numbers of Westerners, the growth of the elite's interest in the mores, fashion and culture of the polities to the West of Russia and a sensed decline in personal morality had started to worry many within the religious-political elite. The clergy were the first to express this worry. The idea of Moscow as the Third Rome, propagated by Filofei in his famous letter to Vasilii III, is commonly regarded as a doctrine for Russia's national identity and foreign policy according to which Russia had a historical sacred duty to defend Orthodoxy in the face of Western Catholicism and then Protestantism. This interpretation is true to a significant extent. However, Filofei's use of this idea also had a domestic political function. Worried by these emerging tendencies, he was warning Vasilii that if moral and cultural Occidentosis infected Russian Orthodoxy God's wrath could be severe given the divine choice of Moscow as the Third Rome.[22] This idea, popular with the ordinary people, was sporadically and cautiously used by the pre-Petrine state since it gave the Church the right to make judgements on and interfere in not just foreign policy but also domestic affairs and particularly the issue of reform.

Another cause of tension between state and church before the launching of Romanov Occidentalism was land, which played a decisive role in their power relationship. The state from the time of Ivan III, short of revenue, maintained its newly established standing army by giving land to those serving. It thus needed increasing amounts of it.[23] Ivan III succeeded in secularizing some church lands. His successor, Ivan IV at the Stoglav Church Council (1551), failed to expand state control of church lands, but the Church was now forbidden to enlarge its land holdings without monarchical permission. Patriarch Filaret expanded greatly the church's political and economic power. On the one hand, thanks to his decisive influence on his son he undermined the practice of *symphonia*, inherited from Byzantium, according to which the state and clergy, while acting in symphony with each other to defend Orthodoxy, were to act only in their own domains, not interfere in the affairs of the other and eschew attempts to dominate the other. On the other hand, he established a vast network of lands, making the Church the largest landowner after the state and established patriarchal administrative, financial and judicial chancelleries to govern these properties. In short, 'Under Patriarch Filaret, who was the defacto ruler of Muscovy from 1619 until his death in 1633, the Orthodox Church and the state itself fused into something of a last bastion of "true Orthodoxy."'[24] Importantly, he had set a precedent that some of his successors sought to follow and Peter I sought to overturn.

Under Aleksei this tension increased. Patriarch Nikon (r.1652–66) initially enjoyed strong relations with the monarch. However, he began to interfere gradually in state affairs and ignore monarchical prerogatives in church matters. In 1654 Aleksei, setting off on a military campaign against the Poles in Ukraine that ultimately lasted about thirty months, charged Nikon with governing the state. The patriarch's active and firm rule provoked the opposition of the nobility and strengthened the tsar's wariness of him. Upon Aleksei's return to Moscow, Nikon relinquished these secular responsibilities. However, he still sought to interfere in state matters that stoked opposition to him and the tsar's concerns about his ultimate aims. Nikon also had the annoying habit of interfering in the people's personal sphere, exhibiting a vigilance against signs of Occidentosis and behaviour he considered to be in contradiction with Orthodoxy. For example, in 1653, having decided that hunting was an Orthodox sin, he wrote to the monarch ordering him and the elite to 'forgo forever the pleasure of hunting' and 'to remove all wild animals, dogs and everything relating to hunting'.[25] This was a heavy blow for Aleksei who was an ardent hunter.

The issue that exercised a decisive influence on their relationship and on that between the state and the clergy was Aleksei's codification of the empire's laws in 1649 which included provisions for the establishment of a state institution charged with managing clerical and church properties and finances, except those belonging to the patriarchy. The measures did not stop there, to the horror of the clergy. The clergy and those souls living on such properties would be subject to the state judicial system whose powers would supersede clerical-run courts. Not surprisingly, Nikon, along with the bulk of the clergy, opposed these moves. A late tsarist-era history textbook, stressing the view of Romanov Occidentalism, argued: 'The clergy was outraged' because it 'was not satisfied' with the power it already enjoyed and wished for more. Nikon 'energetically opposed these reforms and complained to the tsar, stressing that the independence of the clergy' must not be touched.[26]

This tension reached a peak in 1658. Nikon, piqued by Aleksei's brewing discontent with him, abandoned the patriarchy and went to a monastery outside of Moscow expecting the tsar to backdown and request his return. It never happened. Nikon, in self-imposed internal exile but still officially patriarch, in a letter dating from 1662, again attacked these reforms:

> The clergy is a more honored and higher authority than the state. ... The clergy's throne was erected in heaven. ... The tsar is subordinate to the prelate as the body is to the spirit. Tsarist authority resides in the sword that must be used against Orthodoxy's enemies. If the prelates and clergy demand that he defend them from all unrighteousness and violence, then the civil must obey the spiritual.[27]

Finally, on 1 December 1666 a Church Council was convened to try Nikon. In attendance were not only the patriarchs of Antioch and Alexandria but also Aleksei, who delivered a tearful but scathing attack on him. Convicted of abandoning his post, insulting the monarch and inciting rebellion, he was demoted and exiled to a far-off monastery. Nikon with his behaviour and policies had lost the support of not only the tsar and the nobility but also leading clerical figures.

In January 1667 Aleksei, fresh from his victory over Nikon, introduced to the Council the question of the relationship between the state and the clergy. It was announced that the tsar was supreme in civil matters and the patriarch in church affairs. Clerical support of Aleksei in his confrontation with Nikon, however, did not mean clerical opposition to Nikon's stance in regard to those provisions accompanying the codification of law. Metropolitans Pavel of Krutitsi and Ilarion of Ryzan led strong opposition to them. Aleksei backed down and abolished the Department of Church and Monastery Affairs. 'The rebellion of Ilarion and Pavel … showed how stubbornly the clergy would hold onto its rights'.[28] According to the Petrine interpretation of events: 'From that time clerical authorities could judge their own clerics for any crime, even for murder, robbery, and other serious crimes'.[29] In addition, while this Church Council reiterated the tsar's supremacy in secular affairs, it also gave the patriarch the right to rebuke him if he deviated towards heresy as defined by him.[30] The Petrine interpretation stressed: 'Although the clergy seemingly sought isolation and its detachment from lay society, it nonetheless tried to interfere in affairs not touching on the church'.[31] Consequently, during Aleksei's reign, the tension between state and church increased as the state contemplated implementation of aspects of Westernization.[32]

However, the focus on creeping Occidentosis tells only one part of the overall story of fears concerning the loss of identity. Nikon, at the outset of his patriarchy, with Aleksei's support, sought reforms that would return church practices and rituals to their 'authentic' Greek roots and purge distorted 'Russian' elements in the hope of strengthening claims of the Russian Orthodox Church to the position as head of the universal Orthodox Church. Known as the Nikonian reforms, they led to the great schism and are a fitting example of the complications and tensions involved in implementing changes touching on Orthodoxy and elements popularly conceived as part of authentic identity.

The opponents of the Nikonian reforms, led by Archpriest Avvakum, became known as the Old Believers who framed the position subsequently taken by Slavophiles and later Russian conservatives that was 'an indistinguishable blend of opposition to the liturgical reforms, foreign cultural influence, bureaucratic centralism, and social injustice'.[33] Avvakum, calling for the abandonment of these reforms, petitioned the tsar 'to maintain and strengthen his traditional Rus' identity and use his native language: "After all, you are Russian, not a Greek. Speak your native language; do not demean it in church, in your home, or in anything you say."'[34] Petrine pro-West Occidentalism, in response, argued, in the words of a tsarist-era textbook: 'The opposition to Nikon's reforms showed that even the smallest change in church ways already established in Rus' would be portrayed as betrayal of the Orthodox faith itself'.[35] In other words, conceptions of the country's cultural borders had become very rigid, unable even to accept changes that could make Russia the leader of the universal Orthodox Church. In 1682 Avvakum was burnt at the stake for his leadership role in the rebellion against these reforms. Nonetheless, the Old Believers survived this state offensive and increased in number until the demise of the imperial state. Importantly, the experience of Nikon's reforms made a strong impression on Peter's mind.

In sum, the pre-Petrine state was being pulled in two opposing directions. On the one hand, the defence and expansion of the empire's geopolitical borders, along with growing interest among the elite in Western culture, were pushing it in the direction of Westernization. On the other hand, clerical and lay conservatives believed that defence of the country's cultural borders in the face of Western cultural and moral influence was the key to protecting the country's geopolitical borders. In this context, the state implemented piecemeal institutional, educational, military and economic reforms that constituted an embryonic practical process of Westernization. Although aspects of these reforms provoked opposition within the clergy and population, no attempts at Occidentalism, in other words, radical restructuring of popular conceptions of identity and historiography, were made. Yet, in the face of continuing geopolitical challenges posed by the West's great powers and the Ottoman Empire, members of the Russian elite as well as the West increasingly recognized Russian backwardness vis-à-vis the West. In 1670 the German philosopher Gottfried Leibniz, echoing a common belief in Western Europe, predicted that in the future backward Russia would become a colony of Sweden, the hegemon of northern Europe.[36]

Romanov Occidentalism

Peter I, rejecting Krizhanich's views mentioned earlier, argued that the old but distorted Russian identity had to be quickly smashed and its culture fundamentally changed. He initiated the practical process of Westernization and justified it with pro-West Occidentalism. Similar to initial Pahlavi Occidentalism, it had three policy trajectories: (1) anticlericalism; (2) changes in historiography and conceptions of authenticity of native culture and identity that justified this anticlericalism, the monarchy's power and the Romanov cultural revolution; and (3) a cultural revolution designed to create a *homo Romanovicus* who epitomized the key features of Romanov Russian self-representation. These elements underpinned Romanov conceptions of Russian identity and parts of the state's discourse of power and modernization from Peter I's reign to the first shift towards anti-West Occidentalism during Nicholas I's reign (r.1825–55).

Anticlericalism and institutional revolution

Peter I argued that the Byzantine Empire collapsed because it placed too much emphasis on spiritual rituals and the afterlife and too little on the elements needed to sustain a strong army and government. Russia had to avoid this fate. He placed the clerical interpretation of the cause of the occupation of the Second Rome on its head. Years later in private Peter articulated his feelings: 'The bearded ones [monks and priests] are the root of much evil. My father had to deal with one [Nikon] while I with thousands. I want for the common good and yet they are always opposing me'.[37]

Peter's anticlericalism should not be mistaken for antireligious tendencies. He sought to separate religious high culture and doctrine determined by the clergy from Orthodoxy ethics and spirituality in order to save Orthodoxy from what he considered the baleful influence of reactionary, parochial and ignorant clerics. Peter did not see any contradiction between religious identity and ethics and the transformations he sought to implement. The idea that he did not have a significant degree of piety and belief in God is also mistaken. Yet he, similar to Maxim Grek and Malkom Khan, accepted the need to change as the world's conditions evolved.

Peter's carousing with Westerners and their increasing numbers appalled the clergy and conservative elements to the same extent that their opposition to change and parochialism appalled Peter. In 1689-90 Patriarch Joachim expanded the restrictions on foreigners, which included forcing them once again to live in *nemetskaiia sloboda*. His testament stated: 'Our sovereigns should never allow our Orthodox Christians of our kingdom to have close, friendly relations with the heretics and the heterodox, with the Latins, with the Lutherans, with the Calvinists, and the Tatars who don't believe in God'.[38] Some argue that at the time many clerics were not this radical and would have supported a middle path between Romanov Occidentalism and the position of Joachim and his successor Adrian.[39] However, the obscurantism and parochialism of leading Orthodox clerics not only convinced Peter and his successors of the need to contain the clerics but also provided the Romanov state with justifications for Occidentalism and attacks on clerical economic and political interests.

Peter explained the reasons for his moves against church institutions:

> Among the many cases and changes in the performance of our God given power is our people's improvement. ... Having looked at the clerical ranks and seeing in them many faults and great poverty in their affairs, we now have it on our conscience ... that having enacted reforms in the military and civil fields, we neglected the clerical ranks.

In order to face God, he claimed, he was obliged 'to take on the case of reform of the clergy' whose parochial interests must not overshadow the people's and state's welfare.[40] Peter emphasized the people's and state's welfare as the pillar of his rule that overshadowed limited clerical interests. Archbishop Feofan Prokopovich (1681-1736), one of the few leading clerics supportive of Peter, succinctly made the case for change. He stressed that the emperor's deeds held a higher priority than his prayers and if this duty was not fulfilled his prayers would be 'nothing other than sinful'.[41] He justified Peter's Occidentalizing reforms and the supremacy of the state's interests over those of the clergy by claiming that 'no kingdom ever existed that having been under clerical control did not fall'.[42] This was a significant change in the monarchical cosmology.

Peter abolished patriarchal courts and institutionalized the siphoning of church income from its lands to the state in a move common across Europe and beyond as monarchs and states eyed ecclesiastical wealth with impatience and determination to get hold of it. The monarch privately expressed another justification for the attack on church revenue:

> Since ancient times monastic income should have been used for God's affairs and to the state's benefit, and not for parasites and spongers. ... Our clerics have become fat. The gate to heaven is passed due to faith, prayer, and fasting. For them I will pave the road to paradise with water and bread, but not with wine and caviar.[43]

Although Patriarch Adrian supported the idea of a limited division of temporal and religious power, he stressed: 'Genuine pastors do not subordinate themselves to strong men nor do they exhibit shame before rich men, but must denounce, beseech, and censure those who live badly. ... All Orthodox Christians are my sheep and know me and must obey my voice'.[44] In reality he was placing the Orthodox patriarchy above the state and the emperor. His successor Metropolitan Stefan Iavorskii on 17 March 1712 delivered a sermon expressing dissatisfaction with the trends within Petrine Occidentalism. He attacked those who did not follow Orthodox practices and rituals, 'condemning in particular those who did not follow all Orthodox fasts, including implicitly Peter himself, and those who did not keep their wives modestly dressed and out of view'.[45]

The emperor, given increasing clerical opposition and his belief in the efficacy of his transformations and in state supremacy, in 1721 made the church a state-run bureaucratic department, named the Holy Synod, headed by a secular figure appointed by the monarch. He wrote in the *Dukhovnii Reglament* that announced its establishment: 'What is great is that the Holy Synod does not threaten the country with rebellion and confusion, the likes of which come from a single clerical leader since the simple people don't know how clerical power differs from the autocracy'. This body would 'prevent division between the state and the church and perfidious individuals from abusing the people's feelings and opposing the state'.[46] No longer could a patriarch assert, as did Jochim, that 'the tsar must be lower than the prelate and obedient to him, for ... the clergy are the chosen people, anointed by the Holy Ghost'.[47] In this respect Romanov Russia differed from Pahlavi Iran. For example, Shi'ism did not have an institutional quasi-monarchical figure as its head. Briefly put, the Pahlavis, while holding similar sentiments, either could not or did not want to bring the clerical structure and hierarchy into the state. The Romanov state by taking this step ensured that organized opposition to it, either during the reigns of Peter I or Nicholas II, would not come from the clerical class. In Iran the opposite was true. Peter in the *Dukhovnii Reglament* also addressed the charges of heresy being thrown at him and the thought behind his Occidentalism:

> Heresy ... was born not out of study [of Western ways and technology] but from poor understandings and viewpoints of Holy Scripture that grew and strengthened due to malice and pride which did not allow them [those claiming that heresy was born out of study] to change their foolish opinions'.[48]

Catherine II (r.1762–96), who considered herself a student of the Enlightenment, considered the church and its clergy the source of mystical fanaticism and backward superstitions that prevented progress and the construction of *homo Romanovicus*, the new–old person representing the return to Russia's true ancient and claimed European roots. She worked to deprive the clergy of those class privileges that had survived Peter's onslaught. Using justifications provided by pro-West Occidentalism she continued the Petrine offensive by nationalizing church lands. She dealt severely with clerical opposition to these moves, such as that of Metropolitan Arsenius of Rostov and Yaroslavl, whom she had defrocked and sent to distant internal exile. The empress was outraged by reports he had sent to the Holy Synod condemning in provocative language this nationalization of land and comparing Catherine to Judas and the Roman emperor Julian, also known as Julian the Apostate, who had sought to downgrade Christianity, resurrect traditional Roman religious rituals and practices and promote Neoplatonic Hellenism.

The discourses of anticlericalism of Romanov Occidentalism provided the political and ideological means to end the power tension between church and state and establish monarchical supremacy over clerical institutions. The ultimate goal was state determination of the parameters of high culture and identity, steps considered essential for the strengthening of the state and its implementation of reform. At the same time, it weakened the long-standing legitimating liturgical elements of the monarchical cosmology. The consequent ideological vacuum was to be filled by the historiographical discourses of Occidentalism and promises of development to sustain the country's status as a great imperial power.

Importantly, in this discussion of Romanov and Pahlavi Occidentalism the issue of clerical power needs to be separated from that of spiritual power. In other words, the relationship between monarchical and clerical power which overlaps with but is not the same as the relationship between spiritual and secular power because the monarchy in premodern polities and in Russia and Iran before the implementation of pro-West Occidentalism was itself sacred. In the era of pro-West Occidentalism the monarchy sought to expand its spiritual attractiveness and power as it effectively reduced clerical power.

Historiographical revolution

The historiographical paradigm that emerged piecemeal during the reigns of Peter I and Catherine II was implicitly based on the idea that Russians enjoyed unique racial-cultural relations with west Europeans from whom they had culturally fallen behind due to contingent historical events and domestic self-interested reactionaries, the clergy and their supporters. It was argued that centuries of Mongol-Turkic rule had thrown the country from the universal path that would be first travelled by Russia's west-European cousins. Russia needed to return to this lost authenticity in order to go forward and acquire Western forms of power.

Peter, preferring practical matters and action, did not fancy himself a philosopher-king. By contrast, Catherine II considered herself an intellectual and corresponded with Enlightenment thinkers, such as Voltaire, Diderot and Friedrich Grimm. She played a key role in the systematization of Occidentalism and in making explicit these claims of a racial–cultural link with west Europeans. Although Peter did not make explicit statements about a racial link between Russians and west Europeans, his belief in it can be deduced by general statements made by him and his closest advisors and specific policies. For example, in private remarks to nobles, recorded by Frederich Weber, Hanover's representative to Russia, the emperor revealed his understanding of historical processes and implicitly his belief in this link:

> Historians suggest that the cradle of all knowledge is Greece from where over time it was expelled and moved to Italy [Rome]. It was spreading to the rest of Europe

when it was stopped at our borders by the ignorance of our ancestors and thus did not go beyond Poland. ... The circulation of knowledge and science I have just mentioned I equate with the circulation of blood in the human body. It seems to me that with time this science and knowledge will move on from their present location in England, France, and German lands and reside with us for several centuries. Then they will return to their birthplace – Greece.[49]

Peter's understanding was that progress and power that existed at the time in the West were universal and circulatory and therefore no religious or political obstacles to achieving them should exist. Yet, the universal body in which they circulated was made of the different polities and peoples of the white Christian world. The Muslim East, as well as the Far East, was, to use a modern term, Orientalized, since it had greatly fallen behind Europe militarily, economically and technologically.

Peter's view in regard to Russia's link with Europe is also seen in state-sponsored literature. He determined that the political and practical aspects of reform were dependent on transformations in culture and world view that could be achieved through education and books. Consequently, this period witnessed a dramatic increase in the number of books translated from west-European languages and the overall number of books published. Not surprisingly 'publishing was yet another area of Petrine activity where everything had to be done from above: policy was shaped by the tsar's priorities'.[50] The emperor examined all translations and 'almost all books to be published in Russian passed through his hands'.[51] Sometimes, he sat at the desks of editors and authors, reviewing works and making contributions. Therefore, 'the basic characteristic of publishing during the Petrine period was that it was dedicated completely to the service of reforming the country'.[52] Indigenous books were to serve the ideological–political requirements of Petrine Occidentalism while translations were to serve the practical technological requirements of Westernization.

While Peter took great interest in works commemorating and justifying aspects of his foreign or domestic policies, such as *Discourse on the Just Causes of the War between Sweden and Russia* by Peter Shafirov (1717), he also paid attention to more popular genres able to penetrate the middle and lower-middle classes with his vision. The most important and popular of these genres were adventure warrior stories, the majority of which before the Petrine era were translations from west-European languages. The Petrine government ensured that the bulk of such works became Russian. Perhaps the best example in this regard is *The Story of the Russian Sailor Vasilii*, which was printed in large numbers and found popularity among the literate population.[53]

This piece epitomized the vision behind Occidentalism. The choice of a sailor as its protagonist underlined Peter's fascination with and founding of the navy and his policy of sending Russians abroad to study subjects vital for Westernization. Vasilii, an early example of *homo Romanovicus*, having discarded religious superstitions and driven by strong personal initiative and intelligence, decides to serve the state in the navy and thus dedicate his education to it. The young sailor describes his own travels in Russia as he heads towards Western Europe. St. Petersburg, the west-Europeanized city established by Peter that replaced Moscow as the empire's capital, and the positive changes of the Petrine period are paraded in order to provoke feelings of national pride and unity. He then chronicles his travels in Western Europe, providing a firsthand view of its cultural and technical centres. Peter's vision of Russia's place within the world civilizational order is presented in this work. The story begins by stating that Vasilii's family lives 'in the Russia of Europe'. Vasilii, having finished his studies abroad, begins his return to 'Russia of Europe'.[54] This was the first time that Russia had been labelled in this manner, which underlined the claim of a racial–cultural link with the West.

To this dynamic Prokopovich contributed greatly in his writings and speeches. In a major speech in 1718 he compared Russia with contemporaneous and ancient civilizations and polities, placing her within an international context in order to undermine the idea of positive Russian cultural and historical disconnectedness from Western Europe. Peter was glorified as a European monarch of a European country, albeit one that had temporarily fallen culturally behind.[55] By propagating such a belief he was implicitly arguing that Peter's establishment of a centralized absolutist and intrusive state along the lines of the 'enlightened' absolutist states of Western Europe symbolized an important step in Russia's return to Europe. He also placed Peter in the context of classical antiquity, namely imperial Rome and Ancient Christian Rome, substituting 'Orthodox Tsar' with 'Christian monarch' and the Roman title 'imperator'. In 1721 Peter officially replaced the Russian word 'tsar' with this title.

Prokopovich by propagating this position gave voice to an important element of Petrine Occidentalism that assimilated and appropriated into state representations of Russian identity the first 'imperial' Rome and the second universal Christian Rome. The goals were the weakening of the idea of Moscow as the Third Rome, the dispelling of the idea of culturally essentialized opposition between Russian identity and the West and its forms of Christianity, and the unification of Russia's past and present with that of Europe. Thus, conceptions of the country's cultural borders were to be expanded on the basis of the idea of an all-encompassing European Christian identity and not limited by emphasis on Orthodoxy. In line with this was the practice of Peter's successors, up to and including Alexander I (r.1801–25), of representing and portraying themselves in Western clothing or Roman imperial settings. Peter himself demanded and patronized the propagation of such Roman symbols and his inclusion in them.[56]

Dmitri Likhachev (1906–99), the widely respected Russian academic and specialist of Medieval Russia, noted:

> The widespread notion that Peter 'turned' Russia onto the European path of development is very inaccurate. The European character of Russia was formed out of its conversion to Christianity (which was much more important for culture) and not out of Peter's reforms. Russia's ties with Europe were never completely severed, although they grew weak from the thirteenth to the fifteenth centuries, when Russia was under the power of the Golden Horde ... Peter ... did not establish but continued ties with Europe, which had already been strengthened by his father Tsar Aleksei Mikhailovich.[57]

Before him the British diplomat Lord Frederic Hamilton who served in St. Petersburg towards the end of the nineteenth century provided an alternative view popular in the

West and whose fundamental meaning was used by Slavophiles and those opposing Peter's pro-West Occidentalism.

> I cannot help thinking that Peter the Great was one of the worst enemies of his own country. Instead of allowing Russia to develop naturally on lines suited to the racial instincts of her people, he attempted to run the whole country into a West European mould, and to superimpose on it a veneer imported from the France of Louis Quatorze ... it was a foregone failure. It might stand for a time; its ultimate doom was certain.[58]

These two quotes show the complexity of Russia's relationship with the West and the looseness with which race and religion were and can be defined in discussing Russia's relationship with the Occident.

Elizabeth I (r.1741–62), Peter's daughter, modified Occidentalism by adding 'the cult of Peter the Great ... (which) became a major pillar in the ideology of the Russian autocracy'.[59] The example of Peter, implementing radical changes so that Russia could catch up with her west-European cousins, solidified the justification for autocracy rooted in 'enlightened despotism'. Elizabeth and her successor, Catherine II, portrayed themselves as the champion and defender of the Petrine cause, serving as a symbol of 'Western culture and taste. ... These empresses employed Western tastes and manners as signs of imperial rule'.[60] During Elizabeth's reign Petrine institutions were reinvigorated and cultural and intellectual Occidentalism gained momentum, with the empress and Court taking the lead. She also ensured that Orthodoxy and the clergy remained within the boundaries established by Peter, although she was much more religious than her father.

Catherine II further institutionalized the cult of Peter, perhaps best symbolized by her commissioning of the Bronze Horseman, a large equestrian statue of her predecessor that stands in St. Petersburg's Senate Square. In 1766 she fine-tuned Occidentalism's framework by explicitly articulating the claim of Russia's racial–cultural link with polities and peoples to the West of Russia.

> Russia is a European country and the evidence for this is the following. The changes in Russia undertaken by Peter the Great enjoyed great success since the mores existing at that time did not at all correspond to our climate and environment. They had been brought to us by a mixture of different peoples and conquests by foreign countries. Peter I inculcated a European people with European mores and customs with an easiness he himself did not expect.[61]

The empress was arguing that the Mongol Yoke had ripped Russia from the orbit of its European cousins and thrown it from their common historical path. Four years later she underlined, perhaps unwittingly, the challenge Russia continues to face in regard to the place of the West in conceptions of its national identity. In 1768 Abbé Chappe d'Auteroche published his *Voyage en Sibérie* in which he stressed that Russia suffered from a deep and wide-ranging backwardness in comparison with west-European countries and from an intellectual laziness that had resulted in blind imitation of the culture and behaviour of Westerners.⁶² This work outraged Catherine for its message that Russia and Russians were not European. In a response whose length could have constituted a book, Catherine argued that Russia was simultaneously unique and part of the family of Western Europe.⁶³ The problem was where to draw the borders of this uniqueness and similarity as conditions in Russia and the West changed.

During Catherine II's reign Occidentalism was more conceptually pronounced than before in state propaganda, such as poetry, odes, epics and the visual arts. A good example is the works of Vasilii Petrovich Petrov, a favourite of Catherine who was her court poet and personal reader. His officially sponsored works stressed that 'Russians are genuine Europeans, the inheritors of Rome and its imperial glory'.⁶⁴ Continuing wars with the Ottoman Empire during her reign enriched Occidentalism's racial-cultural dynamics by providing opportunities to place Russia in the context of ancient historical events associated with the birthplaces of Western civilization, ancient Greece and imperial Rome. Russia's victories over the Ottoman Empire were situated in the narrative of Europe's struggles against barbarians and darkness dating from the Persians in the days of ancient Greece to the threat of Islam and the Ottomans. In other words, Romanov Occidentalism under Catherine II created new–old heroes, replacing Rome and Greece with Russia. This approach continued into the nineteenth century. It is seen in the propaganda and military songs that accompanied the Russian-Iranian Wars (1804–13) and Russian-Ottoman War of 1828–9.⁶⁵

State discourses also began to flirt with emerging Aryanism to prove its racial link with Western Europe. Imperial propaganda propagated the belief that Crimea was a starting point of the Aryan race. Thus, Russia's acquisition of it at the end of the eighteenth century was a return to one of the empire's points of racial–cultural origin. Moreover, with the annexation of Crimea, Russia claimed a direct link to ancient Greece, the cradle of west-European civilization and therefore primordial membership to the west-European club.⁶⁶ To institutionalize this discourse, Catherine in 1784, having just annexed the peninsula, constructed for herself a new title 'Tsaritsa of Tavricheskii (tauride in English) Cheronesus'. Cheronesus was the name of the first ancient Greek colony on the Crimean peninsula, situated close to today's Sevastopol, while the word 'tavrichiskii' (tauride) is the adjectival form of the Greek name for the entire peninsula, *Tavriia*, *Tavrika* and/or *Tavrida*. In the fifth century these areas became part of the Byzantine Empire. 'Therefore, this title was chosen to underline that the Russian empress became at the same time a "tsaritsa" of [ancient] Greek lands and with them a part of Byzantium. … Obtaining a part of the Roman-Byzantium heritage with the annexation of Crimea, the young Russian Empire obtained its own mythical-historical legitimacy'.⁶⁷ Importantly, while these discourses stressed a Russian link with ancient Greece and Rome via Byzantium, they also stressed Russia's other link with the West, Christianity. According to the medieval narrative dating from the twelfth century *Povest Vremmenikh Let* Grand Prince Vladimir accepted Christianity at Cheronesus in 988.

However, given the temporal differences mentioned earlier, the position of Aryanism in Russian state discourses did not have the same intensity or position it had in those of the Pahlavi state. In addition, Russia lacked the heritage of a great ancient imperial civilization that would have allowed it to claim contributions to the

West's 'universal' civilization. State discourses of the Catherinian period tried to fill this vacuum with attempts to portray Russia as the imperial and civilizational successor of ancient Rome and Greece. Iran, the great enemy of ancient Greece and imperial Rome, had no such need. Russia, in contrast, not constituting the founder of an ancient imperial civilization, had a local pagan culture when it accepted Christianity and became part of an already existing universal civilization.

Given these historical circumstances Alexander I, influenced by the thought of his grandmother, Catherine II, and enjoying a European liberal education under the guidance of the Swiss philosopher, Frederic Cesar La Harpe, expanded this Occidentalism. He strengthened the trajectory of previous discourses by emphasizing, more than Peter or Catherine did, the idea of 'universal Christian principles' that, similarly to the idea of a racial relationship with Western Europe, diluted the idea of Russia as the Third Rome. He sought to reunify Russians with their white west-European cousins through propagation of these universal Christian principles that were to override the feelings of a unique Russian spiritual and cultural identity that had emerged since the schism of 1054. The most prominent example of this was his creation of the Holy Alliance at the Congress of Vienna (1815), whose members included Catholic Habsburg Empire and Protestant Prussia. The Alliance's goal was defence of Christian values and their guardian, traditional monarchy, in the face of the possible contagion of godless revolutionary Jacobinism. Alexander I, embracing these universal Christian values, never showed 'any great personal devotion to the cause of fellow Orthodox Christians in the Balkans, or for that matter, any great interest or sympathy for the Orthodox religion in Russia'.[68]

In sum, Romanov Occidentalism removed the liturgical aspect of monarchical ideology. The legitimacy and justification of the autocratic power of Romanov monarchs was now based on pro-West Occidentalism that would create a *homo Romanovicus*. Through this cultural return to their west-European cousins with whom they shared common Christian links, Russians would attain the forms of power enjoyed by the West and maintain its position as a great power, a bedrock of the dynasty's legitimacy and self-perception.

Cultural revolution

An important dimension of Romanov historiography until the emergence of anti-West Occidentalism was its use of the West's Orientalized views of pre-Petrine Russia to justify Petrine anticlericalism and cultural revolution. Adam Olearius (1603–71) served as secretary to ambassadors sent to Russia and Iran by Frederick III, Duke of Holstein-Gottorp (r.1616–59), to establish trade relations. His description of Russia summarizes the 'orientalized' view of Westerners in regard to Russians dating from the pre-Petrine period.

> When one follows the spiritual characteristics, manners and customs and way of life of Russians, then without a doubt one must consider them barbarians. ... Russians don't love at all the free skills, craftsmanship, high culture and science

and have no desire to study them. And, you know, it is said there 'Good study of skills and crafts soften one's morals and does not allow one to run wild'. And therefore they remain crude and ignorant.[69]

Some two hundred years later a tsarist-era textbook taught:

> A Russian at that [pre-Petrine] time who zealously preserved all given to him by his ancestors in regard to faith, ways, and rituals, could not look indifferently at those bold spirits who abandoned old ways and adapted themselves to new skills and experiences. For example, Orthodox Russians could not watch without loathing at those who used tobacco. They believed that tobacco smell insults religious feelings, that smokers expressed irreverence to icons. With loathing Russians looked upon those who made up their mind to trim or shave their beards. ... A simple Russian thought, 'All that is holy is reflected in beards and those who cut the beard, also distort the figure of God and in the process become similar to a cat or dog'. ... Russian people of the seventeenth century shocked foreigners with their religiosity, strict following of all injunctions of the Church and all rituals of the Orthodox faith. Remaining completely uneducated, the Russian people of that time, or at least, the majority part of them, could not deeply and correctly fathom Christian teaching.

Instead of being interested in new knowledge, 'Orthodox Russians remained entangled in superstitions, fastidiously driving away everything that was incomprehensible to their infantile intellects, considering all "new things" to be satanic delusions and thus they gave no respite to those bold spirits who did not fear to produce scientific experience in such an inhospitable environment'.[70]

The first targets of Romanov Occidentalism in its creation of *homo Romanovicus* were the appearance and behaviour of Russians. The hope was that through imposition of west-European dress they would become west-European, be accepted by the West as civilized and eventually obtain west-European cultural behaviour. Concomitantly, dressing in this style was to convince Russians that they were culturally and racially Europeans. In 1698 Peter, who considered beards a symbol of Orthodox backwardness, ordered the elites to shave their beards and wear Western fashion. He stressed, 'I wish to transform civil fools into citizens ... so they without beards would appear at Court as Europeans'.[71] He also changed female dress, banning traditional clothes such as the *sarafan*, a large long white dress without sleeves that disguised the female figure, and traditional headgear. In place of them came slips, corsets and dresses, to the horror of religious conservatives who regarded these moves as attacks on Orthodox chastity and morality. This social conservatism outside of the Occidentalized sectors of urban society in regard to women continued until the empire's end. In this regard Lord Hamilton noted:

> To grasp the Russian mentality, it must be remembered that they are essentially Orientals. Russia is not the most Eastern outpost of Western civilization; it is the most Western outpost of the East. The Russians have all the qualities of the

> Oriental, his fatalism, his inertness, and, I fear, his innate tendency to pecuniary corruption. ... In a hundred little ways they show their origin: ... in their lack of sense of time; in the reluctance South Russians show in introducing strangers to the ladies of their household, the Oriental peeps out everywhere. ... Easterns they were, Easterns they remained, and that is the secret of Russia, they are not Europeans.[72]

Peter's moves infuriated the clerical leadership whose opposition to them helped bring about the establishment of the Holy Synod. Patriarch Adrian condemned the shaving of beards and the change in female clothing, citing the word and example of God and tradition. He warned Russians to reject all 'newly introduced foreign customs' and 'urged them to protect Orthodoxy from Latin and Lutheran heretics' who were 'enemies of God and defamers of the Church'.[73] In response, Peter became more determined in his belief that negotiation and compromise with clerics were not possible.

After these attacks came attempts to return behaviourally Russians to their west-European cousins. In 1702 Peter in his decree concerning the summoning of West Europeans to Russia argued the need to modernize 'the behavior of our subjects'.[74] Nineteenth-century tsarist textbooks stressed the Petrine view that given Russian detachment from their west-European cousins

> incivility, rudeness, arrogance, street fights, cursing, drunkenness and self-interest were the vices from which many of the citizens of the Muscovite state suffered, including representatives of the Church. These vices shocked foreigners coming to the Muscovite polity from the more cultured, more enlightened countries of Western Europe. Russia, having undertaken rapprochement with the Western world, went from a half-wild, half-Asiatic country, isolated from the enlightened cultural countries of Western Europe, to one that is *re-entering* (italics added) into the family of European nations. Today already a great part of the population of Russia enjoys the benefits of European enlightenment and culture. Judging by their external forms of life, prosperity, environment, comforts, clothing, enlightenment and societal morals, contemporary Russians have moved far ahead of their ancestors.[75]

This view had already been propagated during Peter's reign. Shafirov, incorporating these Orientalized views, in his *Discourses* contrasted Peter's achievements with what existed before his reign: 'Only several decades ago in *other* (italics added) European countries they discussed and wrote about the Russian people and state in the same way in which they did so in regard to Indians, Persians, and other peoples lacking relations with Europe, aside from some trade. Moreover, Russia not only did not have a part in the affairs in Europe, in peace or in war, but also was not included in the ranks of European peoples'.[76] The use of the word 'other' by this official Russian work and references to peoples, such as Persians and Indians, lacking in links with Europe underlines the claims of pro-West Occidentalism of Russia's racial–cultural relationship with Europe.

However, the attempts to return Russians to their west-European cousins provoked severe criticism of the forceful methods used. Towards the end of his reign Peter, frustrated with the epithet 'tyrant' being thrown at him in Western Europe and at home given this cultural revolution, fumed:

> I know that they [Westerners] consider me a strict monarch and tyrant. They are mistaken because they do not understand all the circumstances [of the country]. God knows my heart and conscience. I suffer for my people and wish only good for my homeland. Ignorance, stubbornness, [and] perfidy, have always conspired against me ever since I took the decision to introduce useful reform into the state and to transform savage manners. They, not I, are the tyrants.[77]

Catherine II, while believing in the importance of changing the appearance of Russians, felt that additional energy needed to be given to changes of mass culture and behaviour in order to construct *homo Romanovicus*. Early in her reign she ordered her minister of education, Count Ivan Betskii, to examine how the educational system could be improved to achieve this goal. In his report, which established the framework of the educational system, he argued that schools were to focus on the cultural and moral side of the creation of 'the new person': 'Education since Peter's time … was strictly speaking study and acquisition of European external forms which cloaked old ignorance. These forms alone did not produce the desired civilized European'.[78]

The Romanov monarchy had become secular in practice and Occidentalizing in theory with the goal of replacing the universalism of Orthodoxy with a Western one that was portrayed as a return to authenticity. With the passage of time and the emergence of constitutionalism and republicanism in Western Europe, expectations of constant reform to accommodate perceived socio-economic needs at the heart of Romanov Occidentalism engendered additional expectations among the growing educated classes of moves towards constitutional monarchy. By the middle of the nineteenth century the state found itself competing not only with this Western ideology but also forms of socialism.

Nicholas I and the West

State anti-West Occidentalism emerged during the reign of Nicholas I (r.1825–55). The immediate catalyst for this shift was the Decembrist Revolt (1825). On 26 December a group of leading members of the nobility, many of whom were officers who had served in the Napoleonic Wars and seen Western Europe, launched a rebellion in St. Petersburg in order to prevent Nicholas, Alexander I's brother, from ascending the throne and to establish some form of republic. However, it was also the result of several interrelated developments that emerged during Catherine II's rule and evolved during that of Alexander I.

Peter III (r.January–July 1762) abolished compulsory state service for the nobility which had been established by Peter I. Catherine II institutionalized this measure of Peter III and legalized private property. These steps led to the emergence of a propertied class, free from the burden of service and work, that enjoyed a significant degree of autonomy from the state. Educated and increasingly aware of political and intellectual conditions in Western Europe they came to discuss political and intellectual issues, the country's current situation and forms of its future development. Moreover, during her reign the class of non-noble educated officials and members of the liberal professions grew significantly. Together with the large minority of the nobility engaged in such activities they came to represent educated public opinion with which the state had to reckon increasingly from the late eighteenth century. In short, a salon and print culture similar in form to that of France during the reigns of Louis XV and Louis XVI emerged giving birth to the Russian Enlightenment.

One of the first issues to find expression was a crisis of identity among the educated aristocracy in reaction to pro-West Occidentalism. This crisis, underpinned by a sense of nostalgia for a seemingly lost authenticity, in various corners provoked a questioning of the historiography and cultural politics of Romanov Occidentalism. In 1788 Ivan Boltin, a leading state and military figure and historian, captured these growing feelings:

> When we started to send our youth abroad and gave them the assignment of being educated by foreigners, our morale changed: along with the anticipated enlightenment, in our hearts arrived new biases, new fears, new weaknesses, and wishes unknown to our ancestors. This weakened our love for our homeland. We forgot the old whilst failing to take on board the new.[79]

Princess Ekaterina Romanova Dashkova, head of the St. Petersburg Academy of Sciences and a prominent cultural figure who participated in the coup that brought Catherine II to power, expressed in a conversation with Prince Kauntiz of Austria these growing doubts about pro-West Occidentalism:

> If Peter had possessed the mind of a great lawmaker he would have understood that a good number of the innovations and reforms he introduced by force would have emerged and spread peacefully given time, contacts, trade and commerce and the example of other nations. Also, if he had the capacity to judge the good qualities of our ancestors, he would not have started to destroy the authenticity of their character with the introduction of foreign ways which seemed to him to be far superior to ours.[80]

Describing the 'ways' introduced by Peter as foreign, essentially as signs of Occidentosis, contradicted official views that propagated them as elements of Russian authenticity that pro-West Occidentalism was returning to the Russian people.

Alongside this growing crisis of identity were growing feelings of *ressentiment*. These feelings were initially expressed not at a time of failure but success. By the late Catherinian period Russia had overcome her traditional and immediate enemies, the Ottoman Empire, Sweden and Poland, and had become a great European power playing a decisive role in the continent's state system and in sustaining the balance of power. It was at this time that feelings of *ressentiment* began to emerge. Catherine II showed early signs of it. Russia, 'the star of the East', in her words, had risen and was now outshining the West. Princess Dashkova during her conversation with Prince Kauntiz gave voice to this now-dominant feeling of superiority and empire among the Russian elite:

> A great empire, Prince, having such inexhaustible sources of richness and power, such as Russia, has no need for rapprochement with anyone. A huge mass, such as Russia, correctly governed attracts to it whom it wants. If Russia remained unknown to that point (Peter's reign) and to the extent about which you speak, Your Highness, shows, excuse me Prince, only rudeness or thoughtlessness of European countries to ignore such a strong state.[81]

Yet, these feelings were riddled with doubt about this claimed superiority given Russia's conditions and wrapped in a sensitivity to comparisons between these conditions and those of countries to the west of her. Responding to the negative descriptions of the life of the rustic population provided by Abbé d'Auteroche, Catherine proclaimed in her long response that 'the condition of the ordinary people in Russia is not worse than in other countries. In fact, it is even better in the majority of instances'. In response to Voltaire's unfavourable commentary on peasant living standards, Catherine proudly wrote: 'Russian peasants live better than French peasants. All of them live so well that none of them lives without eating chicken every day. In fact, they are so sick of eating chicken that they now turn to turkeys'.[82] She was not necessarily wrong in material terms. The argument can be made that at the time the diet and health of Russian peasants compared favourably to those of French and English agricultural workers. Boltin as well was taken up by these feelings, as seen in his long and critical attack on the six-volume work about conditions in Russia written by Nicolas-Gabriel Le Clerc who had served as a doctor for the aristocracy. Catherine too was enraged by the work that implicitly stated that Russia was not part of the West.

The image of Russia that outraged the empress and against which she was struggling became dominant in the sixteenth century when, as a result of the expansion of economic and political relations between Muscovy and countries to its West, the increasing numbers of Westerners coming to Moscow subsequently wrote travel memoirs on this seemingly exotic land of the East.[83] Boltin in his work sought to refute the negative essentialist political and legal interpretation of Russia that such memoirs had propagated in the countries to the west of Russia. He argued that ancient and medieval Russia, the period before the Mongol-Tatar invasion, was an authentically European country whose legal culture was equal to that of the West. This position resonates in Putinist Russia. Lavrov in his article mentioned earlier also stressed this point. Boltin was responding to the position that the lack of institutional and legal limits on the monarchy's power and the legal culture behind them prevented a country, such as Russia, from being considered part of enlightened Europe located in 'the West'. Boltin painstakingly tried to show that positive legal developments in Europe of the West had a parallel within Russian legal and political culture. He most probably wrote this piece on the urging of the empress.[84] Yet, while Catherine tried to prove Russia's superiority to the West given a Western standard, intellectual and political figures began to question aspects of Petrine Occidentalism, the spread of Occidentosis as well as the use of this Western standard.

Denis Fonvisin was an influential literary figure and secretary to the head of the Russian Foreign Service, Nikita Panin. Questioning fundamental elements within pro-West Occidentalism, he sought to show that the constitutive elements of authenticity of Russian culture and identity were not inferior to others. In 1777, visiting France, the example of the West for progressive society, he wrote back to Panin's brother, Peter:

> In short, in comparing one [Russia] with the other [the West] I dare confess frankly that if one of our young compatriots, enjoying common sense, becomes indignant when seeing in Russia corruption and disorder and begins in his heart to become alienated from her, in order to appeal to his due love for the homeland, no better path exists than to send him to France. Here, of course, he will quickly realize based on his own experience that all those stories about perfection here are utter lies, that everywhere people are people, that intelligent and honorable people are rare everywhere.[85]

In 1783 Fonvisin sent to the journal *Interlocutor of the Lovers of the Russian Word* (*Sobesyednik Lyubitelei Rossisskogo Slova*) a series of questions on frequently discussed sociopolitical issues. The Academy of Sciences, headed by Princess Dashkova, published this journal to which Catherine herself contributed. He did not sign his contribution in light of his criticism of aspects of Occidentalism. His twentieth question, also posed by Russian figures, in particular Krizhanich, in the sixteenth and seventeenth centuries, is the most important for purposes here: 'How is it possible to destroy two contradictory and harmful prejudices: the first is that everything with us is awful and everything in foreign lands (i.e. Western Europe) is fine and the second that everything in those foreign lands is awful and everything with us is fine and dandy?' Catherine offered a brief defence but concluded with an unresponsive answer that combined the belief in enlightened absolutism and a certain wisdom acquired from ruling: 'with time and knowledge'.[86]

Fonvisin condemned two trends. On the one hand, he bemoaned the historiographical and intellectual basis of pro-West Occidentalism that, in the words of Dashkova, sought to destroy 'the authenticity' of Russian culture and led to the spread of Occidentosis while claiming that the adoption of these ways was a return to Russian authenticity. On the other hand, he was much concerned about the growing chorus of blind national self-worship that was a heightened response to the damage rendered by pro-West Occidentalism on Russian self-respect and self-confidence. The issues he addressed were common to most nations and societies when faced with the challenge of the West and Occidentosis. By attempting to redraw the country's cultural borders on the basis of an alternative conception of authenticity of Russian culture and the place of the West within it, pro-West Occidentalism exacerbated the spread and depth of cultural and civilizational schizophrenia and disorientation that has characterized the experience of non-Western countries in their attempts to respond to the challenge of the West. In the process, it also increased the extent of the intellectual and political backlash to the Occident and consequent various forms of national self-worship that became a fundamental element of the country's intellectual discourses and discourses of power in the domestic political and geopolitical arenas.

The effectiveness of pro-West Occidentalism weakened over time in the face of changing domestic and international conditions and, vitally, the emergence of *ressentiment*. This weakening can be clearly seen in the transformation of the views of Nicholas Karamzin (1766–1826). They provide an excellent example of this trend among a growing number of the Russian elite and of the transition from pro-West Occidentalism, which recognized Russian backwardness vis-à-vis the West while claiming a link with it, to national self-satisfaction, and then ultimately, to national self-worship, which was nonetheless riddled with feelings of self-doubt, and condemnations of the West as a civilization and the spread of Occidentosis.

Karamzin, in addition to being a well-known literary figure and influential publicist, was also a state councillor and official royal historian, a position to which Alexander I appointed him in 1803. In his first major work, *Letters of a Russian Traveler*, published in the 1790s after his travels in Europe he expressed support for Peter's reforms.

> The path of education and enlightenment is the same for all peoples. They all follow each other. Foreigners were smarter than Russians. Thus, borrowing from them, studying them, using their experience is necessary. Is searching for what has been already found really logical? Can not building ships, creating a regular army, opening an academy of sciences and factories really be better for Russians just because they had not originally thought them up? What people have not borrowed from other peoples? Is it not necessary to compare in order to excel? ... Peter the Great ... declared war on our old habits, because, in the first place they were rude, not worthy of our time; secondly, because they hindered the inculcation of different, more important and useful foreign ways and innovations. ... All that is native is nothing in comparison with all that is human and universal. The main point is we must be people, not just Slavic. That which is good for people, cannot be evil for Russians; what the English or the Germans have invented for usefulness and benefit of people is thus mine because I am a person!

In 1802 he wrote in *On Love for the Fatherland and National Pride*:

> Seemingly, we are excessively humble in our thoughts and ideas about our national dignity ... Peter the Great, having united us with Europe and showed us the fruits of enlightenment, for a time humiliated Russian national pride. We glanced at Europe and with one look took on the fruits of its long-standing labors. ... We then showed how to beat the Swedes, the Turks, and finally the French. ... Now we have so much knowledge and taste in life that we can live without ever again asking how they live in Paris or London.

In 1811 he wrote in *Notes on Ancient and New Russia*:

> Peter appeared. ... Posterity rendered enthusiastic praises to that immortal monarch and his personal virtues, and famous achievements. ... But can we

Russians, with history staring us in the face, confirm this opinion of ignorant foreigners and say that Peter is the creator of our country's greatness? ... Shall we forget our Muscovite princes? ... By uprooting ancient practices, presenting them as absurd, and praising and inculcating all that is foreign, the Russian monarch humiliated Russians in their own hearts. ... Russia ... has already existed for some one thousand years ... as a great state, but they repeat to us about all these new things as if we only recently emerged from America's dark jungles.

The ongoing influence of Karamzin's thought on these issues is seen not only in Putinist ideology but also in Putin's statements and remarks.

In recent years, we have been told, we are looking forward to meeting you and welcoming you to our civilized Western family of nations. Well, why would you decide that your civilization is best? There are much more ancient civilizations in the world. Secondly, they tell us, or they hint to us, we are prepared to accept you but our family is a patriarchal family and we are the patriarchs here. ... [The West believes that] they [the Russians] are a little bit savage or they just climbed down from the trees, you know, and probably need to have their hair brushed and their beards trimmed. And have the dirt washed out of their beards and hair.[87]

In 1825 Karamzin wrote to the writer and historian Alexander Turgenev: 'For us, for Russians with a soul, only one kind of true Russia in reality exists, an authentic, original Russia.'[88]

These issues broke into the country's political and intellectual life with Peter Chaadaev's *Philosophical Letters*, written in the period 1829–32 and published in 1836 in the journal *Telescope*.[89] Although revising parts of his argument in subsequent years, Chaadaev questioned the existence of a Russian cultural identity and civilization independent of other great cultures and civilizations. The gauntlet was thrown. Both the autocracy and educated public reacted furiously. Nicholas I called him mad and sent him to a lunatic asylum for a period of time. The journal was immediately shut down and its editor arrested. The ensuing debate that would continue until tsardom's collapse in 1917 would present the state and its power discourses on authenticity and the place of the West within it with both challenges and opportunities.

Slavophilism and subsequent derivative schools of thought were a reaction to Chaadaev and Romanov Occidentalism. Despite the differences in aspects of their thought, leading Slavophile thinkers, such as Konstantin Aksakov (1817–60), Ivan Kireevsky (1806–56), Aleksei Khomyakov (1804–60), Ivan Aksakov (1823–86), who would become a leader of Pan-Slavism, and Yurii Samarin (1819–76), shared broad agreement on most major issues that have a bearing on this work. They rejected the view of Westernizers about the authenticity of Russian culture and identity and the Enlightenment belief in progressive linear history and universal civilization that the West claimed to embody. They argued that Western civilization was characterized by an atomized and selfish people, devoid of traditions on which to lean, engaged in an eternal struggle over mutually antagonistic commercial and personal interests. In contrast to this West stood the authenticity of Russian culture and national identity that, as Aksakov detailed in his work *The Fundamental Beginnings of Russian History*, was based on spirituality, morality, feelings of collectivism and traditions. These elements provided the Slavophile path to the future.[90]

The holder of this authenticity was the peasant class. One of the fundamental contentious issues of both the intellectual discourses on the authenticity of Russian culture and national identity and Romanov Occidentalism was the rustic population. Pro-West Occidentalism held that peasants were a backward, irrational, superstitious, Orthodox group that needed to be transformed into *homo Romanovicus*. They represented the black masses of parochialism, ignorance, stubbornness and blind opposition to change about which Peter bitterly complained. When Peter and Catherine and the nobility looked out from St. Petersburg or their estates they saw only this mass that sporadically and unexpectedly broke into barbaric rebellion. Every reign since that of Mikhail had experienced some form of peasant rebellion or disturbances.

During Catherine's reign the Pugachev Rebellion (1773–5), the largest peasant rebellion in the history of imperial Russia, occurred which counted Old Believers among its active supporters. Yemelyan Pughachev (1740–75), a disenchanted Cossack former army officer, led the rebellion. He claimed to be the deposed and killed emperor, Peter III, Catherine II's husband, in whose name he would establish a new, just government that, among other policies, would abolish serfdom. In reality the rebellion was the culmination of a growing spread of peasant revolts that were taking place during the Russian-Ottoman War of 1768–74. Initially not taken seriously by Catherine, the rebellion spread to many parts of the empire and by 1773 the territory he nominally controlled extended from the Ural mountains to the lower Volga and into parts of today's Kazakhstan. The state finally crushed it in 1775. This rebellion and its goals only solidified these official and urban viewpoints of the peasants and of the need to control them until their transformation into *homo Romanovicus*.

The Slavophiles argued that in the pre-Petrine period a form of social, political and economic evolution distinct and superior to that of the West existed in the peasant commune. This social order was based on those vital elements lost by the West: morality, spirituality, nobleness of character, true Christianity and collective feelings. In this respect they were inspired by European Romanticism and specifically the work of the German thinker August von Haxthausen. Having travelled in Russia (1843–4) he wrote that Russia's peasant commune was similar to the primitive agrarian communism of ancient Germany which he believed represented the beginning of the history of German lands. Konstantin Aksakov wrote that the peasant commune was 'a union of people who have renounced egoism, individuality and work for the common accord and good; this is an act of love, a noble Christian'.[91] Dostoevsky in his *Diary of a Writer* argued that the peasants would 'show us a new road, a new way out of all our seemingly insoluble difficulties. St. Petersburg will not in the end determine Russia's destiny. ... Salvation and the bright light of the future will come from below'.[92] These peasants, so denigrated by the state and the Occidentosis-ridden elite, were, in reality, the bearers of authentic Russian culture and identity.

Therefore, in these discourses the real enemies of the authenticity of Russian culture and national identity were Occidentosis-ridden Russians. They rejected their own history and culture and blindly imitated Western behaviour and mores rooted in materialism, hedonism and Godlessness. The goal of Occidentosis was to separate them from their own culture, religion and heritage to the West's benefit. Claiming that the Romanov elite lived within Russia, but outside of Russian society, Slavophiles and other nativist derivative groups called on them to reconnect with the rustic population – the societal group that had not lost the elements of true Russianness. Dostoevsky summed up this view of the official *homo Romanovicus:* 'This cosmopolitan and Europeanized elite must return to the soil and submit to the people's truth. They would then be able to find true peace and heal their split personality'.[93] Only at that point could such people help Russia take on the challenges confronting her. He had little doubt about Russia's position in the world: 'The entire meaning of Russia is encompassed in Orthodoxy, in this light from the East, which will flow to blind humankind in the West which has lost Christ'.[94]

The Slavophile approach to the question of authenticity of Russian culture and national identity entailed a critical view of the autocracy as it had evolved since Peter's reign. They idealized the pre-Petrine autocracy, the source and defender of Russian authenticity, working in concert with both the church and the Boyar Duma. In the Slavophile view, the old Boyar Duma was a true consultative body of high-ranking nobles that enjoyed legislative, executive and judicial functions. Peter and his successors replaced this authentically Russian Duma with an impersonal, alien bureaucratic state inspired by the West headed by a new form of autocracy set on implementing pro-West Occidentalism. The autocracy had succumbed to Occidentosis which it spread. The Slavophiles sought the autocracy's return to its role as source and defender of Russian authenticity and the country's cultural borders as they defined it. Thus, the state considered them a potential political threat. For example, Samarin, one of the many Slavophiles to find himself facing harassment and imprisonment, was languishing in the Peter and Paul Fortress when he was summoned to the Winter Palace. 'Unshaven and not in his Sunday clothes' he was brought to Nicholas I who explained the reasons behind his arrest:

> I know you were not entertaining bad intentions but you have let loose amongst the masses a dangerous idea. According to it Russian tsars since the time of Peter the Great have acted only on the basis of German suggestions and influence (i.e. soft power). If this idea reaches the masses it will beget horrific calamities.[95]

The broad group of early Westernizers of the first half of the nineteenth century responded to these attacks on Petrine Occidentalism. Vissarion Belinskii, one of the group's leaders, provided the fundamental elements of this defence:

> The spirit of the Russian nation is not in peasant barbarism, but in the social groups that emerged after the reforms of Peter the Great, and adapted civilized life. … Russia understands that its salvation is not dependent on mysticism, asceticism, or pietism but rather on the development of civic and humanitarian values. It needs not sermons, it has heard enough of them, or prayers, it has prattled enough of them. It needs the awakening of human dignity that has been slung through the mud and filth for centuries.[96]

He condemned the jingoism that he believed was at the heart of Slavophile thought, and the attempts to recreate a Slavophile path for development in the name of the preservation of Russian authenticity.[97] He wrote:

> Now only weak, limited minds can think that the success of mankind is harmful to the success of nationality and that a Chinese wall is necessary for its preservation. ... The struggle of the overall human with the national is nothing more than a rhetorical form. ... Even when the progress of one people is completed through the borrowing from another, it is completed by the nation. Otherwise there is no progress.[98]

However, the Westernizers were less ideologically united among themselves than the Slavophiles. They vacillated between liberalism and socialism and between ideas of enlightened absolutism in which the intelligentsia would play the leading role in implementing all-encompassing reform before steps towards constitutionalism, and the periodic glorification of the people.

As these two main groups and a growing number of derivative schools of thought struggled with each other as the nineteenth century progressed, the imperial state was reformulating the place of the West in its concepts of authenticity and national identity. The immediate catalyst for this change was the Decembrist Revolt of 1825. The rebellion was crushed and its participants and organizers thrown into the Peter and Paul Fortress. Nicholas I blamed the spread of Western influences.[99] Such influences had announced themselves on Europe's political, ideological and eventually geopolitical landscape in the forms of the French Revolution, the Terror and Louis XVI's execution.

In the initial stages of the French Revolution, Catherine and most of the nobility were not too concerned with events in France. Progressive nobles, and in particular the younger generation, many of whom would end up fighting Napoleon, discussed events in France, particularly the monarchy's forced steps towards constitutionalism. Attention was paid to the virtues of the two main models of governance in 'the West', the egalitarianism of revolutionary France and the model of England, where a House of Lords, a powerful aristocratic body, gave the landowning nobility a significant degree of representation in relation to both the monarchy and the 'commons'. However, as events unfolded in France, Catherine and the nobility became increasingly sceptical and worried. These feelings can be seen in her reaction to the work *A Journey from St. Petersburg to Moscow* (1790) by Alexander Radishchev.

Written as a travel log of a young Russian travelling between the two capitals, the work targeted two fundamentals of tsarist rule, the autocracy and serfdom, that prevented Russia from becoming part of the West and detailed their baleful consequences while comparing Russia with the seeming progressive history of France. Another target of the work was religious obscurantism. While radical for its time, the work reflected a growing opinion among the progressive nobility that emerged during her reign. For example, the two Panin brothers General Pyotr and Nikita Ivanovich during this period wrote a proposed constitution for Russia that would have ended autocratic capriciousness, included forms of popular, primarily noble, representation and thus placed the country's political system within Western conceptions of political culture.

This project was given to Paul I (r.1796–1801), who did not act on it. Catherine, having read Radishchev's book, was outraged: 'This author is ridden with Frenchosis, seeking and seizing every pretext to undermine respect for authority ... to provoke the masses against their betters and the state'.[100] Radishchev, to the surprise of many, was charged and sentenced to death, which was commuted to ten years' internal exile. Only twenty-five copies of the book were sold; 600 were destroyed when Radishchev was arrested. It was published abroad in the middle of the nineteenth century by opposition groups. Only after the 1905 Revolution was it once again published in Russia. Nonetheless, it circulated in *samizdat* form not long after Radishchev's arrest.

Events in France during 1791–3 gave more reason for worry and concern in St. Petersburg; they were now viewed as potential threats to the empire's stability. Louis's capture at Varennes in June 1791 proved that he had become a prisoner of the revolution and was no longer in reality sovereign. The month before, French revolutionary contagion reached Poland, on Russia's border, where a constitution was proclaimed. This event and Louis's swearing an oath of loyalty to a constitution in September outraged the empress. In the first half of 1792, as events in France seemed to be reeling out of control, Catherine acted to prevent contagion. The Russian ambassador was recalled from Paris while Russians in France were ordered home. All French citizens living in Russia were forced to denounce the Revolution and swear loyalty to the Bourbon monarchy and were put under surveillance. In August of that year the Bourbon monarchy was overthrown.

The execution of Louis XVI and Marie-Antoinette in January 1793 and the launching of the Terror and systematic guillotining of thousands horrified European dynasties and elites from London to St. Petersburg and seemed to signal a new era of barbarism emerging within the Enlightenment's depths. In June 1793 Catherine wrote to Grimm: 'They know only how to pillage and kill' and, in 1794, 'I take it you remember that the late king of Prussia (Frederick II) used to say that Helvetius had confessed to him that the aim of the *philosophes* was to overthrow all European thrones, and that the *Encyclopaedia* was created with the singular aim of destroying all kings and religions'.[101] Consequently, she repudiated her long-standing flirtation with Enlightenment thinkers. Already in 1792 she had ordered the confiscation of a new edition of Voltaire's complete works while piecemeal works by other writers were banned. In 1796 censorship became institutionalized and systematic for the first time during her reign. Private printing presses were confiscated while all books to be published had to be submitted to censorship offices for licences. Books from abroad, in other words, countries to the west of Russia, were to be reviewed at the border. Censorship control offices opened in Odessa, Riga, along the border with Poland, Moscow and, of course, St. Petersburg. Her horror and actions to contain revolutionary contagion were not unique. They were shared by countries across the continent by 1792–3, including Britain.

Domestic developments during the reign of Catherine II, the French Revolution, and the Napoleonic War were the preconditions for the Decembrist Revolt whose immediate cause was the inability and/or unwillingness of Alexander I to act on his intent to grant Russia a constitution, a goal increasingly attractive to a growing number within the progressive aristocracy. At the beginning of his reign he established an unofficial committee composed of young aristocrats to discuss the idea of a constitution for the Russian Empire. His fears about such a step and the Napoleonic Wars put an end to this endeavour. After Napoleon's defeat, he again flirted with it. At the peace congress of 1814/15 he expressed his belief that constitutions should be established in various countries, although he still entertained fears about giving one to his own. Nonetheless, in 1809 he granted one to the Duchy of Finland and in 1815 to the Kingdom of Poland. Both were constituent parts of the Russian Empire.

Alexander, in his speech in 1818 to the Polish *Sejm*, expressed the hope that the constitution he had granted Poland would 'spread a beneficial influence over all the other countries that Providence has committed to my care'.[102] That year in private he told his brother, Constantine, the Grand Duke of Poland, 'Soon this great moment of joy will also arrive for Russia, when I grant a constitution to her'.[103] He also told the French ambassador, the comte de La Ferronnays:

> I love constitutional institutions and think that every decent man should love them, but can they be introduced indiscriminately for all peoples? Not all peoples are ready to the same degree for their acceptance. Of course, freedom and law which can be enjoyed by an enlightened nation such as yours does not suit other ignorant peoples.[104]

Alexander's thought and intentions were fairly known in the aristocratic world and thus raised hopes that he would act. They also raised fears among the conservative nobility. It opposed the idea of constitutionalism while regarding the autocracy as the defender of Russian authenticity but also their rights and property as landowners and serf owners. These nobles feared that constitutions would eventually bring the freeing of the serfs with land. Alexander I too contemplated plans for the liberation of the serfs, as did his successor Nicholas I. The progressive nobility and intelligentsia, meanwhile, believed that moves towards constitutionalism and the liberation of the serfs would eliminate the two most glaring obstacles to Russia's acceptance and/or return to the exclusive civilized club of the West. However, geopolitical and domestic considerations, and specifically Alexander's belief that the Russian people still lacked the cultural and political enlightening benefits of Occidentalism needed for a successful constitutional system, played decisive roles in his unwillingness to grant a constitution to Russia. Nonetheless, given his belief that Russia was a racial–cultural member of the west-European club, the future possibility of constitutionalism was not rejected on the grounds that it was Western and therefore alien to Russia and Russians. While he failed to act on his intentions, Alexander, knowing that constitutionalist secret societies had emerged, did nothing to disband them. They came to play roles in the Decembrist Revolt.[105]

A. N. Muraev, a high-ranking aristocratic officer in the Napoleonic War and one of the founders of the Decembrist Revolt, confessed during his interrogations: 'I obtained my insane liberal ideas during my stay in foreign countries, from the spirit of the age'.[106] In the preamble of the constitution for the governmental system the Decembrists sought to establish he wrote: 'All the European nations are attaining constitutions and freedoms. The Russian nation ... deserves one just as others do'.[107] Prince S. G. Volkonskii, a well-decorated major-general and leading Decembrist stated, 'In general all that we saw in passing through Europe in 1813 and 1814 created the feeling amongst all the young that Russia completely lagged behind in social, international, and political spheres and many more were inspired with the idea of becoming more clearly acquainted with Europe'.[108] In response, Nicholas I refused to pardon the revolt's leaders: 'I am duty-bound to give this lesson to Russia and to Europe'.[109] Several were executed while many were sent into internal exile. Shock waves went through the elite.

In light of the penetration of Russia's cultural borders by political and ideological Occidentosis that caused the Decembrist Revolt, Nicholas I mobilized state resources to defend these borders on two fronts. The security front was to be protected by the Third Section of His Majesty's Own Chancery, established in 1826. As the emperor's secret police, it had the responsibility for ensuring political stability, following and incarcerating political dissidents, and censorship. Publications from the West as well as domestic works that were potentially threatening, such as Catherine's correspondence with Voltaire and other Enlightenment-era figures, were banned and others heavily censored, such as the well-known memoir about Peter I, *The Accounts of Nartov about Peter the Great* (*Pazskazi Nartova o Petre Velikom*). It opened the post in order to monitor public opinion and discover pockets of opposition and revolutionary groups. Appearance also became a concern for Nicholas in his struggle against political Occidentosis. He found subversion in men's beards. In his instructions to the Third Section he ordered that bearded Russians must become 'objects of constant police surveillance, because over there in Europe the beard is the sign of membership in some ill-intentioned and evil political society'.[110]

The second front was moral and cultural. General I. V. Vasilchikov, imperial aide-de-camp and charged by Nicholas I with arresting those in the capital involved in the Decembrist Revolt, summed up the conviction held by the emperor and elite about its root causes: 'The entirety of the new generation is infected', infected with cultural and political Occidentosis. General A. Benckendorff, the Third Section's first chief and head of the national gendarmerie, in describing the duties of these two security organization, noted: 'Now the gendarmerie has become the moral physician of the people'.[111] This revolt and thought behind it were

> not in harmony with the character or feelings of the Russian nation. These Western sentiments had penetrated the country's cultural borders ... but it will never penetrate any farther. Russia's heart has never been, and never will be, infected with this poison.[112]

In 1826 Nicholas, addressing the sources of this sickness, published an announcement in the newspaper, *Severnaiia Pchela*, which for most of its existence (1825–64) was a secret organ of the security services:

> Let parents give complete attention to their children's moral education. Not to enlightenment, but to mental illness, which is more noxious than physical illness since it means the absence of firm principles. Parents must be held responsible for this willfulness of thought, this source of violent passions, this destructive luxury

of semi-knowledge, this urge toward fantastic extremes, whose beginning is the decline of morals and end is perdition. All the government's efforts and sacrifices will be in vain if home education does not cultivate the character of children and young adults and does not correspond with the state's aims.[113]

While parents would deal with this side of moral and cultural education, the state moved to implement reforms within the education system. In 1827 Nicholas issued a decree requiring all pupils between the ages of ten and eighteen to study in Russia. This was to ensure that all children would receive a proper inculcation of the elements of the authenticity of Russian culture and national identity that would immunize them against Occidentosis. The programme of state-subsidized university education in the West was ended, while studying abroad became rare given bureaucratic hurdles. Even regular travel abroad became difficult. In 1851 the issuing of passports for all practical purposes ceased. Nicholas told Prince Gagarin: 'I confess that I do not love sending [people] abroad. Young people return from there with a spirit of criticism'.[114]

The government, in order to immunize people from infection by Occidentosis and mobilize them around the throne, devised a new discourse on the authenticity of Russian culture and national identity. Count Sergei Uvarov, minister of education (1833–49), institutionalized this new discourse in an ideological triad based on 'authentic' Russian elements, *Orthodoxy, Autocracy, Nationality*. This was the first major step in the ideologization of the monarchy in the face of competing ideologies from the West. Before examining these elements it is necessary to review briefly major aspects of Karamzin's political and historiographical thought that played a significant role in the formulation of this triad. Uvarov had obtained this ministerial position thanks to Karamzin's recommendation to the monarch. Karamzin at the beginning of Nicholas' reign became one of the new emperor's closest advisors. Only his poor health prevented him from accepting a formal position.

Karamzin frequently voiced opposition to Alexander's musings about constitutionalism and reform of political institutions. This opposition was based on his understandings of the authenticity of Russian culture and national identity and on the belief that that culture, history and traditions as they had evolved over time determined a country's social imaginary and were reflected in its political system. These justifications for the autocracy came together in his multi-voluminous work, *The History of the Russian State*. He wrote this piece as Court historian, having received an order from the emperor to write an official history of the empire. This work, along with his *Notes on New and Ancient Russia*, played a fundamental role in the emergence of the ideology of conservatism expressed in this triad. He had no doubt that the 'autocracy is the bulwark of Russia; its indivisibility and wholeness is essential for her happiness'.[115]

His interpretation of history argued that the autocracy was the only historically correct and practical form of government for Russia. Anytime the autocracy was weak or modified Russia faced domestic turmoil and chaos and consequent attempts by geopolitical enemies to establish their hegemony over her. He pointed to two events to provide his thesis: the internal weakness of Kieven Rus that led to the Mongol-Tatar occupation and the Time of Troubles. Moreover, the motor of historical development in Russia was the autocratic state. It is for this reason that his book is called the *History of the Russian State* and not the *History of Russia*. In it the autocracy was glorified and sacralized; it was the source and defender of Russian authenticity and catalyst and leader in its march towards the future.

Uvarov, in his memo to Nicholas I, stated that steps needed to be taken in order 'to eliminate and replace so-called European education with the demands and necessities of education for Russia; to cure our new generation from its blind and thoughtless passion for the foreigner's superficiality and inculcate in the young souls respect for all that is native and the conviction that only by adjusting general global enlightenment to our popular culture and spirit can true fruits be brought to all and to each'.

> Given the rapid collapse of religious and civil institutions in Europe and the spread of destructive ideas … it is necessary to strengthen the motherland on solid foundations … to put into one whole the sacred authentic elements of Russian nationality and fasten to them the anchor of our sacred principles without which we cannot prosper, strengthen ourselves, and live. … Without love of the faith of one's ancestors, a people, similar to a private individual, must perish. To weaken the people's faith is to deprive them of their blood and rip out their hearts, to reduce them morally and politically to the lowest level. It would be a betrayal in the full meaning of the word. … A Russian, devoted to the motherland will not agree to the loss of a single dogma of our Orthodoxy [while] … Autocracy represents the indispensable condition of Russia's political existence. The Russian colossus is based on it. … This truth is felt by the majority of Russians. … This truth must be present and developed in national education and upbringing. … Along with these two national beginnings, autocracy and Orthodoxy, is situated a third, no less important, no less strong element: Nationality. For the throne and church to remain powerful, the feeling of nationality, which links all together, must be supported. The question of nationality does not have the type of unity which the question of the autocracy has. But both of them come from the same source and reproduce themselves on each page of the history of the Russian people. … Time, circumstances, love for the motherland, loyalty to the monarchy convince us that it is time that we, in regard to national education and upbringing, turn to the spirit of monarchical institutions and search in them that force, that unity, that firmness of which we have frequently thought to discover in pensive illusions.[116]

The essence of nationality in the triad was that Russia had a unique authentic state, culture and identity that not only differed but also must differ from the West. Importantly, what had to be taught in the schools and universities was that 'through some ridiculous passion for European forms we can harm our own institutions; that passion for innovations [from the West] throws into chaos and confusion the natural relations between all members of the country and state and impedes the peaceful gradual development of her forces'. Therefore, in these early stages of anti-West Occidentalism Russian identity became securitized and the justification of the autocracy became the defence of that identity and the country's cultural borders in the face of Occidentosis. As the state moved to change and control these discourses, criticism of the autocracy became equated with betrayal of the Russian authenticity handed down through the generations.

In accordance with this overturning of elements of pro-West Occidentalism, Nicholas I attempted to mobilize or construct Russian traditions in architecture, writing and culture while having the state propagate these official understandings of Russia's identity in the face of manifestations of Occidentosis.[117] Condemning those who claimed that the West was the model to emulate, Nicholas I stated that given the importance of authenticity of culture and national identity 'Russian imperfection is many times better than their [the West's] perfection'.[118] The state, supported in this regard by the Slavophiles, proclaimed that the West was in a state of perpetual decline and would in the near future collapse. Prince Vladimir Odoevskii in 1844 summed up the views of these two approaches.

> The West is dying. While it gathers its petty, trifling treasures, while it gives way to despair, time goes on. ... Time runs and will soon overtake that old, decrepit Europe – and perhaps drown her with those layers of still ashes, in which the great systems of the peoples of ancient America have drowned. ... We [Russians] are situated at the crossroads of two worlds: the dying world and the future world. We are new and fresh. We are not connected to the crimes of old Europe. ... Great is our system and difficult is our feat. We must revive and give life to everything.[119]

Mikhail Pogodin, a historian at Moscow University, who dominated Russian historiography during the Nicholavean period, along with Stephan Shevyrev, a well-known literary critic, poet and academic, was one of the strongest propagandists of this triad. At a time of strict censorship during Nicholas's reign, he and Shevyrev published the semi-official *Moskivtiyanin* that propagated these views.

Pogodin's thought appearing in this newspaper and his written works that were sanctioned by the state reflect the dynamics of this initial phase of anti-West Occidentalism. He did not condemn the centralization and strengthening of the state during Peter's and Catherine II's rule. He, however, decried the spread of cultural, moral and political Occidentosis. He condemned Peter for having

> instilled in Russians a passion for things foreign ... [which] still predominates and causes much harm ... an English, German, and French person, or whoever else foreign is assumed in our society to embody courtesy, civility, trustworthiness, respect – but on the other hand, one word – Russian – brings to mind untrustworthiness and suspiciousness. I dare to curse Peter the Great for creating this passion, for this insult to the motherland. ... Peter by bringing in Westernization destroyed the native and blocked its natural development.[120]

He propagated the idea that the West, having abandoned religion, turned towards materialism, commercialization and individualistic hedonism and set the conditions for its gradual, inevitable decline into barbarism. Russia, defending its geopolitical and cultural borders, would represent the future and a superior civilization to that of the West given its protection of Slavophile themes of spirituality, morality, religion and collectivism while achieving economic and technological development.[121]

The glorification of these new state conceptions of authenticity and essentialist condemnations of Western civilization at the centre of Nicholavean Occidentalism provoked those political and intellectual figures discontented with the reigning socio-economic circumstances and the autocracy's use of these discourses to justify its power. Chaadaev led the charge, frustrated with the spread of feelings of *ressentiment* that were finding expression in Slavophile and state discourses and, in particular, with the strengthening national self-worship that, in his opinion, could only result in stagnation. He wrote in *Apology of a Madmen*:

> So now emerges a new school [that proclaims] – 'The West is no longer needed, what Peter the Great created must be destroyed, return to the desert wasteland is necessary'. Forgetting what the West has done for us, not having a sense of gratitude toward this great person who civilized us and toward Europe which trained us, they reject Europe. … They ask, 'What good is it for us to search for enlightenment from the peoples of the West? Why should we envy the West? [We should envy] its religious wars, papacy, warring knights, and Inquisition? These are great things indeed! Is the West the birthplace of science and deep works? Of course not. As is known the East is that birthplace'.

He also attacked what seemed to him to be the increasing tendency of the state and the Slavophiles to distort Russian reality.

> I never learned to love my country with closed eyes, a worshipping mind, and clogged ears. I find that a person can be useful to his country only when he sees and judges it clearly. I think the era of blind love has passed. We are obligated to be true to our country. I love my country the way in which Peter the Great taught me to love it. I confess that I find alien to me that blissful patriotism, that patriotism of the lazy that positions one to view everything through rose-colored spectacles and to be obsessed with one's illusions. Unfortunately, many sensible minds suffer from this.[122]

Nicholaevan anti-West Occidentalism increased in intensity in the wake of the Revolutions of 1848 which started in France with the overthrow of King Louis Philippe and spread across Europe. Nicholas I played a decisive role in suppressing the threats to the Austrian and Prussian monarchies during the tumultuous events of 1848–9, and thereby obtained the title of the 'Gendarme of Europe'. This title captures the essence of this anti-West Occidentalism according to which a true Europe existed whose values and authenticity were based on monarchy, aristocracy, spirituality and austere morality. This gendarme would defend this Europe in the face of the existential threats posed by the false Europe, in other words, the 'West', symbolized by Western liberal and radical thought, godless revolutionary movements, and constitutional monarchy and their baleful political consequences and corrupting influence on culture and morality. Pogodin in a part of his report to Nicholas I quoted earlier also described the reasons why the West was an enemy of Russia.

> [They] hate Russia because they consider her the greatest obstacle to the so-called universal historical progress, confident that without Russia moves towards constitutions in Germany and everywhere else will succeed completely. They believe that forward on this path of progress first of all they will encounter Russia. (This is so, noted Nicholas in the margin.) Consequently, any increase in Russian strength which is considered dark, dangerous, and harmful for freedom, development, enlightenment and therefore unacceptable, must be stopped and destroyed in any way possible.[123]

He was underlining the Russian claim to its unique nativist modernity that allowed the preservation of authentic Russianness and the idea of a struggle between these true and false Europes whose outcome would determine the long-term future of Europe.

This binary was not new to Russian discourses. The first such discourses focused on the division in the world Christian Church and then forms of Protestantism. The English word 'Orthodoxy' translated from the Russian word *pravoslavie* fails to convey the full Russian meaning of this word whose literal translation is 'the true belief' whose protection was in the hands of Moscow, 'The Third Rome', that stood in contrast to the 'false' Christianities of the West. Such discourses were integral to official state conceptions of Russian authenticity and national identity until the discourses of pro-West Occidentalism launched by Peter. During the Soviet period this paradigm transformed once again. Russia was the representative of true Europe, the Europe of socialism and communism, while the West represented the false Europe of capitalism, bourgeois culture and republicanism, and mass consumerism whose leaders were the United States and the United Kingdom. The Putinist state revived this approach. Russia became the symbol and defender of true Europe's values, such as patriotism, spirituality, traditional moral values and feelings of collectivism in the face of the false Europe, symbolized by the liberal West, North-Atlanticism and cosmopolitanism.[124]

In summary, Nicholas I launched anti-West Occidentalism to protect the country's cultural and thus geopolitical borders against the threat of Occidentosis. Nicholas believed that in fighting against political and cultural Occidentosis, which had its roots in the liberal and radical tradition of the Enlightenment and the events of 1789 and Jacobinism, he was fighting for the political and cultural values of traditional true Europe. This belief underpinned his strong support for the Holy Alliance. However, as European states throughout the nineteenth-century continued to move, however haphazardly, in the direction of constitutionalism and republican forms of government, these Romanov discourses found this balancing act between concepts of Europe and the West increasingly challenging.

Nicholas's turn to anti-West Occidentalism only confirmed in the West the fundamental Eastern otherness of Russia and its exclusion from civilized Europe. This reconfirmation of west-European views of Russia's relationship to the West was best expressed by the travel memoir *La Russie en 1839* written by the Marquis de Custine which became an international bestseller. It shaped European views in the nineteenth century in regard to Russia.

> Everything about Nicholaeven Russia filled the Frenchman with contempt and dread: the despotism of the Tsar; the servility of the aristocracy, who were themselves no more than slaves; their pretentious European manners, a thin veneer of civilization to hide their Asiatic barbarism from the West; the lack of individual liberty and dignity; the pretense and contempt for the truth that seemed to pervade society.[125]

3

The apogee of Romanov Occidentalism

The Crimean War

In early 1853 Nicholas I sent shock waves across Europe when he confronted the Ottoman sultan, Abdulmajid, with demands that he give St. Petersburg written guarantees that the rights of the Orthodox Church would remain forever untouched by the Ottoman state, and annul his granting to Catholics in 1852 under pressure from the French government the right to hold a key to the Church of the Nativity in Bethlehem that brought with it free access to the Chapel of the Manger. The restored Bonapartist regime took these steps for domestic political reasons. They played a role in Louis Napoleon's plans to transform the Second Republic into the Second Empire and exchange his title of president of the Republic for emperor. Nicholas was infuriated by the Ottoman state's granting of these rights given the long-standing quarrels between Catholics and the followers of Orthodoxy over this access and the signal it sent of weakening Russian influence over the Porte.

The Ottoman government, while assuring St. Petersburg that no plans existed for the revoking of any rights of the Orthodox Church, refused to provide legally binding guarantees. It stressed that taking such a step would be equivalent to a foreign capitulation and to granting Russia the right to interfere in domestic Ottoman affairs. During the next six months, Nicholas increased diplomatic pressure on Constantinople, but to no avail. Frustrated, in July 1853 he decided to apply military pressure and sent troops into the Ottoman provinces of Wallachia and Moldova. He stressed to Vienna, Paris and London that this occupation was temporary until Abdulmajid agreed to his demands and, in any case, was sanctioned by the Treaties of Adrianople (1829) and St. Petersburg (1834). These great powers did not accept his explanations seeing in them a rather clumsy but dangerous attempt to strengthen Russia's influence in the Ottoman Empire. At the same time, a vocal part of public opinion in these countries shared this view but also held the belief that Nicholas's autocracy was a reactionary semi-Asiatic despotism based on a messianic Orthodox ideology set in opposition to Western Christendom and political and cultural ideals that had reached fruition during the Enlightenment. In this context, the sultan, backed by Paris and London, refused to back down and on 4 October declared war on Russia given Nicholas's refusal to pull his forces out of these provinces.

As tensions between St. Petersburg, on the one hand, and Paris, London and Constantinople, on the other, increased in the run-up to the outbreak of war, Russian propaganda stressed that Nicholas, as the most powerful Orthodox monarch, was acting only out of duty to protect Orthodox peoples, especially those living under the yoke of a Muslim polity. The emperor thundered in public declarations: 'Russia has not forgotten God! ... We march in defense of Orthodoxy!'[1] Slavophiles and the clergy welcomed a foreign policy based on defence of Orthodoxy. Russian nationalists, while mobilized by this religious imagery, also saw in this struggle the opportunity to spread Russia's geopolitical reach into the Near East and beyond, into the Mediterranean, confirming the suspicions of Western capitals. In sum, anti-West Occidentalism based on the triad and reflecting Nicholas's beliefs was now expressed in foreign policy.

Nicholas's attempts to portray his confrontations with the Ottomans as a Holy Crusade provoked deep scepticism and fear. Vienna in 1853 in an official statement condemned Russia's position and stressed that Nicholas had no grounds to call for a Holy Crusade since the Ottoman state had done nothing 'in recent times' to oppress the Orthodox.[2] Nicholas's demand for the revocation of the key given to Catholics came across as inflaming sectarianism among Christians which provoked French public opinion to approve military support for the Ottomans. Bishop Antoine de Salinis of Amiens declared Orthodox Russia 'the born enemy of Christian Europe' and a threat to the values and authenticity of Catholicism while Archbishop Marie-Dominique-Auguste Sibour in Paris called for a struggle against the 'barbarism' of the Orthodox world headed by Russia. Napoleon III's foreign minister, Edward Drouyn de Lhuys, in a message to his diplomatic cadres stated that the one saving grace in 'our epoch, however troubled' was its exemption 'from one of the evils that most afflicted the world in former days – I mean the wars of religion'. Now Nicholas's actions which were 'an appeal' to 'fanaticism' that was in contradiction to 'reason' threatened to roll back this one achievement.[3] Queen Victoria in her declaration of war underlined that Britain was entering the war 'in defence of an ally whose territory is invaded, and whose dignity and independence are assailed'. In blunt language she claimed that Nicholas was using the imagery of Orthodoxy and a Holy Crusade in order to mask naked aggression to expand Russian power.[4]

The Russian view can be seen in a secret report sent by Pogodin to Nicholas in December 1853, in the initial stages of the war, in which he condemned, to the monarch's approval, the West's double-standards.

> France takes Algeria from the Turks, England annexes every year a new Indian territory to its colonial holdings in India: these steps don't break [geo-political] equilibrium, but Russia takes Moldova and Wallachia, temporarily in the words of the Russian sovereign (and who dares not believe him) and, they claim, equilibrium is broken.
>
> France in front of the world and in peacetime occupies Rome and remains for several years.[5] That's nothing. But Russia, if it only thinks about Constantinople, then (it is claimed) the entire building of European politics trembles and peace is threatened. England declares war on the Chinese who have supposedly offended the English: no one has the right to intervene.[6] Yet, Russia is obliged to ask Europe for permission even to quarrel with one of its neighbors. England ravages Greece, supporting the false suit of a fugitive Jew, and burns its fleet:[7] this is legal, but

Russia demands a treaty in order to protect the security of millions of Christians: that [the West claims] strengthens too much her influence in the East and disturbs equilibrium.[8]

These remarks also hint at something basic – only having failed to achieve quickly his goals through diplomatic pressure and clearly blundering into an armed conflict with the Ottoman Empire and its allies did Nicholas I turn it into a full-scale Orthodox crusade and, in the process, give full reign to sentiments and ideological forces that would exercise a strong influence on tsarist-era domestic and foreign politics.

France's and Britain's decision to fight with the Muslim Ottoman Empire against Russia and Austria's unwillingness to support Russia despite Nicholas's role in saving, in 1849, Franz Josef's throne fanned the flames of anti-Westernism. Anna Tiutcheva, a young maid-of-honour at Court from a well-known Slavophile family, described in her diary inflamed public sentiment:

A horrible struggle has burst upon us. Great and contradictory forces are now on a collision course: the East and the West, the Slavic and the Latin worlds. … Filled with dread and anguish one asks, what will be the outcome of this struggle between these two worlds? No doubt exists. We, Russia, are on the side of truth and ideals: Russia fights not for material gain and interests of this world, but for eternal ideas.[9]

The political and ideological dimensions of this war strengthened intellectual discourses, and especially Pan-Slavism, that stressed positive Russian cultural distinction from the countries to its West and the need to protect Russian authenticity in the face of the threat of moral and cultural Occidentosis. Pan-Slavism emerged in the 1840s and 1850s and obtained large-scale popular support as a result of this war and gained great momentum at the beginning of the 1870s with the publication of *Russia and Europe* by Nikolai Danilevsky. It underwent several reprints over subsequent years to satisfy public demand. While upholding the superiority of Russian culture, this work argued that Western civilization had reached its cultural peak during the Renaissance and Reformation and was now in moral, cultural and political decline. The cultural and political forces unleashed by the radical liberalism of the Enlightenment, manifested in the Terror of the French Revolution, the 1848 Revolutions and the Paris Commune and the sociocultural consequences of the machine age, materialism and atomistic individualism, had deformed and debased west-European civilization and brought this decline. Russia had to avoid such a fate.

Yet, Pan-Slavism also reflected a form of *ressentiment*, arguing that 'Russia emphatically did not belong to Europe: the best proof of this was that Europe itself did not consider Russia "one of us", and turned its back on Russia in abhorrence'.[10] Evidence of this was Paris's and London's support for the Ottoman Empire and Vienna's neutrality. The admired 'other' refused to recognize the one aspiring to be it. Consequently, race became a determinative factor in distinguishing Russia from polities in the West while protection of Russian authenticity in the face of Occidentosis was portrayed as a national struggle. During this period Fyodor Tiutchev, a diplomat and a well-known Pan-Slavist writer and the father of Anna quoted above, coined the term 'Russophobe' to describe those intellectuals and writers who took inspiration from the West and used Western criteria to judge Russia. They were Occidentosis-ridden Russians who, in his opinion, despised the true authenticity of native culture and national identity.

Pan-Slavism, integrating the triad and Nicholas's motivations in regard to the Ottoman Empire, provided Russia with a new geopolitical doctrine. It proclaimed Russia the big brother and protector of Slavic peoples in the Balkans and the unification of the Slavic races a major geopolitical goal. In other words, its 'aim was to force the tsarist government to adopt a more aggressive and chauvinistic foreign policy … in order to create a powerful federation of Slavic nations under Russian leadership' in the face of the threats of Germany, Austria-Hungary and Britain.[11] The impact of this thought on public opinion and foreign policy was felt in Alexander II's reluctant declaration of war in 1877 against the Ottoman Empire and the assumption of the leadership of a coalition of Orthodox forces that included Bulgaria, Montenegro, Romania and Serbia fighting over Bulgarian independence and the sultan's control over his predominately Orthodox Balkan provinces. Importantly, Pan-Slavism also spread 'the myth of the inevitable clash between Slav and Teuton' which 'was a nonsense, but dangerous and powerful nonsense for all that'.[12] This 'myth' and its influence on educated public opinion exercised a strong influence on foreign-policy decision makers in the years and months leading to the start of the First World War.

Russia's ignominious defeat in its own backyard, symbolized by the loss of its naval base at Sevastopol almost a year after Nicholas I's death in March 1855, disgraced in the eyes of educated public opinion the Nicholavean approach based on anti-West Occidentalism, by proving that the empire had become a giant with clay feet. Nicholas's burgeoning anti-West Occidentalism had intensified Russia's economic and technological backwardness at a time when Russia's neighbours to the West, in particular France and Britain, continued to reap the economic and power benefits of industrialization. This state of affairs under Nicholas I was compared unfavourably to the previous era of forms of pro-West Occidentalism that had transformed Russia into a great power recognized by the West's major powers, evidenced by its role in defeating Napoleon. Grand Duke Constantine bemoaned: 'We cannot deceive ourselves any longer; we must say that we are both weaker and poorer than the first-class powers and furthermore poorer not only in material terms but in mental resources'.[13] The responsibility for this situation was placed on the dead emperor's shoulders. In many quarters, Nicholas's death brought a sense of relief and hope for positive change. Prince Pyotr Dolgorukov noted in his diary: 'We remember … the universal jubilation. With Nicholas's death ended an era of despotism'.[14] Alexander Nikitenko, literary figure and a member of the secret committee for censorship during Nicholas's reign, in his diary noted the rising sentiment that large-scale change was indeed a necessity: 'Many are now discussing the need for legality and openness (*glasnost*)' and reform of governance and 'the current bureaucratic administrative structure'. Focus on internal reform along the lines of pro-West Occidentalism would also have a beneficial influence on Europe's view of Russia since 'up to now we have portrayed ourselves to Europe only as a giant fist threatening European civilization, and not as a great power intent on its own development and improvement'.[15]

Alexander II's reign is key to understanding the political tensions within the discourses of pro-West Occidentalism and the shift to anti-West Occidentalism that characterized the subsequent reigns of Alexander III and Nicholas II. When Alexander II ascended the throne by all indications he was not contemplating a programme of vast reforms. However, the undermining of Russia's status as a great power and dynastic legitimacy brought by defeat in war, economic backwardness and low morale in the educated classes and aristocracy convinced him of the need for change. While Alexander II did not flirt with liberal ideas of constitutionalism, as did his uncle Alexander I, unlike his successors, he did not regard the West as alien to Russia and showed a pragmatism, albeit reluctant at times, in the face of changing domestic and international conditions. Consequently, his reign became known as the Era of Great Reforms during which Russia experienced transformations on a scale and depth not seen since Peter's time. Three of these reforms have particular importance for this study. They were (1) the emancipation of the serfs; (2) judicial reforms that led to the establishment of an independent judiciary; and (3) institutional changes. Interrelated and wide-ranging they represented a new round of the practical process of Westernization within the framework of pro-West Occidentalism that rejected Nicholas's modus operandi. Alexander, as he implemented reforms, 'strove to take on the image of a monarch championing Western ideals that Nicholas I had condemned as alien to the Russian body politic'.[16]

Alexander II concluded that the Nicholavean reliance on the discourses of the triad, the bureaucracy and security apparatus, and the landed elite was not politic and effective. The state needed to regain the confidence of the progressive aristocracy, elements within the intelligentsia and growing educated classes. Behind this conclusion was Alexander II's recognition that Russia needed reform and the state, in turn, needed the support of these groups to implement it. He, therefore, inaugurated a policy of gradual liberalization of the public sphere which included a significant lessening of censorship that culminated in the dissolution of the Supreme Committee for Censorship. These new conditions led to the rapid evolution of educated public opinion, political groups and pseudo-political organizations. These early moves had a positive influence on educated popular opinion and provided the state with the opportunity to garner public opinion for its policies and strengthen its legitimacy. However, these moves also created new challenges for the state. The diversification of this expanding public opinion generated counter narratives on issues such as the constitutive elements of Russian authenticity and national identity, foreign policy and appropriate paths for development, and thereby represented both a threat and an opportunity to the state. This limited opening of the public sphere and implementation of reforms certainly generated educated popular support for the regime. It also fanned expectations for additional change. The danger existed that failure to meet to an extent such expectations could have a deleterious influence on the state's public standing and set the conditions for the emergence of extremism.

The freeing of the serfs in 1861 exercised a powerful and enduring influence on the country's political and economic evolution. The supporters of pro-West Occidentalism considered it a major step in the country's positive political development, bringing the country closer to the progressive West by eliminating one of the clearest examples of Russian backwardness. Another obstacle to Russia's membership to the West was the existence of autocracy. Yet, at the same time, this step strengthened the belief of many liberal reformists in the idea of an enlightened autocracy, dragging the country and population towards Western civilization, implementing enlightened reform in the face of blind resistance to change among the peasant masses and self-interested elite and social groups. After all, Alexander II, after a period of consultation and preparation, freed the serfs and overrode the opposition of the gentry with a stroke of his pen while the young, democratic United States was fighting a bloody civil war to achieve the freedom of its slaves. Lastly, serf emancipation freed up manpower needed for industrialization, a process that began in earnest during Alexander II's reign.

One of the most consequential of his reforms was the establishment in 1864 of *zemstvos*, elected local government councils at provincial and district levels charged with handling local affairs. Their establishment, along with the judicial reforms, were considered essential not only for the overall programme of liberal reform and the capturing of public political opinion but also for effective governance given the expansion of responsibilities handled on a local level after the emancipation of the serfs. While *zemstvos* were tied to the bureaucracy in St. Petersburg, they nonetheless enjoyed the authority to handle local issues, such as property insurance, postal and delivery services, hospitals, primary schools and roads. Their establishment raised hopes that steps would eventually be taken towards constitutional forms of governance in the imperial centre.

In the midst of this reforming period, on 4 April 1866, a former student from the nobility, D. V. Karakozov, tried to assassinate the emperor. This attempt symbolized for Alexander a seeming contradiction. His reforms, particularly the policy of liberalization, were to prevent the emergence of such extremism by providing a public space for debate and create hope for peaceful evolution and development, however ambiguous at the time the final destination of political reform. Yet, his reforms were radicalizing certain elements within the intelligentsia and student population and leading to this use of terrorist violence against the state.

High society, as well as the emperor and the elite, was shocked by this act. Although the group to which Karakozov belonged was not a serious political force, the attempt on Alexander's life played the key role in bringing a conservative turn in government policy. Contributing factors were the insurrection in Poland (1863) that had galvanized Russian conservative and nationalist opinion and the emancipation of the serfs that had caused much resentment among the gentry and the peasantry. This resentment bred fears of class war if the political space was further liberalized and gentry demands for representation were satisfied.

Reformists were removed from leading posts, including the Third Section and Interior Ministry. Since the opposition was being driven by rising student extremism and radicalism, fuelled by political Occidentosis, Dmitrii Tolstoy, a known opponent of reforms, replaced the reform-minded, Alexander Golovin, at the Ministry of Education. Given these changes, aristocrats who had opposed the emancipation of the serfs but lacked any institution to oppose it began to organize themselves in opposition to the progressive aristocracy that had played a key role in Alexander's reforms.

From the early 1870s Alexander's reforming zeal had clearly waned. His reforms and limited opening of the public sphere had led to the growth of radical revolutionary groups inspired by various forms of nativism and political Occidentosis and using terrorist methods. While certainly small in number their influence on state and public opinion was not insignificant. Importantly, their activities helped temper the state's reforming tendency which in turn weakened educated public support for the state. Peter Valuev, minister of internal affairs (1861–8), minister of state property (1872–9) and head of the Council of Ministers (1879–81) in 1877 reported to the emperor:

> What deserves attention is the clear lack of participation of almost the entire educated part of the population in the current struggle of the government with the small number of criminals and plotters who are striving for the overthrow of the fundamental conditions of state, civil, and social order.[17]

The issue was the contradiction between societal expectations in regard to additional political liberalization and Alexander's unwillingness to that point to contemplate institutional and legal constraints on his power and the expansion of the role of educated public in the country's political life. In other words, the policy of liberalization and the establishment of the *zemstvo* initially raised expectations in this regard, but public opinion came to realize that the state was not prepared to engage in a larger dialogue with society and respond positively to these expectations.

In 1879 another assassination attempt only convinced Alexander to continue with the tough approach. Nonetheless, in February 1880 another more serious one took place. This incident involved a bomb in the Winter Palace placed by S. N. Khalturin, who had obtained a job there as a cabinet maker with the goal of killing the emperor. Despite substantial damage to a part of the imperial residence, Alexander survived. Now convinced that the tough approach was a failure he changed tactics. He established a Supreme Executive Commission charged with crushing extremist groups, determining the causes for growing political discontent and developing policies to stop the spread of political violence and terrorism. The man in charge of this commission was Count Mikhail Loris-Melikov. Believing that repressive measures alone could not ensure political stability and tranquillity, he stressed in a report to Alexander:

> Extracting Russia from the current crisis can be achieved only by the strong autocratic will but this challenge cannot be met only through punitive and police measures. … The country's situation became difficult given the pause in reform [and] the apparent refusal to correct those weaknesses in reforms that emerged after their implementation. As a result the youth, not knowing worse times and not having experienced the outrages and disgraces of the period before the reforms, heap all of their discontent on the reformers, while socialist ideas have not endured any serious or convincing criticism in government propaganda.[18]

One of his first steps was the removal of Tolstoy from the Ministry of Education and the dissolution of the Third Section, whose responsibilities were transferred to the Interior Ministry. He lessened greatly censorship and indicated that a new cycle of reforms would be unleashed. Through these steps he sought to deprive the extremists of even passive support of the educated classes and put an end to their apathy in regard to the state. While giving more freedom to the press, he met with editors urging them to work with the state in fighting extremists and in obtaining support from society for the state.

The state had indeed failed to respond to the other competing ideology of the West, socialism and its derivatives as society experienced the initial and quickening stages of industrialization and the deepening of capitalism that the government had initiated in an attempt to catch up with the West's great powers. Socialism began to compete with and then overshadow liberalism and constitutionalism, which, especially after the Revolutions of 1848, was seen as the protector of capitalists' rights and property among the youth and educated classes. For many, socialism offered a developmental path to the West and thus the future that corresponded with conceptions of the elements of authenticity of Russian culture and national identity, such as collectivism, social justice and social harmony, while saving society from the human, social and economic horrors of liberal industrial capitalism.

Given this perceived similarity between elements of Russian culture and socialism, it was assumed that it would be easier to travel its developmental path. Alexander Herzen, the well-known thinker and oppositional figure, in these conditions developed the idea of Russian socialism. He argued that he recognized the form of socialist development in the Russian Orthodox–inspired peasant collective, the commune (*obshchina*). He established a vision of the future that incorporated Western elements within a Russian skin attractive to the masses that also offered a modernity superior to that of the West's liberalism and capitalism and of the state that was turning towards capitalism in order to obtain Western forms of power. Herzen concluded, 'The Western Liberal group will obtain strength and popular support ... only when they have Slavophile themes'.[19]

Extremists found socialism appealing because it offered a clear explanation of the ills of society and a blueprint to the future. It promised in the construction of a worldly socialist utopia avoidance of the mistakes and horrors of the liberal capitalist West. Here the extremists gave little attention to the idea of freedoms and civil societies. 'In other words, they renounced the idea of freedom for the sake of a rapid transition to a socialist structure that would in turn solve quickly all problems'.[20] The imperial state, faced with the challenge of actual governing, had a difficult time combatting such utopian thinking that was detached from social, political, cultural and economic reality.

After the crushing of leading terrorist groups, and specifically 'The Populists', in August 1880 Alexander made Loris-Melikov interior minister while dissolving the Supreme Administrative Commission. In 1881 Loris-Melikov presented the emperor with the results of official research that showed that the lack of political reforms which would allow a greater public say in governing was a main cause of discontent among the educated classes and progressive nobility and of rising extremism, especially among the youth. At the top of the list of policy suggestions was the establishment of two commissions charged with preparing legislation. One would deal with administrative issues, the other financial and economic ones. They would be composed of elected officials from *zemstvos* as well as government officials, academics and well-known publicists. Their proposed legislation would be sent to a General Commission, itself composed of these two commissions as well as elected specialists from *zemstvos* and large urban areas.

Alexander II, faced with this social and political situation, eventually accepted the provisions of this legislation and thereby placed Russia was on the cusp of establishing forms of elected institutions albeit with very limited powers and responsibilities. He told his ministers: 'Gentlemen, that which is proposed to us is the Estates-General of Louis XVI. One must not forget what followed. But, if you judge this to be of benefit of the country. I will not oppose it'.[21] This comment reflects the long-standing fears of Russian monarchs and elite of the possible consequences of opening up the political system and of including the uneducated masses in the political process. Class warfare reminiscent of post-1789 France, but only worse under Alexander II given a growing proletariat and rural–urban migration, seemed a probable result of establishing Western liberal forms of governance. Alongside the possibility of class warfare was the danger of national and ethnic violence that threatened the disintegration of the empire. A taste of this was experienced as recently as 1863 in Poland. After all, one only had to remember that Louis XVI's convocation of the Estates-General in response to growing financial and political pressure led to the unleashing of revolutionary forces, the monarchy's overthrow and the guillotining of him and his wife.

On 13 March 1881 Alexander, having signed the decrees, went to attend the traditional Sunday parade, despite exhortations by Loris-Melikov and others not to attend for security reasons. On his return he stopped by the palace of his cousin, Grand Duchess Catherine, and told her of his decision. On his way to the Winter Palace a student named Rysakov threw a bomb at the imperial carriage. The emperor, not wounded, alighted against his driver's wishes to check the condition of several of his Cossack escort officers who had been wounded. At that time, a Polish student named Hriniewicki threw a bomb at Alexander's legs, shattering them. Bloodied, he was taken to the palace to die. His grandson, the future Nicholas II, witnessed his dying grandfather being carried into the imperial residence.

Apogee of anti-West Occidentalism

Alexander III immediately met with Loris-Melikov to discuss responses to the first assassination of a monarch since the dynasty's founding and the signed decrees. They were scheduled to be announced in the press the next day. He told Loris-Melikov that out of respect for his father the decrees should be published. In the late afternoon the new emperor went to his palace, Gatchina, outside the capital. In the middle of the night, he sent a message to Loris-Melikov ordering that the decrees not be published. The following week at a ministerial meeting he rejected them: 'Russia cannot adapt a national representative body invested with forms taken from the West. These forms are not only foreign to the Russian people, but also could destroy all the foundations of their political conceptions'.[22] Loris-Melikov responded that these institutions 'had nothing in common with Western constitutional forms'.[23] In a private conversation with the conservative Count Stroganov Alexander III was less diplomatic: 'I too feared that this [Alexander II's decree] would have been the first step towards a constitution … constitution!? What is that? So that the Russian tsar can take an oath and swear allegiance to cattle?'[24] The long-term result of Alexander's decision 'was to unite public opinion into a single oppositional camp… and thus ensured the revolutionary explosion of 1905 from which tsarism never recovered'.[25] Alexander III was convinced that his father's political reforms had provided space and incentive to radicals to attack the state, while his spread of educational opportunities to the lower classes only added to this political destabilization. He believed that providing secondary education to the lower classes would lead to 'contempt for parents, dissatisfaction with their own station, bitterness towards the existing and, given the nature of things, inevitable inequality in the moneyed position of various social groups'.[26] This decision, and the thought behind it, set the conditions for the resurgence of the discourses of anti-West Occidentalism while his reign became known as the era of counter-reform.

A finger of responsibility for bringing about Alexander's change of mind has been pointed at Konstantin Pobedonostsev – an influential political figure and head of the Holy Synod and who was tutor to Alexander III and Nicholas II. He argued that the idea of Russians being west-European and of democracy and constitutionalism were 'the great lies of our time'.[27] As debates raged at the state's highest levels about the fate of these decrees he wrote to Alexander:

> If they sing for you the old siren songs that one must calm down, that one must continue pursing the liberal course, that one must make concessions to so-called public opinion, for God's sake don't believe, Your Majesty, don't listen. This spells destruction, the destruction of Russia and yourself; this is as clear as daylight. … The mad villains who killed your father won't be satisfied with any concessions and only grow more savage. … This evil seed can be extracted only in a struggle with them for life and death, with iron and blood. … Only one sure straight path exists … launching, without hesitation, this struggle, the most holy ever fought in Russian history.[28]

He also considered Occidentosis and the West as existential threats to Russia's cultural and geopolitical borders.

> Clearly, from the West comes a systematic approach against Russia … Western armed detachments undermine our strength, nationality and church. Even now a Western company is receiving the right to acquire land and even rent ports. We have already experienced the consequences of allowing these foreigners to obtain real estate. A mass of foreigners owning property in Russia is a great evil that will bring misfortune to our international relations. A foreigner for some reason has always been placed in a privileged position as he enjoys a double security detachment – one provided by Russian law, the other by their embassies and consulates. [Consequently] many difficulties will face our government, especially

in regard to our relations with the USA where, as is well-known, all is based on moneyed interests and bribes, where the peoples' representatives in Congress serve above all else the representatives of private and trading interests and where industrial companies constitute the hegemonic power in that state.[29]

Alexander III and Nicholas II did not share the intensity of Pobedonostsev's views, although they maintained specific conceptions of authenticity of Russian culture and national identity that were reflected in Nicholas's triad.

The rejection of Alexander II's decrees marked the return of anti-West Occidentalism based on the triad and modified to reflect current conditions. They provided cover and justification for Alexander III's significant closing of the public sphere, intensification of censorship and undermining of Alexander's judicial reforms and *zemstvos*. These moves, combined with repression of revolutionary terrorist groups, created a sense of political stability, but social and political discontent continued to spread under the surface as progressive aristocrats, intellectuals and the educated middle class continued to be inspired by Westerns forms of liberalism, constitutionalism and/or socialism and their native derivatives. The threat of socialism noticeably grew as the working class increased in size due to rural–urban migration, the intensification of industrialization and its increasing attractiveness to the educated classes and intelligentsia. When Nicholas II succeeded his father in 1894 that same public opinion expressed quietly hopes that he would revive the approach of his assassinated grandfather, who had rejected his father's anti-West Occidentalism. Nicholas soon dashed these hopes:

> It has come to my attention that recently in some *zemstvos* the voice of certain people is heard, people who are being carried away with foreign senseless dreams about participation of *zemstvo* representatives in domestic governance. Let all know that I, devoting all my strength to the people's benefit, will preserve the autocracy as fiercely and unbendingly as my deceased and unforgettable father.[30]

Given Alexander III's and Nicholas II's world views and the ongoing need to support Russia's claim to be a great international power, two fundamental trajectories characterized their reigns. On the one hand, the state, building on the economic and technological trends initiated by Alexander II, launched a vast programme of infrastructure building, capitalist industrialization and attraction of foreign capital to fund them in order to sustain Russia's position as a great power. Sergei Witte, finance minister (1892–1903) and prime minister (1903–6), who played a decisive role in the policy of industrialization, stressed to Nicholas II that if economic modernization was not expanded and hastened, Russia would face the ignoble destiny as a supplier of natural resources to the advanced countries of the West. While these reforms and policies increased the empire's share of global industrial production, Russia's economy remained underdeveloped in comparison with the economies of Britain, Germany, the United States and France while, 'in per capita terms its wealth and industrial production ranked beside Spain and below Italy'.[31] This economic reality led to relative decline in the international arena.[32] As this rapid economic modernization gained momentum, the professional and commercial classes enlarged, as did pressure for political change.

Political pressure from below also increased as rural migrants arrived in the cities in search for work in the growing industrial sector. Confronted with an alien urban culture, horrific working conditions and insufficient social welfare programmes, they were increasingly attracted to the promises of socialism and inclined to believe that the state sided with factory owners, native as well as Western, against the interests of the simple workers. The second trajectory, therefore, was the intensification of the imagery and discourses of anti-West Occidentalism in order to manage the political and social challenges resulting from the process of Westernization.

By the beginning of the twentieth century signs of social discontent began to take the form of political violence and terrorism. Nikolai Bogolepov, the minister of education who had used harsh measures to deal with rising student activism and radicalism, was the first major figure to be assassinated (1901). The period 1901–3 witnessed five assassination attempts on leading political figures. In the years 1903–5 the number of successful attempts increased. Killed at the hands of revolutionary terrorists were Dmitry Sipyagin, interior minister, Vyacheslav Plehve, former head of the internal police and Sipyagin's successor, Grand Duke Sergei Alexandrovich, Nicholas II's uncle and Moscow's general-governor, the head of the national gendarmerie, the military attorney general and the mayor of St. Petersburg. In the midst of these developments, geopolitics entered the arena.

From the end of the nineteenth century, Japan and Russia sought to spread their influence as the Chinese Empire decayed. Their competing interests in the region created worries about the outbreak of war between them. As early as 1902 Witte wrote to Count Lamsdorff, the foreign minister, that a victory in a war with Japan over Korea would be very costly and generate little societal support. The real threat was society's 'hidden dissatisfaction' already being felt which the war would surely exacerbate.[33] Aleksei Kuropatkin, the minister of war, warned Nicholas in 1902 and 1903 that war with Japan would be very unpopular given current societal discontent and provide anti-state forces an opportunity to whip-up revolutionary fervour, especially if wartime sacrifices were increasingly made on the populace. Nicholas ignored these warnings, limiting himself to the opinion that 'all the same it is a barbarous country' and continued his policy in the Far East that eventually led to the Russo-Japanese War (1904–5).[34]

The 1905 Revolution: Constitutionalism and anti-West Occidentalism

Russian defeats, along with simmering worker discontent set afire on Bloody Sunday when soldiers fired on workers in front of the Winter Palace on 9 January 1905, led to a large-scale rebellion that spread to the countryside as the peasants took advantage of the weakened state to attack the landed nobility and seize land. Concomitantly, discontent emerged in conservative camps over an ineffective autocracy that failed to defeat an Asian country and maintain Russia's status as a great power, while the educated classes and progressive nobility too turned against the state given their long-standing hopes for political change. The state, faced with major naval defeats against the Japanese and spreading rebellion at home, ended the war. This move allowed it to crush eventually the 1905 Revolution through a mixture of concessions, namely the granting of a constitution, and the use of brute force. A political and social revolution was avoided.

In October 1905 Nicholas II signed the October Manifesto that promised a constitution. Many at the time and in subsequent historiographical interpretations have held that the manifesto was the first step towards Western forms of constitutionalism, a step that corresponded with Russian membership in the Western club. Yet, for many at the time and subsequently this constitution represented a break from true Russian authenticity of culture and national identity. These two interpretations were reflected in the Constitution. While it proclaimed the establishment of a representative parliament, the Duma, whose deputies would be popularly elected, albeit on a restricted franchise, its First Article reaffirmed the emperor's autocratic power. Nicholas II defended his insistence on it:

> The Act of 17 October I granted consciously and have resolved to carry it through to its fulfilment. However, I am not convinced that renunciation of my autocratic rights and changing the definition of the Supreme Power is necessary. My conviction is that changing that article … for many reasons is extremely dangerous. I know that if the First Article remains unchanged discontent and entreaties will emerge. But, one must consider from what quarter these reproaches and discontent with come. They will come of course from the so-called educated element, the proletariat, and the third element. I am convinced that eighty percent of the Russian people will be with me, give me support, and be grateful to me for such a decision.[35]

Thus, the constitution, while it gave the Duma legislative powers without precedent in Russian history, also ensured that the monarch remained the pillar of the political system. Duma approval was needed to make a bill law but its ability to initiate legislation was limited. That prerogative resided in the government's hands, in other words, the Council of Ministers and its chairman, all of whom were appointed by the emperor to whom it was responsible. Yet, the government needed a parliamentary working majority to obtain passage of legislation. This state of affairs placed the Russian political order closer to that of imperial Germany than to any Western constitutional forms. This duality of prerogatives was also reflected in the power of the purse. The state budget needed Duma approval but if, for whatever reason, it failed to pass a budget, the previous year's budget would automatically be implemented. Moreover, Court expenditures and certain military expenses were beyond the Duma's purview. The Duma enjoyed the right of interpellation of ministers while ministers enjoyed the right not to answer.

The State Council, the upper house, served as an additional check on the Duma and thus party and emerging mass politics. The emperor appointed half of its members any of whom he could remove at the beginning of every calendar year. The remaining other half were elected based on a limited franchise and from particular socio-economic and cultural institutions. No bill could become a law without its approval. This conservative body was sensitive to the emperor's opinions and beliefs on any bill. Nicholas understood this body's power and increasingly appointed hard-line conservatives to it in order to weaken Stolypin and his growing reformist activities that seemed to threaten the interests of the autocracy and the landowning noble class.

The post-revolutionary period (1906–14) was characterized by economic change and military reform. Defeat in war had shown again Russia's economic, technological and military weaknesses that undermined its position as a great power. Moreover, the state's financial situation was dire, a consequence of wartime expenses and the chaos and suppression of the revolution. Similar to the situation after the defeat in the Crimean War, the state intensified military reform and industrialization, which was greatly fuelled by Western, and in particular, French capital and investment. Moreover, weakening productivity in the agricultural sector, which was one of the greatest sources of surplus capital obtained through the export of agricultural stuffs, and peasant unrest during the 1905 Revolution showed that the state could no longer ignore the issue of land reform.

Peter Stolypin, the prime minister (1906–11) who launched a new cycle of Westernization, envisaged two goals when implementing land reform. The peasants had shown in the 1905 Revolution that they sought land and liberation from the onerous monetary duties placed on them and the commune when the serfs were emancipated to compensate the landowning nobility for the loss of souls and land. Worryingly, peasant dissatisfaction in this revolution had shown that their loyalty to the emperor could not be taken for granted. Through the granting of land, the breaking up of the commune and the cancellation of these monetary duties it was hoped that a bulwark for the monarchy that represented the vast majority of the population would be created. The monarchy could lean on this bulwark as it faced in the urban areas increasing political challenges posed by the working class and liberal and socialist leaning members of educated public opinion. In contrast to Alexander II's approach that placed emphasis on strengthening the link between the state and the progressive autocracy and urban-educated classes, Nicholas II's government looked to the landed nobility and the peasant class. Economically the hope was that the breaking up of the commune would raise agricultural production for both domestic consumption and export. Stolypin in his speech announcing the land reforms stressed:

> The commune more than anything else holds back our political as well as economic development. It hinders the formation of a middle class of small-landed proprietors who, in the most advanced Western countries, comprise their might. What propelled so quickly America into the front rank if not individualism and small landed property? Our landed commune is a rotten anachronism, which prospers only thanks to the artificial, baseless sentimentalism of the past half century which is contrary to common sense and the most important needs of the state.[36]

Thus, the state's discourses portrayed the rural population as the holder of the authenticity of Russian culture and national identity and emphasized its unique link with the tsar as the source and defender of that authenticity, while its economic policies were set on transforming peasants into a rural *homo Romanovicus* based on the West's example. In sum, the goal of capitalist development without succumbing to Western liberal forms of governance remained.

As the state intensified the practical process of Westernization, the socio-economic and political tensions that had played an important role in the coming of the 1905 Revolution continued to confront the state with challenges that it hoped to manage with reliance on this peasant bulwark and the expansion and deepening of the discourses and imagery of anti-West Occidentalism which should not be confused with rejection of Europe or unwillingness to adopt elements from the West needed for economic and technological development. The autocracy, discursively buttressed by the triad conceptions of Orthodoxy and nationality, portrayed itself as essential to Russia's past, as the source and defender of the authenticity of Russian culture and national identity, to its present, as the other force able to hold together this vast empire and protect its geopolitical borders against foreign threats, and to its future, claiming it was Russia's only authentic historical driving force, able to achieve economic and technological development while acting as an above-class force that maintained social unity, rendered justice to all, and prevented societal descent into moral and cultural corruption brought by Occidentosis. Nationality took on a new form and importance, blending the traditional definition of Russianness, Orthodoxy, with a strengthened emphasis on the Russian-Slavic race. The shift was clearly seen in the implementation during the reigns of these last two emperors of a policy of Russianization, particularly in the Baltic German areas, Poland, Finland and Ukraine and dovetailed with the myth of the inevitable racial clash between Slavs, headed by Russia, and the Teuton. Alexander III summed up these roles and the justifications for the autocracy noted earlier: 'The autocracy created the historical uniqueness of Russia. If the autocracy crashes, God forbid, then so does Russia'.[37]

Corresponding changes were made in official symbolism and imagery. It dropped Occidentalist symbols, revived under Alexander II, and replaced them with the imagery and symbolism of true Russianness, rooted in pre-Petrine Muscovite Russia, under the protection of the paternal and patriarchal Holy Tsar and buttressed by Orthodoxy in opposition to the West. In place of 'the emperor' pursuing pro-West Occidentalism came 'the Russian tsar' defending the authenticity of native culture and identity against Occidentosis. The symbolism of the emperor 'underwent an ideological change from emphasis on the "hero-emperor" (an image characteristic of the European imperial tradition) to tsarist traits (an image taking inspiration from Orthodox collectivism and providing the base of the new national myth)'.[38] This change was visible even in clothing. Unlike Peter and Catherine, Alexander III and Nicholas II wore simple 'Russian' clothing and preferred Russian native traditions. Nicholas sat at his work desk in a simple Russian peasant shirt along with peasant-style baggy pants. In fact, Nicholas II mulled over dress reform according to which formal court dress, whose Western style Peter I imposed, would be returned to pre-Petrine fashion. He dropped the idea when he realized the exorbitant cost of the jewels and ornamentation of this 'authentic' Russian dress. Alexander III and Nicholas II, similar to Nicholas I, stressed and propagated Russian traditions, as they deemed them to be, in culture and art. The overall tone of state propaganda reflected this change.

Promotion of constitutionalism, republicanism and/or socialism, portrayed as Western ideologies, was propagated as heresy and treasonous to the authenticity of Russian culture and national identity that had been passed through the generations at great cost. Within these discourses the representations of social groups changed. The urban-educated classes, the products of pro-West Occidentalism, were no longer held up as an example to society. Culturally and politically Occidentosis-ridden, they were portrayed in negative contrast with the group that took its place as the current example of *homo Romanovicus* of anti-West Occidentalism, the rural population. Little discursive effort was made to appeal to this minority, urban-educated and progressive groups. The discourses and symbolism were tailored to appeal to the conservative nobility, radical nationalist and monarchist groups, the bureaucratic and security apparatus, and the rural population, while it was hoped that through the passage of worker legislation the state could de-politicize the workers by showing that the autocracy was indeed the best defender of their rights.

Any understanding of the evolution of anti-West Occidentalism must take into account Nicholas's personality and world views. First, he has been portrayed as weak-willed, lacking the intelligence and stamina to govern the rapidly changing empire, and a determined fatalist. To an extent this is true. At the beginning of his reign he wrote to his mother the dowager empress Alexandra Feodorovna: 'I look submissively and confidently to the future known only to God. He always organizes everything for our good, although at times his trials seem to us unduly heavy'. Therefore, it's necessary to repeat, 'Such will be Your will'.[39] He remarked to Stolypin: 'None of my projects is successful. I do not enjoy success. And besides human will is impotent'.[40]

Yet, in regard to two political issues he showed a resilience of will that belies this characterization. First, he was determined to protect and preserve the autocracy. Faced in 1905 with the possibility of a political and social revolution and pressure to take steps towards a constitutional system in order to avoid it he remarked: 'All this time I have been tormented by the worry as to whether I have the right before my ancestors to change the limits of that power I received from them'. As late as 1916 when public discontent and anger over the war and living conditions, in addition to long-standing political grievances, began to emit the smell of revolution, he rejected the pleas of Grand Duke Paul Alexandrovich to establish a government that enjoyed public confidence: 'I took an oath for the autocracy on the day of my coronation. I must remit this oath in its entirety to my son'.[41]

These were not politically cynical statements oriented to justify a naked hold on power for the sake of power. Alexander III and Nicholas II strongly believed, correctly or not, as did many within the political elite, that only the autocracy was capable of maintaining the social unity threatened by growing class tensions, internal stability of the multinational empire in the age of spreading nationalism, its position within the European and global state system and carrying out the policies needed to support that position. This was the approach formalized by Karamzin. Nicholas told his Interior Minister Prince Svyatapolk-Mirskii in late October 1904 as the winds of the 1905 Revolution began to blow: 'You know I don't hold to the autocracy for my own pleasure. I act in this sense because I am convinced that it is necessary for Russia. If it were simply a question for myself, I would happily get rid of all this'.[42] Nicholas also viewed the autocracy as the repository of Russian authenticity and the heritage of generations over the centuries. Here again is the influence of Karamzin's understanding of Russian history.

Second, Nicholas adhered to conceptions of the authenticity of Russian culture and identity that might seem contradictory but were easily placed next to each other in his mind. No doubt exists that Nicholas considered himself a European. He was even culturally Anglophile to an extent, speaking fluent English which was the language of communication with his wife. Typical for the time, he was related to many leading European dynastic houses. His cousins were George V of Britain and Wilhelm II of Germany and he was related to Queen Victoria. His mother, Alexandra Feodorovna, formerly known as Princess Dagmar, was the daughter of Christian IX of Denmark at whose court he spent many summers in his youth. Her sister was Queen Alexandra, Edward VII's consort. Nicholas's wife, Princess Alix from a minor German duchy, was also a cousin of George V and Wilhelm II.

The problem was defining this Europe, the constitutive elements of its identity and which countries and political systems epitomized it. On one level, the idea of a powerful developed Europe of white peoples in contrast to the rest of the world that it was colonizing provided an effective international identity. However, across the continent divisions and debates remained over the cultural, political and even geographical conceptions of this Europe. The Enlightenment offered a vision that it claimed was the true Europe whose standard bearers in Nicholas II's reign were France and Britain. They represented progressive linear history and the idea of a true Europe made up by a superior and exclusive political and cultural civilization, 'the West'. Countries that rejected Western liberal forms of governance had failed to join this caravan of history and were denied membership to the West that, to repeat, claimed to represent the true Europe.

As mentioned earlier, during Nicholas I's reign, and especially after the 1848 Revolutions, the Russian state employed a discursive and political response that described a false Europe, named 'the West', and a true Europe represented by Russia and defended by its monarchical system. Nicholas II subscribed to this imagery that helped rationalize his continued defense of the monarchy's power in the face of pressure to implement political reforms at a time when the monarchy, compared to Nicholas I's reign, faced a greater number of ideological and political threats and in particular the growing challenge of mass politics. This idea of true and false Europe promised a path for Russia's inclusion in Europe, an inclusion that was essential to the prestige, self-confidence and self-respect of the Romanov dynasty and its elite, while allowing for the propagation of discourses of anti-West Occidentalism.

General Alexander Mosolov, minister of the Imperial Court (1902–16) during the 1903 celebrations marking the two-hundredth anniversary of the founding of St. Petersburg, 'spoke enthusiastically' to Nicholas about Peter I's reforms and heritage. However, Mosolov noted

> the tsar was not supporting my view. Knowing of the tsar's self-restraint, I nonetheless dared to ask him if he sympathized with what I had said. Nicholas was silent for a moment and answered: 'Of course I recognize my famous ancestor's

many services. However, I confess that I would be less than honest if I said that I shared your enthusiasm for him. This ancestor I love less than the others given his passion (*uvlechenie*) for Western (*zapadnii*) culture and his trampling of pure Russian customs and mores. It is impossible to inculcate foreign ways without some form of revision and reshaping. Perhaps it was a transition period, and perhaps it was necessary, but I am not supportive or sympathetic to it'.[43]

Nicholas carefully chose his words. He said 'Western', not European culture. This 'Western' culture was distinct from true European culture and could not speak for all of Europe. It was therefore foreign and alien to the authenticity of Russian culture and national identity. Once again imagery conveyed Nicholas's beliefs. This time at the great ball he hosted at the Winter Palace as part of these celebrations, which, it must be remembered, marked the anniversary of the beginning of imperial Russia and the turn towards pro-West Occidentalism. All invitees were required to don 'authentic' Russian clothes dating from the pre-Petrine period and perform traditional Russian dances dating from that period. For weeks before this gala, they had to learn such dances.

Since the closing years of Catherine II's reign the state had faced a gradually increasing challenge posed by the growing number of competing ideologies from the West and their derivatives and nativist narratives that challenged its Occidentalisms. This challenge took the form of either an amorphous public opinion among the aristocracy, intelligentsia and educated professional classes or revolutionary and terrorist organizations. As a result of the 1905 Revolution and the establishment of the Duma, these ideologies and narratives now competed with those of the state in the form of political parties in electoral politics in a semi-free political arena. The government, lacking its own party, was forced to find a working majority in the Duma in order to govern while it, backed by monarchical power, could check any radical reforms and policies proposed by majorities in the Duma. In other words, its power to block was greater than its power to pass and implement legislation which was dependent on obtaining this majority. To understand the challenges the discourses of anti-West Occidentalism were to manage a brief look at the broad political tendencies in the Duma is necessary. The composition of the first two Dumas (27 April–21 July 1906 and 20 February–2 June 1907) whose deputies were elected on a restricted franchise reflects the complex political situation in which the Russian state found itself in the immediate aftermath of the 1905 Revolution.

The largest party in these two Dumas was the Constitutional Democrat (Kadets). This was the party of Anglophiles who took inspiration from the British constitutional system and its division between the Houses of Lords and Commons. The party's main goals were protecting and expanding the civil and political rights granted by the October Manifesto and moves towards the institutionalization of Western forms of constitutionalism. Another goal was land reform. Following this party in the number of seats in these two Duma were independent deputies and the Labour Party. The Labour Party shared the Kadet's political goals, but with a focus on the rights and interests of the peasant and working classes and the labouring intelligentsia. The speakership and highest governing posts in this Duma were held by Kadets. In this Duma only 10 per cent of deputies supported the autocratic ideal.

The First Duma pushed for land reform, calling for the breaking up of noble estates and the transfer of their property to the peasants. The radical leftists pushed for this land transfer without compensation to noble landowners. The government rejected what it considered a brazen attack on private property and on one of the few social groups loyal to the state, the landed aristocracy. At the same time, it refused to contemplate the Duma's other principal demands, namely ministerial responsibility to the Duma and not the monarch, expansion of the Duma's prerogatives, universal suffrage and a political amnesty for those involved in the 1905 Revolution. As tensions between the Duma and the government and the emperor quickly rose, Prince C. D. Urusov from the Party of Democratic Reform gave a speech in the Duma that devastated the state's repressive measures and unwillingness to work with this new body. It was dissolved that day. The First Duma lasted only seventy-two days.

New elections were held whose results disappointed Nicholas II and the government. On the one hand, the Kadets, considered the main threat to the autocracy given its politically Occidentosis-ridden state, obtained only 98 seats, falling from 154. On the other hand, the Socialist Revolutionary Party, founded in 1902 and is the largest non-Marxist party, and the Russian Social Democratic Workers Party, the largest Marxist party that had two wings, the Mensheviks and the Bolsheviks, obtained a substantial numbers of seats. These two parties had not participated in the elections to the First Duma. They, along with other socialist leaning parties, won 118 seats. The Labour Party won 104 seats, down from 107. These groups held 320 of the Duma's 500 seats and thus pushed this body's political leaning to the left of the First Duma. While they had political and ideological differences on some issues, the government had little hope of putting together a working majority to push legislation. This election also saw the rise of the Octobrist Party which garnered fifty-four votes. The Octobrist Party supported the 1905 Constitution but rejected the position of the Kadets. It saw itself as the government's natural ally, helping it to govern and implement 'sensible' reforms during a turbulent period. However, the duality in the constitution about the powers of the emperor and Duma created a division in this party between a left wing that was closer to the Kadets and a right wing that had more in common with conservative monarchist parties supporting the idea of the autocracy free of constitutional annoyances.

The Second Duma, therefore, suffered the same fate as the first one, although it remained in session several weeks longer. Dissolving it, Nicholas issued an imperial manifesto detailing a new franchise law designed to weaken the parties that together held majorities in the first two Dumas, in other words, the Kadets and socialist parties, seen as ridden with political Occidentosis, and to ensure a rightist conservative majority that would provide the government with a working majority. This change of the electoral law went against the 1905 Constitution according to which no legislative project could become law without the Duma's approval while the manifesto proclaimed that the authority to change the electoral law belonged only to the monarch.

The desired election results for the Third Duma (1907–12) were obtained. The Socialist Revolutionaries obtained no seats while the Russian Socialist Democratic Workers Party saw its number of seats slashed from sixty-five to nineteen. The Labour Party was decimated, reduced to a mere thirteen seats. The Kadets found themselves with only fifty-four. The Octobrists became the largest party with 154 seats. Behind them were various nationalist groups with ninety-seven seats. Over the life of this Duma these groups would come together to create the All-Russian Peoples Union, that in the Fourth Duma (1912–17) became the largest rightist party. In the Third Duma it considered itself Stolypin's natural ally. Yet, this party's ideological approach to the authenticity of Russian culture and national identity, which reflected the discourses of other rightist groups, sought to strengthen the state discourses of anti-West Occidentalism. This party's approach was situated within the triad whose elements they sought to propagate as the Russian form of nationalism, a goal first established by Nicholas I.

According to the discourses of the All-Russian Peoples Union, the autocracy and tsar were portrayed as the source and defender of Russian authenticity. 'True grandeur, sacralized and strong name, an independent tsar, who himself supports Russian truth and thought, and popular belief for the throne, the light of native faith, universal thought, and Christian feelings-these are some of the eternal characteristics of our national idea'. However, unlike the extreme right, this group accepted the constitutional system as it evolved after the 1907 changes to the franchise law, equating it with the old Boyar Duma that had entered the history books with the emergence of the Petrine imperial bureaucratic state. 'The resurgence of the political system we understand as a return to antiquity, openness, while popular representation is a return to authentic Russian truth and the ancient foundations of our life'. Russian nationalists must strive 'for a monarchy revived on ancient Kieven and Muscovite roots'. This belief was based on Slavophile conceptions according to which the autocracy, while protecting the authenticity of Russian culture and identity in the face of Occidentosis, enjoyed a unique relationship with the people whose fundamental rights and cultural authenticity it respected. According to Slavophile thought and derivative schools, the bureaucratic state implementing pro-West Occidentalism was a despotic system, alien to Russian conceptions of governance, and despotically imposing foreign 'Western' ways and culture on the people.[44]

Given the threat posed by the West and the spread of Occidentosis to the authenticity of Russian culture and national identity and its source and defender, the autocracy, this group called for a national mobilization around the Crown. 'Our country and its antiquity appear to be a great hindrance to those people who see the greatest ideal and example in Western European culture, to those people who seek to live according to prepared recipes and prescription without any exception and without consideration if they are appropriate to our circumstances'. These Occidentosis-ridden people and groups sought to spread this disease with Western ideas of cosmopolitanism and internationalism. While manifestations of Occidentosis, these ideas were portrayed by such people as deceitfully attractive universal ideas that would provide some form of utopia in this world. However, under the leadership of the autocracy those true Russians 'who believe in the organic authentic growth of Russia' would be mobilized. For such people 'Russian antiquity and authenticity is an enteral source for the rational creative work' that would provide Russia's path to the future.[45]

The differences between Russians and Russian civilization and Westerners were clear. Unlike Westerners, 'the person with a pure Russian soul is the brother of humanity'. Unlike Russia, Western civilization was in a state of decline as its foundations were corroded by hedonism, atomistic individualism and brutal forms of capitalism and consumerism that forced people into a daily struggle against each other for fulfilment of their materialistic and in most cases superfluous needs while poverty spread among the lower classes. But Russia's conditions were clearly different. 'Inherent to Orthodoxy and the Russian people are gentleness, goodness, kindness, empathy, compassion, love, mercifulness, self-sacrifice, and forgiveness'. In other words, a unique spirituality existed that placed human relationships, collectivism, empathy and an internal peace above all else.[46]

Three radical nationalist and monarchist groups also emerged in the wake of the 1905 Revolution which targeted the seeming emergent threat to Russian authenticity posed by the spread of cultural and political Occidentosis epitomized by the new constitution. They were the Russian Monarchist Party founded by V. A. Gringmut, the Russian Assembly led by Prince Dmitrii Golitsyn, the United Nobility and its governing council that enjoyed close relations with the Court and the State Council, and the Union of the Russian People founded by minor government officials, A. I. Dubrovin and V. M. Purishkevich. Hardcore defenders of the autocracy, the position of the nobility and 'authenticity' of Russian culture, they targeted the politicians and parties supporting any form of liberalism or socialism, those threatening manifestations of Occidentosis. Nicholas I's triad was their motto.[47]

The Union of Russian People is of particular importance since it attracted the personal support of important state and court figures. It advocated a strict interpretation of Uvarov's triad that found favour with Nicholas who had the interior ministry provide it with financial aid for its newspaper, *Russian Banner* (*Russkoe znamya*) and other forms of propaganda and even with arms. By 1907 this party claimed to have some 1,000 paramilitary groups that together had approximately 300,000 members who harassed and attacked liberals, socialists and Jews. Nicholas, not surprisingly, planning for the future, saw this Union as a strong centralized monarchist party dedicated to protecting the autocracy and Russian authenticity against pernicious Western influences and against Jews intent on controlling not only Russia but eventually the world.

Nicholas supported extreme rightist groups and particularly the Black Hundreds which included in its ranks not only the Union of Russian People but also the Union of the Archangel Michael and the All-Dubrovinist Union of the Russian People, among others.[48] Across the country local organizations operating under the umbrella of the Black Hundreds printed newspapers, magazines and other forms of propaganda. They took inspiration from Uvarov's triad while adhering to the international politics of Pan-Slavism which advocated unification of all Slavs under Russian leadership in opposition to the West, and therefore 'visceral opposition to the West'.[49] Westerners were seen as 'practitioners of soulless capitalism whose pernicious revolutionary' and liberal ideologies needed to be combatted. Nicholas exchanged messages with these groups and their leaders while having informal meetings with them arranged outside of regular protocol. Moreover, Nicholas also provided financial help to them. His support was not limited to this. When members of the Black Hundreds assassinated prominent politicians and public figures such as Mikhail Gertsenshtein, a Kadet deputy from Moscow, and were convicted by the courts, Nicholas pardoned them. He provided pardons for other members convicted of lesser crimes. Moreover, General

Paul Kurlov, a favourite of the empress Dowager and Nicholas II, in this period became head of the internal intelligence services. He provided funds and political cover to these extremist rightist groups and their publications propagating discourses of anti-West Occidentalism. Yet, Nicholas's support was dependent on the political interests and circumstances of the monarchy at any point in time. He and his more conservative ministers and officials were equivocal about the revolutionary and anarchist threat inherent in the mass populist right that some of these groups represented. Nicholas and the highest state officials were unwilling to share in any meaningful way power with these rightist groups. Nonetheless, they were prepared to use them when necessary against those political groups infected with political Occidentosis.

Stolypin by 1911, the year he was assassinated in Kiev, was a much-reduced political figure. He and his government found themselves assailed from many directions. His political and economic reforms provoked the opposition of rightist groups and the conservative nobility who not only feared the consequences for their interests of such reforms but also did not want the constitutional system to become institutionalized and independent of the autocracy. Inside the Duma the slowing momentum of reform due to conservative opposition within the Duma and State Council not only weakened the key government–allied party, the Octobrists, but also ensured that left-leaning parties, such as the Kadets, would increase their pressure on the government for change. As the Duma became increasingly paralyzed, Stolypin began to lose the support of the educated urban classes. At the centre of these events was Nicholas and his determination to undermine this system and ensure the centrality of the autocracy and himself in the political system.[50]

During Kokovstev's tenure, which ended in 1914, Nicholas increasingly appointed hard-line conservatives to the cabinet who in turn reported directly to him. Thus, Kokovtsev had little practical control over the Council of Ministers. The idea of a united ministry was dead while individual ministers with Nicholas's support consistently moved policy to the right, suffocating the post-1905 constitutional system. Kokovtsov noted: 'Nominally I was considered the head of government, directing its activities, and responsible for it to public opinion. In reality, one group was conducting a policy clearly hostile to me and weakening gradually my position'.[51] By 1914 the Duma had effectively been reduced to a mere talking shop, enjoying the confidence and support of neither society nor the state led by Nicholas.

At the same time worries about the spread of moral Occidentosis increased greatly as Russia's industrialization and urbanization gathered speed. From 1910 crime grew at an alarming rate, especially in the large urban areas such as St. Petersburg and Moscow. St. Petersburg, the political capital, became known as the crime capital. Along with this sign of a dramatic fall in personal morality, sexual morality too, in the opinion of many, was quickly declining. Freedom of the press allowed by the 1905 Constitution led to an explosion in pornography, erotic magazines and pornographic novels. Prostitution spread and was increasingly visible. In St. Petersburg some forty-seven brothels, many in the city centre, had popped up, reflecting a process in most urban areas, large as well as small. It seemed that the capital of Orthodox Russia was beginning to resemble Western capital cities, Paris and London, where moral corruption was the socially accepted norm and spirituality no longer existed. Lev Tikhomirov, a propagandist of the triad and editor of *Moskovskie Novosti* lamented: 'The Russian people! ... They have lost already their past spirit and spirituality. Their former feelings'.⁵²

Concomitantly concerns emerged about cultural and moral decline in the face of mass consumerism, commercialization and materialism – those pernicious signs of Occidentosis. Members of the intelligentsia and aristocracy held in disdain merchants, whose numbers increased as a result of industrialization and the spread of materialism and consumerism, for their commercialization of society and human relationships and reducing life to the pursuit of money. They decried the influence they had on the masses. The intelligentsia 'worried that the emergence of mass market and urban entertainments encouraged self-indulgent materialism and threatened folk traditions and culture'. Not surprisingly, Slavophiles, neo-Slavophiles and populists were the loudest in this condemnation of Occidentosis and looked to the Crown for action. These groups

> envisioned an economy founded on the peasant commune and held that agriculture, a socially productive form of labor and the primary source of national wealth, rather than industry or commerce, should support Russian society. Following from this worldview, both groups faulted wealthy capitalist entrepreneurs for their purported imitation of the West and adoption of Western ideas, trends they deemed irreconcilable with Russia's traditions of rural community.⁵³

Consequently, a sense of cultural and moral malaise resulting from the spread of Occidentosis continued to grow until the end of Nicholas II's reign.

The year 1913 marked the tricentenary of the founding of the Romanov dynasty. The form of the celebrations, their official symbolism and propaganda and in particular the ceremonies surrounding the imperial couple's tour that traced the path of Mikhail Romanov from his birthplace to the throne in Moscow provide the best examples of the tone of Romanov anti-West Occidentalism. It had three fundamental trajectories.

First, the mythical and sacralized link between the tsar and the people was emphasized. While this approach is expected and natural, the definitions given to the idea of the people hold importance for this study. The emphasis on the word 'tsar' even though the sovereign remained officially known as the emperor underlined the fundamental importance of the pre-Petrine period as the fount of Russian cultural authenticity in anti-West Occidentalism. Flowing from this was the emphasis was on the peasant as genuine Russians people, who maintained this authenticity and loyalty to its source and defender, the autocracy. This group stood in contrast to the Occidentosis-ridden intelligentsia, urbanized educated populace, and aristocratic liberals who advocated various forms of changes rooted in Western models and were critical of the autocracy. During the 1909 celebrations marking the Battle of Poltava during Peter's reign Nicholas remarked to the French military attaché that since they were not in St. Petersburg no one could say that the Russian people did not love their tsar and that he was 'certain that the rustic population, landowners, nobility, and army remain loyal to the Tsar. The revolutionary elements are composed of Jews, students, landless peasants, and some workers'⁵⁴ and the corrupt Occidentosis-ridden urban groups. In October 1905 he had written to his mother: 'The days after the signing of the Manifesto were not bad not only for the Jews but also Russians-engineers, lawyers, political agitators and all other kinds of nasty bad ones'.⁵⁵ Grand Duchess Olga Alexandrovna noted during the imperial steamship's voyage along the Volga in 1913:

> Wherever we went we were met with manifestations of loyalty bordering on frenzy. When our steamer travelled down the Volga we witnessed crowds of peasants wading up to the waist in the water in the hope of catching a glimpse of Nicky. In some towns I saw artisans and workers falling to the ground to kiss his shadow as we passed. Cheers were always deafening.⁵⁶

These scenes convinced the imperial couple that the discourses of anti-West Occidentalism reflected reality. The empress told a lady-in-waiting: 'Now you see for yourself what cowards the ministers are. They are constantly frightening the tsar with threats of revolution and here – you see it yourself – we need merely to show ourselves and immediately their hearts are ours'.⁵⁷

Second, the image of *tsar-batushka* was emphasized – an image that was downplayed during the reigns when pro-West Occidentalism was hegemonic. It was based on the idea of the tsar as the nation's paternal head and differed from the title 'father of the motherland' that had been bestowed upon Peter and portrayed him as the father of a resurgent new Russia who through his enlightened bureaucracy implemented reforms in order to march forward towards grandeur and greatness as a great European imperial power. The image of the *tsar-batushka* was rooted in the pre-Petrine image of the tsar as the country's paternal figure defending the country's cultural and geopolitical borders in the face of corrupting influences coming from the West, and 'the people', in other words, the peasants, from corrupt and malevolent bureaucrats of his own state and the urbanized educated classes all of whom were morally, culturally and/or politically ridden with Occidentosis.

These two competing images of the sovereign symbolize the fundamental trajectory of pro-West and anti-West Occidentalisms whose common and distinguishing theme was the peasants. The father of the homeland and those successors who adhered to and propagated the cult of Peter along with the power of an enlightened bureaucracy regarded the culture and authenticity epitomized by the peasant class as the main cause for Russia's backwardness in comparison with the West. The *tsar-batushka* image proclaimed this peasant as the epitome of Russian authenticity that had to be preserved. For example, during receptions at the Winter Palace in the initial phase of these celebrations the empress 'wore a long Oriental gown of silk brocade and the tall cone-shaped *kokoshnik* worn by Russian empresses before the court was Westernized by Peter the Great'.⁵⁸ Kokovtsov noted in his diary:

> The voyage of the Sovereign was given the meaning of a family celebration of the Romanov House while the state character of this event was not given any place. ... The concept of the government, its role and meaning, were pushed into the background. While the personal character of the Tsar's rule was strongly and clearly underlined, the view that the government constituted some form of barrier between the Tsar and his people, preventing them from getting closer to

each other, was increasingly propagated. [Thus] developing in him [was] the cult of autocratism that obtained increasing strength … [In the years after the 1905 Revolution] the idea of the greatness of the Tsar's personality and belief in the unlimited devotion to him, as God's anointed, of all the people, of their blind belief in him, alongside their belief in God, progressively strengthened, at least amongst those closest to the tsar. The tsar himself undoubtedly increasingly believed that the sovereign can do everything alone because the people were with him, the people knew and understood him, infinitely loved him because they were blindly devoted to him. Ministers not ridden with this understanding of the autocracy, and even more the State Duma … believed that the monarch should understand that governing in the old way was no longer possible, that he should adapt to new conditions that were reducing the previous prestige and darkening the halo of 'the Muscovite Tsar' governing Russia as if it were his own estate.[59]

Lastly, the celebrations intensified the portrayal of the establishment of the Romanov dynasty as a great national moment in the long history of the Russian struggle to protect the authenticity of culture and identity in the face of long-standing and various forms of Occidentosis. This struggle, whose importance grew from the mid-nineteenth century in the face of the spread of Occidentosis, first fully expressed in the Decembrist Revolt, and the German geopolitical threat was to unite the bulk of the real people, those peasants, around the throne and paper over growing socio-economic and cultural differences that were threatening social unity and the state.

Peter Durnovo was a hard-nosed, perceptive conservative top official of the imperial state, serving from 1900 as deputy minister of interior and leading the radical right wing in the State Council from 1907. He was hated by moderate reformists and liberals, including Kadets and left-leaning Octobrists for his belief that Western liberalism, constitutional forms of governance and republicanism would destroy Russia and its empire. While supporting discourses attacking political Occidentosis, he was not a Slavophile and did not idealize the pre-Petrine period. In February 1914, several months after the end of these celebrations, he sent a report to Nicholas. In it he outlined Russia's domestic and geopolitical situation as fears about a war with Germany increased. In this report, Durnovo by providing insight into rightist opinions about the West, symbolized by Britain and France, explains the attractiveness of anti-West Occidentalism.

Durnovo opposed Russia's alignment with France and Britain and the idea of war with Germany:

> A struggle between Russia and Germany is profoundly undesirable to both sides, as it amounts to a weakening of the monarchical principle. It should not be forgotten that Russia and Germany are the representatives of the conservative principle in the civilized world, as opposed to the democratic principle incarnated in England … and France.

Russia's geopolitical interests, the nature of its political system and conceptions of authenticity of culture and identity dictated that Russia not war, but rather align with

Germany in the face of the threat of political Occidentosis and the West's geopolitical power. After all, the leader of this West, Britain, in her foreign relations had been 'the protector of the most demagogical tendencies, invariably encouraging all popular movements aiming at the weakening of the monarchical principle'.

After the Crimean War Russia had resumed its role in sustaining the continent's balance of power and in struggling against revolutionary movements and the spread of political Occidentosis. This policy initially brought Russia closer to Berlin and Vienna in the so-called Three Emperors's League. However, during the last twenty years of the nineteenth century, autocratic Russia established an alliance with Republican France to counter the growing strength of imperial Germany and the geopolitical aspirations of the Austro-Hungarian Empire in the Balkans. In the early 1900s Paris and St. Petersburg aligned with London, also increasingly concerned by Berlin's increasing strength and desire to obtain its place under the sun. Durnovo was calling for a reversal of these alliances so that Russia and Germany, by defending the monarchical principle and combatting Occidentosis, would together serve as the gendarme of the true Europe.

Reflecting anti-West Occidentalism, Durnovo saw two fundamental ideological threats emanating from the West, liberal capitalism latched onto forms of constitutionalism and socialism. In his opinion, socialism was the far more dangerous of the two. 'The masses undoubtedly profess, unconsciously, socialism's principle. ... (W)orkers and peasants are not looking for political rights which they neither want nor comprehend. ... The peasants dream of obtaining a gratuitous share of somebody else's land; the workers, of getting hold of the entire capital and profits of the manufacturer. Beyond this no aspirations'. At the same time, the educated urban middle classes, intellectuals and elements critical of the government in the Duma, such as Kadets and even Octobrists, represented a political threat given their goals to put an end to the autocracy and establish a Western constitutional system. However, they did not enjoy support among the workers or peasants given their Occidentosis-ridden state and airs of intellectual elitism. He predicted that if Russia engaged in a war with Germany, which he stressed would last longer than expected by most people, the country would face a social revolution, even if it won.

Durnovo saw in Germany not only a fellow anti-West conservative power but also an economic partner more reliable and trustworthy than France or England. Moreover, the Germans were not as arrogant and condescending as the French and English, who still showed their contempt for Russia and Russians. He told Nicholas that Western investors and industrialists, namely France and Britain, 'are interested excessively in obtaining the largest possible returns from capital invested in Russia, even at the cost of economic ruin of this country'. This approach contrasted with the more just approach of the Germans and their desire to think and act long term in Russia – an approach that benefitted both sides. The Germans also made efforts to speak Russian, even if often 'with a heavy accent'. Westerners, on the other hand, given their negative view of the non-Western Russians kept their distance. 'Who has not seen French and English who having spent almost their entire lives in Russia and yet still do not speak a word of Russian?'[60] This report was too little too late.

On 2 August 1914 Nicholas II appeared on the balcony of the Winter Palace in St. Petersburg overlooking Palace Square, in whose centre is a large column commemorating the Russian victory over Napoleon, to acknowledge the large crowd of people who had gathered there. They had come to show their support and loyalty to the monarch in the wake of the German declaration of war against Russia. This upsurge in national and monarchical feelings in the face of the Teutonic threat seemed to put to rest the growing political and social tensions increasingly threatening the autocracy. Thirty months later, in February 1917, the Romanov dynasty was overthrown. In 1918 the Bolsheviks executed the imperial family. On the ruins of the Romanov state emerged the Union of Soviet Socialist Republics that, especially from the Stalinist period (1929–53), propagated an intense and universal form of anti-West Occidentalism.

4

Pahlavi Occidentalism: The period of Reza Shah

In 1921 Reza Khan and Seyyed Zia Tabatabai, a well-known Anglophile journalist, launched a coup d'état against the politically paralyzed prime minister Sepahdar. Tabatabai became prime minister while Reza Khan assumed the post of war minister. Ahmad Shah (r.1909–25) was given assurances that these steps did not aim to overthrow, but rather protect, him from the Bolshevik threat. By 1923 Reza Khan became prime minister. Two years later he deposed the Qajar monarch and ascended the Peacock Throne.

The country's situation was catastrophic. The 1906 Constitutional Revolution had failed to create the conditions for state centralization, the implementation of reforms and the end of imperialist exploitation. Educated and elite opinion had coalesced around ideas that transformative action by a decisive leader was needed to preserve Iran and that a country in such circumstances could not be governed by constitutional forms, especially when the illiteracy rate was around 90 per cent. Ali Dashti, a literary and political figure, in his newspaper, *Red Dusk*, noted at the time: 'The best method for achieving this [reforms] is the establishment of an efficient, powerful government that, while enlightened and virtuous, can with the end of the bayonet achieve modernization and welfare and eliminate moral corruption.'[1]

This sentiment had already prevailed in the Berlin Circle – a small group of influential Iranian intellectuals living in Germany's capital where they published under the editorship of Hassan Taqizadeh the well-known journal *Kaveh*. This group consisted of figures such as Hossein Kazemzadeh Iranshahr and Morteza Moshfeq-Kazemi. Given the country's conditions they were able to play an important role in steering 'Iranian nationalism away from liberal constitutionalism and social democracy [and] toward enlightened despotism and spiritual revivalism, flirting even with fascism'.[2] In the words of Ali Akbar Davar, the founder of Iran's secular judicial system during Reza Shah's reign, 'Iranians will not voluntarily and willingly become human [in other words, civilized in the Western sense]. Salvation must be imposed on Iran'.[3]

Official Pahlavi historiography propagated this narrative, stressing the chaotic and dangerous situation in which Iran found itself during and after the First World War and the failure of the constitutional system and its politicians to address it. Mohammad

Reza Shah portrayed his father's forceful measures as the logical manifestation of that period's conditions.

> A gifted and individualistic people, we had disintegrated into lethargy and political and social anarchy. ... Unfortunately, by the time of World War I we were in a great state of decline. The First World War was, as they say, the straw that broke the camel's back and our country was occupied. Foreign powers strove to take advantage of our weakness and achieve and maintain whatever they wanted. After that war, in reality a miracle [his father's emergence] saved us.[4]

These conditions constituted only the latest stage in the country's progressive decline, increasingly obvious from the beginning of the nineteenth century.

The loss of territory and spread of Russian and British economic and political influence prompted intense debates concerning the reasons for the West's rise and Iran's decline. By the end of the nineteenth century, that conclusion that the key to the West's power was culture and race was becoming increasingly popular. Thus, Reza Shah, building on intellectual and political tendencies that emerged during the last half-century of Qajar rule, initiated cultural transformations that would create the conditions for replicating the West's various forms of power. In his son's words, he 'was ... determined to Westernize Iran'.[5] The first Pahlavi monarch in his coronation speech stressed that his rule would be based on the 'implementation of fundamental reforms' in all spheres of life and governance.[6] Vital initial goals were creation of national unity from among Iran's varied ethnic, tribal and confessional groups, countering the geopolitical threat posed by the West's power (including the USSR) and laying claim to the empire's historical right to be a great power. Henceforth, the emergence of the Pahlavi state was portrayed as the beginning of the end of this decline.

The elements defining the dynamics of Pahlavi pro-West Occidentalism are similar to those of the Romanov one: (1) anticlericalism; (2) changes in historiography, conceptions of the constitutive elements of authenticity of Iranian culture and national identity undertaken to justify this anticlericalism, the monarchy's power, and the Pahlavi cultural revolution; and (3) a cultural revolution designed to create a *homo Pahlavicus* who epitomized the key features of Pahlavi Iranian self-representation. These elements underpinned Pahlavi conceptions of the authenticity of Iranian culture and national identity from Reza Shah's reign to the attempt at ideologization of the monarchy in the late 1960s.[7] This Occidentalism existed under the overall Pahlavi triad of God, Shah and Homeland that propagated the idea of the monarch as the patriarchal figure of the Iranian people and source of power and authenticity, of God as the protector and granter of that power and of Homeland that stressed national unity, the sacralized land of Iran and its defence in the face of external and internal enemies.

Anticlericalism and institutional revolution

Similar to pre-Petrine Russia, before the Pahlavi era, periodic tension characterized the dynamic between the state and the clerical establishment despite or because of their symbiotic political and mutually legitimizing relationship. These early episodes of heightened tensions cannot be regarded as attempts by either side to redraw fundamentally the roles each played in society. During the Safavid period conflicts emerged over property and the boundaries of their respective powers. These tensions intensified in the latter period of Qajar rule given the increase in debates over how to respond to the challenge of the West. Clerical and lay figures with vested economic and political interests felt threatened by possible reforms while claiming that Westernization, and in particular educational and cultural reforms, would mark the end of Shi'i authenticity and identity.

Naser al-Din Shah (r.1848–96), no great reformer, faced the spread of British and Russian influence while lacking a coherent vision of change. Leading clerics accused him of neglecting his primary responsibility – the protection of the country's cultural and geopolitical borders. These feelings increased during the reign of his successor, Muzaffar al-Din Shah (r.1896–1906), who died several days after signing the decree accepting a constitution, as he faced a growing revolt. The Qajar state responded to these accusations, implicitly arguing that the clergy, who, in refusing to support reform, and particularly cultural and administrative transformations in the spheres of education and the judiciary in which the clergy were dominant, had contributed to making Iran vulnerable to the West. Ultimately,

> the most prominent reason for the paucity of educational and judicial reforms in the Nasiri era and the resistance to new aspects of Europe's material culture was the Shah's realistic apprehension of intruding into the ùlama's (clergy's) sphere ... the Shah [Naser al-Din] conspicuously avoided confrontation with the ulama on issues of great sensitivity.[8]

Consequently, the state found itself economically and militarily weak and increasingly short of income. Attempts to raise funds by granting trade and monopoly concessions to foreigners and obtaining foreign loans only increased the dependence of the crumbling empire on Western powers, including Russia, that provoked additional clerical and lay outrage.

The clash between the state and the clergy reached new heights in 1891–2. Naser al-Din Shah, having signed a major tobacco concession with a Briton that brought badly needed income, was frustrated with clerical-led opposition: 'Really the mentality of these clerics and the "people" is shocking. They are in such a state of ignorance. They do not understand the contemporary world and situation. They live in the past. Every period has its own exigencies and conditions. It is not possible today to act as in the past'. The role of clerics in what became known as the Tobacco Rebellion, and the subsequent government climb down, infuriated him.

> Still that ignorant clergy of Karbala and Najaf who had come to Tehran and forced poor Fath Ali Shah to wage war on Russia are still around. And now everything from which Iran suffers at the present is the result of these clerical admonitions and exhortations. Today a repeat [of clerical intervention in politics] is not needed at all.[9]

At the same time, educated elite opinion whose numbers, although slowly growing, remained very small and concentrated in a couple of urban areas among a population that was overwhelmingly rural, tribal and illiterate, blamed the shah's autocracy and the clergy, both which feared the consequences of reforms for their power and interests, for the country's decline. The 1906 Constitution, by placing limits on that power and putting a theoretical end to autocracy, had given many the hope that it would be able to create a strong centralized government that would be able to implement needed reforms. However, in the face of clerical and lay opposition and Russian and British intervention, these hopes were dashed.

Reza Shah shared Naser al-Din's opinion about the clergy – an opinion that in the closing decades of Qajar rule was becoming dominant in intellectual and political circles. Nonetheless, during his years as prime minister (1921–25) and the initial two years of his reign as monarch, he maintained a stable relationship with top clerical figures.[10] He understood that he needed clerical support in his struggles with Ahmad Shah and for the establishment of the Pahlavi dynasty, once he abandoned the idea of establishing a republic. Concomitantly, leading clerics were willing to support him out of fear that otherwise he might establish a secular republic, similar to the one founded by Ataturk in Turkey under which the clergy would lose its sociopolitical and economic positions. His seeming willingness to listen to them and intention to resist Western imperialism also played in his favour, as did his pilgrimage to Karbala and Najaf in December 1924.

By the end of 1927 the relationship between Reza Shah and the clergy entered a new phase that ended with its political and economic emasculation which lasted until the close of his reign. In May 1925 he introduced compulsory military service. An exemption for religious students was offered provided that several criteria be met, including passing an examination administered by a government commission. These criteria increasingly angered the clergy for they granted to a secular authority power over it. Moreover, many leading clerics claimed that they were already performing a form of national duty through their defence and propagation of Shi'ism. Given circumstances at the time, the government backed down.

The clergy, by opposing this move, proved to Reza Shah that his belief that clerical obstructionism was inevitable and any negotiations with the clergy and the giving of limited concessions could end only in the state's defeat. By backing down, he had given reason to the clergy to believe that it could limit the state's power and determine the shape and extent of reforms. He thus concluded that the implementation and institutionalization of his reforms were dependent on politically emasculating the clergy. Ehsan Naraqi, a French-trained sociologist with leftist political sympathies, who obtained high positions in the office of Empress Farah, stated a decade after the 1979 Revolution:

> Of course our clergy, the majority of them, during this period were reactionaries. They did not want the people to become enlightened. They couldn't and didn't accept progressive thought or genuine modernization. ... The majority was backward. Reza Shah took advantage of this and crushed the clerics.[11]

This quote is useful not only because of its description of the clergy but also given his role in the 1970s in propagating a return to Islamic authenticity which he defined rather ambiguously.

Consequently, state propaganda stressed clerical resistance to badly needed reforms, the country's modernization and therefore civilization itself. This was one of the starting points of Pahlavi Occidentalism. Reza Shah announced:

> Many people erroneously believe that the acquisition of modern civilisation is identical with abandoning religious principles and the *shar'ia*. ... As a result, they shoved the country into backwardness. Therefore, we face a long-standing stagnation. We must overcome this backwardness and lethargy.[12]

With this speech he underlined that he did not see any contradiction between his transformations and Islam's basic tenets. The problem, in his opinion, was the clergy, the material interests they sought to protect through production of a particular culture and their ignorance of the world. He targeted clerical control over the judicial and educational systems which provided the clerics with both an income and a great degree of sociopolitical power. Deprived of this control the clergy could not oppose state centralization and reforms.

Reform of the educational system was decisive and ambitious. While rapidly expanding the state school system, the state increased its control over religious schools and limited the spheres of their activity. By the early 1930s the state gave itself the right to license and supervise religious schools, establish their syllabi and submit religious students to state examinations. The result was a decrease in the amount of teachers and pupils in religious schools. Moreover, the establishment of the Faculty of Theology at the recently founded Tehran University was the state's first major step towards the creation of a Pahlavist form of Islam. The state also destroyed clerical power over judicial activities as it secularized the judicial system and most aspects of law. In 1926 the justice minister, Ali Akbar Davar transferred the functions of clerical-run courts to the state judicial system and deprived clerical courts of the fee-generating rights to register vital documents such as property titles, powers of attorney and affidavits. In 1930 clerics were banned from becoming judges.

To strengthen state anticlericalism, state propaganda focused on clerical opposition to policies, from seemingly simple issues, such as the inclusion of music in official educational curricula to more thorny issues, such as a strong centralized government and judicial reforms. They were portrayed as parochial ignoramuses who opposed the concept of civilization. The result was a drop in the popularity of clerics in urban areas. Ayatollah Khomeini claimed:

> During Reza Shah's reign cabbies did not accept clerics as fares. The deceased Hajj Abbas Tehrani Ramollah once said 'When I was in Arak I wanted to take a taxi. The driver told me he did not take two kinds of fares – one was *akhunds* [a derogative term for clerics], and the other prostitutes'.[13]

State attacks on the clergy's socio-economic and political positions, however, were not accompanied by direct attacks on and degradation of Islam. Reza Shah sought to ensure that clerics did not interfere in oppositional politics and to overthrow and separate clerical determined forms of religious high culture, superstitions and doctrine from

Islamic ethics.[14] Islamic ethics were to constitute the moral code of *homo Pahlavicus* while his political loyalty belonged to the Pahlavi state. In the words of Mohammad Reza Shah: 'My father made the clergy confine themselves primarily to religious matters which, by definition, have constituted their basic function'.[15] Achieving this was a prerequisite for the creation of *homo Pahlavicus*.

Historiographical revolution

This revolution sought the transformation of common perceptions of authenticity of culture and local and national identities in order to create a *homo Pahlavicus*. It was the theoretical catalyst for the cultural and institutional revolutions launched by Reza Shah while providing the state with the political and ideological justification to establish its supremacy over clerical institutions and determine the constitutive elements of the authenticity of culture and national identity. It served an additional, but equally important, purpose. Reza Shah's political and personal anticlericalism created a political–ideological vacuum that undermined the long-standing legitimating liturgical elements of Iran's monarchical cosmology. Therefore, changes in historiography and in the monarchy's legitimating underpinnings were needed. Broadly speaking, the historiography of pro-West Occidentalism and nationalism, along with promises of material and social benefits, would fill this vacuum. Fundamental elements of this historiography played important roles in Pahlavi ideology until the dynasty's collapse.

When Reza Shah established his dynasty, racial theories explaining differences in civilizational progress were at their apogee with one of the leading racial theories in the West explaining that its civilizational success was Aryanism.[16] The historiography of Pahlavi Occidentalism claimed a racial link between Iranians and West Europeans by propagating the idea that Iran's pre-Islamic Achaemenid and Sasanian Empires were the first examples of Aryan polities. Already in the closing decades of Qajar rule Aryanism was becoming popular among the educated and elite classes. It was not solely a Pahlavi invention. Aryanism rationalized and justified the technical programme of Pahlavi Westernization by portraying it not as the imposition of a foreign civilization, but rather as a return to Iranian greatness and authenticity that had been corrupted by contingent historical events, such as the Arab and Mongol invasions. In other words, Aryanism explained Iran's past greatness and was an augury of its future while constituting the foundational element of the authenticity of culture and national identity that included Islam, but was not subject to it and clerical-produced culture.

This emphasis on the return to authenticity of culture and national identity was a major theme of Pahlavi discourses. In the words of Isfahan's governor at the time:

> History teaches us that any people in the world who once lived with authority, power and greatness due to losing cultural authenticity slowly lost their independence and greatness. … A people's progress and decline have a direct and unique link with their culture and only that culture. If we examine the history of our ancient pre-Islamic Iran and take into account the sorrowful and depressing era before the coup d'état (of Reza Khan) in order to find the cause for these varying eras we

will see that the determinative element of this misfortune was the loss and lack of authentic culture. Look at the masses – they are deprived of literacy. ... How can they strive to restore our ancient but destroyed power and greatness or even have the chance to think of paths out of their current misery and chaos?[17]

Aryanism and pre-Islamic Iranian Empire were evident in a myriad of areas from literature and print media to architecture and official symbols. State secondary-education textbooks proclaimed: 'History now belongs to the narrative of the people of the white race. The white race has several branches the most important of which is the Aryan one', to which 'the peoples of Iran and Europe belong'.[18] In this context much attention was given to the race of the Pahlavis. Mohammad Ali Foruqi, Reza Shah's first prime minister, at his coronation proclaimed: 'The Iranian people know that today they have a monarch born of pure Iranian race (*padeshahi pakzad va Iraninezhad*)'.[19] Official publications explained why the new imperial family was of pure racial stock.

> The inhabitants of that area of Iran in which our great Shahanshah was born are representatives of the pure Iranian race because this region, given its natural setting and mountain ranges, was not subject to a multitude of foreign invasions. Consequently, their race did not mix with other races.[20]

As this quote indicates, Iran's multiracial dynamic was the result of both its imperial heritage and numerous foreign occupations, starting with Alexander the Great. This historical legacy posed ideological and political challenges to emerging Pahlavi racial discourses on national identity and authenticity. The state's solution was explained by Ali Asqar Hekmat, minister of culture (1933–40), who along with Issa Sadeq and Ismail Marat played a major role in this period's politics of culture and the writing of primary and secondary official textbooks.[21]

> The Iranian people constitute a society that emerged on the base of the pure and great Aryan race. During a large part of our 2,500-year history different racial groups were gradually dissolved in it. ... Newly arrived Arab, Turkish, and Mongol elements were assimilated into the Aryan race. In the end Iran never lost its authenticity and uniqueness. ... Reza Shah ... understood the importance of Iran's racial unity and from the beginning of his reign worked toward the strengthening of this part of national unity.[22]

Unity was a major goal of the policies and discourses of this period. Imperial Iran, similar to other multi-ethnic and multi-confessional polities, faced the emergence of local ethnic nationalism within its borders that challenged a traditional source of unity – allegiance to dynasty. The power of ethnic nationalism was confirmed by the break-up at the end of the First World War of the Russian, Austro-Hungarian and Ottoman Empires and the spread of the idea of national self-determination at the heart of Wilsonianism. At the same time the belief, popular since the French Revolution and the transformation of a seemingly lethargic France under Louis XVI into a major military power under Napoleon, that nationalism and patriotism were the keys to national revival and great power complimented the conviction that race was the determinative factor explaining the West's rise and success.[23]

In these domestic and international contexts emerged Pahlavi discourses aimed at creating national unity through an Iranian identity based on the Aryan race or, as it was sometimes called, the Iranian race (*nezhad-e Irani*) to which local ethnic, tribal and confessional loyalties would be transferred.[24] These early discourses stressed that Pahlavi conceptions of race and unity were not a new phenomenon in the history of the Iranian plateau. Unlike Hashemite Iraq and Jordan, Syria, Saudi Arabia and Lebanon, Iran was not a new state or nation. 'The unity of Iran, in other words, the national unity of this land's people, reaches back some three thousand years. The majority of the peoples who have become and been part of this motherland are from the Aryan race ... the oldest race' of this land. Any other peoples and races living within its borders and in the region before the Aryans arrived were 'simple and embryonic civilizations' that had merged into Iranian civilization.[25] By contrast, these new states 'despite having an old culture and civilization and long history became composed of different races' and created a 'fake people and established therefore an artificial and unnatural government'.[26] Iran had avoided such a fate given its historical and organic racial unity. These claims belied a reality in which regional, tribal and local ethnic and religious identities were strong and an overall concept of modern Iranian national identity and nationalism remained weak among the masses. State educational and linguistic policy, propaganda, obligatory national military service and policy of sedentarization of the tribes, along with Occidentalism, aimed to strengthen among the masses Pahlavi concepts of national identity and nationalism.

One of the key challenges facing the Pahlavi state was to bolster national self-confidence and self-respect, specifically among the elite, educated classes and intelligentsia, which had been severely shaken by the country's decline and great susceptibility to the West's imperialism. Mirza Fath-Ali Akhundzadeh (1812–78), an influential thinker and publicist, compared Iran's past imperial glory with its decadent state under the Qajars and described the increasing feelings of nostalgia held by these classes: 'Oh Iran my heart bleeds for you! What happened to your grandeur, prosperity, and good fortune? Where is that honor? What happened to that divine empire, renown strength and power?'[27] *The Travels of Ibrahim Beig*, written at the beginning of the twentieth century, similarly oozed nostalgia and distraughtness over Iran's decline. Obtaining great popularity among the small literate urban population, it helped mobilize people during the Constitutional Revolution.[28] The work tells of a young Iranian brought up in Egypt who, upon the death of his merchant father, travels for the first time to Iran. He compares the images of Iran generated by his reading of the greatness of pre-Islamic Iranian Empires with the backwardness, poverty, desperation, lawlessness and chaos he witnesses in Qajar Iran. This work is a call to arms in the struggle for a return to authenticity of culture and thus civilizational greatness and power. Issa Sadeq shared the sentiments expressed by this work and, in describing them, made a comment on the mentality of those driving Reza Shah's Occidentalism.

> What caused me the most pain during that period [of study in France in the first decade of the twentieth century] was that the French considered us

uncivilized and our country amongst the ranks of colonies since Iran was subjugated to foreign forces and imperialists. This defeat was the source of shame and cause of humiliation. … At the time when Russia had dominance over Iranian affairs and the influence of the English was very high, a feeling of inferiority and wretchedness spread amongst the people. And I was not an exception in this regard. Europeans with their science and industry that was the cause and process by which they gained superiority over Asia seemed to be superior.[29]

These feelings could have only been exacerbated by Pahlavi official recognition of the West's superiority. Here again Aryanism fulfilled an important role. The claimed Aryan racial link between Iran and the West sought the liberation of Iran from the dark world of 'Oriental' peoples wallowing in barbarity, inertia, ignorance and weakness, who offered themselves up as easy prey to the West. Certainly, Iran had fallen behind it due to historical and geopolitical contingencies. However, unlike true 'Orientals', its Aryan racial and cultural heritage, given the right leadership, would return the country to its rightful place in the pantheon of its racial cousins in the West.

Pahlavi Aryanism initially focused on propagating a racial and thus primordial cultural link with the West while accepting Iranian backwardness vis-à-vis the West. By the mid-1930s a new element emphasized the idea that Iran with its universal culture was not only the founder of civilization in antiquity but also a civilizational source for this contemporary West, now regarded as the bearer of universal civilization. This element became more pronounced in the closing years of Reza Shah's reign with the establishment of the Organization of Public Enlightenment (OPE) in 1938, the last great step in Pahlavi cultural policy of this period.

Understanding OPE's goals requires a brief examination of additional elements exercising an influence on Pahlavi discourses, namely the competing ideologies of constitutional monarchy, epitomized by Britain, and communism, symbolized by the USSR, and the search for an advanced Western country to aid in the modernization of the economy and military. Given the record of British and Russian imperialism in Iran and the ideological threats they posed the Pahlavi state turned to Germany, probably the most industrialized and economically advanced country in Europe, despite its defeat in the First World War.

During the Weimar period economic relations between the two countries began to develop. After Hitler's rise to power, they quickly and greatly expanded. Underpinning and providing momentum to them was Aryanism and a common desire to limit British and Soviet power. Both polities while proclaiming shared Aryan roots issued calls for a national cultural resurgence and preservation of native authenticity that justified state power. Reza Shah in a private conversation in 1935 with Wilhelm von Blücher, the German envoy in Tehran, welcomed the expansion of these ties and revealed one of his justifications for authoritarianism.

> Right now, authoritarian government is the only possible variant. Otherwise the people will sink into communism. The previous German government did not satisfy the Iranians' well-founded wishes and hopes. … But the present German

government understands Iran's interests. With its coming to power began the fruitful development of Iranian-German relations.[30]

As Iranian-German relations expanded and deepened, German propaganda activities in Iran too expanded and deepened. Importantly, the Pahlavi state tolerated them at a time when it arrested communists and leftist sympathizers and banned in the 1930s the use of the word 'democracy' in official language and mass media.[31] German propaganda in Iran took the form of books, journals, magazines, newspapers and pamphlets – the bulk of which were written in Persian. They were distributed by German businesses operating in the country and German government venues, such as consulates and cultural offices. German organizations involved in the creation and spread of such propaganda were the Nazi Party's Department of Foreign Affairs, the foreign division of the propaganda ministry, the Ministry of Foreign Affairs, and finally the *Abwher*, German military intelligence. In addition, German companies placed large amounts of advertisements in native Iranian publications, such as *Iran-e Bastan*, that championed Iranian-German relations as well as the resurgent Germany under Hitler's leadership. These propaganda efforts were accompanied by visits of high-ranking Nazi officials involved in ideological indoctrination and political propaganda. For example, in December 1937 Baldur von Schirach, the head of the Hitler Youth (1931–40), made a visit to Iran that received wide coverage in the Iranian press. He held talks with Hekmat, the minister of culture, and met with Reza Shah. In official ceremonies Iranian youth giving the Nazi salute were paraded in front of him.

German propaganda in Iran had two broad trajectories. One glorified Hitler and Nazi ideology while stressing the spiritual resurgence of the German people under his leadership that brought with it economic and military strength. The other trajectory propagated the idea of strong German sympathies for Iranians. Occupying this propaganda's centre was the theory of the common Aryan origins of the German and Iranian peoples. Before Hitler's geopolitical interest in Iran, Nazi classification of races provided no place for Iranians and any other Eastern peoples. However, Iranians were now told that Hitler maintained a strong and special sympathy for Germany's Aryan cousins, the Iranians and, to prove German sincerity in this regard, he exempted Iranians from the Nuremburg Race Laws. In 1935 the Reichstag had enacted these laws that sought the protection of the purity of German Aryan blood. It prohibited marriage and even sexual relations between Germans and Semitic peoples. Islam, however, posed a challenge to this unifying paradigm of Aryanism. It was quickly solved. Nazi propaganda inside Iran disseminated the idea that Shi'ism was a true Aryan religion in opposition to Arab Islam coined 'Semitic Sunnism'.[32]

Iranian propaganda spread pro-German sentiments and underlined common Iranian and German geopolitical world views while maintaining attacks on communism and the 'liberal' West. On the day von Schirach returned to Berlin, Iranian newspapers in an organized move ran an editorial that showed that the state had determined which country represented for it the true West. Titled 'The West and the East' it proclaimed: 'The West is in need of a resurgence (*rastakhiz*) along the lines of contemporary Iran, while the East is in need of a West, a West epitomized by the German Reich. At the same time Iran is the cradle of the Aryan race, just like Germany'.[33] The formulation is craftily succinct. Britain and France, constituting the fake West, needed a moral and spiritual resurgence similar to the one initiated by Reza Shah that was culturally returning Iranians to their Aryan roots. Germany defined and represented the real West. It was economically, technologically and militarily strong, and culturally and civilizationally independent of the modernities based on inauthentic Enlightenment thought, liberal capitalist democracy and communism. Iran needed to take example from this West to which it primordially belonged given its and Germany's common Aryan roots. As noted earlier, for these same reasons imperial Germany's developmental trajectory was attractive to Russian conservatives in the late tsarist period. It had achieved high levels of economic and technological progress and built a powerful military while preserving authentic Germaness and rejecting Western liberalism. This editorial's message and its simultaneous publication in several newspapers attracted the attention of Soviet agents in Iran who included it in their analysis reports for Moscow.

This dynamic is seen in the Iranian positions in regard to the Spanish Civil War that mirrored those of Germany. For example, *Ettela'at* wrote in summer 1936: 'The military intervention [in Spain] shows that the people are ill-disposed to the Republic, or rather, republicanism is not an appropriate and effective form of governing'. Six months later it wrote: 'Spain has always been the best starting point for communist penetration. ... Communism has always sought to control a base for revolution on Europe's outskirts from where Marxism can spread to Africa'.[34] Yet, Reza Shah and the political elite maintained a suspicion about the extent to which lesser powers could rely on and have confidence in Europe's great powers. TASS (the official Soviet news and telegraph agency) in a secret bulletin sent to Moscow noted: 'Iranian political figures are expressing fears about the Munich Conference, underlining that this agreement is a lesson and warning for all small states'.[35]

In this context, the OPE was founded and situated within the Ministry of Culture. Its first director was Ahmad Matin Daftari who, at the time of his appointment, was justice minister and subsequently served as prime minister (November 1939–July 1940). He had studied at the German school in Tehran that was established in 1907 by imperial Germany and then worked in the German embassy as a secretary and a translator. Not surprisingly, Daftari was a leading Germanophile, a point highlighted by Soviet intelligence which also reported on what it described as a strong relationship between this organization and Nazi German institutions of propaganda.[36]

The organization's goals were twofold. Its cultivation and direction of public opinion was to strengthen the state's legitimacy and mobilizational capacity and to create *homo Pahlavicus*, the builder and product of the practical process of Westernization. The OPE represented the first coordinated effort by the Pahlavi state to cultivate the elements of pro-West Occidentalism among the youth. The Rastakhiz Party, after a long interregnum, would resume these efforts. Importantly, the founding of OPE was initially part of a plan to establish an all-encompassing national political party that would be 'similar to the People's Party of Turkey'.[37] This organization's generous budget and large purview of activities reflected the great political and ideological role it was to play. Its importance was underlined when Reza Shah, Crown Prince Mohammad Reza, the speaker of the parliament, ministers and parliament deputies, among others, attended its First Annual Festival held in April 1939.

The year 1940 saw changes in Reza Shah's approach to Germany. In February 1940 the leader of the Iranian Fascist Youth Mohsen Jahansuz and his colleagues were charged with attempting to launch a coup d'état. After the fall of France and in the face of growing German sympathies among, according to Soviet intelligence analysis, the Iranian bourgeoisie, military and state officials, Reza Shah instituted personnel and institutional changes. In June he removed Daftari as prime minister and threw him in prison, charged with spying for Germany. His successor at OPE was Issa Sadeq. Soviet intelligence welcomed this change, reporting that Sadeq, having studied in Britain and France had little sympathy for Nazi Germany. That same month in a speech he made to the editors of the leading newspapers, Majles deputies and state officials, he announced that the means of propaganda were not working effectively and ordered their strengthening across the country. To achieve this, he established a Central Directorate of Propaganda under whose purview fell cinemas, print mass media, radio and Pars, the national telegraph agency. The OPE fell into its structure. The goal was not only centralization and improved efficiency but also changes in discursive tone and specifically the ending of ideological flirting with Nazi Germany.

The OPE at its founding consisted of a central committee and six working councils: (1) Council of Speeches, (2) Radio Council, (3) Council for Textbook Preparation, (4) Arts Council, (5) Music Council and (6) Council of Print Media. The Central Committee held responsibility for coordination of decision making and harmonization of the activities and messaging of the various councils. Its membership included well-known political and state intellectuals such as Said Nafisi, Ismail Marat, Hekmat, Reza Shafaq and Gholam Reza Yasemi.

The Council of Print Media supervised the publication of newspapers and journals, focused on improving the technical quality of print media and directed the propagation of pro-West Occidentalism. Mohammad Hejazi, its director, reported at the Festival that approximately one thousand articles on these issues, and specifically elements of Occidentalism, had been placed in various newspapers. Alongside the Council of Print Media worked the Radio Council. In a country where illiteracy was above 90 per cent radio was the only means for propagating the Pahlavi message across the country. Given the lack of radios in private possession one of its primary goals was the installation of loud speakers in public places.

The Council of Speeches coordinated public political speeches held at regular intervals across the country. High school and university students and government officials on all levels across the country were forced to attend these speeches which were published by the newspaper *Ettela'at*. It determined the topics of these speeches that were delivered by national and local political, military and cultural figures, as well as the organization's cadres. At the First Annual Festival it was reported that 6,644 such speeches were held.[38] In order to improve these speeches' quality and effectiveness the organization established 'learning centres' where cadres and other figures could acquaint themselves with the art of speech and, more importantly, undergo a political education about speech topics. These lessons focused on the following topics, among others: (1) cultivation of public enlightenment through the use of Pahlavi interpretations of Iranian history; (2) explaining the importance of Iran's ancient and national ruins and monuments; (3) the struggle against superstitions and foolish (*sakhif*) beliefs; (4) Iran's service and contributions to universal (Western) civilization; (5) patriotism and monarchism; (6) the patriotism of ancient Iranians; (7) Iran's conditions at the time of Reza Khan's coup d'état; (8) Iran's progress in the Pahlavi era; (9) national identity and unity; (10) hygiene; (11) morality; (12) the principles and advantages of enlightenment and the new civilization; (13) national duty and interests; and (14) principles of progressive change.[39]

The theme of the universal character of pre-Islamic Iranian Empire and civilization, its contributions to contemporary Western civilization and the cult of the personality of Cyrus the Great reached new heights during this period. This shift of emphasis was an attempt to overcome the West's hegemonic Orientalist discourses that placed Iran within the camp of the 'barbaric backward Orient'. Certainly, Pahlavi pro-West Occidentalism accepted Orientalist understandings of the causes behind Iran's decline in light of the West's rise in the eighteenth and nineteenth centuries. However, it could not accept ancient Greek forms of Orientalization initiated by Herodotus that propagated the idea of primordial Iranian barbarity, backwardness and moral corruption that had mutated into modern Orientalism.

Lasan Sepahr, governor of Kashan and head of that province's public enlightenment, in a major speech 'The Monarchy of Three Thousand Years or the Seniority of Iranian Civilization' described the discursive trends of Pahlavi pro-West Occidentalism of the late 1930s. 'Iran's ancient empire prepared humankind for the spread of progress and civilization. ... The roots of today's civilization (i.e. the West) ... initially emerged in the land of Iran'.[40] Stressing the historical inability of foreign conquerors to destroy Iranian independence, greatness and civilization, he proclaimed that 'the current generation must take example only from these ancient Iranians as the country moves forward'.[41]

Pahlavi pro-West Occidentalism now proposed a historiography that clashed with Western historiographical forms, dominant since at least the Enlightenment, and targeted the West's ideas of its exceptionalism. At stake was an interpretation not only of the genesis of the unique characteristics attributed to Western civilization that led to its modernity and power with global reach but also of the fundamentals of the West's conception of itself and of the Orient that emerged with Herodotus and was philosophically, historically and ideologically integrated in the thought produced during the Enlightenment's long eighteenth century.[42]

At the centre of this historiographical and ultimately political debate was the figure of Alexander the Great and the Achaemenid Empire.[43] According to Enlightenment historiography this empire was the first in a long-line of stagnant, despotic and uncivilized Oriental polities that were in need of rescue from their barbarity, backwardness and seemingly eternal societal lethargy and moral corruption. It portrayed Alexander as the first enlightened conqueror from the West who destroyed a despotic, backward 'Oriental' empire and bestowed to its long-suffering peoples Western enlightenment, civilization and just government that respected the rights of ethnic and confessional groups, and, vitally, hope for renewal. Enlightenment historiography based on this binary of civilized West and barbaric East fed into Orientalism and provided the West's imperial powers, such as Britain and France, with a justification for their vast maritime empires.

Pahlavi Occidentalism, in response, argued that it was Cyrus and not Alexander, who established the idea of human rights and just government that respected the rights of ethnic and confessional groups. This was a direct strike at a fundamental element of the West's claims to exceptionalism. The basis for these claims was the Cylinder of Cyrus, which the Pahlavi state, as well as some scholars, claimed was the first declaration of universal human rights, given Cyrus's policy of repatriation of Jews after their Babylonian captivity. According to the cylinder, Cyrus condemns Nabonidus, the last Babylonian king (r.556–539 BC), for mistreating his empire's subjects, specifically Jews and Babylonians themselves: 'He committed evil in regard to his subjects. Every day ... [he tortured his people]. Under a merciless yoke of power he crushed them all'. Cyrus introduces himself as a just ruler who re-established civil and religious structures destroyed by this tyrannical Babylonian state.

> Examination of Cyrus' charter and ancient Jewish texts can indeed give the impression that the privileges and autonomy bestowed by Cyrus were exceptional when compared with traditional relations between other monarchs of the Near East and an ethno-religious group. Along with the Babylonized Cyrus of the cylinder such a portrayal has played a significant role in creating an image of the Achaemenid conqueror as a peaceful and tolerant monarch who had made a decisive break with the 'barbarous and oppressive' praxis of the Assyrian-Babylonian state. Today, Cyrus is propagated by his modern supporters as the founder of 'human rights'.[44]

From a scholarly point of view, the meaning and function of Cyrus's charter is debatable. However, the historical record provided enough evidence to allow the Pahlavi state to present Iran and not the West as 'the founder of human rights' and appropriate for itself one of the fundamental criteria used by the West to prove its exceptionalism and superiority. This Pahlavi historiographical interpretation sought to turn the idea of the genesis of Western civilization on its head. Yet, in doing so, it also sought to prove both Iran's primordial racial and cultural link with the West and its avant-garde role in establishing elements the West utilized to distinguish itself from the East and claim its primordial superiority to it. These claims while surely politicized became reflections of historiographical trends later in the twentieth century.

By the end of Reza Shah's reign this approach had obtained a prominent position in state discourses. The official publication commemorating the wedding in 1939 of the crown prince to Princess Fawzia, the sister of Farouk I, the king of Egypt, articulated this historiography:

> The first great service of this land's shahs provided human civilization (in reality they implemented in that old world a form of moral revolution) was their proper approach to and just behavior with conquered peoples. Until the Achaemenid Empire, conquerors, when they vanquished a country and made it part of their empire, dealt brutally and mercilessly with the defeated peoples, subjecting them to ruin and genocide. This brutal approach and unacceptable behavior was even considered a source of pride and glory. ... But Cyrus the Great dealt with

conquered countries and peoples with respect and restraint, refusing to destroy them and their towns ... [and] working toward their reconstruction ... [while] respecting their local religions, traditions and elites.

The Achaemenid Empire was 'the bright torch of Iranian civilization and culture (and) universal humankind'.[45]

> This civilizational and industrial greatness flowed into the Sasanian and Safavid periods. The extent of Iran's universal civilization and culture during these brilliant and shining periods was so great that today we can see all over, in every field related to matters of thought and genius and finally the sources of human life the attractive and alluring traces and beautiful offspring of the Aryans.[46]

A policy integral to this approach was the state drive to restore and preserve ancient monuments, giving greater momentum to an issue to which the Society of National Monuments founded by Abdolhossein Teymourtash in 1921 had been dedicated. In the words of Isfahan's governor: 'Every country's identity is dependent on the preservation of its historical monuments. These monuments show the truth of our ancient shahs' great works and power'.[47] Equally important was the state's strengthening of the cult of Ferdowsi and the *Shahnameh*.

This emphasis on Iran's ancient civilizational and imperial greatness and its contribution to the development and power of Western civilization was not uniquely Iranian or particular to the Pahlavi Shahs. Those countries, even geographically inside Europe, that could claim in one way or another ancient civilizational greatness, such as Italy and Greece, while finding themselves in the nineteenth and twentieth centuries unable to respond to the challenge of the West, adopted similar discursive and ideological responses.

In this respect the Savoy Dynasty in Italy, especially during the Mussolini period (1922–43), provides a good point of comparison. It emphasized the Roman classical past to strengthen claims of civilizational primacy and justify Italy's inclusion alongside Europe's great powers, namely France and Britain, despite Italy's economic, technological and military backwardness, which was considered the consequence of cultural and racial backwardness. This period experienced an intensification and institutionalization of the cult of ancient Rome, *Romanità*, within state discourses on *Italianità* (Italianess), a long-standing dominant theme from before unification, and the place of the West within it.

Giuseppe Maggiore, a leading judicial figure and propagandist in fascist Italy and friend of Giovanni Gentile, a leading fascist ideologue who was Mussolini's first minister of culture, wrote:

> There is nothing in the patrimony of European civilization that does not bear the stamp of Romanità. From the alphabet to language, from ways of thinking and reasoning to ways of building; from materials ... to architectural structures; to tools ... to domestic furnishing, everything originates from Rome: political, social, municipal institutions ... religious rites and athletics.

Europe's common Roman heritage underpinned Italian claims to cultural pre-eminence and dominant role in establishing the universal civilization that began with Rome and would again be centred in Italy. In these discourses on the authenticity of Italian culture, the state discarded the notion of backwardness and its role of pupil to the West's one as mentor and claimed the mantle of civilizational primacy. For example, France was presented as a barbarian backwater à la Asterix prior to the arrival of Caesar's legionaries. The discourse flipped the dynamic between the two countries. Italy was the parent and France was the progeny. 'Similarly, Britain (originally home to a race of "cannibals") had only become part of the civilized world through the Roman conquest'. Mussolini proudly proclaimed: 'Anything that it is still strong and vibrant today has a Roman origin'.[48]

The Universal Exposition of Rome was an international fair scheduled for 1942 to honour the twentieth anniversary of the Fascist March on Rome. Given the outbreak of war it was not held. Nonetheless, its themes provide a succinct example of these discourses. Its main theme was 'universality ... in space, time and subject. All peoples, of all centuries, in all forms of activity should be represented, so as to achieve the synthesis of Italian and universal civilization in Rome'. According to this emphasis on antiquity, Romanità was a universal civilization that built the great Roman Empire and then provided to future generations of humankind the pillars and criteria of civilization. Similar to Pahlavi glorification of Cyrus's charter, Mussolini's monarchical Italy proclaimed that Roman law was 'a measure of the genius' of the Italian race and 'a gift to and of the Roman world'.[49] According to Count Ciano, the Italian leader's rhetoric was based on his belief that Westerners had persuaded Italians that 'they were not a race, but a faint-hearted medley of people born to serve and please the nations on the other side of the mountains'.[50]

Italy during this period, building on tendencies of the Risorgemento (resurgence) era that led to Italian unification, focused on the creation of a new man. 'This new man Italian fascism sought to create was not just the opposite of the individualist man of liberal civilization', but also 'the opposite of that type of Italian who had inhabited the peninsula for centuries'.[51] Thus, at the same time Italy and Iran, looking to the splendour and greatness of their imperial heritage, sought to create an idealized and romanticized person of the ancient past who had been corrupted over the centuries and caused their backwardness relative to the West. This old–new person would symbolize these countries' future.

The Iranian and Italian states hoped that through this use of their imperial heritage they could bolster national self-confidence injured by these feelings of backwardness and strengthen national unity in this period of national resurgence. Moreover, they sought to project Iran and Italy in the international arena as members of this superior West, to whose emergence as a universal civilization, they claimed, ancient Rome and Iran had made great lasting contributions. Thus, Italy and Iran, despite challenges in regard to development and the power differential between them and the West's leading powers, sought to repatriate the modern achievements of the West to themselves. Mohammad Reza Shah expressed frankly the feelings behind this historiography: 'If you Europeans think yourselves superior, we have no complexes. Don't ever forget that whatever you have, we taught you three thousand years ago'.[52] He told this to Oriana Fallaci, an Italian journalist.

The OPE, in addition to these historiographical discourses, included in speeches themes that emphasized the cultivation and strengthening of spirituality, the feelings and emotions of the people and the spirit of the Iranian people. The goal was to establish spiritual bonds between the Pahlavi state and the masses and place them in an emotive historiographical framework that historicized and sacralized this relationship. Daftari in his first speech as OPE head noted: 'The topic that receives the bulk of our attention is that of the spirit of the people. ... For the time we are not dealing with physical cultivation. ... The Organization of Public Enlightenment strives to cultivate the people's ... feelings and emotions'.[53] These themes are important to this study since they re-emerged in Rastakhiz discourses.

Cultural revolution

These institutional and historiographical changes played key roles in the implementation and justification of a cultural revolution that would return Iranians behaviourally and culturally to their west-European cousins and create *homo Pahlavicus*. Reza Shah in a speech to students stressed:

> Our basic goal in sending you to Europe is that you undergo moral education because we see that Western countries have obtained a high level [of culture and power] because their moral education is complete and comprehensive. If the goal were only scientific education we would not have to send you abroad. We could have easily employed foreign teachers and professors.[54]

The last shah noted about his own education: 'Since my father was so determined to Westernize Iran, no one was surprised when he decided to send me to school in the West'.[55]

One of the first stages of the Pahlavi cultural revolution was the transformation of the appearance and clothing of Iranians. Several elements fed into this goal. Reza Shah himself privately expressed shame at seeing his Aryan subjects 'backwardly' dressed in front of Westerners. For example, when chastising one of his ministers for not wearing a sufficiently Western fedora, he stressed that he wanted Iranians to be like Westerners, to dress as Westerners, so that they would not be mocked.[56] He believed that Western clothes by accentuating differences in appearances between Westerners and Iranians were a key cause for an Iranian inferiority complex. Change in appearance would provide self-confidence:

> Iranians must recognize themselves as equal to these Westerners and thus they will become enthusiastic for and approving of development and progress and know that from the point of view of spirit, physical character, and talent they are not different from Westerners. The only difference is this hat [i.e. appearance and clothing], and this difference must be removed.[57]

The Romanov and Pahlavi attacks on dress are not surprising. The relationship between clothing, authenticity of identity and ultimately ideas of cultural superiority had existed since ancient times in polities such as the Roman and Persian Empires.[58]

Said Nafisi, who had been a leading figure in the OPE, in his official history of the Reza Shah period published before the emergence of Pahlavism explained the monarch's motives: 'As long as Iranians saw Europeans wearing clothes so different from their own, they would believe that Westerners enjoyed a unique superiority over them. Thus, they would consider themselves inferior, vassals, even stooges, willing to follow the orders of Westerners'.[59] This belief that clothes created an inferiority complex among Iranians reflected Reza Shah's conviction that Iranian clothes were symbols and reminders of Iranian backwardness. An essential element of this new politics of clothing and return to authenticity was the implementation of a policy according to which 'traditional Iranian clothing was introduced and propagated as being in opposition to development, civilization, welfare, and prosperity of the Iranian people'.[60] An official history of the Pahlavi period explained: 'Reza Shah understood very well that Iranian clothes ... belonged to past eras and people must wear new clothes similar to those of advanced countries. [These new clothes] would destroy the traces of backwardness and decline'.[61] Thus, the transformation of clothing was considered the first essential step towards the reform of behaviour and morals and the creation of *homo Pahlavicus*. The hope was that through imposition of European dress they would become Western European, be accepted by the West as civilized and eventually obtain west-European cultural behaviour. At the same time, dressing in this style was to convince Iranians that they were culturally and racially Europeans.

Underlining this official approach were moves to memorialize traditional clothing by displaying them in museums and specifically the Iranian Museum of Anthropology, founded in 1935. It was dedicated to the study of the customs, culture and clothing of the Iranian peoples during the premodern Qajar era. These traditional clothes, although regarded a part of the flow of Iranian history, were to be confined to exhibitions detailing the past and to the study of folklore and folkways. They had little room in the new Iran. The motives behind the creation of this museum say much about the thinking driving the dress policy of Pahlavi Occidentalism:

> From the time that the doors of the West's brilliant civilization were opened to us and until 1929 when with the law concerning the homogenization of the various forms of dress was passed, societal groups and tribes from the urban population to the nomadic groups transformed into a normal international society while the signs and remnants of our old culture and civilization were slowly being destroyed. But, Shahanshah Pahlavi, himself the catalyst for these national changes and transformations, given his God-given luminous intelligence recognized this ongoing loss and the need for the preservation and safeguarding of these ancient remnants [in museums].[62]

Pahlavi clothing policy also played an integral part in attempts to create a single Iranian people and national unity from Iran's myriad ethnic, tribal and confessional. Nafisi in the same official history wrote:

> One of the most important benefits of the new clothing laws and their implementation was the transformation of Iranians into a single national unit and people through removal of all external and superficial differences that frequently

ended with real domestic differences, disunity, and conflict. These changes in clothes exercised a great influence on the unity of the Iranian national spirit. It is not for nothing that from the days of yore it has been said that the exterior is a window into the interior. Any population whose peoples have differences in appearance (based on tribal, religious, and/or regional loyalties and heritage) without doubt, willingly or unwillingly, will not enjoy domestic harmony. This will lead to external disunity and tension. ... Without a doubt any person who sees a group wearing clothes different from his will not consider that group one of his own and will consider it alien and foreign.[63]

This unity was naturally seen as the key weapon in obtaining other goal of Pahlavi Iran, the struggle against imperialism. Hekmat argued: 'The defeat of the Achaemenids was not due to the strength of the Greeks, but rather the weaknesses in Iran's national unity'.[64]

In the decades before the establishment of the Pahlavi dynasty and the introduction of laws imposing changes in dress, an organic and gradual Westernization of menswear was taking place among the educated and political classes, for one of two reasons. Some who adopted such Western dress sought to project a difference and superiority in regard to the masses, while others sought to project ideas of Westernization and progress and their recognition and rejection of Iranian backwardness vis-à-vis the West. During this time the wearing of Western clothing, but not hats 'spread down the social scale from the Court and aristocracy to the educated urban strata, but men's clothes did not become a political issue'.[65]

By the late 1920s the issue of dress became political. In 1927 the government made the 'Pahlavi hat', the official hat for men that was similar to French army and police officer hats. Opposition to it was due to its visor which some clerics and their lay supporters claimed impeded touching the ground during prayer. The state responded that the hat symbolized a return to authenticity: 'Pahlavi caps now common are similar to the caps of ancient [pre-Islamic] Iran'.[66] A year later the Seventh Majles passed the first dress code and fines for not following it. Its first article required anyone working for the state to wear Western suits and the Pahlavi hat. Article 2 provided exceptions for clerics, various regional religious figures and Sunni muftis. Khomeini during the reign of Mohammad Reza decried these moves: 'This horrific [Pahlavi] cap was a source of shame for an Islamic country and blackened our independence'. He denounced the Pahlavi imposition of European clothing that was 'based on the idea that ... everyone must be the same in order to be part of the civilized world!' and rejected the idea that Iranians had to dress as Europeans 'in order to enjoy greatness in this world'.[67]

The politics of dress obtained additional momentum after Reza Shah's return from his visit to Ataturk's Turkey. Impressed by that country's development, in late May 1935 he told his ministers that Iranians had to become Western in appearance as well as culturally. Fundamental reform of male and female dress was again addressed. The first step in this renewed process was the wearing of Western felt hats that were to replace the Pahlavi cap. By July 1935 a decree made it obligatory. State employees had to wear it or be put on unpaid leave. Even rubbish collectors and carriage drivers were subject to it. In Tehran and some other larger cities these policies were met with a degree of support among the middle and upper classes, shamed by Iranian backwardness. These felt hats, in contrast to the Pahlavi hat, were called international, a sign of the conflation of Western civilization with internationalism. Nonetheless, these hats were too propagated as a return to authenticity of culture given the claim that Iran was a racial and thus primordial cultural member of the West.

The extent of the politicization of male clothing paled in comparison to that of female clothing, and specifically the veil. Female veiling, politicized after the 1906 Constitutional Revolution, too was a vital element of pro-West Occidentalism and the politics of identity. Given the patriarchal nature of Iranian society sustained by the social conservatism of Islam the issue of veiling referred 'not merely to the piece of clothing that protects women from the gaze of men, but also to the proper mode of interaction between unrelated men and women and has visual, acoustic and behavioral dimensions'.[68] During this time the number of urbanized educated Iranians opposing the imposition of the veil increased, as did calls for its removal in the burgeoning press. For these groups, the veil symbolized political, social and cultural backwardness and constituted a major obstacle to reforming the country and returning it to its cultural authenticity.

In 1928 the shah's female relatives decided to celebrate the Iranian New Year (21 March) and the twenty-seventh day of Ramadan (they coincided with each other that year) at the Holy Shrine in Qom dressed in transparent veils. A number of clerics voiced strong criticism. In particular, Ayatollah Mohammad Bafghi sent a message upon their arrival: 'If you are indeed a Muslim, why have you come here in such a state? And if you are not a Muslim why have you come at all?' He called for their departure. Reza Shah was immediately informed via telegram about these remarks. Infuriated, he, along with his minister of court, Abdolhossein Teymourtash, left for Qom. Violating the tradition of removing footwear, he entered the shrine, pulled the cleric down from his pulpit and arrested him. Bafghi was imprisoned and then banned from ever returning to Qom.

Later that year Reza Shah issued an order that gave permission to women to appear in public places without a veil. His momentum in this regard then temporarily slowed in light of growing clerical opposition and, more importantly, the overthrow of King Amanullah of Afghanistan in 1929 by forces opposing his policy of Westernization.[69] When in mid-1930 Reza Shah received a petition from thirty-five women from the elite asking him to discard imposition of the veil he demurred, stressing that given Amanullah's overthrow the time was not yet ripe for such a step.[70] However, the impression Turkey's social and economic development made on him during his visit convinced Reza Shah to accelerate his Westernizing reforms, especially in regard to the role of women in society and veiling.[71] At a ministerial meeting in the summer of 1934 the monarch remarked: 'I once ordered an education official to take steps toward the ending of the face and head covering worn by women. He either did not want to or could not do this. Now you with tact and sang-froid will take action so that this old custom which is in conflict with civilization is eliminated'. The minister of education promised immediate action and stressed that veiling was 'in conflict with civilization'.[72] In other words, the veiling of women was in contradiction with Iranian authenticity. The state began to prepare public opinion for this step through unofficial propaganda campaigns and gradual informal loosening of rules governing the veil. The measures included having the wives of leading government officials attend functions without the veil, the establishment in late spring 1935 of the Society of Women dedicated to female rights and the elimination of the veil and increasing restrictions on the wearing of the veil by teachers and schoolgirls.

The impression that the state intended to allow women to unveil increasingly worried the clergy. As clerical opposition grew, Reza Shah and the political elite became more convinced of the dangers posed by the clergy to the entire project of pro-West Occidentalism. This clerical opposition inspired protests in Tabriz, Qom and Shiraz, among other areas that, rather than giving cause to the state to pause, strengthened the shah's sense of purpose to implement these reforms and eliminate clerical opposition. The breaking point came in Mashad where Ayatollah Aqa Hussein Qomi openly condemned the shah's policies of Westernization of male dress, in particular the Western hat, and unveiling. He travelled to Tehran to convince the monarch to abandon his Westernizing plans that undermined Shi'i cultural authenticity. Not only did he fail to make contact with the shah or any top officials, he also was forced into exile in Najaf. This prompted a revolt in Mashad.[73]

Starting on 10 July 1935 rallies and meetings were held around the Gowharshad Mosque, a part of the Imam Reza shrine. Clerics and lay preachers condemned the Westernization of dress and the forced exile of Qomi. The next day, protesters, radicalized by speeches, grew in number. On 13 July military forces attacked the shrine and mosque and killed some demonstrators. Nonetheless, the protesters remained in the shrine. As news of this attempted suppression spread more people flocked to it. The next day the military established control over the city, seized the mosque and crushed the revolt. Many were killed and buried in unmarked graves while Mashad's senior clerics were arrested. The revolt confirmed the shah's belief that the clergy, its lay supporters and the 'uncivilized' masses were culturally unable to reconcile themselves to pro-West Occidentalism and the return of authenticity. Both camps could not coexist. Convinced that no compromise could be reached, the shah took steps towards forced unveiling.

In January 1936 Reza Shah attended the opening ceremonies of Tehran's Teacher Training College. Accompanying him were the queen and his two daughters, Shams and Ashraf. They, along with the other attending women, were unveiled. The queen, not the shah, distributed the diplomas.[74] Almost four decades later in 1974 the queen mother told the Minister of Court Assadollah Alam that as she and Reza Shah were on their way to this ceremony he confessed that perhaps death was better than a life 'in which he was forced to show his wife bare-headed in front of strangers. However, he had no choice. If he did not take this step Iranians would be seen as backward and barbaric'.[75] Even he, despite his determination to implement his programme, was periodically torn between the new and the old.

A month later, on 1 February, Reza Shah issued a decree banning the veil. Local authorities were instructed to arrest and punish anyone, in particular clerics, protesting the policy, and to prevent veiled women from entering shops, cinemas, public bath houses, riding in carriages and cars. In sum, 'Reza Shah insisted on complete Westernization of dress' in regard to female clothing.[76] State propaganda increasingly spread the idea that what some reactionary elements condemned as Westernization of dress was in reality a return to Iranian authenticity: 'This veil and what it symbolizes is in no way linked or related to the Aryan racial peoples'.[77] In a move that further angered and convinced clerics of the anti-Islamic thrust of the Pahlavi state, prostitutes were not allowed to unveil. This step was taken in order to ensure that unveiling would be associated with progress and civilization and not with the spread of prostitution and moral decline.

By the time Reza Shah abdicated in 1941 in face of the Anglo-Soviet invasion of the country, Iranians had indeed experienced a great deal of change. Whatever his successes and failures, the issue of change became the dominant political topic, overshadowing, or at least forming, debates about political reform. However coherent and incoherent this pro-West Occidentalism was in its attempt to justify Westernization, the elite recognized that on a mass level Occidentalism encountered problems in achieving mass valorization of reforms and in effectively limiting their fear, trepidation and wariness in regard to change, whatever its shape.

The problem was that for the masses the calls of return to authenticity of culture and ancient forms that rationalized Pahlavi Westernization did not strike a personal chord. The state's conception of authenticity was an ancient one that did not form part of the masses' everyday culture and norms. Thus, towards the end of the 1930s state propaganda placed additional emphasis on the popular inculcation of the valorization of reforms and on countering negative feelings towards change. The lead was taken by the OPE, and specifically in radio broadcasts and in the official illustrated journal *Iran Today* (*Iran-e Emruz*). Under the editorship of Mohammad Hejazi, it was considered a leading showcase and propagator of Pahlavi discourses on Iranian authenticity and the practical achievements, such as the construction of factories and infrastructure, sports and physical education, the increasing role of women in society, and the military, among other issues. Memos from the Ministry of Culture and OPE, including its regional branches, show concerted efforts to spread this journal across the country.[78] For example, the prime minister's office sent out circulars to governors ordering them to provide lists of people who were to be given subscriptions while pressuring civil servants to buy one.[79]

This journal provides an excellent textual and visual representation of the Iran sought by the Pahlavi elite, the pillars of Pahlavi propaganda and its attempts to obtain popular acceptance and valorization of change. Setting the tone was the inaugural issue's editorial titled *Modernity* (*Tajaddod*) written by Gholam Reza Yasemi. Very active on the organization's speaking circuit, he was a member of the organization's central committee as well as a well-known historian, writer/poet and one of the first professors of Tehran University. It shows that by the end of Reza Shah's reign members of the elite had a realistic understanding of the psychological and social issues associated with change.

> It is not the allure of habit and familiarity that makes a person believe only in stability and the permanency of things. Rather human instinct creates in people the fear to abandon those things to which they are accustomed, forcing them to regret the passing of old ways. ... Why do people so fear the passing of their old existing habits, customs, thoughts and do not easily become prepared to accept

new things in the place of old things? The reason is that a person does not fully know himself.

The soul of a person has an essence that is prone to habit and routine ... it always becomes attached to something and since it has become accustomed to it, it unites with it ... a person becomes one with it and with all of its energy and power strives to maintain it because the changing of such habits and customs in reality means that a part of him passes away. Thus, humans have a fear of the progressive change of customs, thought, habits, traditions, and rituals and therefore say that the same old forms and customs are sufficient for us. ... From this dynamic emerges the corruption of morals and thought and the weakening of will.

The conclusion of the discussion here is that all the elements and atoms making up the world are in constant progressive change. There is no permanency and respite from change. In this world inertia, in other words the constant repeating of the past, does not in reality exist. Only humans out of fear of the decline of old well-known forms and appearances seek to preserve them. But in the end they cannot prevent their corruption and decline. ... The people who accept the logic of progressive change and modernity are the fortunate ones. ... Unfortunately, some people confuse modernity (*tajadud*), which is the elimination of corruption and corruptive elements with *tabaddol*, which means the complete change of some thing. *Tabaddol* means to remove something and replace it with something else while *tajadud* means the removal of old corruptive elements from something and putting, step-by-step, in their place something new. These two words have two completely different meanings.[80]

These propaganda efforts within the framework of pro-West Occidentalism were abandoned due to the political and economic destabilization created by the abdication of Reza Shah on 16 September 1941 in the wake of the Anglo-Soviet invasion. He died in 1944 in exile in far-off South Africa.

5

Pahlavism

Mohammad Reza, young and inexperienced, found the reins of power thrust into his hands at a time of growing political and economic turmoil. He struggled to make the Crown, whose hold over the state and political arena had weakened as result of the abdication and Allied occupation, a relevant proactive political force. His frustration over its weakening was coupled by the chaos dominating the country's political life. In his first book *Mission for My Country*, he recalled:

> Their [British and Soviet] continual interference in our political life and affairs thoroughly disgusted me and my people. ... On every side I saw the miseries and sufferings of our citizens brought on by the economic and other policies adopted, and at the same time I was revolted by the way in which some wealthy Persians become yet more bloated, in utter disregard of the welfare of their country. In Parliament ... no coherent programme emerged.[1]

With the end of the Second World War, the country's occupation and Stalin's geopolitical adventurism in Iranian Kurdistan and Azerbaijan, the shah sought to strengthen Iran internationally as the Cold War heated up. He believed that the greatest geopolitical threat was the USSR, with its ideology that found support inside Iran and avaricious eyes focused on the country's northern provinces. Concomitantly, Britain still sought to protect its large oil and economic interests in the country. He, similar to this father, sought a third power able to neutralize the geopolitical ambitions of these two countries and provide military, economic and technological aid to his practical process of Westernization. While his father's gaze had turned to Berlin, he looked across the Atlantic to Washington. The choice was logical. The United States was not only the world's superpower dedicated to struggling against Soviet ideological and geopolitical expansionism but also a standard bearer of anti-imperialism with no history of exploitation in Iran. The shah noted in *Mission for My Country*:

> Some extremists claim that the United States has revived the old imperialist tradition of exploitation. ... I must say that this has not been our experience. We demand and receive complete equality of treatment. ... America has never tried to dominate us as the old imperialists did, nor would we tolerate that; and the same applies to our relations with other countries.[2]

Published in the early 1960s this opinion would change during the Rastakhiz period. The shah also intensified his struggle to strengthen the monarchy's power and authority. His father's example and the country's chaotic and deteriorating conditions and political paralysis seemingly demanded that he rule and not just reign.³ In 1947 George Allen, the US ambassador, noted that the shah, despite being 'by far the most powerful figure in Iran' was unable to 'to do very much of a positive nature' although he could 'prevent almost any action he does not like'.⁴ A fluid relationship between domestic and international factors made achieving this goal difficult.

In the period leading to Mossadegh's overthrow in 1953 and afterwards, the shah, broadly speaking, was challenged by three ideological–political threats: constitutionalism/democracy, socialism/communism and various forms of nationalism. The varied nationalist groups integrated elements of socialism, democracy and/or constitutionalism while some, such as the Pan-Iranist Party and Sumka, used neo-fascist and/or racist themes. However, unlike his father, he faced a growing Islamist threat whose forces ranged from politically active clerics such as Ayatollah Kashani to the violent organization *Fedayeen-e Islam* founded by Navab Safavi which carried out several high-profile assassinations that made a lasting impression on the monarch.⁵

From the other side of the political spectrum communism and the Iranian communist party, Tudeh, challenged the monarchy. Backed by Moscow, this party was founded by Iraj Iskandari, along with a group of educated youth, who after Reza Shah's abdication were released from prison to where they had been sent in the mid-1930s for propagating communist thought. 'By 1945-46, Tudeh had become the party of the masses in more than name' with six seats in the Majles, three ministries, and, it claimed, 50,000 core members. The party 'drew most of its support from urban wage earners and from the salaried middle class – especially the intelligentsia'.⁶ However, Tudeh's popularity was damaged by Stalin's adventurism in Azerbaijan and Kurdistan, and his demands for oil concessions in the north of the country. Splits emerged within the party's leadership and rank-and-file between supporters of Soviet claims of proletarian internationalism and nationalists with leftist economic and social sympathies.⁷ In February 1949 the shah, taking advantage of public sympathy arising from a failed attempt on his life at Tehran University, moved to finish his campaign against Tudeh. Declaring martial law, he outlawed the party, arrested many of its leaders and shut down its propaganda organs. Until the 1979 Revolution, the state maintained a relatively effective struggle against communist-inspired movements while various ideological themes within Marxism and socialism continued to influence to an extent some intellectual and political thought and methods.

The third challenge came from the secular nationalist cause, represented by the National Front and its standard bearer, Mohammad Mossadegh. Supporting the political ideals of the 1906 constitutionalist movement, it advocated modernization and an open struggle against imperialism, and specifically Soviet and British ambitions. This movement's struggle for the nationalization of Iran's oil industry which Britain had effectively controlled since the beginning of the twentieth century came to define it. This struggle came to a head with the UK-/US-inspired royalist coup that resulted in Mossadegh's overthrow and the shah's return to the country in August 1953. The greatest lesson the shah took from this experience was never to allow a prime minister or any political figure to become popular and possibly overshadow him.

After Mossadegh's overthrow, the shah focused on stabilizing his political position. Backed by Washington, he strengthened the state's monopoly over violence and thus its autonomy over socio-economic groups. Concomitantly, he worked to re-establish political links with the Crown's traditional allies, the clergy, merchants and landowning class who controlled the eighteenth and nineteenth Majles (1954, 1956), while also relying on the state bureaucracy. The discovery in 1954 of a large Soviet-backed Tudeh network in the armed forces, which reflected the continuing attraction of leftist and communist thought, and the Qarani plot, foiled in 1958, whose seeming aim was to launch a coup and force the shah to act as a constitutional monarch, represented the kind of challenges the shah faced in the post-Mossadegh period. The consequence of these two plots was the strengthening of the security services and close monitoring of relations between members of the military and security services and discouragement and following of any unusual links between them and the staff of the Soviet, British and US embassies.[8]

In 1957 the shah allowed the establishment of two official political parties, the National (*Melliyun*) Party, headed by Manuchehr Eqbal, and People's (*Mardom*) Party, headed by Assadollah Alam. The shah had several motivations. He sought to attract the support of the growing educated urban class, which was increasingly discontented with socio-economic conditions and the closed political space. Achievement of this required implementation of reforms that would also have a deleterious influence on the interests of the Crown's traditional allies. However, the shah, in light of this political pressure for reform and the growth in the state's bureaucratic, military and security apparatus, saw less benefit in preserving links with these allies.

During this period (1941–60) the state lacked determined and coherent cultural policies dedicated to the raising of mass culture, in the broad sense of the word, and to achieving the ultimate goal, the construction of *homo Pahlavicus*, and did not systematically propagate the elements of pro-West Occidentalism reminiscent of the Reza Shah period, particularly in its closing years when the OPE was active. *The Cultural Organization of Iran*, published in 1958, drew attention to and decried this rudderless cultural policy. Emphasizing elements of the Berlin Circle's thought and Pahlavi discourses of that period, it called for a revival of the activist and enlightened roles of the state and intellectuals in creating *homo Pahlavicus*. In this regard, it argued that two fundamental challenges had to be addressed when formulating state cultural policy.

The first challenge, while simply stated, was complex, requiring effective state planning and foresight. 'The reason for attention to cultural problems ... and the greater study of systems dedicated to the youth's education and cultivation is the transition ... and evolution of simple rustic life to a new scientific and industrial one.' The other challenge was the protection of the authenticity of culture and national identity threatened by Westernization. This authenticity, which fundamentally and positively differed from Western culture, was predicated on (a) an 'interconnected' Iranian spirituality composed of its poetry, history and philosophy; (b) a sense of morality superior to the West's; (c) the Iranian influence on Islam which was 'brimming with Iranian political, social, and scholarly thought' and; (d) flexibility and willingness to borrow from other world cultures despite Iran's long, rich and deep philosophical and intellectual heritage. These elements played key roles in the evolving discourses of Occidentalism from the late 1960s. Its concluding remarks too became a precursor of both the causes for, and elements of, reformed discourses of Rastakhiz-era Occidentalism.

> The Iranian people, despite great strivings and attempts, have not been able to create a respectable, comfortable life. ... What is shocking is that what our so-called modernizers call Western civilization has failed to construct and secure a good life for Western peoples and has spread to Middle Eastern peoples its political problems, internal disorders, confusion and chaos of thought, its unproven economic philosophies and hypotheses, destructive views, and relentless, merciless bloodletting. In the West governments and peoples face economic problems and industrial revolutions while in the East in addition to economic problems, its peoples and governments must engage in a war and crusade against the imperialism and imperialists of the West!

The state needed to have an effective cultural policy defending the authenticity of Iranian culture and national identity since, '(u)nfortunately, one of the bests tools of these imperialists (is) the destruction of authentic culture' and 'in this way they create people wholly representative of Western culture'. These threats to authenticity were particularly dangerous given state inaction: 'Today the Iranian people have never been so pessimistic about their culture and cultural problems. ... The country's cultural condition is weak and declining ... [while] chaos and disorder, lack of discipline and overall policymaking' characterized state cultural institutions.[9]

In conclusion, in this period the shah's approach to domestic politics was a mixture of hard power exemplified by the military and security apparatus and attempted courting of particular groups within the urban middle class and elite. Efforts at creating soft power and mass mobilization through a coherent propaganda were negligible while systematic propagation of pro-West Occidentalism reminiscent of the Reza Shah period did not exist. However, changing domestic and international conditions would force the shah to give more attention to ways of strengthening Pahlavi soft power.

By the late 1950s socio-economic discontent was intensifying. This development was not lost on Washington and Moscow. A 1958 US national intelligence report concluded that 'the present political situation in Iran is unlikely to last very long. The most probable development is an attempt by certain military elements possibly in collaboration with civilian elements desiring liberal reforms to force the shah back into the role of a constitutional monarch'.[10] The Eisenhower administration increasingly stressed to him the need for reform in order to address this rising discontent. The CIA even initiated a covert operation that placed articles in the Iranian press demanding reforms and warning of the consequences if nothing was done. It let the monarch know that its operatives were behind the articles.

The Kennedy administration was more insistent about the need for reform. While the shah, citing the Soviet threat, continued to press for more military aid, the administration stressed the need to alleviate the socio-economic problems that were feeding this public discontent, threatening political destabilization and raised the possibility of a social revolution. Washington argued that relying on the military and security forces to maintain the regime was, in the long term, not tenable. The shah, at least publicly, accepted this viewpoint, writing in *Mission for My Country*:

> In late 1949 I went to America to plead for increased economic and military aid for my country. I received a friendly reception, but returned home empty-handed. ... The failure of my mission was certainly in part our own fault, because the Americans realized that we were not yet handling our internal affairs with the necessary firmness. ... Immediately upon my return, I redoubled my efforts at reform.[11]

The USSR too believed this growing domestic discontent would soon be expressed on the streets. Khrushchev told Walter Lippmann in 1961: 'The misery of the masses and the government's corruption added up to certain revolution'.[12] Indeed during 1960–2 the state increasingly faced unrest, such as the various teacher and student riots in 1961 and the invasion of Tehran University's campus by security forces in January 1962. Parviz Sabeti, the head of SAVAK's Third Division, the internal intelligence section, at the time wrote reports to the shah that the United States had a role in the riots in order to pressure him accept the administration's recommendations for domestic policy. The prime minister Jafar Sharif-Emami (1960–1) told him the same.[13] The shah had contemplated only piecemeal reforms, perhaps best symbolized by his attempts at land reform in the late 1950s that failed given the opposition of the traditional classes in the Majles.

In 1962 the monarch grasped the nettle. Set on exceeding his father's reforming zeal in transforming the country and under growing domestic and international pressure he launched the White Revolution of Shah and People, with himself as the 'Leader of the Revolution' (*rahbar-e engelab*). Privately he also expressed commitment to reform: 'I am going to go faster than the left. ... You're all going to have to run to keep up with me. All the old economic and political feudalism is over and done with'.[14] By launching a revolution and proclaiming himself its leader, the shah, seemingly, had decided that in the face of socio-economic discontent and the attractiveness of the three competing ideologies, the monarchy could not solely rely on a dry triad of God, Shah and Homeland and could not afford to be relatively depoliticized and without ideological trappings. Similar to the approaches of the OPE in the last years of his father's reign, the shah sought to establish an emotionally charged link between the people and the monarchy while the monarchy would receive the credit for the Revolution's successes. Yet, the shah, by proclaiming himself its leader, effectively erased the political and ideological boundary between the Crown and the government, headed by the prime minister, and the Majles and placed the Crown in direct competition with other ideologies, to whose elements and prescriptions for the future it would have to respond and provide alternatives. Surely, the monarchy could benefit from any successes of the White Revolution. Conversely, the danger existed that any failures would also be attributed to it at a time when it faced increasing ideological challenges. One needs only to remember the words of the essayist Walter Bagehot written in the time of Queen Victoria when various groups sought the monarchy's politicization: 'We must not bring the Queen into the combat of politics or she will cease to be reverenced by all combatants; she will become one combatant among many. ... Its [the monarchy's] mystery is its life. We must not let daylight in upon the magic'.[15]

Certainly, Iran was not Britain. The dominant belief within the elite and society that deep reforms were needed, although their type and model remained contentious issues, and the conviction of the shah and many within the elite that only a centralized, powerful and self-proclaimed enlightened monarchy could overcome petty personal and class interests in the name of a national resurgence ensured the decision for the Crown's politicization. The shah's push for the excessive politicization of the monarchy was also determined by his unwillingness to tolerate any popular political figures. The experience of Mossadegh and the humiliation he endured during the first thirteen years of his reign continued to loom large. This politicization helped create the conditions for subsequent attempts at the ideologization of the monarchy that would characterize the Pahlavi state until 1979.

The principles of the White Revolution, initially numbering six but climbing to nineteen by 1978, along with the developmental plans drawn up and implemented by the Plan and Budget Organization founded in 1947, brought great economic, social and technological changes. These changes, although preventing a communist Red Revolution exacerbated a number of existing political challenges facing the state while creating new ones. At the centre of the original six principles was the shah's much-touted land reform that was fairly successful in breaking the landowning class' back and in providing some land and opportunity to small and mid-sized famers to develop. However, it also helped create the conditions for increasing levels of rural–urban migration prompted by the search for work as the agricultural sector shrank. The urban workforce in the period 1966–76 grew by 54 per cent, while agriculture's share of GDP declined from 37 per cent in 1968 to 8 per cent by 1977. This growing number of rural migrants in urban areas such as Isfahan, Tabriz, Mashad and especially Tehran posed serious challenges to the state, especially the absorption of these newly arrived migrants. Similar to rustics newly arrived in urban areas across the globe, they found themselves to varying degrees appalled, fascinated, disoriented, enchanted, attracted and alienated by the urban environment.

In urban areas these migrants felt the extent of economic and class differences between themselves and the urban middle and upper classes, many of whom during the 1960s and 1970s were *nouveau riche*. These new rich tended to be ostentatious and arrogant with a strong sense of entitlement, characteristics that only added to class tension. Rural migrants also felt the stark contrast between their own mores and behaviour and that of the new rich urban class which was considered corrupt and Occidentosis-ridden. This theme would come to occupy an important place in Rastakhiz rhetoric. Importantly, the state's original discourses on identity propagated the idea that to obtain civilization one had to become culturally Westernized. Those who became this *homo Pahlavicus* were the holders of an identity and position superior to those who had not yet obtained the markings of this civilization or refused the very criteria making up *homo Pahlavicus*. This dynamic also meant that within the established urban population a sociocultural cleavage grew between the technocratic and professional middle and upper class, who were popularly recognized as the Occidentosis-ridden products of Pahlavi Occidentalism, and the old bazaari and urban working class and clergy who rejected *homo Pahlavicus* which they considered Occidentosis-ridden.

With the implementation of the White Revolution, primary, secondary and higher education quickly expanded. In the period 1966–76 the student population quadrupled. At a time of rising student activism in the West that influenced Iranian students, the increasing numbers of students constituted a growing political threat to the state. Moreover, with the expansion of the student population came a vast increase in the number of students from villages and small towns moving to the large urban areas. They shared many of the same feelings of their working-class brethren newly arrived from these areas. The difference between them, however, was the students' ability to articulate their feelings and outrage and the academic environment in which they operated. As noted earlier towards the end of Reza Shah's reign, the state became increasingly concerned with the youth's ideological and political cultivation. By the mid-1960s the state would begin to address again this issue.

A central element of this second round of pro-West Occidentalism was the expansion of Reza Shah's attempts to enlarge the role of women in society. Educational opportunities for them were greatly expanded, as were their civil rights, of course within the framework of Pahlavi authoritarianism. Granted the right to vote in the run-up to the referendum on the White Revolution, they also obtained the right to run in elections and hold public office. By the time of the passage of the Family Protection Act of 1967 they received the right to sue for divorce while the state limited the conditions under which a man could sue for divorce, have multiple wives and obtain custody of children in the case of divorce. The increasing presence of women, unveiled, in higher education, the professions, the entertainment industry and even in politics constituted another major social change that many found for varying reasons discomforting and disorienting.

In this context, the period between the launching of the White Revolution and the 1971 celebrations marking the 2,500th anniversary of the founding of the Achaemenid Empire experienced two major developments at the centre of this study that emerged due to a myriad of factors. This chapter examines the first of these developments, the shah's initial moves, however opaque and cautionary, towards the ideologization of the monarchy. The other development, the emergence of anti-West Occidentalism and specifically the changes in the shah's and the empress's views on the authenticity of Iranian culture and national identity and the place of the West within it are covered in the following chapter. Although these two developments are presented in different chapters they emerged and evolved, albeit in less than cohesive ways, in the same time period. Together they provide the backdrop to the ideology and discourses of the Rastakhiz Party.

Ideology and Pahlavism

By the early 1960s the state faced not only the challenge of the three main competing secular ideologies, democracy, nationalism and socialism, but also forms of

Islamist thought that began to crystallize in opposition to the discourses of Pahlavi Occidentalism. This Islamist thought also targeted the other competing ideologies.

> The dominance of the secular triumvirate of nationalism, democracy, and socialism appealed to a significant minority in the Iranian political community that, in turn, became a significant Other in terms of which religious ideologies began to re-define and relocate themselves.[16]

Given the increasing intellectual and popular appeal of these competing ideologies, the Pahlavi state began to redefine and relocate itself ideologically in regard to them approximately at the same time clerical and lay religious figures, such as Mehdi Bazargan, Ayatollah Mahmud Taliqani and Ayatollah Mortaza Motahari, among others, decided to do the same for Islam.[17] In other words, from the early 1960s the two traditional sources of power and legitimacy in Iran, the monarchy and the clergy, independent of, and in competition with, each other gave greater attention than before to rearticulating themselves ideologically in reaction to the threat of these three competing ideologies. Both state and Islamists discourses portrayed these ideologies as alien and threatening to their respective conceptions of authenticity. At the same time, the shah had fleeting concerns about the effectiveness of the official two-party system in mobilizing both mass and educated popular opinion.

In these circumstances the shah contemplated systematic ideologization of the monarchy. Certainly, discourses of the White Revolution had ideological elements but they were piecemeal and not integrated into a tight ideological framework similar to modern ideologies. The ideology named Pahlavism and introduced in the four-volume series *Pahlavism* published in the immediate run-up to the shah's coronation in 1967 was presented as a new–old Iranian cosmology, a total ideology, that established the theoretical elements common to modern ideologies, namely politicized historiography, comparative political systems, a world view, economic theory, sociology and a programme for rapid modernization. These elements were to constitute the ideological school of Pahlavism and justify the monarchy in historical and contemporary terms. These books combined within Pahlavism equally the imagery of a past golden age and the construction of a golden future. As the initial attempt at the ideologization of the monarchy, Pahlavism played an important role in setting the ideological and discursive framework of the Rastakhiz Party.

The author of *Pahlavism*, Manuchehr Honarmand, was born in 1927 in Zanjan. After secondary education he entered the burgeoning civil service. His initial post was auditor for the Organization of Social Insurance. He quickly advanced through it, becoming special auditor, chief of auditing and then director of the department for organizational integrity (*sarparast-e edare-ye hefazat*). According to his SAVAK file, from his early youth he was politically active and a fervent nationalist supporter of the Pahlavi state. Although he entertained some leftist sympathies he was an ardent anti-communist and opponent of the Tudeh Party. Thus, in the chaotic period after the end of the Allied Occupation, he was active in political parties that opposed Tudeh, such as the Democratic Party (*Hezb-e Demokrat*), which had been headed by Qavam al-Saltaneh, and the Party of the Toilers of Iran (*Hezb-e Zahmatkeshan-e Iran*) founded in 1951 by Mozaffar Baghai Kermani.

The Party of Toilers was initially a coalition of anti-Tudeh forces that had two broad wings. One, headed by Khalil Maleki, consisted of the working class, some white-collar workers and intellectuals sympathetic to its concerns and the other, headed by Baghai himself, that consisted of moderate intellectuals, small and mid-sized merchants and business people and a portion of white-collar workers. They were the nucleus of Baghai's previous party, the Organization of the Guardians of Freedom, that championed the institutionalization of electoral transparency and the concept of free and fair elections. Baghai and his wing joined the National Front, the coalition that constituted Mossadegh's political base, since he supported the prime minister's struggle for oil nationalization and the supremacy of the 1906 Constitution while opposing absolutist royalists who resisted Mossadegh. Honarmand was personally close to Baghai and his wing. As the struggle between Mossadegh and the shah intensified and the Tudeh Party seemed to be increasingly behind the nationalist prime minister, Baghai in 1952 pulled his support from the National Front, as did Honarmand. This move in turn created a break with Maliki and his supporters who remained loyal to the prime minister.

Honarmand's timely break with Mossadegh, his strong opposition to Tudeh and enduring loyalty to the dynasty ensured the shah's confidence in him. According to SAVAK documents this confidence led him to charge Honarmand with writing *Pahlavism*.[18] Soon after the publication of the first volume of *Pahlavism*, Honarmand received a congratulatory letter from Senator Javad Bushehri who headed the official committee overseeing the arrangements for the celebrations marking the 2,500th anniversary of the founding of the Iranian Empire by Cyrus the Great. *Pahlavism* was immediately placed high on this event's list of official publications that was distributed within the government. After the publication of subsequent volumes more positive references in regard to him and these writings were recorded by SAVAK in his individual file.[19] In 1970 the shah had him join the newly found and officially supported pan-Iran party, Party of the Iranians (*Hezb-e Iranian*).

The book's introduction provided the reasons behind the shah's decision for the theorization of Pahlavism.

> Now that the country's active forces have sprung into action ... and the empire is quickly moving in the direction of a bright future it is necessary to theorize the political and economic ideology and school of the ... shah, name it 'Pahlavism', and compare it with the contemporary world's other progressive schools from the economic and political points of view in order to show its superiority.

Accepting the Enlightenment understanding of progressive history and implicitly using Hegelian and Marxian conceptions of linear historical development, Honarmand stressed that one goal of these works was to show the superiority of Pahlavism over these Western conceptions. Thus, Pahlavism greatly expanded the attempts of the late Reza Shah period to make a discursive shift in regard to Iran's position vis-à-vis the

West, from student of the West to its mentor. This shift reached new heights in the Rastakhiz period.

> With great pride it is possible to say that in the world where [the political systems] of a majority of countries are based on various political schools whose roots are found in the five principles of feudalism, imperialism, liberalism, democracy and socialism, the shahanshah has unveiled a new school. Its creative power is greater than that of socialism, its freedom and equality of rights is superior to those of democracy, and its method of action is stronger and more effective than those of radical liberals. It tramples the bases of the bourgeoisie and feudalism while eliminating the anarchism that emerges from liberalism. ... It must be registered as a political culture under the name of Pahlavism. ... In a world where theories and idealistic theorists are registered under the rubric of political cultures, what is the problem with the progressive School of Pahlavism, whose teachings are improving the world's situation, also being recognized as a political culture and school?[20]

Figure 1 Amir Abbas Hoveyda. *Rastakhiz*, author's collection.

Another reason behind this attempt at the monarchy's ideologization was the lacklustre performance of the political parties. By the time of *Pahlavism*'s publication two officially sanctioned political parties existed, New Iran (*Iran-e Novin*), the party in power and headed by the prime minister, Amir Abbas Hoveyda, and the People's Party (*Mardom*). The shah created the New Iran Party in 1963 in order to mobilize and expand popular support, and in particular that of the educated middle classes and technocrats, as the monarchy became increasingly politicized as a result of the White Revolution. The books *Pahlavism* articulated the shah's disappointment with their performance. 'Unfortunately, *Iran-e Novin*, despite great efforts ... and given its lack of specialization in institutional affairs' had failed to establish a strong link between Pahlavism and the people. It lacked a 'proper social infrastructure and institutions' and 'real connections with the people'. Without 'these essential elements' a party 'is not able to choose real deputies' and thus help the country's development.[21] Worryingly, despite the attractiveness of the White Revolution, these official political parties, and specifically *Iran-e Novin*, had failed to create a modern national ideology which was essential to generating popular hope and mobilization behind this Revolution (Figure 1).[22]

Historiography

Historiography is a vital element of ideology that supports a state by rooting it in the past or presenting it as the final inevitable result of historical forces. Pahlavism integrated both. Pahlavist historiography was more than simple glorification of the Pahlavi dynasty based on a claimed link between it and pre-Islamic Iranian Empire. Rather, building on elements within the Occidentalism of the Reza Shah period, it sought in pre-Islamic Iranian Empire a comprehension of Iran's past and an augury of its future. Pahlavism combined a Romantic interpretation of imperial history that was subjective and impassioned with a deterministic conception that identified it with the inevitable golden and progressive age of Iran's modern future. Vitally, this history, more clearly and systematically articulated than during Reza Shah's reign, was to be a substitute for religion and, more importantly, clericalism, and a mechanism for inculcating a common political culture, creating national unity and establishing new sources of monarchical legitimacy.

Pahlavism re-introduced the main themes of the Occidentalism of the Reza Shah period, Aryanism, and the idea of Iran as a source of Western civilization. Thus, Westernizing reforms constituted not the imposition of a foreign culture, but rather a return to lost Iranian authenticity. Pahlavism however pushed the tone of Pahlavi discourses towards anti-West Occidentalism. Rejecting the West's historiography and Orientalized portrayal of Iran since the time of Herodotus, it called for the writing of a new historiography for Iran: 'The time for change in historiography has arrived. The true history of imperial Iran must and is starting to be written'.[23] This would become a common Rastakhiz theme. Pahlavism condemned the West's attempts to 'dry out the root of the richness of Iranian culture' through Orientalist discourses while bemoaning the relative success of these attempts. But 'the roots [of Iranian culture and civilization] were so strong and deep that they re-energized and laid seeds, bringing into existence the current dynamism'.

The base of Pahlavism's historiography was the idea of continuous Iranian history originating with the establishment of the Achaemenid polity. 'Thanks to this empire, the world's largest, and particularly its customs and societal traditions, Iran, during its 2500-year-old history, survived waves of foreign invasions, charlatans, and conquests, and especially the Arab invasion.' Survival was due to the strength of Iranian culture to seduce conquerors, such as Alexander's successors, 'who accepted Iranian traditions and way of life and gradually melted into that culture'. While recognizing military defeat at the hands of Arabs, Pahlavism stressed that 'Arabs, although destroying pillars of Iranian civilization, accepted its greatness and deep philosophy. Here is the influence of genuine Iranian customs on Islam'.[24] Iran therefore possessed an ancient imperial civilization that despite military defeat and conquest remained a victor in civilizational terms. Its soft power was greater than Arab and Mongol hard power. Yet, Pahlavism decried: 'Despite all this history and glory they still call us backward and deprived'.[25]

To counter this Orientalist interpretation, a goal first set towards the end of Reza Shah's reign, Pahlavism took aim at Western historiography that portrayed ancient Greece, and specifically Athens, as the pioneer in the development of the philosophy of governance. Pahlavism claimed that in reality the political and philosophical leaders of the Iranian Empire first seriously debated the strengths and weaknesses of various forms of government, even if their conclusion differed from that of ancient Greece. 'In times long gone the Iranian people had thinkers who were able to distinguish the forms of government and clearly articulate their characteristics.'

The historical evidence for this claim was the inscriptions of Darius (r.522–486 BCE) at Behestun, among other areas, detailing the overthrow of Gaumata, a Magian priest whom Darius accused of falsely claiming to be Bardiya, the deceased son of Cyrus the Great. On 11 March 522 BCE this 'false' Bardiya launched a successful revolt against Cambyses II (r.525–522 BCE). Cambyses II, on a military campaign in Egypt, died during his return to the imperial heartland to crush the revolt. Gaumata found broad support for his rebellion given the tyranny of Cambyses II who failed to rule as his father, and the popular belief that Gaumata was indeed the real Bardiya. Darius claimed that unknown to the population Cambyses had killed some time before the real Bardiya, thus the willingness of the elite and people to believe that Gaumata was indeed the real Bardiya. On 1 July Gaumata proclaimed himself shahanshah. He ruled for approximately seven months before Darius and a group of aristocratic supporters, the most important of whom for purposes here are Otanes and Megabyzus, overthrew him.[26]

With the overthrow of the 'false' Bardiya, Darius convened a meeting with the realm's leading thinkers to debate the empire's political future. Pahlavism, to back up its historiographical claims in this regard utilized Herodotus' *The Histories*. 'Even Herodotus with all of his rancor and hostility toward Iranians in his third book detailed the formation of a committee to choose a successor to the throne after Gumata's overthrow.' The committee had seven members, including Darius. Otanes, urging democracy, argued

> that we should put an end to the system whereby one of us is the sole ruler. Monarchy is neither an attractive nor a noble institution. You have seen how vicious Cambyses became. ... [Democracy] has the best of all names to describe

it – equality before the law. ... It is free of the vices of monarchy. It is government by lot, it is accountable government, and it refers all decisions to the common people. So I propose that we abandon monarchy and increase the power of the people.

After him, Megabyzus spoke in favour of oligarchy:

Otanes' arguments for abolishing monarchy represent my own views too. However, in so far as he was recommending the transference of power to the general populace, his argument is flawed. A mob is ineffective, and there is nothing more stupid or more given to brutality. ... The approach of the general populace is that of a river swollen with winter rain: they rush blindly forward and sweep things before them. Let us leave democracy to Persia's enemies, while we choose a number of the best men and put power in their hands.

Darius then spoke. He agreed with Megabyzus's poor estimation of democracy and stressed the inevitably of the spread of corruption within democracy. He however did not accept the idea of oligarchic government. 'In an oligarchy ... a number of people are trying to benefit the community, and in this situation violent personal feuds tend to arise' as each one of them strives to be the victor. Factional struggles bring a violent antagonism, 'which lead(s) to bloodshed'. He argued that monarchy had to be preserved because it obtained and guaranteed the country's cultural and geopolitical independence. 'And I would add that we should not abolish our ancestral customs, which serve us well. That is not the way to improve matters.' Four members endorsed Darius' view and the monarchy remained.[27]

Pahlavism showcased a Persian translation of this text and praised the Iranians' choice of monarchy because 'it combines the experience and expertise of the oligarchy while looking out for the people's interests and welfare'. This conversation summarizes the fundamental elements of Pahlavi discourses of power that came to an ideological fruition during the Rastakhiz period. On the one hand, the imperial monarchy was the epitome, source and defender of Iranian cultural geopolitical independence. On the other hand, it was portrayed as an above-class agent protecting the welfare of all classes while preventing the claimed excesses and probable chaos of democratic systems, oligarchic rule and of course bloody social and political revolution. In the nineteenth and early twentieth centuries these elements constituted the traditional defence of monarchy in Europe in the face of competing modernism that emerged as a result of the Enlightenment. As the shah told an American writer in the early 1960s: 'Any government, of any form, if it is to be a serious government, must have someone above politics-above petty jealousies, above parties, cartels, trusts, the financial powers- who must and should make fundamental decisions'.[28] Pahlavism concluded that the decisive role played by the monarchy in the power and grandeur of the Achaemenid and Sasanian Empires showed the wisdom of this choice. Importantly, it argued that Achaemenid emperors transformed monarchical virtues into 'a true ideology founded on distinct moral, social and economic bases that remain to this day, albeit in a changed form'.[29] Pahlavism therefore proclaimed that it was resuscitating an authentic Iranian ideology dating from the Achaemenid period.

The use of this ancient imperial heritage by an Iranian dynasty, whose appeal was based on the continued existence through the centuries after the Arab-Islamic invasions of an Iranian cultural identity rooted in the Persian language and its literature, Ferdowsi's *Shahnameh*, the Iranian solar calendar, and popular adherence to traditional Iranian holidays and festivals, had a long history dating at least from the rule of the Safavid dynasty. What was new under Pahlavism was the use of this imperial historiography in pursuit of a modern ideological goal – the establishment from above of a brilliant golden age through the creation of a new person, *homo Pahlavicus*, imbued with authentic Iranian elements. Pahlavism, similar to other modern ideologies emerging during and after the era of the French Revolution, determined to create a new person that embodied its historiography and political goals.

Three elements made up *homo Pahlavicus*. The first element was primordial and eternal faith in the imperial system.[30] Second was the concept of empire that symbolized the golden ages of the past and the future. At a time of decline and weakness relative to the West, Iran could regain self-confidence from the pages of its imperial history. The Achaemenid Empire 'took Iranian culture, art and civilization to the lands of Europe and Africa', where 'they were accepted and adapted'.[31] The 'two superpowers of the ancient world' were Rome and the Iranian Sasanian Empire, a millennium before the superpower rivalry of the United States and the USSR. This past and future greatness of Iran was directly linked to the monarchy since it and empire were synonymous. Pahlavism's third emphasis was on Aryanism.

Revolutionary ideological regimes, into which the shah was hoping to transform the state within the framework of traditional monarchy, must attack the past in order to justify the present. According to *Pahlavism* the ancient past, from which it was claimed the ideology Pahlavism emerged, provided the grounds to attack the relatively immediate past. In other words, the glory and might of Iran's ancient empires were compared to its shame and weakness in the nineteenth and early twentieth centuries. This comparison was vital to the ongoing attempts to revive life of this ancient heritage and strengthen nostalgia for it. Pahlavism articulated four causes for Iran's temporary ejection from the club of civilization builders and universal history and loss of grandeur and power whose restoration it aimed to obtain.

First, it directed its ire at the Qajar dynasty. 'From 1800 to 1900 Europe and America ran in the direction of exploration, industry, trade and power while the Qajar government occupied itself with fun-making (*khoshgozarani*).' Despite military defeats and the obvious need for reform 'the Qajars, in an attempt to protect their regime, encouraged the people to indifference and licentiousness ... and worked only to serve their own personal interests, forgetting those of the Iranian Empire'.[32] Second, Pahlavism blamed imperialism of Britain and Russia. These empires through military action, interference in Iranian domestic affairs, and 'aid to forces of reaction within the country', namely clerics and Qajar officials, undermined the Iranian Empire. Third, a weak central government and monarchy, having created the conditions for imperialism's spread, became 'a puppet of foreign powers'. It allowed the country's unity to crack as tribes and regional leaders governed as they saw fit with no or little regard of the central government. Particular attention was given to the alliance of some local tribal leaders with foreign powers.[33] Fourth, Pahlavism held reactionary clerics and the religious culture they produced responsible for blocking the limited moves of the Qajar government towards modernization and for fatally damaging the constitutional movement and its plans for national rejuvenation.

Religion and anticlericalism

Pahlavism's understanding of the causes of decline and goals to establish centralized power and initiate Westernization determined that clerical power and institutions and the culture they produced would be main objects of its political attack. One goal was the overthrowing of clerics and their interpretation of religion, which had determined public cultural forms and high culture. Achieving it was a prerequisite for the creation of *homo Pahlavicus*.

Pahlavism sought to justify in historical and contemporary terms this goal of 'separating religion from politics'. It claimed that attacks on clerics and their institutions were a return to an authentic Iranian method of governing dating from its pre-Islamic imperial period and that the separation of church and state was a natural universal process and necessity. The theorization began with a contorted historical outline of the separation of church and state in the West from St. Augustine to Jean Bodin. It concluded with outlines of the anticlericalism and separation of church and state in Western political schools, namely democracy and forms of totalitarianism, such as fascism and Nazism.[34] The relevance of the Western experience in this regard was based on Pahlavism's claim that Iran enjoyed ancient racial–cultural links with the West.

Attention was then turned to the history of church-state relations in pre-Islamic Iran. Zoroastrianism was presented as one of the main pillars of Iranian identity that bequeathed a rich intellectual, religious and moral heritage to Iranians and the world. Pahlavism argued that the place of Zoroastrianism in pre-Islamic Iranian Empire had lessons for the present. 'The oldest government about which we have sufficient historical information is that of the Sasanian emperors in whose time Zoroastrianism and Manichaeism were popular religions. These emperors, while respecting religions and their followers, ensured the complete separation of state matters from those of religion.' But, in some reigns this separation was not strictly followed. 'In Iran when religion had the opportunity to mix with politics and interfere in it, as under Hormuz Shah (r.270–271), the result was disastrous. He lost his government.' However, 'in the time of Khosrow (r.531–579), the last powerful Sasanian emperor, full respect was given to all religions. Since no law was based on a single religion and justice was administered for all, the empire enjoyed prosperity and the government profited from stability and popular support'.[35] The historical lesson was clear.

Pahlavism, having extolled the greatness and virtues of Zoroastrianism, was faced with the need to explain why Iranians lost faith in this authentically Iranian religion and accepted Islam brought to them by the Arabs.

> The lack of attention to the genuine bases of religion and the politically motivated changing of those bases distorted that religion's spirit, which had been [based on] the people's freedom. This spirit's destruction led to the emergence of despotism

and tyranny that replaced justice and fairness. So, a majority of people, who once believed in this religion, were attracted to Islam which held the same beliefs of old Iran.[36]

The reasons for this attraction were rooted in the actions of a reactionary Zoroastrian clergy that, having forgotten the religion's true essence in order to pursue their worldly interests, set in motion the collapse of the Sasanian Empire. Yet, Islam's success and attractiveness to Iranians was due to its derivation from this lost authenticity of Iran's own religion. 'Zoroastrianism's foundations, which were passed onto Islam, included compassion, graciousness, hospitality, forbearance, peace and friendship, respect for the rights of others and freedom. All of these were in our religious books before Islam'.[37]

While Arab domination of Iran was the consequence of the baleful mixing of religion with politics, it also subsequently provoked a strong passion among Iranians for their authenticity and identity. 'After the Arab conquest of Iran the puppets of the Umayyad and Abbasid Caliphates established religious government. This move was one of the fundamental causes for the emergence of national Iranian governments such as the Safarians and others. Eventually, state power split from religious influence.' Pahlavism, in its historical review of the Safavid, Zand and Qajar periods, sought to prove that its separation of religion from politics had been the praiseworthy goal of previous dynasties, which only the Pahlavi dynasty succeeded in achieving.

Pahlavism charged clerics with damaging state interests under the Qajar monarchy and the 'popular constitutionalist' movement. It claimed that this movement's greatest achievement was not the limitation of monarchical power but rather 'separating legally and forever religion from politics. But because of clerical opposition and influence these two elements were not separated as they should and must be.' The tension between these two forces grew until Reza Shah destroyed clerical power over the educational and judicial systems and ended their influence in public affairs. State interests were to predominate over the clergy's parochial interests.[38] These steps were taken in order to create *homo Pahlavicus* and return culturally Iranians to their Aryan racial cousins, West Europeans.

According to Pahlavism in the anarchy that emerged in the wake of Reza Shah's abdication, 'power-hungry clerics found the opportunity for political exhibitionism. They included Ayatollah Kashani who interfered in politics during the time of Mossadegh's government'.[39] Condemning clerical interference in state affairs, it provided the definition of a genuine cleric: 'Real clerics remain in religious establishments dealing with religious study. … The latest attempt by power-hungry, ambitious clerics was seen only a couple of years ago and was suppressed. Never again shall they raise their heads'.[40] This 'latest attempt' was a rebellion in 1962 led by Ayatollah Khomeini who opposed the White Revolution and the granting of extraterritorial status to US government and military officials and their families. The state crushed the demonstrations and exiled Khomeini. In its wake the shah echoed sentiments made by Peter I some 250 years ago.

> A number of ignoramuses and reactionaries has always existed whose brains have not moved and who are always placing obstacles in our path. … Their brains are not capable of moving. This black [clerical] reaction … over the past thousand

years has not witnessed any progress in its thought. It thinks that life is made up of obtaining something for nothing and sponging off others, of idleness, eating and sleeping. In the six points [of the White Revolution] an idea exists for everyone. ... But who opposes it? Black reaction, stupid men who understand nothing and are ill-intentioned.[41] They are similar to depressed, motionless snakes and, similar to them, float in their own filth. ... If these sordid, vile elements ... do not wake from their sleep of ignorance the justice's fist, like thunder, will strike their heads in whatever cloth they are, perhaps to terminate their filthy, shameful lives.[42] ... They don't want the country to prosper and develop. They think of their own interests. They are against reforms because they won't be able to trick anyone anymore ... and trick anyone into revolting against the government.[43]

He ended his attempts initiated in the 1940s and 1950s to maintain some form of political relationship with the clergy. Sabeti noted that with the implementation of the White Revolution it was recognized that the clergy had become 'one of the fundamental opposition groups'.[44]

Pahlavism, taking inspiration from Reza Shah, called for the weakening of clerical institutions and influence over public cultural forms. In order to achieve these goals it advocated state interference in ecclesiastical affairs and the creation of a Pahlavist Islam that neutralized the reactionary Islam propagated by clerics.

> No doubt exists that in the near future in the education and cultivation of the future generations steps will be made by genuine national religious leaders to establish authentic Islamic rituals and moral principles worthy of Islam and to save religion from superstition and personal interests.

A body of 'genuine' clerics and a state-run religious corps would propagate the values of Pahlavist Islam and bringing it 'to the people in the countryside and small cities'.[45] Only this Islam could have a presence in the political arena, serving state interests. Moreover, Pahlavism advocated stripping Islamic ethics from Islamic doctrine. The shah in his speeches spoke of an ethical and spiritual Islam confined to the private sphere that, as we shall see in the chapters on the Rastakhiz period, constituted the best defence to godless communism, the West's consumerism, materialism and decline in morals.[46] In other words, Iranians, no longer under the doctrinal influence of clerics and 'black reaction', would live morally good Islamic lives while adhering to the principles of Pahlavism.

Competing 'unauthentic' ideologies

The use of historiography to justify the present is not enough to constitute an ideology and obtain ideological hegemony. It must also show superiority to competing ideological systems which, in the case of Pahlavism, were Western capitalism and nationalist constitutionalism, various forms of socialism and eventually Islamism. The first political issue with which Pahlavism contended was tension between its emphasis on the regime's implicit desire for absolute power, portrayed by it as a form of enlightened absolutism, and the spirit and provisions of the 1906 Constitutional Revolution that subordinated monarchical power to the popularly elected Majles to which the prime minister and cabinet were responsible, and not to the shah. Pahlavism's response was a historiography that emphasized the failure of the constitutional system to implement the long-standing goal of modernization in the face of the West's imperialism.

> In Iran the words constitutionalism and political parties, having simultaneously come into existence, are synonyms. The emergence of political parties and fronts was due to the desire of foreign governments to exercise limitless influence in pursuit of their own interests in Iran and the thought of intellectuals and the reactionary elite who acted on the basis of their personal and/or collective interests. No doubt exists that intellectuals had very limited room for maneuver in their struggle with reactionaries. These two classes with the encouragement and incitement of foreign governments gradually lined up against each other. As a result, two parties, one constitutionalist and one dictatorial came into existence. England's policy was to strengthen the constitutionalists and that of tsarist Russia to aid the supporters of tyranny.[47]

These political parties from their inception were tainted, having abandoned national interests and become the playthings of imperialist powers and instruments for the realization of personal interests. This approach seen in subsequent volumes of Pahlavism referred back to Darius's admonitions about democratic forms of government.

Pahlavism, while casting doubt on the intentions and ability of constitutionalist parties, lauded the socio-economic goals driving the idea of constitutionalism. 'The constitutionalist agenda was clear: the separation of political power from clerics, obligatory military service, distribution of land to the peasants and farmers, obligatory national education, (and) creation of an agricultural bank to help peasants and farmers'.[48] However, 'these goals united against the democrats clerics and landowners who used the Majles to attack and oppose reforms. The reactionaries attacked the democrats with the claim that they sought to use a constitutional, semi-socialist government to push the country away from religion. This rhetoric was effective since the separation of religion from politics is one of the principles of democrats.' Therefore, the democrats were unable to overcome reactionary elements.

This political narrative, however, did not provide Pahlavism with sufficient grounds to delegitimize the democrats and their ideology. They had to be tainted as agents of foreign powers.

> The democratic party had good relations with England and enjoyed the material and intellectual support of the English government. ... But when Russia and England became allies in World War I, the democratic party was left without support. ... Thus, in the face of reactionary elements they were defeated along with their socio-economic agenda.

According to this interpretation, the democrats, given their lack of domestic political power and popular support, were forced to rely on the support of a Western power. They therefore found themselves dependent on London's changing international interests. Once the democrats were deprived of this conditional and foreign support, reactionary clerics and landowners through effective use of propaganda that warned about the loss of religion were able to use the democratic system established by the constitutionalists to block modernization.

If democrats suffered because of their links with the British, leftist parties, after the Bolshevik Revolution, were in the hands of the USSR. 'In the Fourth Majles (1921-1923), the socialist party was linked to Russia. This party with its slogans of freedom fought against reactionary obstructionism and provoked reactionary forces and clericalism (*akhundbazi*) to attack it'.[49] In sum, this interpretation referred back to Megabyzus who wished democracy onto Iran's enemies given its inherent weaknesses, inability to create national unity and susceptibility to foreign interference. The remedy to this situation was clear. The Pahlavi dynasty and Pahlavism constituted the only true and authentic national modernizing forces that refused to be a plaything of imperialist powers.

According to Pahlavism the establishment of the Pahlavi dynasty was a manifestation of a popular desire for a strong just hand, independent of imperialist forces to transform and save the country. 'By examining the process by which parties were established and dissolved before 1921 it can be clearly recognized that these parties knowingly or unknowingly were the agents of foreign powers.' Thus, 'it is natural that they, politicians of such quality, before thinking about implementing the party's agenda, which in any case always had a deceitfully seductive appearance, were thinking of enrichment of their own personal interests'.[50] A strong centralized authority, the monarchy, hovering above petty factional and personal interests, was needed. During Reza Shah's reign 'these political puppet shows and their players could no longer remain in any form'. He was 'stronger than any political party. With a spirit greater than that of any politician he saved the country from certain collapse and gave it real independence and international credit, and established the genuine principle of constitutionalism'.[51]

The truthfulness of this interpretation was seen in the country's conditions when in the wake of Reza Shah's abdication the monarchy weakened and political parties and individual politicians again sought, and were sought by, foreign interests.[52] Although these parties used 'nice slogans' and 'spoke of improving the people's welfare', they ultimately served foreign or narrow personal interests. The consequence was misfortune for the people and general chaos. Yet, once again the monarchy, faced with the handing over of the country to foreign powers by these incompetent, selfish and/ or traitorous domestic elements, moved to consolidate power in the period 1946-53. Pahlavism's claim in this regard was severely undermined by the role of the United States and the United Kingdom in overthrowing Mossadegh and strengthening the monarchy. Combatting this aspect of popular historical memory was a theme of the Rastakhiz period and the shah's pronouncements marking Mossadegh's overthrow, coined in official parlance as the national rebellion and resurgence (*rastakhiz*).

Given the Constitutional Revolution and the era's political realities in which the Pahlavi state existed, a constitutional veneer was maintained. Pahlavism professed the importance of the 1906 Constitution but did not advocate the type of free elections characterizing the West's liberal democracies. Parties' actions had to conform to Pahlavism's basic political principle, coined 'Constitutional Monarchical Parliamentarianism'. According to it, given the country's socio-economic challenges and the tendency of parties to follow either foreign or their personal interests, the shah would set policy and modernizing goals which deputies elected by the people would carry out. The deputies and parties could debate the best methods for achieving these goals, but would not be permitted to undermine Pahlavism's principles. Honarmand, laying the principles behind the Rastakhiz Party some eight years before its establishment, stated:

> A political party's most important challenge is to propagate the national ideology, Pahlavism, and make it its pillar. A party's only possible path is the ideology of Pahlavism and strengthening of its philosophical authenticity. ... No deputy can be outside this ideology's framework. Pahlavism needs to be actively propagated so that the people know the direction in which the shah wants to take the country and thus become mobilized around this ideology.

Pahlavism's interpretation of constitutionalism stressed achievement of its 'socio-constitutional principles [that] aim for the development of, and progress toward, clean and completely free elections, which will eventually come as the result of the people becoming literate, the raising of popular culture and the elimination of deficiencies in the electoral process'. In other words, state-established criteria had to be met before full implementation of the 1906 Constitution. The raising of political culture included importantly, in the words of the shah, 'the removal of [religious] superstitions and foreign elements that have soiled our ancient culture'.[53] Alongside these political and cultural criteria were economic ones. His term 'economic democracy', first floated in *Mission for My Country*, stressed that the vast reduction in poverty and raising of living standards were prerequisites for political democracy. Pahlavism's political principle, taking a page from Marxism-Leninism, saw democracy first in socio-economic, and not in political, terms which justified its hold on power.

Pahlavism also codified the significant changes in the conceptions of the monarchy and justifications for its power implicitly introduced during Reza Shah's reign. Before the establishment of the Pahlavi dynasty, the legitimacy and justification of monarchical power were based on the preservation of religion, maintenance of order, defence of the borders and rendering of justice. These monarchical responsibilities were static in practice and liturgical in theory. Having fundamentally changed the liturgical aspect of the monarchy, Pahlavism became statist and anticlerical in nature and transformative in action. These elements became the base of its legitimacy and justification for its power. However, as the next chapter shows, when *Pahlavism* was published, the state was also initiating changes in conceptions of the authenticity of culture and national identity that propagated the Crown as the source and defender of that authenticity in the face of Occidentosis. This mission too became a justification of its power.

Superiority and universality

At the centre of the 'Economic Philosophy of Pahlavism' was the White Revolution that

> began a social course … whose result was the rapid advance in the direction of science and civilization of today's world. … White revolution means that a leader without thinking of his personal interests and without fear of possible political dangers on his path rises against despotic laws and useless, hollow traditions and moves in the direction of reform and the people's welfare.[54]

This section began with a brief history of 'economic philosophy in America and Europe' and of Iran since the pre-Islamic period. Pahlavism's interpretation of Iranian economic history followed the premise of its interpretation of Iranian political history. The pre-Islamic Iranian empires were praised for their infrastructure, economic dynamism and prosperity while the economic system under 'Arab domination' was condemned.[55] Under the Safavids, who put an end to Turkic rule, another form of foreign domination of Iran, 'the economy of Iran advanced along a new progressive path'. However, this trajectory ended during the Qajar period, which 'can be called the period of real economic decline in Iran'.[56]

'The main pillar of Pahlavism's economy consisted of nine elements' which were the principles of the White Revolution: '(1) land reform; (2) worker profit sharing; (3) enfranchisement of women; (4) privatization of state industries and factories which will help with the costs of land reform; (5) literacy corps; (6) nationalization of forests; (7) establishment of guilds; (8) health corps; and (9) development corps.' These principles were expanded to eighteen during the Rastakhiz period to include worker, social and old-age insurance, health care and partial worker control of factories. The other basis of Economic Pahlavism was the five-year economic development plans that focused on infrastructure, industrialization and the agricultural sector. Overall, the White Revolution and the development plans emphasized social welfare programmes, which were at the base of what the shah called his 'pink' path, a middle route superior to 'dark' capitalism and 'red' communism. In other words, Pahlavism, emphasizing a past golden era that provided the elements for the future golden age, claimed superiority to all existing politico-economic schools and thus universal appeal. In a 'world of chaos, the antiquity of Iran under the guidance of Pahlavism is an island of stability in these rapidly changing times. The transformation of this old country under the shah's leadership makes the world turn to his philosophy'.[57]

A vital element of Pahlavism's claim to superiority was its interpretation of the idea of a social contract between the state and the people. After briefly and rather superficially reviewing the idea of the social contract in the works of Western thinkers such as St Augustine and Thomas Hobbes, Pahlavism critiqued the shape and form of the social contract in the modern polities of the West. 'In communism a social contract exists but no freedom; people have no role' while 'in developing and some developed countries, the elite through propaganda and abuse of the electoral system use the democratic system to protect themselves from threats to their interests. Iran suffered from this at one point'. Pahlavism claimed to offer a superior path. The shah had 'established a new social contract that has in reality two sides. The people are the creators of the government which has the duty to fulfill the people's needs. It is a bilateral social contract'.[58] Once again it was emphasized that the monarchy, hovering above petty individual and collective class/group interests, would implement this social contract but not undertake a social revolution, similar to other revolutionary ideologies, whose consequences were dangerous, unpredictable and frequently bloody as they broke national unity. The shah stated:

> The basis of our ideology and revolution, and thus the progress of our thought is that our work would be based on the security of the majority's interests. But who are the majority? Without doubt, farmers and workers and other classes, classes with low incomes. I hope in the future that an affluent class comes into existence and a middle class takes shape. But this is not a reason to be against the kingdom's other classes.[59]

This position created a challenge to Pahlavism's attempts to reap the benefits of popular mobilization accompanying a modern ideology that targets specific social groups in its attempt to implement a 'revolution' and/or to preserve an authoritarian or totalitarian system. Even Pahlavism's use of the clerical and landowning class in this regard was limited.

Pahlavism claimed another element of superiority, that of speed. It promised quick, painless modernization. 'Pahlavism is a school that takes society along a shortcut from feudalism to a level higher than that of social parliamentary democracy. ... Pahlavism is a school that with unimaginable speed is taking the people from the dark world in the direction of a bright future'.[60] Here once again it is seen an acceptance of the Enlightenment idea of progressive history wrapped in a Pahlavist skin. In 1976 during the Rastakhiz period the shah predicted: 'If today's situation continues and is characterized by the same level of development we will reach the level of development of today's Europe in twelve years ... within twenty-five years we will be one of the world's developed countries'.[61] One can hear Nikita Khrushchev's promise made at the XXII Party Congress in 1961 that the present generation of Soviet citizens would live under communism by 1980.

The proclamation that Pahlavism had discovered a new path of socio-economic development, the shah's 'pink path', was not unique. Other ideological regimes in the Middle East too claimed they had found such a path. However, Pahlavism, unlike them, claimed that its path had universal appeal for it answered the needs of other countries alienated by the deficiencies of '–isms' of 'the Old World', namely liberal democratic capitalism and communism. This would become a major theme of the Rastakhiz period.

> In Pahlavism's philosophy, capitalism, in other words workers in the service of capitalists, has undergone fundamental and real change with the sale of shares of government factories to the people. Pahlavism also weakens socialism. Since workers are becoming shareholders of the profits of factory owners and industrialists, a level superior to socialism is coming into existence.[62]

While using essentially Marxist-Leninist critiques of capitalism, Pahlavism also attacked the socialist/communist models in the USSR, Eastern Europe and developing countries.

> Under socialist governments private property has no meaning. All capital belongs to the state and the people are servants of the state on which they are dependent for their wages. Simply put, in socialist states the capitalist is the government. In imperialistic capitalist states, a small number of people [similar to the socialist state] control the agricultural and industrial parts of the economy.[63] Pahlavism breaks these philosophies. By distributing land it breaks feudal capitalism, and with profit sharing for workers, the sale of government factories and industries and official recognition of workers' unions, it destroys the state capitalism of socialism. At the same time, it truly fulfills the goal of the people's welfare and regulates wealth without spilling blood or the creation of negative opposition.[64]

The long-standing threat of the West's imperialism only increased as Iran marched on the path of development that would protect the country's sovereignty and independence. 'Over the last several years the tentacles of parasitic economic imperialism of the great powers, hidden from view, have latched onto the strength and capability of our ancient culture.' This imperialism, strengthened by the devious attractiveness of Western economic thought 'seeks to destroy Iran's ancient culture because that culture is the enemy' of materialism and imperialism. But, Pahlavism claimed, the West's materialism and economic thought could not render fatal damage to 'this authentic culture'. Rather 'after a short period of darkness' authentic culture will become 'stronger, more productive, and brilliant. ... The White Revolution ... is the beginning of the elimination of these political tentacles from Iranian cultural life'.

These pronouncements were the prelude to topics expanded in subsequent volumes of *Pahlavism*. Pahlavism proclaimed that the White Revolution, having set the path towards practical Westernization based on economic and technological development, now by the end of the 1960s had to give more attention to cultural authenticity, including humanistic and spiritual issues. Volumes two and four are devoted to them. Underlining the failure of every political party to address the increasing cultural threat posed by the West, *Pahlavism* emphasized the protection and strengthening of spirituality and morality that were primordial elements of Iranian authenticity. It called for 'greater popular awareness of Iran's authentic and ancient culture' which would prevent the emergence and spread of Western materialism and culture. This determination to ensure the preservation and spread of authenticity would ensure that 'the economy will be in the service of the people' and not vice versa.

The title of the fourth volume *The First and Last Universal Government or Spiritual Governance* constitutes the first attempt of ideological codification of a main theme of the Rastakhiz period, Iranian spirituality and morality, its place in conceptions of Iranian culture and identity, and the necessity of protecting them in the face of the threats posed by Western imperialism. According to it 'spirituality creates a strong and enduring family' in whose milieu reigns supreme respect for elders and 'brotherly advice and commands'. Spirituality also ensures links between families across and within social, ethnic and tribal groups. 'This ancient culture of the Iranian people has made our country in the current sea of materialism an island situated on genuine human feelings and affection.' The West, by definition, destroyed such virtues. Naturally, Iranians, having 'earlier than any other people in the world discovered and protected the belief in a single God (Zoroaster)' and through its urban culture, created 'the world's first spirituality-based government' under the leadership of Cyrus the Great.[65] This spirituality and morality ensured openness to all peoples, regardless of race or religion and stood in contrast to Western 'Christian nations' that 'face disorder and chaos emerging from racial and religious discrimination.'[66]

Pahlavism stressed that the materialism and consumerism of Western culture were integral to the plans of Western imperialism for the spreading of its hegemony and a domestic brutality that denied people social and human justice. It denounced Western imperialism for 'trampling the human rights of small nations' through a geopolitical and economic exploitation that deprived these nations' lower socio-economic classes of food and access to 'the advantages of the contemporary world'. This assertion contradicted the official position of only six years prior:

> Everywhere you find that the outmoded capitalistic imperialist exploitation of less developed peoples is giving way to new co-operative relationships symbolized by the work of the United Nations technical assistance agencies.[67]

These attacks on Western imperialism and warnings about the spread of Western culture and values in Iran were accompanied by direct condemnations of the West as a civilization. It could and should not be the model for the future for other countries such as Iran. Any objective study of the foundations and current circumstances of Western civilization showed that it created conditions in which Western peoples suffered from 'fear and trepidation throughout their lives' given 'the pursuit of individual economic gain and benefit', and consequent lack of spirituality, humanism and equality. Pahlavism promised an effective blending of Iranian authenticity based on this unique spirituality and morality with economic development. In light of this authentic approach Pahlavism 'must become a global goal in the face of Western materialism and culture'. However, while Pahlavism claimed the formulation of a practical Iranian alternative to the West's modernities, the Pahlavi state, as it emerged during the time of Reza Shah, came to symbolize the Westernization of the economy, culture, morals and society in the minds of most Iranians.[68] This hurt the legitimacy of Pahlavism's claim to be an authentic Iranian school. Rastakhiz discourses would strive to change this popular perception.

Pahlavism, nationalism and the world

Pahlavism's international relations were based on the idea of a 'globalizing world' and on the rejection of isolationism. But the Pahlavist idea of globalization differed from that propagated by the capitalist West under the slogan of liberal cosmopolitanism, and from the Soviet one, coined international proletarianism. The shah argued: 'First the era of

Pax Irannica existed which was followed by Pax Romana. Recently, we witnessed Pax Britannica. But, today only one kind of pax can exist and that is global peace' based on the principle that international relations were rooted in 'the deep interdependence of the fate of all countries and peoples of the world' in which 'the rights of countries are respected' and the great powers had no right to interfere in the internal affairs of lesser powers. Within this framework, 'all countries would work together to ensure peace and economic growth'. Therefore, 'Pahlavism is a genuine supporter of the UN, rejects isolationism and autarky and strives for peaceful co-existence with its neighbors'.[69] However, Pahlavism, unlike other dominant ideologies of the Middle East, was wary of Third Worldism mainly because it considered Iran a primordial member of the elite 'Western' club.

Similar to many ideologies, Pahlavism was nationalistic, emphasizing Aryan roots to prove Iranian superiority to its neighbours and strengthened the symbols of national independence. Moreover, a major constitutive element of modern ideologies justifying the power of authoritarian or semi-authoritarian systems is the image of a specific foreign enemy. The state, by claiming to defend the country's cultural and geopolitical borders in the face of this enemy construct, and placing blame for its own failures on it, can strengthen its legitimacy and ideological hold. Pahlavism not only lacked this powerful ideological tool but faced the popular memory of the US and UK role in overthrowing Mossadegh and the shah's close relationship with these powers. Thus, despite Pahlavism's rhetoric, the public perception of the shah as an agent of the West, whose interests he served before those of Iran, remained. Pahlavism's claims to be the defender of Iranian independence rang hollow for some. Rastakhiz discourses aimed to change this perception.

The contradictory nature between Soviet ideology and the monarchy, and the shah's great fear of Soviet intentions, meant that the Pahlavi state would place itself in the camp of the West during the Cold War, even if it did not share the belief in liberal democracy. At the same time, the atheism of Soviet ideology offered Pahlavism the role of defender of the faith. History also provided cause for making the USSR an ideological enemy construct. Tsarist and Soviet intervention in domestic Iranian politics along with successful and unsuccessful attempts to seize Iranian territory left a strong negative popular impression that remains to this day. Despite these issues, Pahlavism did not use systematically the Soviet Union as a specific enemy construct, which could have limited the damage to its legitimacy rendered by the perceived and actual role of the United States in the country. Nonetheless, Pahlavism initiated state discourses warning about the plots of the imperialism of both the capitalist West and communist East against Iran. It stressed that the Pahlavi project particularly provoked Western imperialism given its claims to universality and superiority to the West. 'Since this ideology [Pahlavism] will become dominant and victorious and is not a puppet in the hands of the [communist] East or [liberal capitalist] West (*nokar-e sharq va qarb nist*), the peoples of the East, Asia and western Asia will follow it. For the interests of Western imperialism this situation is dangerous'.[70] Prior to the emergence of Pahlavism, state discourses, while including rhetoric about the injustices done to the country by the imperialism of Russia and Britain and indications about Iran's desire to be a great regional power, did not warn of ongoing threats of Western imperialism to Iran's ongoing economic development and geopolitical aspirations.

In sum, Pahlavism was an attempt at the ideologization of monarchy. It combined a modern transformative ideology based on the construction of a revolutionary utopia and a political conservatism dedicated to preserving the ancient monarchy with a Romantic interpretation of imperial history that was impassioned, subjective and rooted in a deterministic conception identifying the Pahlavi dynasty with the inevitable golden age of Iran's modern future. But Pahlavism was to be an Iranian ideology that rejected ideology and the '–isms' of the West and thus could be considered a non-ideological ideology. The shah implicitly summarized this aspect of *Pahlavism* in a conversation with an American writer at the end of the 1960s. 'Some things might look communistic to you, or socialistic to people in European countries – or liberalistic. Our ideology is an amalgam of whatever we thought would suit best our interests and needs. So, you cannot put a trademark on us'.[71] However, the shah did not expend much energy on the propagation of the Pahlavism of these books, despite its efforts to attain ideological and political unity. Nonetheless, Pahlavism served as an initial framework for the ideologization of the monarchy and provided many elements to Rastakhiz's ideological framework, as will become apparent in the following chapters. The steps towards the monarchy's ideologization accompanied an evolution in the shah's and the empress's views in regard to the authenticity of Iranian culture and national identity and the place and imagery of the West within it which is the topic of the following chapter.

6

The shah and the imagery of the Occident

In 1961 the shah published, *Mission for My Country*, which was ghost-written by Dr Donald Wilhelm, Jr., a visiting US professor of political science at Tehran University.[1] In it, the shah portrayed himself as a forward-looking transformative ruler determined to broaden the reformist path opened by his father and fine-tune the approach to Westernization and pro-West Occidentalism his predecessor initiated.

> Certainly no one can doubt that our culture is more akin to that of the West than is either the Chinese or that of our neighbors the Arabs. Iran was an early home of the Aryan race from whom most Americans and the peoples of European are descended. On the whole from the point of view of race we are separate and distinct from the Arabs who are Semites. Our language belongs to the Indo-European family which includes English, French, German and other major Western tongues. ... Of course Iranians over the centuries married with other peoples from other races. When the Arabs conquered Iran a great number of Arab words entered the language but the authenticity of race and the characteristics of the language did not change; it has remained. ... Our culture is the oldest continuous one racially and linguistically linked to that of the West.[2]

The shah's views of history that formed under the influence of Reza Shah's pro-West Occidentalism, along with his feelings of insecurity resulting from Iranian backwardness relative to the West which come across strongly in this book, made Aryanism and Iran's role in Western civilization essential elements in his conceptions of Iranian identity.

Mission for My Country showed that pro-West Occidentalism remained hegemonic and that the practical process of Westernization remained a positive albeit challenging path to the future. In the conclusion to the chapter 'Westernization: Our Welcome Ordeal', he wrote:

> In a country such as our Iran with all of its ancient heritage and customs, fundamental and rapid changes naturally bring difficulties and hardships. But these struggles and difficulties must be tolerated and handled in order to achieve Westernization. But I will never accept that we lose our rich ancient heritage.[3] On the contrary, I have every confidence that we can enrich it. ... Selective and judicious Westernization can help us towards the goal of democracy and shared prosperity; that is why I refer to it as our welcome ordeal.[4]

Yet, the shah also hinted at the differences in Iran's and the West's cultural characteristics that would be included in *Pahlavism* and *Rastakhiz* discourses.

> When I travelled to the Far East in 1958, I was reminded of a sagacious remark by Mr. Lester Pearson, Canada's former Minister of External Affairs. 'Coca-Cola,' he said, 'is no substitute for Confucius'. I think that suggests the dilemma of many of the world's economically less-developed countries that have encountered difficulties in implementing Westernization. Iran is an example of a land with a culture that is much older, and in some ways deeper and mature, than the countries of the West. In some ways Western countries can teach us the principles of their new civilization while perhaps Iran can acquaint them with its significant and influential ancient civilization and teach them some vital elements.[5]

The shah juxtaposed a popular conception of the West based on consumerism and materialism with a recurring conception of the East, and in this case Iran, that stressed a long rich history, ancient culture and deep spirituality. This claimed cultural difference has been propagated by nativist groups, from German Romantics and Russian Slavophiles to Rabindranath Tagore in India and Kakuzō Okakura in Japan. The shah, however, articulated this difference while claiming that Iran was a racial–cultural member of the West. Therefore, this perceived cultural binary between the West and Iran is not portrayed in essentialist terms while Western culture is not propagated as an existential threat to Iranian authenticity. Rather, this difference was presented as an opportunity for both sides, coexisting under the West's civilizational umbrella, to reach a higher stage of the human condition by adopting the best each side had culturally to offer.

> We are both adjusting the technology to our culture and our culture to technology. And here lies a clue to a new kind of pioneering ... I foresee that my country may help provide leadership in the world-wide quest for a fresh synthesis of East and West, old and new.

This synthesis would not only bring Iran to the level of the West but also set the conditions in which 'we will rise to a higher level' of development and civilization than that attained by the West.[6] Despite this mention of a unique role for Iran and cultural binaries between the conceived West and East, the shah's main emphasis remained on the racial–cultural link with the West that rendered secondary the other discursive elements of identity:

> Our cultural links with the Western democracies have a record that is centuries old and is not similar to fleeting flames of love. The people of the West during the many past centuries have borrowed much from our culture and we too have integrated some elements of their new culture and civilization into our own and today our goals and those of the democratic countries of the West are identical and this equality of ideals is a source of pride for us and for the countries of the West. ... Whenever I look at the ancient and rich history of my country several

unique points attract my attention. For example, Iranians are known for having personal independence. ... In this respect we are similar to the French ... (and) the Americans. It is for this reason that Americans and Iranians are compatible with each other.[7]

Such comparisons with the French and Americans and emphasis on this link were also a reflection of the Cold War and the shah's desire since the end of the Second World War to attract and maintain strong Western and, in particular, US support.[8] During his state visit to the United States in 1961 the shah, hoping to obtain additional US military aid, tailored his speeches for his US audience. Utilizing themes from *Mission for My Country* in his remarks at a state dinner in the White House, to a joint session of Congress, and at the National Press Club, he stressed the link between Iran and the West, Iran's contributions to the West's civilization and his role as a reformist. The Kennedy administration, however, was not swayed and continued to emphasize the importance of socio-economic reforms in order to achieve domestic political stability.

As the shah propagated these views, beginning in the early 1960s, the state was confronted with intellectual and social trends that posed new political and ideological challenges. First, views of the West among the growing intellectual and educated classes evolved. These classes during Reza Shah's reign and, roughly, the first fifteen years of Mohammad Reza's reign themselves as 'agents of the West and saw their role as bringing the positive West to the people'. Moreover, state intellectuals and technocrats, believing in the masses' cultural backwardness, had faith in the benefits of enlightened absolutism implementing Westernization. By the early 1960s intellectuals and publicists, many of whom began to suffer from an identity crisis, ' now saw it as their duty to inform the masses of the decay and spiritual difficulties facing the West'. They claimed that a spiritual and moral vacuum had emerged in Western societies in which people now led atomized and mechanized lives. The narratives coming out of these discourses underlined the need to find 'an alternative to the West in the sense of moral values. Now that the West had a moral vacuum, the Eastern utopia must be characterized by its spirituality and morality'.[9]

These intellectuals and publicists also stressed that Western political systems suffered from such a vacuum and therefore could not be an example of the future for non-Western peoples. In the international arena these political systems too had much for which they had to answer. The West's geopolitical games were responsible for horrific global wars while its imperialism presented constant threats to the cultural, economic and geopolitical independence of non-Western countries. The most vivid examples were French resistance to Algerian independence, the escalating war in Vietnam and Western support for Israel. Last but not least was the US–UK-inspired coup d'état against Mossadegh.

Second, the sociocultural and moral changes resulting from Pahlavi Westernization were increasingly felt on individual and societal levels. Unease grew about the direction in which society was moving while these changes were increasingly disorientating. Intellectuals and publicists bemoaned a sensed precipitous decline in personal, and, in particular, sexual, morality and spirituality and the spread of conspicuous consumerism and materialism. Consequently, debates about the constitutive elements of Iranian authenticity intensified and began to compete with Pahlavi pro-West Occidentalism. These debates were dominated by (a) a belief in a crisis of identity resulting from Pahlavi Occidentalism; (b) the necessity to provide a definition of authenticity of Iranian culture and national identity as a counter-discourse to Pahlavi Occidentalism; (c) the need to return to such authenticity and identity; and (d) the achievement of social justice that communism and capitalism seemingly failed to provide.

Lastly, an underlying theme of these discourses was the need for political reform. On the one hand, a growing number of intellectuals and professionals saw in the absolutist Pahlavi state a force destroying Iranian authenticity and exploiting the country to its benefit and that of its Western allies. Here the legacy of Mossadegh's overthrow as well as the close geopolitical relationship between the shah and the West, particularly the United States, loomed large. On the other hand, the growth of the state bureaucracy and security apparatus had resulted in a closed political space that prevented direct criticism of the shah's domestic and foreign policies. Thus, non-state intellectuals, including those producing new Islamist discourses, in pursuit of political change believed that the 'most feasible weapon against the regime' was 'attacking its lack of authenticity'.[10] This intellectual anti-Westernism and anti-Americanism that grew from the early 1960s was expressed in films, books, scholarly articles and pieces in the popular press. Unable to criticize political conditions, intellectuals, publicists and activist journalists turned attention to domestic cultural and moral conditions emerging as a result of Westernization and to undermining the idea of the West's civilizational superiority.

Two works in this genre, Jalal Al-e Ahmad's *Occidentosis: A Plague from the West* (*Qarbzadegi*) and Ehsan Naraqi's *Atomization and Loneliness in the West* (*Qorbat-e Qarb*), are briefly examined here given their influence on Rastakhiz discourses of anti-West Occidentalism.[11] The choice of these two works is not reflective of a belief that only they exercised a strong influence on educated opinion and party discourses. Al-e Ahmad's work is well known and any discussion of this topic rise must include it. Worthy of note is the fact that not he but Ahmad Fardid first coined the term. Fardid, a strong follower of Heidigger, 'claimed a neo-mystical reading of Islam corresponding to Martin Heidigger's critique of Western modernity'.[12] Nonetheless, al-e Ahmad's work made the term famous and thus has been frequently covered in the literature, especially in the search for the causes of the 1979 Revolution. Naraqi's work, although relatively unknown outside of Iran and within the existing literature, exercised a strong direct and indirect influence on state discourses and educated opinion. First, Naraqi was a cultural advisor to the empress and a member of the committee charged with writing the Philosophy of the Revolution established by the shah. These positions brought his views close to the centre of power. In addition, at the end of the 1960s he joined the UNESCO World Heritage Project in Iran whose goal was the preservation of material culture which was regarded as a repository of cultural authenticity. Second, his work was serialized in Rastakhiz publications. Third, Rastakhiz publications frequently solicited articles and editorials from him and published his remarks made in other public venues. Al-eAhmad never enjoyed such official links and platform.

Al-e Ahmad in 1944, turning his back on his Islamic identity despite or because of his father's religiosity, joined the Tudeh Party. By 1948 he abandoned Tudeh over its willingness to tow Moscow's political and ideological lines and subsequently supported Mossadegh. During the 1950s he started an intellectual return to Islam as the source of authenticity of culture and national identity. This journey's result can be seen in the themes he included in a research paper on the Goals of Iranian Education delivered at the Congress held in 1961. Its proceedings were published the following year but without his report. This infuriated Ahmad: 'The Ministry of Culture was neither worthy nor capable of publishing this report. The time had not yet come for one of the office of the Ministry of Culture to publish a report like this one officially'.[13]

Disappointed and infuriated by this omission, al-e Ahmad in 1962 privately published the first edition of *Occidentosis*, which he gave to friends and colleagues. Later that year the journal, *Ketab-e Mah*, intended to publish excerpts from it. The state prevented this. He then wrote a second edition. SAVAK raided the publishing house, confiscating all copies. Nonetheless, from the middle of the 1960s *Occidentosis* spread in *samizdat* form among the educated classes and the youth. The work 'was read and discussed in high schools and universities as the first bibliographical item on a hidden syllabus with which the Iranian youth of the 1960s came to political self-consciousness. You were accepted into cliques of political activists by virtue of your ability to quote passages from it verbatim'.[14]

Al-e Ahmad in *Occidentosis* launched a broad attack on the foundations of Western civilization and the historiographical pillar of Pahlavi pro-West Occidentalism that, he claimed, created a crisis of identity by spreading Western culture – a process coined Occidentosis. Ahmad argued that the imperialist West 'awakened only one passion, that for ancient Iran. Passion for, ... (and) belief in, the pre-Islamic history of Iran.' It propagated a view of Iranian identity and history as if 'from the Sassanian Empire until the government of [Reza Shah's] coup d'état only two and a half days had elapsed, and even then in a sleep'. Underlining the influence of Western historiography on pro-West Pahlavi Occidentalism, he claimed that a consequence of this approach was 'to create confusion in the nation's historical consciousness' by connecting 'directly the power of the coup d'état' to pre-Islamic Iranian Empires 'as if there were no distance of some 1,300 years between them'. For him the motivations behind pro-West Occidentalism were clear. Only 'by loosening the religious-cultural background of the contemporary man' and changing the elements constituting national identity 'would the onslaught of Westernization be possible'.

From the work's first page, al-e Ahmad diagnosed the disease from which he believed Iranian society, and in particular educated Iranians and the Pahlavi system, were suffering:

> *Occidentosis* is surrender and enslavement to the West. *Occidentosis* is like cholera. If this seems distasteful I could say it is like heatstroke or frostbite. But no. It is at least as bad as sawflies in the wheat fields. Have you ever seen how they infest wheat? From within. ... We're talking about a disease. A disease that comes from without fostered in an environment made for breeding or causes, and if possible, a cure. This *Occidentosis* has two heads. One is the West, the other is ourselves who are taken with the West. By us, I mean a part of the East.

This work's title, *Occidentosis*, at first glance gives the impression that the target is the capitalist West, in keeping in line with Ahmad's previous leftist background. But, he provided a broad definition of the West.

> One pole is the Occident, by which I mean all of Europe, Soviet Russia, and North America, the developed and industrialized nations that can use machines to turn raw materials into more complex forms that can be marketed as goods. These raw materials are not only iron ore and oil, or gut, cotton, and gum tragacanthin; they are also myths, dogmas, music, and the higher worlds. The other pole is Asia and Africa, or the backward, developing or nonindustrial nations that have been made into consumers of Western goods. ... Our age is one of these two worlds: one producing and exporting machines, the other importing and consuming them and wearing them.[15]

He rejected the idea that the West's modernities, liberal democratic capitalism and communism symbolized the developmental and historical destination of the world's peoples. In denouncing the universalist claims of Western civilization, he called for a return to authenticity and the implementation of nativist solutions and policies.

Yet, al-e Ahmad understood the geopolitical and domestic requisites for change and opposed preserving those cultural and religious characteristics he believed were an obstacle to development. However, he failed to articulate clearly the constitutive elements of this authenticity that needed to be protected. Thus, he could not provide guidance on how to combine its preservation with achievement of needed technological and economic change. What remained was a clear rejection of the West and an ambiguous solution to Iran's economic and technological backwardness.

> Technology we are forced to import. We must also learn the science that comes with it. That (the technology) is not Western; it is universal. ... Now we, as a developing nation, have come face to face with the machine and technology, and without our volition. That is, we have resigned ourselves to whatever may come. What are we to do? Must we remain the mere consumers we are today or are we to shut our doors to the machine and technology and retreat into the depths of our ancient ways, our national and religious traditions? Or is there a third possibility?[16]

The importation of this technology was linked to machines that too constituted a serious threat to Iranian society and cultural authenticity. 'History has fated the world to fall prey to the machine. It is a question of how to encounter the machine and technology ... [So far] we have been unable to preserve our own historiocultural character in the face of the machine and its fateful onslaught. Rather we have been routed'. The key was, he believed, placing the machine and technology in the service of the individual and not vice versa. This rhetorically attractive theme that was poorly defined and ambiguous in regard to solutions for the problem it described would be subsequently co-opted by the shah and the Rastakhiz Party.

While agreeing that 'we need to take certain things from the West', he drew red lines. 'The social sciences and the humanities' had to remain native since 'at the moment do we have anything other than these as symbols of our Iranian identity?' The threat to these symbols and Iranian authenticity was not only rooted in the West; it was also within Iran's borders and, he implicitly charged, the state itself.

> Our schools make occidentotics, people with no more substance than ripples on the surface of the water. They supply the cultural milieu for the breeding of occidentosis. This is the greatest threat posed by our schools and educational system.[17]

The agent spreading Occidentosis was obvious.

> Our schools, our universities, our whole educational system, whether by design or through the unfortunate logic of the age, raise such people and deliver them to the nation's leadership – occidentotics standing on thin air who disbelieve in any basis for belief. They have no party, share in no hopes for humanity, know no traditions or myths. They retreat into a certain kind of vulgar Epicureanism. They grow corrupted and stupefied by corporeal pleasures. They fasten their eyes onto the lower members and onto superficialities. They care nothing for tomorrow, only for today. And all this is only reinforced by the radio, publications, textbooks, the closed laboratories, the occidentosis of the leadership, the twisted thinking of those returning from Europe.

The attack on the characteristics of the Occidentosis-ridden person was scathing and wide. It is quoted extensively here in order to provide an understanding of the dynamics of al-e Ahmad's work and the basis for its comparison with Rastakhiz discourses.

> An occidentotic who is a member of the nation's leadership is standing on thin air; he is like a particle of dust suspended in the void, or a shaving floating on the water. He has severed his ties with the depths of society, culture, and tradition. ... According to the rule that one must follow the West, here to attain to leadership one must be unscrupulous, must not be steadfast or principled, cannot have roots or have his feet planted on the ground of this land.[18]
>
> The occidentotic is a man totally without belief or conviction, to such an extent that he not only believes in nothing, but also does not actively disbelieve in anything – you might call him a syncretist. He is a timeserver. Once he gets across the bridge, he doesn't care if it stands or falls. He has no faith, no direction, no aim, no belief, neither in God nor in humanity. ... The occidentotic has no character. He is a thing without authenticity.[19]

While the state and its educational system were responsible for grooming Occidentosis-ridden Iranians, the cities and the urban environment were their breeding grounds. 'The cities, these cancerous members that grow by the day with no pattern, with no authenticity, daily demand more food processed by Western industry. Daily they sink further into decline, rootlessness, and ugliness'.[20] Architecture and urban design were not the only issues. The very urban atmosphere spread Occidentosis.

> Our cinemas do not instruct or aid in the intellectual transformation of our people. Every cinema in this part of the world is nothing more than a child's bank into which every city resident drops two or three tumans a week so that the principal stockholders in Metro-Goldwyn-Mayer will become millionaires. Our city dwellers' thoughts are molded by these cinemas, by the government radio, or by the illustrated weeklies. These all follow a road that leads to conformism, everyone turned into carbon copies: identical houses, identical clothes, identical luggage, identical plastic tableware, identical airs, and worst of all, identical ways of thinking. This is the greatest danger in our new wave of urbanization.[21]

Such a society underpinned by consumerism, materialism, commercialization and homogenization would lose any understanding of what constituted a 'real hero' and 'genuine human'.

> Another of the problems of Western societies is that, besides making submissive and tractable people, as machine tenders, they are making a new kind of people one might call 'prefabricated heroes', like prefabricated houses. One sees this in the lavish lives of the film stars and in the lives of the astronauts, and this is logical enough: when you have homogenized all the people so that no one stands higher than anyone else, you have no choice but to break this uniform pattern of human mediocrity now and then with a prefabricated hero, to show that all is not hopeless. Accordingly, just as, for instance, Ford Motor Company places its annual order with a given American university for so many mechanical and electrical engineers with certain qualifications, a given film studio builds heroes according to plan. ... As a result, another hero has been added to the ranks of the heroes of the silver screen. That is, another historical or legendary hero has been bled dry of any dignity or credibility. ... In this age of transformation, we need people of character, expert, ardent, principled people – not occidentotic people, not people who are sacks full of human knowledge, jacks-of-all-trades and masters of none, or who are merely decent, good natured, pliant, and earnest, or adaptable and placid, or meek and angelic. It is such people who have written our history up to now, and we've had enough.[22]

The consequence of this cultural Occidentosis was the spread of Western imperialism. 'Today it is by relying on these occidentotic intellectuals participating in the government that the West's political representatives and the body of consultants behave toward us just as the British ambassadors (once) behaved.'

In conclusion, al-e Ahamd's Occidentosis was an amalgam of conspicuous consumption, commercialization, the enslavement of humans to the machine and technology, the dominance of Western-trained technocrats, commercialized pop culture and a spiritless existence. One could say that al-e Ahmad's *Occidentosis* was fundamentally a furious and ranty expression of Third Worldism that spoke romantically of scientific and technological modernity emerging and existing within a traditional nativist moral and spiritual framework. This rosy rhetorical synthesis of Western modernity with native authenticity was easier to propagate than implement for it did not provide a path to its achievement. It was deceitfully attractive, evidenced by the work's popularity and the spread of the terms Occidentosis and Occidentosis-ridden. This attractiveness would be reflected in the emergence of many of this book's critical themes in official discourses that came to constitute Pahlavi anti-West Occidentalism.

The shah was not unaware of the trends that contributed to, and obtained inspiration from, al-e Ahmad's *Occidentosis*. When this work became popular and a much discussed topic in intellectual and educated circles, seemingly the Court gave the green light for an article to be placed in *Ferdowsi*, the most popular sociopolitical magazine in the country according to SAVAK.[23] Titled 'Occidentosis or Arabosis?' (*Qarbzadegi ya Arabzadegi?*), it responded to al-e Ahmad's thesis and articulated Pahlavi understandings of the Iranian crisis of identity.[24]

> Given our long tumultuous history of wars, pandemonium, and ups and downs nothing for us really exists except for Arabtosis (*Arabzadegi*). ... I use the term Arabtosis because of the false and laughable term Occidentosis. ... According to al-e Ahmad the Occidentosis-ridden person pretends to be religious and to follow religious customs, but is hollow inside. This person has no real beliefs. ... The Occidentosis-ridden person is trashy, an opportunist, he is indifferent to everything as long as he can achieve his goals, he has no faith, principles, ideology, or faith in God and mankind. ... The Occidentosis-ridden person has no real character and lacks authenticity. ... The Occidentosis-ridden person is a dandy who takes care of only himself. ... He is the West's malicious face.
>
> I don't know how al-e Ahmad could have corrupted the Machine Age with these big accusations. ... No Mr. al-e Ahmad this negligent, thoughtless person lacking in beliefs and principles who is a liar and sycophant, broken, ignorant, and country-less appeared some 1,200 years ago on this soil. ... It is now 1,200 years we have had such people on our soil. They have no confidence or trust in each other. They hide their real beliefs. Because they are always suspicious they never open their hearts. You'll never hear the cry of objection, or a but or a why ... I say that the Occidentosis-ridden described by al-e Ahmad is ... in reality Arabtosis-ridden. ... I skim the pages of the last one thousand years of our history and count all the instances of superficiality, fakeness, spiritual instability, opportunism and misfortune so that everyone knows that what came and what became of us after the invasion of the [Arab] bedouins of this land and their attack on our morality, racial authenticity, bravery, and steadfastness. ... What wretchedness struck our spirit and race and the Iranian genealogy over the last 1,200 years! ... And with this examination al-e Ahmad's terms Occidentosis and specifically the Occidentosis-ridden person are shown not to be worth a penny![25]

While al-e Ahmad's work focused on the spread of Occidentosis and the crisis of identity, Naraqi's book, published at a time when the problem of Occidentosis was recognized on an official level, paid primary attention to the myriad social and moral problems facing the West and their fundamental causes. By bringing the reality of the negative West to Iranians he could strengthen the struggle against the spread of Occidentosis inside Iran. These problems not only signalled the West's decline but also negated it as a positive example for other countries. 'Our country given a myriad of causes, flowing from one dam, had a condition in which a great number of people – those who have travelled to the West as well as those who have not travelled there – was overtaken by an intense passion for the West, its culture and civilization.' By examining the West's current state the battle against this influence could be successful. Its spread was just as serious as Al-e Ahmad described.

Naraqi's definition of the West also encompassed both the capitalist and communist worlds. These two warring sides in the Cold War that constituted the West were united by civilizational similarities, namely a 'horrific, cold, and spiritless hegemony of materialism and conspicuous consumerism that is increasing everyday'. The only philosophical issue dividing them and driving this civil war within Western civilization was the way in which they manifested this materialism and consumerism while their shared materialism and slavish subordination of the individual to technology and the machine had created serious social crises in both sides of the Cold War. 'Western civilization, given its reliance on the increase of economic production and prioritization of life's external forms and individual materialistic demands, has neglected human spiritual and inner needs.' The constant struggle between people for the advancement of their individual materialistic needs brought the instrumentalization and commercialization of social and familial relationships and spread an emotionally unfulfilling atomistic individualism. Only a few perceptive Westerners understood what horrified Iranians and Easterners about the dynamics of Western civilization: 'In today's West, products, consumer goods, machine-produced goods determine the social framework and social relations' in which people live and exercise a determinative influence on the trajectory of one's worldly existence. Little possibility, if any, remained for an individual in the West to lead a spiritual and solaceful life based on altruism and genuine family and social relationships. Freedom of choice had been taken from them.

Individuals in the West, therefore, were suffering from 'loneliness and atomization'. But the malaise afflicting the West was not limited to these feelings. Given the destruction of the sense of family and friendship, individuals 'feel that life itself is empty and barren. Therefore, they are deeply afflicted by a fatigue with life and alienation from everything and everyone.' These sentiments manifested themselves in a myriad of social crises facing the West, from drug and alcohol addiction and family breakdown to robbery, murder and violence. These social crises, clear to all, proved that the West was not the worldly utopia many in the Western and non-Western worlds believed and that the East was indeed superior to it.

Any doubters about such a conclusion only had to examine the state of the West's youth. This social malaise and 'spiritual poverty' that had overtaken the West ensured that in the West one's youth, 'instead of being a time of hope and optimism, was a period dominated by feelings of hopelessness and depression'. These feelings were 'expressed in their behavior – hippieism, lax sexual morals, drug addiction'. If the West were the worldly utopia, as claimed by Occidentosis-ridden Iranians, the suicide rate would be decreasing. However, statistics showed the opposite. This 'lack of ideals in life in the West, a sense of a vacuum in life and depression' was pushing increasing numbers of Westerners towards ending their lives.

The antidote to Occidentosis and the malaise afflicting the West was the East. Naraqi took his book's title from the eighth-century work of the Iranian thinker Hakim Aliqadr Sahrudi, *Al-qarbeh al-qaribeh*, which was based on this binary of the East and the West.

> In this meaning the East is the world of life and the epitome of a new brilliant dawn, the home of privileged divine angels while the West is the world of oppression and a symbol of darkness. The angel Gabriel has two wings in Sahrudi's opinion, the right one is the East and the left wing is the West ... Sahrudi's book tells the story of an individual's collapse in the West's materialistic world or, in other words, the story of a self-exiled individual in the West. This occurred while the authentic spiritual base of an individual survives in the East.[26]

Thus, one of the main themes of Naraqi's book that occupied a prominent position within Rastakhiz discourses was the sub-narrative stressing the idea of an essentialist and primordial binary of the West and the East. The causes of the current state of the West's decline in the late twentieth century as well as the spiritual and moral superiority of the East, now facing the threat of Occidentosis, had to be viewed also through this prism of the ancient past.

Al-e Ahmad and Naraqi differed from each other in language, research mythology and approach. Al-e Ahmad

> was a man who after two decades of thought and experimentation had discovered an important and fundamental truth concerning his society – its disastrous subordination to the West in all areas – and was in a hurry to communicate this discovery to others. He had neither the time nor the patience to engage in careful historical research. ... The chapters of the book that purport to analyze the historical roots of occidentosis contain a number of errors, some of them significant enough to undermine his argument.[27]

Naraqi, who obtained his doctorate in Sociology from the Sorbonne, used academic research methods and language to advance his argument whereas even 'Al-e Ahmad was particularly conscious of the fact that he wrote in a hurried and inaccurate discourse' that lacked any methodological discipline or historiographical rigour.[28]

Nonetheless, both men called attention to the issue of a crisis of identity in the face of Occidentosis. In al-e Ahmad's work,

> Islam is presented above all as the essential and defining attribute of a civilizational sphere, to which Iran belongs, that has been at war with the West for more than a millennium. Within the context of this fundamental contradiction, Islam is seen to be the ultimate defense against the encroachments of Occidentosis.[29]

Naraqi too argued that the binary of the East and the West was primordial and antagonistic. Underlining Islam's spiritual and moral dimensions, he saw in that religion a defence against Occidentosis, but within the framework of the imperial system and Rastakhiz discourses. Al-e Ahmad did not subscribe to this opinion. Naraqi's acceptance of the Pahlavi state and willingness to work within it most probably was due to his scepticism in regard to the clergy.

In the period 1964–73 SAVAK directed the shah's attention to the growing popular appeal of these discourses as they increasingly appeared in the print media. In this regard it considered the weekly magazine *Ferdowsi* particularly worrying.[30] In 1966 SAVAK warned that *Ferdowsi*'s articles attacking the West for geopolitical and cultural imperialism 'can turn severely public opinion against the US and the West'.[31] Reports dating from 1967 and 1968 confirmed this prediction.

> There is a rapidly growing readership of *Ferdowsi* amongst students of Tehran University ... [given] the anti-Westernism of its articles and condemnations of US foreign and domestic policy. ... Students and a large part of the educated class welcome any criticism of the USA because they consider US policy in Iran a deadly poison. ... [*Ferdowsi*] has created support for itself amongst the educated and intellectual classes thanks to its anti-Americanism. ... This journal for some time has entertained this anti-US stance.[32]

In 1971 SAVAK stressed that *Ferdowsi*, 'in order to increase its sales and maintain its popularity among the intellectual and educated classes, some of whom for whatever reason are frustrated and disillusioned, tries to publish severe and extreme criticism of the West. Many articles come from those with extreme anti-West views'.[33] In the same year, interrogations of student and political activists across the country showed that 'the magazine *Ferdowsi*, with its articles on socialism, Western imperialism, anti-Americanism and Vietnam had incited them'.[34]

The shah, sensing the changes reflected in these reports, took steps to manage these new competing discourses of intellectual anti-West Occidentalism. The ideologization of the monarchy, initially expressed in the White Revolution and Pahlavism, was thus accompanied by initial moves towards anti-West Occidentalism. However, to attribute solely political motives to the shah's and the empress's evolving views in regard to the authenticity of Iranian culture and identity would be a mistake. They, along with state intellectuals, too became increasingly concerned by the cultural, moral and even aesthetic transformations resulting from Westernization and the spread of Occidentosis. In this context for the first time since the abdication of Reza Shah, the Pahlavi state took steps towards the formulation and implementation of a cohesive cultural policy integrated in an ideological framework detailing Pahlavi conceptions of authenticity of culture and national identity.

In the wake of the announcement of the White Revolution, the government of Ali Mansur in 1964–5 increased its number of ministries from twelve to twenty, a move reflecting the state's growing duties resulting from the implementation of the Revolution. It also introduced a bill proposing the establishment of a new Ministry of Culture and Art (MCA). Until this point cultural policies concerning, in the words of Mansur, 'protection, development, and recognition of our ancient heritage and civilization of the country' had been handled in a piecemeal fashion across several ministries. This bill reflected the state's emerging concern over the issues of authenticity of cultural and national identity. Mansur, on the one hand, stated that the bill reflected the shah's desire 'to redouble efforts in the guiding and reforming of society. ... The creation of a new person is the real issue.' On the other hand, its preamble stated that a goal was 'the development and recognition of the country's authentic civilizational heritage'.[35] He stressed: 'One of the progressive programs taking inspiration from the shah is that we must be proud of the culture and achievements of our ancient pre-Islamic Iranian civilization and strengthen and defend them'.[36] These two trends created the momentum for the creation of institutions to propagate new official discourses on the West and Occidentosis and develop policies to combat them and acculturate the masses. The most important of these institutions were the MCA, the Supreme Council of Culture and Art (SCCA) and National Iranian Television, becoming National Iranian Radio and Television (NIRT) in 1971. Before examining these institutional and policy changes, an examination of the shah's evolving remarks in this regard is necessary.

The shah's rhetorical flirtation with Western democracy attached to the idea of an Iranian racial–cultural link with the West ended. Joining his public denouncements and criticism of communism that dated back to the 1940s was intense criticism of the West's political and economic systems. He now portrayed both liberal democracy and communism as deceitfully attractive ideologies of the West incompatible with Iranian authenticity.

> In many of your democratic countries ... money controls everything, that dead people have voted. ... What I want to say is that we will not imitate any foreign form of government or modernization. ... We will never make ourselves prisoner to specific pre-existing foreign ideologies and frameworks. ... The epoch of dry inflexible ideologies [emanating from the West] is over. They are unable to answer the varied needs of society. Many of the principles and philosophies and '–isms' taught to us in the past as 'eternal truths' and unchanging are now old and outdated.[37]

Iranians who supported either of these two forms of Western modernity suffered from political Occidentosis.

Second, he added to this political anti-West Occidentosis a sociocultural element that focused on claims of the West's spiritual and cultural collapse that was portrayed as the consequence of Western liberal political systems that propagated a deceitfully attractive understanding of freedom based on hedonism, consumerism and materialism situated within a brutal capitalist framework. People, overtaken by consumerism and materialism, engaged in a daily struggle to advance their own interests, while sacrificing spirituality and social and familial relationships. This system deprived people of genuine freedom by forcing them to abandon spirituality and morals in order to survive and satisfy increasing consumerist appetites. Those who could not survive in this system either committed suicide or turned to a life of violence and crime while those who enjoyed the fruits of this system, having discarded spirituality and morality, engaged in hedonism. As a whole, these elements making up Western society ultimately begot political, moral and spiritual collapse and chaos. The shah asked: 'What does freedom mean? Does it mean being able to commit violence, robbery, steal? Is that democracy? Is that human rights? This is ridiculous. What is this democracy? (Does it mean) only cursing? Stealing? Hedonism? Murdering?'[38] One could claim that these statements were political rhetoric. But he also privately expressed such sentiments to both Iranians and Westerners. For example, he told Jimmy Carter in late 1977: 'Growing terrorism, permissive societies, democracy collapsing through lack of law and order. If things continue on the present track, the disintegration of Western societies will occur much sooner than you think. ... Freedom is not something that does not have a breaking point'.[39]

From the late 1960s the view of the West from the outside was indeed increasingly critical, as it was even in the West itself. Domestic forms of organized political violence, such as the Red Brigades in West Germany, the Red Brigade in Italy, the IRA in the United Kingdom and groups such the Liberation Army and Weather Underground in the United States, which bombed the US Capitol building, and growing student and public unrest over Vietnam symbolized by the killing of protesters at Kent State, seemed to underline a growing sickness within Western societies. At the same time, rates of violent and sex crime in major Western countries and specifically the United States were rising quickly. For example, the murder rate in the United States in 1974 hit a new record of 20,000 reported homicides. In the UK the situation was similar. The type of crimes being committed horrified not only the shah, Pahlavi elite and Iranian public opinion but also the public in those countries. From the late 1960s the Iranian press gave significant coverage to these issues, bringing into the homes and minds of Iranians the horrors of Charles Manson, the Zodiac Killer, Dean Coril and the Houston Mass Murders, John Wayne Gacy, the Son of Sam, David McGreavy, Mary Bell and forms of homegrown terrorism in Western societies. As the shah increasingly spoke in negative terms about these conditions in the West, Western commentators decried 'crime waves' overtaking parts of the West and debated the causes behind the rapid rise in violence and murder which seemed to underline a particular sickness and decline of the West. The Iranian fear was that the process of Westernization would create the same crises at home.

In this context, the shah's previous references to a cultural difference between the materialistic consumerist West and a spiritual and moral Iran, once propagated as an opportunity for the two racial cousins to learn from each other, evolved into an existential threat to the reformulated conceptions of Iranian authenticity he now propagated.

> We know that today's world must, given the extraordinary development of science, industry, and technology, on a daily basis create increasing levels of societal material welfare and comfort. But we also believe that material progress alone cannot ensure genuine happiness for society. This is because the human spirit, the highest example of divine spiritual manifestation, must be nourished to the same extent as the physical body. To achieve this no path exists other than paying

attention to spirituality and the authenticity of culture. ... The spirituality of Islam and the philosophy, Gnosticism and customs of the East which are the principles of spirituality, must be protected. ... We must protect and combine this great spiritual heritage with the changes that are required of today's society.[40]

Overall,

> we expect that the Iranian character and its culture, civilization, and exquisiteness of its spirit, all of which has survived over the centuries, will be preserved, despite today's era of violence in life and the materialistic conditions that exist. [They must be preserved] so that spiritual and materialistic elements combine and create a balanced person ... a new Iranian person.[41]

The shah believed that the loss of spirituality and morality would have grave social consequences similar to those causing the West's decline. In state discourses, as well as the shah's statements, those Iranians who lost this spirituality and morality suffered from cultural and moral Occidentosis. The best defence, the monarch stressed, was a personal, privatized Islam, independent of clerical influence.

> Our future cannot be exclusively materialistic and technological. My attachment to religion ... has a personal character. The Islam needed by society is now under threat by materialism (*madeparasti*). ... Despite our technological and economic advances, I am giving attention [to current conditions] so that our future is based on strong spiritual principles that will prevent society from falling into materialism.[42]

His anticlericalism however remained. In response to a question as to whether Islam was an obstacle to progress the shah stressed:

> But which Islam? That [reactionary form of] Islam that clerics (*mollahs*) in the past propagated since for them power and influence could only be based on nothing else than the people's ignorance, a state in which they strove to hold the people. It [change] was indeed difficult since 90-99% of the population was illiterate, and education was rare.[43]

In this vein, the shah and the state intensified the propagation of a spiritual declericalized Islam as a major element in this struggle against Occidentosis.

Third, having linked his political anti-West Occidentalism with new attention to the issue of the authenticity, he claimed that the Pahlavi form of democracy was 'authentically [Iranian] and constructive ... [and] responsive to the needs and the spirit of Iranian society' because it was 'based on the principles of the ancient civilization and culture' of Iranians. Therefore, 'we have no need to imitate foreign principles and procedures because the best inspiring element for us is our own authenticity of thought, civility, and culture'.[44] This new Iran, under imperial leadership, would retain 'spiritual, social, and cultural authenticity'.[45]

Within this discursive context the shah began to address frequently the issue of a crisis of identity. To that point no official recognition had been made that such a crisis existed and that the sociocultural phenomenon called Occidentosis was a threat to the authenticity of culture and national identity. The shah proclaimed: 'We want to say to the youth that their thoughts must focus on what elements from the West cannot be accepted by Iranianess'.[46] The 'new identity' of *homo Pahlavicus* 'is forged with ideological and political authenticity – an authenticity of identity accentuating the difference between East and West'.[47] This emphasis on the accentuation of these differences represented a shift from his position of the early 1960s according to which Iran would be in the avant-garde of creating 'a fresh synthesis of East and West'.[48]

The shah's rhetorical association of Iran with the East beginning in the early 1970s had a limited political–ideological use within Pahlavi anti-West Occidentalism that was not similar to Eastern political–ideological responses, such as Pan-Islamism or Pan-Asianism, to the challenge of Westernization/modernization and Occidentosis. They emerged in the late nineteenth century when the West, rejecting 'its own claims to the universality of modern civilization and inclusiveness of the world order', turned to discourses attributing its superiority either to Christianity or, more often, to unique characteristics of the white race.[49] However, a consistent theme of Pahlavi conceptions of identity was the Aryan racial link between Iran and the West. The elements Pahlavi anti-West Occidentalism shared with Eastern ideological responses to the West were anti-imperialism and emphasis on claimed Eastern superiority of spirituality and morals wrapped in the rhetoric of authenticity.

The shah's emerging anti-West Occidentalism therefore was an ideological-political hybrid that placed Iran at a juncture from where it claimed to be attached simultaneously to the imagined East and West while not being a full member of either. He stated that 'for me [crisis of identity] is not an issue. Perhaps one day we can create a path linking the cultures of the West and East'.[50] Here again is his new emphasis on a cultural divide between the East and the West that placed Iran in the East. However, in the following statement, he stressed: 'But we should not forget that today's civilization (i.e. the West) began with our country.' Iran remained a primordial racial and cultural member of the West, which owed the initial sources of its success to ancient Iranian civilization, despite these emergent discourses of anti-West Occidentalism. He insisted: 'We are not part of the developing world'.[51] His remarks made in 1972 succinctly summarize this evolution.

> Until a couple of years ago, our single hope and aim was to become similar to the West. … But now we, while still recognizing the West's positive characteristics, seek to adopt and adapt them to Iranian morality and spirituality. After all, we must have our own spiritual and philosophical principles.[52]

The empress too addressed this topic in similar tones. 'Without recognizing cultural and spiritual issues the understanding of our national identity is not possible. … In current conditions every people has no other option but … to protect national identity on the base of its own cultural authenticity (*esalat-e farhangi*)'.[53] Implicitly criticizing past government inaction on these issues she stressed: 'We must pay more attention to defending culture and authenticity that face attacks by elements of the so-called new civilization".[54] By 1975 her remarks had become more direct:

> For the third time we face a foreign cultural attack (*hojum-e farhangi-ye biganeh*). We cannot allow ourselves to succumb to this attack. ... We must be very active in the struggle to protect our cultural authenticity (*farhang-e asil-e Irani*) and Iran's natural spirit.[55]

Similar to the shah she paid attention to the claimed divide between a materialistic West and spiritual East.

> Universities must be the guardians of the [authenticity] of eternal Iranian culture. ... Material wealth alone cannot make decent, proper people. ... We must return national authenticity to the people ... I stress that that the national mission and national authenticity do not mean not borrowing the best elements of other cultures and civilizations because since the beginning Iranian culture and civilization have had the ability to borrow. ... This talent of mixing and acquiring is the secret to its development. However, given the spread of materialism, consumerism, and technology, and the world's current conditions, society is confronting a spiritual crisis and increasing social tensions. Thus, efforts to protect national and spiritual values are increasing. ... Our society in order to remain faithful to its national identity needs men and women, especially in management and leadership positions, who maintain national beliefs. ... In the past great thinkers and educated people were always the faithful, loyal guardians of our national identity and cultural existence.[56]

The imperial couple's comments reflected the belief that economic and technological change could be achieved and maintained while preserving conceptions of traditional authenticity of culture and national identity. Yet, while speaking of the flexibility of Iranian culture to borrow from other cultures in order to survive, they revealed concerns that the threat of Occidentosis was existential and differed from other cultural and moral threats in recent history.

These claimed concerns about the existential threat of Western culture to the authenticity of culture and national identity became part of a new justification for the monarchy's power. Under Reza Shah the need to implement Westernization, in the face of domestic reactionary forces and threatening imperialist powers, justified its power while pro-West Occidentalism provided a justification for this Westernization. In this framework, monarchical power was an enlightening force that, through the raising of mass culture and taste, would return Iranians to their lost authenticity rooted in common Aryan racial and cultural links with Westerners. Now, however, that same Western culture and its by-product, Occidentosis, constituted an existential threat to that authenticity. These existential threats were not only cultural; they were political as well, represented by the competing ideologies of the West, liberal democratic capitalism and communism. The current state of societies in the capitalist and communist worlds showed that these modernities were fundamentally flawed and could not be an example to follow. However, they retained their deceitfully attractive appearance in order to play their role as instruments of Western imperialism. The monarchy, the sacred source and defender of Iranian authenticity, now led the struggle against this imperialism and Occidentosis in order to justify its power.

The offensive against political and cultural Occidentosis took place on two fronts. SAVAK and other security forces using hard power constituted the first front. The second front, based on soft power, was staffed by organizations charged with implementing these new discourses on authenticity. For example, in 1964 the shah established the Foundation of the Culture of Iran whose goals were 'the struggle for the cultivation, fulfilment, and propagation of the Persian language and the protection and preservation of Iran's rich and great culture'. The empress was the chairwoman, while Princess Ashraf was her deputy. Parviz Natel-Khanlari became its general secretary and managing director. A main feature of this organization was the annual holding of The Festival of Culture and Art whose goal was to acquaint people with authentic Iranian culture and art and to increase their participation in that world. The ultimate goal was 'to strengthen national unity and sense of uniqueness'.[57]

The SCCA, established by the shah in 1967, was to play the leading role in the implementation of cultural policies, the acculturation of the masses and the crusade for the preservation of Iranian authenticity. Its membership consisted of the ministers of culture and art, education, and intelligence, the heads of the Iranian Academy of Arts, Tehran University, and the Royal Council on Culture. Eight to fourteen figures from the Iranian world of art and culture nominated by the minister of culture and approved by the shah also sat on it. These latter members would serve four-year terms that could be once renewed.[58] The minister of culture was its head while a general secretary ran it (Figure 2).

At the time of the SCCA's founding the shah told its members: 'It is necessary that the people are acquainted with the authentic spirit of Iranian culture through cinema, television, publications and other forms of mass media. ... The country's authentic old culture must be promoted across the kingdom.' He stressed that it had been founded in order to find solutions to the cultural crises facing the country and to strengthen the people's authentic 'cultural spirit'.[59] A year later at a meeting dedicated to approval of the 'Cultural Policy of Iran' he spoke once again of the 'progress of the authentic culture of Iran' and 'spirit of the authentic Iranian culture'.[60] One of the SCCA's early projects was the interviewing of the residents of 151 villages. These interviews showed the SCCA had much to accomplish. While 'villagers knew about the Vietnam War' they 'knew nothing about Shah Abbas. Those who knew something about him, knew very little else about history. They had radios and were interested in foreign news but bypassed national broadcasting via radio or television'.[61]

By the end of the 1960s across the state's upper levels, including the Iran Novin Party, it was increasingly clear that protection of Iranian authenticity had become a rhetorical and policy priority for the shah.[62] Alam in his diaries mentioned this in 1968–9, while pointing a finger at those he held responsible for the sense of malaise in cultural policy:

> At five in the evening the empress chaired a commission meeting dedicated to harmonizing the country's cultural activities. The prime minister [Hoveyda] and

Figure 2 The shah with members of the Supreme Council of Culture and Art. Mehrdad Pahlbod, far right. *Ferdowsi*, author's collection.

I were present. The prime minister strongly criticized the state of culture and the lack of a program to deal with it. I said to myself you have been prime minister for three years now and nothing has been done. All these criticisms come back to you.[63]

He also provided in another entry insight into the strengthening feelings of nativism among the highest echelons of the state. 'There was a meeting of the Foundation of the Culture of Iran attended by the empress. It is working very well indeed. Natel-Khanlari was minister of culture in my cabinet. … He wants to remove from foreign hands research about Iran'.[64]

The SCCA's first general secretary was Jamshid Behnam, a renowned Iranian sociologist who received his doctorate from the Sorbonne. He was the founder and first head of the Faculty of Social Sciences at Tehran University and had been a member of Ali Mansur's Progressive Circle until it transformed into the Iran Novin Party. He left the group as he did not wish to be involved in politics. However, the SCCA offered him the possibility to influence cultural policy and counter the influence of Western-educated technocrats involved in the implementation of the White Revolution. In his opinion these technocrats 'completely forgot in their planning cultural development'. Consequently, 'crises have emerged in both material development and culture'. These crises were a consequence of 'rapid modernization'.[65]

Behnam's background and opinion in regard to the issue of authenticity and the West made him an ideal candidate for this post. Believing in the idea of mass access to culture and acculturation from above, he sought to coordinate cultural and economic development in order to avoid the type of crises that Iranian society was facing as the socio-economic consequences of the White Revolution increased their influence on society and individuals. Behnam also believed in protecting traditional forms in Iranian arts in the face of cultural Occidentosis and Occidentosis-ridden Iranian artists.[66] In 1971 he was succeeded by Zabihollah Safa who retained the post until the Revolution. He shared Behnam's concerns about the threat of Occidentosis to Iranian authenticity and sought to make the protection of Iranian authenticity the SCCA's primary duty. However, he did not believe in prioritizing mass access to culture to the same extent that Behnam did.

One of Behnam's first moves was to attract non-state intellectuals and cultural figures by inviting them to participate in SCCA meetings. The attractiveness of these rhetorical changes and increased state attention to the issue of moral and cultural Occidentosis was described by Masoud Behnud in a series of articles published in *Ferdowsi* a year after the SCCA's founding. Having participated in all the meetings that he could attend he expressed great enthusiasm about its activities and the issues it sought to address. His feelings were not unique. A significant number of those non-state intellectuals not advocating the system's overthrow and not interested in political action were relatively attracted to these changes in Pahlavi discourses. They were particularly tempted by the possibility to exercise to influence the state's new emerging cultural policy at a time when their worries about the threat of Occidentosis were growing.

Behnud in his report on SCCA activities noted that during the first year of its existence its members had failed to agree on the definition of culture. This failure is not surprising. Providing a definition of culture has been a contentious topic in scholarly circles for more than a century. Flowing from the lack of resolution on this issue emerged a lack of agreement in regard to the constitutive elements of the authenticity of Iranian culture and identity. These questions, fundamental to the struggle against Occidentosis, were difficult to answer not only in a scholarly context but also in the context of policymaking, given factors such as politics, geopolitics and human agency. In particular, the opinions of the shah and the empress and the extent of the attention they paid to these issues strongly influenced the trajectory of the politics of authenticity.

However, the SCCA, unsurprisingly, easily achieved agreement about the threat facing Iranian authenticity. All agreed that the spread of materialism and consumerism, those pernicious manifestations of Occidentosis, was undermining Iranian spirituality and authenticity and that 'the West's culture is attacking blitzkrieg style and shoving our unique societies into a dangerous situation'. Western culture was also undermining Iranian morality: 'Long hair, odd and revealing clothes, promiscuity, licentiousness, and forms of drug abuse are spreading amongst the youth.' The SCCA, as well as state and non-state intellectuals, spoke with one voice:

> All are convinced that although Iran over the centuries of its history has taken from other civilizations, it had not lost its authenticity. Therefore, given our long record of civilizational authenticity we must not adapt excessively Western culture. We must ensure that the acceptance [of elements of] Western culture does not render damage to our existing cultural values.

Despite the exhortations about the need to preserve authenticity and expressed state and societal concerns, the reality of the West's power, and the necessity for other countries to confront and compete with it, posed complex questions: 'But in reality what should we do? Is it necessary to be a follower of Western civilization or not? It is clear that the answer cannot be a categorical "no" given the need for Western technology and the current global economic system'.[67] The fundamental issue remained: how to integrate the need for economic and technological development with this authenticity. The SCCA position was not a rabid essentialist anti-West Occidentalism – this was not the goal of the Pahlavi state: 'The conclusion of all is that we must accept Western civilization but only by taking its positive elements, and not its bad ones.' However, before any effective and coherent steps in this regard could be taken fundamental questions had to be answered: What was culture? What constituted Iranian cultures? What was Western culture and its relationship with scientific and technological modernity?

To debate and answer such questions and propagate the state's growing concerns about the authenticity of Iranian culture and national identity the SCCA published a journal, *Culture and Life* (*Farhang va Zendegi*) from January 1970 to December 1978 for a total of twenty-seven issues. This journal was a forum in which state and non-state intellectuals could debate these questions whose answers were essential to promoting cultural policies for the protection of authenticity in the face of Occidentosis. By opening this important channel of communication with non-state intellectuals the state was also trying to initiate a policy of inclusionary politics. Behind this decision were two aims.

The first aim was primarily political. The Pahlavi state sought to split the varied groups of intellectuals propagating discourses critical of its pro-West Occidentalism and thus questioning its claim to be the defender of Iranian authenticity. Through its new struggle against Occidentosis it sought to attract those intellectuals who were not politically active and not flirting with ideas in fundamental contradiction with the imperial system. While seeking to attract these intellectuals with the possibility of influencing cultural policy, the state also sought to co-opt and integrate elements of their anti-West Occidentalism into official discourses. The second aim dealt with actual policy. The state was seeking specialist advice and practical help in formulating discourses and policies to deal with the threat Occidentosis posed to this newly defined authenticity. The lack of concerted state approaches to cultural policy during the first decades of the shah's reign had resulted in a dearth of strong institutions, experienced bureaucrats and a broad understanding of the goals and methods of cultural policy. Initially the state's attempts were relatively successful. Non-state intellectuals who, despite scepticism in regard to the state, initially positively but cautiously responded and contributed articles to this journal included Dariush Ashuri, Reza Davari, Hezhir Darvish, Nader Ebrahimi, Cyrus Parham, Parviz Sayyad, Dariush Shaigan, Houshang Golshiri and Mohammad Khoshnam.

Given this goal of attracting non-state intellectuals, the journal, although published by this state body, stressed in every issue that the views expressed in its articles were not necessarily reflections of official policy and viewpoints.[68] Therefore, this publication cannot be considered solely the SCCA's mouthpiece. However, the topics chosen for discussion on its pages reflected concerns and aims the SCCA sought to express in cultural policy. This publication's importance was that it constituted an important move towards the formation of cohesive and unified policies in regard to the authenticity of culture and national identity and the challenge of Occidentosis. Policymaking in this regard was entering a new multidimensional phase that included state solicitation of input on these issues from non-state specialists and intellectuals who, in the light of state censorship, did not have the opportunity to express their opinions in regard to state cultural policies and the spread of Occidentosis, as evidenced by the earlier state reaction to al-e Ahmad's book.

The journal's first issue set its overall tone and public mission:

> The journal *Culture and Life* is the result of the search and strivings of a group that believes in the necessity of the blending and interweaving of culture and life and the creation of more momentum and creativity in this regard. This belief is the incentive for close intense co-operation with the Supreme Council of Art and Culture which approaches the issue of taking decisions in regard to contemporary cultural problems without any predetermined claims or frameworks. The goal of these studies – which take shape on the basis of the principle of Iran's cultural policy – is the search for paths and methods to acquaint better and deeply our society of tomorrow with itself and the world.[69]

A review of the themes and topics addressed by this journal, especially in the period leading up to the establishment of the Rastakhiz Party, shows that the SCCA sought approaches for dealing with Occidentosis and the creation of a new cultural atmosphere. Each issue of the journal was dedicated to a specific topic. Listed below in order of publication, they included (1) culture; (2) language, linguistics and national unity; (3) the individual and culture; (4 and 5) tradition and heritage; (6) the culture of Iran; (7) culture of the East; (8 and 9) cultural anarchy and disarray; (10 and 11) technology and culture; (13) cinema; (14) cultural policy; (15 and 16) culture and the family; (17) workers and the houses of culture; (18) Iranian cinema; (19 and 20) women in the culture of Iran and the world; (21 and 22) language and literature; (24) Cultural development; and (25 and 26) culture and national unity. These topics flowed easily into Rastakhiz discourses. Sub-narratives of many of these topics focused on crises in the West that were portrayed as harbingers of the West's slow but ineluctable decline: spiritual and moral collapse, atomistic individualism, sexual promiscuity and hedonism, the spread of pornography, a lost youth drowning in drugs and sex, and unchecked materialism and conspicuous consumerism that had become goals of one's existence in the West.

An excerpt from a speech by the shah adorned the inaugural issue's first page. In it he articulated the main themes of his evolving discourses in regard to the authenticity of culture and national identity and the place of the West within it. He emphasized the fundamental cultural and civilizational differences between the East and the West that were based on the binary of a spiritual and moral East and a materialistic but economically and technologically advanced West. The East, while striving to obtain similar levels of economic and technological development, had to defend its superior levels of spirituality and morality in order to provide meaning and sense to one's existence in this world. His words were a call for a struggle against Occidentosis.[70]

An accompanying lead article written by Behnam described the tone of the emerging new state discourses on the West. Stressing the civilizational binary between the West and Iran, he argued that the West, due to its hedonism, materialism and consumerism, was now in a state of decline. The liberal capitalist system, based on increasing levels of materialism and consumerism, ensured that Westerners were always in a state of confusion and anxiety about the present and the future. Consequently,

> the Western person is exhausted. At the peak of its power, he has become confused and anxious. The taking of tranquilizers and sleeping pills, while part of their daily routine, cannot cure their disquiet, anxiety and sense of uneasiness. The addiction to these drugs is a sign of the desire and search for peacefulness, tranquility, and solitude.[71]

Moreover, the dominance of hedonism in the West had resulted in 'the rejection of moral customs and taboos' clearly evidenced by sexual revolutions and deviation, nudity in films, the commercialization of sex and the spread of pornographic magazines. Therefore, the West could not serve as an example for Iran while the spirituality and morality of the East, and specifically Iran, were the cure to the ills causing the West's internal decay and decline. These themes became dominant in the Rastakhiz period.

Using a method that would reach its peak during the Rastakhiz period, Behnam, in order to prove these points about the West and show Iranians that in reality they were the holders of a superior civilization, cited the opinions of Western writers and thinkers critical of Western civilization. While Western technological and economic advances were, to an extent, praiseworthy, these thinkers and writers, as well as non-Western observers, clearly saw spreading internal rot in the West. The reality was that 'a great number of groups of the young in whose hands the West's future resides is worried. They have doubts about the bases of Western civilization and even reject them.' Disappointed by and losing faith in Western civilization, the West's youth 'turn to Eastern religions, such as Buddhaism, Hippieism, Zehn religion' in search for a lost spirituality and greater meaning of life.

In light of these criticisms of the West, the journal published pieces calling for a struggle against Occidentosis. The first salvo was an article penned by the SCCA itself that, echoing the shah's opinion, called for the protection of authenticity since 'technology and economic development cannot stand alone without culture and morality'. The current and continuing crisis of Western civilization proved the veracity of this assertion. However, the SCCA stressed that its search to protect this authenticity was not a call for the sacralization of the past, but 'rather a path between Occidentosis and blind traditionalism (*sonnatzadegi*)'. It admitted that a crisis of identity existed and implicitly confessed that the negative backlash to the cultural and moral consequences of Pahlavi Westernization played an important role in changing state policy and discourses:

> In a world where human life is becoming void of spirituality, finding new paths so that spirituality can provide more values to human life is necessary. ... Today, if not all the people, at least the educated classes, feel that our culture is afflicted

with a crisis and it is in this feeling that the discussion about the values of cultural heritage has been put forth.

Therefore, despite the call for a path between Occidentosis and sacralization of the past, primary focus remained on warnings about the existential threat of the West to Iranian authenticity, although the threat need not be exaggerated.

> No need to worry about this identity and cultural crisis exists since Iranian culture over the centuries has taken from other civilizations. We must not be fearful of taking values, amongst other things, from other cultures. The West's technology cannot destroy this spirituality – in the past it has not, these two elements need not be in contradiction with each other (if properly amalgamated). ... In any case, in principle this very science (of the West) has been adopted from Iranian culture in the first place.

Yet, the supporters of *sonnatizadegi* did have reason to be concerned since 'the unique nature of contemporary Western civilization and its attack on us with the goal of establishing hegemony ... in the end means the destruction of national and local cultures'. Therefore 'any adaption of some values of Western culture must be undertaken in such a way that Iranian culture is not destroyed and eliminated'.[72] Thus, in light of and despite the calls for a middle path between Westernization and *sonnatizadegi* 'a majority opinion exists inside Iran that Western civilization is facing a serious even existential crisis. Can we in the East provide a path of salvation for them?'

The following issue's editorial identified the changes resulting from the practical process of Westernization that were feeding into the growing concerns about Occidentosis which would, if left unchecked, force individuals in the East to exist in a framework devised by the West.

> The great economic and social changes in today's Iran have overturned the way of life, the needs and means, and even perceptions, of life. Material welfare has produced new wants for people while the turn toward the machine civilization has created more leisure and free time. These changes are generating fears that our society will become progressively anonymous and nameless and will lose its unique features while our society's members will feel increasingly alone and separated from each other.[73]

The state needed to take more steps to deal with these issues.[74] Echoing al-e Ahmad, the article stressed that one of the pillars of state cultural policy was to ensure that, unlike in the West, where 'the person is in the service of technology', in Iran 'technology is to be in the service of the person and thus the country will "avoid the West's mistakes"'.[75]

In a subsequent issue, Dariush Homayoun, who would become a leading state and party figure, expanded on these issues. He condemned the West's atomistic individualism in which life was dominated by the 'ongoing struggle of individuals to obtain material goods' whose 'acquisition had become a goal of life'. This 'push for ever more material goods' had resulted in the loss of the true meaning of one's existence in this world. However, in the East, people who lived with a material standard of living lower than that of West but also with the hope for its improvement, retained the real meaning of one's existence in the world, an existence based on spirituality, human relationships and love. In sum, 'we can describe Western culture as "materialistic" because its pillars are based on it ... [while] the culture of the East can be called spiritual'.

To be sure, Homayoun did not deviate into essentialist discourses of anti-West Occidentalism; he did not allow his argument to evolve into an Ahmadesque rant. However, he issued a call to arms to deal with the threat of Occidentosis. 'A materialistic base of culture, the spirit of consumerism for the sake of consumerism, excessive individualism, and other deficiencies of Western culture have been transferred to the countless masses of the East'. Action needed to be taken to protect Iranian authenticity. If steps were not taken, Iran would face the same social and moral crises that confronted the West.[76]

In spite of these opinions and establishment of various institutions charged with the implementation of the imperial couple's evolved views on authenticity, until the Rastakhiz period, bureaucratic confusion and infighting dogged efforts for the implementation of a united cultural policy. According to Behnam, some bureaucratic tension existed between the MCA and the SCCA over who would have the last word in creating cultural policy. Despite this tension, coordination between the SCCA and the MCA was relatively good. But other bodies 'implicitly did not accept the purview and powers of the Supreme Council or just superficially coordinated with it'. The SCCA's head just did not have the power to impose coordination on other institutions.[77] According to some claims, the shah, the empress, Hoveyda, Pahlbod and Reza Qotbi, head of NIRT and the empress's cousin, frequently made decisions affecting policy with little, if any, attention paid to the SCCA (Figure 3).

> An individual could visit any one of them without regard to what the Supreme Council of Culture was doing, and say 'yes that is good, do that' and then help that individual do that. ... Their intervention had a personal dimension, in other words [it was dependent on] what were their personal interests and opinions.[78]

At the same time, this subgroup was also afflicted with factional tendencies. Tension existed between the MCA, which enjoyed great institutional power and coverage in regard to cultural policy, and the empress's office which lacked it. In addition, according to Pahlbod, serious differences about the direction of cultural policy existed between him and Qotbi. As a result Qotbi and NIRT as a whole paid no serious attention to the SCCA.[79] This tension was so great that according to Hossein Nasr, a SCCA member, 'if Pahlbod had not been the shah's brother-in-law, the empress many years [before the Revolution] would have brought enough pressure to have him removed'.[80] One example of the rancour touched on the licensing and censoring of films which was under the MCA's purview. Films that had been banned or heavily censored by Pahlbod's ministry, such as Mehrjui's *The Cow* (1969) and *Dayereh-ye Mina* (1974) and Naser Taqvai's

Figure 3 Empress Farah and her cousin Reza Ghotbi, head of National Iranian Radio and Television, author's collection.

Tranquility in the Presence of Others (*Aramesh dar Hozur-e digaran*, 1973) were shown at the Shiraz Festival of Art and Culture started by the empress in 1967.[81]

In sum, although in principle the SCCA was to be the coordinating institution for the creation and implementation of cultural policy, in reality it did not enjoy full power and influence over other cultural institutions, like NIRT. Pahlbod confessed: 'The Supreme Council failed to fulfill its duties'.[82] During the Rastakhiz period the failures of the government and specifically the SCCA to deal with these cultural problems became a major target of party rhetoric.

Censorship policy

Changing sensitivities in regard to topics subject to censorship is another indicator of the evolution of state discourses on Iranian authenticity. SAVAK's Third Department, made up of nine divisions, was the most (in)famous since it dealt with internal security. As mentioned earlier, Parviz Sabeti headed this department during the period covered in this work. Its Fifth Division named Operational Support had five offices, the second of which was called 'Censorship'. The Censorship Office had three groups: Action, Inspectorate of Publications and Translation Control. Press monitoring was centralized within this office. Only it, with the approval of the head of the third department, along with the prime minister's office, had the right to close and reopen publications. During the tenure of SAVAK's first head, General Teymour Bakhtiar (1957–61), systematic censorship was established.[83] Only it could approve licences for newspapers and magazines after a security check was completed on proposed editorial leadership and writers. The Censorship Office kept files on such figures, as well as a list of those banned from writing or publishing. Lists of banned expressions were also kept. Those individuals and periodicals considered dangerous were subject to telephone bugging and post monitoring. For example, several requests were made for monitoring Ferdowsi's telephones and post throughout the 1960s.

SAVAK's approach to censorship evolved in the 1960s. At the beginning of the decade officials gathered copies of magazines after publication but before distribution and newspapers after the publication of the first edition and sent them to the Censorship Office where they were quickly reviewed. By the late 1960s this practice was abandoned when figures on SAVAK's payroll sat on the editorial boards of publications to ensure that inappropriate items did not appear. During this decade censorship and self-censorship progressively increased in intensity, although as the following samples show, sensitivities to topics changed. This was a reflection of evolving state discourses on the West as a civilizational and geopolitical concept. This sampling also provides a sense of the dynamics of the growing intellectual and popular anti-West Occidentalism.

In the context of tightening censorship of the 1960s *Ferdowsi*, reflecting emerging intellectual trends, turned its rhetorical guns on Western civilization and issues of culture and morality in Iran. In this way, the magazine could criticize the state by implicitly questioning its authenticity given its programme of Westernization. An early example was a major article published in 1962, 'Warning Bell: The Young in the Grip of Moral Corruption and Corrosion'.[84]

> Young school girls during recess smoke and relate to each other their nocturnal escapades. ... An unhealthy society and environment is driving our young boys and girls into the arms of immorality, corruption and decay. ... Mothers, instead of paying attention to their children's correct spiritual upbringing and husbands' requests, think about vulgar make-up and their own repulsive social life and intercourse ... [and] husbands, primarily occupied with having a good time with other women, ... repay the love of their wives and children with betrayal and cruelty. ... They are producing morally corrupt children.

The article quoted letters of high school girls attending the Anoushirvan Girl's School. One girl narrated how she visited a boy whose family was not at home.

> Several times we danced the Cha-Cha-Cha. Since it was hot he told me, 'Take off your shirt. I'll take mine off.' We then danced some more. I then stretched out on his bed. He laid next to me. My body was hot ... I am not such a fool to lose myself. By the way, Pari, [the addressee] that son-of-gun Behrang [her dancing partner] is shrewd and slick. He always has in his pocket a package [of condoms].

The article blamed this moral corruption and the negative changes in parents' behaviour on Occidentosis. The main culprits were sexy parts in Western films allowed by the government to be shown, Western clothing and emphasis on external appearances, and hedonism. The article challenged the premise that this lifestyle was modern and progressive.

Six days after its publication, SAVAK reported that since 'this topic completely contradicts morality and virtue' the magazine was to be temporary closed. SAVAK worried that this piece would provoke clerical elements and turn public opinion against the state over cultural and moral issues.[85] SAVAK reopened it after having received promises that articles against public morality would not be printed. Another condition for its reopening was the sacking of the editorial manager, Naser Nirmohammadi, who would become of the SCCA's leading members advocating for the political and cultural struggle against Occidentosis and the editor of its journal. General Hassan Pakravan, SAVAK director at the time, understanding that this article had been originally approved or overlooked by the Censorship Office wrote a report to both it and the MCA, in which he explained this issue's potential to damage the government's standing and why the issue of morality was important.[86]

SAVAK's warning had the desired, albeit temporary, effect. The magazine continued to publish articles on this topic, but without the severity and implications of this one. However, two years later *Ferdowsi* attracted SAVAK's attention with another article, 'The Degradation and Decadence of a Generation' that was accompanied by a picture of a Western female stripper wearing only a G-string dancing for gawking Western young men in a smoke-filled cabaret.[87]

> Immorality has awakened and taken over everywhere. … Any place you go, any person to whom you listen you notice that its impact is everywhere. Virtue and piety no longer have any meaning. … Corruption without any pity or mercy is advancing and destroying virtue. … Every day the number of those struggling against it becomes smaller as the waves of immorality attack. … Virtue, honesty, work and service are being eliminated from Iran's social fabric while the weight of immorality has become heavy. … This decadent generation sees no future and has no hope. It is insurgent. It is mad. … In this land governed by the laws of immorality and criminality those wishing to combat this process are being destroyed. Where are we going with this immorality? One day a great rain will come (and) an ocean will devour this red sea of immorality.

This article contained the same implicit condemnation of Pahlavi cultural policy that allowed the spread of Occidentosis and the same condemnations of the West as the source of moral and spiritual corruption. SAVAK reported:

> *Ferdowsi* has published an article, which in the most wicked way attacked the social morality and self-esteem of Iran and Iranians, and a picture of a semi-naked woman. … Given the description over the dramatic penetration of immorality in Iranian society which the writer, with emotion or anger, has provided and the way in which he portrays Iran it is necessary to be objective. First, any foreign person

or government who reads it has grounds not to have confidence in political, social or economic transactions with Iran and Iranians. Second, the article and others similar to it damage any actions [in regard to bringing up the youth] and transforms their hopes into despair. ... This article damages public morality.[88]

SAVAK, reprimanding the managing editor, again feared that the discussion of socio-moral corruption would damage public perception and state legitimacy and undermine pro-West Occidentalism. The warnings had the desired effect. In the period 1964–6, articles on the issue of morality and spirituality continued to appear, but lacked this one's severity and intensity. Moreover, they did not portray the issue as a struggle between the positive forces of moral tradition and the decadence of the new morals created by Pahlavi Westernization.

By 1968 the theme of the link between Western culture and moral and spiritual decay became more common and condemning of the West. However, SAVAK no longer showed sensitivity to moral and cultural issues and their potential to damage state legitimacy. In a 1968 lead article 'Dirty Tehran', *Ferdowsi* reported the closing of two clubs in Tehran because of immorality and vice.[89] The issue's cover was adorned with young Western girls with their Western boyfriends passionately kissing. The article 'The Playthings of Tehran' stressed that regular people and *Ferdowsi* 'had consistently complained about the debauchery and immorality in these places but were ignored by the authorities or faced with official denials that anything was wrong in these places'. The implicit conclusion was that the state or rather elements within it, if not supported, at least turned a blind eye to the spread of moral Occidentosis.

This issue was covered in another article 'The Immorality of Society and the Fall of the Youth'. These recently closed clubs/cafes 'are not the last sites of debauchery. ... Their closing will not limit the immorality going on inside and outside the walls of such places.' *Ferdowsi* argued that 'the spread of immorality among the youth' is a major problem that demands official action from a state that had ignored it. Emphasizing that this vice was a phenomenon of the West, it warned about moral and cultural Occidentosis and provided the causes of its spread:

> The decadent bourgeoisie and the absence in these new conditions of strict classification [of norms] and social limits ... [have resulted in] our youth lacking aptness and competence. ... [Consequently] in their encounters with the external appearances of the West's so-called advanced culture they lose themselves, make many mistakes and forget much.

Condemning the haste of the spread of this 'modern life', the article implicitly claimed it was being encouraged by the state. The result was that 'moral corruption is growing' which is 'wide-spread and unnatural'. Despite this article's anti-Westernism, criticism of government inaction and its articulation of a nostalgia for a real and imagined morally pure past, SAVAK did not record negative comments.

Probably the best example of *Ferdowsi*'s approach to, and implicit condemnation of, the cultural elements of Pahlavi Westernization and the spread of Occidentosis and its progeny, the Occidentosis-ridden *nouveau riche*, was its coverage of the suicide of the celebrated and widely respected wrestler, Gholam Reza Takhti (1930–68). The coverage's tone was also an accurate reflection of the growing public reaction to Occidentosis and Occidentosis-ridden people. He hailed from south Tehran, a region that had come to be popularly regarded as the bastion of traditional and authentic Iranian culture set in opposition to the northern parts of the city, the habitat of the Occidentosis-ridden *nouveau riche*. In this series of articles one senses the growing feelings of disorientation and nostalgia for a lost and imagined Iran that was disappearing as the manifestations of Occidentosis spread.

'Why did Takhti choose death?' one article asked. 'He grew up with certain customs, beliefs, and traditions and unfortunately he could not adapt himself to the habits, customs, and behavior of the young class from which his wife came.' Thus, 'his suicide was a national reflection' of the battle between the Occidentosis-ridden classes and 'society's socially and morally authentic parts'.[90]

> His internal reality that created his character, values, and being had its roots in tradition and the past. The current reality is the negation of all that and therefore solving this contradiction was not possible. ... He chose defeat so that the reality of his being and values would be strengthened. ... Suicide is the last resort of a person seeking to ensure that the reality of his being can triumph over society's outward reality. ... Takhti was the last example of moral behavior, of a tradition and matrix of values which had deep, ancient roots that are intensely in contradiction with the current situation. This contradiction he could not solve. Because being other than this meant for him his becoming an alien, a foreigner. ... His family and those of the environment in which he grew up were beholden by their own traditions, culture, and behavior and have had the good fortune not to doubt their values and enjoyed the power to defend them.

The antagonist of this tale was Takhti's wife, Shahla, who was introduced in another article 'The Death of a Modest and True Human'.[91] She had stressed, 'I didn't get along with Takhti's sisters who also could not get along with me. Our families belonged to two completely different classes and these class differences brought serious differences in thought and a disconnect in taste.' These two people became representatives of the perceived sociocultural conflict between genuine Iranians and those ridden with Occidentosis. Takhti, quoted in this article, described the behaviour he found unacceptable: 'Shahla in front of her family curses at me. ... Her father yells at me: "You do not fit into our family's culture."' The undertone was clear. Occidentosis-ridden Iranians not only believed in their cultural superiority but also insisted on demeaning those Iranians clinging to traditional conceptions of culture and morality that these examples of *homo Pahlavicus* considered backward. Yet, Occidentosis-ridden Iranians needed this 'traditional' and 'backward' Iranian to exist since demeaning and mocking this person was essential for stabilization of their conceptions of their identity. Their identity, in turn during the Rastakhiz period, would be attacked and described as 'the lack of identity'.

Takhti in response to the remarks and actions of his wife's family wrote in his suicide note: 'I became very upset when hearing these words. ... Shahla is on a weight-reducing diet and is not breast-feeding Babak [their new born son]. I am upset. I fear that my child will go without milk. ... Today, Shahla, in front of her mother and brother, pelted me with her fists and called me a jerk and a bum ... I'm not on speaking terms with her and the rest of the family. I came to this hotel. I will not return home.' There he killed himself.

The article then focused its attention on the causes of the behaviour of this Pahlavi-created group symbolized by Shahla. It had fallen under the influence of 'government television programming that continually beams Western movies and the Western lifestyle' which stress that the 'new figure' [*homo Pahlavicus*] symbolized the desired future. This new figure sought Western-style dancing clubs and casinos, and accepted 'the Western obsession with the person's external appearance to the detriment of spiritual health'. Shahla's decision to go on a diet soon after giving birth and thus depriving her newborn of his mother's milk was presented as an example of the superficial behaviour of the Occidentosis-ridden Iranian. The Takhti-Shahla saga as it was described in these articles underlined not only growing social disorientation resulting from rapid socio-economic changes and growing outrage with the bourgeois Occidentosis-ridden *nouveau riche*. It also reflected a rapidly spreading nostalgia for an authentic Iranian past: 'Old values have lost their color.' The figure of Takhti crystallized sympathy for those fighting against Occidentosis: 'I love and respect those people who are facing off these other [i.e. Occidentosis-ridden] groups. I wish that this group in its evolutionary direction does not fall into the moral sludge of their corrupted neighboring class.'

Wrestling is considered the ancient sport of Iran. Inevitably therefore Takhti's great fame as a wrestler provided another arena in which to portray this clash of civilizations. *Ferdowsi*, contrasting Iran's good traditional moral values with the West's corruptive forces, propagated or at least tolerated by the state, saw in sport the difference between this spiritually superior East, Iran and the West. 'Our traditional sports are different from those of the West because (for us) cultivation of the body is a means for the cultivation of the spirit and of a system of morals and values that enable one to lay claim to the title of hero (*pahlavan*)'.[92] It underlined that the common word for hero 'qahraman' represented the Western sportsperson who while showing great skill and physical strength was in reality a spiritual and moral vacuum. The Iranian hero, *pahlavan*, however, used this physical side to enrich the spiritual one in order to create a complete human and genuine hero from whom all should take example. Takhti 'was the perfect example of *pahlavan* and not *qahraman*'.

SAVAK reports on the press in the aftermath of Takhti's suicide did not address these issues.[93] This lack of reaction underlined the state's decreasing sensitivity to claims of moral and spiritual decline attributed to Occidentosis. In the period 1969–74 *Ferdowsi* intensified its condemnation of the ongoing spread of sexual deviance (*enherafi*), lack of a belief system among the youth (*biimani*) and licentiousness (*bibandobari*) due to Occidentosis. The following sampling of articles show the type of rhetoric and topics used to portray Occidentosis as an existential threat to the authenticity of Iranian culture, morality and spirituality. These articles also attacked in essentialist terms Western civilization that, it was stressed, was experiencing a steep decline in morality and spirituality that presaged its overall collapse. These articles did not prompt closings or condemnation by SAVAK.

While the West was exporting to Iran technology, consumer goods and arms, *Ferdowsi*, among others, focused on the more dangerous 'exports of the West', namely elements pushing civilization into cultural obscenity and moral corruption from which the West itself was suffering.[94] Articles reported on the spread among the West's underage youth, and specifically the United States, of sexual activity and their engaging in sex with adults. They also focused on adults who preyed on underage youth. 'Underage girls are bait in the sexual revolution of advanced nations. ... Mimi is a fifteen-year-old pupil. She states, "In the last three years I have slept with nine older guys. It is completely natural. It is great. It's really great to destroy [old] beliefs."'[95] Another article 'Young Girls and Sex' adorned with provocative pictures, focused on the spreading fashion in the United States, of older men going after young and underaged girls.[96] Concentrating on the causes of this moral decline an article 'Amorality, Hollowness, and the Fall of the West' told Iranians that 'many values in the West have gone with the wind and Christian spirituality has given way to licentiousness'. These unfortunate developments, 'combined with Western consumerism and atomization, will lead to the collapse of Western civilization'.[97] 'The Fall of the Youth', the title of another article, stressed that one had only to look at the West's young to understand that Western culture 'destroys but does not build' while 'the hollow models of the West's youth are poisoning the minds of the Third World's youth'. These hollow models were based on a loss of hope whose source was 'decline, callousness, lethargy, and excessive sex'.[98] Action needed to be taken to ensure that Iran did not fall into this same cesspool.

Excessive sex and the decline of sexuality morality were common themes. Typical of this approach was the cover of one issue that exhibited a provocative picture of the bottom half of a young girl in tight jeans in whose hand was a half-eaten apple with the caption 'The Desires of the Forbidden Fruit'.[99] The article associated with this picture 'Sex and Consumption' argued that sex, consumerism and human exploitation, in other words, the pillars of Western civilization, 'have combined with the political system' and together will lead to the West's fall. The pictures associated with the article brought home the article's message. One woman, naked with her hands over her bare breasts, stares sexily into the camera. In another, a partially naked young boy and naked girls embrace each other in a collective exhibit of licentiousness.

Four weeks later *Ferdowsi* declared: 'The spirit of Western civilization from the beginning has been based on hostility, oppressiveness, exploitation, and aggression'.[100] It is 'dehumanizing' and 'the most inhumane civilization' in history. Science, the original basis of Western civilization, was flawed and had led to the current undesired situation in the world: 'Science without any modesty claims it will save us. But the result of its work is an inhuman and unwieldy clutter' that cannot provide the basis for happiness. *Ferdowsi* predicted that Western society 'with its limitless freedom of sex is dragging itself down to destruction' while the rapid spread of pornography in the West showed that 'sex had become a form of exercise with spectators'.[101] People were being reduced to animals. Until its closing in 1974 that was part of an overall cull of the press, *Ferdowsi* continued the onslaught. An article titled 'Immorality' claimed that Western civilization represented the 'violent storm of a new but not superior society' that was intent on destroying old societies.[102] Recognizing the centrality of morality to the cultural authenticity of Iran and non-Western countries, 'Western culture first attacks morals'. Its goal was 'the death of classic morals' but, unfortunately, it had no desire 'to create new morals'. One month later the magazine reported on the moral and sexual corruption of Iranian youth resulting from studying in the West. Parents were warned about sending their children there to study.[103]

The anti-West Occidentalism that appeared on the pages of *Ferdowsi* is probably best summed up by one of its own editorials:

> The hollow and empty ideas of the West's youth are poisoning the minds of the young of the Third World. ... The world has been shaking for thirty years. This Western world every day destroys values and the people pay their respects to the corpse of traditions. Values have become crushed, broken into little pieces. Many traditions have been buried to the shame of the East.

The result was manifestations of Occidentosis, 'an indifference [to spirituality] that has dried people's brains, sexual extremism, hippieism, and search for effortless material welfare'.[104] SAVAK recorded these articles but did not react.

Westerners living in Iran, portrayed as the agents of Occidentosis, too faced condemnations. The shah's modernization programme and military cooperation with the West, and in particular the United States, led to thousands of foreign advisors and their dependents pouring into the country. For example, the number of Americans alone reached 50,000 by 1972. The presence of these foreigners, seen by the public as an extension of the state, created frequent cultural conflict. From the late 1950s until the late 1960s criticism of the presence of foreigners was not permitted. Typical of the articles on this issue was *Ferdowsi*'s, 'An Agent of the Relocation of the Obscene and the Vulgar Appearance of the Western Hussy', that summed up growing popular feelings in regard to this presence.[105] It had one picture of a Western girl stripping to her bikini on a beach, while another showed a group of young Western guys and girls hanging out in a small pool. While only their heads, hands and knees are visible, it can be assumed that they are all naked. The author Dr Hoshiyar attacked 'unsavory Westerners who pay no attention to our national and religious customs, practices, and traditions'. He condemned the practice of foreign bars and cabarets in Iran to post a sign, 'No entrance to Iranians'. While denouncing the feelings of racial and cultural superiority held by Westerners that led to the posting of such signs, it was stressed that Iranians, in the first place, had no need for such places since they had neither the moral turpitude nor patience for such places.

These signs, however, were part of a larger issue – the arrogant, irreverent and provocative behaviour of Westerners in Iran who were unable to disabuse themselves of the sense of their civilizational and racial superiority over Iranians. One could see this arrogance everywhere. Hoshiyar complained: 'These drunken foreigners on the streets curse loudly, harass Iranian women, and they fight', destroying public tranquillity and offending the Iranian sense of proper behaviour. He condemned 'half-naked Western boys and girls who publicly play with each other's bodies' and 'act like animals in heat. They do things that even a disgraced dog would be embarrassed to do. ... They make love with spectators and in front of the noble and innocent Iranian youth.' Hoshiyar, while claiming he is not 'a conservative traditionalist' stressed that many people felt the way he did and waited for government action. After all, he emphasized, we 'worry about the future of our sons and daughters who encounter this [licentiousness]', in their own country. He implicitly charged that this large presence of Westerners in the country, the spread of Occidentosis and the crumbling of Iranian morality were the consequences of mistaken state policies, namely the implementation of Westernization and the creation of the Occidentosis-ridden *homo Pahlavicus*. 'Our mentality of loving all things Western is the cause for allowing this.' The article ended with an announcement: 'Entrance to unwanted foreigners is forbidden!' SAVAK did not respond.

By the late 1960s these essentialist condemnations were accompanied by condemnations of the West's geopolitics and political ideologies. 'Liberalism, the pillar of Western civilization, is a false freedom since only those with economic power enjoy it. They use this so-called freedom to impose their interests on society'.[106] In a society undergoing rapid urbanization where the gap between the rich and the poor seemed to be growing such rhetoric found a ready audience. Western liberalism did not represent freedom because it promoted a hegemonic discourse of the wealthy classes and supported institutionalized racism. The natural target of this attack was the Occidentosis-ridden bourgeois *nouveau riche*.[107]

The geopolitical pillar of liberalism was the West's old and new imperialism, one of the most frequent targets of *Ferdowsi*. This imperialism, interested only in the expansion and protection of the West's political and economic interests, prevented the development of the Third World in order to ensure it remained in a cycle of backwardness, poverty and hunger.[108] 'In the countries of Asia and Africa foreign elements preventing natural and historical change have always existed. ... These foreign elements have used intervention and established puppet governments' in order to achieve their goals. Direct old imperialism was fading from the pages of geopolitics, but 'the new imperialist systems have created a fresh network in the international arena that links together their collective interests'.[109] This imperialism's worst aspect was its approach to the issue of world hunger and starvation: 'The Westerners' view in regard to hunger is a mash of imperialism' that caused and maintained this situation. Pieces also periodically appeared whose tone implicitly or explicitly supported dimensions of the rhetoric of Soviet foreign policy that took aim at Westernization, and shared elements of Third Worldism. 'The emergence of the USSR and the ideology of communism have dislocated world imperialism. ... It is also a new effective agent in the encouragement and mobilization of revolutionary agents across the Third World and a direct and indirect danger to the position and influence of imperialist countries'.[110]

These changes in the topics considered sensitive and integrated in censorship policy show that the state from the close of the 1960s to the establishment of the Rastakhiz Party permitted publicists and public intellectuals to fan the flames of cultural and geopolitical anti-West Occidentalism. The state had recognized that elements within intellectual and public opinion were progressively becoming more critical of the West as a civilization and geopolitical actor. In many cases, this anti-West Occidentalism was also being used to question the state's authenticity and legitimacy given its close geopolitical and economic links with the West and its policy of Westernization. At the same time, large sections of intellectual and political opinion took inspiration from Western political norms that they hoped to see established in Iran. Countering this tendency required the intensification of state discourses of anti-West Occidentalism.

Within this period, the shah and members of the Pahlavi elite were also becoming increasingly sceptical of fundamental cultural and moral elements of Western civilization, concerned about the loss of Iranian authenticity, as defined by the state, and confident about Iran's future. This confidence was expressed in the grand celebrations held in 1971 in Persepolis marking the 2,500th anniversary of the founding of ancient pre-Islamic Iranian Empire by Cyrus the Great. *The Economist* summed up the message the shah wanted to send: 'The whole thing was a declaration that Iran is well on the way to becoming the strongest economic and military power in the Middle East. ... Iran will be nobody's vassal.' *TIME* was more blunt: 'The Shah was determined to stage his show of shows [a play on his title Shahanshah, Shah of Shahs] as a sign to the rest of the world that Iran is again a nation equal to all the others-and much finer than many'.[111] These celebrations, while reflecting the shah's growing confidence about Iran's prospects and belief in an Iranian modernity superior to those on offer from the West, also disguised his growing concern about specific dynamics of the political system.

7

The Rastakhiz Party: Ideology and structure

The shah, having returned from his month-long working holiday in St. Moritz, on 24 February 1975 told Alam to summon the cabinet, members of the Majles and Senate and the media to a news conference at which he would make a major announcement. Alam noted that he had been pensive since his return.[1] On 1 March they made their way to the architecturally modern palace, situated high in north Tehran, overlooking the sprawling capital.[2]

Brimming with confidence, the monarch appeared. He began by underlining the great developmental success Iran had achieved which he attributed to his own revolutionary leadership. Now, he stressed, the time had come for all Iranians to participate in, and take credit for, the steps in the kingdom's march towards the Great Civilization. To achieve this, he announced the dissolution of all political parties and the establishment of the Rastakhiz Party. Iran became a single-party state. According to the shah the Party would provide the theoretical and practical framework for this participation and be the conduit for opinions and criticisms channelled in the political system from the bottom to the top and vice versa.

Yet, the shah deemed that the Party's founding required all Iranians to make clear their political preferences. Simplifying decision making for the masses, he determined the three groups from which to choose. The first group consisted of people who accepted the Party and its three fundamental guiding principles: the imperial system, the 1906 Constitution and the White Revolution. These people would enjoy the opportunity to participate in this great march forward. Apolitical people constituted the second group. While not enthusiastically supporting the Party, they were also not advocating the regime's overthrow. They could reap the benefits of the country's economic and social development, but could not expect to participate in the political arena now demarcated by the Party. A small minority fell into the third group. They were 'traitors' who, linked either 'to an illegal organization or … the outlawed Tudeh Party', opposed this 'national resurgence'. Given their illegal activities such people should be in prison or, alternatively, could 'leave the country tomorrow, without even paying exit fees and can go anywhere' … since they 'had no nation' and were 'not Iranian'.[3]

This move seemingly signalled the monarch's increasing confidence while confirming conclusions made inside and outside the country that he, sensing domestic and international successes, had ascended to a new height of power and influence. Seemingly, he was no longer the tepid indecisive monarch of 1953 when he fled the country, but rather a strong visionary revolutionary leader leading his grateful people to the gates of the Great Civilization while playing a major role in international politics, enjoying the respect of both Washington and Moscow. The shah's hubris and its expression in state propaganda are reflected in concomitant changes in the design of Iranian currency.

In the year of the Party's establishment the twelfth currency series of the shah's reign was released. The obverse of banknotes of the first eleven series was adorned with relatively small portraits of the shah, usually contained within some form of frame. In the new twelfth series the size of the shah's portrait more than doubled, dominating nearly one-half of each bill type and constrained no longer by any frame.[4] The grandiosity surrounding the Party's establishment and the new domineering position of the shah's portrait on the currency belied the monarch's limited, but growing, concern about aspects of the political system that had in the late 1960s prompted limited steps towards the ideologization of the monarchy.

On that chilly Sunday in March only a few people had an inkling about the contents of the shah's announcement. One of them was Abdulmajid Majidi, the head of the Plan and Budget Organization who had audience with him in Switzerland to discuss economic matters. At its end the shah changed the subject. Expanding on the concerns about the two-party system expressed in *Pahlavism*, he told Majidi of his intention to change the party system since it had failed to sufficiently mobilize people behind the state. The new system would provide 'for criticism from within and for its own reform and improvement. Thus, we want to change the country's political structures so that the system itself can have a mechanism for internal criticism'.[5] However, as one of the shah's most recent biographers noted: 'No one knows exactly how the Shah got the idea of the Rastakhiz Party.' One cannot but agree with him that 'Rastakhiz was a stream many tributaries fed'.[6] However, the idea of the establishment of a single-party state was not new. The shah had flirted with it in the late 1950s along the lines that began to emerge at the end of his father's reign with the establishment of the Organization of Public Enlightenment (OPE).

The following passages from *Mission for My Country* provide a glimpse into the shah's thinking at the beginning of the 1960s. In the first passage, he hinted that he once had doubts about democratic forms of governance but nonetheless remained loyal to them.

> One of my first acts as king had been to affirm the rebirth of constitutional democracy. Yet such chaos had come to the country's political life that perhaps it would have been understandable if, at that juncture, I had become permanently disillusioned with the democratic process. Fortunately for the country and for me, my political convictions had by then become firmly rooted, so that threatening developments could not easily scare me into abandoning the principles of such men as Thomas Jefferson, principles I was determined to follow.

Having affirmed his belief in democratic systems, he condemned single-party systems.

> Communist dictators resemble Fascist ones in that they enjoy holding elections. They hope to give the ordinary working man the idea that he has a voice in the

Government of his country. But Communist rules allow only one political party; anybody who tries to start another, or who speaks against the ruling party, is likely to be liquidated. In the elections (if you can call them by that name), the voter has no choice, for the only candidates listed are those of the ruling party ... I wonder how many intelligent people are fooled by that sort of thing.

So I consider that my role as King requires that I encourage parties. If I were a dictator rather than a constitutional monarch, then I might be tempted to sponsor a single dominant party such as Hitler organized or such as you find today in Communist countries. But as a constitutional monarch I can afford to encourage large-scale party activity free from the strait-jacket of one party rule or the one-party state. As a symbol of the unity of my people, I can promote two or more parties without directly associating myself with any.[7]

Another recent biographer of the shah dates his discontent with the existing party system to October 1972 when he turned to Mehdi Samii, a well-respected technocrat to discuss the idea of establishing a new party that would breathe life into the stagnating two-party system.[8] The shah had for some time before this step expressed worry about declining popular interest and participation in the existing two-party system and asked for the reasons for this tendency. SAVAK reports dating from 1970 to 1971 too warned about this decline and growing discontent with Iran Novin and the government headed by Hoveyda.

Generally, the people are convinced that executive organs everyday create and deepen the divide and gap between the shah and the people and thus make the people progressively disinterested with state organs in general. Not only has the struggle against corruption, theft, and factional fighting within the government produced no results, it has in reality paralyzed government organs.[9]

The shah sought a new political party that could mobilize the young and the growing educated classes around the state by playing the role of loyal opposition to the government. It would be 'a centrist party with hints of social democratic ideas in its proposed platform'. Such a party could to an extent rebuild the political wall between the state, headed by him, and the government, head by the prime minister, and run by the bureaucracy, that he had undermined when he proclaimed himself Leader of the Revolution. In this regard, the shah provided a simple example 'of what he envisioned loyal opposition could do. He suggested that the police, for example, had recently "found that the dynamite used by saboteurs was sold to them by people of our railroad administration. We would give the tip to [the new party] to attack the government."'[10] The shah was contemplating a modus operandi used by authoritarian leaders, from monarchs to presidents and 'national leaders' seeking to deflect criticism from themselves and strengthen their image as the defender of the nation's and people's interests by declaring war on self-serving, corrupt and/or incompetent bureaucrats and high-ranking officials, including ministers.

The shah was not entertaining ideas of a true opposition party that criticized not only the government's implementation of policies and administrative efficiency but also the main policy trajectories established by him. Nonetheless, he continued to underline that he was against a one-party system since it would lead to dictatorship. He insisted that he wanted 'democracy' but 'the real, not the fake, not the American type'. He did indeed find the politics of democratic polities rather repulsing – 'dirty, one has to tell lies and enter into all kinds of deals with all kinds of people ... [and] the spiritual and moral corruption is everywhere'.[11] Wary of the type of politicking required in democratic and parliamentary politics and fearing the consequences of mass politics and the decentralization of power, he confessed to a US author: 'Whatever parliamentary democracy we have, it must adapt itself to the nature of Iran'.[12] Such a position begged the questions of who would determine 'the nature of Iran' and whether such a determination would reflect to a significant degree the country's conditions. He had real doubts about the efficacy of democracy. In the immediate aftermath of the military coup d'etat in Pakistan against Zulfikar Ali Bhutto the shah remarked to Alam: 'This only goes to show how democracy is unsuited to certain countries. ... How can you hope to build up a nation by fragmenting its politics into opposing camps? ... Whatever one group builds, the other will endeavour to destroy'.[13]

The shah's remarks are not unusual or a reflection of just a need to protect his power. They were genuinely felt interpretations of parliamentary politics held not only by political figures and those holding power in most countries faced with the soft political power of the West. For example, Thomas Mann, the famous German writer, noted in his book, *Reflections of a Non-Political Man*: 'I don't want the Parliamentary Party horse-trading that poisons the whole of the national life of politics ... I don't want politics. I want objectivity, order and decency. If that is Philistine, then I want to be a Philistine. If that is German, then I want in God's name, to be called a German'.[14] This passage captures well the long-held and common doubts about democratic liberalism held not only in Germany, but in many societies and polities of the non-Western world. The argument being made by figures such as the shah and Mann was that politics and development could be achieved and managed without the moral and political corruption that seemed to prosper and spread under democratic liberalism. They stressed that

> there was more to the life-world than the Parliamentary politics of France and Britain. ... But they tended to wrap up their political beliefs in a metaphysical language that liberals found deeply disconcerting. That which they found disconcerting were the values propagated by Mann in his youth: 'the collective against aggressive individualism; the rejection of liberal elitism; the celebration of the "non-political": the rejection of the "poison" of Parliamentary factionalism; a return to the community's roots'.[15]

These feelings were fundamental to Pahlavi and Romanov anti-West Occidentalism. Despite his views about parliamentary politics and liberal society, the shah in his discussions with Samii, along with the earlier publication of *Pahlavism*, showed that for some time he had recognized the weaknesses of the official two-party system and increasing political tension it was creating while it faced competition from ideologies of the West. However, he ended the Samii project. Yet, this step did not mean that the shah had somehow assuaged his concerns about the existing political situation and the dynamics of the official two-party system.

On the heels of the abandonment of the Samii project emerged a new committee that expanded the channels of debate about this issue. In February 1973, Hushang Nahavandi, at the time the head of Tehran University (1971–6) and subsequently the chief of the empress's personal office (1976–8)[16] submitted a plan to her that led to the creation of an increasingly influential committee, 'The Analysis Group of the Issues of Iran in the Aura of the Revolution of Shah and People'. Its initial leading members included Nosrat Moinian, head of the shah's personal office and one-time head of Iranian National Radio, Pahlbod; Hossein Nasr, at the time head of Aryamehr University; Qotbi and Sabeti. It existed until the regime's collapse. The exact number of its members is not known, but the estimates of Alam and others place it around 500 to 600 individuals occupied with research and analysis. The shah told Alam:

> Recently we have wanted a number of academics and thinkers to compare and evaluate our Revolution however they please and if they have a recommendation they should give it. If their recommendation is accurate and right then we will accept and add it to the principles of the Revolution of Iran or substitute it with one of them. To this extent we are now giving freedom of thought to new thoughts and ideas.[17]

The shah maintained a positive opinion of this group, whose analysis he described as 'food for thought', even after the Party's establishment.[18] He also considered it a vital source of analysis on Rastakhiz's performance.[19]

An important element of this report was the group's survey of popular opinion that underlined the growing dilemma facing the state. On the one hand, a majority of those surveyed acknowledged the rise in living standards. On the other hand, political apathy was on the increase due to the stagnation and artificiality of the two-party system and closed political space. The educated and the youth were particularly disconnected from the government and increasingly attracted to Western ideologies, liberalism and communism, and their derivatives. Nahavandi and this initially small group with the shah's support explored ways to combat them. Similar to the conclusions expressed in *Pahlavism* this group concluded that the current two-party system and Hoveyda's modus operandi were failing to mobilize sufficiently mass support for the monarchy and creating a sense of stagnation in the country's political life, despite the White Revolution's economic and social successes.

Discontent among the youth and the intellectual class was growing while violent leftist-inspired groups such as *Fedayeen-e Islam* and *Mojahedin-e Khalq* increasingly made their presence felt. For example, during 1971–4, General Ziaudinn Farisou, the chief of staff of the military tribunal that tried political prisoners was assassinated; in 1973 US Colonel Lewis Hawkins was assassinated; small-scale guerrilla warfare emerged in Gilan; an attempt was made to kidnap the US ambassador, Douglas MacArthur II; and student unrest increased across university campuses, in particular, in 1973 at Tabriz University and in 1974 at Tehran University. Between 1971 and 1974 some four hundred bombing incidents were recorded.[20] While limited, these incidents were seen as symptomatic of a growing problem. The emergence of anti-shah student organizations in Western Europe and the United States added to these concerns. At the same time, educated public opinion seemed worryingly detached from the state's travails and apathetic in regard to the political system. Alexander II had faced the same dilemma which he sought to manage with limited political changes he approved on the day he was assassinated.

One element vital to achieving victory in this struggle was limited reform of the party system that would mobilize the support of moderate political opinion by allowing for more freedom of expression and criticism of the government's performance while not threatening the state's security and stability. Even within SAVAK some sympathy for limited changes existed. Sabeti, during these discussions, voiced support for the expansion of freedom of expression and criticism as long as it was gradual, judicious and controlled. He argued for the initial granting of such freedoms to those individuals and groups loyal to the regime. Enjoying this opportunity, they could recognize and debate challenges facing the state. Once they had succeeded in solving or at least managing the bulk of them, these freedoms could be given gradually and slowly to the rest of society.[21] The goal was much easier to state than to achieve.

This group headed by Nahavandi, having expanded its numbers and the range of issues it discussed, published a journal *The New Society* (*Jame'e-ye Novin*) whose first issue appeared in summer 1974. It ceased publication in summer 1978, having produced a total of thirteen issues. It tackled the same issues addressed by *Culture and Life*, particularly the West's position in the authenticity of Iranian culture and identity. A list of the leading members of the journal's governing writers' council reflected its political and intellectual weight: Jamshid Behnam, Mohammad Reza Jalili, Kazem Vadiei, a well-known academic who would occupy ministerial and high party posts, Hossein Nasr, Nahavandi, Manuchehr Ganji, minister of education in the last Hoveyda cabinet, Mohammad Ismail Razvani, a well-respected historian and professor at Tehran University, Ahmad Hushang Sharifi, Ganji's predecessor at the Ministry of Education, who also held posts in the MCA and in academia, and Karim Motamedi, minister of telegraph and post in Hoveyda's 1973 cabinet. *The New Society*, unlike *Culture and Life*, was an official state journal. Although it sought to broaden the state's contact with non-state intellectuals within the purview of the Analysis Group, it nonetheless published articles reflecting the concerns and positions of this group and then the Party.

In 1974 another group, smaller than the one headed by Nahavandi, was convened by Ganji whose members included Ahmad Qoreishi, Gholam Reza Afkhami and Ali Alimard. Their report too underscored the White Revolution's social, economic and technological achievements that had created new political and administrative challenges. If left unchecked, 'the political system would become dangerously underdeveloped relative to other social subsystems, and consequently increasingly vulnerable'.[22] The proposed solution was the establishment of

> a political movement, not a party, called the Resurrection Movement of the Iranian Nation, or Rastakhiz ... within which individuals would be free to join associations, unions, cooperatives, and political parties of their choice. Simultaneously, steps

would be taken to decentralize the bureaucracy and empower local councils through appropriate legislation.[23]

The shah rejected this proposal. The monarch's dislike of this idea was conveyed by Hoveyda to Qoreishi at a celebration marking the anniversary of the Constitutional Revolution. The prime minister made his way towards him and remarked: 'What was that rubbish (*mozakhraf*)? His Majesty wondered if you had read his book in which he said that a single-party system is against the principles of democracy'.[24]

In sum, by the end of the 1960s and into the early 1970s a veneer of publicly projected hubris rather successively concealed the shah's simmering concerns about the dynamics of the stagnating two-party state. At the same time, a growing number within the elite were convinced that the existing two-party system had to be reformed. One problem was determining what steps needed to be taken and their management at a time when socio-economic conditions were rapidly changing. The fundamental problem was the shah, who seemed to be alternating between two fears, the fear of the consequences of not reforming this system and the fear of the consequences of such reform.

The conclusion should not be made that the shah was not optimistic about Iran's future. He frequently was, especially in the wake of the White Revolution's sensed successes, steady economic growth and the dramatic rise in oil income in the early 1970s. But that optimism was subject to gnawing concerns about aspects of the country's political situation. These alternating feelings reflected and exacerbated his contradictory fears concerning how and to what extent to reform the two-party system.

The shah's realization in 1974 that he had cancer also played an important role. Even before this realization, he spoke privately and publicly of the need to ensure a smooth succession for his son Reza, the crown prince.

> Of course, until now whatever ... I have implemented was an order from the top to the bottom. But I am not eternal. For the security of the country's future I must have structures and institutions that not only preserve and institutionalize the revolution's fruits but also make them deep-rooted.[25]

These remarks did not just have a rhetorical value. He had endured a rough transition caused by the Allied occupation and effective collapse of state institutions built by his father.

Another cited factor in the decision to establish the Party was the shah's increasing worry about Hoveyda's political aspirations and his patronage network in the Iran Novin Party. Alam believed that the establishment of the Analysis Group was one of the first steps taken by the shah to limit the power of Hoveyda and Iran Novin.[26] Alam, however, was not an impartial observer. He and Hoveyda were factional rivals. Nonetheless, his suspicions in this regard were shared by Hoveyda: 'The Prime Minister does not care very much for Nahavandi. He fears that one day his group of thinkers will create problems for the supremacy of his party's rule'.[27] In a conversation with Alam the shah alluded to his worries about Hoveyda.

> Again the conversation turned to the Party. I mentioned that the people's welcoming of the Party is astonishing while the prime minister is very sad. He

asked: 'Why?' I said that in the end Iran Novin had claims to be the decisive majority among the people, and perhaps it had different calculations as well ... who knows. The shah responded: 'Of course he [Hoveyda] is an intelligent person and I am convinced that he knows that he never can be (the voice of the decisive majority of the people), but perhaps he had entertained the construction of some castles in the sky for himself.' This was the first time that I heard such a thing from the shah.[28]

Dariush Homayoun too argued that 'one of the goals for the establishment of the Rastakhiz Party was to break down Hoveyda's Iran Novin party'.[29] According to Qoreishi, 'Hoveyda understood that the Party was not his creature and was used to crush Iran Novin'.[30] The issue was not that Hoveyda, backed by the Iran Novin Party, could in any way compete with the shah. The monarch said as much to Alam. What perhaps worried him was that a political force, such as Hoveyda or the Iran Novin Party, could destabilize his modus operandi of divide and rule within the increasingly fractious elite. The dominance of any one political faction could raise resentment among other elite groups and make his management of them more difficult, while their consequent hallowing would increase his reliance on Iran Novin and its network within the bureaucracy.

The shah alluded to these issues in his public statements. In particular, he believed that Hoveyda and the Iran Novin Party sought to take credit for his successes in order to increase their popularity and power and weaken fatally the opposition party.

> Before we proposed the Rastakhiz Party, the structure was based on ... two different parties. We hoped to have one majority and one minority party. Democratic methods, in other words the people, would appoint those in power. In the event that the people become dissatisfied with those in power the minority and majority parties would switch positions. However, things did not work out that way. Since the country was experiencing amazing development and everyday it was possible to show the people ten examples of positive policies, the party in power was naturally able to take political advantage of the country's development and the party that was in the minority and whose members were equally patriotic and dedicated to modernization was slowly deprived of any political activity since anyone when asked is the country developing or not could not say 'no' and had to say 'of course' a thousand times.[31]

He repeated these reasons on several occasions. But with the Party's establishment 'the political figures and activists [of this minority party] would also have the opportunity' to participate in the development and success of the country and 'co-operate with the government'.[32]

Whatever roles these various factors played in the decision to establish the Rastakhiz Party and its timing, the shah already by the end of the 1960s had concerns about the ineffectiveness of the two-party system. These concerns, as well as remedy, were articulated by the first academic and theoretical book on the Party, *Single-Party Systems and the Rastakhiz Party of the People of Iran* that was serialized in party publications. The parties that were active until Rastakhiz's establishment

> despite sharing the same goals and ideals, did not enjoy success in mobilizing the people for participation in political and patriotic affairs. In reality the contradictory discourses of these parties' leaders and some of their cadres created doubts, ambivalence, and finally indifference among the urban classes and even amongst the educated and leaders of society.

The consequent stagnancy was 'a cancer' preventing

> the realization of the goals of the Revolution of Shah and People. These parties forgot the people and their opinions and instead focused on their own petty issues and interests. This development coincided with society's quick transformation that created new conditions and challenges for the state.

The shah recognized this reality and the 'necessity to clarify the people's role' and concluded that 'it was necessary that everyone's thoughts become one and their hands and brains be consolidated on the path to unified goals'. Rastakhiz's aim was 'to mobilize the people to attain national goals as part of the Revolution'.[33]

Homayoun stressed that the Party's establishment was a good idea

> for giving life to elections and attracting people to them (because) Iran's party system had become a laughing stock. ... It was only a name. There was the political machine of Iran Novin while the heads of the Mardom Party were chosen by the prime minister. What kind of party system is that? The people had no dealing with or care for them.[34]

It had become a laughing stock given its dynamics and the shah's great sensitivity to criticism. Having proclaimed himself the Revolution's leader and thus excessively politicized the Crown, the government and its ministers became mere appendages of the Crown, simply executing its wishes. The political border between the head of state and the head of government became dangerously blurred. The shah's desire to have the Revolution's successes attributed to him also created a situation in which any failure would also be attributed to it by public opinion. In this context the two official parties did not enjoy the political space or practical opportunity to offer manifestos and compete electorally with each other. Any criticism, even by these parties during controlled elections, 'reflected ultimately on the shah' who 'believed that any form of criticism of the government (in other words the prime minister and the cabinet) was in reality a criticism' directed at him.[35] The shah, by not allowing the party in opposition to criticize government performance and the party in power, ensured that the electorate would become progressively cynical and alienated from the political system. The Mardom Party, consequently, became an empty shell of a political organization, deprived of cadres and funding.

These issues came to a head in the early 1970s. Dr Yahya Adl, a friend of Hoveyda, headed Mardom from 1960, when Alam resigned the top party post, until 1971 when he resigned due to increasing party discontent with Mardom's ongoing status as the minority party. He was succeeded by Dr Alinaqi Kani, a political opponent of Hoveyda close to Alam. During a 1972 electoral his criticisms of the Hoveyda government began to upset the shah, while the Mardom Party began to attract popularity, a development that reflected the growing discontent and fatigue with that government. Sabeti has claimed that given Kani's approach during this election the Mardom Party began to evolve into a real opposition party. Hoveyda, who accepted the idea of limited criticism of the government, became increasingly frustrated as Kani's criticisms intensified.[36] In particular in Tehran and Qom he made aggressive speeches, even at one point likening the 'ruling party' to a 'dirty environment'. In some campaign stops he asked the monarch to end 'the rule of a handful of profiteers, egotists, and contemptuous enemies of freedom'. Hoveyda, determined to end these attacks, placed all of Kani's critical remarks in a dossier he submitted to the shah. As Hoveyda surely hoped and predicted, the monarch ordered Kani's resignation. It was the end of July 1972. Hoveyda, determined to put an end to attempts to transform Mardom into a true opposition party, succeeded in using the shah's fury over Kani to obtain the return of Adl to the post as party head. He remained in that post until the end of June 1973. Hoveyda chose as his successor Naser Ameri, who had been suggested by Adl. Ameri, although a long-time member of the Mardom Party, had a cordial relationship with Hoveyda. *The Economist*'s analysis written at the time of Kani's removal is telling:

> Although the Shah of Iran remains as anxious as ever he was for popular participation in government, all the signs are that the country is moving towards a one-party state. Last week's local elections confirmed the trend and underlined the fact that there is a long way to go if the Shah's intention of 10 years ago to create a two-party system is to be fulfilled. One stumbling block has been public apathy towards parliament and local councils because effective power is seen to reside with the Shah and his nominees. Another has been apathy towards the parties amongst a public which sees no real difference between them.[37]

Thus, while Hoveyda's short-term problem was resolved and his position secured, the regime's political challenges increased. In fact, the relationship between Hoveyda and Ameri too fell apart as he tried to reinvigorate the Mardom Party by attacking the government's performance. Towards the end of Ameri's tenure, Alam noted:

> In the evening ... Naser Ameri ... stopped by. He said he does not have money and no one is giving him any money. 'I don't have permission to talk. The newspapers should be supporting us – in these conditions how can I attract members? There is nothing to offer. Please tell the shah!'[38]

The reason was clear. In another entry Alam noted:

> His Imperial Majesty is furious over a recent speech by Naser Ameri, leader of the Mardom Party, in which he called for state-funded health care and university

education for all ... 'Why, he asked, should the children of wealthy parents be exempted from paying university tuition?'... He [the shah] had made clear in his address at the education conference in Ramsar that he fully supports merit-based state scholarships, regardless of family background. 'Why don't those damned politicians ever read my speeches? ... Why in God's name do they not make the effort to grasp the principles behind the policies we've implemented?' That is all very well, but what on earth is the role of an opposition leader if he cannot criticize government performance and promise a better way of doing things? ... If the opposition is merely window-dressing, I see no reason to have it.[39]

Ameri too suffered the same fate as Kani at the hands of Hoveyda and the shah. He was removed as party head in the closing days of December 1974.

The consequent increasing levels of public apathy and discontent and youth activism were not lost on the imperial couple and SAVAK. As the political and ideological tendencies among the youth increasingly worried the shah, he came to the conclusion that what he eventually called publicly Occidentosis arising from the youth's crisis of identity was to blame. Occidentosis-ridden, they would deliver themselves into the hands of Western imperialist groups and ideologies. The shah had emphasized to Samii during their meetings that his goal was to build up 'self-confidence and self-respect in the people, a belief in our own power and ability ... to fight the tendency of the people, especially the youth, to deny, denigrate, and to reject'. These fears were expressed in Rastakhiz's manifesto: 'The youth are the most influential and important defender of all achievements and guarantor of the Revolution's continuation. The youth will one day occupy management positions and be the creators of the strong and prosperous society of tomorrow's Iran.'[40] His concern about this social group dominated the trajectory of Rastakhiz ideology and propaganda.

Ideology

The Rastakhiz Party, as any political party and particularly a single all-encompassing governing one, needed a relatively cohesive and coherent ideology that demarcated a system of philosophical ideas, beliefs, historiography and even myths that targeted specific social constituencies and could mobilize them to preserve and revere an existing sociopolitical order. A state ideology must have a world view that articulates its place in the global civilizational order, socio-economic and political strategies for the present and the future, and domestic and international allies and enemies, ideological, cultural and/or geopolitical.

Ultimately, an ideology must establish its superiority to other competing ideologies in order to achieve and maintain hegemony. Theoretically, this superiority frequently rests on one of two pillars. They are the imagery of, and return to, a past golden age, which, for example, is dominant in Islamism and Slavophilism, and/or the promise of a future golden age, which is characteristic of the liberalism of the early French Revolution and Leninism. Fascism, however, to varying degrees, integrates both pillars. The achievement of this hegemony requires some form of ideological integration of the interests of a number of social groups and their political and cultural expressions. Achieving and sustaining this hegemony also requires contextualization of the ideology in regard to time and space and the relative integration of some common practices and recognized historical and political viewpoints, religious beliefs, values systems and symbols underpinned by a relatively cohesive and coherent historiography and philosophy. In this regard the series *Pahlavism* laid the ground for Rastakhiz ideology.

The Rastakhiz Party's record on this account is mixed. Such a record should not be surprising or unexpected since the shah announced its establishment without taking preliminary steps towards the construction of party ideology, regulations and institutions, while Rastakhiz existed for only three and a half years. Nonetheless, progress was made. The Party's fundamental guiding ideological principles were clear. According to party doctrine, which was approved at the First Party Congress (21 April–1 May 1975) the Party had three such principles that the shah had articulated in his speech announcing Rastakhiz's establishment.[41] Topping this list was the imperial system which was the 'the secret of the continuation and the expression of all cultural, political, and social characteristics of the Iranian people'. It was 'the authentic and natural form of governance across the sway of Iran's ancient history that has ... preserved the country's independence, boundaries and the authentic values of the people of Iran'.

The second principle was the 1906 Constitution. The Party did not emphasize the constitutional limits of monarchical power, described as Western-inspired. Rather, it propagated the idea that 'Iran's Constitution is the heritage of a national blood struggle against imperialism and exploitation'. The Constitution was both a consequence of Iran's encounter with imperialism and vital weapon in the struggle against it. The contradiction between its spirit and legal provisions, on the one hand, and the Party's establishment and the reality of the nature of the shah's rule, on the other hand, was justified not only by this struggle but also claims of the nativization of the political system undertaken to reflect the reality of Iran's authenticity and socio-economic and political conditions.

Underpinning the shah's propagation of the nativization of the political system was his concern that the country's political, social and cultural conditions were not appropriate for a Western-style constitutional system. In his first book the shah, in addressing criticism that the two-party system was artificial and imposed from above and therefore a puppet in the monarchy's hands, argued that in a country where the vast majority of people was illiterate and parliamentary and party politics were a fundamentally new phenomena, controlled steps, such as the official two-party system, were needed while conditions for true constitutionalism were created.[42] He was more blunt in an interview in the year that it was published: 'When the Iranians learn to behave like Swedes, I will behave like (the) King of Sweden'.[43]

During the Rastakhiz period it was stressed that the establishment of a genuine constitutional system 'requires the training and education of several generations of fathers, mothers, schools, and societal conditioning'.[44] Inevitably, this line of reasoning became an element of party discourses: 'Until the educated professional middle class develops and takes shape and thus becomes a force, we must not allow repetitious chaos in the name of party politics (*hezbbazi*)'.[45] Here is not the place to discuss the merits, weaknesses and possible political expediency of this belief and rhetoric. It has little direct bearing on the arguments being made in this work. What is important is that the shah, probably sincerely believing his expressed opinions, sought to find an 'authentically' Iranian form of democracy, eventually called 'democracy of the imperial system' by the Party. Subsequent chapters show that the difference in this system's nature with that of the 1906 Constitution that placed real limits on the Crown's power helped create the conditions for Rastakhiz discourses of anti-West Occidentalism.[46] The last principle was the White Revolution.[47]

These principles were not particularly new; they had been propagated piecemeal since the launching of the White Revolution. However, they were now part of an official ideological school. The primary theme was the need for mass mobilization behind the monarchy in the crusade to defend the country's cultural and geopolitical borders in the face of Occidentosis and implement the White Revolution in the march towards the Great Civilization. Thus, at the centre of party ideology and discourses was emphasis on a return to, and protection of, the authenticity of culture and national identity within the framework constituted by the shah's and the empress's evolved views in which one element looked to the past and provided legitimacy to the regime's claim to authenticity. In this vein, the Party's establishment and the institutionalization of the three fundamental guiding principles were propagated as the final stage in the nativization of the political system. In the early 1960s the shah told an American writer,

> The Constitution was brought to us by the British, and it was a defense against Czarist Russia. It was never really Iranian. It had been copied from the Belgian Constitution, with the powers of the king stripped. It was an amalgam of various reasoning and methods. ... 'In the Shah's view, it seemed, the Constitution was being "Iranianized", despite its Western origins, and without drastically modifying its text'.[48]

This was a long-held belief. On 22 May 1975 at a meeting of Nahavandi's Analysis Group he stressed that he considered the Party's establishment a necessary step in this nativization, arguing that the 1906 Constitution was an example of blind imitation of the West that had to be rectified.[49] One year after Rastakhiz's founding on the occasion of the anniversary of the 1906 Constitutional Revolution the shah characterized the dynamics of Iranian democracy:

> The base of this real democracy responds to the Iranian people's material and spiritual needs and is in accordance with our country's spiritual and cultural values and standards. ... This democracy cannot be and is not the blind imitation of foreign ways because many of them are not compatible with the ancient traditions of Iranian culture and civilization. These ways are not even compatible with the traditions and culture of the very societies that have them. Even there [the West] the people are frequently discontented with these ways. This new system is the guarantor of the daily growth of morals and culture of all Iranians and the preservation of individual and social freedoms. It is not synonymous with unbridled perverse chaos [produced by these ways in the West].[50]

This emphasis on nativization was at the core of the regime's new ideological crusade against the West's modernities and ideologies. It sought to free itself from them and provide a nativist ideology that promised a modernity based on the authenticity of native culture and identity and thus superior to those propagated by the West. Rastakhiz proclaimed:

> Since we are not enslaved to the limits of any one 'ism' or ideology that is the result of the thought of a minority and groups that backed foreign beliefs and are interested only in protecting their dogmatic beliefs. We act only in the general interest and on the basis of respect for individuals, individual freedoms, and non-exploitation of people.[51]

The Great Civilization, therefore, promised the Iranian people a worldly modernist paradise that replicated Western economic and technological development but within the ancient framework of Iranian authenticity. This paradise would be constructed by the ancient imperial monarchy under the shah's revolutionary leadership.

On a political level the shah hoped that these three principles and their supporting discourses would provide the framework for his attainment of two goals that were to a degree contradictory given the overall nature of his rule. On the one hand, Rastakhiz, propagating the march towards the Great Civilization and the struggle against the West's imperialism, was to strengthen unity and mobilize the masses behind the imperial system. On the other hand, the shah, hoping to lessen political discontent, sought to provide an enlarged political space that allowed for criticism of socio-economic and cultural issues and discussions about their causes and possible management and resolution. He even stated: 'We are gradually moving towards a society in which the people will be able to choose their leaders', meanwhile the Party would be 'the largest representative of the belief in the people's participation in the country's affairs'.[52] Yet, the shah, by stressing that 'the Party must struggle against any negative tendencies and extremism', also underlined the tensions between these two goals and the boundaries of that popular participation and criticism whose fluidity was determined by him.[53]

The shah was attempting to find a middle path between genuine constitutionalism and hard authoritarianism and manage the growing challenge of mass politics. Finding this panacea would be difficult. A vital step in this process was reform of the meaning of loaded terms, such as 'democracy'. The shah implicitly confessed to this:

> As I have said, within the Party debates and discussions are taking place. Democracy, what does this word mean? If I correctly remember when the Greeks invented democracy, the meaning was public debate and discussions in the city's public arena. These public discussions right now take place not only in base of the Party, but also in the public arena. ... This is democracy.[54]

Yet, he also announced: 'The Party will follow my views. ... We are in the process of creating a political party and administration of the kingdom that will study my opinions and ideology, and the Party, accordingly, ... will implement my opinions and ideology'.[55] Certainly, this remark did not mean the monarch was abandoning the transformative goals behind the Party's establishment. Rather, it shows that he was not prepared to tolerate criticism of his overall policies, the direction in which he was taking the country, and the extent of his power. The remark also reflects the powerful and comprehensive role the shah envisaged for the Party.

Hoping to counter foreign criticism of his one-party system and possible private misgivings held by Iranians, the shah emphasized that given his special role, his one-party system fundamentally differed from other one-party systems, especially in the USSR and communist bloc.

> You know that in my country I do not occupy a political position. I am the country's leader and my position is higher than any political party. I have the ability to enforce objective competition amongst the people. In other political systems when a political figure imposes a one-party system the conditions emerge which you consider dictatorial or oppression of the people, etc. But a king is superior and beyond these things.

In other words, the shah, enjoying a spiritual emotive link with the people and history and hovering above society, free from attachment to any specific socio-economic or political group, would defend the interests and rights of all, ensuring social justice while protecting the country's cultural and geopolitical borders. He added that another reason for the superiority of this system over those of the West was its capacity 'to prevent the outbreak of political and social chaos' and 'licentiousness'.[56]

In an attempt to reconcile these two goals or rather blunt these contradictions, the shah, after the spring 1975 elections to the 24th Majles, the first of the Rastakhiz period, announced the establishment of two competing wings under the Rastakhiz umbrella. Hoveyda, as party head, held a working conference (8–9 July 1975) at the Hotel Intercontinental (today's Laleh International Hotel) to work out the details. In his conference speech he outlined the dynamics of these wings.

> Within the party framework these wings will be representatives of the variations of popular thought and opinion. Any thought or opinion that has a root in our culture will be respected within these wings. ... But it is necessary that I underline that the Party's general secretary, given his responsibility to preserve party unity, will not belong to or be dependent on any particular wing; nor will the prime minister ... since according to the Constitution he is chosen by the shah. Clearly, the arena of these wings' activities, whose goals are the country's progress, will be within the Party so that the Party can take inspiration from the interaction and confrontation of these competing ideas and beliefs. ... In the Party's opinion none of the wings is superior or enjoys privileges that the other does not. These wings' fundamental duty is the intellectual and mental mobilization of the people within the party framework and the strengthening and development of constructive and fundamental dialogue. ... But don't forget, not even for a moment, that having a position in a wing will not divide us against each other but rather increase and strengthen our bonds on the basis of respect for each other's opinions and to the benefit of Iranian society.[57]

This limited opportunity to participate in criticism, recognize publicly problems and make policy recommendations was to mobilize the youth and the increasingly large educated and urban classes around the monarchy. At the same time the Party's proclaimed duty of recognizing and discussing problems and bringing them to the government's attention was to strengthen the state's link with society and prove to the masses that a channel for conveying their concerns and problems and a mechanism to pressure the government to act, at least in theory, existed.

Jamshid Amuzegar became head of 'The Progressive Wing' (*Jenah-e Taraqikhah*) and Hushang Ansari, head of 'The Liberal Constructive Wing' (*Jenah-e Liberal-e Sazande*). At the time, Amuzegar was interior minister while Ansari was minister of the economy. When Amuzegar subsequently became party leader he was replaced by Abdolmajid Majidi. Ansari remained in his position until late spring 1978. Sometime later these names changed, becoming just the Progressive Wing (*Jenah-e Pishro*) and Constructive Wing (*Jenah-e Saazande*). It took these wings several months to organize and become active. The policy differences between the two while minimal reflected official attempts to include various streams in public opinion. According to party publications, the Constructive Wing opted for a liberal economic policy that privileged industrialization, technological advancement and economic growth, while the Progressive one pushed for a socially progressive agenda that privileged social welfare and justice with an emphasis on mass political participation. By winter 1975 they were regular actors on the political scene. Rastakhiz publications show that the wings' political activity and policy recommendations, when they were made, were not substantive; they were slight variations on overall party themes and positions. These publications devoted much more space to all-Party activities and announcements, such as the membership drive, the expansion of party groups and committees, the anti-profiteering campaign and the struggle against Occidentosis. However, on the occasion of important party gatherings and meetings and in response to specific events the wings' leaders expressed strong views situated within the Party's overall approach.

The existence of these two wings, nonetheless, created worries about unity. The fear was that they would provide momentum and an institutional framework to factional fighting between the increasingly rancorous elite groups. Factional infighting was certainly exacerbated with the appointment of these two men: 'Both Amuzegar and Ansari, with little if any regard to party issues or manifestos immediately set about trying to attract well-known people to their respective wings'.[58] The shah, having noticed this increase in factional fighting, ordered that the wings could not constitute political factions within the Majles and take opposing positions on bills. Party divisions on bills and policy were not to be expressed in the Majles. Rather, they would first debate legislative bills only within the party. The shah stated:

> The Party's wings and their names are there so that dialogue takes place. Otherwise, if you want the truth, I would say that perhaps 10, 15 or even 100 different forms of opinion and thought exist – they can be expressed them within the Party and party groups. But all these thoughts cannot form a majority. For example, 10 different beliefs cannot comb together a majority of several million. Differences in thought, ideas, opinions and taste must gradually become more brief and abridged

so that they are expressed within the confines of the two wings and the shape of two opinions. This is a natural process. Even in those countries which we say are so-called democratic more than two main parties don't exist. We want this within the confines of the Rastakhiz Party that is inclusive of the Iranian people. In other words, just as in a big family debate and wrangling takes place, the Party is one big national family. Within the limits of that family it is possible and necessary to debate and discuss without drawing swords and chopping each other's heads off.[59]

Institutions

Soon after the announcement of the Party's establishment, a recruitment campaign was launched. Criteria were simple and straightforward: Iranian nationality, eighteen years of age and a clean legal record. Rastakhiz publications proclaimed ever new victories in this recruitment drive. It was strongest in mid-sized and large urban areas and places of work, while it was weakest in rural areas and among the various tribes. By 1976 the Party claimed a membership of six million. After this initial period, membership numbers increased, but more slowly. Registration was the only proof of being a member. Interestingly, membership cards were not issued. Therefore, 'it was not clear who was a member and who was not'. According to Homayoun membership procedures were neither forced nor needed.[60]

The shah, pleased with these statistics, nonetheless modified his initial opinion.

> The issue of quantity of members is not relevant because everyone making up the Iranian nation must become a member. Thus, I don't accept the word 'quantity'. The Party is all-encompassing. We must recognize all Iranians as its members. In any case, any person who does not accept party principles and the Revolution's provisions have, in my opinion, a defective brain or a wish for the country's domination by foreigners. No healthy and logical person, I imagine, would reject the importance of the country's continued existence.[61]

The First Party Congress approved the Party's institutional structure that was organized as a pyramid. The shah stood above the central governing organs – the Central Committee, Executive Committee, Political Office and General Secretaryship. They, in turn, stood over local party committees and organizations whose numbers were greater given their countrywide coverage (Figure 4).[62]

The institution in which the top and successively lower levels of this pyramid came together was the party Congress held every four years. Deputies were chosen by local party cells. However, three congresses were held in the period 1975–8 due to changing political and social conditions. The Congress was, in principle, the highest party organ, determining the overall course and content of party policies and procedures and approving changes to party doctrine and constitution. Theoretically it elected the general secretary to four-year terms. In reality the shah chose him and the Congress rubber-stamped the appointment. It was a mechanism for the political education of

Figure 4 Opening ceremony of the Party's Central Committee. Conducting the inaugural prayer is Majles deputy and cleric Gholamhossein Daneshi. He was executed after the Revolution.

cadres, their mobilization and propagating the Party's activities and populist character. Ultimately, similar to party congresses in the USSR and other communist countries, it was to be a showcase of party and national unity and an expression of support for the country's leadership while its pronouncements and promises were to mobilize the cadres and the masses in defence of the imperial system in the face of Western conspiracies and Occidentosis-ridden fifth columnists.

The Central Committee was made up of selected members of local party committees who served two-year terms. Its chairman, who was elected by its members, had the responsibility for convening it meetings, although the general secretary had the power to call special sessions. At least two sessions a year were to be held. The Central Committee's main duty was the approval of the code of ethics and procedures of local committees and the supervision of their activities which included the propagation of party activities and discourses, local mass mobilization, and the holding of dialogue sessions with socio-economic and professional groups about local issues and problems.

The Executive Committee, whose membership included the general secretary, his deputies and fifteen members from the Central Committee, met once a month. It was the highest all-Party organ operating between party congresses and convenings of the Central Committee. One of its more vital functions was setting the political and policy framework in which the Political Office carried out its duties. The Executive Committee also chose the fifteen party members, other than the general secretary, who sat in this office. Given its links with the Central Committee and lower party organizations the Executive Committee provided the Political Office with data on problems and challenges needing party and government attention. Given these varied responsibilities, the Executive Committee had to meet at least once a month. Amuzegar chaired its regular meetings. When he became Party head, Ahmad Qoreishi assumed this position.

The Political Office had two major responsibilities. It was charged with the establishment and supervision of party commissions and committees that dealt with internal party issues and/or issues that had made their way up from local party organizations. The Political Office was also responsible for the harmonization and coordination of policy positions of the party and government. Chaired by the prime minister and convened at least once a month, its membership included the party general secretary and his deputies, several cabinet ministers, two deputies from the Majles and the imperial senate who were charged with harmonizing activities between the Party and the legislative branch, and sixteen members of the Executive Committee. The Party held a slight majority over government representatives in order to ensure party hegemony. In sum, the Political Office was the most important party organ responsible for policy and decision making.

The general secretary, according to the Rastakhiz constitution, was 'responsible for all party administration and the highest party executive'. The maximum number of terms that could be served was two. One issue that dogged this post was whether one person should simultaneously be party head and prime minister. Resolution of this issue was important in determining the dynamic of the relationship between the government and the Party. Was the Party to be only the government's cheerleader or should the Party criticize it and be the public conduit through which public discontent should be expressed? This is discussed below.

Local party centres, village councils, city councils and larger province councils (*kanun*) were the backbone of the Party's countrywide coverage. They were to play a key role in the expansion of the links between the centralized state and the population by holding dialogue sessions on a local level with the masses to identity problems and offer policy recommendations. They were also the backbone for local mass mobilization. They became active in this regard towards the end of 1977 with varying degrees of success.

At the forefront of party activities and propaganda were the special party committees and seminars. They were formed to great fanfare, frequently after local dialogue sessions, to deal with concerns and problems expressed by public opinion. Their role was key in proving the Party's responsiveness to public opinion and role as leader in bringing issues causing discontent to the government's attention. In this last capacity these committees assumed the responsibility not only of criticism of government performance but also of the implicit supervision of its response to these issues. Committees were established to deal with issues ranging from profiteering and corruption to traffic and education. Within the first eight months of the Party's existence ninety-two such committees were established. By the middle of 1976 they had increased to 140.[63] Given their prominent public role and the public support these committees could generate, the wings initially struggled with each other over control of them. Eventually Hoveyda issued a directive that these committees could not be attached to any wing.[64]

The shah in an interview with *Rastakhiz* two weeks after it started publication stressed that the Party had to pay special attention to the youth:

> I consider it necessary that the Iranian people and particularly the youth can imagine and picture for themselves the scenic panorama of the Great Civilization. … Dialogue with the young must start. The Party can have youth organizations and many (of the members of such organizations) can become linked to the Rastakhiz Party, even those who have not yet reached the age criteria for full membership.[65]

The Party therefore had several organizations devoted to this group: The Congress of Pupils, made up of high school students who would eventually become party members, the student organization was devoted to university students and the youth organization was open to young urban and agricultural workers. On the one hand, the Party portrayed itself as not only a representative and defender of youth interests in society and the educational system but also a mechanism for the recognition and amelioration of problems afflicting them, from education to personal issues. On the other hand, the Party dedicated itself to the youth's proper political education and mobilization around the state and its immunization in the face of competing Western ideologies and, in the opinion of the shah, reactionary clerics.

Hoveyda was appointed to a two-year term as the first general secretary, while remaining prime minister. However, after eighteen months in October 1976, the shah removed him from this party post. He remained prime minister until August 1977. Several reasons prompted this move. Hoveyda had jumped into party activities, although he did not wish to see the Party become a strong political force. Nonetheless, while trying to strengthen party institutions, he also sought to mould them to bolster and institutionalize his power position. His appointment of his loyal cadres from Iran Novin to top Rastakhiz positions created the impression that he was striving to transform it into his own fiefdom. The shah, SAVAK and others in the elite became increasingly concerned. The fear was that the same inertia that played a key role in the decision to establish the Rastakhiz Party would once again emerge.

SAVAK, which provided the shah every three months (unless circumstances dictated otherwise) analysis about the Party, on 22 May 1975 noted:

> The selection of Mr. (Fereydoun) Mahdavi to the position of deputy general secretary of Rastakhiz by the prime minister shows that he is again filling the top positions of the Rastakhiz Party with his former Iran Novin colleagues. The people expected that Rastakhiz's leadership positions would be filled with new people from academic, cultural, education spheres. However, again these groups have been forgotten, as they were in the past. One dare says that the Iran Novin Party is in reality wearing the clothes of the Rastakhiz Party. Mr. Mahdavi has no

background in politics. The people believe that the prime minister wants only to protect his face and keep up appearances.⁶⁶

SAVAK reports to the shah frequently spoke of 'the Hoveyda faction' (*band-e aqa-ye Hoveyda*). Similar complaints from other people also reached the monarch. In autumn 1975, Mohammad Baheri, a close political ally of Alam, his deputy in the Ministry of the Court and the Court's representative to the Political Office, wrote in his report to Alam and the shah that the Party and particularly its Political Office were not performing well. Fundamental organizational and ideological issues were not being addressed while the activities of the top party leadership could be summed up as 'all for show and deception and charlatanism (*suratbazi va hoqebazi*)'. This report infuriated the shah since his new project was already showing signs of stagnation and traditional factional politicking, led by Hoveyda and his clique from Iran Novin. Through Alam the monarch ordered Baheri 'to go on the attack and deal with these issues'.⁶⁷ In a subsequent report, one among a growing chorus of complaints about Hoveyda, Baheri wrote to the shah: 'Since the head of the Rastakhiz Party unfortunately still thinks he is the head of the Iran Novin Party ... he is unwilling to understand and accept the new needed ways of constructing and managing the Rastakhiz Party'.⁶⁸ Alam, not willing to pass an opportunity to weaken his old rival, tactfully urged on the shah the opinion that 'those old ringleaders of the Iran Novin Party must abandon' the Rastakhiz Party because 'they neither have a good name or popularity among the people'.⁶⁹

Alam, Baheri and SAVAK did have a point. The Party had been established with the hope of strengthening popular interest and participation in politics by offering channels for ground-level activity and criticism of government (in)action. However, the emergence of old political faces, particularly from the Iran Novin Party, created the impression that perhaps the old politics and approach had just been wrapped in new Rastakhiz packaging. Another major SAVAK report was particularly condemning of Hoveyda's management style.

> Before the establishment of the Rastakhiz Party, the people had become desperate due to the oppression, unfairness and prejudices and favoritism of the Iran Novin Party. A large number of the youth and intellectuals were thoroughly dissatisfied with these conditions and thus went into a form of solitude and seemingly had no [political] refuge or home. Jobs and responsibilities were divided among a well-known group of members of the [Iran Novin] party. [Thus] cynicism, disappointment and despair imposed themselves on the people's hearts. However, the establishment of the Rastakhiz movement gave hope to those seeking to serve the Shah. ... They were prepared, with complete interest and desire, to place their expertise and experience at the disposal of their compatriots. But, with full regret, events are evolving in such a way that in the Rastakhiz era those same cadres of the Iran Novin Party have taken over to such a great extent that now a large number of youth and intellectuals hold the belief that the Rastakhiz Party is the old Iran Novin Party, but with a fancy new name, therefore in reality nothing has changed. After all, now both posts and jobs are in the hands of the cadres of the old Iran Novin Party.

This analysis was approved higher up the SAVAK chain:

> The excessive degree of the presence and influence of cadres of the dissolved Iran Novin Party in the Rastakhiz Party has led to old programs and approaches being repeated and thus a large number of people, wishing to serve shah and country, now seek refuge in political solitude and periphery. In this regard it is necessary to draw the attention of those with high-office to this issue so that the horrific ogre (*hayoola-ye vashatnak*) of the Iran Novin Party does not consume and engulf the society of Rastakhiz.[70]

Faced with this situation the shah removed Hoveyda. He explained his decision by announcing that political effectiveness required that one person must not simultaneously be prime minister and party leader.

Hoveyda's replacement was Jamshid Amuzegar whose first term lasted from September 1976 to August 1977. Amuzegar, educated in the United States, was a member of Mansur's Progressive Circle and thus was an early member of Iran Novin. He nonetheless was never an ally of Hoveyda, while Hoveyda from the beginning of the 1970s increasingly viewed him as a serious threat to his position as prime minister. In 1965 he was appointed finance minister, a position he held until 1974 when he became interior minister. According to SAVAK documents he had a reputation for being very pro-American. He was a leading member of the Council of American-Educated (Iranians) that concentrated on the strengthening of economic and cultural ties with the United States and sought to use these ties to advance members' positions in factional struggles. He enjoyed a special relationship with the US ambassador to Iran, Armin Meyer (1965–9). SAVAK, which referred to this group as the American faction (*band-e Amrikaii*) expressed worry about these ties. The shah therefore entertained some early concerns that played a role in damaging Amuzegar's chances to replace Hoveyda at the end of the 1960s.[71] Nonetheless, Amuzegar from 1965 was an advisor to the shah and Iran's representative to OPEC, a position that came with the post of finance minister. He played a key role in implementing the shah's plans for increases in oil prices in 1971, 1973 and 1974. As a result, the shah awarded him the Order of the Crown, First Class and allowed him to remain the country's OPEC representative despite his move to the Interior Ministry. Amuzegar's position on the oil question and attacks on Western, and in particular United States, opposition to rises in the price of oil, which included charges of imperialism, positively influenced the shah's views of him in the early 1970s.[72]

Amuzegar, who had entertained hopes to become prime minister, was surprised by his appointment to the party chairmanship. He was also fearful of assuming this responsibility. In a private conversation with Sabeti, held on Amuzegar's initiative, he confessed his worries: 'I have no experience or background in a political party'.[73] This was an implicit confession that he was a technocrat, not a politician. Many in the elite held this opinion of him.[74] In response to Amuzegar's solicitation for advice, Sabeti stated that the Rastakhiz Party was a nationalist party designed to mobilize the people around the throne and state: 'The raising of nationalism must be the Party's ideological pillar.' One of the key approaches to mobilizing nationalist feelings in this framework was 'to recognize and publicly discuss society's problems' in order to strengthen the link between the state and the masses.[75] Once the people felt that the state was responsive to their concerns and problems, political tensions would lower. However, Sabeti's opinion of him and his management style was not high: He was 'arrogant, selfish, and generally unpleasant'. He was unable to connect with people. Sabeti also notes that their relationship was not good since Amuzegar, unfairly, considered him part of the Hoveyda faction.[76]

Whether Amuzegar acted on this advice or not, his first tenure as party head saw an increase in the propagation of discourses of anti-West Occidentalism that had emerged during the Hoveyda period. Amuzegar himself took aim at the West's ideologies, stressing that they had exhausted themselves and could not provide an example for Iran. In his first public speech as party head he announced: 'Today's world is no longer the world of ideology [of the West], but rather of technology.' '–isms' no longer ruled. As prime minister he would explicitly blame the West for the country's economic problems.

In early August 1977 the shah removed Hoveyda as prime minister and replaced him with Amuzegar. Hoveyda became minister of court, taking over from the dying Alam. By this time the Pahlavi state was facing increasing domestic economic and political problems. Expectations were that Amuzegar's deputy, Homayoun, would assume the top party post. However, the monarch's choice fell on Mohammad Baheri who was not a party deputy leader. This created a problem that was solved with bureaucratic fudging.

Baheri's background in party politics and organization brought much to this position. A native of Shiraz, in his youth he was a member of the Shiraz Tudeh Party when it emerged in the mid-1940s. During his time in Tudeh he played a leading role in the management of its publications. In the aftermath of the party's banning, he went to Paris to study law. He returned to Iran in the summer of 1953. During his time abroad the author and politician Rasul Parvizi, a close friend from his Tudeh days, became close to Alam.[77] Through this connection Baheri was able to establish a close political and personal relationship with this powerful figure at the top of the power pyramid that lasted until Alam's death in 1977 (Figure 5).

Upon his return Baheri became a professor at Tehran University and an active member of Alam's Mardom Party, holding responsibility for the party's youth organization, propaganda and newspaper. As director of the Imperial Inspectorate for Higher Education and Research, a post he obtained in 1970, he was deeply involved in trying to shape and reform higher education policy, professionalize the educational system and improve relations between the state and the burgeoning student population. For example, he was known for writing extensive reports for the annual Conferences on the Revolution in Education presided over by the imperial couple.[78]

During Alam's premiership (1962–4) he served as his deputy and minister of justice. When Alam became minister of court he moved with him, serving as his deputy. From the mid-1960s to his appointment to head of the Rastakhiz Party he held several posts that influenced his politics in Rastakhiz. From 1962 he was a cultural and social advisor to the Pahlavi Foundation and from 1970 he was a member of the Executive Committee of the Foundation of the Culture of Iran, among other posts.

Figure 5 Mohammad Baheri, centre, Hushang Nahavandi, right. Rastakhiz, author's collection.

From 1977 he was senior advisor to the empress, and representative of the Ministry of Court to the Supreme Council of the Guardians of the Revolution. In sum, Baheri was a state ideologue and technocrat with leftist tendencies and deep experience with party matters. He was intensely loyal to the shah. For example, when he joined the Party's Political Office he asked the shah about the wing he should join. The monarch responded that he did not care; it was his own decision.[79] Both the question and answer show the degree of importance given to these wings.

The appointment to the top party post surprised Baheri. He initially thought that Alam had persuaded the monarch to select him. However, he told Baheri that he had played no role in the shah's choice.[80] The shah voluntarily told Baheri that he chose him because he was 'not affiliated or dependent on any faction or person'.[81] This was a strange remark since Baheri was a leading member of the Alam faction and did not have a good relationship with Hoveyda whom he blamed for the stagnation of the two-party system and for failing to provide effective leadership to the Rastakhiz Party.[82] For example, Baheri who attended the monthly meetings of the Executive Committee and the Political Office stressed in a post-revolutionary interview that during the Hoveyda period these meetings and thus institutions were only small talking shops: 'Nothing really happened at these meetings'.[83]

The shah, seemingly recognizing these institutional bottlenecks and even inertia, told Baheri that he should solicit advice from Parviz Nikkhah in regard to the Party's organization, management and ideological issues.[84] This is another telling example of the Pahlavi state's use of repentant leftists. Nikkhah, who completed his medical studies in Britain, had been a leading member of the Confederation of Iranian Students that had emerged in Western Europe and the United States, and of the Marxist Revolutionary Organization. He was sent to prison for distant links to the plot to assassinate the shah in 1965. Once he renunciated his leftist past, thanks to familial links with the elite he was able to obtain a meeting with the monarch and then early release from prison in 1968. The shah remarked after seeing him that he did not think Nikkah was a killer. During his time in prison he became a revolutionary hero among leftists, a position he lost when he became a political analyst with NIRT, criticized Soviet Marxism, Maoism and leftist revolutionaryism in broadcasts and, specifically, urged the young to abandon revolutionary opposition and cooperate with the Pahlavi state in building a new Iran.

Baheri also had little time for Amuzegar. When Amuzegar, just appointed prime minister, contacted him, he believed that perhaps the new prime minister wanted him to enter his cabinet. After the Revolution Baheri underlined that he would not have accepted any position in the Amuzegar government because 'I just did not like him.' His problems with Amuzegar were, seemingly, political and factional. When the two wings were established Alam asked Baheri to help Ansari in strengthening his wing in opposition to that of Amuzegar. Baheri, who had little, if any, confidence in these two men nonetheless obliged since seemingly Alam was moving towards Ansari given Amuzegar's seeming ascendency.[85]

Baheri had a poor estimation of Amuzegar's tenure as party head. 'Amuzegar was not at all suitable for party work and felt no commitment to party issues. He also did not have any confidence in the people' which was a prerequisite for party work.[86] In this regard Sabeti voiced a similar opinion: 'Amuzegar himself understood he had little of the capabilities needed for the position and did not have the necessary talent. ... He was not a social person.'[87] According to Baheri, during this period, 'the Party transformed into a set of administrative institutions, into a bureaucratic entity' that in his view could not play the mobilizing force the shah wanted.[88] Qoreishi, deputy of the Executive Committee, agreed: 'Amuzegar was not a political or social person. He granted very limited access to Rastakhiz members, deputies, and the people. ... He sat there and read OPEC files and did OPEC-related work. He never took the Party seriously and never took Party work seriously.'[89] The Party was becoming relatively rudderless.

Baheri seeking to portray his appointment as the beginning of a new active period in the Party's life as party leader did not solicit advice from his two predecessors.[90] With implicit criticism of his predecessors, he implemented institutional changes designed to make the party administratively effective and expand its links with the people. According to Qoreishi, 'Baheri was political and liked going after the government and was a good speaker, as well as a social person. He established contact with the people.'[91] Importantly, he paid great attention to the infrastructure and content of party propaganda and publications and appeared more frequently at public meetings, rallies and on television than did Hoveyda or Amuzegar. During his tenure Rastakhiz publications increased the number and intensity of the discourses of anti-West Occidentalism that focused on the threat of Occidentosis and Western imperialism.

Baheri noted that at the time he believed in 'an effective propaganda machine and campaign' that paid 'more attention to Iran's history, the role of the imperial system in national unity and the role of the shahs in the production and representation of the characteristics of Iranian culture'.[92] In other words, cultural borders constituted the first front in the struggle against the West's imperialism. His attention to this front was framed by his belief, common among the Pahlavi elite, that 'foreign countries' played key roles in provoking Iranian students and creating disturbances across the country's campuses.[93]

In order to create this effective propaganda mechanism Baheri established the Committee for Leadership of Education and Propaganda (*Komite-ye rahbari-ye Amuzesh va Tabliq*). Headed by one of Baheri's deputies, Vadiei, its duty, as indicated by its title, was 'the determination and guiding of the Party's political education and propaganda'. It was to meet at least once a month. Its membership included leading party and non-party figures.[94] This committee had several sub-committees: (a) committee for propaganda planning; (b) committee for theoretical issues and those related to political education; (c) committee for domestic policy; (d) committee for foreign policy; and (e) committee for cultural and art policy. They were incorporated into a coordinating council.[95]

One of the key practical political issues was the determination of the relationship between the government, headed by the prime minister, and the Party, headed by the general secretary. The shah did not envisage that the Party's executive and institutional power would exceed that of the government headed by the prime minister. Yet, he indicated that the Party would hover above and encapsulate society, representing a whole while the government would be limited to politics and policy implementation. Rastakhiz would play the key role in promoting national unity and mobilizing the masses while being a conduit for public concerns and grievances to the government. Moreover, its programmes of political and ideological education would be the production line of *homo Pahlavicus* and thus of correctly politicized and ideologized state cadres. In the meantime, it would also be a source for policymaking and recommendations. When the shah stressed that 'the government belongs to the Rastakhiz Party' whose main goal and duty is the strengthening of 'national unity' he was not talking about their power relationship.[96] Rather, he was stating that the Party, through its programmes of political and ideological education, would come to own the government ideologically and politically. However, to a significant extent the discussion was academic since the Crown was the supreme leader of both party and government. Nonetheless, the framework outlining the theoretical and practical relationship between these two institutions needed to be established. Was the Party to be critic or cheerleader? The shah never made a final decision in this regard and therefore gave additional momentum to factional and personal struggles.

Hoveyda was not receptive to the idea of serious and directed Rastakhiz criticism of government performance. In a speech to the Majles he stressed that the government was above the Party and added that it did not have a major role to play either in policy or administration. He considered the Party a mechanism limited to mobilizing people around the government.[97] In other words, Hoveyda's position mirrored that of his approach to the role of the Mardom Party under the old system. In this respect Baheri offered a telling example. During Hoveyda's tenure, Baheri took a lead in organizing party meetings dedicated to recognizing problems and the government's policy reaction to them. Hoveyda became angry. Telephoning Baheri, he ordered a cessation of these activities. Baheri too became angry: 'This is not correct or proper and is in reality fractious and divergent (from the Party's goals and duties).' Despite these remonstrances, Hoveyda continued to insist he put an end to these meetings. Baheri relented but stressed that Hoveyda as head of government could order their closure, but not as party head since Baheri was acting only on the basis of the party's duties and responsibilities.[98] In the opinion of Baheri, Hoveyda's approach to this issue hampered the Party's effectiveness in mobilizing people and serving as a conduit between them and the state.

Amuzegar during his first tenure as party leader sympathized with Hoveyda's position. He argued that the Party and the government did not have parallel relations (*ravabet-e mavazi*). The government was certainly prepared to listen to the Party's opinions on some issues. After all, everyone in the cabinet and government were party members. Yet, the Party was not to interfere in executive and even legislative matters.[99] Importantly, Amuzegar, despite becoming Party leader, accepted Hoveyda's offer to remain in the cabinet as interior minister. Hoveyda understood that through retention of Amuzegar in the cabinet he could limit any party moves to assume the role as critic of the government. At the same time, Amuzegar's acceptance of the offer showed the extent to which he took the Party seriously.

However, during Amuzegar's tenure the Committee of Political Education, of which Baheri was a member, announced that the Party 'as the voice of the people and organization that includes all will have supervisory powers over the government while the government maintains its constitutional executive powers and on that basis would perform its duties'.[100] In this respect the Party established an *Ombudsman* that would solicit popular complaints about government performance, among other issues, review them and then pass them onto the government. Amuzegar, not pleased with these moves, sought to contain party criticism of the government. He feared the emergence of political divisions and even competition between party and government and was wary of whipping up public opinion by drawing attention to problems and issues the government had not sufficiently addressed. In this regard he and his party deputy Homayoun had a difference of opinion.

Homayoun believed that the Party, in order to enjoy political and popular relevance, had to be critical when discussing government performance.[101] This position, however, did not mean that Homayoun believed that the Party should involve itself in the inner workings of the government and Majles: 'The Party is not the successor of the government or Majles.' He nonetheless envisioned a supervisory and nationally unifying role for the Party that required it act as a conduit between the people and government. It would also review the actions of the government and the Majles, ensuring that deviations from the will of the shah and people, as determined by the Party, were corrected. Lastly, he believed that the Party had to lead the fight against corruption and inefficient and incompetent bureaucrats since in the previous decades the bureaucracy and executive institutions had failed to carry out their duties in this regard.[102] If the Party played these roles political tension and discontent would decrease while criticism of conditions would be deflected from the monarchy onto the government, strengthening the monarchy's position as a seeming supra-political positive force.

Baheri's position on this issue also differed from that of Amuzegar.

> The Rastakhiz Party is a political organization that has no similarity with the world's other political organizations. Therefore, the example of the relationship between the Rastakhiz Party and government and Majles also cannot have any similarity with the relationship between these government institutions and political parties in other countries. ... The fundamental principle is that the Party can in no way share with the government responsibility for governing or interfere in the work of the Majles. The Party must be only a mechanism for the transfer of popular wishes, thoughts and opinions to governmental institutions-executive as well as legislative.

He left open the possibility that bills put forth in the Majles could be initially proposed by the Party. Baheri believed that while the role of policy implementation was beneath the Party's dignity, it did have the responsibility for debating and offering legislative proposals. Moreover, he was a strong supporter of the idea that the Party was the only path for transferring to the government the people's wishes and opinions. In such conditions, no need existed for the Party to interfere directly in the work of the Majles or government.[103]

Baheri's understanding of the Party's role and responsibilities created tension in his relationship with Amuzegar. Looking back at that period Baheri noted:

> The Party was to provide inspiration and guidance to the government and parliament. Majles members needed to take guidance from the Party. ... [However] we didn't see one government decision or policy for which the Party had been asked to provide an opinion. None. ... The prime minister did not want it. ... The government did not want someone or something to become its partner.[104]

Frustrated with this approach of the Amuzegar government, Baheri went to the shah and argued that the government should, at least at the level of the Political Office, discuss with the Party bills and legislation before their being sent to the Majles. The shah agreed. However, several days later Moinian telephoned Baheri, informing him that the decision had been made that the government would send legislation to the Party leadership on the same day it would be sent to the Majles. Baheri, annoyed, asked: 'Where is the usefulness in this? Just to inform us?' Moinian responded that Baheri had to agree that anything the shah said was correct. Baheri naturally accepted this but ended the conversation by saying: 'If we really want to have a Party and have it act as a Party, the Party must discuss it [legislation] before it goes to the Parliament.'

According to Baheri, due to this issue his relationship with the Amuzegar government continued to deteriorate: 'Amuzegar and the government were upset over this position. They were upset that the Party wanted to do something, to become effective, play a role.' Amuzegar was also critical of Baheri's support of seminars devoted to discussing and identifying problems and the Party's role in propagating these issues and informing and pressuring the government in regard to them.[105] SAVAK chimed in on this issue in reports to the shah as tension between Baheri and Amuzegar began to rise. It argued that if the people did not believe that the Party was exercising an influence on government activities it would fail to achieve its primary goals, namely influence in society and garnering of popular support.[106] SAVAK therefore supported Baheri's understanding of the party role. In this context Amuzegar, Hoveyda and Ansari conspired together and orchestrated Baheri's removal and Amuzegar's re-appointment as party head in January 1978. Once again one person held simultaneously the positions of head of party and government.

Rastakhiz publications

A variety of party publications began to appear approximately two months after the Party's establishment. Its official newspaper, *Rastakhiz*, was established on 3 May 1975 under the editorship of Dr Mehdi Semsar (1929–2003). He had completed studies in both pharmacology and journalism at Tehran University. He then obtained a master's degree in political science from the University of Paris and his doctorate in the history of journalism from the University of Toulouse. He had worked for the newspaper *Keyhan* since 1949, eventually becoming its editor in 1967. In 1974 Hovedya pushed him out.[107] The shah, meeting with the newspaper's staff before publication of the first edition, stressed that *Rastakhiz* was the official mouthpiece of his all-encompassing political party, dedicated to propagating his thought and that of his Revolution.[108] Officials and ministers were told that since Rastakhiz publications belonged to the official single Party they needed to respond to requests for interviews and give 'scoops' to them.[109] The newspaper was professionally run and known for a quality that, in the opinion of many, placed it above the two other leading dailies, *Keyhan* and *Ettela'at*.[110] Even a study of the Party recently published in the IRI admitted that 'from the point of view of official interests of that time, this newspaper acquired a notable qualitative and quantitative success'.[111]

The primary mission of *Rastakhiz* was coverage of party activities, goals and ideology. Nonetheless, each issue, containing on average twenty-six pages, offered comparatively in-depth coverage of national and international news, analysis, economic issues, art and culture, sport and a daily page with updates on events and exhibitions, a television guide, cinema listings and crosswords. Pages were also dedicated to politics, party editorial and opinion, and special reports on domestic and international developments and anniversaries, such as the announcement of the White Revolution, the US Bicentennial or important elections in other countries. It was a complete daily newspaper that blended well coverage of the Party with the vast array of areas covered by professional papers not serving as an organ of a political party.

The second publication at the centre of this work is the periodical *The Youth of Rastakhiz (Javanan-e Rastakhiz)* which published its first issue on 22 May 1975. According to party documents it was to be the leading popular intellectual publication, targeting university students as well as intellectuals and the educated class. In its advertisements the magazine introduced itself as 'the journal for intellectuals and the youth'.[112] Dr Mohamamd Ali Zerangar was its director throughout the Rastakhiz period. Having studied medicine and journalism in India and Pakistan he eventually became head of the public relations division of the Iranian consulate in Karachi before returning to Iran. He translated works from Urdu into Persian for the Iranian media and wrote pieces on events such as the shah's visit to Pakistan in 1962. He also became head of the party publishing house and its department for relations with Iranian media.

The magazine however had several editors. The first, Hushang Pourshariati, had experience in journalism dating back to 1957. He started his journalistic career at *Ettela'at* and moved to *Ayandegan* in 1970. His tenure at *The Youth of Rastakhiz* lasted only five months at which time he became head of NIRT's Pars News Agency.[113] He was replaced by Hesam al-din Ashrafizadeh. In the late 1960s he sporadically contributed pieces to *Ferdowsi*. In 1972, while studying medicine at Tehran University, he began to work as a translator of foreign news for NIRT.[114] His arrival at *The Youth of Rastakhiz* was accompanied by changes in its name, which became *Rastakhiz of the Young* (*Rastakhiz-e Javan*) and format.

In August 1977, Baheri as party head replaced Ashrafizadeh with Hossein Sarfaraz. Having studied, but not receiving, his degree in history and geography at the University of Tehran, he entered the world of Iranian journalism in 1956. He soon became the editor of *Omid-e Iran*. During the 1960s he was editor of *Sepide va Siah*, *Khandaniha* and *Tehran Mossaver*, well-known and popular magazines. He was also a poet.[115] Sarfaraz had been a member of the Mardom Party and deputy editor of the party's newspaper. He had failed to become a Majles deputy from his native town, Darab, in the 1971 elections. After the Party's establishment, he joined the staff of *Rastakhiz* as editor of its section on society and social issues. When he became editor the name changed again, reverting to *The Youth of Rastakhiz*.

The Rastakhiz Party also published weekly magazines that targeted other socio-economic groups. *Rastakhiz of the Countryside* (*Rastakhiz-e Rusta*) focused on the peasant and farming class and *Rastakhiz of the Workers* (*Rastakhiz-e Kargaran*) on the working class. These two publications have little importance for this study given their overwhelming attention to issues and challenges the Party considered vital to these socio-economic groups and state interests. Among these issues were not debates over Iranian authenticity. A review of the issues of *Rastakhiz of the Countryside* shows that emphasis was placed on personal hygiene, farming techniques, state agricultural policies, drug addiction, and the activities of Rastakhiz cadres and members of various corps established by the shah to aid in the development of the countryside. The language and syntax were more simple than those of *The Youth of Rastakhiz* – a reflection of the overall education and literacy level of the rustic class.

In place of debates about Iranian authenticity and the West, *Rastakhiz of the Countryside* published articles focusing on members of the imperial family, specifically the shah, the empress, and the crown prince, in a bid to strengthen the cult of the monarchy. Certainly, *The Youth of Rastakhiz* focused on the Pahlavi dynasty, but its monarchical indoctrination was subtle. One noticeable difference between the two was that *Rastakhiz of the Countryside* much more frequently than *The Youth of Rastakhiz* published pictures of the imperial family. Except for several issues during the first six months of its publication, *The Youth of Rastakhiz* did not adorn its covers with photographs of the shah and/or other members of the imperial family.

Rastakhiz of the Workers sporadically and rarely touched on issues of identity – a topic that was discussed primarily in the context of criticism and condemnation of communism. Overwhelming focus was on propagating the shah's socio-economic policies and achievements in raising this class' working and living conditions. Photographs of the shah and/or the imperial family decorated the cover of this publication more often than the cover of *The Youth of Rastakhiz* but less often than that of *Rastakhiz of the Countryside*. Despite these differences, all three publications placed great emphasis on their role and that of party cadres in identifying and relaying the concerns and problems of these socio-economics groups to the government.[116] Fundamentally these two journals were designed to establish 'civilized' norms, teaching good hygiene, civilized public behaviour, proper child rearing and the aesthetic side of everyday life.

The Thought of Rastakhiz (*Andisheha-ye Rastakhiz*), a tri-monthly journal first published in August 1976, targeted party cadres. Adapting a philosophical character, it devoted its articles to theoretical and abstract issues touching on the Party. It had the lowest print run of any party publication. It had a total of eight issues. Similar in character was the monthly publication *The Philosophical Foundation of Rastakhiz* (*Mabna-ye falsafe-ye Rastakhiz*) that began publication at the end of January 1978. It has a run of only several issues before being closed down. The journal *Talash*, which before the Rastakhiz period was published under Hoveyda's guidance, fell under party supervision in September 1975. *Talash*, however, was not a specific party publication dedicated to propagation of the official ideology as were the newspaper *Rastakhiz* and *The Youth of Rastakhiz*. It never achieved any degree of popularity.[117]

The following chapters examine Rastakhiz discourses on the authenticity of Iranian culture and national identity and the place of the West within it that appeared in these publications. Farhang Mehr, member of the Executive Committee and head of Pahlavi University in Shiraz, in an editorial for *Rastakhiz* outlined the party approach to this issue. Encapsulating elements of previous chapters, it helps set the tone for this study's remaining chapters.

> The main cause for the confusion and disorder in the period between the (1906) Constitutional Revolution and the Revolution of Shah and People was the lack of clear recognition of national objectives and poverty of political ideology. ... The White Revolution is an Iranian Revolution born of Iranian thought and implemented by Iranian hands and is not derivative of any foreign example.

While it was 'possible to adapt technology and industry from the West', objectives, aspirations, culture and mores had to remain Iranian. Given this requirement,

> our ideology must be linked to common national thought, feelings, culture, history and characteristics. Such elements cannot and must not be adapted from other peoples. ... This ideology ... is a unified philosophical system that encompasses all aspects of life-political, economic, cultural, moral, and societal. The fundamental

base of this ideology and national aspirations is national culture and heritage. One of the most important elements of this base was the issue of human rights. Contrary to the West's opinion individual freedoms and respect for human dignity and rights that first appeared in the charter of Cyrus the Great some 2,500 years ago are promised also by the 1906 Constitution and by the character of the Revolution of Shah and People.

The imperial system and the Rastakhiz Party were the vanguard in the crusade against Occidentosis. 'Within this ideological framework non-economic dynamics and human, religious and spiritual characteristics have a special and unique place' in contrast with the materialism, consumerism and atomistic individualism of the West. Looking to the past and the future, 'we do not believe in economic determinism, namely liberal capitalism and communism, in history that is the foundation of Western thought. We believe in the importance of the people's role in history. ... [Thus] we do not subscribe to the idea of the unity of historical processes [in other words in the thesis of the end of history].' The authentically Iranian modernity was the Great Civilization.

> This imperial system is the expression of the [national] characteristics of political culture, social culture and the aspirations and wishes of the Iranian people. In Aryan culture a law named 'Asha' [that is integral to the Zoroastrian faith] teaches us that with authenticity of thought, speaking the truth, and working honestly we will step on the path of truth and development.[118]

8

Rastakhiz Occidentalism: Identity crisis and preservation of authenticity

Hossein Nasr in early March 1978, at ceremonies at Golestan Palace marking the centenary of Reza Shah's birth, delivered a speech about the Pahlavi role in Iran's cultural history. He praised specifically the changes in policy in regard to the issue of authenticity of culture and national identity implemented by the imperial couple during the Rastakhiz period.

> The protection and preservation of culture, along the lines articulated by the shahanshah, are today receiving greater attention from writers, poets, journalists, and artists. ... Cultural activities have been greatly expanded at a time when, as a result of the encounter and clash of Iran's national culture with the West's civilization, culture, and thought a crisis had emerged that necessitated the doubling of strivings in the preservation and resurgence of the authenticity of national culture.

These cultural activities ordered by the shah were to create the conditions that would 'return Iranian society to that authenticity'.[1]

This mission was the Party's since its establishment: 'In our country we have entered a new era in our national resurgence, during which one of the most vital elements is the recognition and protection of our national heritage and authenticity'.[2] Similar to Nasr, Rastakhiz confessed that 'only over recent years has the importance and priority of cultural policy and protection of authenticity greatly increased'.[3] The reasons for this were clear:

> The Revolution and the production of the new Iranian person who, with the preservation of the values and traditions of the past, in the contemporary period work for and look to the future. ... The Revolution of Shah and People over the last fifteen years has given the Iranian people a new fresh spirituality and morale based on Iran's special nationalism and a clear view of the future. Before the Revolution the view of Iranian [identity] was often focused on the past. We lived with and in our past, our pride was that of ancient pre-Islamic Iran. This view to the past was laden with regret and nostalgia which shook the national consciousness. After the Revolution we realized that living only with and in the past was not possible, that it

is necessary to have a new condition. This new consciousness became the catalyst for Iran's economic development whose rate became the fastest in the world. During the Revolution's first ten years this consciousness expired, it came to pass. The slogan of work and only work surely gave strength to the new consciousness, but by the time of the Revolution's second decade this consciousness evolved and became vitally concerned with the preservation of our heritage.[4]

The Rastakhiz period thus was marked not only by economic and developmental resurgence symbolized by the White Revolution but now also by a resurgence of Iranian spirituality and authenticity: 'A revolutionary society more than anything else must enjoy strong spirituality. … The Leader of the Revolution, even before launching it, gave great attention and thought to identity – "Who were we? Who are we? And what shall we become?" … The Revolution of Iran, from its inception, was based on the correct path toward modernization of the ancient society of Iran which is founded on its ancient and accepted traditions and values' in opposition to those of the West.[5]

The tone of Rastakhiz discourses on the authenticity of culture and national identity was set by the shah's and the empress's varied pronouncements and statements while three written works *The Philosophy of the Revolution and Party*, *Single-Party Systems and the Rastakhiz Party of the People of Iran* and *Toward the Great Civilization* expanded and gave them a systematic coherency integrated in a framework common to other modern ideologies. The historiography, philosophy and ideology, including the struggle against imperialism and Occidentosis, propagated by these texts also provided the fundamental elements of new textbooks used in the military forces and civilian bureaucratic institutions.[6] At the centre of these evolved discourses remained the idea of *homo Pahlavicus* whose historical, cultural and social elements underwent revision.

The first change touched on the official meaning of an identity crisis. The cultural revolution initiated by Reza Shah and continued by his son until the early 1960s with the launching of the White Revolution took aim at claimed cultural and social distortions in conceptions of Iranian identity resulting from Arabtosis (*arabzadegi*) and its by-product, the reactionary clergy. These distortions had created a crisis of identity by culturally separating Iranians from their racial cousins, West Europeans. In the Rastakhiz period, however, the cause and consequence of an Iranian identity crisis was Occidentosis. Occupying a central position in Rastakhiz ideology, Occidentosis was propagated as a multifaceted and existential threat to the authenticity of Iranian culture and national identity.[7] Importantly, the Pahlavi state did not retreat from implementation of many elements of the practical process of Westernization that was still regarded as the only path to transforming Iran into a great regional power although the term itself fell out of use.

This chapter examines the narratives surrounding this official recognition of a crisis of identity resulting from Occidentosis, starting with the imperial couple's pronouncements, and including the themes of these three written works. Together they provide a discursive and ideological context for the examination of overall Rastakhiz discourses in subsequent chapters. Without a doubt the shah, and to a lesser extent the empress, played a decisive role in setting the tone and approach of these discourses. However, they could not, nor did they try to, dictate the specific themes, content and tone of the pieces appearing in Rastakhiz publications and speeches made by leading party leaders. Institutions also played a role in either setting the tone of such discourses, such as the Party's Political Office, SCCA, the MCA and the Ministry of Education, or exercising a security role, such as SAVAK. Certainly, the evidence suggests that direct coordination of discourses and policy between them was not fully institutionalized and effective, given bureaucratic and personality clashes. Nonetheless, they acted within the discursive framework established first by the shah and then the empress. On the front line were individual party-state intellectuals and publicists who played key roles in the content, formulation and propagation of these new discourses. The content and tone of the pieces in Rastakhiz publications examined in the following chapters might at times come across as extreme and as having more in common with the rhetoric of the IRI than with perceptions of the Pahlavi state. One could even guess that the shah and the empress would not have agreed with all dimensions of Rastakhiz discourses on these issues. Nonetheless, that Rastakhiz publications would propagate opinions and discourses examined in the following chapters without broad and clear signals from the shah is inconceivable.

Occidentosis and the crisis of identity

Hamid Enayat, in *Culture and Life*, some fifteen months before the Party's establishment noted:

> The cultural war on Occidentosis that over the past decade has become a slogan of intellectuals as well as political figures, has turned into a rationale to stymy attempts to learn or educate about the West. But the definition of Occidentosis is never made clear. ... [Given this] we must at least recognize that struggling against the West's claimed dangerous moral influence requires a correct understanding of the West's culture and civilization. Otherwise, we will be fighting an unknown enemy.[8]

In the Rastakhiz period attempts were undertaken to define officially this Occidentosis. Soon after the Party's establishment the shah sent a directive to Hoveyda in which he stressed that given 'the great social and economic success' achieved by the White Revolution, 'it was now time to focus on philosophy, political education, and the preservation of authenticity'. Having confessed for the first time that an identity crisis resulting from Occidentosis existed, the shah announced:

> I am giving much attention to the issue that our future cannot be based on materialism and technology, but rather on strong spiritual principles that will prevent society from falling into consumerism and materialism. ... The clergy must work on the strengthening of spirituality and belief in God and distinguishing them from the materialistic world.

He held that 'society's material progress must be accompanied by humanistic and spiritual aspects' that together constituted the unique 'Iranian spirituality' (*manaviat-i*

Irani) and a pillar of the authenticity of culture and national identity.[9] In a subsequent speech at Tehran University marking the beginning of the 1976 academic year he elaborated:

> One of the most important goals of the Revolution of Iran is the glorification and exaltation of spirituality and elements belonging to the other world in order to prevent Occidentosis (*qarbzadegi*) and the praise of foreign ways, which the West's era of the machine brings with it, from destroying the essence of Iranian society, turning us into aliens in our own country and ultimately creating non-Iranians from Iranians.[10]

In sum, spirituality and morality, the claimed bases of Iranian authenticity, were threatened by Occidentosis, defined as deceitfully attractive materialism and consumerism spread and underpinned by rampant commercialization that created atomistic individualism and hedonism. Rastakhiz proclaimed: 'We will prevent the emergence of a consumerist and hedonistic society'.[11]

The shah also argued that Western technology represented a threat to spirituality and morality.

> Iranian society and, as whole, societies of the East are reliant on ancient traditions and morals. Now that technology is struggling against some of these traditions and morals, how is it possible to accommodate this technology with them? ... As long as the imperial system exists – it is not some *parvenu* system – technology will be in the service of the people. ... Our traditions will not allow Iranians to become captive and slaves of technology and machines. If people become captives of technology they will become spiritless and unable to understand anything in their life. They will be a lifeless machine. They will resemble Frankenstein. Such a situation means of course the end of civilization and humankind as we know it. ... The thousands of students who go abroad for education and return are subjected to the civilization of foreign countries. We want to say to our youth that they must be able to decide what things are possible to adopt, what things are tolerable to an extent, but, most importantly, what things our Iranianess and innate Iranian characteristics cannot accept. This is the reality – we should take those things that make our lives more comfortable and easy from Western countries without taking on the bad and ugly characteristics of these foreign societies.[12]

In this struggle against Occidentosis, 'one of the benefits we have is our customs and traditions that will not allow an Iranian to become a prisoner of technology', as people had become in the West.[13] 'The taking of modern technology ... does not mean adopting its [the West's] moral characteristics, customs, and rituals'.[14] The shah also repeated the theme increasingly propagated since the second half of the 1960s that the imperial system was both the source and the defender of Iranian spirituality and morality. In its absence Iran would become ridden with Occidentosis and find itself a victim of indirect economic and political imperialism.

The empress too spoke to these themes, issuing warnings about 'the cultural invasion of the foreigner (*hojum-e farhangi-ye biganeh*)' and underlining 'the necessity to protect and strengthen Iranian authenticity (*esalat-e Irani*)'. Stressing this new interpretation of authenticity she argued: 'The more we become familiar with our country's old cultural roots, the more we rely on ourselves and the less we are influenced by different cultures that attack us'.[15] Speaking at the Farah Pahlavi Foundation she pushed for practical action: 'This foundation must devise more plans for the protection of cultural values, Iranian morality, and implement measures for the spread of its recognition among social groups'.[16] After all

> This authenticity has enjoyed an amazing durability and continuation that over the last fifty generations has passed from one generation to another. ... This heritage allows the adoption of limited concepts of modernization while protecting the spiritual essence of Iranians. ... At the time of material progress and development our moral values and cultural heritage have a special position in national development.[17]

The imperial couple's warnings and exhortations were portrayed as their timely recognition of the threat of Occidentosis. In the words of the empress: 'Luckily, we still have the opportunity to preserve our ancient cultural, literary, moral and cultural traditions, traditions that people still respect'.[18] Yet the challenge was formidable. She was clear about the first step in facing this onslaught: 'In confronting the culture of the West self-awareness is a necessity'.[19] Focusing on her remarks, *Rastakhiz of the Young* argued:

> Humankind, which has never faced such a complete whirlpool of changes as it does today, is in need of new multi-disciplinary understandings and innovative thought. ... Today it is increasingly clear that our era's material accomplishments are coming at the cost of the gradual destruction of our cultural heritage that is the culmination of centuries of struggles and efforts. ... The expansion of communication links and the universal tendency toward homogenization of the forms of life have thrown into danger cultural distinctions and differences that are the sources of creativity and development.[20]

Following the directive to Hoveyda, the shah and the empress attended the first meeting of the Party's Executive Committee where they emphasized the need for the expansion and refinement of party cultural publications, regarded as the avant-garde in the struggle for the protection of this authenticity. This cultural education was considered integral to the strengthening of the party programme of political education since, according to the shah at this first meeting, 'we still do not know well our country. We must be vigilant in knowing our country. This is the Party's duty'.[21] *Rastakhiz*, commenting on the shah's remarks, condemned previous state inaction:

> His statements show that in the recent past we have neglected knowing our country and cultural authenticity. We must as soon as possible strive to correct this issue.

... The speech of the Leader of the Revolution of Iran must be taken to heart by all responsible authorities and Iranians in order to correct this issue. Authenticity must be recognized and protected in the face of Occidentosis.[22]

The Youth of Rastakhiz echoed these themes in a corresponding lead editorial titled 'The Revolution and Spirituality'.[23]

A telling example of the changes in state discourses on national identity and the shah's moves to anti-West Occidentalism is the evolution of the terms Occidentosis (*qarbzadegi*) and Occidentosis-ridden (*qarbzadeh budan*). Earlier was covered the negative reaction of the Pahlavi state to al-e Ahmad's *Occidentosis*. During the Rastakhiz period these terms became part of state lexicon. Party publications attacked those it described as *qarbzadeh*, condemning 'their blind imitation of the worthless superficial behavior of Westerners' and 'glorification of the West's so-called attractiveness'. While stressing the need for Western technology, it argued that by becoming *qarbzadeh* one 'fell on the path toward oppression by the West'. It warned people 'not to lose their identity'.[24]

These terms also became part of the shah's political lexicon: 'We must prevent the penetration into our society of undesirable foreign elements and the spread of moral, social, and political corruption. ... We must not become ridden with Occidentosis (*qarbzadeh nabashim*)'. Yet, concerned that his political and cultural anti-West Occidentalism could be used by those clerics and their lay supporters who opposed his social and economic changes, he added: 'We must not assume that struggling against Occidentosis is synonymous with enmity with the West or any form of modernization. ... We must give full attention to [the authenticity] of national culture, [but] we must not recognize this as being synonymous with reactionary schools of thought'.[25] Picking up on this theme, the Party proclaimed: 'We must once again know ourselves and our authenticity'.[26]

In summary, the imperial couple's statements provided a broad definition of the negative West and thus unmasked 'the unknown enemy' about which Enayat warned. Given this negative West Westernization had lost positive meaning in the shah's and the state's lexicon. The term 'modernization' was now a positive practical process that was accompanied by a struggle against Occidentosis which was propagated as a process initiated by the West to weaken the country's independence. However, only in late 1978 did the state allow publication of al-e Ahmad's *Occidentosis*. Despite the Pahlavi state's gradual co-opting of discourses of anti-West Occidentalism from the early 1970s his work was a dangerous intellectual discourse that implicitly portrayed the Pahlavi state as an agent of this disease.

Broadly speaking, Rastakhiz discourses that took shape within this broad definition propagated the idea of two forms of identity crisis and Occidentosis-ridden Iranians. The first group, the subject of the following chapter, was ridden with cultural and moral Occidentosis. The second group consisted of people ridden with political Occidentosis. They took inspiration from competing ideologies of the West, liberal democratic capitalism and/or communism, and their offshoots. This group is examined in Chapter 11. Both groups were regarded as politically and culturally existential threats whose causes were international as well as domestic.

Single-party systems and the Rastakhiz Party of the people of Iran

Mehdi Mozaffari, a Party member and an associate professor at Tehran University, authored this text. It was completed with Nahavandi's support as part of the work of his Analysis Group. Serialized in Rastakhiz publications, it played an important role in the propagation of the Party's ideological and specifically historiographical dynamics until the publication of the two other 'sacred texts'.[27]

A major goal of this work was to cultivate among party cadres and society the importance of authenticity of culture and national identity and the threat posed by Occidentosis. Proclaiming the existence of 'the new national identity',[28] it argued:

> National identity in the current era is one of the most fundamental political and sociological discourses and debates. How is it possible for a people to lose its identity or authenticity? What conditions are necessary for a lost national identity to be resurrected? This is the most fundamental question with which a large number of societies are dealing.

Unwittingly predicting the debates over authenticity of national culture and identity in the West in the second decade of the twenty-first century, exemplified by the vote for Brexit, the election of Donald Trump to the US presidency, and growing tensions within the European Union, he argued:

> Even in industrialized, advanced countries they also strive to prevent the destruction of national characteristics and uniqueness and not to allow an alien culture to dominate native culture. The causes of these strivings are clear – a country's independence is predicated on authentic national identity. ... To say that cultural hegemony is the most dangerous and deep manifestation of hegemony is not an exaggeration. Cultural hegemony delicately and calmly appears ... then firmly establishes a foothold as it spreads. It exercises intense influence on the language, culture, customs and traditions of a people and fundamentally changes them.[29]

The emphasis on the universal concern about the authenticity of national culture and identity was to give Western approval of the party crusade against manifestations of Occidentosis.

The answer to this challenge was the construction of *homo Pahlavicus*:

> Is it possible to equate our ideals with the return to Islam at the time of its emergence and become Salafi? We have tried such paths and it is clear they are mistaken, they were paths to nowhere. We want a person who, while remaining loyal to the past's positive values and customs, creates within himself the momentum [for the achievement of technological and economic modernity]. ... Should we, with hands tied, surrender ourselves to Western technology and ignore our history,

culture, and values and special features and become a faceless, colorless society? ... No, we want to remain ourselves.[30]

This was another exhortation for the ever-elusive combination of economic and technological modernity with authentic nativist culture and identity.

Turning his attention to Occidentosis-ridden Iranians, Mozaffari stressed that 'one's following of the trends of a foreign culture', a culture that sought 'hegemony', was 'in reality only cheap flaunting and exhibitionism'. The Occidentosis-ridden ones, engaged in this type of behavior in order to feel superior, argued 'that which they have is "complete and perfect" and that which is one's own is defective and very much incomplete'. One can hear the condemnations of such people in Russia made by Fonvisin at the end of the eighteenth century, Pogodin in the early nineteenth century and Dostoevsky in the second-half of the nineteenth century. The behaviour of these Occidentosis-ridden people was certainly offensive and even repulsive, but it also posed serious threats to Iran's cultural and eventually geopolitical borders.

> [In the establishment of alien cultural hegemony] society's aristocracy and so-called 'elite' play a key role. First, they attract alien culture to themselves. Since their position is superior to other societal groups they exercise a strong influence. They then flaunt this alien culture and make an impression on society. In this way, they establish the hegemony of foreign culture over native culture. ... This cultural hegemony is the prerequisite for the establishment of foreign economic and political hegemony. [Thanks to this group] this cultural hegemony easily and without encountering opposition establishes itself over societal conditions and maintains its squeeze on society. ... This has been repeated several times in Iran.[31]

Mozaffari stressed that historically 'over the centuries this [foreign cultural hegemony] has retarded and hollowed our progress and development'. During the time of Alexander the Great 'Greek culture was hegemonic because the upper Iranian classes were enthralled with it'. Then came the Ashkanians (Parthians).[32]

> The rustic Ashkanians were the guardians of Iranian culture and identity. ... Far from these corrupted urban elements they were provoked by the damage wrought by this foreign culture. If they had not rebelled, it is possible to conceive that today we would be speaking Greek and acting as Greeks.

The next great threat to Iran's cultural borders came from the Bedouin Arabs.

> Arab hegemony over Iranians manifested itself differently. It was not hegemony of one race over another. Rather it was a new system of beliefs, enjoying momentum and youthful vigor, that become victorious over an old, worn-out system that due to various powerful strikes and domestic corruption could not rejuvenate itself. In this victory the Iranian people perhaps played a role bigger than that of Islam's soldiers.

He was stressing the belief that Islam had become significantly Iranianized. In this narrative the Iranians through the establishment of the Abbasid Caliphate (750–1258) revitalized Islam when it too began to suffer from political and intellectual inertia. But in the end 'Islamic identity became the successor to Iranian identity' but did not completely destroy it. Under the Safavids Iranian identity experienced a resurgence. However, foreign enemies again conspired against Iran. 'It was not long before the West arrived and, with its shrewd and devious methods, blocked this road to independence. In this way we came close to independence before it was taken from us' during the Qajar period.

This historiography portrayed the Rastakhiz crusade against Occidentosis as an existential struggle for the preservation of authenticity that had characterized Iranian history since the Achaemenid period. This historical crusade, and the current Pahlavi one against Occidentosis, had a geopolitical aspect whose arena was not limited to arms and military encounters. History had shown that those Iranians enthralled with any alien culture had played vital roles in undermining the country's cultural borders that inevitably led to the weakening of the country's geopolitical borders and ultimately the establishment of foreign economic and political hegemony.

Mohammad Reza Ameli-Tehrani, party head for Tehran and Central Province and deputy party head during Amuzegar's second tenure, outlined the contemporary forms of this traditional threat. He had been a strong supporter of Mossadegh and member of the Pan-Iran Party. He, similar to Manuchehr Honarmand, distanced himself in time from the embattled prime minister before his overthrow.

> We know that in today's world a war of belief and ideologies between governmental systems is a way of life. None of us is immune to the possible influence of other social and political thoughts and ideas of one of these philosophical camps [the liberal capitalist West and communist East] because unfortunately until now political thought, similar to the West's industrialized goods, we imported from the West. Thus, naturally the views of our educators have been influenced by imported thought and these foreign ideas are taught to our youth. Given the Iranian Revolution and, particularly, the beginning of the Rastakhiz period our society clearly cannot and must not be under the influence of such thoughts and ideas that are in contradiction with the national path and not in Iran's interests or benefit.

Occidentosis, the Party warned, specifically targeted the youth because their 'essence is similar to raw dough and therefore they are easy bait for foreigners. Thus, we must arm them with national ideas and thought and not with non-Iranian thinking' of the imperialist West.[33] In sum,

> The Rastakhiz Party within the framework of the three fundamental principles propagates this authentic national identity and places this identity within the Party's features and characteristics. The Party has the mission to make the impossible possible in the clarification, formulation, and propagation of Iranian identity. ... This will not be possible unless those who hold responsibility in the

Party leadership devote all their energies to the formulation and interpretation of the authenticity of national identity and ensure that they themselves are the best examples of Iranian authenticity and national identity.[34]

The Philosophy of the Revolution and Party

On 20 November 1975 the shah issued an order to Hoveyda for the establishment of a commission charged with the writing of *The Philosophy of the Revolution and Party* that 'would justify and rationalize the Revolution's principles'.[35]

> Now that the desired brilliant results ... of the Revolution of Shah and People in the social and economic condition of the Iranian people have become obvious, the time has come to compose a philosophy in the shape of a comprehensive ideological conceptual system on the basis of a forward-looking dialectic and scientific view. This is to be done in order to illuminate and propagate the logic of the changes that are on the trajectory of the nation's cultural and spiritual life. I give the mission to the Rastakhiz Party to form a committee made up of the best minds who will complete this assignment on the basis of comprehensive study and research and present their ultimate product to me.[36]

Hoveyda, decree in hand, announced at a meeting of the Political Office that the practical task of writing this philosophy was, in reality, not his job. Rather his role was one of 'leadership and guidance'. Baheri eventually assumed the responsibility for running the weekly meetings of the writing committee and drafting of the philosophy. Other members of this writing committee included Naser Yeganeh, Shahpour Zandanian, Hossein Nasr, Ahmad Fardid, Ehsan Naraqi, Amuzegar, Nahavandi, Ameli-Tehrani, Amir Taheri and Enayatollah Reza. A cleric also participated to ensure that antireligious elements were not included in the Philosophy. According to Baheri and others, members' attendance was irregular.

Yeganeh, chief justice of the Supreme Court (1975–9), was Hoveyda's political ally. So too was Amir Taheri who at the time was editor of the daily *Keyhan*, a post he obtained as a result of Hoveyda's factional politicking that ended in the removal of his predecessor, Semsar, the editor of *Rastakhiz*.[37] Enayatollah Reza had been an army officer and member of the Tudeh Party who ended up living in the USSR for approximately twenty years and in China given his role in the Azerbaijan crisis. He returned to Iran in 1967, having abandoned his communist beliefs. In addition to scholarly work in the National Library and an academic post at Pahlavi University, he found doors open to him within the Pahlavi elite as an effective publicist in the struggle against various forms of Marxist and Maoist thought. Shahpur Zandania was a fervent nationalist who had been the spokesperson for the Sumka Party. He was the editor of the short-lived party publication, *The Philosophical Foundation of Rastakhiz*.

The shah ordered that the *Philosophy* be written on the basis of dialecticism which he had added sometime before in his speeches about the Revolution. To help in integrating the concept of dialectics into the philosophy Baheri recruited Kuroush

Lashai, who was formally invited by Hoveyda. Lashai had been a Maoist hoping to raise a rebellion in Iranian Kurdistan. He was eventually imprisoned. Once he repented Maoism, his sister Fereshte, who was a supervisor of protocol in the Ministry of the Court, approached Alam about her brother's plight. Lashai, after meeting with Alam and then eventually the shah found some doors at Court open to him. He became an advisor to the court and head of the Legion of the Servants of Mankind. A strong public critic of both the USSR and the West, Rastakhiz publications, especially during Baheri's tenure, reported his major speeches that targeted Western imperialism.[38]

Lashai, decades after the Revolution, recalled that 'because of his leftist background' it was assumed he knew 'something about dialectics' and thus could help the committee fulfil the shah's wish.[39] Baheri, Lashai and several others spent over one thousand hours debating and writing the text of the philosophy. According to Baheri in this text dialectics were portrayed as a 'divine tradition' (*sonnat-e elhai*) in order to distinguish Pahlavi Philosophy from Marx's dialectical materialism. 'The dialectics we introduced was a divine tradition … a change that emerges in society, a change that emerges in nature, a change that, in reality, must be called a tradition (*sonnat*) and this tradition is divine (*khodai*) change. This is where and how we introduced dialectics.' This definition of dialectics was used to explain and justify the reforms of the White Revolution and other transformative policies unleashed by the Pahlavi state.[40]

Baheri, having finished a draft on the basis of these 'divine dialectics' by-passed Hoveyda and delivered a copy to the shah via Alam. On 1 August 1976 the shah, having read it, expressed satisfaction but noted that the text was 'too complex', especially its first pages, for ordinary people to understand. He ordered that 'they more simply write' it. He nonetheless concluded that 'in any case the issues were well handled'.[41] Baheri took these remarks as a sign that 'all was fine in the text's preparation. After all, the shah had said it was acceptable'.[42] At this point, ideological differences and factional struggles began to influence this process.

The ideological and political issue that fed into existing factional politics was the place and meaning of dialectics and the extent of the use of 'leftist' terminology. Baheri faced not only this challenge. The shah's establishment of the Party was not preceded by a period of preparatory work. Therefore, party cadres faced a daunting task in quickly creating party ideology and institutions. Sources existed for party historiography and philosophy, namely the elements of Pahlavi Occidentalism of the Reza Shah period, the shah's two books *Mission for My Country* and *The White Revolution*, in addition to his numerous speeches and remarks, and finally the ideological elements included in the trial balloon named Pahlavism. However, the problem was deciding what elements from these works needed to be included in Rastakhiz philosophy and ideology and to what extent, if any, should each of these elements be modified to reflect political conditions and the shah's concerns.

These theoretical and political challenges were made more difficult by the influence of human agency and faction, driven by political and/or personal animosities and disagreements. For example, Baheri, as a member of the Alam political network, would inevitably face criticism from the Hoveyda faction. At the same time, Nahavandi and Baheri, despite their common leftist sympathies, had personal and political differences.[43] This friction was particularly troublesome for Baheri since Nahavandi tended to consider himself the Party's theorist while he and the work of the Analysis Group had direct access to the shah. At the same time, Baheri's leftist background not only influenced how he approached the writing of the philosophy but also how other committee members approached his draft proposals. Lastly, Baheri had to deal with the shah's role, whose values and world views he had to ensure were accurately reflected. This was particularly difficult since the shah had little idea of the elements that should be included, aside from the three fundamental guiding principles, and a vague understanding of dialectics on whose inclusion he insisted. This would not have been a serious problem if the shah had paid little attention to the details of the philosophy. However, he diligently followed its drafting.

The first real signs of trouble came some twenty days after the shah's initial praise of Baheri's draft. During an audience with Alam the shah suddenly complained: 'By the way, tell Baheri that all his writings have the mark of Marxism, as well as its terminology. We clearly understand!' Terms such as 'dialectic' had, for some reason, provoked him despite his insistence on its inclusion. Alam responded:

> It was your order and wish that we raise a hand against the Communists and use their language to crush them. Secondly, in regard to this issue you have brought up, I am forced to mention that Baheri is stuck between the Party's two wings, one is the intellectuals, the other is the Freemasons. Baheri is managing the intellectuals since he knows their language. With their language he has created discourses that are acceptable and approvable by you.[44]

One could surmise that according to Alam's paradigm, the Freemasons were those sympathetic with the capitalist West and the intellectuals were those with leftist and socialist sympathies. Alam's response sheds light on the understanding of the political and intellectual dynamics within the Party. Decades later Qotbi in a discussion about the Pahlavi state's lack of propaganda against Khomeini's idea of Islamic Government, unintentionally backed Alam: 'The shah ... proposed that we should develop our dialectic against the communists' dialectic'.[45]

One of the elements playing into the shah's increasing use of the term 'dialectics of the revolution' and his insistence that it be included in the *Philosophy* was the rise of what he and Pahlavi discourses called 'the imperialism of black reactionaries' and related terms such as 'the imperialism of the Red and Black', 'Marxist Islamism' or 'Islamist Marxism'. The seeming threat posed by this increased by the end of the 1960s and early 1970s. The figure that played a powerful role in making this paradigm popular was Ali Shariati whose thought stressed an ideologized Islamic identity that offered a path to the future along with a return to authenticity and self. Thus, the *homo Pahlavicus* sought by the state was an artificial Iranian inspired and implicitly constructed by the West's imperialism.

Shariati's idea of Shi'ism as a complete political party was similar to the monarchical Rastakhiz Party. These two parties propagated themselves not only as the epitome and holders of the authenticity of culture and identity but also the framework for revolutionary activity dedicated to the construction of a millenarian project. Shariati 'sought to use an already established "ideology" in the Islamic world in order to create the necessary political apparatus, party, slogan, banner and popular force to achieve' revolutionary ends, namely social justice.[46] In a similar vein the series *Pahlavism* concluded that Achaemenid emperors transformed monarchical virtues into 'a true ideology founded on distinct moral, social and economic bases that remains to this day, albeit in a changed form'.[47] Thus, Pahlavism argued that it was pursuing the resuscitation and updating of an authentic Iranian ideology that dated from the Achaemenid period that was now called the Rastakhiz Party. Shariati also shared elements of Pahlavi anticlericalism and criticism of the current inertial and even backward state of Islamic thought and culture produced by the clerical class. Shariati

> consciously believed and propagated the idea that his version of Islam, the 'true Islam' was the way forward in a revolutionary way. ... As a revolutionary ideology, Shariati's, the true, Islam was to mobilize the masses, challenge the authorities that be, compete and fight with other ideologies on their own ground and on their own terms. ... Shariati's vision of Islam was to transform it, quintessentially, into what it was: a political statement best suited for particular revolutionary objectives in this or in any other age.

His opposition to the existing Islam that he sought to transform into the 'true' authentic Islam was 'manifested in a number of directions: first against its intellectual, spiritual, and theological aspects; second, against the operative Islam, particularly its submission to a divine will as a religious doctrine'.[48] The shah, on the other hand, sought to struggle against this existing Islam and the clergy with the *Philosophy of the Revolution* that while stressing protection of the imperial system as the source and defender of the country's cultural and geopolitical borders portrayed that system, backed by the Rastakhiz Party, as the historical motor of positive change and development and a modern revolutionary force.

In sum, to a significant extent the form and aims of Shariati's rhetorical mixture, but not its substance, of a utopia in this world built by a united revolutionary party operating on the principles of a revised revolutionary Shi'ism underpinned by a return to a historicized authenticity of culture and identity mirrored the discourses of the late Pahlavi state, especially during the Rastakhiz period. Importantly, these discourses and in particular the *Philosophy of the Revolution* were not just dedicated to attacking the idea of this Marxist Islam. They were used to attack the liberal West. Marxist Islam and liberal West constituted the threat of Occidentosis. The dual targets were identified by the shah on the occasion of *aid-e qadir* in 1977, the Muslim holiday marking the anniversary of the official proclamation of the Prophet Mohammad's successor: 'Real religion and not Islamic Marxism protects society. Islam is to protect spiritual Iran from the lost of spirituality, a spirituality that the West has already lost'.[49]

A couple of weeks later, Baheri submitted the Philosophy's final draft that only slightly differed from the text accepted by the shah. A caveat had been added according to which if and when extraordinary events occur, such as war, or serious domestic unrest, this divine dialectic movement may be suspended for a period of time. Hoveyda, having read it, expressed unease and stressed that this issue had to be decided by the shah at a special meeting. Baheri was surprised by Hoveyda's opposition. To his mind, suspending temporarily the divine dialectics in such circumstances was politic and essential. Once a crisis had been averted and stabilization achieved, the march towards the Great Civilization would resume. However, as Baheri subsequently realized, Hoveyda had ulterior motives. The seeming monopoly of the Alam faction in the writing of the *Philosophy* as well as the language being used by it had provoked political and ideological concerns among those, who, if not aligned with Hoveyda, were not in the Alam camp. Baheri at the time did not fear a meeting with the shah since he had already approved the text.

On the day of the meeting, the committee members arrived, including Naraqi, Yeganeh, Ameli-Tehrani, Enayatollah Reza and 'others', according to Lashai. A good number of them had a record of only sporadic attendance. Baheri and Lashai arrived together. Then Manuchehr Azmun, at the time a Majles deputy and member of the Executive Committee and Political Office, arrived. Baheri upon seeing him turned to Lashai and said: 'The security service has sent their own person as well.'

In the early 1950s Azmun started university study in West Germany. However, when the Mossadegh government cut funding for students studying abroad, he eventually applied for scholarships given by the East German government. In 1958 he received his doctorate in Political Economy from the University of Leipzig. During his time there he took specialized courses in the philosophy of communism and the principles of communist parties at the Faculty of Karl Marx. However, the extent of his leftist sympathies is unclear. Having completed his education, he entered SAVAK where he worked until 1969. After serving in SAVAK he worked his way through the corridors of power. As a member of the Iran Novin Party, he became close to Hoveyda, having served as his deputy in his last cabinet before the Party's establishment. In the immediate aftermath of the shah's announcement about Rastakhiz's founding he was charged with creating a blueprint for the party structure. He

> came up with a perfectly fascist plan, according to which each profession – farmers, workers, teachers, students, shopkeepers, doctors, and so on – was organized internally and joined at the tope by the party's command organs. … This conception of the party, a hybrid construct of the Italian and Spanish schools of fascism, met with widespread opposition and was withdrawn once the queen sided with its opponents.[50]

He thus was a perfect figure to attack Baheri's draft and the Alam faction. Soon after his performance in this meeting Hoveyda brought him into the cabinet, making him minister for employment and social affairs.

At the meeting, the Hoveyda and Alam/Baheri groups sat on opposing sides of the long table, to the shah's left and right. After some introductory remarks by Lashai, the shah sarcastically said, 'Well it seems that we in reality had not made the Revolution.'[51] The monarch had taken affront at the understanding of divine dialectics that downplayed the role of human agency, specifically his role, in the White Revolution. At issue was not only this caveat but rather the entire approach to the writing of the Philosophy. Baheri, pretending not to have noticed the shah's seeming anger, placed a copy of the text in front of him. The monarch, puzzled, asked: 'What is this?' Baheri responded that it was the part of the text causing disagreement among the committee's members whose resolution was in the monarch's hands. Once Baheri had finished reading it, Azmun started 'and forcefully attacked Lashai' as well as the text. Baheri and those around him quickly realized that Azmun had for some time prepared for this offensive. Attacking the idea of dialectics of the Revolution Azmun thundered: '"This is a Marxist text placed in the framework of the imperial system and in principle has a destructive, sabotaging goal and aim." A couple of people shook their heads in agreement and approved of his words'.[52]

The attack launched by Azmun and his supporters focused on the meaning of the term 'dialectics' according to which, in the words of Lashai, 'that every phenomenon has a beginning, a period of development, and then end and that the philosophy of the dialectics has nothing to offer except this meaning'. Azmun situated 'the Revolution and the future of the monarchy' within this framework. In other words, the final result of this divine dialectical movement was clear: 'If the Revolution is the beginning of a phenomenon, and according to the philosophy of dialectics every phenomenon has a beginning, period of development, and ultimately end, then the Revolution begins to work against itself and must come to an end. In this respect, therefore, the monarchy too faced nothing other than this', an end.[53]

After Azmun

> Enayat spoke in favor of the use [of dialectics], stressing that Islamic Shi'i theory of gnosis too has dialectics. Marxism, a modern ideological school, did not have a monopoly on the idea and meaning of dialectics. He pointed to several old Iranian philosophers [whose works contained dialectics]. He concluded and insisted ... that the prepared text had nothing to do with Marxism.

The meeting collapsed into arguing. In the midst of this ruckus in the monarch's presence, Baheri, once he obtained a turn to speak, stressed: 'I swear that this text has no links with Marxism.' Defending the text, he increasingly used leftist terminology. According to Lashai, in the midst of this the shah, turning to Hoveyda, with anger and frustration asked: '*What* is he saying?'

> Once he said that the room became quiet. Despite this it became clear that the Shah did not believe that the meeting finished. Then a couple of people cautiously picked up the discussion. The issue of dialectics again became the center of attention. As the discussion continued about dialectics the Shah with frustration asked, 'Then what happens with the crown prince?' I remember, these were the exact words he used.

The shah worried about the future of the monarchy and the fate of his heir.

> It was clear that before the meeting he (the shah) had been already set-off by these issues. ... Hoveyda had a victorious smirk on his face, sensing that he had defeated us. Of course, in the meeting he took no sides and without a doubt it was to his

benefit not to interfere openly. If Alam had been there, the meeting would not have evolved in such a way. But it was inevitable because Baheri did not have the position and stature that Alam enjoyed with the shah.⁵⁴

Baheri, while accepting the idea that Hoveyda used this issue to advance factional interests, suspected that Nasr too played a role in turning the shah against the text and in the attack on him and Lashai given their leftist background. Nasr did indeed believe that too many Iranian intellectuals had become leftist.⁵⁵ The meeting went on for ninety minutes. At its end the shah ordered Hoveyda to address this issue and decide which of the two sides was right. Baheri told Lashai as they left the palace after the meeting, 'We were close to losing our heads'.⁵⁶ The shah expressed his feelings during Alam's next audience.

> The shah received the party members charged with writing the Philosophy of the Party. I was not at the meeting since I have no post in it. Around dinnertime the prime minister, flustered, telephoned me. He said the meeting went very badly. In the Shah's presence the opposing sides went after each other. In particular, Manuchehr Azmun, the leading Majles deputy from Tehran who was not scheduled to be at the meeting, attacked Baheri. He said that 'This philosophy you have written, all of its terminology and even the text are communist.' Baheri became angry. The shah said: 'Yes, it was not a pretty scene. Baheri also said silly stuff'. I gently said that the doctrine [of dialectics] that the shah wanted for the Party is the one Baheri has written. It is appropriate and ideal. Nonetheless, the meeting produced no agreement about the party's philosophy. The prime minister asked that I tell Baheri to compromise and have a draft prepared that included the concerns and worldview of the others. I told him I would try. But in reality this entire episode, including the fight at the meeting, is the result of the bungling and shoddy character of the prime minister's activities. It is not possible to reconcile lightness and darkness. Those opposing Baheri believe he and his colleagues are Marxists when in reality the draft delivered to the shah was in accordance with his orders and wishes. [This belief that Baheri is a Marxist] has been strengthened since Kuroush Lashai, who until recently was a member of the Tudeh Party, entered Baheri's circle.⁵⁷

Complaining about the text, the shah thundered: 'I am the creator of the Revolution. It is I. I want that which is in my heart to be implemented, not that which floats around in the limited thought of Baheri and his colleagues.'

Although the shah had used the term 'dialectic' in the decree establishing this committee and sought to use such terminology to combat the growing attractiveness of Islamist Marxism, he seemingly did not understand fully either the meaning and implications of it or how it would fit into party philosophy. The fundamental Marxian meaning of the term, 'constant revolution and constant revolutionary movement forward' was also the meaning used by Baheri in coming up with the Pahlavi term, 'divine dialectics'. Alam repeatedly mentioned to the monarch that Baheri's use of this definition corresponded to the shah's own use. After all, Alam reminded him, he himself had stressed that 'there must always be a revolution ... if there was no such movement forward, the revolution [and the party's ideology] would petrify and decay'.[58] Continuing his defence of Baheri, Alam repeated that not only did Baheri's use of this term and its definition correspond with the shah's own articulated meaning of the word but Baheri had also fulfilled the shah's own orders that the philosophy reflect his own thinking and beliefs.

A fundamental theoretical problem facing Baheri, and reflected in the shah's frustration, was the attempt to reconcile varied and somewhat conflicting elements within the same ideological and philosophical framework. It also draws out the ideological and philosophical tensions inherent not only to the ideologization of the monarchy but also to the idea of a revolutionary monarchy. On the one hand, the shah, through the three fundamental guiding principles, stressed the eternal quality of the ancient monarchy and the imperial system. On the other hand, his position as Leader of the Revolution and the use of the word dialectic promised constant change and revolution.

The shah gave great importance to this project, seeing in the writing of the official philosophy and historiography a fundamental 'sacred' text that would attract the people to the Party, create lasting popular loyalty to the imperial system and constitute the framework not only for party activities but also the training for its cadres from local organizations to its central governing organs. In his words

> The real question is one of quality [of party members] and not quantity [since all Iranians will become members of the Party]. The fundamental issue is quality. Thus, we must as soon as possible and in better terms explain the Philosophy of the Party and Revolution in order to strengthen the people's belief in it. At the same time [on the basis of this philosophy] the Party must produce cadres. It is for this reason a party faculty must be established and administered where belief, discipline, and faith will be greater than in any other place.[59]

The Philosophy of the Revolution was finally published in mid-autumn 1976. In addition to its official mini-book form, it was serialized in all Rastakhiz publications, although *Rastakhiz* and *Rastakhiz of the Young* provided the greatest coverage, publishing over several issues the entire philosophy.[60] The mini-book consisted of thirty pages divided into five chapters: (1) Society before the Revolution; (2) The Logic of the Revolution and National Exigencies; (3) Preparation for the Revolution; (4) The Rebuilding of Unity and National Independence; and (5) The Philosophical Values of the Revolution.[61] The word 'dialectic' was used three times in the first two chapters in order to place, according to the shah's original decree, the Revolution and the monarchy's role in 'a comprehensive ideological conceptual system on the basis of a forward-looking dialectic and scientific view'. In reality, the first chapters of the *Philosophy* dealt with an issue that also faced Soviet historiography and ideology: Reconciliation of the idea of dialectics, in other words, the inevitability of revolutionary changes emerging from a society's superstructure, with the role of the revolutionary leader, be it Lenin or Mohammad Reza Pahlavi, in bringing about such changes.

Rastakhiz's response to this question, to an extent reflecting the divisions over the use of 'divine dialectical movement' and strikingly similar to Soviet historiography, first underlined the increasing need for change and domestic political forces opposing change, such as the clergy, that produced the great revolutionary leader.

> At points in every nation's history some social institutions that had played a role in the survival of the essence of a society's existence evolve into forms opposing societal development. In such conditions dealing with these forces is a necessity. … In these substructural circumstances emerges a great transformative leader with his unique abilities who becomes a catalyst for the revolutionary and positive changes needed for the country's development … [and] survival of the essence of society's existence.

According to Marx the modes of production and the contradictions within each one of them leading to communism constituted the dialectics of history. Pahlavi philosophy, not to be outdone and with an eye on the formulations of Shariati and conceptions of Islamist Marxism, provided the elements of its dialectics that constituted 'a special method for the discovery of the laws of movement and of the relationship of the principles of the Revolution of Iran that in fact make up' its dialectics. The logic constituting this revolutionary dialectic and party philosophy was based on three elements: (1) Iran's special geographical conditions; (2) Iranian civilization and culture; and (3) the empire of Iran and the imperial system.

It presented these geographical conditions as both a curse and blessing. Iran's position was excellent for trade and the country was rich with vast natural resources which created the ideal conditions for national progress and development since ancient times. But, this rich position made Iran a frequent target of invasions and imperialism as enemies sought to plunder these riches for themselves. This threat became more acute with the spread of the West's imperialism. Throughout history, these attempts to impose and maintain hegemony on Iran started with attacks on the country's cultural borders: 'In every society, the fundamental goal is the protection and safeguarding of society's unique essence. This essence of our society is the survival and continuance of a flourishing national identity.'

However, a rigid interpretation of authenticity that did not allow for the timely borrowing from other civilizations as part of national resurgence was not propagated. Rather, cultural flexibility was portrayed as an ancient authentic part of Iranian civilization. In other words, the shah sought an Iranian modernity: 'Iran's civilization and culture, in accordance with the nature of its society, enjoys the unique power to be accepting and flexible while, at the same time, protecting its cultural authenticity and national identity.' Many passages focused on defining this authenticity that alternated between this flexibility and 'a unique spirituality and traditional morality' that would be preserved in the face of changes.[62]

Protection of this spirituality and traditional austere morality, fundamental elements of Iranian authenticity, was one of the vital goals of the Party as determined by the shah: 'Any review of the thought and philosophy of the Commander of the Revolution teaches us that before undertaking transformative changes he believes that three questions must be answered: "who were we? who are we? what should we become?"'. Yet, only one answer could be given. 'The Revolution of Iran, from its beginning, chose the path of development and rejuvenation paved with ancient and accepted traditions and values'.[63] While Iranian culture was flexible and able to absorb elements from other cultures and civilizations, it also

> protects its cultural principles and national identity. Humanism, deep intellectual and philosophical traditions, an absence of reactionary obstructionism and stagnation, distance from any form of philosophical fanaticism and made this civilization and culture rich, productive, and generative. ... The unique nature and authenticity of this culture and civilization is based on continuous creativity coupled with stress on its authentic characteristics. ... At the same time the authentic foundations of Iranian culture and civilization are veneration and reverence of spirituality, avoidance of materialism, and the shunning of drowning oneself in carnality and conspicuous consumerism. ... According to the shahanshah, one of the principles of the Revolution of Iran is preservation of these elements of this authenticity.

The source and defender of this authenticity over the 2,500 years of Iranian history was the imperial system, 'the most authentically Iranian institution and form of governance'. It 'is the epitome of the highest forms of humanism, classless thought, and the relationship between a father and his child'. The totality of the monarchy's role envisaged by this Philosophy underlined the political contradictions at the heart of the Rastakhiz experiment: 'It is true to say that the Iranian monarch is not only the kingdom's political leader. He is also a teacher and mentor. He is a figure who for his people not only builds dams, bridges and water systems but also guides their spirit, thought and hearts'.[64]

The shah, the Leader of the Revolution, having in a timely manner recognized the laws of movement and national exigencies, sought to unleash changes as the dialectics demanded. He faced daunting domestic and international obstacles:

> (1) the contradiction between the interests of the landowning class and those of the farming peasant class that made up the bulk of the population; (2) the contradiction between national interests and those of imperialism that had throughout Iranian history sought to plunder the nation's riches; (3) the contradiction between the strict restrictions on the participation of women in society and the fact that they made up some 50% of the country's population; (4) the contradiction between the interests of the workers and those of management and owners; (5) reactionary [clerical] forces.

Fortunate for the Iranian people, history had given the mission of overcoming these obstacles and implementing changes to a knowledgeable leader, the shah. Proclaiming the end of the '–isms' of the modernities of the West, he would guide the people towards the Great Civilization, the authentically Iranian modernity superior to those on offer by the West.[65]

Towards the Great Civilization

The last 'sacred Pahlavi text' *Towards the Great Civilization* was published at the beginning of 1978 and serialized in Rastakhiz publications. In its preparation participated Shoja al-Din Shafa, a nationalist cultural figure, who was the head of Pahlavi National Library and deputy minister for culture in the Ministry of Court. In 1958 he had suggested to the shah the idea of holding celebrations marking the 2,500th anniversary of the founding of the Achaemenid Empire. He also played an important role in replacing the Islamic Iranian solar calendar with the imperial calendar based on that anniversary on the occasion in 1976 of the fiftieth anniversary of the founding of the Pahlavi dynasty. The date went from 1355 to 2535. The extra thirty-five years accounted for the time the shah had been on the throne. This book was a re-articulation and fine-tuning of elements already introduced in his first two books and, more importantly, *Pahlavism* and *The Philosophy of the Revolution*.

Broadly speaking this book had two main discursive trajectories. One outlined the shah's grandiose plans to implement this millenarian project. The other touched on the issue of the authenticity of Iranian culture and national identity and the place of the West within it. In the wake of its publication Hossein Nasr gave a televised interview in which he outlined the work's anti-West Occidentalism.

> If we put aside the fact that this book's author is Iran's leader who reigns over the spirit, heart, and body of the Iranian people ... the point worthy of attention is that in this book we have an invaluable view of the overall situation in today's world. It is possible to say that this book is in reality a perfect mirror of all views of today's world. It is possible to say that economic agents, the complexity of the economic relationship between the East and the West, the North and the South, that have come into existence, military issues and problems in various places of the world, are the consequence and result of the domination and hegemony of Westerners in the era of imperialism not only in our country but in the remaining countries of the world.[66]

The shah, in the introduction, stressed that the book's major goal was to address the social, political, economic and cultural changes engendered by the White Revolution. At their centre was the issue of the authenticity of culture and national identity in the face of Occidentosis which, reflecting Rastakhiz discourses, was portrayed as a struggle between Iranian morality and spirituality and Western materialism, consumerism and hedonism.[67] 'Being Iranian means the necessity of freely accepting the mission that the ancient history of this people and its eternal spiritual, moral and civil values have placed on the shoulders of every Iranian'.[68] This mission deemed that the Iranian people were 'both the historical founder and guardians' of the 'authenticity of civilization and culture'.[69] At the top of this structure stood the ultimate source and protector of this authenticity in all its aspects, the ancient imperial system that would construct the Great Civilization. The other 'eternal element of this authenticity' was a 'love for, and deep commitment to, the land of Iran and the defence of authentic national identity and characteristics' under the aegis of the imperial system.[70]

Occidentosis, however, challenged these elements. 'I hope that in the future with the preservation of the characteristics and values of Iranian civilization, with reliance on our authentic national identity, with the support of the richness of our spirit and cultural heritage we can prevent our youth from falling into various forms of deficiencies and confusion'.[71] In this respect, the shah detailed the dimensions of cultural education and its importance in managing the crisis of identity.[72] He expressed optimism that this struggle with this identity crisis and Occidentosis would be victorious since 'Iranians historically have not been prepared to betray the authenticity of their national culture and identity'.[73] Of course, this also meant loyalty to the imperial system, the source and defender of that authenticity.

The shah recognized that a main cause for the identity crisis and the spread of Occidentosis was a sense of Iranian inferiority in regard to the West. To help combat this, he utilized the historical observations of Westerners in regard to Iran. He quoted from Napoleon's letter to Fath-Ali Shah: 'When Cyrus the Great in Iran was founding the firm method of governance from which other governments of the world took example our ancestors were still living in the jungles and deserts'.[74] François-René Chateaubriand (1768–1848), the great French writer, historian and politician, too made an appearance: 'When in the history of the world we approach the Iranian era, we feel that we have placed a foot on the scene of great history'.[75]

He reiterated, moreover, long-standing themes from the historiography of Pahlavi Occidentalism. 'In regard to the art of governance, Iranians established their own empire, which was the first Aryan government in world history. At the same time it was the first world empire in history governed on the basis of principles of justice and humanitarianism whose supreme example is the famous charter of Cyrus the Great'.[76] This repeated emphasis on the cult of Cyrus the Great was a renewed rebuttal of the West's claims to exceptionalism based on the idea that it was the first to promote human rights and tolerance and repeating of claims that Iran was a source of Western culture. The shah argued that given this civilizational heritage and the Revolution's successes, Iranians should and must abandon 'feelings of inferiority' in regard to the West.[77]

While maintaining Aryanism and the racial link between Westerners and Iranians, he argued that the West, made up of communism and the liberal West, was incompatible with the authenticity of Iranian culture and national identity. Offering wide-ranging criticisms of Western civilization, he saved his greatest ire for Western imperialism and racial and religious prejudices. These three elements at the base of Western civilization had resulted in the continued economic and social deprivation of the non-Western world and the West's unwillingness to grant civil and basic human rights to non-Western peoples. Even within Western societies this idea of democracy was a chimera, limited to the political arena, where people had the right to vote for politicians devoted to populism and the dominant tendency was to say anything but the truth in order to win an election and to the legal arena, in which everyone was only theoretically equal before the law. The elites of the liberal capitalist West, who portrayed their system as worthy of emulation, did not in any serious manner address social and economic equality. 'Inside the developed countries of the West a majority exists who, similar to the colonized non-Western peoples-although of course to a lesser extent-were and are only in the service of elite interests.'

In contrast was 'Iran's economic, social, and political democracy' that in addition to its strength and stability was a 'healthy democracy' led by the monarch who protected the socio-economic and political interests of all Iranians. Exploitation of man by man would disappear with the construction of the Great Civilization. This superior Iranian system enjoyed another great virtue, it was not based 'on the West's constructed and bought democracies. Rather it takes inspiration directly from the spiritual and earthly conditions and circumstances of Iranian society'.[78]

Iranians could not take inspiration from the West. Consumerism, materialism and commercialization had overtaken Western society and brought about the 'collapse of ancient spiritual values, the spread of licentiousness, chaos, a striving for excess convenience, carelessness, and indiscretion' and overall 'social and moral corruption'.[79] The manifestations of corrupting and dominant hedonism, such as 'drug addiction, hippies, sexual deviances', were destroying the West's societies.[80] The speed of this decline was increasing because 'the restraining forces of religion, morality, spirituality and culture' were 'no longer tempering and controlling perversity and wild instincts'.[81]

These remarks and others made by the shah about licentiousness, the decline of morals, and the pernicious influence of hippieism and attributing them to Occidentosis were reflections of his personal beliefs and reactions to developments within Western and Iranian societies. For example in early 1970 Alam reported the police's closing of a controversial club in Tehran:

> The club was suspected of being a centre for drug dealing and the police were perfectly justified in closing it down, especially since the proprietor was a member of Princess Ashraf's set and gossip had begun to spread. His Imperial Majesty went so far as to express himself delighted by the raid and personally commended the chief of police for taking a stand against a den of hippy decadence.[82]

Moreover, these beliefs were also a reflection of issues the shah faced in his family life.

His eldest daughter, Shahnaz, from his first marriage to Princess Fawzia of Egypt, divorced from her first husband, Ardeshir Zahedi (1964), and soon after abandoning her next fiancée (1969) fell in love with Khosrow Jahanbani who was from an elite family. The shah did not approve of him, considering him a hippy and a bad moral influence on his daughter. He was convinced that as a part of Jahanbani's hippy lifestyle he was a drug-user who had made Shahnaz a LSD addict. Consequently, he had the man, who at the time was fulfilling his obligatory military service (1969), tried and thrown into jail for three years for derelection of duty. Alam, working as mediator between the monarch and his daughter, finally obtained his release from jail and the shah's permission for them to marry, although the shah refused to attend the engagement and allow him access to court. Alam noted in his diary in late 1970:

> Once again the issue of Princess Shahnaz came up. The shah is greatly upset over the guy she has chosen to marry. Her husband, or rather future husband, is a hippy and entertains strange and bizarre ideas and opinions. ... The shah said: 'As a father I could possibly forgive her when she makes mistakes but as Shahanshah of Iran I could never accept a good-for-nothing hippy as my son-in-law. If I did accept

him it would mean that I am fostering and propagating in the country the spread of licentiousness and worthless, empty convictions and thought in regard to life'.[83]

The shah allowed them to marry, but abroad in Europe where he told them they were to live.

In *Towards the Great Civilization*, just as examples were chosen from Western historiography to back claims about Iran's ancient grandeur and civilization, Western critics of Western civilization were included to strengthen the official discourses on the West's contemporary state. Centre stage was given to the French thinker and poet Jules Romain (1885–1972), the founder of the Unanimism literary movement, which was to be a response to atomistic individualism and, in some interpretations, Western-style hedonism, or rather the glorification of individual desires and wants. The best example of his thought is his series *Les Hommes de bonne volonté*. According to Romain, 'If our epoch, if our civilization is moving in the direction of a catastrophe it is not because of lack of attention to dangers or ignoring of it, but rather because of hedonism, lack of moral spirit and courage for dealing with these dangers'.[84]

The shah therefore concluded 'the adaption of today's Western civilization as a unified example for other peoples of the world is not acceptable and any attempt by the West to impose [its culture and civilization on other peoples] cannot have a positive consequence'.[85] Mixing personal beliefs with political interests he stressed: 'From the point of view of our Revolution ideology is not something that can be imported. The principles under the name of capitalism, socialism, and communism and the dozens of other "-isms" ... cannot answer the needs, spirit, and conditions of our country'.[86] Increasingly frustrated with growing Western criticisms of his rule and the state of human rights inside the country, an issue detailed in the following chapters, he proclaimed that 'countries such as Iran have the right to and must find and travel their own path to the future'.[87] Travelling along this path however was dangerous since the West's new imperialism was determined to establish its indirect hegemony over Iran and the rest of the non-Western world.

The only way by which Iran could achieve the Great Civilization was the path paved by the Revolution, which, he stressed, had 'no foreign inspiration and influence, it is completely Iranian, it is authentic'.[88] This path, however, was threatened by the spread of Occidentosis. The people had to strive for the protection of the authenticity of Iranian culture and national identity and its source and defender, the imperial system.[89]

> Culture is one of the main principles of the infrastructure of the Great Civilization. Since without the solid support of cultural values no civilization, no matter how developed, can long exist. Of course, my understanding of culture is a broad one. In this meaning culture is synonymous with all the spiritual values, moral characteristics, human emotions and sensitivities, art, and, above all else, the spirit of patriotism and self-sacrifice, devotion, and forbearance in the service of social interests. ... These values of national culture and traditions linked to them have for us such a high position in life that we do not equate them with any form of material wealth, and all the accomplishments of Western civilization. We attract the knowledge and technology of the West and we will increasingly do this but we

will not allow any unhealthy intellectual phenomena that is not compatible with our cultural authenticity to infect and spread in society. A main goal is and will remain the defense of this authenticity.[90]

The cultural element ... is the deterrent force in the face of the danger of the rise of a materialistic monstrous society that could as a result of increasing industrialization come into existence. We know that this state of affairs has already happened in the developed countries. In these societies technology places a human under its own command and hegemony and makes the human, who in reality is the inventor of technology, an element and member of technology itself. ... But our 'Great Civilization' will not face this danger because we are careful to ensure that we base our civilization on an appropriate balance between industrial development and spiritual growth. I believe that in this way and under the rays of the richness of our culture and heritage of our deep-rooted cultural and moral values we will avoid collapse into the abyss which now threatens these material and materialistic civilizations. Thus, a main pillar of official policy is protection of these values, culture and national identity.[91]

Importantly, the shah stressed the importance of Islam in this struggle against Occidentosis, while continuing to preach anticlericalism, charging members of the clergy of being either reactionary or self-interested populists.[92]

Summarizing the civilizational and cultural achievements of Iran over twenty-five centuries he provided a broad definition of his millenarian project in language reminiscent of *Pahlavism*: 'Why should we not place such a country and people on the path of the Great Civilization?' This uniquely Iranian social imaginary and form of modernity with universalist aspirations were superior to the modernities offered by the West. But

What is the Great Civilization? It is a civilization in which the best elements of knowledge and human insight are combined in the path of the attainment of the highest levels of spiritual and civil life for all members of society. It is the civilization in which the new accomplishments of science and industry and technology are combined with the highest spiritual values and advanced standards of social justice.[93]

Iranians and their authentic culture have the unique capacity

to use the scientific and industrial advances of the developed world in order to benefit from material welfare and accomplishments of the new form of life without placing their soul and spirit in the service of the devil of technology and fall into its trap of melancholic disorientation and confusion that has afflicted many of the young' in Western societies.[94]

In conclusion, 'a fundamental element of our Revolution is the steady adaption [of social and economic changes] to unique Iranian cultural and civil values and spirituality [and] the preservation of the balance of the multisided material progress with the humanistic and moral values of Iranian society'.[95]

9

Occidentosis: Culture and the arts

Discourses attacking manifestations of Occidentosis were broadly divided into two forms. One form, examined in this and the next chapter, propagated Occidentosis as a domestic sociocultural threat. The other form, the subject of Chapter 11, focused on the idea of Occidentosis as an instrument of Western imperialism designed to achieve and maintain indirect political and economic hegemony. Both forms sought to change the popular image of the Pahlavi state as an agent of Occidentosis and portray it as the source and defender of this redefined authenticity in the face of this disease, a role that justified its power.

Hoveyda, in an interview for *Rastakhiz*'s first issue, underlined that in line with the shah's wishes the Party, while focusing on social justice, prosperity and movement towards the Great Civilization, would pay special attention to 'the protection of national uniqueness and authenticity'.[1] Therefore, 'one of the Party's main goals is to protect Iranian identity and culture ... which has for more than sixty centuries provided service to humankind. ... We will defend our authenticity'.[2] He announced that the Party sought to mobilize the population for 'a spiritual resurgence' (*rastakhiz-e ma'navi*) that would ensure that people 'shun the appearances and mien of Occidentosis and focus on spiritual issues, the internal person, including morals' and that 'we will ... avoid the moral and spiritual crises of Western industrialized nations'.[3] He created a party committee charged with creating the conditions for this resurgence while the Party also assumed the activities of another committee previously established by the shah which he had charged with determining the characteristics of the Great Civilization, including the articulation and protection of 'national cultural values, identity and authenticity'.[4]

This spiritual resurgence and protection of authenticity of culture faced a formidable foe in Western imperialism that, Hoveyda warned, purposely spread materialism and conspicuous consumerism by dangling in front of people its fashion, luxury items and consumer goods. This strategy, which he labelled 'consumerist imperialism', sought to create Occidentosis-ridden classes inculcated with the belief that materialism and conspicuous consumerism were the goals of one's existence in this world. It baited in particular the youth, impressionable and inexperienced, in whose hands the country's future would fall. Expressing worry about the speed with which Occidentosis was infecting society, he stressed that 'society must be prepared to adhere to spiritual non-materialistic ideas'.[5] Proclaiming that 'the Revolution of Iran rejects and repudiates consumerist imperialism', he underlined that the Party's aim was 'to reach the highest levels of technical and economic progress while protecting our cultural and moral traditions, and to avoid the schisms from which the industrialized countries suffer' that emerged due to materialism and consumerism.[6] These elements constituted, according to him, the starting point for the Party's main mission: 'That which is unchangeable for us is the complete cultivation of the Iranian person (*ensan-e irani*)', who rejected all manifestations of Occidentosis and was the builder and product of the Revolution in the march towards the Great Civilization.[7]

Ostentatious *nouveau riche*, whose numbers were increasing due to rapid economic growth, the rises in oil prices and expansion of educational opportunities, were a core target as they were widely recognized as the most ridden with Occidentosis given their slavish following of Western fashion, personal behaviour corrupted by Western immorality, passion for conspicuous consumerism and philistinish approach to culture.[8] In the minds of increasing numbers of people this group was the direct result of Pahlavi policies. This group's characteristics first fuelled the intellectual discourses on the need to define and protect Iranian authenticity in the face of Occidentosis.

Party discourses targeted this group because of the sense it represented a threat with cultural and social dimensions to political stability and social unity. This group's monied status and tendency to flaunt its wealth could only exacerbate social tensions among the lower classes by serving as a constant reminder to these classes of what they did not and could most probably ever have. This flaunting, moreover, was inclusive of the belief that those with wealth were superior. This group's culture and moral Westernization, which it also flaunted, too played into the message that the *nouveau riche* were superior. The *Ferdowsi* articles written on the occasion of Takhti's suicide quoted earlier succinctly described the social and political tension and discontent this group could cause. The fear existed that these lower classes, alienated by this group's Occidentosis-ridden state, and increasingly outraged by its ostentation that only underlined class differences, could become increasingly susceptible to leftist and communist ideologies. These were not the only issues weakening social unity and driving discontent. Among the growing rural migrant population in the cities, and particularly young workers and students, was also sexual envy and/or outrage. These wealthy classes not only provided their youth with the material opportunities and, in some cases, cultural flexibility to date and enjoy a libertine youth, but also seemingly weakened traditional cultural and moral barriers to the spread, in the shah's and Party's lexicon, of licentiousness.[9]

Kazem Vadiei, in a long piece in *Rastakhiz*, outlined the Party's concerns in this regard and its approach to them. This approach portrayed the characteristics of the Occidentosis-ridden *nouveau riche* as alien and warned that that this group increased the threat of class welfare. To counter this threat the Party was leading the struggle against this Occidentosis and for social justice.[10] Leading Party members and publicists, responding to those imperial questions of 'Who were we? Who are we? and What are we to become?' and therefore determining true Iranians from false ones, clearly drew society's battle lines in this struggle. On one side stood deceitfully attractive hedonism, materialism and imperialist consumerism spread by the West and attractive to the country's *nouveau riche*, a prime target of this struggle. This was the first element of the Iranian identity crisis. On the other side stood the authenticity of Iranian culture and national identity based on spirituality, proper morality and appreciation of the non-materialistic aspect of one's existence in this world.

The offensive against the urban Occidentosis-ridden *nouveau riche* had two fronts. The first one combatted this group's symptoms of Occidentosis, namely conspicuous consumerism, materialism and hedonism. The other front consisted of systematic condemnations of this group's attempts to create its identity and prove its superiority over others by flaunting possessions and goods from the West as well as mimicking Western behaviour. Certainly, this group's offensive, even grotesque, exhibitionism provoked abiding resentment among not only party-state intellectuals and publicists but also non-state intellectuals. However, for those situated on the lower rungs of the socio-economic ladder, this behaviour served as a daily reminder not only of the reality of class differences but also of their practical inability to obtain what these Occidentosis-ridden groups enjoyed and flaunted.

Rastakhiz of the Youth early on joined this struggle and targeted students and young professionals. 'The West's examples of life and behaviour drags individuals and especially the young toward the destruction of authenticity and traditions and transforms them into aliens in regard to their own identity and society.' This cultural Occidentosis created groups of Occidentosis-ridden 'bourgeois dancers', who had abandoned traditional austere morality and social duties and conscience in order to drown themselves in consumerism and hedonism. They were superfluous people, leeches on society devoid of understandings and goals above and beyond their personal materialistic interests.

> Consider the way these so-called future educated ones and upper-class brats spend their time. These Occidentosis-ridden ones don't really work. They get money from their parents and spend hour upon hour emptying their brains as they focus solely on having a good time. ... Even in cars they dance and have a good time. This is the result of Occidentosis that brings the degradation and unbalancing of logic, thoughts and intelligence.

Their parents who 'work maybe only four hours a day and then they too, similar to their children, waste their time. ... This empty shameful consumerist life is devoid of humanitarianism.' These people by abandoning humanitarianism had lost fundamental sentiments constituting the authenticity of Iranian identity. This loss of identity,

> where will it lead us? We must teach today's young that they are the generation of the Revolution, that they must go to the school of the Party and Revolution and on the basis of the education provided by this school they can converse about social problems, politics, economics, and even have, sometimes, productive, beneficial recreation.

In order to advance the Revolution's goals 'all these foreign elements and threats to authentic culture must be destroyed'.[11]

These urban Occidentosis-ridden *nouveau riche* stood in stark contrast to the population of small towns and rural areas who 'remains the epitome of culture, authenticity, and national identity and thus the guardians of Iranian traditions, customs, and moral values'.[12] They had not abandoned religion, 'one of the best ways' to immunize people against 'Western materialism and consumerism'.[13] Rastakhiz discourses comparing the 'Occidentosis-ridden state of the youth of the middle and upper classes' with 'the youth of the villages and small urban areas' mirrored ideological and popular tendencies in other societies undergoing Westernization and specifically urbanization and industrialization. They also reflected large swathes of Iranian public and intellectual opinion. This trend was clearly visible in film. Beginning in the late 1950s and gaining momentum in the 1960s and early 1970s was a broad village film genre that expressed this anti-urban and thus anti-Occidentosis theme. These films contained the same fundamental message: 'praise for indigenous values of rural folk and criticism both of distorted Western values and the moral corruption of city dwellers'.[14] As mentioned earlier, this binary view was an axiom of Rastakhiz historiography of Iran according to which urban classes since the Selecuid Empire had excessively indulged in adaption of foreign ways that distanced them from the authentically Iranian population in small urban and rustic areas and primed the country for foreign domination.[15]

The empress claimed that she too found authenticity in this group: 'Foreign culture must not be imposed on the rustic population' while implicitly criticizing those urbanites with a sense of superiority: 'Wearing a coat and trousers is not necessarily a sign of being civilized'.[16] This comment also signalled two emerging changes in the official view of dress. Under Reza Shah Western forms of male and female dress were considered the first and vital step towards being and being seen as civilized. In the later Pahlavi period, in light of the growing negative reaction to *nouveau riche*, this Western dress was also increasingly regarded as a cover for behaviour considered uncivilized and in opposition to the authenticity of Iranian culture. At the same time, this group used the issue of Western dress to denigrate and portray as backward those Iranians who, given either considerations of ethnic or local identities or poverty, did not wear the clothes of the civilized West. Believing that loss of national dress would lead to loss of cultural authenticity, the empress sought to inspire a return to and development of Iranian fashion based on nativist designs and motifs. She supported fashion shows introducing such clothing and wore Iranian-inspired dress at official ceremonies, such as the 1976 celebrations marking the fiftieth anniversary of the Pahlavi dynasty. Keyvan Khosrovani, her chief designer of such clothes, expressed similar statements in his interviews with *The Youth of Rastakhiz*:

> We can revive our old clothes. I take such pleasure in seeing people of the provinces wearing the clothes particular to their region. I myself at times wear baggy Kurdish or Lur pants. However much people laugh at me or look at me with surprise, I pay no attention. But, I do become piqued because they are in reality mocking their own identity and nationality.[17]

Rastakhiz's discursive crusade was not limited to these specific Occidentosis-ridden groups. Occidentosis had infected many areas of the country's social and culture life from where it spread to social groups.[18] The Party held that the most obvious and pernicious forms of Occidentosis could be seen in the fields of cinema, television, music and architecture. It worried that these increasingly Occidentosis-ridden fields would infect the population given their daily contact with them. Therefore, the crusade against Occidentosis, if it was to succeed, had to defeat its manifestations in these fields.

This Party struggle against Occidentosis in those fields faced long-standing complex questions that had to be addressed in order to conceive a coherent, cohesive state cultural policy in the context of the practical process of Westernization and to determine the parameters of the struggle against Occidentosis. First, what cultural and moral standards should the state through censorship and funding propagate and uphold in the arts? The didactic and entertainment value of films and television programmes should be based on what cultural and social bases? Second, should these forms of arts reflect and cater to mass culture or rather should they have as their goal the progressive development of mass culture? If yes, on what should this progressive development be based? Third, what is the role of the state and intellectuals, state as well as non-state, and censorship in this process? Lastly, what were the manifestations of Occidentosis? This question touched on two additional issues. Were such manifestations of Occidentosis limited to the commercialization of the arts and the emergence of pop culture? Or were other forms and specifically avant-garde forms in the arts too a form of Occidentosis that had to be combatted or rather were they didactic, progressive forms of art to be supported? The following two sections, by touching, respectively, on the Party view of cinema and music, give an indication of how the Party approached the struggle with Occidentosis. The following chapter examines these issues deeper by examining the Party approach to the Shiraz Arts Festival and placing it in a limited comparative context.

Filmfarsi

Toghrol Afshar (1933–56) was a well-known albeit young journalist and film critic. His early knowledge of foreign and Iranian cinema was the result of the influence of his mother, Behjat Esfandiari who, along with her brother, Nima Yooshij, the founder of the school of New Iranian Poetry, regularly watched silent movies in hotel cinemas. By the age of seventeen he was already writing a column about cinema in the major daily *Keyhan* and the popular magazine *sepid va Siah*. He subsequently published in the early 1950s a magazine called *The Cinema Courier* at a time when Iranian cinema began to increase its production. At the age of twenty-three he died in a drowning accident.

The importance of this young intellectual to this study lies in his introduction of the terms *ebtezal*, or its adjectival form, *mobtazal*, which can be translated as 'culturally obscene', to categorize and condemn a growing number of commercially made Iranian films that instead of attempting to raise mass taste and recognition of true art catered to and even lowered such taste and recognition in order to be commercially successful. To counter the spread of *mobtazal* films, Afshar, a short time before his accidental drowning, stated his support for a censorship body. When he introduced these terms he surely did not conceive of the long-standing influence he would exercise on discourses about Iranian cinema. From the early 1950s to this day these terms and meanings set the framework for political and social debates about not only film but also music and theatre. Rastakhiz discourses were no exception in this regard. The Party declared war against the spread of *ebtezal* in film and music which it attributed to the spread of the infection of cultural and moral Occidentosis.

The second term essential not only to debates about Iranian cinema but also to Party discourses in this regard was *filmfarsi*. In 1955 in *Ferdowsi* Hushang Kavusi, a well-known film critic and cultural figure, coined it.[19] Following in Afshar's footsteps, the term described commercially made Persian-language films whose production began in the 1950s and increased greatly in popularity and numbers in the 1960s and 1970s. During this period in the opinion of state and non-state intellectuals, the clergy, and educated popular opinion the fundamental characteristic of *filmfarsi* was its catering to and strengthening of mass popular taste rather than assuming cinema's didactic role and raising mass culture. This growing group of critics decried what they described as the cultural obscenity (*ebtezal*), banality and vacuousness of the storylines of *filmfarsi* that paraded in front of the viewer various forms of fist and knife fights, named 'velvet-hat' films because of the fedora worn by the knife-wielding and fist-flying action guys in these films, provocative singing and dancing in cabarets, and varying degrees of silly comedy and comic melodrama.

A colloquial term frequently used to describe such films was *abgushti* or *stewpot*. *Abgusht* is a heavy stew containing mutton, potatoes and fat that is eaten with thick bread. At the time it was a favourite meal among the working and lower classes. The negative meaning of *abgushti* is similar to that of the English term *stewpot*: 'Although many regard stew as an absolutely delicious repast, it formerly was considered a dish far inferior to a large roast, for into the stewpot went small, leftover scraps of meat and vegetables'.[20] *Abgushti* films, similarly, were vastly inferior being made up by scraps of third-rate stories, performances and scenes all thrown together into a cinematic stewpot.

While the proliferation of culturally obscene, stewpot films created growing criticism of government cultural policy, the spread within this so-called genre of 'sexy films' made the issue of cinema politically important. They contained scenes of partial nudity, sexy dancing and suggestive looks and songs performed in front of male audiences in cabarets or downscale nightclubs, and women clothed only in underwear and a bra, negligée and/or bikinis. At the time many people believed that such cabarets and nightclubs were breeding grounds for moral corruption and the women performing in them were little better than prostitutes. Enflaming greatly public opinion were scenes in these films that bordered on the Western conception of soft-core pornography. They did not contain scenes of hardcore pornography.

The spread of *filmfarsi* as an industry was linked to socio-economic changes whose speed increased with the White Revolution. Economic growth, rural–urban migration, urbanization and the expansion of the middle class presented new opportunities to the entertainment industry. In short, increasing numbers of people with increasing amounts of free time and money sought both ways to spend them and forms of escapism. To the horror of intellectuals, socially conservative as well as leftist, and the religious establishment the private commercial sector recognized these opportunities and by the mid-1960s was producing increasing numbers of *filmfarsi* that through mass appeal had the ability to satisfy this growing market. Despite the ideological and philosophical differences between these groups, 'both sides were suspicious of pleasure (as symbolized and provided by *filmfarsi*) for they regarded any type of leisure activity engaged in for its own sake as either socially harmful or religiously harmful'.[21] In the 1960s these groups believed that the spread of the 'culturally obscene' *filmfarsi* genre was a consequence of manifestations of Occidentosis, the most important of which was the commercialization of cinema. The drive for ever-increasing profits was leading to the abandonment of production of films with didactic or artistic value and the spread of two forms of *filmfarsi*. One was the *mobtazal* 'culturally obscene' films and sexy films. The other exercised a deleterious influence on society through its positive portrayal of libertine Western lifestyles. In both cases the fear was a decline in sexual mores and social culture, and an increase in juvenile delinquency and escapism. The Pahlavi state from the mid-1960s found itself under increasing attack by these two groups and public opinion for an ineffective cultural and cinema policy that allowed *filmfarsi* and thus Occidentosis to spread.

In 1964 the MCA was given complete control over matters dealing with the production and supervision of films as well as censorship which had been transferred from the Interior Ministry. These broad responsibilities were consolidated in the Directorate of Supervision and Exhibition (*Edareh-ye nazarat va namaesh*). Its first head was Kavusi who was succeeded in 1967 by Seyyed Ebrahimi Saleh who held this post until 1979. Saleh's arrival brought institutional changes. Under this department's purview two new bodies were established. One, the initial committee, colloquially known as the 'lower committee' because it was housed on the MCA's ground floor, gave initial permission for filming and made decisions about cutting scenes from films and granting licences for their showing. This body included representatives from the MCA, Ministry of Information, Interior Ministry, National Gendarme and SAVAK. Appeals by filmmakers and disagreements within this body were referred to the Supreme Council for Exhibitions of the Arts (*Shura-ye ali-ye honarha-ye namaeshi*), known colloquially as the 'upper commission' whose membership included figures such as Majid Majidi, Baheri, Fereydoun Hoveyda, the prime minister's brother, representatives from SAVAK and the Interior Ministry, among others (Figure 6).[22]

Kavusi, soon after accepting this position, stated his goals and those of state and non-state intellectuals in regard to censorship in an interview with the magazine, *Bahar*.

> Censorship in my opinion is sometimes necessary and sometimes unnecessary. Of course it would be better that censorship as we know it today did not exist but that is dependent on the people. Any time social understanding and education has reached a certain point [and thus people are not prone to imitate and mimic behavior in films] then censorship is unnecessary. We see that in more developed societies censorship is much weaker than in societies that have fallen behind. In any case, in my opinion, the best form of censorship that is necessary is valued-based. One must prevent the spread of cultural obscenity (*ebtezal*) in any of its forms – music, literature, cinema, theatre, art. Easy profits from simple works is a danger to society's cultural and educational progress.[23]

Figure 6 Hushang Kavusi, author's collection.

Years before he was more blunt: 'A dictatorship of art must be established in order to acquaint people with what art of value is and to throw to the waste side forms of pseudo-art'.[24] His remarks mirrored those made by Mohammad Ali Samii, head of the Exhibition Commission that played a decisive role in censorship at the end of the 1950s: 'Since the growth of the intellectual thought of the Iranian people has not been significant and [thus] they often cannot understand well a film's story and comprehend its finer points, it is necessary that censorship be severe, in particular in regard to *filmfarsi* since a majority of Iranians imitate others'.[25] Kavusi's and Samii's remarks show that a number of state and non-state intellectuals, while finding political censorship illegitimate to varying degrees, considered censorship in the arts legitimate given their negative appraisal of mass culture and their claims to be the bearers of enlightenment and therefore responsible for the people's acculturation.

Acting on these sentiments, Kavusi issued new censorship guidelines in order to combat the spread of *filmfarsi* and specifically 'culturally obscene' films and provide a framework for the moralism, didacticism and high culture he and others believed had to be at the centre of Iranian cinema. Some of the scenes and themes that were banned are summarized in order to provide a sense of the conditions in which Iranian cinema found itself:

> (a) Insulting religions and anything held religiously sacred; (b) defaming the shah or the imperial family; (c) scenes showing revolt and rebellion against state security, police, and military forces; (d) defaming state officials; (e) Propagation of illegal ideologies and schools of thought; (f) scenes showing the assassination of state officials; (g) Encouraging despicable, wretched, vile and inhumane acts such as betrayal, criminality, espionage, adultery, homosexuality, theft, bribery, and violation of other peoples' rights in such a way that lacks a positive and humanist ending; (h) Sex scenes seeking either to satisfy lewd desires or attract viewers; and (i) Revealing body parts of men, women, boys, and girls that should remain covered and thus offends public morality.

The last two points dealt with 'sexy films'. Point twenty of these guidelines addressed the fundamental nature of *filmfarsi* that had to be censored or banned: 'Films that in totality or in parts, as a result of lacking value (*biarzeshi*), create conditions for the spread of acceptance of cultural obscenity (*mobtazalpasandi*) amongst viewers must be censored and/or prevented from being shown'.[26]

Despite attempts to ensure adherence to these guidelines, the spread of *filmfarsi* continued during the last fifteen years of Pahlavi rule and exercised a negative influence on public attitudes towards the government given its responsibility for issuing film licences. Hoveyda did not interfere in the workings of the MCA and this department and limited himself to rhetoric about the need to protect authenticity of culture and national identity in the face of Occidentosis.[27] Yet, from the late 1960s a growing number within the elite recognized that this failure in combatting 'culturally obscene' *filmfarsi* was beginning to damage state legitimacy in religious and intellectual circles and within public opinion. At the same time many within the elite too expressed discontent and outrage over the spread of 'sexy films'. Given state control over licensing and censorship many within these circles began to consider 'commercial cinema as a conspiracy staged by a powerful yet fearful government in collaboration with a profit-hungry commercial movie business to dupe Iranians by means of fantasy, sex, and violence'.[28] Moreover, attacks on government cultural and cinema policy effectively undermined state claims to be the guardian of authenticity and strengthened the impression that it was the leading spreader of Occidentosis. Kavusi, soon after abandoning this post, noted:

> I wanted to establish new criteria for the cutting of film scenes. Unfortunately, I was only about twenty percent successful. In any case Article 20 of the censorship guidelines … is my legacy. In general I am against censorship. However, I am for it only in those cases that censorship and control are used in regard to values. A film that lacks value and is a cultural obscenity (*mobtazal*) must without fear or hesitation be rejected.[29]

One problem faced by the government and the critics of *filmfarsi* is that it was indeed a popular genre as evidenced by statistics published by the MCA in 1973 and 1976. Thus, many producers of *filmfarsi* claimed that they were only responding to mass tastes. On the contrary, state and non-state intellectuals and the religious establishment charged that the producers of *filmfarsi*, materialistic and commercially driven, in other words, Occidentosis-ridden, inculcated and spread the taste for culturally obscene *filmfarsi* in society instead of trying to raise the moral, cultural and spiritual levels of the masses. For many in the artistic and intellectual elite, as well as state intellectuals, *filmfarsi* and societal preference for it were indicative of the mutually reinforcing elements of Occidentosis.

A key reason for the spread of *filmfarsi* was also censorship. During Saleh's tenure, sensitivity to implicit political issues and themes in films significantly increased. This policy move played a decisive role in creating the conditions for the 'production of more violent and sexually charged but politically safe, escapist, and melodramatic commercial movies, such as the stewpot and tough-guy films'[30] that in the increasingly commercialized cinema industry offered the prospect of profitmaking given the inability to make socially and politically meaningful films that might cross the state's political and ideological red lines. Additionally, the state failed to have a cohesive, well-funded film policy that created the financial and artistic conditions for the flowering of the moral, artistic and didactic films that were supported by state and non-state intellectuals. Lastly but just as importantly, a major problem faced by the department was differences of opinion over what constituted 'cultural obscenity' (*mobtazal*).

Adding to the spread of *filmfarsi* was the increased importation of US films by the end of the 1960s by which time the majority of major US film studios had opened offices in Tehran: Columbia, MGM, Paramount, 20th Century Fox, United Artists and Warner Brothers. 'The flooding of the top markets with foreign action and sex movies forced domestic commercial producers to join the deluge. Film markets became saturated with foreign movies and their local imitations. Signs of crisis began to surface'.[31] The increase in such US films greatly stoked fears about the spread of moral and cultural Occidentosis, whose consequence, Rastakhiz warned, was

> the Hollywoodization of the youth. ... A group of our youth is moving in the direction of Hollywood culture. ... They adapt the music, language, and forms of recreation and consumerism from these Western films. Foreign cigarettes with foreign brands, foreign clothes with foreign labels, foreign dances with foreign music and orchestra – our youth must eradicate Western culture from themselves. They can allow Western culture to touch them lightly but they must not permit themselves to be duped and deceived by it![32]

In the immediate years before the Party's establishment, growing negative perceptions and worries in public opinion about *filmfarsi* were increasingly expressed in books and mass media. Not surprisingly, concern and outrage focused on the increasing production of 'sexy films' that, as described at the time, were 'a new form of perversion and seduction that has spread everywhere, even into the home'. These works decried that 'Iranian cinema has been a follower of European and Western cinema and imitates all of their corrupted and corrupting elements'.[33] In the words of one contemporary researcher on this issue, at that time 'directors would find any flimsy excuse to include otherwise incongruous sexual scenes'.[34] The increasing public and intellectual discontent over these issues is reflected in the book *Negative Viewing* published in 1974. A compilation of quotations and commentaries from Iranian periodicals and newspapers condemning the sex, violence and immorality in cinema and NIRT television programming, it issued a direct message to the government to act.[35]

One of the best contemporaneous sources for coverage on the evolution of the topic of sex in *filmfarsi* is the monthly journal *This Week* (*In hafte*). It began publication in 1966 as an English-language magazine for tourists that offered articles about Tehran, cultural news, and listings of events, cinema showings, theatre and cabaret performances, and a television guide. In 1971 Javad Allamirdolu, who had studied in Belgium and France and had been a journalist for *Ettela'at, L'Express* and *Le Monde*, obtained the right to publish it. He transformed it into a Persian-language erotic magazine, the first in Iran, to the outrage of the clergy and public opinion. With pictures of semi-nude women and articles on aspects of sex, it provided regular updates on *filmfarsi* movies with such scenes and the actresses and actors performing in them. Since this magazine claimed to focus also on social issues, it sought to give the impression that it was touching on these topics in a serious manner. Even it confessed in its 1972 Iranian New Year edition: 'Sex over the last year has placed Iranian cinema, as well as world cinema, under its influence. Given the attraction of sex in films people come. Thus, producers have found more reason to include these themes and scenes because their first goal is profit'.[36] The commercialization of cinema that led to the spread of 'sex' in films was openly admitted. For example, *This Week* reported

> Nematollah Aqassi, the well-known singer [a male singer in down-scale clubs known for singing *abgushti* songs] is now filming the last scene of his first film, *Eivallah*. Originally the film was supposed to be a drama but in the light of success of sexy films the producer, [Manuchehr] Nouzari, has sought refuge in sex and wants to ensure commercial success with this spice (Figures 7 and 8).[37]

The film did indeed enjoy success. The magazine's continuing coverage explained the success of such films: 'The market for sex is hot! ... Iranian filmmakers, in the footsteps of Western filmmakers, have discovered for themselves a tendency for sex in films while a number of stars of Iranian cinema has shown great audacity in engaging in sex scenes'.[38] To place these changes in perspective, in 1959 some twenty minutes of Parviz Khatibi's film *The Enemy of Woman* (*Doshman-e Zan*) were censored since the male hero, a teacher, taught in a girls' school.[39]

At the end of 1973 *Culture and Society*, the journal of the SCCA, issued a special edition devoted to the condition of cinema and theatre. The lead article 'Prelude to the Sociology of Cinema', examined the link between sociological and cinematic trends, and specifically the rapid growth in production of Iranian erotic films, over the last couple of years:

> Until the closing years of the last decade [1970-1971] *filmfarsi* did not contain much sex. But gradually Persian-language cinema in light of the wave of sex in world cinema did not allow itself to be left behind. The consequence of this new

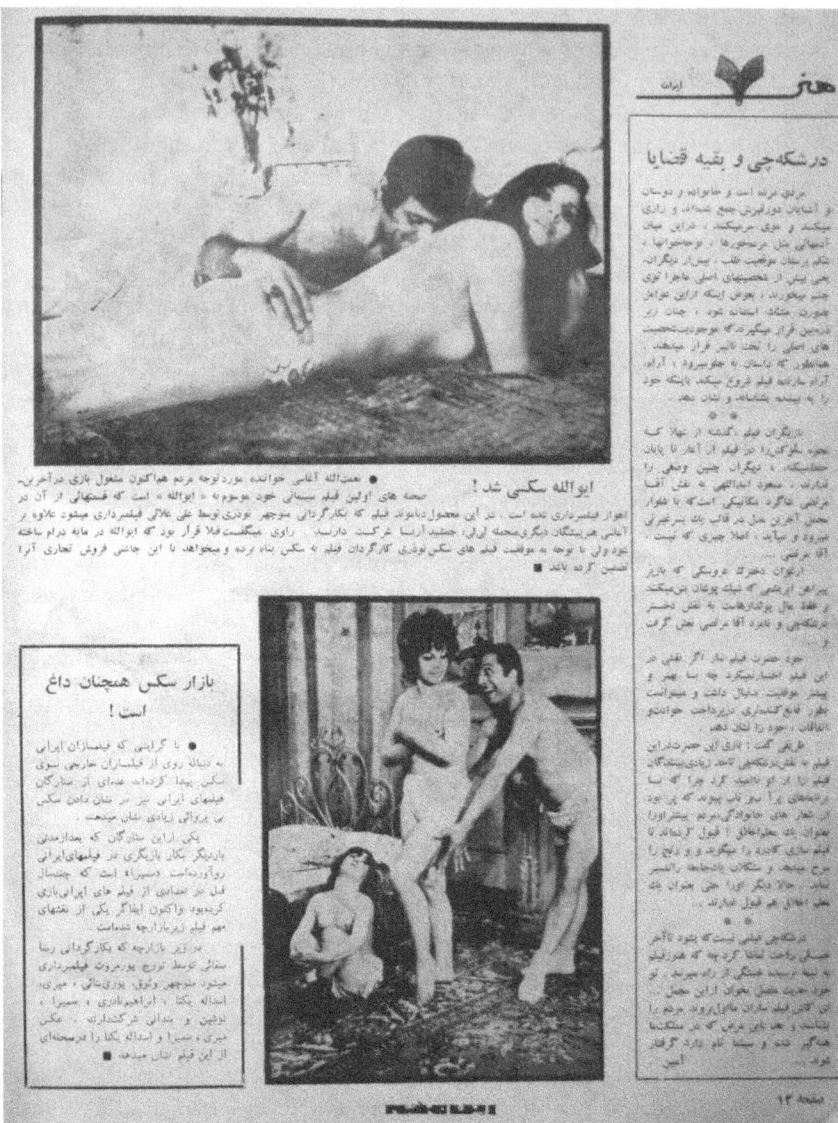

Figure 7 Top: Scenes from the film *Eivallah* starring Nematollah Aqassi. The headline reads: 'Eivallah has gone sexy!' Bottom left headline reads: 'The market of sex remains hot!'. *In Hafte*, author's collection.

wave in *filmfarsi* is the emergence of sex stars (*setarehha-ye sex*) or the Goddesses of sex (*Elaheha-ye sex*). It has become such that at the present one of the principle trends of *filmfarsi* is sex.[40]

The cult of celebrity that followed the better-known stars of *filmfarsi* emerged alongside the rapid growth in the coverage of the country's mass media and advertising

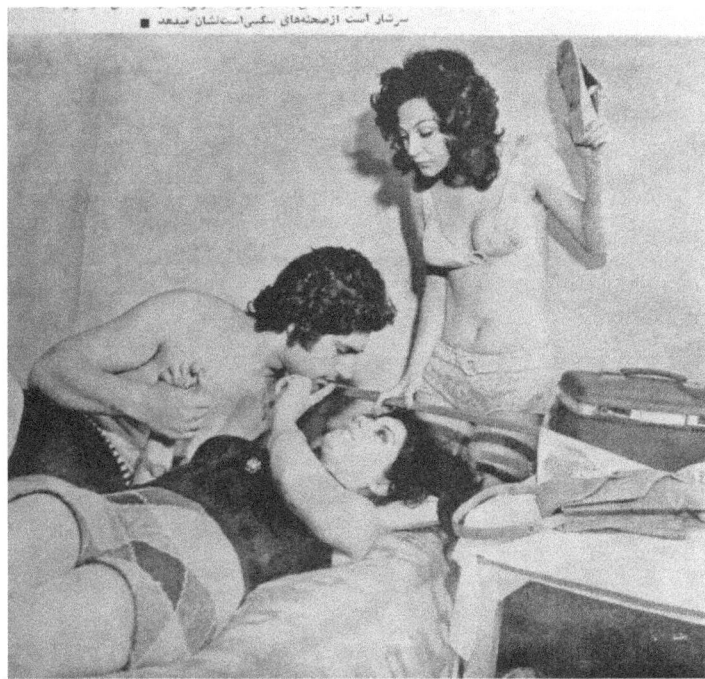

Figure 8 Scene from film *Sunday's Woman (Zan-e yekshanbe)*. In *Hafte*, author's collection.

industry that now stretched across the country. The cult of celebrity inevitably came to be an instrument of the advertising industry which used these stars to promote consumer goods, from refrigerators to clothes and shoes. However, the sexual themes and the transformation of women into sex stars within *filmfarsi* that accompanied the expansion of advertising added to growing public frustration. The newspaper and magazine advertisements of the Iranian manufacturer of durable consumer goods, *Azmaesh*, provides just one example of this growing tendency. The advertisements for its refrigerator contained a picture of a beautiful woman leering at the reader while her bare breasts were partially covered by her hands that nonetheless showed enough bare skin to allow imaginations to run, especially after reading the text placed between her and the refrigerator: 'A sexy woman is hot, hot hot, but an *Azmaesh* refrigerator is cold, cold, cold!' (Figure 9)

On 2 May 1972 the armed opposition group *Fallah* bombed the offices of *This Week* located on Ferdowsi Street in the centre of Tehran. Mortaza Alviri, who headed the bombing, described his reasons and, implicitly, the growing discontent over moral Occidentosis.

> In that magazine (*This Week*) sexy pictures were published. It was the only magazine in the country doing this. I had great sensitivity in regard to this journal. I felt a responsibility to struggle against it. ... [I believed] that this type of magazine was very noxious and deleterious to the youth who were the future fighters and

Figure 9 'What is the difference between a sexy woman and an Azmaesh refrigerator?', author's collection.

militants. Therefore we had to struggle against this form of magazine and prevent our youth from following the path to which this form of publication wanted to push them.[41]

The following month SAVAK permanently closed this magazine.[42]

Complicating the government's situation were intellectual films and specifically Iranian New Wave cinema that had emerged in the mid-1960s in the wake of French New Wave cinema. This genre, dedicated to exploring various forms of social conditions and thus making implicit social and political criticisms, posed particular challenges to the state. On the one hand, it represented the didactic films theoretically sought but, on the other hand, tried to use social themes to make implicit social and/or political criticism. Moreover, some of these films, in the footsteps of the West's New Wave cinema, used the theme of sex and scenes of partial nudity that had the potential to enflame religious and socially conservative elite and mass opinion about the spread of moral Occidentosis. In this regard, Khosrow Haritash's film *The Turmoil of Love* (*Qiamat-e Eshq*, 1972) is a good example. Its portrayal of a man's struggle between, on the one hand, his belief in religion and thus austere sexual morality and, on the other, sexual passion was geared to appeal to an educated audience. However, scenes of partial nudity in which the actress Fereshte Jenabi played the key role and the love scene between the son of the film's main character and the girl in question subjected this film to criticism from certain circles for signs of moral Occidentosis.[43]

The Story of Mahan (*Qesse-ye Mahan*) released in 1973 represented a film genre situated between stewpot and highbrow intellectual films. On the one hand, it sought to provide a moral lesson.[44] On the other hand, it also created controversy. In it Noush Afarin (Fateme Abdi), only seventeen at the time, had a nude scene. She played in five more *filmfarsi* that year. Once she became famous in *filmfarsi*, she went on to become a pop singer. Her path into *filmfarsi* and to notoriety that included such scenes was increasingly offered by *filmfarsi* companies and producers to young aspiring actresses. *The Youth of Rastakhiz*, following in the footsteps of critical media attention to this issue before the Party's establishment, published numerous articles condemning this path. At the same time it decried the infection of the youth by Occidentosis which tore them away from traditional Iranian morality and threw them into the arms of these Occidentosis-ridden figures and into such sexy scenes. *Ferdowsi* succinctly summarized the feelings held by many when it decried 'prostitution in *filmfarsi*' (Figure 10).[45]

The state's growing sensitivity to political themes and symbolism and to social criticism about the spread of moral Occidentosis in cinema is seen in another of Haritash's films, *Speeding Naked Till Noon*, released in 1976. The film's story is simple. Perhaps taking inspiration from Dostoevsky's Rodion Raskolnikov in *Crime and Punishment*, it is about a young student heavily indebted to a money-changer whom he kills. He is then forced to abandon the girl he loves and enter into a relationship with an older woman who had witnessed the killing. The film contained nudity and scenes of soft porn in which the actresses Fereshte Jenabi and Eren played alongside Faramarz Sadiqi who played the role of the student. Government censors had three fundamental problems with it. First, 'because a loathsome money-charger's business was called Imperial' censors believed that this figure 'could be interpreted as referencing the

Figure 10 Snapshot from sexy *filmfarsi* 'Three-person Bed' (Takht-e Khab-e Senafare) published in *Ferdowsi* with condemning article 'The Naked Women of *filmfarsi*'. *Ferdowsi*, author's collection.

government'. Second, according to Haritash himself the theme of a university student and his socio-economic plight had dangerous 'political overtures'.[46] Lastly, the nudity and scenes of soft porn were considered too much in light of public opinion. After a long process the film was cut by thirty minutes.[47] Public opinion regarded this film with such scenes as another manifestation of moral Occidentosis. Rastakhiz criticized this film. However, as a whole Rastakhiz publications did not attack these intellectual films and in fact provided a good deal of coverage to filmmakers within this genre, including Haritash, that included multi-part interviews in which, among other themes, he frequently condemned the commercialization of *filmfarsi*.

'Sexy films' in *filmfarsi*, therefore, was one of the first targets of Rastakhiz publications. 'In *our* history people have never looked upon a human as a commodity, a piece of merchandise', to be degraded in such films in order to obtain profits.

> *Filmfarsi* producers and particularly those making 'sexy' films must either voluntarily become national [and adhere to Iranian authenticity] or be brought under government control. ... Why is it that our filmmakers, actors, and actresses instead of making historical films, films strong with proud historical themes, for the sake of a few thousand rials are prepared to corrupt public morality? ... The majority of our filmmakers has some kind of sexual sickness. With stripping women naked in films they humiliate and degrade them. ... The youth provide momentum to this tendency because they are, unfortunately, infatuated with the West.[48]

In 1974 the MCA issued addendums to censorship guidelines in an attempt to respond to growing public criticism. It once again banned 'the showing of naked organs of both males and females (and) sexual details (*joziat-e jensi*)'. *The Youth of Rastakhiz*, reviewing previous government (in)action on this issue, argued that these 1974 new guidelines, which the government had announced with fanfare, were in reality nothing more than reiteration of earlier guidelines that had banned such scenes. Rastakhiz argued that the problem was not in the guidelines but rather government enforcement. Moreover, the 1974 addendums were

> unclear and ambiguous. What organs, what parts of the body should not be shown naked? …What does the term 'sexual details' in these guidelines mean? … In any case the producers of *filmfarsi* place a very small black spot on the related areas. Of course, they do this not to satisfy the MCA, but rather to attract and entice filmgoers with the label: '*Entrance forbidden to those under 18*' in the hope of raising ticket sales.

Despite this 1974 directive, the government failed to stem the spread not only of *filmfarsi* that contained these 'sexual details' but also public discontent by indirectly drawing attention to its laxity in enforcing these regulations. 'Those responsible have never taken seriously their duty in dealing with *filmfarsi*. In reality, along with the agents of *filmfarsi*, they too are only fooling and juggling about and making a spectacle'.[49]

Rastakhiz by focusing on this issue reflected public opinion and co-opted themes increasingly covered by the print media in the years leading to the Party's establishment. *Sepide va Siah*, a long-running and popular magazine dedicated to social, cultural issues, published in 1972 a letter supposedly penned by a teenager to his mother who was following the path subsequently taken by Noush Afarin into the 'culturally obscene' world of *filmfarsi*. It reflects the tone of the media and public opinion.

> Mother, you are good. I love you so much. … The work you do to an extent has an effect on me, it is linked to me. If your income increases, my appearance and clothing become better, my financial situation becomes better. I know all of your efforts are for my well-being and good fortune. If I ask you why you are naked in *filmfarsi*, without a doubt you will stress the rise in living costs and say that you get naked because they give you more money. However, that answer will not satisfy me. I prefer that you become a simple pure actress and that your income remains little. Instead of my going to one of the best schools in Europe I can go to a small school in our country. Don't expect that if I study in Europe where nudity is not an important issue I will become similar to Westerners. No! I will not change my morals and worldview. … If I see your pictures in magazines in which you are naked and in the arms of different men, what kind of feeling do you think I would have?[50]

In this context Rastakhiz provided its definition of *filmfarsi* and determined what constituted 'cultural obscenity'. They were films characterized by 'inappropriate scenes of violence and sex' and 'a collection of unrelated and illogical events … *Filmfarsi* is a form of hocus pokus … *Filmfarsi* producers are only merchants with only one goal, money. Consequently, they pay no attention to culture and authenticity of culture'.[51] At the same time, 'velvet-hat films are not true National Iranian cinema'.[52] Both types had to be censored and banned. It needs to be mentioned that films, 'simple films' that had purely entertainment value but lacked 'corrupted morality' and 'cultural obscenity' were not considered *filmfarsi* (Figure 11).

Figure 11 Cover of *The Youth of Rastakhiz* providing illustrations of the condemned themes of *filmfarsi* that are cancelled by a big 'X'. *Javanan-e Rastakhiz*, author's collection.

Rastakhiz regarded the commercialization of cinema and the spread of *filmfarsi* as the consequences of Occidentosis:

> The reality is that … the distinguished groups of high-quality filmmakers … face constant attacks by *filmfarsi* and will remain so, without doubt, far into the future. The justifications *filmfarsi* producers make in order to defend themselves are more ridiculous and comical than the films they make. Their most commonly

cited excuse is capital used in film production that must be returned with a profit. At first glance this premise is correct. However, the fundamental issue is whether they have the right and license to produce whatever they want in order to recoup their capital and obtain a profit. They imagine that they have this right and license. Therefore, if they throw human dignity and the reality of human existence in this world into the gutter in order to obtain a return on their capital and simultaneously hollow and empty societal values and beliefs – it is no big deal.[53]

Without doubt, 'the only result of the production of *filmfarsi* is the filling of the pockets and wallets of the profit seekers' who produce these films while 'the majority of *filmfarsi* producers believe that cinema and filmmaking are similar to the selling of second-hand cars and jerry-building ... [they] are traders peddling fundamentally corrupted goods'.[54] These people were portrayed in essentialist terms, so thoroughly Occidentosis-ridden that their redemption and return to Iranian authenticity was almost an impossibility:

Any attacks we make on these film producers, whom we blame for the problems facing us, cannot go any farther than 'moral' advice and even then no guarantee exists that such advice would work since if from the outset they were concerned about preservation of national morality and respect for national culture and traditions and even for cinema-goers themselves they would never have made such films in the first place. They are merchants selling corruption.[55]

They had created a 'cultureless movement ... [based on] 'cultural obscenity, demagogy' that had 'became rooted in Iranian cinema and grew'. This movement through the 'trick' of the cultivation of mass culture's base elements sought only to increase its commercial success.[56]

Rastakhiz publications, as part of the party campaign against Occidentosis, frequently interviewed leading intellectuals and cultural figures to discuss the current state of the arts, art forms and their role in society. Such interviews not only gave legitimacy and gravitas to the crusade against *filmfarsi* but also, it was hoped, strengthen the Party's standing in intellectual circles and public opinion. For example, Haritash in a series of interviews he gave to *The Youth of Rastakhiz* echoed Rastakhiz concerns:

In *filmfarsi* everything must be built anew. ... The spread of cinemas in the various places of the city [Tehran] was only for the showing of *filmfarsi*. ... Businessmen placed cinema in a coffin. ... Because of the search for profit by producers, an illiterate group of screenwriters became famous. ... *Filmfarsi* producers are cultureless and greedy profiteers. They have never used any capital to create a film with cultural value. ... If you give *filmfarsi* makers all the necessary tools and capital, they will once again make bad films. ... Those who defend *filmfarsi* are the same ones who are searching for an opportunity to make such films and money.[57]

Rastakhiz warned that the people under its leadership would recognize and reject the cultural obscenity of *filmfarsi*. 'The producers of *filmfarsi* forgot that you can fool some of the people some of the time, but not all the people all of the time'. With the Party's help, the masses would lament, just as intellectuals, educated people and the Party, that 'Iranian cinema began with the ideas of "mission", "truth" and "healthiness" and was continuing to evolve along this path when the thoughts and ideas of money-makers, the destroyers of creativity, and other purveyors of "the so-called inevitable cultures (*farhangha-ye nagorizi*)" of the West infected this process and brought Iranian cinema "to the abyss of collapse, death, and breakdown"'.[58] It proclaimed: '*Filmfarsi*–cancelled, *filmfarsi*–voided'.[59] This expression was a play on that used by Hossein Yazdanian in his attack on *filmfarsi* in his book published in 1968:

> Without a doubt the day will come that the people as a result of such films and television programming will become infuriated and through the burning of films express their disgust. … Without a doubt the day will come that the masses will bring pressure to their own authorities to close these places of deceit and seduction.[60]

Yazdanian's book, known only among intellectuals and parts of educated society, and the increasing worry about the spread of *filmfarsi* among state and non-state intellectuals are both seen in the 1973 popular film *Bita* directed by a leading figure in progressive Iranian cinema, Hezhir Dariush. Kavusi himself appears in one scene as a reporter. In a meeting with co-workers he is supposed to discuss a proposed exposé showing a link between commercialization and cinema. Their expressed serious concerns about the possible reactions to publishing it implicitly refers to the idea of powerful groups pushing this commercialization. In another scene the rather young and somewhat naïve Bita, played by Gugush, who is in love with a journalist in the field of economics, goes to a bookstore to buy him a gift. After she poses several questions that reflect her naïve world view, the bookseller suggests Yazdanian's book.[61]

Rastakhiz pointed a finger of responsibility for the spread of *filmfarsi* at government maladministration and took particular aim at the Directorate of Supervision and Exhibition:

> This office's duty is to judge and gauge these films' quality and moral appropriateness. Its duty is to censor those films that are determined to be harmful to society's culture. This office's duty is to prevent the spread and distribution of films that harm and render damage to cultural and national dignity and the country's status. Does this office fulfil this duty?

In order to answer this question *The Youth of Rastakhiz* in the course of several issues examined this directorate's activities and government performance. It reported that 'from 1972 to now (1976) some 289 *filmfarsi* haven been produced' and that 75 of the 132 cinemas in Tehran were showing 'sexy films'. Only one conclusion could be made. The MCA and this directorate were not performing their duties.[62]

The more dangerous culprit was the influence of Western films and television programming. Rastakhiz believed that the success of its campaign against the spread of Occidentosis in Iranian cinema was contingent on obtaining government action limiting severely their import. The import of Western films was increasing since the late 1960s. By 1974 some 40 per cent of television programmes were imports, primarily from the United States, while by 1976 the ratio of foreign imports to domestically produced television programmes increased by three to one. By the mid-1970s, when Rastakhiz began its campaign, it was even becoming cheaper to import Western programmes than to make domestic ones given rising production costs and tax structure. The danger these Western films posed was clear:

> Film is a form of indoctrination, an actor's every movement, every word that is said in the film, its very setting makes an impression on the viewer, and especially the young. The film's very foreignness impresses itself on the viewer. [Thus] the youth become separated from their national culture. They abandon their traditions slowly and unwittingly and accept the West's culture as the example and standard of behavior. … It is traitorous if we strengthen [through these films] elements of Western culture. It is traitorous if we remain silent. We will be satisfied when we protect national culture and no longer propagate Western culture.[63]

Armed with these statistics Rastakhiz publications broadened their attacks on government inaction and maladministration that allowed the spread of Western films and television programmes it described as 'the culmination of an anti-cultural movement inspired by the West'.[64] Stressing that such films and television programmes culturally polluted viewers and created the conditions for the further spread of commercialization of cinema Rastakhiz asked: 'Those responsible, do not they see these imported pornographic and culturally obscene films? These films are an attack not only on traditional Iranian values but also cultural authenticity. The Party's goal therefore is to purify Iranian films of this influence'.[65]

While Rastakhiz certainly decried government inaction on this issue, its discursive ire was equally, if not more intense, in regard to the role of Westerners and the West's civilizational attributes, namely rampant commercialization and culturelessness. Party discourses were premised on the belief that 'Western filmmakers came, sold pictures, got their money and scuttled off'.[66] These Western film producers and studios epitomized the commercialization of cinema and had little concern for authentically artistic and didactic films and no care for the damage they did to the cinema of the non-Western world. Ultimately, *filmfarsi*, in order to remain commercially viable was forced to replicate the forms and methods of these increasingly popular US and west-European, particularly Italian 'B', films. Yet, *filmfarsi* producers were not innocent. 'The narrow-minded and short-sighted producers of *filmfarsi*, thinking only of box-office receipts, have been engaged in the most weak and pithy work'.[67]

Another target of Rastakhiz publications was cinema owners who were portrayed as Occidentosis-ridden and thus indifferent to the artistic or didactic role of authentic Iranian films. In this regard it referred to statistics published by the MCA that showed that Hollywood films dominated the cinemas in upper-class northern Tehran while the cinemas of the city's southern poorer areas showed genuine Iranian films. Using these statistics Rastakhiz made more effective its discourses of Occidentosis by adding a socio-economic dynamic. Unlike the true Iranians living 'around Shush Square' and the rustic youth who, it was claimed, appreciated true Iranian films, the Occidentosis-ridden youth of the *nouveau riche* were a major reason for the popularity of Western films and television programmes. 'These "upper-class" brats must accept that one high-culture Iranian film is worth hundreds of such non-Iranian films'.[68] These cinemas showed these Western films in order to cater to the 'brats' of the Occidentosis-ridden *nouveau riche*. Rastakhiz publications charged that these cinema owners were 'evil-minded, malevolent people [who] don't give good Iranian films the opportunity to succeed. ... These cinema proprietors don't pay any attention to one issue – the duty and responsibility to propagate authentic culture and thought.' Instead they focus on 'culturally obscene, superficial, worthless Western films'. The Party called for the MCA to force cinemas, and especially in those 'fancy areas' of northern Tehran, 'to show good Iranian films and drop the focus on Western films'.[69] Farrokh Ghaffari, a well-known cultural intellectual involved in cinema and close to the empress, in an interview at the end of 1977 with *Rastakhiz of the Youth* summed up these party themes: 'Culturelessness is the unifying element of *filmfarsi*. ... The government must act [to create the conditions] for the production and exhibition of good films.' He too blamed cinema owners whom he described as ' merchants who do not take into account cultural issues'. But they were not solely responsible. 'Bad American films ruined the people's view [of cinema]'.[70]

The Party in early 1977 established to great fanfare a special committee that, in response to public opinion, would examine the causes for the spread of *filmfarsi* and Occidentosis and the financial and moral crises in Iranian cinema while *The Youth of Rastakhiz* promised ongoing coverage of its work whose results would be presented to the government. The Party promised to secure government action. Ali Reza Meybodi chaired this committee. It held its first dialogue sessions on 8 June 1977. It attendees included Homayoun, the deputy party head; Majidi, representatives from the MCA; Ministry of Economy and Finance; Tehran City Hall; Abbas Shabaaviz, Secretary of Society of Producers; Hashem Khermand, advisor to the minister of culture and deputy responsible for cinema in the MCA; Ali Abbas, film producer; Said Matlabi, film director and representative from the film director's guild, among others.

The first issue addressed was the causes for the current state of Iranian cinema and the spread of *filmfarsi* and sexy films. Shabaaviz argued that 'all those involved have led cinema to its death' while Mohammad Ibrahimi, a well-known film critic, rejected the idea that the current lamentable state of Iranian cinema was in fact a new condition: 'We don't have a cinema over whose corpse we should mourn. Everybody knows this. ... Cultural obscenity after cultural obscenity piled up one after another' had sometime before destroyed the body of Iranian cinema that resulted in no cinema. Meybodi, fulfilling the Party's role, led the attack on the government's role in this matter.

> As a filmmaker, and not as this meeting's moderator, I have a question for Mr. Khermand and an entreaty to which he and the other responsible figures in the Ministry of Culture and Art need to answer. Today ninety percent of the movie screens in Iran are at the disposal of culturally obscene Western films. These films exercise a very bad influence on the people's culture, mentality, and common sense. I want to see if Iranian filmmakers make Iranian copies of such films

would you allow them to be shown? No way exists for us to separate Western culturally obscene films from domestic ones. Any culturally obscene film must be ostracized. ... However, why does the Ministry make distinctions between these culturally obscene films? In this way it has created a situation in which it seems to be supporting propagation of culturally obscene foreign films in the country. Seemingly, such cultural obscenity has a right to make its impression on the people's mentality and common sense while Iranian cultural obscenity does not enjoy such a right.

Khermand, in the face of this and other criticisms sought to defend the MCA's performance. He stressed that the MCA's approach to licensing and censorship was based on the idea that 'between Iranian and Western cultural obscenity no difference exists'. Seeking to blunt this criticism, he stressed that some 25 per cent of foreign films brought into the country end up in the MCA's 'rubbish bin'. He admitted that implementation of guidelines that dictated what constituted cultural obscenity had been at times weak and inconsistent given problems in the training of MCA cadres. Consequently, a number of culturally obscene films, Iranian as well as Western, had obtained licences. His response to charges that the government and specifically the MCA had played a determinative role in the spread of *filmfarsi* reflected the standard party-state approach: 'To those people who now criticize us I must say that Iranian cinema, from its inception, 100% of the time followed only commercial goals.' Thus they spread popular acceptance of cultural obscenity and low taste.

In another series of meetings Khermand's attempt to place blame on figures in Iranian cinema for the spread of *filmfarsi* was criticized with relatively forceful language. The government and its policy of censorship were charged with playing a leading role in the spread of cultural obscenity in *filmfarsi*. Shabaaviz led this attack. The nature of this censorship and, he implied, excessive sensitivity to topics and scenes that could seemingly be considered political had 'forced Iranian filmmakers to film stories about prostitutes and those with the velvet hats' since little was left to attract viewers.[71] Moreover, the censorship process itself had gradually and unintentionally pushed filmmakers in the direction of sexy and velvet-hat films by teaching two valuable lessons. First, they had to avoid politically sensitive issues and not cross political red lines. Second, implementation of the guidelines dealing with 'cultural obscenity' and themes such as nudity and violence was patchy.

During these meetings the government was also attacked for allowing a flood of foreign, and in particular Western films, to enter the country. That which provoked particularly strong criticism was tax policy that imposed a higher rate on the showing of Iranian films than on Western ones. At the same time, the government had not allowed the price of tickets for Iranian films to rise despite growing costs of production. This had not only pushed filmmakers to make increasingly 'culturally obscene' films in the hope of covering costs and achieving a profit but had also led many to abandon film-making.

The MCA, in response to these criticisms and growing public and party pressure, prepared a new package of measures. It announced new directives that banned any form of nudity, sex scenes and 'such scenes considered an insult to public decency'.

In February 1978 in the face of continued party pressure it issued a blanket ban on sex themes in films, domestic as well as international.[72] It also promised more strict interpretation of what constituted culturally obscene foreign films and linked permission for showing by cinemas of foreign films with the purchase of Iranian ones. The Party while claiming a victory, noted again that the real issue was whether the government would ensure their enforcement. It promised updates on the extent of government enforcement of these guidelines.

Determining the causes of the MCA's failure to address these growing concerns about *filmfarsi*, particularly sexy films and film imports, especially from the West and the delay in responding to such concerns is difficult and would require a separate research monograph. After the Revolution, Pahlbod confessed that, although censorship and the institutions for it were housed in his ministry, 'We were entangled in amazingly diverse and mercurial trends and currents of thought. Coordinating and handling them was completely impossible'.[73] His remarks leave many questions unanswered. Yet, the Rastakhiz Party had seized this issue and made some progress in forcing the government to address the issues that had provoked intellectual and public criticism of government performance.

Rastakhiz also frequently attacked NIRT programming for which Qotbi was responsible as NIRT head. After the Revolution his management at NIRT has been frequently criticized by members of the Pahlavi-era elite for programming that exercised a negative political influence on public perceptions of the general trajectory of state cultural policy. One problem, underlined by Sabeti, was that coordinating cultural policy was difficult given Qotbi's links with the empress that allowed him to ignore organs such as SAVAK, which was sensitive to trends in public opinion and perceptions, and the SCCA, which advocated a more conservative approach and sought to coordinate and harmonize state cultural policy. Sabeti has praised Qotbi's ability in establishing countrywide television coverage and in producing a good number of programmes of pure entertainment. However, 'he failed in creating effective cultural and political programs' that were sensitive to popular culture and world view. In addition, Qotbi's unwillingness to coordinate with the SCCA has been noted by its members while Pahlbod too was critical of Qotbi's broadcasting, believing it was too liberal and Westernized, promoting ideals, art and culture at odds with the authenticity of Iranian culture and national identity.[74]

The issues driving Rastakhiz criticism were familiar and clear. The Party proclaimed that as a whole 'current TV production and programming are an experiment in cultural obscenity. The current Iranian and Western banal and culturally obscene compilation of TV programs has left no room for Iranian culture.' Radio 2 was frequently attacked: 'Every time you turn it on Western music is being played … Rastakhiz demands an answer to the question: Why all this Western programming? … The majority of programs on TV Channel 2 are Western and they show the vacuous side of Western life.' While TV and radio programmes must 'protect authentic cultural values', NIRT continued to broadcast Western programmes that 'are inculcating us with the characteristics of Western society'.[75] Rastakhiz publications demanded to know why this tendency was allowed to spread.

Rastakhiz attacked the writers of NIRT television series, arguing that they were Occidentosis-ridden and 'don't believe in the richness of Iranian culture, or are ignorant of it and/or are simply in search of money'. The problem was that themes, storylines and settings of these television series glamorized Western culture: 'Is it really necessary to imitate the destructive scenes of Western films and programs and, to boot, in a weak and obviously borrowed form?' At the same time, these writers refused to reflect authenticity in television programmes. This approach was interpreted as rejection of that authenticity: 'Iranian TV series do not reflect figures and values from Iran's contemporary social life'.[76] More worryingly were the manifestations of Occidentosis in children's programming. 'Why are Iranian children allowed to watch tobacco-chewing cowboys instead of the Seven Ordeals of Rostam (*Haftkhan-e Rostam*)?'[77] Rasul Parvizi bemoaned to *The Youth of Rastakhiz* that 'the older generation grew up with Rostam and Sohrab, Siavush, and Esfandiar (heroes from the *Shahnameh*). Today they grow up with cowboy shows' and, as a result of Occidentosis, suffered 'a lack of family discipline'.[78] Overall, NIRT was condemned for following a policy that brought 'displays of Western culture and civilization to rain down on our minds. ... Our minds are bombarded with these displays and in the end they destroy our confidence in our society's authentic culture and traditions'.[79] Rastakhiz's message was simple: 'The Party calls for more NIRT action [against Occidentosis]. This is needed in order to protect authenticity'.[80]

NIRT did to an extent respond to these criticisms. The showing of Western series and films continued on Channel 3, the international channel dedicated to broadcasting in foreign languages. However, specific programmes were designed to deal with the issue of Occidentosis and the creation of *homo Pahlavicus*. Prominent among these programmes were series such as Ahmad Sharofi's *The Builders of the Future* (*Ayandihsazan*) and Bahram Firihvishi's *The Land of Iran* (*Iran-e zamin*). Another programme, *This and That Side of Time* (*In sui va an sui-ye zaman*) was a series of discussions between Naraqi, Ahmad Fardid and others about the 'Western person' and 'Eastern person'. These discussions were to be transformed into a book published by Sorush Press, NIRT's publishing house.[81] Nonetheless, Rastakhiz until the summer of 1978 continued its condemnations given what it considered insufficient changes in NIRT broadcasting.

'The Occidentosis' of music

The world of Iranian pop music too was at the top of the list of the Party's targets. *Rastakhiz* and *The Youth of Rastakhiz* regularly published pieces detailing the ways in which Occidentosis had infected it and its pernicious moral and sociocultural consequences. As forms of pop music, itself seen as the result of Occidentosis, became increasingly popular in a progressively commercialized music industry, older forms of Iranian music were seemingly under attack and faced, in the more hyperbolic articles, cultural annihilation. Alongside and within articles detailing this loss of musical authenticity were exhortations to mindfulness and protection of traditional forms of Iranian national and regional music. These sacralized forms of music were portrayed as one of the most important repositories of Iranian authenticity.

State and non-state intellectuals, as well as figures from the music and art world, were increasingly worried about the youth's growing infatuation with Western pop and rock music and the expression of its forms in Iranian music. The fundamental problem from which additional challenges flowed was that 'our youth are ignorant of authentic Iranian culture of music and dance. … They have turned to the West. … The youth must know that our country has no need for Western art or music.' A youth infatuated with Western music and desiring the spread of its forms in Iranian music would inevitably exhibit other signs of Occidentosis in their world view and behaviour that would have dire consequences for the country's future. Thus, the Occidentosis-ridden state of Iranian music had an important place in the party struggle to secure protection of cultural authenticity and the country's future.[82]

According to party discourses, Occidentosis had infected this world in two broad ways. First, it brought a 'negative' technology that changed a singer's voice and created an artificial music not reflective of a performer's talent. This technology created 'valueless pop music' that lacked authenticity, philosophical meaning and/or artistic value. This music's artificiality, in fundamental contradiction with the authenticity of Iranian music, was symbolic of Western civilization.[83] This infection's other form was a triad consisting of cult of celebrity, a culturally obscene pop culture and materialism. Rastakhiz condemned the writings of Occidentosis-ridden Iranians in the mass media who glamorized this triad and portrayed it as worthy of emulation.

The immediate catalyst for the launching by Rastakhiz publications of an enduring full-scale offensive against the infection of music by Occidentosis was a scandal surrounding the pop singer Dariush, considered one of the most popular pop singers at the time, and a woman called Maryam. Several issues associated with this scandal were portrayed as the clearest manifestations of the spread of Occidentosis. The first article on the scandal set the tone: 'How and where does moral decline begin?' The story itself was simple.

> The story of a married woman's love for a cheap merry maker (*amale tarb*) from the social point of view is examined here. Maryam was married with children when she fell in love with Dariush. They began to have 'relations'. She left her six children and husband for him. She made her decision. However, after a short period their relationship – as one can only expect from such a relationship – turned cold.[84]

He distanced himself from her … [and] began looking for more bait to satisfy his appetite.' Maryam, outraged and depressed by this rejection, in search of revenge, 'poured acid on Dariush while he was performing. … Part of his face, neck, and body were burned.' Not surprisingly the gossipy and celebrity press covered in detail this story and sensationalized it, provoking party outrage.

This first article condemned Maryam's actions. However, she was also portrayed as a hapless, unwitting victim of Occidentosis that cultivated in her an infatuation for celebrities. Having succumbed to it, she was willing to betray traditional Iranian morals in order to be with him. She was 'simple, naïve, credulous. The glossy glamourous pictures in newspapers and magazines that feed the celebrity of these pop singers led her to fall in love with this cheap performer (*motreb*). The use of the word *motreb* instead of the word *khanandeh* (singer) is illustrative of the overall tone of the article and the Rastakhiz approach towards pop singers. Since at least the early twentieth century the meaning of the word *motreb* has been negative, emphasizing doubtfulness of talent, banality of music and cultural obscenity. Rastakhiz publications argued that this scandal could not be considered a one-off, the result of the madness caused by Occidentosis of one gullible young woman. Her infatuation with celebrity and the pseudo-religious 'cult' following of a pop star were already a dangerous common and spreading symptom of Occidentosis. 'We'll see – when Gugush [another very popular singer and actress of this period described below] cuts her hair, the day after most girls will cut their hair'.[85]

Rastakhiz publications stressed that the infection of Occidentosis could also be seen in the reaction of newspapers and magazines that condemned Maryam while denying that Dariush was responsible. *The Youth of Rastakhiz* argued that the infection of people by Occidentosis, such as Maryam, would not have played a determinative role if Occidentosis-ridden pop singers, such as Dariush, had not infected the world of Iranian music. 'Pity those young people when a cultureless singer, a pop icon appears. ... What morals and morality can we expect from such performers? What do we know of Dariush's moral health before we make judgment' in regard to who is really guilty?[86] This conclusion was the salvo in the expansion of the Rastakhiz campaign.

The campaign's theme was boldly proclaimed. Splashed across the cover of the first series of articles in *The Youth of Rastakhiz* were pictures of well-known pop singers, including Dariush, Sattar, Hayedeh, Mahasti and Gugush. Across their faces was drawn a large red 'X' accompanied by a dramatic proclamation: 'The Disseminators of Cultural Obscenity (*mobtazal*)'. Paraphrasing Marx, Rastakhiz proclaimed that they, not religion, constituted 'the opium of society'.[87] While the cover was to inflame popular opinion, the articles provided a popular sociological analysis of this scandal. They pointed the figure of responsibility at Occidentosis.

> When a woman from amongst this land's females wistfully and easily abandons her husband, six children, and home, goes after a so-called celebrity, eventually throws acid on his face, and ends up in prison, in reality we, as a society, are to blame. Families are to blame for failing to teach young children the old standards and criteria that constitute a proper social life. These fathers and mothers believe that their responsibility and duty are just to provide food and clothing, material things, to their children and send them off to school. ... Why are parents not teaching proper social norms and morality to their children or that the thirst for celebrity based on questionable talent and methods is not a proper model to be followed? ... What kind of society have we become if these figures are praised and admired? Schools too are responsible. ... They do not teach them what life's goal is or their position in history [and] their responsibilities and duties in society.[88]

Occidentosis was leading people, and particularly the youth, to choose role models and heroes with undeserved celebrity created by a commercialized world of music that emphasized style over substance, glossy materialism over meaningful spirituality and immorality over proper austere morals.

> Why are our youth not familiar with Hafiz and Saadi? Do you really want to know? The answer is clear and simple. Our pampered children, mine and yours, as soon as they open their eyes and see television and hear radio, as soon as they become impressionable in regard to everything out there, what do they see and hear? ... The scenes screaming out from the television and native cinema, the glossy pictures of magazines, and the noise from the radio all pay great attention to the behavior, mannerisms, voice, and news of this type of person, such as the 'respectable, honorable and chaste' Ms. Gugush. That poor unfortunate Gugush, the very same one who for a time remained in her father's clutches and then became captive of her dear husband and then before freeing herself from him, found her next dear lover. One tires of the scandalous stories coming from these 'cultureless figures'. If today it is Dariush, yesterday it was Gugush and before that Aghassi, and before that Susan. Of course, tomorrow there will be others.[89]

The use of Gugush as part of the attack on Occidentosis is telling. Before discussing it, putting into context these remarks about her is necessary. Her father, Sabir Atashin, an immigrant from Soviet Azerbaijan, was a travelling actor and street performer. Gugush's birth name is Faeqeh Atashin. Her parents divorced when she was three. By the age of four she was a part of her father's act. As a teenager she started singing in cabarets. At the age of seven she began to obtain parts in films; by the late 1960s she was a fairly well-known singer and *filmfarsi* actress. By the time of the Dariush scandal, her personal life too had been a subject of public and press attention.

In 1973 she married one-time boxer and cabaret owner, Mohammad Qorbani. Rumours about their troubled relationship, his violent behaviour towards her and other female performers in his cabarets, and Gugush's wish to be divorced and his refusals visited the pages of those newspapers focusing on celebrity gossip and scandals. Her eventual divorce from him, it has been claimed, was due to Hoveyda's direct intervention. This did not end her media presence. Her affair and then marriage to the well-known actor Behruz Vosuqi (implicitly mentioned in the quote above) the year after her divorce and their separation a year later provided more fodder for the gossipy press.

Abbas Milani, in providing a perhaps nostalgic but fair view of the image of Gugush's role in this period, also offers insight into the reasons behind Rastakhiz attacks on her and portrayal of her as a product and disseminator of Occidentosis.

> For a generation of Iranians, she embodied the frivolous joys, the reckless abandon, the exuberant air of social experimentation, the defiant desire to debunk tradition and its taboos, and the vigor and vitality of youth. ... Her artistic prime coincided with the age when a culture of celebrity, modeled on the celebrity cult of the West, was beginning to take hold of the public imagination in Iran. She was the biggest celebrity of 1970s Iran. ... Her every move and mood, her every affair

and appearance, her hairstyle and taste in decoration, were grist for the mill of gossipmongers and celebrity hounds.[90]

The Youth of Rastakhiz, four months after its first issue, published a feature on Gugush that included a long interview with her and discussion of the manifestations of Occidentosis she supposedly exhibited. The image that emerged from this interview was one of a controversial Occidentosis-ridden figure who perhaps was deserving of some sympathy. It was followed by commentaries by the doyens of the Iranian world of music and cinema whose dominance in these fields emerged decades before Gugush became well known. It is here that the negative side of the Gugush factor and its implicit link with Occidentosis comes out.

Delkash (Esmat Baboli, 1925–2004), one of the best-known singers from the mid-1940s to late-1960s when she retired, whose popularity nonetheless remained great until the end of the Pahlavi dynasty, commented:

> Gugush is given to the people as their daily nourishment of music. They have created a strong public relations campaign around her that is beamed constantly. Unfortunately, people eat this food given them because of appearances, but not its substance. Gugush is not trained and, in fact, does not have a good voice. Only her looks and gyrating (*halatbazi*) during performances excite and provoke people. … One important point about Gugush is that her 'singing' is accompanied by many innuendos of sex, affectation, histrionics, and attempts to set fashion trends. The slaves of fashion gather around Gugush who, with her understanding of them, everyday adds to her collection of clothes.

Golpa (Akbar Golpayegani, b.1934), one of the most popular singers of traditional Iranian music, too expressed a negative opinion of her voice and stressed 'another regret about Gugush is that she associates the profession and role of singer with gyrating, fancy clothes, and good make-up'. Touraj Negahban (1932–2008), a well-known traditional songwriter and poet, commented: 'Gugush, in my opinion, would be better as an actress or a showgirl.' Even Fereydoun Farrokhzad, who appeared with her in televised music programmes, was critical. Following this section were comments, reflecting, it was claimed, public opinion in regard not only to Gugush but the overall state of the Iranian world of music.

> Ahmad Rahmani, a second-year student at the Higher School of Political Science: 'Gugush's voice is completely regular, there is nothing special about it. You hear such a voice in every home where people hum tunes to their children. In my opinion other elements, not her voice, are the cause for her popularity. Whatever these elements are, I consider her a sign of the collapse of national culture.' Nasrin Sharifi-Haqiqi, a junior college student in Qazvin: 'I like her voice … however I am convinced that today's singers (such as Gugush) do not do anything positive for the economy. In fact the opposite. They send a significant part of their money to the West and nobody can do anything about it.' Ali Ashkan, an office worker: 'The world of these singers differs greatly from that of real people. Today's singers, (such

as Gugush), probably think that in reality they aren't from or part of the regular people, the very people who made them popular. Today's singers have yet to express any gratification for or recognition of the people's role in their popularity.' Another group of four students stressed: 'Gugush's voice and personality for us doesn't hold any importance or anything special for us. With deceitful and false PR she finds popularity. Gugush is not the example of a woman of life but rather a woman built on rumors and PR.'

Winding up this feature on Gugush was a discussion about the causes for her popularity which was attributed to negative trends in culture resulting from the spread of Occidentosis. Its subtitles describe Rastakhiz's approach: 'Gugush and Dead Culture', 'The Collapse of Morals' and 'The Agents and Elements' behind the death of culture.[91]

In party discourses, the Gugush or Dariush 'issue' was a manifestation of Occidentosis and prompted the need to pose and answer vital questions: 'What is happening to our society? Who and what carries the greatest blame for this situation?' In the first instance fingers were pointed at the sensationalist press that thrived on glamorizing the lives and behaviour of celebrities and spreading rumours about them in order to maximize profits through sales and advertising revenue. This excessive commercialization of journalism was a consequence of Occidentosis. However, this press would not have attracted so easily subscribers and subjects for its writings if society had been immunized from Occidentosis. In other words, the success and influence of the Occidentosis-ridden press was regarded as both cause and symptom of the infection of society by Occidentosis.

Great blame was placed on pop music figures who were portrayed as carriers and spreaders of Occidentosis. 'Hayedeh, Dariush, Mahasti – they are the opium of society. They are cultureless and depraved disseminators of cultural obscenity (*mobtazal*) and immorality. … Today's singers are tugboats christened "Absolute Culturelessness".' They were disseminators of 'cultureless products' given their doubtful talent, poor music and banal melodies and lyrics that were existential threats to Iranian musical traditions. They enjoyed an undeserved celebrity and notoriety: 'With what criteria did they become so-called singers?'[92] Claiming that 'many of today's singers need to go to night school in order to learn how to read and write Persian' Rastakhiz publications argued that Occidentosis-ridden commercialized forces in the music industry, slick Western-style public relations and the yellow press had worked together to promote practically 'illiterate, uncultured' singers who 'are only agents of money and wealth', disinterested in genuine beauty and art and the didactic dimension that should be associated with their profession.[93] These pop figures were also condemned for leading corrupt and corrupting Occidentosis-ridden lives and for mocking authentically Iranian austere morality and proper values. It was feared that the cult of celebrity, glamorized by the yellow press, would lead to the infection of the youth by moral and cultural Occidentosis. Rastakhiz proclaimed: 'The outbreak and spread of this opium is and must be forbidden.' (Figure 12)[94]

As these manifestations of Occidentosis spread within the Iranian world of music and produced the cult of celebrity, Rastakhiz argued that now more than ever genuine Iranian heroes, symbolizing and protecting Iranian authenticity, needed to

Figure 12 *The Youth of Rastakhiz*: 'The disseminators of cultural obscenity and culturelessness'. Included on the cover are pictures of Sattar, Mahasti, Dariush, Gugush and Hayedeh. *Javanan-e Rastakhiz*, author's collection.

be propagated and that the youth had no need for figures 'adapting Western forms of celebrity' such as Gugush and Dariush. Unfortunately, 'the tugboats of cultureless celebrity' had pushed into the periphery of the popular consciousness figures who had preserved and contributed to the authenticity of culture and national identity over the course of Iranian history. Looking to that history, Rastakhiz publications provided examples of such heroes who could be held up in the face of Occidentosis: 'Ferdowsi, Mousavi, Hafez, Ibn Sinna, Razi, Dehkhoda, Alame Qazvini, Moin, Eqbal Ashtiani.' Rastakhiz publications decried the sense of superiority of the Occidentosis-ridden Iranians who fawned over these pop Iranian figures and Western culture and negatively compared such Iranians with those Iranians loyal to their authenticity whom this group degraded. The conclusion was clear – these older traditional Iranians were superior: 'Our illiterate grandmothers, with all their illiteracy, could recite Hafez from memory. Now what kind of situation is it that our children frown upon hearing the name of Hafez.' The Party, leading the campaign to restore authenticity, 'condemns this scandal and catastrophe'.[95]

The offensive against Occidentosis also targeted lyric writers. They were charged with being 'the agents of the chaos and collapse of songwriting' who were producing the 'drivel' and 'cultural obscenity (*mobtazal*)' performed by these singers. This offensive too began in the party's early days and increased in intensity. Two weeks after the original feature on Gugush *The Youth of Rastakhiz* opened up this front. Rather than propagating its own opinion in the form of an editorial or critical article, it reported public attitudes and specifically the viewpoints of the respected older generation of singers. For example, once again Delkash emerged, unwittingly echoing Rastakhiz's tone.

> In those days our verse writers were specialists in language and expression. They were literary, such as Moeini Kermanshahi, Rahi Moayyeri and Abdolhassan Varzi. They were poets. From their hearts and on the basis of their feelings they wrote songs and verses that are eternal. They are always worthy of hearing. But today's 'songs' are available in kilos, similar to onions and potatoes, bought and sold in a commercial market. ... In my opinion song verses are one of the most important didactic methods. They teach in Persian to our young lessons in morality.[96]

Decrying the 'cultural obscenity and scandalous work of cultureless songwriters' Rastakhiz called for a return to 'authentic Iranian music'.[97] Similar to pop singers these 'songwriters are illiterate ... and don't even know Persian grammar'.[98] The songs they wrote had no artistic, spiritual or didactic value. They were only banal and simplistic lyrics backed up by artificial electronic music. Again, only one conclusion could be made: 'The problem is the commercialization' of the music world that catered to the lowest common denominator in mass culture in order to increase popularity and profits.

At the same time, Rastakhiz publications gave attention to the influence of cultural Occidentosis and commercialization on the authenticity of the country's local music cultures. 'Our local songs are on the verge of being destroyed' at the hands of these pop singers and 'the agents of the weakening and collapse of songwriting'.[99] An illustrative example of the article's tone was the splashing across its first page of more unflattering pictures of Sattar, Hayedeh, Mahasti and Dariush. 'If thought is not given to national and regional music, it is curtains for it.' It called on the government to implement educational and cultural policies against the 'cultural obscenity' brought by the spread of these manifestations of Occidentosis.[100]

These themes did not float in the periphery of party discourses. The Second Party Congress held in October 1976 paid particular attention to them. Preparing for it, *The Youth of Rastakhiz* published a special edition dedicated to summarizing these manifestations of Occidentosis and providing paths for the crusade against it. The problem to which this conference was dedicated was clear: 'Our culture is facing an attack of destructive forces.' This Congress repeated the claim that excessive commercialization – a consequence and symptom of Occidentosis – carried the bulk of responsibility for the forces destroying the authenticity of Iranian music and personal and social culture. Singers, song writers and journalists were again condemned for pandering to the least common denominator in order to gain as much profit as possible and for failing to maintain, let alone raise, authentic cultural standards. While yellow journalists, the masses, such as Dariush's Maryam, and songwriters all had varying degrees of personal responsibility, singers, their materialism and love of celebrity driven by commercialization carried the most blame.

The current pop singers were 'unprofessional' and since 'their only goal is to sing and put money in their own pockets' they pay 'no regard to the cultural and artistic quality of their songs'. The result was 'the sudden birth of cultural obscenity. ... In reality we don't have singers or, more correctly perhaps, you could count on one hand the number of real singers we have'.[101] Rastakhiz bemoaned:

> These so-called artists, and others like them, could they not have provided a positive example in the social sphere? Would it not have been better and is it not better that they before entering the world of art learn the basics of the culture of art? In this way, they could have been in the service of art rather than being deviants of its authentic values.

The conclusion was grim:

> The world is crowded [with culturally obscene, artless music because] it lacks standards, fresh ideas, and boundaries. It is a world in which one can do whatever one wants to do and no one takes issue. ... Therefore, it is crowded, crowded with cultureless, useless things. The so-called cultural world being created could be summed up: 'Hey idiot. How much for this junk?' We here of course are talking about the sad unprofessional world of our artists and musicians.[102]

Rastakhiz, while pledging to continue the crusade against the agents spreading this Occidentosis, set a slogan for the Congress: 'Don't transform authenticity into cultural obscenity (*mobtazal*)'.[103]

This Rastakhiz campaign, however, suffered from a fundamental contradiction that weakened its effectiveness. Not only were singers such as Gugush, Dariush, Hayedeh, Mahasti, among others, popular among certain social groups, they also enjoyed access to the public and private parties of the top Pahlavi elite where they sang. It has been claimed that at the majority of formal and informal dinner parties held by the imperial couple 'the popular singers of the day' performed while 'there was no sign of authentic Iranian music'.[104] The best visual testimony to this contradiction is a video of Gugush singing in late 1978 in Niavaran Palace at the crown prince's eighteenth birthday. The imperial couple and leading members of the Pahlavi elite were present while she sang a variety of songs that ended with the Persian-language version of 'Happy Birthday to You' as the cake was cut. Outside the Revolution was gaining momentum. Yet the sentiments Rastakhiz publications expressed were certainly held by certain social groups. In sum, the state found itself caught between two large camps holding opposing views about music and its link with authenticity of culture.

Occidentosis and the commercial sector

The commercial sector was another target of the party campaign against the infection of Occidentosis. Hashemi Hairi in an article titled 'The Persian Language and the Sickness of Occidentosis' fired the opening salvo. He decried the increasingly popular practice of using Western languages and terms in signs and billboards and questioned the rationale behind it. Seeing in this practice an 'attack of the Occidentosis-ridden ones' on the Persian language, he called for party pressure on the government to restrict this practice.

The problem however, to his chagrin, did not stop here. Restaurants were increasingly writing their menus in English or French, especially those serving foreign food. The regretful consequence of this practice was the inability of many 'regular' Iranians to order food in restaurants and 'to enjoy an evening out'. They increasingly felt as aliens in their own country. This linguistic and culinary practice spread because it gave the Occidentosis-ridden Iranians another sought-after opportunity to prove their superiority to those not yet infected with the disease and show themselves at home with Occidental languages and cuisines. While these linguistic issues might seem trite and insignificant, of concern to only reactionary nativists, it was claimed that in reality they posed a long-term threat to the country's independence. The struggle against this linguistic Occidentosis was a necessity because 'the reality is that the historical trajectory of the West's imperialism and the imperialists tells us that one of the main methods for the stabilization and strengthening of this imperialism is the spread of foreign language and culture'.[105]

Occidentosis too infected authentic Iranian cuisine and eating habits. A series of articles expressed outrage over statistics showing that of the 176 restaurants surveyed in Tehran only 11 served Iranian food. 'Unfortunately, over the last several years the great wave of those gawking at the West threatens not only our art and literature but also our culture of food.' As part of the party campaign against Occidentosis, Rastakhiz announced that it 'will have regular articles reporting on the quality and quantity of Iranian food and the number of places serving Western food and the challenges of cuisine culture in today's Iran' and the establishment of a party committee to deal with this issue. Subsequent reports showed that this form of Occidentosis continued unabated. Rastakhiz complained that finding a restaurant serving Iranian food was increasingly difficult while the bulk of eateries newly opened served only foreign food. Iranian cuisine was under attack. The cause for this debacle was the culinary preferences at home of Occidentosis-ridden Iranians. Rastakhiz decried their fawning over 'French mustard, Dutch cheese, and French fish'. From the party point of view, equally outrageous was the cost paid by 'real' Iranians and the exchequer for the importation of these expensive foreign food products to satisfy the other passion of the Occidentosis-ridden ones, Western luxury goods. They created through their tastes 'an inflation of imports' and strengthened the West's 'consumerist imperialism'. The Party called for a campaign against consumption: 'Stop importation of foreign cars, especially luxury ones. Stop imports of expensive foreign food'.[106] Rastakhiz action in this regard brought limited practical results.

In party narratives an additional area suffering from Occidentosis and thus contributing to the spreading identity crisis was architecture. In a series of articles Rastakhiz lamented that Iranian architecture 'has lost to Western architecture. It has been humiliated. It has lost its authenticity'.[107] Vartan Hovanessian (1896–1982), a famous Iranian-Armenian architect who designed well-known buildings such as the Sa'adabad Palace, Tehran Officers' Club and Ferdowsi Hotel, was given prominent coverage. He bemoaned the influence of Western architecture and commercialization that had led to the destruction of Iranian architecture.[108] Mohsen Moqadam, one of the founders of the Faculty of Fine Arts at Tehran University, made a damning conclusion: 'The art of architecture in Iran is dead'.[109] Commercialized contractors, local city councils and ultimately the government were blamed for allowing the fall of Iranian architecture and the proliferation of Western-style apartment buildings with small living quarters that did not correspond with either authentic Iranian architecture or living styles.[110] In the words of Hovanessian: 'The authenticity of our architectural culture ... has been destroyed. ... That which the West did with our architectural heritage was in reality the work of a plunderer and ravager'.[111] The infection of architecture by Occidentosis was propagated as particularly worrying since 'architecture is the living memory of every people and nation ... [it] maintains within itself the flame of the people's history'.[112]

Figures close to the empress were prominent on this issue. For example, Keyvan Khosrovani in his interviews with *The Youth of Rastakhiz* stated:

> Today all of my activities are focused on showing the importance of the old design and architecture of Iranian towns and cities. The problem of destruction of these old urban designs and architecture is now spreading [from Tehran] to the provinces. In my opinion this is a national catastrophe. Every old brick that is ripped down is the ripping down of a piece of our culture.[113]

His attempts to reinvigorate Iranian architecture can be seen in the Nain Inn, the Kanun Library and his family home in north Tehran which was destroyed after the Revolution. Hossein Nasr in a prominent article titled 'In Memory of the Iranian Home' stressed that Western architecture, which served as the framework for the construction of new homes and apartments, was a major cause of the loss of cultural and national identity. He warned: 'The transformation of our urban fabric is breaking our psychological and physical links with our cultural life'.[114] The empress in the regard was unequivocal.

> We must defend and protect our culture's roots. The national technology that we had and with which the people for centuries lived must be preserved. ... The way of doing things corresponded to the life, climate, and traditions and customs of Iran. For example, the traditional forms of buildings in Iran were simultaneously beautiful and inexpensive and corresponded to the climate, way of life and regional conditions and temperament of the people. At the same time many of the new buildings of today do not have such advantages. I have said several times more attention must be paid to this issue.[115]

Without a doubt Western architecture was exercising and continues to exercise a decisive influence on the construction of homes and apartments in the country's urban areas. However, the rapidly growing urban population, especially in large cities such as Tehran, whose population shot up from 2.7 million in 1966 to 4.5 million in 1976, made necessary not only quick construction of housing units but also smaller living spaces to accommodate these growing numbers and make them affordable as property and housing costs, especially from the early 1970s, began to skyrocket. All of these issues and troubles were blamed in blanket form on Occidentosis.

Lamenting the passage of Iranian architecture, the Party stressed: 'This form of life is part of our national culture' that had to be protected. This threatened form of life consisted of not only architecture but also the traditional Iranian concept of the urban neighbourhood. The creation of apartment buildings and the rapid construction of new homes in old neighbourhoods, as well as the emergence of new neighbourhoods, seemed to leave, in the words of party publications, little, if any room, for the old customs and traditions of authentic Iranian neighbourhoods in which everyone knew and helped each other, the older generations were respected by the young and everyone knew her or his place. A party committee dealing with this issue declared that, contrary to unfortunate trends, 'Iran's architecture must be in harmony with authentic Iranian culture'.[116]

In this regard, the Party, claiming it was responding to popular demands for a return to the authenticity of Iranian architecture, proclaimed a victory. *Shahestan-e Pahlavi* was a massive development project covering a large area of today's Abbasabad whose construction was first proposed in 1968. It was to become the new centre of Tehran with an enormous square named *Meidan-e Shah va Mellat*. This region would be architecturally modern and, according to its US and UK planners 'a national centre for the twentieth century'.[117] However, the Party, claiming that it was responding to popular demands, brought pressure on the government to lead a movement for the strengthening of authentic Iranian architecture. The result was, according to a major piece in *Rastakhiz*, that '*Shahestan-e Pahlavi* will be constructed according to Iranian architectural methods and styles'. No details about the constitutive elements of these methods and style were given.[118] The Revolution put an end to this project. However, it was only a drop in the bucket, as the Party itself admitted.

Rastakhiz attacks on the infection of Iranian architecture by Occidentosis and emphasis on overall return to authenticity reflected and symbolized the growing feelings of nostalgia that intensified as the rate of socio-economic changes and consequent popular disorientation and anxiety increased. As Rastakhiz published pieces on this growing feeling of nostalgia Haritash in 1977 made a film *To the Memory of* (*Beh Yad*) that focused on vintage doors and archways that invoked 'the deep nostalgic longing of modern Iranians for the fast disappearing past and their fraying connection with it'.[119]

The list of these changes prompting disorientation and nostalgia can be large and include, for example, industrialization, rural–urban migration and the consequent breakdown of traditional family structures, the growth of cities that brought the destruction of old neighbourhoods and the spread of slums, the commercialization of culture, the spread of the cult of celebrity, changing public appearances and behaviour, a sense of decline in personal and sexual morality, and perceived growth in class differences. Of course, the individual importance and role of each of these, and others not listed, in adding to the quite natural feelings of nostalgia that grow as one ages, were dependent on the socio-economic position, education and personal history of every individual. Yet, that which is important is that increasing numbers of people across the socio-economic spectrum were suffering from a nostalgia for a partially imagined and partially real simpler, happier past in which morals were traditional, social and kinship relations was genuine, free of any instrumentalization that seemed to come with Occidentosis and commercialization, and life was stable and predictable, providing a warm sense of security and sense of belonging. As the individual faced and endured increasingly rapid change impacting on his personal life, the more he sought stability and security in this past that, it was felt, was superior to the conditions being created by Occidentosis, the slayer of this past.

The one topic that Rastakhiz publications used to address and sympathize with these feelings was the process of urban growth, especially in Tehran, that was bringing the destruction of these old neighbourhoods and putting in their place apartment complexes and Western-style homes for the superficial Occidentosis-ridden *nouveau riche* who were perceived as beings without an identity and a past. However, the focus on the infection of architecture by Occidentosis creates the impression that the cries for a return to authenticity in architecture were to a significant extent emerging from a search for the seeming stability and familiarity these old neighbourhoods represented as society faced ever-increasing rates of change and disorientation.[120]

> The person of today (in Iran and specifically Tehran) seemingly no longer belongs to a local neighborhood but rather has become mobile and urbanized and even seeks to go beyond this situation – he seeks the same new mode of life of the West. This desire has created many difficulties and problems that have their roots in the spirit and psyche of a person.

The traditional neighbourhood now disappearing was portrayed not just as locality in which people lived, but a social unit that generated and preserved genuine social relations, and Iranian spirituality and morality. Lamenting the passing of such areas, Rastakhiz published articles about them and 'the memories of friendships, and closeness that have been lost' in the face of Westernization and Occidentosis. It decried that 'today homes are [physically] closer together than ever before' while, in seeming contradiction, 'people [in the same neighborhood] are distant from each other like never before'. The lead in this process was Tehran that 'has lost its identity. ... Its inhabitants are strangers to each other and seemingly have no desire to put an end to the sense of alienation between them.' In the past these close-knit neighbourhoods were not only the scene of genuine and close social and kinship relations, but also provided a sense of stability and security to people in a hostile world. This was defined as authenticity of Iranian culture and national identity.

This atomization and individualism brought by the spread of Occidentosis, especially in architecture, had only one antidote: 'Native culture is the only refuge of a lonely individual'.[121] All Iranians had to comprehend that 'to be cut off from Iran's culture is [spiritual, moral and personal] collapse'.[122] Now however, Rastakhiz warned,

'With the destruction of these localities and neighborhoods comes the destruction of moral values and cohesive comforting characteristics. ... Only regret and remorse is left.' It exhorted that 'the characteristics and values of one's areas (*mahali*) must be held'. If not, a superior form of life would be destroyed and replaced by the hollow one epitomized by the Occidentosis-ridden *nouveau riche*.[123] This was the future awaiting other Iranian cities unless something was done. This was the fear expressed by figures such as the empress, Khosrovani and Nasr. The Pahlavi state, the original agent of the practical process of Westernization, was held responsible by many for the destruction of this perceived simple and genuine life. While Rastakhiz sought to change this perception of the Pahlavi state, it also mourned: 'To the memory of traditions now being forgotten'.[124]

10

Occidentosis and the Shiraz Arts Festival

The Shiraz Arts Festival, held annually from 1967 to 1977, was founded by the empress who was also the head of its board of trustees. A sampling of its thirty-one members shows an attempt in principle to have broad elite representation in this grand event: Alam, Moinian, Qotbi, Farrokh Ghaffari, Mehdi Bushehri, the prime minister and seven ministers. Yet, the festival's programming and execution were in the hands of Farah and political and intellectual figures close to her. Qotbi served as executive manager, while Ghaffari served as his deputy and, importantly, programming director. Busheri, Princess Ashraf's third husband and director of Le Maison de l'Iran in Paris, directed its managerial committee. At the first festival the empress stated that its main goals were cultural exchange and enlightenment and acquainting Iranians and foreigners with old and new forms of Iranian art and introducing foreign forms of art to Iranians.

Despite these goals, or because of them, the festival, 'though artistically successful, became politically an issue of considerable consequence for the regime and a strain on the dynamic of art and politics in the country'.[1] Given this, the politics surrounding this festival provide a suitable concluding commentary on (a) the Party approach to the crusade against Occidentosis; (b) the politicized dilemma of determining the specific manifestations of Occidentosis in the arts; and (c) the normality of the Iranian experience in this regard in a comparative context.

In the years before the Party's establishment the festival was increasingly charged with having a growing and undue emphasis on performances using avant-garde forms that were portrayed as signs of Occidentosis or simply insulting to national pride. Nudity in some performances provoked particularly strong popular and press criticism. What made the festival politically dangerous was the state's moral and financial support of it. Consequently, the impression strengthened that Occidentosis-ridden intellectuals who considered themselves the social and cultural vanguard and therefore superior to the masses sought with state support to impose these Western art forms and their underpinning world view on them. The festival's sympathizers argued that these boisterous critics 'singled out' the various forms of avant-garde performances and unfairly portrayed the festival as a manifestation of Occidentosis while ignoring the many performances dedicated to traditional forms of Iranian art from poetry and music to theatre, including its religious form, *taghize*. A review of the performances made over the eleven years of the festival's existence shows that the Iranian cultural presence grew as a result of these criticisms and by the time of the Party's establishment had indeed become strong.[2] Nonetheless, avant-garde forms and scenes of nudity overshadowed this presence and, according to a 1972 SAVAK report summing up public and media opinion, led 'the majority' to conclude 'that the festival's intention is the elimination of Iranian national cultural pride so that the people become accustomed to Western and European traditions and customs'.[3]

By the time Rastakhiz was established this public perception remained. Post-revolutionary interviews with members of the Pahlavi elite show that in the upper echelons of the state and the court concern existed about the increasing discontent provoked by the festival and the damage rendered to the state's political and cultural authority by aspects of the empress's cultural policy, such as the festival, seen as artistically too 'liberal'[4] or Occidentosis-ridden. Pahlbod noted in a post-revolutionary interview: 'We had people who returned from Europe and wanted to propagate in Iran European ways of thinking and perspectives in regard to [avant-garde forms of] art'.[5] Additionally, many within the elite and society objected to these avant-garde forms on aesthetic grounds. Alam perhaps best expressed this sentiment: 'This festival is nothing special. A French group playing strange ragtime instruments makes strange sounds with strange machinery, such as cooking pots, in a way that only makes a European and an Iranian a laughing stock'.[6]

As these elite divisions remained and criticism of the festival's avant-garde forms increased, which were reported and enflamed by the media, such as *Ferdowsi*, concerns about the ongoing damage to the state's political and cultural authority grew. At the same time, the festival's supporters were increasingly frustrated and began to believe that some conspiracy against them existed. At the 1973 festival Ghaffari was pressed at a news conference to respond to these criticisms. A reporter, prefacing his question, stated that while the festival's original theme was contemporary forms of art that also encapsulated traditional forms, any review of the last several festivals showed that the focus was on avant-garde art. Consequently, he posited, the festival 'had greatly increased its distance from the people' who no longer were part of the festival or understood it and its performances. What, therefore, was the purpose of this festival that used public money? Ghaffari, seemingly piqued by these comments, responded: 'Any programme that is performed in the world, the Shiraz Festival will invite so that the Iranian people know what is going on in the art world. ... The festival doesn't have the duty to teach art.' While acknowledging these criticisms he underlined: 'The festival has nothing to do with classic art and will not return to it. What we want to see is the modern world'.[7] His comments, rather than mollifying, only provoked public opinion and proved to the festival's critics its overall Occidentosis-ridden trajectory.

In these circumstances the Rastakhiz Party, having launched its crusade against Occidentosis, in early autumn 1975 turned its attention to the trajectories of various state-sponsored festivals in the period before its establishment and the role they were to play in this crusade. Naming specific festivals – the Shiraz Arts Festival, Tehran Film Festival, Tus Festival, Tehran International Art Exhibition and the Festival of Art and Culture – Rastakhiz underlined that when they were founded 'attention to and emphasis on national culture, knowledge and authenticity were perhaps not among their priorities. But now that knowledge of our traditional Iranian values, history, nationality and culture is one of the necessities of our sociopolitical life, these festivals can and must perform this function' in the propagation and protection of authenticity in the face of Occidentosis.[8]

The Party, having implicitly acknowledged previous criticisms of the Shiraz Festival, claimed a role in ensuring that the festival played this function. However, this grand proclamation came to nothing. No subsequent mention of this role was made in regard to the Shiraz Festival or any other festival. In regard only to the eleventh and last festival held in 1977 did Rastakhiz publications make mildly critical remarks. In one instance the official poster was criticized for being an imitation of a piece done by the US graphic designer Milton Glaser.[9] The other instance had a shade of the struggle against Occidentosis. The festival had published a book on the sociology of *siahbazi*, an Iranian performing comical tradition, penned by an American anthropologist specializing in Iran, William Beeman. Rastakhiz denounced the book: 'Are we to believe that among all the researchers we don't have one with the qualifications to write such a book and thus it was necessary to get a foreigner to write on this Iranian topic?'[10]

The nature of the relationship between the empress and her supporters and the Party and its campaign against Occidentosis came into relief during this 1977 festival. It became (in)famous for scandals surrounding the performance by an avant-garde Hungarian émigré theatre group called Squat of its play *Pig, Child, Fire!* that sought to decry the injustice and overall state of the modern world. Ghaffari, having heard or seen it in Paris (differing accounts exist), along with a handful of other festival organizers, decided it would be a suitable contribution to the festival.[11]

The play was performed on Ferdowsi Street, a main Shiraz throughway, and in a large-windowed store front on that street. Its scenes of male and female nudity, violence and simulated rape and suicide provoked outrage and condemnations from the press, local clergy and onlookers. After the Revolution both supporters and opponents of the Pahlavis claimed that this public outrage played an important role in setting the preconditions for revolutionary mobilization. The extent to which such claims are true is not of primal importance here. What is important is how this outrage played out, the Party's reaction to it, and what commentary it can make about the politics of Occidentalism. The initial outrage over the play resulted in a confrontation at the festival between Maryam Kharazmi, a journalist for *Keyhan International*, *Keyhan*'s English-language version, and Arby Ovanessian, a well-known young Iranian-Armenian playwright, screenwriter and director who had been active in the festival in the past and recommended this piece. This confrontation became known as 'The 7-UP scandal' (Figure 13).

Kharazmi, after Squat's first performance, wrote a short piece for her paper condemning those scenes she considered culturally and morally obscene and thus not corresponding to public conceptions of morality and art. Ovanessian during his flight to Shiraz read the piece, already cognizant of other critical articles, and specifically one written by Janet Lazarian, another Iranian-Armenian, for the English-language newspaper *Tehran Journal*, published by *Ettela'at*. Although both journalists, according to him, had written pieces defending his work, he was convinced that again attempts, similar in content and intent to those that had targeted him in the past given his use of avant-garde methods, were being made to blacken the festival and avant-garde art in general.[12] For example, at the 1971 festival Ovanessian directed a restructured

Figure 13 Arby Ovanessian, centre, author's collection.

enactment of *Vis and Ramin* by the eleventh-century Persian poet Fakhr Gorgani. The main character is a woman who falls in love with her husband's brother. However, in contrast to Gorgani's portrayal of this character as a treacherous adulteress, this version positively portrayed her as a slayer of traditions, fleeing from forms of social obligations and agreements. Public opinion considered this interpretation a reflection of radical Western feminism and of cultural self-alienation on the part of the Occidentosis-ridden intelligentsia.[13]

Ovanessian and Kharazmi and her supporters have different versions of what transpired. The version presented here comes from Kharazmi's article, 'The "art" of emptying a bottle of 7-UP on a reporter's head', published in *Keyhan* the day after the incident. It enjoyed the greatest influence on public opinion since its narrative formed the base of reporting by the national print media, including *Ettela'at* and *Ayandegan*. In her article Kharazmi before describing the incident repeated her objections to the play: 'In this performance the actors and actresses either denigrate each other's chastity or simulate suicide with fake bullets.' Condemning these avant-garde forms she sarcastically noted: 'The art of Europe's elites for us "backward" Easterners is still not digestible. We are a "prejudiced" and "ignorant people" and thus we don't like to see sex scenes on the theatre stage.' In contrast was the Occidentosis-ridden Ovanessian who 'believes that *Pig, Child, Fire!* is a great piece of art that must not be criticized'.[14]

Having provided the backdrop, she turned the reader's attention to the main feature. Ovanessian on the day of his arrival to Shiraz saw Kharazmi in the foyer of Pahlavi University's concert hall. Then, in Kharazmi's words,

> This artist, yelling in a Chelsea English accent, approaches me. He then shouts at me, 'Hey art ignoramus! Know that I have no manners! I am rude. Take this in order to understand!' And with that he poured a bottle of 7-UP over my head. The curtain then dropped on this performance. However, no one applauded.

Continuing the portrayal of the confrontation between her and Ovanessian as a confrontation between Occidentosis and Iranian authenticity, she recounted her steps after this incident. 'I returned to my hotel room, took a shower, changed my clothes and set off to Hafez's tomb to listen to traditional Iranian music. I had a very pleasant and comforting time indeed.' The Chelsea-accented, Occidentosis-ridden, self-proclaimed progressive art intellectual, who, in the words of Amir Taheri, *Keyhan*'s editor, lacked self-control and had become a follower of 'the tradition of intellectual terrorism' and 'art and literary despotism', stood in stark contrast to this Iranian journalist who remained calm and sought solace in traditional Iranian environments, poetry and music.

Taheri's commentary was published a day after another incident between the two that took place the day after the 7-UP scandal. According to witness reports detailed in *Keyhan*, *Ettela'at* and *Ayandegan*, Ovanessian, seeing Kharazmi in the lobby of the Koroush Hotel, initiated another altercation and, becoming increasingly angry, attempted physically to attack her but was prevented by bystanders, most of whom were other journalists. Now the scandal entered a new phase. Kharazmi filed an official police complaint and Ovanessian was arrested and then released on bail. In chronological order, on 21 August the 7-UP incident occurred, on 22 August Kharazmi's '7-UP' article was published, the incident at the hotel took place and Ovanessian was arrested, and on 23 August Ovanessian, facing a growing outcry, issued a formal apology. He 'confessed that his behavior was unbecoming and uncivilized'. Kharazmi accepted his apology and retracted her police complaint, while maintaining her condemnations of the play and Ovanessian's behaviour.[15] After the second incident, Qotbi issued a statement condemning Ovanessian's behaviour and stressing that he had no official position or responsibility in that year's festival. By this time, the festival's authorities under pressure from the security forces had already removed the offensive scenes from *Pig, Child, Fire!* in order to calm public and media reaction.

Media criticism of the play reached new heights after this second incident. *Keyhan* ran another article outlining the reasons for outrage: 'Empty intellectuals who are attempting to be representatives of progressive art and European "avant garde" have been subjected to intense criticism by the people of Shiraz and the attendees of the Shiraz Arts Festival.' The Occidentosis-ridden intellectuals failed to understand that 'the fundamental reason for the people's objections and protests to this play' is that its 'elements are empty, without meaning and contain filthy re-enactments of sexual acts – all in the most reprehensible way'. To prove these points, *Keyhan* provided readers with a detailed description of the play's controversial scenes which were not included in its original reporting dating from only two days before. This initial reporting was mild, speaking only of 'horrific and frightening images and scenes of violence and killing' and 'scenes of bedroom activities'.[16] The revised description was raw. 'In one scene a man is naked from the waist down' while in another 'an actress shockingly spreads her legs while sitting on a chair and a camera in live-stream shows the area between her legs and provides a complete color picture of her "female area"' (*madegi-ye zan*) on a twenty-four-inch television. Can you guess the reaction of regular viewers and the people of the street and market-place in the face of such a representation of European progressive art? (In another scene) 'a guy pulls up a woman's skirt and in a vulgar and brazen way performs a sexual act in a deviant way'. That this play was performed on a major throughway and in a large shop window in front of the 'shocked eyes' of children, elderly women and the youth was particularly incendiary. *Keyhan*, dismissing the belated cutting of some scenes, demanded to know: 'On the basis of what human and moral standards and what concept of authentic Iranian culture, morality, and values' are such pieces chosen and performed? 'Do authentically Iranian values and culture allow for such performances?'[17]

In this same issue another editorial 'Monsieur Ovanessian' using Rastakhiz language made a stinging attack on Ovanessian and Occidentosis-ridden figures in general charging them with being in opposition to the authenticity of Iranian culture and national identity. 'Supporting a play that from start to finish is a reflection of sexual obsessions and scenes made up of a man, woman, child and pig in the streets of Shiraz' meant that Ovanessian was 'not an Iranian'. A real Iranian would not have defended 'this foreign disgrace' and would not have attacked an art critic who was 'performing her duty as a patriot in exposing these disgraces and filth'. Addressing Ovanessian: 'Let's assume that you are not Iranian – and you are not Iranian – come with those foreign standards of yours, which you flaunt, and their filth, which you respect, and let's have a little talk, that is if you aren't an intellectual terrorist, if you aren't an art fascist. Those very foreign standards of your friends state that you have the right to speak and I have the right to speak. You have the right to put on a ridiculous and disgusting play, such as *Savari dar amad* (one of Ovanessian's controversial avant-garde works) while we have the right to write that this play is ridiculous and disgusting. Of course you also have the right to respond' to our criticisms.

The editorial attacked the idea that Occidentosis-ridden intellectuals and those involved in art had the right to determine what was art and 'civilized' and impose it on the people: 'Our society is not in need of you, or people like you. Our society does not need these foreign educated ones.' Ovanessian and others like him believed they were the 'gendarme of art'. This arrogance and belief might not be their fault since '"they" allow you to deliver to society any old garbage and call it art' and 'you get huge amounts of money. ... You who have used the people's money to travel abroad, you who with the people's money have cast anchor in the most expensive foreign cafes, what have you done to make you believe that this land and era are indebted to you?' Referencing 'they' was an implicit attack on the aspect of state cultural policy behind the holding of the Shiraz Arts Festival by the empress and those close to her.

Ovanessian and this 'they' were charged with spreading cultural and moral Occidentosis while the idea that these forms were didactic, progressive and the standard of civilization was rejected.

> *Agha-ye* Ovanessian, or, excuse me, monsieur or mister Ovanessian ... or monsieur love-of-all-things-foreign, how surprising that again we are forced to admonish and ask you, 'who are you and *what* are you doing?' ... I'm not concerned with your art, I won't speak of it again. I correctly know that sooner or later our society, which has not accepted to this point your art, will throw you and your art into history's trashbin, if it has not done so already. Arts with roots in foreign blood and culture are not and cannot be ours.[18]

An interesting sidenote adding to the context is *Keyhan*'s publication one day before the incident between Ovanessian and Kharazmi of an interview with the Iranian Samarkand-born and Soviet-trained composer Aminollah Hossein who had, for the second time in his life, visited Iran to attend the festival. The piece's headline, a quote from the interview proclaimed: 'Iranian musicians, composers and song-writers are Occidentosis-ridden (*qarbzadeh*)'.[19]

Ettelaʾat's reporting of these confrontations and commentary was similar in tone, denouncing 'the dirty scenes of sexual intercourse between the performers' of *Pig, Child, Fire!* and 'childish Iranian artists (*jujehonarmandha-ye Irani*)' who 'had sold out national [cultural defences] so that this garbage is forced-fed to the people through the use of the bludgeon and 7-UP'. *Ettelaʾat* stressed that one of the reasons Ovanessian was infuriated with Kharazmi's criticism was that he had intended to bring the Hungarian group and its play to his theatre in Tehran. It reported that according to witnesses Ovanessian yelled at her that his father, having read her piece, had told him that he must not do this and 'participate in an indecent operation. ... My father believes that I wanted to bring a pornographic play to Tehran.' The editorial, stressing that the people wanted to feel an artistic and personal link between themselves and the festival and thus state cultural policy, gave some advice: 'Mr.Ovanessian, our people, similar to your own father, who has objections to this performance, hate this play. If you wish to know and understand our people, first you must get to know and understand your own father! That is all!'[20] This call for a return to authenticity on the part of the Occidentosis-ridden intellectuals involved in the arts and others could have easily appeared in Rastakhiz publications.

The reaction of Rastakhiz publications significantly differed from that of *Keyhan*, *Ettelaʾat* and *Ayandegan*. Rastakhiz reporting on the public and press reaction to the play and the confrontations between Ovanessian and Kharazmi was delayed by days. Only and finally on 24 August did *Rastakhiz* publish a news item that summarized the events starting with the 7-UP event (21 August) and ending with Ovanessian's issuance of a public apology. It was the first time that a Rastakhiz publication mentioned public criticism of the play. The language it used was relatively neutral and muted: 'The writer of *Keyhan*'s English version had criticized *Pig, Child, Fire!* for offensive scenes (*sahneha-ye zanandeh*) depicting sexual relations.' Her criticisms were 'unpalatable for Arby Ovanessian' who, wanting to put on the play in Tehran 'believed that her criticism in high probability could harm his interests'. In a strict narrative form it mentioned his emptying of the 7-UP bottle on her head and made reference to 'his attack on her the following day with the intention of intensifying his unacceptable behavior'. Consequently, 'Kharazmi lodged an official complaint with the police'. No other mention in *Rastakhiz* was made about Ovanessian and the condemnations of him and Occidentosis-ridden intellectuals by the other three leading daily newspapers did not find any echo in it. *The Youth of Rastakhiz* made no mention of this story or these incidents.[21]

In regard to the play itself and the 1977 festival, Rastakhiz publications were positive. *Rastakhiz*, two weeks after the play's last performance, three weeks after the first performance that sparked these various scandals and nine days after the festival's end, published a review of *Pig, Fire, Child!* It was described as a 'unique exhibition' and 'masterpiece' (*shahkar*) whose artistic contribution had not been seen 'in the country over the last several years'.²² *The Youth of Rastakhiz* at the festival's conclusion ran a feature article. At the end of its glowing narrative it concluded: 'In the Eleventh Shiraz Festival everything was chic. ... In Shiraz a person is forced to be chic'.²³ No mention of the play, the altercation between those two individuals, or the larger issue of who determines what is art was made.

The Party's reaction to the dynamics of the 7-UP scandal – the play, public and press reaction to it, Ovanessian's behaviour and the reaction to that behaviour – was subject to particular influences. One was the empress's sponsorship of the festival and the closeness to her of intellectuals involved in it. The shah's official party could not criticize the empress's activities. Moreover, at the time of the 1977 festival the Party was undergoing internal changes. Ten days before the festival's opening, the shah on 17 August appointed Amuzegar as prime minister and Baheri became party head.

A vital issue was the reaction of the clergy. Even before the performances of *Pig, Child, Fire!*, the Shiraz clergy in their sermons strongly criticized the festival's dates which coincided with the beginning of the holy month of Ramadan. Ayatollah Abdolhossein Dastgheib, reported SAVAK, 'severely criticized the festival and called on God to curse those who inaugurated and participated in it'. Ayatollah Sheikh Bahae al-Din Mahallati echoed this remarks. Ayatollah Sayyed Ahmad Pishva thundered that unfortunately 'today's artists are similar to Gugush' and for them 'a source of national pride' was those political and intellectual figures, 'also [culturally and morally] similar to Gugush' who established and ran the festival. 'The masses must not go these festivals so that those like Gugush are forced to desist from putting on such festivals.' On the day after the first showing of the play (18 August) but before details of the contentious scenes were widely reported in the press, Ayatollah Dastgheib in a sermon declared that the festival was outrageous and incendiary and condemned its organizers because 'they bring to Iran from non-Muslim Western lands dancers' who only spread corruption and scandal. Importantly, the national media, except for Rastakhiz publications, criticized this issue of timing. The following week the scandal over the play broke and the state was put on the defensive.²⁴

At 9.00 pm in the evening on 25 August 1977, after the 7-UP scandal and the publishing of the details of the pornographic scenes from *Pig, Child, Fire!* by *Keyhan* and *Ettela'at*, a group of leading clerics and merchants from Shiraz and its environs visited Ayatollah Mahallati. They brought copies of newspaper articles about the play and the scandal. According to SAVAK, they informed Mahallati that 'during the days and nights of Ramadan in public they commit acts that contradict public morality and in front of people they show a woman's genital area (*alat-e zani*) and perform ugly vile acts. In other words, at night they invite the masses to corruption (*fesad*) and debauchery and fornication (*fesgh-o fojor*).' Hearing this, Mahallati then read the newspaper pieces. Outraged, he called on all clerics and Friday Prayer Leaders to close in protest their mosques' doors from Saturday. A telegram was also sent to Tehran urging the immediate closing of this Eleventh Festival and the permanent dissolution of the Shiraz Arts Festival.

On the day of this meeting the deputy head of police counter-intelligence, a Colonel Soltani, telephoned Mahallati asking him not to allow the closing of the mosques.

He also pointedly asked 'why were these people [clerics and preachers] cursing the empress from the pulpit?' The cleric responded that 'they had become very upset given this festival's "programme of nudity"', especially during the month of Ramadan. Ayatollah Dastgheib's public remarks embodied the general clerical reaction: 'I have heard something. The Festival of the Pig. … What a name it has! Those who go there, males and females, are more disgusting and vile than a pig. A curse upon them! … When will you stop corrupting and perverting our youth and handing them over to imperialism!' In the words of SAVAK: 'It had been agreed that all clerics, preachers, and Friday Prayer Leaders in their mosques over these last couple of days to speak of the festival's moral corruption and to forbid people from attending it.' In fact, up to a month after the first showing of *Pig, Child, Fire!* clerics continued their condemnations of the nature and timing of the festival and those responsible for holding it.

SAVAK analysis of these rolling events shows a relatively objective understanding of their causes. It confessed that initial clerical criticism of the festival and of those responsible for its holding due to the festival's timing had influenced public opinion to the state's detriment. One of the first steps it suggested was the issuing of private warnings to critical clerics.[25] However, as the criticisms rapidly expanded to include the play and its incendiary scenes SAVAK analysis turned to the causes of this growing scandal and threat. One analysis dated 29 August stressed that the root problem was the festival's timing and allowing performances 'with scenes clearly in contradiction with religious principles'. Despite the legitimacy of this negative reaction to these two issues, 'extremist clerics and opportunists' used them in order to inflame greater public opinion. SAVAK also pointed a finger of responsibility at the critical articles in *Keyhan* and *Ettela'at* which the clerics integrated in their attacks on the festival and those managing it. Higher up the SAVAK chain of command a point was added that in fact it was these critical articles that had excessively provoked not only clerics and preachers but also public opinion. 'The reaction of the people and religious zealots to this programme (*Pig, Child, Fire!*) has indeed been very intense and the public criticism of it in the newspapers also prompted Shiraz's leading clerics in conjunction with provocations of religious zealots to make such sharp condemnations of the festival.'[26] SAVAK noted that if criticism of the festival had come only from the mosques steps could have been taken to neutralize it and 'no big issue' would have come out of it. However, the scale of the public and newspaper outcry and clerical condemnations had made the situation unusually complex.

Some three weeks after the scandal SAVAK provided a retrospective analysis. It reported that the play performed by foreigners did indeed have sex scenes (*eshqbazi*) and pornographic acts (*a'mal-e rakik*), particularly the 'exhibition of sexual relations between a man and woman' and 'the showing of female genital areas' that could not but provoke large-scale negative public reaction and condemnations which then spread to the mosques and sermons. However, the articles in the national media, and in particular *Keyhan* and *Ettela'at* in the aftermath of the 7-UP scandal and their continued criticism of the festival's timing during Ramadan had intensified and spread public outrage. These developments in turn caused the extreme and ongoing clerical condemnations of the festival, the state's leading figures and overall state cultural policy. Consequently, 'cynicism' among the people in regard to the state and its top officials had grown.

Moreover, while recognizing that large numbers of young and old had been provoked and angered by the festival, it predicted that 'with the passing of time slowly the youth will emerge from under clerical influence' although a not insignificant number will remain under their influence for the foreseeable future. Given these conditions SAVAK concluded:

> It seems that these parts of the program that have created such heated discussions were an unintentional mistake the blame for which belongs to those responsible for the festival. In order to prevent the repeat of such events it is necessary that from now on those responsible for the festival must use tactfulness and perceptiveness when choosing pieces that are to be performed and take into account the dates of religious holidays, Ramadan and Moharram when setting the festival's dates.

Unsurprisingly, given Pahlavi anticlericalism this clerical reaction exercised a strong influence on the party response on several levels. Baheri, soon after becoming party head, attended a funeral ceremony in central Tehran. The presiding cleric was Abdolreza Hejazi, who in his programme on Radio Iran which ran every day from 1.00 pm to 4.00 pm during Ramadan had been openly critical of the timing of the festival and those scenes. Naturally, his critical rhetoric was not similar to that of the Shiraz clergy and even *Keyhan* or *Ettela'at*. Nonetheless, he was recognized as a leading albeit moderate, critic.

SAVAK reported on the ceremony

> In the presence of Baheri Hejazi officially announced his objections in regard to these two issues [the play and the holding of the festival during Ramadan] and said that in the first instance the government (*dolat*) acted improperly and that those who had done this were communists who had recently returned to the country and, so to say, had become repentant. It was they who were undermining the kingdom. Since Dr. Baheri was participating in the ceremony, (Hejazi), in order to avoid any offense, modified his comments and said of course a number of them and, then addressing him (Baheri), said that I do not know you well but I have heard that you are a believer and pious and thus you recognize that it is your duty not to allow the moral and cultural collapse of our society and the violation of the rights of Islam and the clergy.

This experience only confirmed the understanding held by Baheri and a number of party officials and publicists of the way in which the Shiraz Arts Festival had become 'politically an issue of considerable consequence for the regime' and now for the Party. Baheri in post-revolution interviews noted that at the time he opposed on political and cultural grounds the festival's avant-garde trajectory. In this context he implemented changes in party propaganda, one of which was staff changes at *The Youth of Rastakhiz* including the replacement of its editor, Ashrafizadeh, with Hossein Sarfaraz. This reformed and re-energized *The Youth of Rastakhiz*, which in Baheri's opinion was a chief weapon in the propaganda arsenal, could not directly criticize the festival. The optics of the Party criticizing directly the festival's timing and *Pig, Child, Fire!* would have been dreadful for the Pahlavi state, even if the Party would have been seen as reflecting public opinion. Public opinion would have detected in such criticism a humiliating government climbdown in the face of clerical opposition. Moreover, the image of the monarch's party and the clergy criticizing on the same grounds a state-sponsored event so closely associated with the empress, and at a time when clerics had implicitly denounced her, could not be accepted by the shah and the state-party elite.

The Party, therefore, faced an important political and intellectual dilemma. The non-party press reaction had brought into relief achievements of the party campaign against Occidentosis. Party rhetoric had played a key role in normalizing the terms 'Occidentosis-ridden' and 'Occidentosis' in intellectual and public discourses while the Party's frequent use of these terms gave them an official standing and licence to be used. Moreover, these attacks showed that the party campaign not only reflected growing intellectual and political concerns about the spread of Occidentosis but also intensified them. Yet, the Party had to remain silent on the scandals swirling around the Shiraz Arts Festival. However, this possible optics was not the only issue influencing the Party's approach.

The Party response to the 7-UP scandal also brought into relief the political–ideological limits of its understanding at that time of the manifestations of cultural and moral Occidentosis in the face of mass opinion. The shah and the Party spoke of an Iranianess (*Iraniyat*), as the base of *homo Pahlavicus*, and of the need to determine what elements of the West corresponded to it and what elements could not be accepted by it. As the previous chapters showed, the Party provided a broad understanding of what it considered to be the manifestations of cultural and moral Occidentosis. However, these party interpretations, to an extent influenced by the view of the empress and those close to her, drew a line between these manifestations and Western avant-garde forms of art which they considered a sign of civilization. It is here that the party's interpretation showed its political limits and weaknesses. Another example is the party approach to *filmfarsi* and particularly sexy films. Many intellectuals condemned *filmfarsi* and specifically its use of nudity and sex scenes. In this respect they accurately reflected swathes of public opinion. However, nudity in new wave films and in avant-garde forms did not provoke them in the same way given the belief in the progressive and didactic dimensions of such forms of art that were increasingly used in the West. Yet, for a large part of public opinion, the clergy and in quarters of the political and intellectual elite these forms remained manifestations of cultural and moral Occidentosis and even civilizational regression.

The Party under Baheri recognized that the effectiveness and legitimacy of the Party's campaign against Occidentosis and the role it played in mobilizing public support for the Pahlavi state were dependent on greater correlation between its understandings of the manifestations of cultural and moral Occidentosis, and specifically avant-garde forms in art, and those of public opinion. This scandal about such forms at the festival the Party could not ignore. Yet, direct criticism of the festival was not politically possible. A way however was found. *The Youth of Rastakhiz* two weeks after the end of the festival and one week before its special and positive review of the festival published two feature articles on art that indirectly signalled party support for the critics of avant-garde art and *Pig, Fire, Child!*. The headline of the first piece, an interview with

Reza Saffari, a Mashad sculptor, set the tone: 'Art lacking national authenticity is a form of debauchery'.[27]

The year 1977, therefore, can be regarded as pivotal to the party approach to cultural and moral Occidentosis. As noted in the previous chapter, in the closing months of Amuzegar's first tenure as party head, the government, under party pressure, took steps to deal with the issue of nudity and sex in *filmfarsi* and by that autumn the Party modified its approach to avant-garde forms. By late spring 1978 party members became openly critical of this festival and avant-garde forms. As the state faced increasing public dissatisfaction, by early summer 1978 party figures and publications began to call for the cancelling of the festival scheduled to be held in August in order to prevent the inflaming of public opinion. It was indeed cancelled. Yet, already in the immediate aftermath of the 1977 festival lessons had been learned about the limits that should be respected when allowing avant-garde art to be performed and about popular conceptions of the manifestations of cultural and moral Occidentosis.

The festival's sympathizers, who exercised significant influence in the Party, divided broadly its critics into two groups: 'The clerics were anti-art on religious grounds, the leftists on ideological grounds; the one attacked it as a signature of infidelity, the other disparaged it as bourgeois and anti-people'. Certainly, this interpretation is true to a significant extent, although it was specifically avant-garde art forms that greatly provoked these groups and placed them close to mass opinion. This interpretation of the festival's critics, however, minimizes the importance of several interrelated issues, namely sociocultural realities in Iran in quarters that cannot be simply labelled overly religious or leftist, the growing importance of the question of authenticity of nativist culture and identity, and criticism on aesthetic grounds of the festival and its avant-garde dimensions. These issues provoked divisions within the political and intellectual classes over this aspect of the empress's cultural policy and its support of avant-garde forms. This interpretation also shows a poor understanding of the historical trajectory of and reaction to avant-garde forms in the arts in the West. A brief review of examples from France and the USSR helps to place these intellectual and political conditions in late Pahlavi Iran in a broad historical context and to normalize the criticism of avant-garde art forms in Iran and specifically of the Shiraz Art Festivals. They show that the public reaction in Iran to avant-garde forms in the arts was not unique and cannot be reduced only to these two groups. Lastly, in addressing these issues, one must not downplay the purposeful controversial intention of intellectuals involved in the arts, driven by philosophical–ideological, financial and/or personal motives that were underpinned by a sense of cultural and intellectual superiority in regard to the masses and belief in their avant-garde role.

The original meaning of avant-garde is military, describing those units first sent into battle to prepare the way for the advance of other units. In 1825 Claude de Saint-Simon, an early influential socialist thinker, in his treatise *Literary, Philosophical and Industrial Opinions* transformed the term, giving it an art and social meaning. He considered artists to be the avant-garde in the transformation of society that would put an end to social and political injustice and oppression.

> We the artists will serve as the avant-garde for amongst all the arms at our disposal, the power of the arts is the surest and most expeditious. When we wish to spread

new ideas amongst men, we use the lyre, ode or song, story or novel; we inscribe these ideas on marble or canvas. ... We aim for the heart and imagination, and hence our effort is the most vivid and most decisive.[28]

By the beginning of the twentieth century the meaning of term avant-garde evolved. 'It now designated self-proclaimed art movements whose admitted objective ... is the break with traditional and acquired tendencies and forms' in the arts while maintaining, if not implicitly, its radical social role.[29] Additionally, it came to address more directly than before the link between art and morality, and in particular sexual morality, a frequent target of intellectuals and pseudo-intellectuals since at least the Enlightenment. The creativity and sovereignty of the artist, if avant-gardism was the goal, had to be liberated from conceptions of this morality and socially accepted behaviour. A person concerned with them could never achieve personal and artistic freedom. 'Morality, as the avant-garde was wont to say' was 'the invention of the hideous and revenge of the ugly'.[30]

Iranian leftist criticisms of the festival's avant-garde performances had their roots in Stalinist cultural policy that overturned the modernist, avant-garde forms that flourished during the early years of Soviet power, and sought a return to cultural and moral forms rooted in socialist realism, a form portrayed as close to the people. Dmitrii Shostakovich, the Soviet composer and pianist, starting with his Second Symphony (1927) increasingly used avant-garde and experimental methods in his composing to the praise of other intellectuals. In early 1936, the year the Soviet government launched its war on avant-garde art, which it called 'formalism', Stalin visited Moscow's Bolshoi Theatre to see Shostakovich's newest avant-garde piece *Lady Macbeth of the Mtsensk District*.

Stalin and his entourage were not pleased. They did not like its avant-garde music and mocked the love scene between the opera's two main characters, Katerina and Sergei. The following day, *Pravda*, the CPSU's official newspaper, in its editorial informed the country of Stalin's and thus the official view of not only Shostakovich's work but also all avant-garde forms.

> The audience from the first minute is shocked and flabbergasted by this opera whose music is made up of intentionally unstructured, confused and chaotic sounds. The snatches of melody, those embryos of musical phrases sink, burst out and then once again grinding and screeching disappear in a crash. ... The deformity and abnormality (*urodstvo*) in this opera comes from that same source as that of [avant-garde] deformity and abnormality. This petit bourgeois 'innovation' will lead to the rupture of authentic art, science, and literature. ... This is a game of unintelligible esoteric things that can only end very badly.[31]

'Petit bourgeois innovation' naturally meant the cultural influence of the capitalist liberal West that was considered a direct threat to Soviet civilization. Platon Kerzhentsev, the culture minister, told Shostakovich that he had to abandon avant-garde's mistaken methods and 'achieve something that the masses could understand'. In the following week *Pravda* continued the offensive, signalling to the intelligentsia that avant-garde forms would no longer be accepted. Attacking not only this opera but also

Shostakovich's recent ballet, *The Limpid Stream* (*Svetlii Puchei*), a light-hearted comedy about peasant life on a collective farm, the newspaper stated: 'Both these productions are far from the clear, simple, true language that Soviet art must speak'.[32] Shostakovich and the rest of the art intelligentsia, understanding that the Soviet state had launched a campaign in the name of the people against avant-garde forms, abandoned them.

Avant-garde forms in the arts have frequently provoked negative reactions on simple aesthetic and moral grounds by individuals and social groups which were not clerical, religious or, as sarcastically characterized by Kharazmi, 'backward' looking 'Easterners'. Probably the best example of this is the premiere of Igor Stravinsky's *The Rite of Spring* (*Le Sacre du printemps*) in May 1913 in Paris by the Ballets russes with choreography by Vaslav Nijinsky. The Ballets russes, founded by Sergei Diaghliev and performing in the French capital since 1909, had become known for using avant-garde forms that for a time generated excitement. However, Daghilev through intensification of eroticism in performances pushed society's accepted moral norms. For example, the year before *The Rite of Spring* the company performed Debussy's *L'Après-midi d'un femme*. Nijinsky was both its choreographer and dancer while the sets and costumes too were avant-garde. The story is about a man-like rural deity with horns and a tail who falls in love with a wood nymph. 'Nijinsky, dressed in leotards at a time when skin-tight costumes were still thought to be improper, provoked in the audience a collective salivation and swallowing as he descended, hips undulating, over the nymph's scarf, and quivered in simulated orgasm. That was simply the culmination of a ballet that broke all the rules of traditional taste.' *Le Figaro*'s editor condemned the piece on the paper's first page, calling the ballet 'neither a pretty pastoral nor a work of profound meaning. We are shown a lecherous faun, whose movements are filthy and bestial in their eroticism, and whose gestures are as crude as they are indecent'.[33] Scenes were changed in order to alleviate the outcry.

The Rite of Spring, however, was the breaking point. Its avant-garde forms in music, namely dissonance and asymmetrical rhythms, and in the dancing, described by Stravinsky as 'a group of knock-kneed and long braided Lolitas jumping up and down' and 'it seems, the willful ugliness and lumpiness of Nijinsky's evocation of Russian prehistory' that depicted a sacrifice of a virgin from Russia's pagan history, caused 'the storm' to break.[34] While accounts of what happened differ, no doubt existed that 'the event provoked a seismic response'.[35] The storm had started with critical whistling, then yells of 'shut up' from the audience, followed by shouts and jeers that became so loud that the music was drowned out. Realizing that the dancers could no longer hear the music, Nijinsky, in the wings, mounted a chair and shouted out directions to the hapless dancers. Food and drink were then thrown at both the orchestra and stage. The audience turned on itself between those who hated and those who supported these avant-garde forms. Scuffles broke out. Some claimed that around fifty people were eventually thrown out. Henri Quittard, *Le Figaro*'s music critic, described this debut and its avant-garde quality as an example of 'puerile barbarity'. In the United States the piece met the same reception.

In France after the First World War a significant swathe of public opinion increasingly condemned avant-garde forms not only on aesthetic grounds, but also as part of a return to authenticity of culture and national identity. This postwar societal and intellectual backlash to these forms to an extent reflects trends in late Pahlavi Iran. Paris in the decades before the war's outbreak was regarded as the centre of avant-garde art, in whose development an influx of immigrants from Eastern Europe, Spain and Italy played a decisive role. The best example of this development is the art of Pablo Picasso. He, along with Georges Braque, at the beginning of the twentieth century founded a new avant-garde art form known as Cubism, inspired by Picasso's *Le Bordel d'Avignon* (renamed *Les Demoiselles d'Avignon*). Called Cubism given its method of painting by and within cubes, it represented the desire of these two painters to break completely with traditional methods and forms in Western and particularly French art. Its depiction of subject matter too broke with all traditions of representation. In the words of Picasso, 'A head is a matter of eyes, nose, and mouth which can be distributed in any way you like'.[36]

Cubism became the dominant avant-garde school in the period 1905–19. It gave birth to additional 'Cubinist' schools, including, importantly, Cubo-Futurism. The official founding of this school came in 1909 with an article for *Le Figaro* written by an Italian, Filippo Marinetti. Taking Cubism and avant-garde art to its logical philosophical conclusion, he called for a futuristic art, the end of respect and admiration for previous art forms and the destruction of art museums where they were exhibited. This school was established and developed predominately by Italians and Russians, such as Luigi Russalo, who also played an important role in avant-garde music, Giacomo Bella, Kazimir Malevich and Vasilii Kandinsky.

This foreign influence in the emergence of Cubism, a form adapted by French artists, mirrored the growing presence of foreigners in France's cultural life that provoked concerns about conceptions of authenticity of French culture and national identity. Indeed, at the time when Cubism was taking off, in all cultural and art fields 'Paris seemed to be far more entranced by foreign culture than its own'. Exhibitions and festivals were dedicated to foreign arts and culture from Italy to Russia and the Austro-Hungarian Empire. Certainly, important native French contributions, usually limited to Alexandre Charpentier, Debussy, Gabriel Fauré, Maurice Ravel and Florent Schmitt, received accolades, yet 'all the recent stir and excitement seems to have been generated by foreign composers and artists'. This sense was palatable and fed a foreign sense of superiority and hubris and even 'imperious pretensions to ultimate art'. Alexander Nikolayevich Benois, the costume and stage designer for Diaghliev's Ballets russes, in 1909 in Paris summarized these feelings held by non-French intellectuals and artists: 'We have shown the Parisians what theatre should be. ... This trip was clearly an historic necessity. We are in this contemporary civilization the ingredient without which it would corrode entirely'.[37] In a striking, but unsurprising parallel with late Pahlavi Iran, while aspects of the innovative art of foreigners could provoke a degree of interest, native artists rebelling against traditional nativist forms ultimately 'were likely to be denounced as agents of anarchy and decomposition' committing a form of artistic betrayal to the country's cultural and artistic authenticity. The popular and widely read critic and writer Samuel Rocheblave described the parameters of this growing backlash that decried the infection of native French arts by foreign forms: 'Impressionism, which broke down color and light, and cubism, which broke down solid form, were not French styles but something approaching "barbarism"'.[38]

The unexpected outbreak of war in 1914 and its horrors, from life in the trenches to the new forms of weaponry for mass killing, prompted deep doubts about the path Western civilization had taken and its future. In Germany Oswald Splenger's *The Decline of the West* expressed this malaise overtaking the West. One of the best examples in France of this trend was the popular works of Georges Duhamel (1884–1966), a physician and writer who volunteered to serve as an army doctor on the front during the First World War. His wartime experience undermined his belief in the West's conception of progressive history represented by urbanization, industrialization and mechanization that was supposedly underpinned by a Western intellectual and political rationality. This transformation, shared by many as a result of that war, is felt in his wartime memoir, *Civilisation*, published in 1918 and awarded the Prix Goncourt.

This malaise about the fundamentals of Western civilization fed into concerns about French decline. Although France had emerged from the First World War a victor, it found itself economically and financially weak. To an extent the country's mood was similar to that after the shocking defeat of Napoleon III's Second Empire at the hands of Prussia and the horrors of the Paris Commune (1871). This sense of lost grandeur and glory, the search for the causes of this decline and consequent questions about authenticity of culture and national identity set the political and intellectual context and political polarization for the post-war Third Republic.

Generating intellectual and political momentum behind these trends were domestic socio-economic transformations. France, lagging industrially behind Britain and Germany, entered industrialization's second phase only after the war. Thus, in the postwar period the consequences of this process, particularly rapid urbanization linked to the enlargement of the working class and rural–urban migration, exercised an increasingly strong influence on French society and intensified debates and concerns about authenticity of culture and national identity. To put this in perspective, only in the 1930s did France's urban population begin to outnumber its rural one. Relatedly, debates intensified about the direction in which social and moral conditions were moving and about the future of human identity.

In this context Lucien Romier, a leading French journalist, editor of *Le Figaro* (1925–7, 1934–42), and later minister in the Vichy government, expressed these fears about the future of the authenticity of French culture and intensified worries about Americanosis in his popular work *Who will be the master? Europe or America?* (*Qui sera le maître? Europe ou Amérique?*) published in 1927. What he saw in the United States horrified him, although he believed that Europe and France in particular had to adopt some US practices in order to preserve their cultural and geopolitical independence. But the age of the machine and consumerism taken to extremity in the United States and the image of Europe possibly succumbing to a future already existing across the Atlantic Ocean directed attention to a fundamental problem of so-called modern civilization, namely the relationship between humans and the machine. 'This problem consists of mastering the power of the machine without sacrificing the human identity of man. ... The world's master will be the "civilized" man who knows how to employ the machine to his own ends, and not the "proletarian" seeking civilization's secret in the machine'.[39] He expanded these themes in his other popular work *The New Man:*

sketch of the consequences of progress (*L'Homme nouveau: esquisse des conséquences du progress*) published in 1929.

This work was followed by Duhamel's phenomenally popular book *Scènes de la vie future* published in 1930 (by 1931 it had gone through 243 editions) and in English translation, *America: The Menace-scenes from the Life of the Future* (1931), that, as its title indicated, looked with trepidation, doubt and anxiety to the future. It railed against the US way of life, from the deceitfully attractive promises made by glamourous Hollywood films and advertising to the commercialization of culture, the spread of materialism and consumerism underpinned by a machine society. 'No nation has surrendered itself to such a willful extent to the excesses of industrial civilization than the United States. ... This is our future! All the stigmata of this devouring civilization, we shall be able – less than twenty years from now-to see them on the body of Europe'.[40]

As Duhamel's book continued to fly off the shelves, in 1931 Robert Aron and Arnaud Dandieu published *Le Cancer américain* that shared one major theme with al-e Ahmad's *Occidentosis*, although in French discourses Americanosis was the key term. Warning about US financial and cultural imperialism, they argued: 'Americanism was not simply a political or economic disease, but a disease of the very spirit that, like a cancer, had grafted itself onto other nations.' The downfall of this spirit 'would be the downfall of Europe'.[41]

What is interesting here is the similarities not only with al-e Ahmad's Occidentosis but also with Russian state discourses on the binary of a true and a false Europe. French discourses portrayed the United States and the threat it posed to French cultural authenticity with language and imagery reminiscent of Romanov and Pahlavi anti-West Occidentalism. The struggle against Americanosis was in defence of not only the authenticity of French culture and identity but also individuals and humanist values. In short, the crusade against Americanosis was founded on the ideas of philosophical humanism.[42] In this context, political and intellectual discourses in the 1920s and 1930s increasingly argued that only a return to French cultural and moral authenticity would enable France to overcome these crises, defend itself from Americanosis and build for itself an appropriate future.

This French authenticity was located in the rural areas and way of life: 'France's dual glorification of peasant and the countryside acted as a compensation for the ever growing rural exodus' that seemed to underline the spread of the 'American cancer' under the guise of massive industrialization, rural–urban migration and consumerism. The peasants were portrayed 'as the backbone of the nation' and thus the leaders in the country's postwar reconstruction. The themes of anti-industrialization and anti-urbanism condemned the sucking of young rustics to the urban areas, and particularly Paris, whose cosmopolitan and morally corrupt environment infected them while making them slaves to the machine and followers of conspicuous consumerism.

The return to authenticity of culture and national identity necessitated such a return in the arts that, it was claimed, emphasized the human and stood in positive contrast with Americanosis. Landscape painting, the native French form of art, placed the real human at its centre but particularly the peasant and peasant lifestyle that epitomized French authenticity. Many French artists who had exclusively used avant-garde forms such as Cubism and Cubo-Futurism abandoned them, having been provoked by 'the notion of an interrupted genealogy in the recent history of French art, a broken link with nature in need of restoration, [that] would rally artists and critics alike in the 1920s'.[43] By the mid-1920s 'a critical consensus would maintain that the resurgence of landscape painting signaled a deliberate realignment with a particularly French tradition'. Examples of such artists were Roger de la Fresnaye, André Derain, Maurice de Vlaminck, André Dunoyer de Segonzac, Albert Gleizes, Jean Metzinger, Auguste Herbin and the poet André Salmon. 'It is they who would be cast as the true followers of France's centuries-old artistic tradition.' This shift was helped and supported not only by a large cadre of influential critics, such as Louis Vauxcelles, but also by public opinion.[44] In summary, in architecture, art, writing and France's overall approach to the world in an era of reconstruction after the ravages of the First World War, weakening self-confidence and the threat of Americanosis, the rallying cry became, 'It is yesterday's France that shall be born tomorrow!'[45]

These intellectual and political trends in 1920s and 1930s France played an important role in the ideology of Vichy France governed by the hero of the First World War, Marshal Philippe Pétain. He replaced the republican motto that represented the ideals of the Western exclusive political civilization, *liberté, égalité, fraternité* with *travail, famille, patrie* (work, family, fatherland), proclaiming that they represented true French values to which the French had to return.

11

Occidentosis and the challenge of imperialism

The discourses on the struggle against Occidentosis were also a reflection of two trends in the shah's geopolitical world view. He was increasingly confident about Iran's international and regional position due to the sense that the economic benefits of the White Revolution and the progressive rise in oil prices gave the country the capacity to pursue what he called in his first book 'an independent national foreign policy'. Yet, according to these discourses, the shah's attempts to follow such a foreign policy and transform Iran into a great power provoked the West's imperialism to strive to weaken and subdue Iran culturally and geopolitically.

The shah's increased assertiveness had three main and interrelated trajectories. He sought (a) to increase the price of oil to finance his domestic economic and social policies and to expand his military build-up; (b) to contain Soviet influence in the region; and (c) to establish Iran as the guardian of the interests of the Persian Gulf in the wake of the British withdrawal from the region. The achievement of the first goal ensured the creation of tension in Tehran's relations with the West, particularly the United States. However, the realization of the other two goals required a strengthening and transformation of the US–Iran relationship.

In the closing years of the Johnson administration the shah pushed for increased military aid and sales, a goal he had pursued since the end of the Second World War. In this respect he enjoyed little success. The administration remained loyal to the policy coined 'the twin pillars' according to which stability in the Persian Gulf and containment of Soviet influence in the Middle East would be achieved through a relative military and geopolitical equilibrium between Washington's two main allies, Saudi Arabia and Iran which were also potential rivals. Thus, logic dictated that arms sales to Iran could not exceed a certain rate. In early 1968 the US National Security Council determined that the administration must continue preservation of this equilibrium 'by avoiding an undue military build-up by the Gulf littoral states'.[1] The shah, however, remained committed to his goal of convincing Washington to view Iran, and not Saudi Arabia, as the natural guardian of the security and stability of the Persian Gulf region. This position was not some imperial fantasy held by an increasingly megalomaniac monarch; it flowed from basic conceptions of Iran's geopolitics. Any power, other than Iran, dominant in the Persian Gulf region could, in theory, not only constitute a threat to the country's long coast but also impede its oil exports through the narrow Straits of Hormuz.

At the beginning of 1968, UK prime minister Harold Wilson forced to reduce state expenditures, announced the withdrawal in 1971 of British forces from the Persian Gulf. Since the end of the Second World War Washington had effectively left this region's security in London's hands given it long-standing presence there. The shah, in response to British attempts to encourage the Saudis to play a greater regional role and the small Arab littoral mini-states to unite in order to limit Tehran's regional aspirations, increased his lobbying efforts in Washington. Yet, at the same time the shah and Saudi Arabia were worried by the gathering strength of Nasserism in Egypt and Iraq's Ba'athist regime that enjoyed strong links with the USSR. He feared that these radical secular regimes could with Moscow's aid destabilize the littoral Arab states and perhaps establish communist regimes there. The shah's goal became the overturning of the 'twin pillars' policy and obtaining US recognition of Iran as the natural guarantor of stability of the Persian Gulf and defender of US interests in the region. The Johnson administration, however, remained committed to the twin pillars.

With the arrival of Richard Nixon to the White House in 1969 the US approach to the twin pillars policy began slowly to change. The relationship between the shah and Nixon, who were old friends and enjoyed a personal chemistry that did not characterize the monarch's relationship with any of Nixon's predecessors or successors, and geopolitical realities, specifically the quagmire of Vietnam, coupled with growing US economic difficulties, played the leading roles in the establishment of the Nixon Doctrine. According to it, Washington would rely on friendly regional powers to be the guardians of US and Western interests in various areas of the world. This doctrine strengthened the shah's attempts to make Iran the Persian Gulf's gendarme after the British withdrawal. Consequently, 'the Shah forged a partnership' with Nixon and Kissinger 'to contain Soviet influence and to establish Iran's primacy in the Persian Gulf. ... Under the Nixon Doctrine, Iran evolved from a client to a partner of the United States in the Cold War'.[2] This change in the relationship resulted in the shah's ability to purchase in large quantities the best in US military hardware, with the exception of nuclear arms. Nixon and Kissinger overrode concerns in the Pentagon about Iran's ability to absorb large infusions of new military technology and the shah's ultimate geopolitical aims. They also abandoned the emphasis of three previous administrations on the importance of economic and social development over that of military purchases. Probably the best example of the shah's increasing assertiveness in foreign policy and the transformation of the relationship between Tehran and Washington was their joint Kurdish adventure in Iraq.[3]

By the time of the Party's establishment and after Nixon's resignation several dynamics were exercising a negative impact on this relationship. Intellectual and popular anti-Westernism and anti-Americanism, on the rise in Iran since the 1960s, were reflected from 1975 in Rastakhiz discourses while Nixon's exit from the political scene under a cloud of scandal and the threat of impeachment modified aspects of the US approach to Tehran. His successor Gerald Ford was an unknown figure in Iran with whom the shah did not enjoy strong personal chemistry. Moreover, Nixon's disgrace led to attacks on many aspects of his foreign policy, and specifically his unquestioning support for the shah. Even before his resignation, public and political criticisms of the

Pahlavi state were growing. The state's character, the issue of political prisoners and use of torture and general violations of human rights by it had frequently placed pressure on the US–Iran relationship. However, Nixon and Kissinger, along with pro-shah politicians, were able to protect and expand the relationship. In the new administration only Kissinger strongly advocated maintaining this geopolitical partnership, while others, such as Secretary of Defence James Schlesinger and his successor Donald Rumsfeld and Secretary of Treasury William Simon, who in July 1974 called the shah 'a nut', pushed for changes that would regulate Iran to a 'privileged client position'.[4]

At the same time, Congress, where criticisms of US policy toward Iran were increasingly heard in Nixon's twilight years, initiated in the autumn of 1976 investigations into the state of human rights in Iran and the sale of US arms to the country.[5] Along with criticism from Congress, organizations such as Amnesty International, the International Commission of Jurists and the increasingly radical Confederation of Iranian Students and Western media hammered at the shah's image. In the end, many of the relationship's fundamentals remained although tension was rising. Importantly, the relationship's rhetorical dimension had changed, not only in the United States but, as this chapter shows, in Iran as well, reflecting in both countries an evolution of the relationship from where it had been during the Nixon administration. Schlesinger stressed that in spite of this '"difference in tone" in US policy toward Iran, "President Ford tended to follow the commitments of his predecessor and the advice of Secretary Kissinger … [However] when it came to new commitments to the shah, Ford was more responsive than Nixon had been to critics of the shah within his administration and in Congress'.[6] This change in tone in regard to Iran coming from the US halls of power and media along with the changed personal dynamic between the occupants of the White House and Niavaran Palace exercised a strong influence not only on the shah's view of the relationship but also on Rastakhiz-era discourses of anti-West Occidentalism.

The threat and reality of imperialism had been part of popular intellectual and political discourses since the nineteenth century as Iran, frequently portrayed as a woman, the motherland, found herself a chaste victim of British and Russian imperialism. A common discursive theme of the early decades of Pahlavi rule was anti-imperialism with implicit references to the perpetrators of that imperialism and emphasis on their past injustices. This theme however was accompanied by a cultural pro-West Occidentalism. During the early stages of the ideologization of monarchy in the 1960s, state discourses on imperialism began to evolve in a piecemeal fashion, becoming more intense and specific in its targets, which, importantly, came to include the United States. In the Rastakhiz period they obtained a theoretical form and became systematic. The linking of the two forms of anti-West Occidentalism, geopolitical and cultural, emerged from evolved Pahlavi understandings and discourses on imperialism that borrowed heavily from postcolonial literature, the ideology of Third Worldism and a growing chorus of Western critics of Western civilization and its geopolitics.

Rastakhiz discourses propagated two forms of imperialism. The first form, hegemonic from the nineteenth to the mid-twentieth centuries, but remaining a danger was direct 'old' imperialism. 'For many years the West's imperialism with its new technology, swords, daggers, and guns brought new geo-political adventurism' to the non-Western world and specifically Iran. This geopolitical imperialism was 'rationalized by a new idea – the complete superiority of Western civilization' and the backwardness of the East, portrayed in essentialist terms. The West's claims to civilizational superiority rationalized and justified its imperialism and exploitation of other countries.

From this old imperialism of the West flowed its second form, 'the new cultural imperialism', that was 'created in order to safeguard the [original] bases of [the old] imperialism' if and when 'from a political and economic point of view it started to crumble or become vulnerable'. Faced with the declining possibility to use military force and establish direct control, Western imperialism considered it 'vital that national native cultures be destroyed and the West's culture, named *the* civilization, would consciously and unconsciously penetrate non-Western lands'.[7] This new imperialism by undermining the confidence of Iranians in their own history and authenticity of culture and national identity would then be able to establish indirect Western economic and geopolitical hegemony. But, proclaimed party historiography, this new imperialism was a method new only in the arsenal of the West. Since the time of the Ashkanians it had been used by imperial powers seeking to impose hegemony over Iran.

By creating an Occidentosis-ridden elite class whose viewpoints and interests would be tied to the West, imperialism would ensure indirectly its economic and geopolitical hegemony. Thus, the crisis of identity resulting from Occidentosis created by this neo-imperialism was a direct threat to the country's independence. This approach included many elements from Third Worldism and the viewpoints of Fritz Fanon in *The Wretched of the Earth*. However, the initial and perhaps greater influence in this regard was played by Soviet cultural policy, and in particular the Stalinist *Zhdanovshchina* given the Tudeh and leftist background of many party publicists and high-ranking members, who, in the opinion of Hossein Nasr, had retained a 'leftist intellectual infrastructure'.

Faced with the emergence of the Cold War, Stalin launched a new cycle of anti-West Occidentalism. In August 1946 the CPSU announced the start of a new campaign against cosmopolitanism, the other term for ideology of the liberal democratic and capitalist West. The following year Stalin initiated the 'struggle against kowtowing to the West'. In 1948 Andrei Zhdanov, Politburo member dealing with ideological issues, using music as an example, outlined the steps for the purification of culture that would lead to the creation of *homo Sovieticus* and destruction of the sensed increase in Western cultural influences.

> The main challenge is to develop and perfect Soviet music. Another challenge is to defend Soviet music from elements of bourgeois decomposition. It must not be forgotten that the USSR is the true defender of the musical culture common to all humankind just as it is the bulwark of human civilization and culture against bourgeois disintegration and degeneration of culture. It must be taken into account that other bourgeois influences from abroad will have common cause with the remnants of capitalism in the consciousness of some representatives of the Soviet intelligentsia. This is expressed in silly and wild attempts to replace the treasure house of Soviet musical culture with the pitiful rags of contemporary bourgeois

music. And thus not only the musical, but also political ear of Soviet composers must be very sharp and quick.[8]

This speech marked the beginning of the *Zhdanovshchina*. These postwar campaigns were to purge signs of Western influences in all cultural and moral fields and thus neutralize negative political consequences they might hold. The CPSU was worried by the spread of Western cultural influences among the urban-educated classes and youth that threatened to undermine claims to the superiority of Soviet civilization not only in economics and living conditions but also in culture and the arts. After all, the cultural war between the USSR and the West was integral to the geopolitical and ideological Cold War. Protection of the authenticity of Soviet culture, as defined by the Soviet state at any point in time, provided the justification for the CPSU's power and handling of political dissidents. In the United States this cultural dimension was just as vital while leftist tendencies were portrayed as a betrayal of the authenticity of US culture and national identity.[9]

Rastakhiz claimed that events in Iran proved the veracity of its interpretation of these forms of the West's imperialism and the shift to neo-imperialism. 'Under Reza Shah the country tried to achieve economic and geo-political independence' at a time when old imperialism still maintained its hold on the international system. But, 'during World War II this imperialism of the West again militarily invaded the country'. Old imperialism in the 1960s and 1970s, realizing Iran's increasing strength as a result of the White Revolution, transformed into neo-imperialism that now was 'trying to invade culturally. ... The penetration of the West's culture into our country started immediately after the emergence of the first sparks of our anti-imperialist struggle'.[10] The point repeatedly underlined was that this anti-imperialist struggle dated from the emergence of the Pahlavi dynasty given its anti-imperialist oil policy and emphasis on Iranian geopolitical, economic and cultural independence.

The inclusion of oil policy in these discourses was integral to attempts to portray Mossadegh's overthrow as a national rebellion led by the shah against this imperialism. In the immediate years after that event the Pahlavi state in a piecemeal fashion began the search for elements of an official narrative of these events.[11] With the publication of *Mission for My Country* these official narratives were codified and propagated within a discursive framework in which the shah's 'positive nationalism' was in opposition to the 'negative nationalism' of Mossadegh and his sympathizers.[12] In the Rastakhiz period, the idea of a concerted effort by the West's imperialism that now implicitly included the United States to retard Iranian development and independence reached its height. For example, the shah on the anniversary of Mossadegh's overthrow, the second after the Party's founding, claimed that if the people had not rebelled against the foreign-inspired groups inside Iran

> in all probability the world's superpowers, every single one of them, would have placed a part of our homeland under their control ... [If these groups had succeeded] our cultural heritage which is made up of the fundamental values of our society, in other words the flowering of national identity that is inseparable from the imperial system, would have been destroyed.[13]

Nonetheless, popular historical memory continued to hold a different interpretation of Mossadegh's overthrow that until the collapse of the Pahlavi state limited the effectiveness of this aspect of anti-West Occidentalism.

The shah during his 1975 state visit to Mexico and Venezuela emphasized this rhetoric of Western imperialism and drew similarities between the actions of the West's imperialism in Latin America and its actions in Iran. The comparison targeted equally the United States and the USSR.

> Any place on which these imperialists have set their feet was faced with the destruction and elimination of national foundations. They strove to separate peoples subjected to this imperialism from their culture and national knowledge. In place of everything nationally authentic they tried to bring into existence a fake and empty phantom individual. They seek to occupy the imperialized peoples with their own appearances and external features. ... But finally in the face of the will power and resurgence (*rastakhiz*) of imperialized peoples, this imperialism and imperialists, in whatever shape they had, have been forced step-by-step to retreat to the extent that today its last remnants are being destroyed.[14]

Given such rhetoric the shah was asked during this trip if he sought the West's decline and collapse. His answer, splashed across the first page of *Rastakhiz*, was an assurance that he did not seek the end of the West, but rather the end of its imperialism.

This rhetoric was not the result solely of the new dynamics of the Rastakhiz period. The shah had already started to speak increasingly of US imperialism by the end of the 1960s. For example, in late March 1970 the Soviet president Nikolai Podgorny accompanied by a large delegation visited Iran. At the state dinner at the Niavaran Palace, Alam noted: 'The shahanshah made a very good general speech but he excessively attacked US imperialism which in my opinion was not good'.[15] At the same time, as mentioned earlier, the state, and specifically SAVAK, from the late 1960s allowed increasing criticism of the United States in the press and portrayals of it as an imperialist power, similar to the other great imperialist powers from Great Britain and France in the west to USSR in the east. To repeat, a reason for this was to respond to the increasing anti-Westernism, and specifically anti-Americanism, among sections of the professional and intellectual middle class and the rapidly growing student population. These feelings threatened the shah's standing given the close relationship between Iran and the West, and specifically its leader, the United States. Simply put, the shah, with this censorship policy and speeches similar to the one given to the Soviet delegation, sought to distance himself from a West that was increasingly under domestic intellectual and popular criticism and attack. At the same time he was advocating policies that did not correspond with the West's interests, such as the rise in oil prices, and the idea of Iran as a great power acting only on the basis of its interests. To be sure, the intensity of the shah's rhetoric varied, depending on circumstances at any one point time.

Yet, in the period before and after the Party's establishment the Iranian press, and specifically Rastakhiz publications, continued to give great attention to the relationship between the shah and leading Western capitals, and especially with Washington. Front pages reported on visits of Western dignitaries and conversations between the shah and Western leaders and high-ranking officials. The tone of the reporting was not solely designed to underscore the West's and specifically Washington's continued support of the Pahlavi state and thus dissuade opposition groups and disgruntled elements of any thought of rebellion, as many have claimed. It also sought to inculcate the idea that Iran, thanks to the shah's leadership, had attained great international prestige and become a powerful regional actor, recognized and respected by the West and importantly the United States. This achievement in international politics and specifically the courting of Iran by the United States and the USSR were propagated in order to provide concrete evidence of the geopolitical success of the Pahlavi state and thus strengthen the shah's domestic political legitimacy. This approach was not unique. For example, one of the reasons for Leonid Brezhnev's support of détente with the Nixon administration was Washington's recognition of the Soviet Union as a superpower equal to that of the United States it brought. The CPSU could now claim that, thanks to its leadership, it had transformed the lethargic tsarist polity into a recognized superpower.[16]

In this context, the Rastakhiz Party stressed that the overall goal from which its other campaigns flowed was the struggle against cultural and political Occidentosis. The West's new imperialism through its spread of Occidentosis targeted the Crown given its position as source and defender of the authenticity of Iranian culture and national identity and determination to ensure Iranian geopolitical independence and fulfil the country's role as a great regional power. The Party issued the West a warning: 'In the new culture of the Revolution of Iran the word imperialism has no meaning'.[17]

> The Iranian Revolution of Shah and People and its pillars are the defense against the imperialism of the East and West, in other words neo-imperialism, and the imperialism of black reactionaries. ... This neo-imperialism that consistently and always turns to (domestic) groups and parties supporting its imported ideologies to obtain influence inside these countries.

This imperialism was the new greatest threat to Iran which, according to Rastakhiz, would increase in proportion to Pahlavi Iran's commitment to its independence and regional role. It called on the people to be vigilant.[18]

This conception of new imperialism included changes in the discourses on the elements constituting the imperialist threats to the country. The first major change was the conflation of communism with the liberal democratic capitalist order of the West.

> Communism is not an ideology or a goal, but rather a means, a tool of overall imperialism. Every historical period has varied forms of imperialism. The shapes only differ. ... Two shapes exist today. ... Communism is one shape. In another shape, groups attempt to subordinate the economies of other countries. This imperialism wants our economy to be dependent [and] laughs at our economic progress. They say you haven't progressed, you can't produce a needle or a locomotive, you have only cheap copies. Why does the West engage in such

propaganda? ... They want to say to Iran, to Iranians, that we cannot achieve the capacity for development or management, or even the ability to govern ourselves.[19]

In other words, Communism was an ideological tool used by a greater entity, the imperialist West. This imperialist West, defined as both sides of the Cold War, threatened the stability and independence of those countries, such as Iran, seeking to defend their national interests. Communism was an effective tool in struggling against such polities given its false promises of the quick construction of a worldly paradise. Ameli-Tehrani at the Third Party Congress stated:

> Communism wants to plunge this land into darkness [while] imperialism of the West seeks to tell Iranians that they do not have the capacity to rule themselves. ... A thing called internationalism and a thing called communism do not separately exist. Communism is a mechanism, not a goal or ideology. It is imperialism's instrument. ... This imperialism of the West seeks to subordinate our economy. It seeks the closing of our universities. It laughs at our economic prosperity and says you have not developed ... you can't manufacture a needle or a locomotive, that what you have is only a pathetic *muntazh*, only the assembly of [industrial and consumer] goods with parts from abroad. ... What is the goal of this propaganda? ... They forget the development of the last fifteen years. ... In the end, they want to say to Iranians that you don't have the capacity for development or self-government. ... The imperialism of capitalism wants to control Iran.[20]

In sum, the Party propagated the idea that communism and liberal democracy were two sides of the same coin minted by the imperialist West.[21]

Along these lines attacks were launched on the political systems of these two sides of the West. The Cold War was propagated not as an ideological war but rather a struggle within Western imperialism over the division of the rest of the world between the two warring sides. What united them was an insouciant and essentialized contempt for the non-Western world that had to remain under its hegemony.

> In Iran when the West is discussed attention is often given to only one of its aspects with which we have contact and experience. This aspect we can summarize with the word 'liberalism'. Liberalism has not only an economic meaning but also a cultural one with its own traditions. This liberalism of the liberal West is only for the West and not for the rest of the world's societies. They branded us and stole from us. With this in mind and with the passage of time a point that needs attention is that Marxism is also a part and product of the West. It is surprising that in some developing societies the belief exists that if they become Marxist, communist, they can escape the West's cultural hegemony. But in reality this is not true. The owners of liberalism and Marxism are the same – the West. ... The war between them is a civil war and it is a mistake to conceive of it as our own struggle or to sacrifice ourselves for the sake of it. ... Perhaps elements could have been adopted from them but the West's geopolitics did not allow it. ... The point is that these two schools, both of them, have been imposed on us by superpowers

with which we have not had positive experiences, while [these culture and political systems] are not compatible with us and our culture.²²

This imperialism, determined to ensure the wealth of these two sides at the expense of non-Western countries, such as Iran, created resentment: 'The feelings of revenge against the imperialists grow: a warning to the individuals of the prosperous societies'.²³

Several months after the Party's establishment a special committee was formed under Baheri's chairmanship to analyse the current political situation and devise policies to manage any ideological and political threats coming from the West: 'In the meeting issues were discussed, the most important of which was the ideologies of the hegemonic tendencies of the superpowers'.²⁴ Their conclusions underscored these discursive trends. Its conclusions, while condemning communism and black reaction, drew particular attention to the weaknesses and dangers of the democratic liberal capitalist West.²⁵ In line with the monarch's rhetoric that blended the defence of identity and authenticity with rejection of liberalism, Rastakhiz propagated the idea that 'Western democracy does not answer the needs of Iran' and condemned the idea of 'exportable democracy (*demokrasi-ye vaaredaati*)'.²⁶ Rastakhiz announced the existence of an authentic Iranian political regime named 'democracy of the imperial system' that, in the shah's words, ensured that Iran would not face political 'chaos' and would avoid 'the licentiousness and promiscuity' characteristic of Western civilization.²⁷ It was therefore superior to the West's democracies where spiritual and moral decline was obvious and whose political chaos at times had led to the horrors of fascism, racism and military and/or political dictatorships. Without a doubt, 'the Revolution of Iran is superior to capitalism and communism'. Alam commented to the shah that with the launching of the Revolution and Party discourses, he had 'liberated himself from the West's "isms" and thus "had a free hand"'.²⁸ The shah agreed.

This conflation also included the negation of cosmopolitanism, the term used to describe the liberal democratic capitalist form of globalization, and internationalism, shorthand for proletarian internationalism, the label used to portray the Leninist-Marxist form of globalization. Baheri, having reworked aspects of party ideological discourses that constituted the base of party political education and public enlightenment, announced in April 1976 these results at this party special committee. These results say much about the direction in which the Pahlavi state was moving.

> Every individual belongs to a society that has its own interests from which that individual benefits. Therefore, an individual, given the unique interests of his own society, cannot belong to global society. Humanity, humankind, human rights, human dignity, by themselves are correct. However, they are relative to the land and population that lives and works together. These related elements create a form of uniqueness that creates a sense of foreignness in regard to other societies. We must pay attention and have strong attachment to the uniqueness of the society in which we live. Our minds must be aware and cognizant of this foreignness. To combine societies so that the unique interests of each one of them are eliminated and the leaders of all societies obtain collective interests is not possible. In some cases the idea of common interests could be true, but in any case every society

has its own unique interests and identity that it must protect. With attention to this reality we must in our program of political education abstain from the idea of cosmopolitanism (*jahanvatani*). Historically, when and where cosmopolitanism is found, it turned out to be a method of deception. Cosmopolitanism on all levels and in all viewpoints is not acceptable. ... Those societies that make claims about internationalism are also lying. Cosmopolitanism and internationalism are not to be relied on. Therefore, that which must be in political education ... is emphasis on the superiority of national authentic culture, ancient history, the Great Civilization, the future.[29]

The Iranian response to these deceitfully attractive forms of Western universalist modernities, portrayed as plots to undermine Iranian independence and sovereignty, was the authenticity of culture and national culture epitomized by the imperial system and the constitutive elements of the Great Civilization the march towards which was taking place 'under the banner of the White Revolution of Shah and People'.[30] To neutralize this threat of Western imperialism, the Party consistently called for the purification of Iranian authenticity. 'We need to become proud [of our identity and culture]' and 'transform our motherland into a sacred icon. ... It is correct that our culture is rich but this culture constitutes a form of [social] capital and, similar to any other capital, if it is not recognized, it is rendered useless. ... As the shahanshah has ordered: "I seek to preserve Iranian identity, Iranian thought, and the Iranian spirit."'[31] The people had to be politically educated about the importance of authenticity of culture and national identity and immunized from Western provocations against the monarchy, the source and defender of that authenticity: 'The myriad foreign conspiracies against Iran have understood, based on the experience of their organizers, that as long as the imperial bulwark exists, they will never succeed in achieving their goals'.[32]

This discursive defensive aggressiveness however included a proviso. 'We are not at war with the culture of "the inclusive world or universalism" or with "the authenticity of humankind" which is humanism. However, as long as this Western humanism and universalism do not pay attention to our national, cultural and ethnic characteristics they are nothing other than imperialism'.[33] This was in reality a postmodern call that rejected the claims of the modernities of Western civilization to universalism and superiority and attempts to impose them on other countries. This proviso, however, left enough ideological space for anti-West Occidentalism. At the ceremony of the 1975 *aid-e fetr*, the holiday marking the end of Ramadan, the shah emphasized: 'The developed nations of the West must recognize that the era of imperialism is over'.[34] Rastakhiz's conclusion was more blunt: 'Imperialism must understand that Iran is a chunk that will stick in the throat and suffocate it' if it attempted to impose its beliefs and hegemony.[35]

12

The curing and preventing of Occidentosis

The Rastakhiz Party, having identified the threats posed by Occidentosis, initiated, broadly speaking, three policy approaches: (1) The Revolution in Education; (2) Party Political Education; and (3) debunking of the idea that the '–isms' and corresponding modernities of the West were superior and universally applicable.

The Revolution in Education

By the late 1960s the state concluded that the quality and conditions of higher education and lack of systematic political cultivation of the youth based on the revised conceptions of authenticity of culture and national identity fuelled growing student discontent. The shah, in order to deal with these issues, established in 1968 a yearly conference 'The Revolution in Education', as part of the White Revolution. Presided over by him and the empress, these conferences determined reforms of the educational system and trajectories of the youth's political–cultural cultivation within the educational system. The shah, similar to the leaders of modern states in the Western and non-Western world since at least the nineteenth century, saw a link between education and patriotism; the former should be dedicated to producing the latter. This was the broad overarching theme of the first two conferences. However, from the Third Conference (1970), the shah, strengthening the themes articulated by Pahlavism and the SCCA, began to stress the need to protect the authenticity of culture and national identity at a time when the West had already discarded, in his words, 'moral and spiritual values'.[1] This initial stress, according to Rastakhiz interpretations of the evolution of these conferences, became more prominent in the Sixth Conference (1974). It 'was the beginning of a new era in the Revolution in Education'. The monarch 'complained about weaknesses across the entire educational system in teaching the youth the realities of the country's situation and shortcomings and derelictions in how families bring up children. These are the main true causes for the emergence of some of the political and cultural deviancies appearing in society'.[2]

With the Party's establishment and the intensification and systemization of the discourses of anti-West Occidentalism, the tone of these conferences and their policy initiatives to a significant degree differed in emphasis from earlier conferences. A major theme that characterized the conferences of the Rastakhiz period was the struggle against the manifestations of Occidentosis across the educational system. The problem was clear, according to Naraqi at the time: 'Contact over the last hundred years with the West and deviations in thought about our national past distanced us from our own culture.' One consequence and cause of this phenomenon was that Occidentosis-ridden people who 'sought to transform the entire world into a west-European system' had established the educational system.[3] Thus, the system was creating if not a Occidentosis-ridden youth, at least a youth susceptible to infection by it. Nafisi's official history of the Reza Shah period, quoted in Chapter 4, is a good example of the tendency criticized by Naraqi. This work, published when calls for reform of historiography were emerging, argued:

> A great powerful force with surprising speed spreads across the globe. Nothing is able to withstand it. Willingly or unwillingly the world's peoples, far and near, are following speedily this [Westernizing] process. All human forces are located within this force, process of civilization. ... The single cause for Iran's debasement, humiliation, shame and disgrace in the previous era was its lagging behind this caravan of civilization. ... It was necessary during this era to accept unquestionably all the sources and symbols of this new civilization and prepare and equip oneself for this new life. Of all the world's peoples the expectation had been that Iran and Iranians, given their 7,000 year-old history and civilizational leadership in every historical era and role as one of the most important founders of human civilization [would play a leading role]. ... However, the Pahlavi dynasty ... returned to Iran this historical role.[4]

This historiographical approach become a major target of Rastakhiz discourses that argued that 'the history that has been written for us' by Westerners was in reality based on the Orientalist paradigm that concluded that Iranians had to become Westerners in order to attain civilizational greatness. The Party therefore pressured the government for the nativization of historiography that rejected this Orientalist-based history. In this vein, Naraqi introduced the term 'cultural terrorism', complementing the Rastakhiz historiographical narrative introduced in Mozaffari's book. '[Cultural] terrorists often become acquainted with the upper classes of Eastern societies and then transform them into bullhorns that accuse countries of the East of lacking culture'.[5] These human bullhorns were the Occidentosis-ridden technocrats, who 'not knowing [authentic] culture, use Western criteria and standards' when devising and implementing policies, and 'thus cannot strengthen Eastern culture'.[6] Such people were incapable of curing the educational system that had been infected with Occidentosis and defending Iran's cultural and thus geopolitical borders in the face of the threat of the West.

Naraqi's position was not a peripheral musing. It was party discourse. For example, Hushang Ansari in the early days of Rastakhiz stressed that 'the youth need to become acquainted with Iranian history' so that they understand what elements from the West were not compatible with the new definitions of Iranianess and how to reject them. Importantly, 'those exposed to foreign education and especially those in government must also be taught to make correctly this distinction'.[7] Rastakhiz publications argued that to achieve this 'national goal' history textbooks, penned by these 'cultural terrorists', had to be fundamentally re-written. These textbooks 'lacked the spirit of nationalism' and focused too much on the West and its claims of superiority. 'What they teach in the history textbooks no enemy could have taught'.[8]

The Seventh Conference (1975), the first after the Party's establishment, addressed these issues. Several months before it the shah in his last speech to the 23rd Majles mentioned them, emphasizing that more efforts were needed so that 'the cultivation and progress of the youth is accompanied by moral and spiritual purity' that reflected Iranian authenticity.[9] Picking up on these signals, in the run-up to the conference party publications severely criticized the government for inaction that had allowed Occidentosis to spread within the educational system and maintain its hold over Iranian historiography, despite the imperial couple's exhortations.

At the conference the shah underlined these shortcomings and deficiencies in the government's handling of the revolution in education.[10] Citing these imperial rebukes, the Party introduced into the conference's proceedings a detailed report, in whose preparation Baheri played an important role, on the many weaknesses in the education system that fuelled student discontent and lowered educational quality at all levels, but particularly in higher education. Hoveyda, stung by the report, sought to alleviate dissatisfaction over it within his ranks by stressing that it was not aimed at any particular group or political figures but rather was a framework for educational reform. In reality it was only the first salvo fired by the Party at the government on this issue.

Rastakhiz stressed that the Seventh Conference would lead to sweeping changes in the educational system and make up for previous government inaction. Thus it would fundamentally differ from all previous conferences. The reason for this was clear – The Party had assumed a supervisory role in the revolution in education that would ensure the government's implementation of the imperial couple's and the conference's policies.[11] Rastakhiz would play this role through newly established committees that, in addition to supervision, would offer policy recommendations.[12]

> The Rastakhiz Party with its unique identity can be the infrastructure for a great cultural movement – culture in the sense of the construction of people tied to authentic national moral principles and foundations. To achieve this a revolution in teaching and education is needed. ... Any country that quickly towards industrialization faces the danger that it will distance itself from spirituality which is an Iranian uniqueness. ... Remaining faithful to one's beliefs and principles is a necessity. ... In regard to cultural challenges we have a long path to follow in light of the crisis of identity. However, the Rastakhiz Party while pursuing economic modernization will also strengthen our cultural infrastructure in the educational system [since] the infection by Occidentosis of the youth is the result of lack of attention to native moral principles and foundations in education curriculum from primary to higher education.[13]

Hoveyda was not pleased.

Continuing its offensive, the Party argued that faulty curricula at all education levels had created an intellectual vacuum in which young people 'are ignorant of national identity' and thus unwittingly 'allow themselves to be deceived' by the '–isms' of the

West, derivative of 'either Marx or Hegel'. Echoing the principles of postmodernism Rastakhiz stressed:

> The youth must understand that every society lives with its own constitution, culture, and national identity. We need to start at a young age proper education about these '–isms' and place the Revolution's charter in opposition to these '–isms' and show the Revolution's superiority. ... Every young Iranian must know the national identity.[14]

Rastakhiz rhetoric stressed that national security and independence demanded that this revolution in education be implemented quickly and effectively in order to compensate for previous government inaction and mismanagement. Hoveyda, forced to play along with these discourses despite the unspoken recognition that these were implicit condemnations of his performance, asked in his conference speech: 'To what extent is our educational system able and prepared to create and cultivate the new individuals for the era of the Great Civilization?' He confessed that much work needed to be done.

One immediate result of these attacks was the publication by the Ministry of Education of revised teaching guides. They were essentially textbooks for teachers and administrators working within the education system that explained the framework and historiographical and ideological elements of party education rooted in discourses of anti-West Occidentalism. Teachers were told to stress that 'the Revolution of Iran is not a capitalist liberal revolution or a so-called socialist revolution'. It was authentically Iranian. They were to emphasize that Iranian authenticity was based on spirituality and austere morality in whose protection in the face of Occidentosis Islam played a key role.[15] Except for this, little other practical action was taken during the year leading to the 1976 conference. The Party was preoccupied with parliamentary elections and ideological and organizational issues as it tried to institutionalize itself. However, the rhetoric of the 1975 conference set the stage for the 1976 one.

The city of Ramsar, located on the Caspian coast, in August 1976 hosted the Eighth Conference to fanfare exceeding that of previous conferences. Following the lead of the imperial couple Rastakhiz publications portrayed it as the turning point in the Revolution in Education and specifically the crusade against the Occidentosis-ridden educational system. Previously unseen levels of coverage were given to the imperial couple's speeches and remarks. Vadiei, writing in *Rastakhiz*, summed up the meaning of the shah's speech, the conference's centrepiece and framework for party action: 'What are we? What do we want to become? What must we become? These are the questions this conference faces and with which it must deal. These are the shah's questions'.[16] Hoveyda was forced to give lip service to these themes:

> The educational system must protect national moral, social and cultural values that are increasingly threatened in the current era of changes ... [and] more time needs to be spent on the protection of spiritual and moral values and authenticity. ... What is not subject to revision is the complete cultivation [of this authenticity] within the new Iranian person. ... With this genuine Iranian person ..., [who is]

based on our own morals and without any imitation of other examples, we must and shall go forward.[17]

Rastakhiz's lead article, 'Education and Imported Culture', while outlining the conference's main themes and proceedings, was frank in its description of the struggle against Occidentosis.

> To say that the problem and challenge of our educational system is that it is still under the complete influence of the West's culture is perhaps difficult. It is difficult because we are in a situation in which all of our struggles are concentrated on eliminating the West's various influences. ... It is necessary to say that the West's cultural influence is a form of spiritual and moral imperialism. ... The first penetration of Western culture into our country started immediately after the first sparks of our anti-imperialist struggles. At first it took the shape of cultural exchange given the belief in [Western] civilization. Although our culture had a unique spiritual depth it could not initially repel this penetration of Western culture. ... Consequently, today Iranian children and youth in primary and high schools are losing the spirit of nationalism. They are feeding on vain foreign Western cultures and suddenly when they reach our age at which they have to determine the country's fate, they do not even know what constitutes the country's spirit and psychology.[18]

Thus, a grave national crisis was brewing that required immediate attention. Rastakhiz's position was a telling confession and condemnation not only of initial Pahlavi Occidentalism but also the educational policies over the previous decades. It could have been easily written by al-e Ahmad or the IRI.

In the discussion about proper curricula the conference, unsurprisingly, concluded: 'Science and technology must be taught in a global context, they are global.' The Revolution in Education in regard to these fields would focus on improving teaching methods and equipment, while curricula and knowledge would remain Western or rather global. However, 'education dealing with history, culture and literature must completely be purged of Western influence. In this regard, the excuse of "Western civilization" as a superior civilization to be imitated is no longer justified and acceptable.' At stake was the country's independence and future. Naraqi warned:

> The imperialist enemy who yesterday was dressed and armed with cannon and guns, now comes, attacking, armed with science, culture, and customs. ... It is not only a question of economic and political imperialism. ... At the present time cultural influence is the greatest and most powerful strategic trick (*tarfand*) used by imperialist countries.

If Occidentosis succeeded in spreading the result would be 'a lack of culture' that was a precondition for Western domination. Rastakhiz publications therefore proclaimed that Iran under party leadership would ensure that 'imperialism no longer has a path [into the realm of education and culture]', and thus the country would be in a position 'to eliminate all signs of imperialism'. The front line for this struggle was primary and secondary education. At these educational levels, culture, literature, morals and history, the native expressions of Iranian authenticity were to be firewalled. 'We must have an independent authentic culture and our educational system must be based on it and its preservation'.[19]

Despite the fanfare and rhetoric of the 1976 conference, the Party judged subsequent government action to be lax. Rastakhiz went public with its grievances, complaining that the shah's concerns had not been addressed: 'Pupils [at the primary and secondary levels of education] are still not being taught about national culture and authenticity'.[20] Focus remained on teaching the West's cultural heritage and history as a superior civilization to be imitated while 'the teaching of Iranian cultural heritage and Persian literature in schools continues to be hollow'.[21] Looking for those responsible for this failure, Rastakhiz fingered government officials: 'Many of our educated, even those occupying sensitive state posts, consciously or unconsciously think more of the interests of Westerners than those of our motherland'.[22] They could not be trusted to carry out the Revolution. These criticisms of government performance remained a continuous theme of Rastakhiz publications throughout 1977 and 1978. The fundamental theme that prompted varied debated topics can be summed up by the questioned posed by *The Youth of Rastakhiz*: 'Why is it that education policy continues to cultivate in today's Iran a youth that knows Shakespeare, Molière, and Chekov better than the gazelles of Saadi, Hafiz and Molavi?'[23]

This question drew attention to language and literature, seen as the repository of national identity and culture, which continued to play an integral role in these discussions. From Reza Shah's reign the nationalized history of Iran with focus on its pre-Islamic imperial heritage and the Persian language, the lingua franca in a multilingual polity and link to this heritage, were considered essential building blocks for national identity and unity. By the time of Rastakhiz, the linguistic concerns, as expressed by the Party, dealt with the spread of the study of Western languages and literature.[24] At issue was not the study of foreign languages, but rather the seemingly growing emphasis on the learning of Western languages at the expense of Persian language and literature. Rastakhiz, in addition to its own discursive focus on the infection of language by Occidentosis, published open letters from the public to the minister of education that decried an education system that supported, or at least tolerated, such tendencies among the youth at all levels of education. The public, therefore, and not the Party, was condemning the government for playing a decisive role in creating a youth 'lacking in identity' and a situation in which one could ask: How is it possible that 'a child whose mother and father are Iranian speaks Persian with an accent?'[25]

The threat of these Occidentosis-ridden schools paled in comparison, however, to dual-language schools that were the favourite of these families. These schools, completely alien in structure, curricula and language of instruction, were in the avant-garde in the cultivation of an Occidentosis-ridden Iranian youth. Although the number of such schools was small relative to the overall amount of schools run by the Education Ministry, the Party took particular aim at them: 'In the Rastakhiz era our education is the creative substructure of tomorrow's generation. Thus, this infrastructure must from its base upwards be Iranian – just as our policy of national independence.' The Party, again stressing its role as the popular-supported vanguard in the struggle against Occidentosis, argued: 'The Education Ministry must act as soon as possible' and make up for its past inaction and poor management.[26]

Rastakhiz pointed the finger of responsibility and blame not only at the 'Occidentosis-ridden' curricula or Occidentosis-ridden education officials. At the top of the party list were parents and families, infected with and spreading Occidentosis, who accepted the West's propaganda that its civilization was superior. They posed a particularly difficult problem to manage. Rastakhiz warned that only in the state educational system could the struggle against this familial-inspired Occidentosis be waged. However, this part of the crusade remained in its infancy since these Occidentosis-ridden families and similarly infected elements within the educational system ensured the privileged position of foreign languages in schools and 'the importation of teaching methods' all of which 'corrupt and pollute national authentic culture'.[27]

Unsurprisingly, the sending of youth for study abroad at the secondary and university levels too came in for criticism. The fear was that living and studying in the West would lead to the infection of young Iranians with moral and political Occidentosis. Rastakhiz headlines ran: 'Spoiled brats go to the West to obtain an education in sex and debauchery – Read this if you want to send your children abroad for study.' Parents were warned about the pernicious moral, cultural and political influence on Iranian youth resulting from 'so-called studying' in the West. Those who nonetheless sent their children to the West were charged with abandoning 'the responsibility for bringing up your children'. The youth's thirst for study in the West was in reality the thirst for hedonism: 'The primary reason to go to the West to study is sex, debauchery, and roaming around aimlessly.' Given these real motivations, Rastakhiz asked 'what are the justifications and rationale for the loss of our riches' to these Western countries, riches paid so that the youth can experience licentiousness?'[28]

The Party proposed that one way of dealing with this was improvement of the quality of education inside Iran. Even when the Revolution in Education achieved this goal, these 'spoiled brats' would still go after the debauchery and licentiousness offered by the West. The problem was that the educational system was no longer teaching proper morality. Consequently, Occidentosis had infected Iranian morality and specifically sexual morality. 'In schools no sign of moral cultivation and intellectual teaching can be seen. ... The breaking of traditions by the East's youth is more than anything else the result of cultural confusion and aimlessness between new values [emerging as a result of Occidentosis] and old ones.' The Party would lead efforts to bolster this front in the struggle.[29]

However the problem of familial-inspired Occidentosis remained. Some parents of these 'brats', having abandoned Iranian spirituality and morality, sought to shun their parental responsibilities by sending their children to the West. Others believed in the superiority of Western civilization and education. In their opinion, the West needed to be brought to Iran. Such people regarded Western education as a class and civilizational status symbol, a means to prove their superiority to other Iranians and a vital weapon in 'keeping up with the Joneses'. Showing signs of Occidentosis, a great number of 'mothers and fathers have become poseurs, enjoying every opportunity to flaunt that their children are studying abroad'. These two trends had resulted in a tendency that was destructive for both the youth and the country's future:

> Sending these young people abroad to study, especially from the high school level, creates a serious identity crisis because these students and pupils who have not yet obtained a complete understanding of Iranian culture and morality and the authenticity of their birth places, go to the West whose culture and morality are completely different.

It was asked, how could these youth once again integrate into society. In this context one had to ask the ultimate question about studying in the West: 'Is it *really* worth it?'[30]

Rastakhiz's answer was clear:

> They return from the West infected with Occidentosis. They believe that whatever is there, and only there, symbolizes culture and civilization. They even believe that our poetry is nothing in comparison with the West's poetry!.. The most correct terms describing the state of today's youth and identity are confusion. ... This crisis of identity [is manifested in] the youth's distancing of themselves from Iranian literature and culture.

Rastakhiz wondered how could such a youth in the future hold responsible positions in the public and private sectors. But this was not the only danger emanating from them. This Occidentosis-ridden youth upon their return to their native land after a period of study became unwitting and in many cases witting disseminators of this disease. Consequently, 'today's hot topic is preservation of authenticity of Iranian culture'. Combatting the infection of Occidentosis required a revolution for the nativization of the educational system: 'Those youth who are sent abroad for education we must first acquaint with and educate about Iran. ... Those who know their culture do not succumb to Occidentosis'.[31]

The Youth of Rastakhiz gave frequent coverage to the views of Rasul Parvizi in this regard who as a well-known writer and a member of the Imperial Senate provided intellectual and political weight to the party's campaign. 'My blood boils when I ask a family ... how can you send this land's human capital land to foreign countries for schooling?'[32] The answer was simple. The Occidentosis-ridden *nouveau riche* sought to ensure the infection of their progeny with this illness and denigrate genuine Iranianess. He too argued that this unfortunate trend to flaunt degrees from the West and to affect the behaviour and mores of Westerners were the fundamental elements these Occidentosis-ridden individuals used to create their social identity and sense of superiority over those Iranians who studied in country. 'These pansy dandies (*juje-fokoliha*)' were a blot on national life, 'returning from the West and darkening our life'. The term 'fokoli', a derivative of the French expression, *faux-col*, had been coined by the thinker Fakhr al-Din Shadman to describe those Iranians who flaunted Occidentosis-ridden appearance and behaviour but were true philistines.[33]

According to Parvizi, these *fokolis* were a blot for two basis reasons. First, they purposely created a sense of inferiority among those Iranians who studied in country through claims that Western civilization and education were superior to anything native. This was maddening for Parvizi since those who studied in country were the ones in a position to protect Iranian authenticity while 'many of those returning' from study in the West 'are illiterate'. Their cultural and scholarly illiteracy, poorly disguised by the veneer of Occidentosis, had 'created a vacuum of thought in Iran'. While they flaunted their Western degrees and spoke of 'how things are done in the West' they were unable to produce appropriate solutions to the country's problems since, by studying abroad and becoming infected with Occidentosis, they could not understand their own country and used Western thought and criteria in finding solutions and policies. Second, these Occidentosis-ridden pansy dandies were spreaders of the manifestations of their sickness-conspicuous consumerism, materialism and hedonism. 'Ninety percent of Occidentosis is the result of material hedonism of this young generation'.[34]

Despite the tone coming from Rastakhiz publications, the Party did agree that national development demanded that students be sent abroad for technical and scientific education. However, such students at the primary and secondary education had to be immunized from the disease of Occidentosis through proper political and cultural cultivation. It also argued that students choosing the humanities and social sciences study had to study in country. The Party set up a special committee to provide guidelines to the Ministry of Education and MCA for this inculcation that would produce the desired *homo Pahlavicus*.

In sum, the Revolution in Education constituted a fundamental element in the Rastakhiz crusade against Occidentosis and the creation of national unity around the Crown. Through the struggle against Occidentosis and reform of conditions in the educational system it was hoped that rising youth discontent and activism could be managed and minimized. However, the attacks on those classes the party described as Occidentosis-ridden and *nouveau riche* were a politically risky move for popular opinion continued to view the state as an agent of this Occidentosis – especially since the two groups subject to this criticism were seen as products of the state. The gamble was that these discourses would transform the popular image of the Pahlavi state as a spreader of Occidentosis.

Political Education

Party Political Education was the other production line of *homo Pahlavicus*. The shah and party leadership considered it the most effective mechanism for the political and cultural cultivation of party cadres, in the first instance, and then the population at large with the three party principles, party sacred texts, and the shah's writings and, vitally, for preparing them for the crusade against Occidentosis: 'The goal of Political Education … is the inculcation of the people with Rastakhiz philosophy and guiding of the people's behaviour, beliefs, judgement'.[35] Given the short time the Rastakhiz Party existed limited steps were taken to fulfil these expectations.

Leading party members underlined that the protection of authenticity of culture and national identity constituted the pillar of this political education from which all other elements flowed. In the words of Ameli-Tehrani:

> The spirit of authentic Iran must manifest itself in national life. ... One of the unique characteristics and missions of the Rastakhiz Party is the correct and accurate recognition of the cultural identity of the Iranian people. ... In other words we, as a Party, don't want external elements in Iranian culture. ... The authentic Iranian spirit must be portrayed and preserved.[36]

Mahmoud Jafarian, deputy party head and first deputy of NIRT, at the first meeting dedicated to the political education of party cadres and the Guardians of the Revolution, outlined the framework in which they were to act.[37] He emphasized 'a united culture that is always only Iranian' and a 'cultural return to the past' from which Iranians 'must take inspiration' in light of 'the era of deep and quick movement in the direction of a new Iran'. Admitting that 'we have no choice but to adopt technology from the West in order to advance the Revolution of Iran' he insisted that 'Western culture, morals, and behaviour are not adoptable'.[38] In other words, 'although we are forced to adopt Western technology for the advancement of economic and social goals, we will not take on Western morals, culture and political behaviour. ... It is a question not only of today's Iran but also the country's heritage and future. ... Everything comes and goes, what must remain is authentic Iranian identity'. Warning about the danger posed by Occidentosis-ridden Iranians he stated:

> Today we see that we need [Iranian authenticity] as much as we need air and water. ... This requires that all of us in our activities and work, in programs, words and decisions, strengthen [conceptions of national authentic culture and identity]. ... We are in need of new Iranians who are aware of their authentic Iranian identity and serve Iran and the eternal imperial system.[39]

Calling for all Iranians 'to be vigilant in the face of the West's cultural imperialism' he stressed that concomitantly party cadres and the Guardians of the Revolution through political education 'will deliver to us unity through its protection of Iranian identity ... [and] cultural authenticity'.[40] The danger was indeed real as Hossein Sarfaraz argued in *Rastakhiz*: 'It is not a lie that the youth are Occidentosis-ridden'.[41]

The Guardians of the Revolution was an organization integral to the White Revolution. Eventually made up of the Literacy Corps, Hygiene Corps and Development Corps, the Guardians were staffed by educated young men and women who, instead of fulfilling their obligatory military service in the armed forces, served in these development corps.[42] This institution underwent organizational changes with the establishment of the Rastakhiz Party. In accordance with an imperial decree dated 5 August 1976 the Party integrated and gave it the additional responsibility of providing political education to the masses. This step included the establishment of a party university that would prepare these cadres for the spreading of this political education.[43] In addition to the Guardians of the Revolution, local party societies and groups under the direction of central party leadership would provide this political education to rank-and-file party members. Rastakhiz publications, and the newspaper *Rastakhiz* in particular, provided coverage of sessions held by party organizations dedicated to political education and provided materials for study and debate for such sessions, such as the serialization of party sacred texts and the shah's writings. [44]

During Hoveyda's tenure as party head the development of political education was slow given his lack of interest and the great organizational, practical and ideological challenges facing the party at its establishment. While Amuzegar during his first tenure gave some attention to it, figures such as Baheri and Homayoun, among others, tried to generate real momentum behind it. One of the consequences of these attempts was the creation in December 1976 of a super committee dedicated to organizing the process of political education. Its membership included the party head, although other high-ranking members pursued this goal. In keeping with party tradition, its announcement included a reiteration that at the centre of this political education was the issue of authenticity of culture and national identity in the face of Occidentosis.[45] By spring 1977 these efforts began to bear some fruit.

Baheri, in contrast to his predecessors, devoted much time and energy to the development of political education. During his tenure it became one of the most important party activities as Rastakhiz discourses of anti-West Occidentalism intensified. After the Revolution Baheri explained:

> The political regime in Iran at the time was facing doubts and the challenges of different ideologies, of political doctrines at a time when the masses in reality had no real awareness or understanding of these doctrines and ideologies. I believed that it was necessary to establish political education and defend the state's legitimacy and say and prove that the regime was the best form for Iran's development.[46]

At the time, Baheri publicly stressed that the struggle against Occidentosis required that 'political education emphasize that the Iranian people must know their own national interests in the international arena'.[47]

Determining the effectiveness of party political education is difficult given the short period of the party's existence and even shorter duration of its active implementation. What is important is the simultaneous expansion of political education and the discourses of anti-West Occidentalism. Together they are principle indicators of the direction of the late Pahlavi state and its approach to the West.

The corruption and eclipse of the West

The effectiveness of the Revolution in Education and Party Political Education was dependent on propagation of plausible and persuasive discourses portraying Western civilization and modernities as politically and economically in decline and morally and spiritually bankrupt. Debunking of the West's modernities was a foundational element in the propagation of the claims of the Pahlavi system and its modernity, the

Great Civilization, to superiority. The Party continued the long-standing state assault on communist thought and its derivatives while greatly expanding the attack on the liberal democratic capitalist West that began before its establishment. The intensity and extent of this attack not only became equivalent to that against communism, but also frequently exceeded it, especially from early 1976.

This intense offensive against the West's liberal democratic and capitalist systems was the party-state response to several challenges. As noted earlier, cultural and geopolitical anti-Westernism was increasingly popular among the growing middle classes and the student intelligentsia. Their ire was projected onto the authoritarian Pahlavi state that seemed to be a spreader of cultural and moral Occidentosis while enjoying a close geopolitical relationship with the leader of that West, the United States. The Party sought through its debunking of this West and discourses of anti-West Occidentalism to project the Crown as the defender of Iranian authenticity in the face of Occidentosis and thereby overturn the negative public perception of it as a carrier of this cultural and moral disease. The Party attacked the West also because of the sense that the ideas behind Western liberalism constituted a threat to the Pahlavi state that was equal to and perhaps even greater than the threats posed by communism and its derivative forms in Iran. Lastly, as discussed earlier, this debunking was also a result of the shah's and the empress's evolved views about the place of the West in their conceptions of the authenticity of Iranian culture and national identity and of Iran's path of development.

International events and geopolitics also fed into this policy of debunking. As the previous chapter showed, Nixon's departure prompted a change in the tone of the relationship between Iran and the United States, the leader of the West. Central to this change was increased Western criticism of the state of human rights in the country and the establishment of a single-party state in 1975. Parallel to this development was the shah's increasing confidence and independence in foreign affairs that led to a rise in tension between the countries, an evolution the CIA had predicted in the late 1960s.[48]

Thus, Rastakhiz publications from their inception took aim at this West, condemning 'the false paradises of the capitalist West and communist East' and the 'deceptive character of the West's civilization'.[49] It declared that 'the West is not synonymous with civilization or progress'.[50] The second issue of *Rastakhiz* published a major article titled 'The Loneliness of the West' that was a summary of Naraqi's book with the same title discussed earlier. The paper exhorted Iranians, and others in the East, to read it while the Party placed it on the list of required reading for political education.[51] This article, published at the outset of the activities of party publications, provides another strong example of the party approach to the West.

> The view of the West in the closing decades of this century has seriously changed. In the past those returning from the West, without wishing it, were infected with the sickness of Occidentosis. The West as it emerged in and evolved from the sixteenth century was a civilization based on liberalism. This made it attractive. This attractiveness relentlessly dragged every one of its viewers and spectators first into confusion and anxiety and then into enchantment and captivation. Therefore, Taqizadeh at one point said that everyone had to become Western

from head to toe.⁵² These Occidentosis-ridden people easily showed their hurried understandings of the victorious West, the ambitious West, the West of technology, a technology that whetted their appetites. ... During earlier periods these people, believing the transformation of the East into the West was possible, initiated the destruction of traditions and institutions. They believed that only with their destruction could order and progress emerge. They held onto this one principle. In order to implement these plans they chanted one slogan: to become civilized one must become Western. In their own other words, the West and civilization were synonymous. These two words are inseparable. Wherever civilization exists, there is the West, any place the West exists, there is civilization.

It also addressed the frequently debated question, 'What is the West?'.

> It is a demon monster... that scowls and greedily glares at the East, it [the West] ridiculously considers the East barbaric since ancient times. ... The one link, the one treaty, which was imposed by one on the other is imperialism. ... What is surprising is that these Occidentosis-ridden people prepare the ground for this imperialism. ... To a degree it is possible to pardon the Occidentosis of people such as Malkom Khan, the early Occidentosis-ridden ones, given conditions at the time. ... The West was attractive. But today the signs of this attractiveness are no longer. The demon-monster is writhing in pain. The civilization the West constructed, similar to Frankenstein with it steel-hard arms, is crushing the creators of regeneration. ... The West is sick, diseased. The members of the West's older generation too feel a sense of alienation and strangeness in regard to the current West. Seemingly, the West's negative dynamics have triumphed over whatever ones it might have had. ... People are increasingly not enchanted with the West. ... In order to be civilized it is no longer required to follow unquestionably the West. ... These worshippers of the imitation of the West have ended up in a cul-de-sac. What is needed is spirituality that stands in opposition to the West's emphasis on appearances, production, [and] materialism.

The shah propagated this interpretation. A decade after launching his White Revolution that emphasized 'the material problems and well-being of the people' he announced:

> I am giving much attention to the issue that our future cannot be based on materialism and technology, but rather on strong spiritual principles that will prevent society from falling into consumerism and materialism ... material progress of society must be accompanied by humanistic and spiritual aspects.⁵³

Warning about the transformation of Iranians into a 'Frankenstein', he announced, 'I am determined to protect Iranian philosophy, culture, and identity. We do not want to resemble a machine, a robot.' The empress echoed these sentiments: 'With the acquisition and use of technology we do not want to lose human virtues.'⁵⁴

Centred around this idea of Frankenstein several elements, covered in previous chapters, constituted the framework of discourses of anti-West Occidentalism.

Conceptions and exhortations for spirituality were set in opposition to what was perceived as the instrumentalization and commercialization of familial and social relationships in the West. This spirituality that underpinned genuine human relationships was portrayed as the only way to avoid the corrupted situation in the West where, it was claimed, material wealth was the determinative factor in social, political and legal spheres. The result was a structurally and culturally imposed perennial struggle waged by atomized individuals for increasing amounts of money and consumer goods at the expense of others that left a society at war with itself. Moreover, what kind of freedom and democracy, it was asked, allowed money to play a determinative role in these fields while imposing a social, political and even legal oppression on those without such wealth.

This implicit oppression was not limited to these fields. The capitalist West's materialistic dynamic denied people real freedom to determine their fate and find true meaning in life by forcing them to engage constantly in this unwanted struggle to the detriment of everything else. These fundamentals of Western civilization while denying people the freedom of mind and spirituality also destroyed the power of true creativity with its slavish glorification of 'cheap celebrity' that produced imitative behaviour within society and 'fashion' that homogenized mores and appearances on the base of common and thus debased morality and appearances. Equally catastrophic was communism under which

> owning of property is banned and the exploitation of others is not allowed, hegemony takes the form of political power and the possession of information. In countries where the means of production and private property have been eliminated and others do not have the right and opportunity to exploit others, domestic situation moves in the direction of political absolutism power and possessing information.[55]

To give discursive bite to the elements of anti-West Occidentalism Rastakhiz publications frequently utilized the works of Western critics of Western civilization, such as Jean Paul Sartre, Simone de Beauvoir, Levi Strauss, Arnold Toynbee, Jacques Derrida, Oswald Spengler, René Guénon, among others. Such critics influenced the growing intellectual criticisms of the West in Iran while providing inspiration and supporting elements to the discourses of anti-West Occidentalism.[56] This approach differed from that of from the mid-1960s to the early 1970s when the state's primary focus was on the propagation of Western thinkers critical and condemning of communism and, in particular, the USSR, such as Raymond Aaron, and Iranians with first-hand negative experience of the communist bloc, such as Enayatollah Reza.[57]

The first stage of these discourses through its negative portrayal of conditions in the West and underlining the criticisms of Western thinkers of Western civilization sought to debunk in the eyes of Iranians not only current Western civilization but its recent historical trajectory.

> Fascism, Nazism, Communism and dictatorial and police governments that emerged after World War I shook our world as it was moving in the direction

of democracy and plunged it into the purgatory of political crisis, violence, and contradictions emerging from consumerism and materialism. Democracy that was developing in the nineteenth century and the social contracts which Rousseau predicated found themselves in disarray and chaos by the end of the nineteenth century in the West. ... The rise in crime and betrayal, suicide and divorce, and moral corruption, the lack of human emotion and spirituality, the lack of feelings of mercy, the lack of deep human relationships and self-sacrifice terrified sociologists at the time. These issues convinced Western thinkers to find a solution but the West continued to evolve in this negative way and to sink deeper into moral and spiritual decline. ... This tired West was starting to rebel, people sought a great humanist ideology, an ideology far from materialism and consumerism ... and compatible with human emotions ... [Nonetheless that which exists] are crises and a materialistic purgatory in the West.[58]

The following stage was characterized by attempts to prove the need and importance of the party goal of preserving Iranian authenticity by citing the thought of Western thinkers. 'One of the largest issues and pains of our era is the attempted transformation of authenticities. ... However, that which is authentic does not change its essence and in fact protects it [its essence].'[59] In this regard the work of the Frankfurt School of Critical Theory and particularly the thought of Erich Fromm (1900–80), the German thinker and democrat socialist, received great coverage. Articles focused on his work dedicated to the issue of identity crisis in the modern era and his brand of social democracy that rejected Western capitalism and Soviet communism: 'The West is now suffering from a crisis of identity and seeks solutions from the East. After the West's imposition on the East, the West is now under the influence of the cultural heritages of the East.' According to Rastakhiz's interpretation of Fromm's thought Occidentosis from which some Iranians were suffering constituted a step backward at a time when the West itself, facing a crisis of identity resulting from its lack of spirituality and morality, was looking to the East as a mentor in this regard. Calling for a new revitalized cultural policy dedicated to the struggle against Occidentosis, it was stressed that 'attention to modernism must not become a mechanism for the destruction of cultural authenticity'.[60]

A great number of the contemporary works Rastakhiz publications cited belonged to French thinkers. Among them was Henri Labroit (1914–95). Over a series of articles his works were used to prove that 'consumerism and the race for money, the base of the West's economic system, overshadowed morality and spirituality'. In an interview he stated: 'The goal of Western society is the creation of superfluous needs. ... The West's entire social structure is based on competition and rivalry, anger, resentment and possessing of things. ... Where is this Western society going? It faces a horror.'[61] The cause for this moral and spiritual catastrophe was Western capitalism supported by its so-called democratic political system that benefitted only the very wealthy. Rastakhiz lamented: 'In the West the possession of things is how humans identify themselves and create their identity'.[62] This was a disaster for the concept of civilization. Labroit predicted: 'If the creation of consumerism in the West is not overturned, its current civilization will march toward its death'.[63]

The thought of René Dumont (1904–2001) French sociologist and ideological founder of France's Green Party, was also frequently cited. He proclaimed: 'If immediate and effective steps are not taken to check the lifestyle and the patterns of consumerism in the West, its entire civilization will collapse. All the signs are there'.[64] George Mathieu (1921–2012), a French abstract painter, specialist in art theory and member of the Academie des Beaux-Arts, was featured in an article, 'Evil forces, from sex and violence, weave an ominous web in the West', because 'his fury is directed at those who destroy culture.' He saw the direction in which Western civilization was going: 'Have the people of the West, all of them, become deaf and mute? … If things don't change in the not so far future not only great people but also regular people will no longer exist. The world will be made up of great masses devoid of any form of live individuality.' Mirroring Rastakhiz discourses about the infection of the world of Iranian cinema by Occidentosis, he criticized the direction in which the West's so-called arts were going: 'Ninety percent of the world's art and cultural exhibitions are made up of products peddled by merchants of sex and violence'.[65] Summarizing his work, Rastakhiz continued to beat the drum that in the West the result was 'isolated, atomized and mechanical lives'.[66] The Party concluded that 'Western civilization consists of atomization, suffocation, oppression, and hedonism'[67] and proclaimed, 'The triteness and corruption of culture is worthy of the West, but not of us!'[68]

Occidentosis was not limited to consumerism and materialism; it was an all-encompassing cancer that, if left unchecked, would destroy all signs of native authenticity. The centrepiece of this element of Rastakhiz narratives was the work of the French anthropologist, Robert Jaulin (1928–96) titled *Introduction à l'ethnocide*.[69] In it Jaulin provided a new understanding of ethnocide. Having lived among the Bari people in Latin America, located between Venezuela and Colombia, he witnessed the death of its culture due to Occidentosis. Therefore, he claimed, the definition of ethnocide included the spiritual and cultural extermination of a people: 'Praise of Westernization issues the death sentence to other civilizations.' The article asked: 'How is it possible that a negative civilization, such as the West's, can succeed in becoming hegemonic and exterminate other civilizations?' The answer was simple. Once the urbanized elite and educated classes became ridden with Occidentosis they infected the entire society and thus brought the destruction of nativist authenticity. This was confirmation of Rastakhiz historiography. Consequently, a warning was issued: 'As long as we believe that only one civilization and future awaits all of humankind we will destroy creativity in life'.[70] Iran had dangerously and blindly set out on the path travelled by the Bali people: 'Our unbridled enchantment with the West over the past one hundred years ruined and corrupted us. We thought anything that comes from the West is a divine message from above and anything the West says is correct and nothing else is left to say'.[71] However, under the shah's leadership a crusade against Occidentosis had started.

A contributing, but not main, reason for this concentration on French critics of Western civilization and modernity was the presence in Paris of a Rastakhiz journalist Hossein Mehri who was working towards his doctorate. He had contributed many articles with this tone to *Ferdowsi* in the late 1960s and early 1970s. Articles such as his prompted SAVAK at the time to note the rise of anti-West Occidentalism among the youth and educated classes. During the Rastakhiz period he was portrayed as someone in a special position to blend the contemporary Western criticisms in regard to Western civilization and modernity with party discourses for domestic consumption. His statements in his long-running series of articles in *The Youth of Rastakhiz* were sharp even if encased in a scholarly language: 'Western civilization is corrosive and unsuccessful. ... The attractive assumptions of the Western person incorrectly negate the history-making elements of the world. ... Bullying behaviour and irreligiosity have plunged the West into cultural decline'.[72] Whatever came of the West, and even if the West would be able to overcome these problems, Iran had to shun its path. Those who were Occidentosis-ridden had failed to understand the West's current catastrophic conditions and its civilization's destructive essence. Moreover, the West was guilty not only of the spiritual and moral death of itself and other cultures. It had also devised efficient instruments of the physical killing of people, as seen in the horrors of the two world wars and nuclear weapons: 'One must not praise the West's knowledge given its inventions of death'.[73] Rastakhiz publications, sensing the possible political utility of Mehri's works, announced that a book summarizing his writings on the West titled *The Destructive Ideology* would be published.[74]

Rastakhiz publications also gave much space to nativist state and non-state intellectuals whose thought to varying degrees corresponded to the discourses of anti-West Occidentalism. Among those who adorned the pages of these publications were Nasr and Naraqi. They played important roles in strengthening these discursive tones. Their views have been well covered in the existing literature and thus need no deep examination here. What is important is that Rastakhiz publications actively propagated their views. The intensity of their criticisms of Western civilization and Occidentosis along with calls for a return to an Iranian Islamic authenticity led some members of the deposed Pahlavi elite, such as Homayoun, to charge that they played an important role in creating the ideological conditions for the Islamic Revolution. Homayoun was particularly critical of Nasr whom he described as 'one of the fundamental theoreticians of the Revolution ... he propagated the idea of Islamic authenticity, he even wanted an Islamic physics'. His 'mentality' and those thinkers propagating such thought and 'opinions were Islam-ridden (*islamzadeh*)'. Nasr denies this accusation.[75] The question of whether Nasr's critics are right or not is of little relevance here. That which is important is that Rastakhiz publications propagated his views as part of its struggle against Occidentosis.

Naraqi, in his comments reported in Rastakhiz publications, propagated and expanded the themes he had articulated in his book *Qorbat-e Qarb*. He took particular aim at Occidentosis-ridden Iranians since they propagated the idea 'that we must become foreigners in body and soul ... because the secret of progress is the complete body of thought of the West.' Society, and these people in particular, needed to undergo a spiritual resurgence. He was equally outraged by the West's claims to universal superiority of its civilization and consequent direct and indirect belittling of other civilizations and cultures. 'Often Westerners imagine that if a country and people are not personifications and manifestations of Western culture, that people and country are without any culture'.[76] His criticisms of Western civilization were based on the hegemonic binary of a West based on materialism and conspicuous consumerism and a spiritual and moral Iran: 'The current crisis of the West has shown us that the consumerist society, given its bases of greed and avarice, will always face the increasing rhythm of production and consumption.' Iran had to be aware of these problems and avoid them. 'Fortunately, the old peoples of the East, including Iran, have still not been overtaken by greed, avarice, and consumerism'.[77]

One of his main contributions to not only party discourses but also those of the shah and the empress dealt with the negative role Western technology could play in society. In this regard he was influenced by the thought of Jacques Attali, a well-known French economic and social theorist who became an adviser to French president Francois Mitterrand. His criticisms of the West were articulated in his book *La Parole et l'outil* to which Rastakhiz publications gave attention.[78] Having examined 'the daily increasing dominance of the machine on the body and the spirit of the Western person' he concluded that the person in an industrialized society would no longer have anything based on his own personal initiative. The imperial warnings about the emergence of Frankensteins that would replace authentic Iranians echoed these sentiments. The question was asked: 'Will the clear and straight adaptation of Western technology by non-Western countries place them on the same path [now travelled by the West]?'[79]

Naraqi feared a similar outcome for Iran. He insisted that science and technology had to be in the service of, and not enslave, the individual. The Occidentosis-ridden ones, who, he claimed, believed that technology and science provided the framework for life, if left unchecked, would lead Iran into a catastrophe: 'Science and technology no longer can be the harbinger of a golden age since as soon as success is made in these areas, complicated challenges appear. Technology cannot solve these challenges'.[80] Technology was also undermining morality, a process Rastakhiz promised to prevent.[81]

Nasr's criticisms of the West, while parallel in form to the dominating themes of Naraqi's thought, in substance differed from it.[82] The bulk of his statements and remarks appearing in Rastakhiz publications propagated the idea of the inevitable decline and collapse of the West and of a resurgent East:

> Given the blows we have suffered at the hands of the West in the decades over the last century we think that because, for example, they can send a missile into space, they know everything. This is not true. They themselves are now in search for new thinking.[83]

This search was prompted by the myriad social, cultural and moral crises the West faced due to the spread of materialism, conspicuous consumerism and commercialization. Unfortunately, at the same time Occidentosis was spreading in Iran and the East. While the West sought new thinking, 'the East had forgotten its philosophy'.[84]

However, he argued, the West's decline, clear for all to see, was not a new development. It had started centuries before. Contrary to the convictions of the Occidentosis-ridden Iranians 'the work of Western civilization is finished and over. ... The Renaissance was the first step of the West's crisis. ... Westerners have so much killed each other that they cannot but speak less of the clean human character. ... In Western civilization the human will not have a future.' In his lexicon the West included the liberal capitalist West and the communist East. He claimed that Westerners 'in regard to philosophy and philosophical systems are amateurs. ... In any case one can divide the collapse of Western civilization into stages and perhaps that last phase, the collapse, is the cesspool of "sex."'[85]

The issue of sex in the West in Rastakhiz publications had three dimensions – moral, cultural and socio-economic – that underscored the West's overall decline into a pool of licentiousness to the horror and pity of the East and Iranians. The tone of Rastakhiz reporting on these issues was similar of that of other printed media, such as *Ferdowsi*, in the decade before the Party's establishment.

Given the overall thrust of Rastakhiz anti-West Occidentalism, the spread of prostitution in the West was a frequent theme in party publications. Coverage of female prostitution was a common and perhaps expected theme in pieces describing moral and economic conditions in any society. This too was true for Rastakhiz publications. *The Youth of Rastakhiz*, however, expanded coverage to include both child and male prostitution in the West and specifically the United States, the recognized leader of the West. Reporting on the spread of child prostitution raised the question of how was it possible that the West, with its great wealth and political systems that were portrayed by it as models for the rest of the world, proved unable to cope with this fundamental issue. The moral side of this issue, in other words, the abundance of adult clients and paedophiles, who were feeding this 'industry' and making it lucrative, was yet another sign of the West's decline. Rastakhiz, emphasizing that this Western economic and cultural system destroyed family structure and morality in the United States, reported that 'both teenage boys and girls are prostituting themselves' while their dealers 'searching for profit exhibit these teenagers on the streets as if they were zoo animals'.[86]

Another series of articles focused on the rapid rise of male prostitution in the United States. This issue brought to the Iranian reader an additional dimension of the cultural decline of the West, the spread of homosexuality. 'Any place that has gays there emerges male prostitution.' Reporting about males, some as young as 'eight and ten' being pimped out underscored the great extent of family breakdown, homelessness and poverty. The lining up of male customers in places such as Times Square in New York or in seedy places of London, whose scenes were replicated in other large and middle-sized cities, to enjoy these children only graphically showed a moral and cultural vacuum at the centre of Western civilization. The desperation of these male prostitutes, from the children to older ones, was evidenced by their low cost. Articles claimed that the price of these human beings started at $15. Statistics were also provided. '40% of prostitutes arrested in Los Angeles are male prostitutes, while in New York and Chicago the rate was 30%.' More galling for the Iranian observer was the obviousness of male and child prostitutes in the West's cities that bizarrely did not provoke a public outcry or government action. 'The problem is clearly seen in Manhattan on the streets … Third Avenue is full of boys and young men selling themselves.' In these cities as well as other major cities of the West, 'male prostitution is seen everywhere. ... [Thus] there is a large selection' offering plenty of opportunity for 'bargaining'.[87]

To understand the impact of such stories on public opinion more than religiosity and social conservatism of the population needs to be taken into account, important as they are. In February 1946 Hedayatollah Hakim-Elahi, a vocal social critic, political publicist and activist, and history teacher at the well-known Zorastrian school in Tehran, Firuz Bahram, published a two-volume work, *Come with Me to the Red Light District (Ba man be shahr-e nou biaid)*. Going through six editions, this work, the first of its kind to be published in Iran, created a long-standing sensation. In addition to a vivid description of the lives of the pimps and owners of houses of ill-repute and the type of guys taking advantage of the services offered, it provided a harrowing description in emotive language of the males and females aged from ten prostituting themselves in this Tehran district. Woven into this narrative non-fiction were condemnations of both society and state for not addressing the moral and socio-economic issues driving this phenomenon. The introduction of the book included a caustic open letter to Princess Ashraf and government officials that exhorted them 'to take immediate and all necessary steps for the curing of this misfortune', and called on the people's social conscience.[88] The book's success in drawing attention to the social and moral consequences of poverty and the moral and social corruption of those willing and able to take advantage of the misfortunes of those males and females prostituting themselves opened the way for additional works on this topic that played vital roles in raising the social awareness and moral outrage of the reading public during the Pahlavi period. In comparative terms, the role played by his book is similar to that of Jacob Riis's *How the Other Half Lives* or Henry Mayhew's *London Labour and the London Poor* that detailed poverty in these cities in the nineteenth century.

Remedying poverty and successfully struggling against prostitution required an effective model of economic and social development. At the time of the book's publication eyes were on the broadly defined West. However, by the Rastakhiz period these reports about the spread of prostitution showed that the Western model was not worthy of emulation given its clear failure not only to reduce rates of poverty but also to prevent its spread. Moreover, the spread of conspicuous consumerism and rampant hedonism, considered defining elements of the West's civilization, had conspired to create the conditions for the spread of child and male prostitution that was geared to satisfy sexual deviancies, paedophilia and homosexuality. The focus on these three issues in Rastakhiz publications, and not female prostitution, was natural since once the Pahlavi state had destroyed the old *shahr-e nou* described in Hakim-Elahi's book, a new *shahr-e nou* emerged in which female prostitution was regulated in order to ensure hygiene and public health. According to statistics dating from the early 1970s approximately 1,500 working women lived there.[89]

The issue of sex in the West in Rastakhiz publications dealt not only with prostitution and sexual deviancy. Reports on the progressive increase in sexual promiscuity and hedonism of the West's youth frequently visited the pages of *The Youth of Rastakhiz* and to a lesser extent, *Rastakhiz*. Articles with titles such as 'Report on the Collapse of Morals and Tradition in the West' portrayed this youth as 'lost', having ditched austere morality and respect for one's own body in order to satisfy sexual hedonism. These people were becoming a hallow shell of a human. 'In France moral codes are dying. … That which worries France is the licentiousness and promiscuity of the youth.' It was claimed that this was common to all Western countries. The West's moral rot was clearly seen in the rate of teenage promiscuity and pregnancy. The number of teenage pregnancies 'has become a catastrophe. … More than one million teenagers aged between 12 and 16 in the USA are pregnant'.⁹⁰ But this problem was not limited to the leader of the free world. The essence and future of Western civilization could be seen in this state of its youth who were 'in a downward spiral of social and moral collapse'.⁹¹ While they engaged in licentiousness their social morality had also collapsed. They 'have no care for family or morals. ... Moral and cultural catastrophe faces the West's countries.' Family structure and links and personal responsibility were entering the trash bin of history. The West's slide into this catastrophe was a clear example of the future that awaited Iran's youth if steps were not taken to combat the spread of Occidentosis.

Yet, at the same time pity and sympathy was expressed for the West's youth. Just as Maryam, the young naïve housewife who fell victim to Occidentosis and the Occidentosis-ridden Dariush, the West's youth too were victims of that civilization's materialistic and consumerist society in which all relationships were instrumentalized at a time when economic opportunities and standards of living were declining. The consequences were clear: 'Prostitution, drug addiction, hunger, poverty, these are the things in which the West's youth are entrapped. They are in search for the panacea of the spiritual East and an escape from their lives in the West.' This reality had to be conveyed to Iran's youth.⁹² Having provided over several issues an examination of the state of the West's youth, Rastakhiz proclaimed its goal: 'We must not allow the licentiousness of Western youth to influence our society'.⁹³ The reporting also had a harsh dimension that examined this issue from a historical point of view tinged with schadenfreude. In looking at how 'indigence, drug addiction, and massive hedonism [were] killing the youth of the West' Rastakhiz rhetorically asked, 'Is the West now paying for its centuries of imperialism?' Whatever the answer, one reality, Rastakhiz claimed, could not be denied: 'The bullying behavior and hypocrisy of Western civilization have caused cultural collapse in the West'.⁹⁴

Another attack in Rastakhiz's war on the West's soft power was the West's socio-economic structure, once portrayed by the Pahlavi state as an example to follow. Just as its discursive attack on the state of morality and spirituality in the West was, to an arguable extent, a reflection of the dynamics of the condition of Western civilization, so was the attack on the West's socio-economic conditions. In the immediate postwar period the US economy dominated most of the world, making up some 50 per cent of global industrial output. Behind it was the United Kingdom, only recently the world's largest empire. Its economy, despite heavy wartime debts and loss of empire, remained the largest in Europe and the second largest in the capitalist world. UK prime minister, Harold Macmillan, in a speech in July 1957 described well the situation in the United Kingdom and indirectly the United States at the end of the 1950s and the view of it from the outside: 'Go around the country, go to the industrial towns, go to the farms and you will see a state of prosperity such as we have never had in my lifetime – nor indeed in the history of this country'.⁹⁵ For many in Iran looking for a model to adapt in the hope of transforming the country into a strong economic and military power and decreasing the rate of poverty and minimizing the social and moral consequences of that poverty only one example had existed in the 1950s and 1960s. This was why Westernization had been called a welcome ordeal.

By the end of the 1960s and the beginning of the 1970s the West's leading economies had entered a decade of recession whose consequences undermined the soft power of the West's economic model. The two examples that obtained the most attention were the United Kingdom and the United States. Rising unemployment and inflation, stagnation and growing financial and budgetary problems came to characterize the UK economy. By 1976 the UK's financial crisis had become so serious that it had to apply for an IMF loan in the amount of $3.9 billion, the largest such loan in the institution's history. Already by the end of the 1960s the decline was clear, symbolized by the removal of the British military presence in the Persian Gulf.

In the United States the economic situation too was weakening, although its economy remained the world's largest. In 1971 Nixon was forced to announce a 'New Economic Policy' that included the end of the convertibility of the US dollar to gold, a move that put an end to the Bretton Woods system. The US economy was suffering from gradual deindustrialization, rising unemployment and inflation which also brought the temporary imposition of wage and price controls. These problems continued to plague the US economy during the Ford and Carter administrations. In addition, despite the West's economic and technological advances, it had seemingly failed to manage successfully the issue of social inequality and poverty while the 1973 oil crisis that intensified the economic recession in these countries underlined its dependency on oil-producing nations.[96] Rastakhiz's conclusion was grim: 'The West's economy is like a hospital that is overflowing with patients – no work, underemployment, while its base is the struggle between people driven by materialism and consumerism.'[97] Such a conclusion was a reflection of the growing confidence in Iran's economic future created by economic policies since the 1960s and the rise in oil prices. The West's economic model, once viewed on an official level as an example and model for the future, was now portrayed as the anti-example, but less so than that of the Soviet Union.

Concomitantly, Rastakhiz claimed that the West's culture and the weakening of the hold of its imperialism played key roles in the West's economic decline: 'The West's economic problems are the result of lack of discipline and will in working' while the shah stressed: 'The dialogue between the North and South has not progressed because in the West your prosperity is completely dependent on the exploitation of the resources of other countries'.[98] An exploitation that the shah had ended with his push for the dramatic rise in oil prices in the early 1970s. This move, Rastakhiz claimed, had provoked Western imperialism to target the Pahlavi state. These publicly expressed feelings were not just instrumentalized political rhetoric. The shah did indeed believe them. In private he told Alam, who had mentioned London's request for an IMF loan: 'That amount is not enough for them. Their problem is laziness, idleness and lack of initiative and given this their problem is not solvable'.[99]

Thus, the West's economic model was condemned for not eradicating poverty and establishing social justice which played a key role in its moral and spiritual collapse. Taking a leaf out of Marxist-Leninist thought, the West's economic model was portrayed as exacerbating poverty and inherently unable to achieve social justice.[100] Rastakhiz publications tried to counter the positive impressions of economic and social life in the West and the criticisms that the Pahlavi state was failing to deal with the issue of social justice. A *Rastakhiz* editorial concluded, 'There the crisis [of poverty] becomes greater every day'.[101] While Iran was continuing to develop quickly to the benefit of all Iranians, in the West, such as France there was 'an outpouring of mental illness in the cities' that accompanied the collapse of morals and opportunities among the youth.[102] Rastakhiz discourses focused on the chasm between the West's projection of prosperity and superiority of its economic system and the equally visible spreading poverty. By the early 1970s New York, Chicago and London, once showcases of the West's superiority, faced economic decline and the spread of poverty and serious crime, such as theft, robbery and prostitution. The problems faced by these cities were reported in detail by Rastakhiz publications.[103]

The Revolution in Education, Rastakhiz Political Education and the attempts at debunking the West's soft power show that the Pahlavi state during the Rastakhiz period had initiated a concentrated and relatively cohesive discursive and practical campaign against the West as a civilization, and Occidentosis, the manifestation of this civilization within Iran's cultural and geopolitical borders. Responding to changed sociocultural circumstances and intellectual trends in Iran and reflecting both the evolved views of the imperial couple in regard to the West and the growing intellectual criticism of the West by Westerners, these party approaches are additional indicators of the direction in which state and society in the Rastakhiz period had taken off.

13

The apogee of Pahlavi Occidentalism

Previous chapters examined the initial elements driving the emergence and evolution of the discourses of anti-West Occidentalism and their ideologization during the Rastakhiz period. Yet, during this period additional issues, such as the West's growing criticism of the state of human rights in Iran, the shah's plans for the acquisition of nuclear power, domestic economic problems and increasing domestic disturbances from the end of 1977 influenced this evolution.

The West's criticisms of the state of human rights, which were heard in the 1960s and early 1970s, reached a new peak in November 1976 with a report written by Amnesty International. Its introduction underlined that 'the following human rights issues ... are of particular concern: (a) arbitrary arrest of suspected political opponents who are held incommunicado for long periods before being charged or tried; (b) the use of torture; (c) lack of legal safeguards and unsatisfactory trial procedures; (d) executions and unofficial deaths'.[1] It stressed: 'The suppression of political opposition is carried out by SAVAK with extreme ruthlessness using a system of informers which permeates all levels of Iranian society and which has created an atmosphere of fear remarked on by visitors to Iran and emphasized by opponents of the regime outside the country.' Iranian society is suffering from 'extreme political repression. In 1975 the last pretense of political freedom was removed by the abolition of the token opposition Mardom Party and the introduction of a one-party system.'

While mentioning the shah's and Sabeti's comments that political prisoners in the country numbered around three thousand, Amnesty International noted that 'foreign journalists and Iranian exile groups' claimed that the range is from 25,000 to 100,000. The report provided a grim description of prison conditions. In graphic detail it listed the alleged forms of torture which included 'whipping and beating, electric shocks, the extraction of nails and teeth, boiling water pumped into the rectum, heavy weights hung on the testicles, tying the prisoner to a metal table heated to white heat, inserting a broken bottle into the anus, and rape'.

Included in the report was a description by Reza Baraheni of his time in prison, which was subsequently a source of contention, even by former political prisoners.[2] His bestselling book *The Crowned Cannibals: Writings on Repression in Iran* published in late 1976 'depicted the Shah's rule as a period of macabre palace orgies and prisons brimming with dissident youth. ... [This book] feted by America's literati and reprinted in part by the *New York Review of Books*, contained many fabrications'.[3] While the fabrications came to light years after the Revolution, it exercised a strong negative influence on Western public and elite opinion in regard to the shah and on his and the Pahlavi elite's opinion in regard to the West.

In the immediate aftermath of the report's release, *Rastakhiz* published its response, 'A new sign of imperialism's conspiracies against Iran' that initiated an intensification of attacks on the West's imperialism.[4] The West, through Amnesty International, had unleashed a 'full-frontal anti-Iran propaganda crusade' based on fabrications that 'many political prisoners are held in Iran' while the state engages in 'the use of brutality and torture'. The West's geopolitical interests prompted this crusade:

> Amnesty International has created an international network to launch at any time a propaganda war against any Third World country seeking to protect its national interests in the face of imperialism. ... In this way the old imperialists have shown that they are learning their lesson from the methods used by new imperialism. Therefore, they prefer the use of attractive labels, such as Amnesty International, to the use of direct political and military pressure to achieve their goals. These methods used by the West are similar to those of communists and saboteurs, and, similar to them, Amnesty International works against our motherland.

The empress was more direct:

> Why do we allow the enemies of Iran to try to harm us? ... Our policies are clear – no one takes orders from abroad. Our independence is a reality. These conditions infuriate some foreigners who try to create divisions within our country. These attacks against Iran are unfortunate and regretful since now conditions in Iran are good. After years of backwardness, Iran is traveling the path of progress and development. ... They really don't see any weak points in Iran. ... Therefore, the only claim they can make is that Iran is tough in dealing with its enemies. Iran is a wealthy country, rich in natural resources with a unique geo-political position. Iran today and in the past has been targeted by many foreign countries and their charlatanism. ... We won't allow anyone to interfere in our domestic affairs and become an obstacle to the country's development and progress. ... There are countries whose governmental system and philosophy differ from ours. We have good relations with them. ... The problem is that these countries, nonetheless, seek the government's overthrow in order to establish one politically and ideologically closer to them. Moreover, Iran's policy in regard to oil and its pricing upsets Western countries and thus they have additional reasons to launch such attacks on Iran. ... If Iran's situation destabilizes, the world's great powers can achieve their goals in Iran. This is why they struggle to create domestic troubles.

She stressed that the best method for defeating imperialism's plots and preserving the country's independence was to strengthen authenticity of Iranian culture and identity.[5]

The shah attributed the West's geopolitical interests to these moves: 'Any time we take steps in regard to oil, some form of monkey-business (*bambuli*) ... starts up'.[6] This *bambuli* began, the shah privately noted, months before the Amnesty report when *The Times* and the *New York Times* simultaneously published pieces critical of the Pahlavi state. *Rastakhiz* summed up the reactions of the imperial couple: 'The attack on Iran launched in the name of the defense of human rights is spiteful and malicious. These attacks have clear goals – namely damaging our national interests.' Following the party approach, Ansari stated: 'Amnesty International is a puppet of international politics.' Iran's position as 'the standard bearer of the struggle against economic imperialism' and the West's 'fear of its independent national policies' caused the West to resort to such conspiracies'.[7] It is worth remembering that Iran's relationship with its prime Western partner, the United States, had retreated during the Ford administration from its highs of the Nixon years. Even if Ford did not modify fundamentally the US–Iran relationship, the tone coming out of the US halls of power and media had changed, becoming more critical and, in Tehran's opinion, more threatening. In summary, the shah and Pahlavi elite interpreted this report and other mediums of Western criticism of human rights as a form of the West's geopolitical imperialism.

Rastakhiz publications in the following weeks intensified the idea of a Western conspiracy against Iran. 'In West Berlin a secret document was published detailing a plan of a struggle against Iran. ... These documents show that secret anti-Iranian activities were being conducted by the pressure group Amnesty International' with the support of other entities. According to the plan from January 1977 'an international struggle against Iran is to begin' based on 'the active cooperation of Amnesty International with anti-Iran groups and individuals'. They intended 'to use the "fake" issue of political prisoners to attack Iran'. These secret documents stressed that claims that thousands of prisoners are languishing in captivity needed to be propagated, even if, they confessed, these numbers were not accurate. Lastly, 'the plan calls for finding so-called political prisoners from Iran who will go to different Western countries and say they were brutally tortured and actively participate in anti-Iran organizations'.[8] Rastakhiz publications repeated the narrative, dating back to the publication of *Pahlavism*, that the imperialist West was hatching such conspiracies against the Pahlavi state given its dedication to an independent foreign policy.

Integral to the discursive response to this report and overall criticism of the state of human rights were accusations of double standards in the West's approach:

> The shahanshah asks how is it that the loud speakers of the imperialists who cry crocodile tears over human rights [in Iran] say nothing about the 1,000,000 Cambodians killed. ... What about the USA and its violations of human rights? ... If human rights are to be defended, they must be defended everywhere and applicable to everyone.[9]

The negative press coverage in the West of this issue and criticisms of Amnesty International or the Hoover commission, combined with the growing sense of double standards, frustrated the shah. According to Sir Anthony Parsons, the British ambassador to Iran at the time:

> He (the shah) used to say very often, 'Why is it that I get such a rotten press and Iraq does not?' – Saddam's Iraq. I used to say, and I still believe this, 'You get this bad press Your Majesty because you expect to be treated as one of us, as part of the Western world whereas we don't treat Iraq as part of the Western world'.[10]

The US Embassy in Tehran reported back to Washington that the shah

> has been stung by a rash of unfavorable publicity appearing in US and Western media about human rights conditions in Iran. Basically, he considers it unfair, unwarranted, and lacking in recognition of major socioeconomic advances his country has achieved during his reign. He wondered why Saudi Arabia, Washington's chief ally in OPEC, received a free pass on human rights?[11]

The Pahlavi elite was indeed puzzled by the West's official and unofficial criticism of Iran and concomitant silence on the issue of human rights in Saudi Arabia. Privately the shah fumed to Alam: 'The Saudis have never shown any respect for human rights, not now and not in the past. Even the hand of a petty thief is chopped off. The liberal press in the US ignores all this, yet they don't hesitate to blacken Iran's reputation.'[12] Parson's remarks might be correct to an extent. Saudi political discourses never claimed a link with the West while the West, given Saudi realities, some of them noted by the shah, never has considered Saudi Arabia part of the Western 'civilized' world. At the same time Pahlavi references to Aryanism and claims to be part of the West set the stage for Parson's remark. Yet, in the opinion of the Pahlavi elite, the real reason for the West's silence in regard to Saudi violations of human rights remained Riyadh's obsequiousness in regard to the West's geopolitical and oil interests. After all, the shah privately referred to the Saudi kingdom as 'an American colony'.[13]

Amuzegar, party leader but still not yet prime minister, was even more scathing in his repeated attacks on the West (Figure 14). While reiterating the charges that the criticisms of the state of human rights were the West's response to Iran's attempts to be independent and protective of its national interests, he saved the most stinging criticism for the United States.[14] He pointedly started his remarks with reference to both British behaviour in Iran when London controlled Iran's oil and the more recent scandals about Western clubs in Tehran banning entrance to Iranians that had once been decried by *Ferdowsi*: 'Those who trampled on our interests and in our own country and wrote that entrance is forbidden to Iranians and dogs now do not have the right to beat the drum about human rights'.[15] This set the tone for the rest of his speech.

> A society whose emergence and existence came with the deprivation of the freedom of that land's native peoples, a society in which entrance to university is dependent on skin color, religion and race is considered rational, a society in which people still because of the sin of having brown or black skin, cannot enjoy, as others, public places, is the same society and people giving themselves the right and permission to criticize others. In Western societies in the name of the defense of individual rights and freedom of the individual the situation has become such that they are legalizing homosexuality when a majority of people are against it. We also see that hundreds of thousands of peoples were killed when these Western countries came into conflict with each other over their competing global hegemonies and dragged the rest of the world into war during which hundreds of thousands of people were killed. In other words, not only do they deprive people of freedom but also the right to life. So, is it fair that such countries have the right

Figure 14 Jamshid Amuzegar. *Rastakhiz*, author's collection.

to criticize us? These societies, where were they when Cyrus the Great introduced to the world the charter of human freedoms? Our kingdom, our culture has a spiritual and sacred meaning of freedom and the meaning has a simple language – freedom must be accompanied by responsibility.[16]

Kazem Vadiei too published a lead article responding to these criticisms. What is noteworthy is the way his piece enlarged and intensified the imagery and language of party discourses of anti-West Occidentalism as the state, increasingly on the defensive, during Amuzegar's premiership implemented limited liberalization, a policy called 'open political space'. Vadiei first laid the discursive framework: 'What must be the basis of debate is Western imperialism's role, various modi operandi, changing shape, and local, regional, and global ruses and ploys' in order to establish and maintain its hegemony over the non-Western world.

> Imperialism fools people with ideas of false democracy in order to undermine political systems seeking to defend their national interests. ... The main target of imperialism's ruses and ploys is the youth's brains and the destruction of [nativist] thought so that it can directly or indirectly open up the path for its political and economic hegemony in Iran.

This destruction of nativist thought and spread of Occidentosis brought signs of 'hippieism and spiritual and moral decline to Iran, the same elements causing the West's decline'.

The Iranian state and people had to be vigilant given the tactical flexibility of the West's imperialism.

> It uses different methods to achieve its goals [and] … changes the form and color of its ruses and ploys. … Everyday it takes a new deceitfully attractive shape and form. One day the slogan is *fraternité, égalité,* and *liberté* [the French Revolution] the next day, democracy [the American Revolution], the following day, freedom of trade [Western economic liberalism], and next, the defense of the rights of workers and farmers [the Bolshevik Revolution], and finally human rights [the West of the post-World War II era].
>
> But these slogans are hollow, a veneer for the real exploitative goals of imperialism. In reality, imperialism is the snakes on Zohak's shoulders.[17] It eats nothing else except the brains of our young – however imperialism never becomes full. It eyes the people's property and wealth and has its hands in their pockets. … It tries to turn the world to its benefit. For imperialism the world is for its taking.

To the outrage of the non-Western world, 'the West plundered the world in the name of progress'.

Unfortunately, he continued, some people ignored this reality of Western civilization and imperialism. In order to prevent their becoming the unwitting agents of imperialism, they needed to be reminded of the reality behind the West's seductive slogans.

> In the claws of the West's industrialist capitalists are the slogans of political freedom, economic freedom and human rights, instruments for sucking in and attracting others. Political freedom means for them freedom to interfere [in the internal affairs of other countries], freedom of trade and economic freedom means their dominance over other countries' material and financial reserves. They arm themselves to the teeth in order to ensure and guarantee their freedom to attack other countries and economic and material dominance over others. For what other reason does the 'democratic and freedom-loving' West arm itself in such a way?

This attack also portrayed Western imperialism as intensely and inherently exploitative of the masses of the West. Seemingly influenced by both Marx's interpretation of the dynamics of capitalist society and Lenin's *Imperialism: The Highest State of Capitalism* Vadiei sought to undermine the belief that Western societies were a source of emulation. The idea that real freedom existed in the West was a chimera:

> Imperialism has pushed and dragged its own peoples into personal indulgence and hedonistic individualism, filled their heads with visions of false democracy … and false civilization, and provides them with bribes under the name of welfare and freedom [in order to keep them subdued]. But these methods cannot eternally

maintain the control of imperialism, [that] inherent part of the bourgeois West and extreme developed capitalism.[18]

The second trend in the Rastakhiz response was the strengthening of the cult of Cyrus the Great. This had already started in 1975. In the Party's early days Rahmat Mostafavi, a well-known cultural figure and publicist who owned and ran until 1974 the well-known weekly magazine *The Intellectual* (*Rowshanfekr*) summarized this cult's meaning and place in party ideology in a major piece, 'The Call of History': 'Cyrus the Great was the founder of the school of Humanism' and thus Iran, not the West, bestowed to world civilization the idea of human rights and values.[19] In light of the Amnesty report, Baheri repeatedly stressed: 'We are the oldest people in the world from the point of view of the belief in human rights. ... [Thus] Iran never accepts the idea that the slogan of human rights can be used for intervention in the internal affairs of others'.[20] A Rastakhiz leader, 'Individual Rights have Deep Roots in Iran', referencing Farah's speech quoted earlier, elaborated these points: 'The empress's speech will surprise many Westerners. It shows that our country and people were the first in the world to shine the light of freedom and equality.' Iran with the charter of Cyrus the Great 'taught the lesson to the world of the necessity of the protection and preservation of human rights'.[21] The question therefore was simple: What right did the West have to criticize Iran and the imperial system? Given this historical fact, the only reason for the West's unfair criticism of the state of human rights in Iran was imperialism's attempt to weaken and subdue any country determined to protect its interests and authenticity.

The issue of human rights took on greater importance in Rastakhiz discourses with the election of Jimmy Carter as US president. From the Iranian point of view, this issue was evolving from a conspiracy of Western imperialism under the guise of Amnesty International and mass media propaganda, to official discourses, albeit in general terms that did not explicitly single out Iran. Nonetheless, Carter's campaign rhetoric that emphasized the importance of human rights in US foreign policy and the infamous delay in his response to the shah's message of congratulations did create concern within the elite and energize the shah's opponents.[22] Parviz Radji, the Iranian ambassador to the UK noted in his diary:

> Sunday, May 22, 1977: President Carter makes a speech at Notre Dame University and says America must abandon its inordinate fear of Communism and its attempts to contain it world-wide. That policy, he says, has led America to embrace any dictator who opposed Communism. Vietnam is cited as an example. Bloody hell! What does HIM think of these remarks, I wonder?[23]

The reality of these changed US discourses hit the shah less than two months later on 6 July 1977 when he and Cyrus Vance, Carter's secretary of state, met. Vance diplomatically delivered the message that the issue of human rights had become an important element in US policymaking. According to Radji, the shah was taken aback.[24] In response, the monarch took limited measures in the hope of calming this growing criticism, such as allowing the Red Cross to visit prisons, issuing a decree banning the use of torture, and talk of limited opening of the political space. Sabeti has stressed that the shah, in the context of the Cold War, was not prepared to enter into open opposition with Washington on this issue and thus made such concessions.[25]

The shah with these moves created the impression that he was no longer the invincible figure once imagined. Opposition figures and groups, taking inspiration from this conflux of circumstances, sought to push the limits of these concessions, especially in light of seeming US pressure on the shah. This reason for this intensification was cited by Sabeti who early in the Carter administration wrote a report for the shah. In it he stressed that in the context of the signals coming out of the White House 'opposition figures every day are becoming more hopeful. We must predict social events and review "elements" linked to America, including military or civilian agents and put them under surveillance.' Initially the shah responded: 'This fear and suspicion are illogical and baseless. They (the Americans) are not mad. They will not begin action against the regime.' But one week later he ordered 'that American agents be recognized and put under surveillance'.[26] Concomitantly, Rastakhiz, in response to these new circumstances, intensified its discourses of anti-West Occidentalism.

In the midst of these events came the proposed sale of AWACS to Iran. Despite the rhetoric on human rights, the Carter administration supported the shah's purchase of these technologically advanced radar airplanes. However, in July 1977 the administration failed to push the sale through Congress because of public and political attention to the state of human rights in Iran, the character of the one-party state and the shah's autocratic power that had emerged in Congress during the Ford administration. Certainly, other issues played into this defeat, such as concerns about the militarization of the Persian Gulf area, excessive spending on military hardware by the monarch, and the possible loss of its technology to the USSR.

The shah, nonetheless, focused on what he considered the dominant theme in the debates about the sale, namely the implicit claims that his rule was inherently unstable given its authoritarian nature and the state of human rights. US ambassador to Iran, William Sullivan, intensified this impression when, in explaining to the monarch the reason for this defeat, he cited the use of Washington lobbying groups of the shah's human rights record to generate opposition to the sale. To be fair, Sullivan also blamed Carter's mishandling of the relationship between the two branches of government when he insisted on determining the congressional calendar.[27] The sale was finally approved in October 1977, but the open debate about the nature of power and the state of human rights in Iran exercised a strong influence on party discourses and opposition groups and figures.

At the same time, the US reaction to the shah's nuclear ambitions provided additional momentum to discourses of anti-West Occidentalism. In the early 1970s the shah began to express his desire to establish a civil nuclear programme that, he insisted, would ensure Iran's energy needs for the future when its oil and gas reserves were depleted.[28] US recalcitrance to establish a strong civilian nuclear relationship with Tehran infuriated the shah and added to his impressions about the trajectory of the US–Iran relationship and Washington's ultimate intentions in regard to Iran.[29]

Washington had several concerns. Despite the shah's announcements that Iran would not seek nuclear weapons, some worry about his ultimate motives lingered. That he wanted to develop uranium enrichment capabilities and possess an Iranian, and not a multinational, uranium reprocessing facility was interpreted by the United States as a sign of Iranian 'unwillingness to submit their plants to foreign surveillance'.[30] Therefore, the Ford administration while agreeing in principle to offer Iran the opportunity to purchase a US nuclear reactor sought to establish controls to ensure that US-supplied nuclear materials would be used only for peaceful purposes. Even if he did not want nuclear weapons at this time, worry was expressed that 'an aggressive successor to the shah might consider nuclear weapons the final item needed to establish Iran's complete military dominance of the region'.[31] Given some but rising doubt about the political stability of the shah's regime, it could not be discounted that 'domestic dissidents or foreign terrorists might easily be able to seize any special nuclear material stored in Iran for use in bombs'. In sum, three issues bedeviled Tehran's attempts to establish nuclear cooperation with the United States: (1) Washington's insistence on a multinational presence in reprocessing; (2) the amount of enriched uranium supplied by the United States that could be stored in the country; and (3) Iran's right to reprocess US-supplied fuel without prior US approval. These issues were not formally resolved by the time of the revolution.

Washington's reticence was criticized in party discourses. For example, Rastakhiz publications reported in detail the proceedings of the Twentieth Conference of the International Atomic Energy Agency held in Rio de Janeiro (21–28 September 1976). Summarizing the position of Iran's conference delegation that heavily criticized the United States, it ran the headline 'Iran's Warning to the New Imperialism'.[32] Party publications stressed that the shah and Iran 'give priority to the vast use of nuclear power' as the essential step in 'achieving energy independence' despite Washington's opposition.[33] Akbar Etemad, the head of Iran's nuclear agency, equated 'the successful transfer of nuclear technology to Iran' to 'a technological resurgence (*rastakhiz-e tiknuluzhik*)' that would strengthen Iran's geopolitical independence and its ability to protect itself in the face of the threats of the new imperialism.[34] As US hesitation in advancing nuclear cooperation with Iran continued, the shah and the Pahlavi elite were arriving at the conclusion that Washington was seeking ways to rein in Iranian economic aspirations and independence. Rastakhiz publications rhetorically asked: 'Is not the monopoly of nuclear technology an imperialist act and move?'[35]

The year 1977, in summary, experienced an intensification of the discourses of anti-West Occidentalism in light of both domestic and international developments. Importantly, this intensification occurred in parallel with the expansion of limited liberalization. Seeking to deflect public criticism of social, political and economic conditions and mobilize the people around the Crown, the discourses of anti-West Occidentalism increasingly propagated the enemy image of Western imperialism and its witting and unwitting quislings as the reasons for domestic problems. Warnings about the threat of the West's new imperialism became more direct and frequent, while articles detailed its new and evolving plots to undermine the imperial system. The fundamental theme was clear: 'A worldwide struggle against Iran is based in the West' because 'Iran's progress provokes Western imperialism to create conspiracies against Iran'.[36] The pillar of these discourses were repeated claims that the 'West's geopolitical and economic interests require that the West keep countries such as Iran developmentally backward. It is part of new imperialism's grand plan'.[37] But to achieve

Iran's relegation to this backward state, the West had to overthrow the Pahlavi state, the source and defender of Iranian authenticity: 'Those behind the foreign conspiracies against Iran have understood, based on their own experience, that as long as the imperial bulwark exists, they will never succeed in achieving their goals'.[38]

These warnings about Western imperialism's plots and conspiracies against the Pahlavi system were not solely a reflection of the situation as it evolved during 1977. They predated this period. For example, Hoveyda, during the 1975 Majles elections, the first to be held after the Party's establishment, argued on the campaign trail: 'Foreigners do not want Iran to be united, ambitious, and developed and thus are now spreading rumors and conspiracies.' He emphasized that the imperial system and the Party were struggling against 'the imperialism of the great powers' and despite 'the delusional furor and uproar of foreigners' the kingdom was moving forward and would hold these elections.[39] These tendencies in official discourses were noticed in July 1976 by John Stempel, a US foreign service officer in Iran, who knew Persian.

> The GOI (government of Iran) is likely to blame foreigners for their failure to correctly impart Western techniques and methods. This is already taking place – there are charges of communist intrigue with domestic opponents of the regime; assertions that foreigners are polluting Iran's culture; and increasing expressions of belief that Western technology is ineffective and not worth the social price being paid for its presence. ... The inevitable criticism of foreigners means that the re-orientation of Persian values that must take place if Iran is to operate its modern industrial structure will have at least a modest anti-foreign animus.[40]

He underestimated the full extent of these discourses as they touched both domestic and geopolitical issues and the extent to which these feelings were genuinely felt by parts of the Pahlavi elite. He was also mistaken in believing that these tendencies constituted a new approach in official discourses rather than their intensification. Stempel was correct, however, in noting the growing tendency to place blame for domestic problems on the West's shoulders.

By the time of the Party's founding, the Pahlavi state faced increasing public discontent over its handling of corruption and the economy, specifically inflation. The immediate cause for the dramatic spike in inflation and corruption was the jump in oil prices in 1973. By 1974 they had quadrupled to $12 a barrel. The state's oil income reached levels about which the shah had only dreamed. The Fifth Development Plan (1973–7), the most ambitious to date, initially envisioned oil revenues of $24.6 billion over five years. By 1974 Iran was bringing in $18.5 billion annually. The question facing the shah and the government was how to manage this skyrocketing income. In March 1974 the monarch held a meeting in Ramsar with members of the government and the Planning and Budget Organization to discuss this huge windfall. He ignored the warning that pouring this oil income into the economy would create strong inflationary pressures, retorting that 'if inflation were to pick up, then Iran would deal with this crisis in an innovative manner'.[41] He told those present: 'The Great Civilization we promised you is not a utopia either. We will reach it much sooner than we thought. We said we will reach the gates in twelve years; but in some fields we have already crossed the frontiers'.⁴² Privately he told Alam: 'We have the money. Now we must use it to build the Great Civilization'.⁴³

Predictably, the infusion of such large amounts of money destabilized the economy. Public spending rose by 142 per cent. GNP grew at rates never seen – in 1973/4, 34 per cent; 1974/5, 42 per cent; and 1975/6, 17 per cent. The rate of imports skyrocketed given the increase in the number and purchasing power of the *nouveau riche* and developmental projects while the country's infrastructure could not handle these increased demands. Shortages emerged while expectations continued to grow. Inflation hit every sector of the economy. Official statistics put the inflation rate of 1974 and 1975 at 18 per cent and 24 per cent, respectively. However, real inflation was probably much higher, especially in the housing sector. In any case, the result was general discontent, especially among the lower and middle urban classes, hit particularly hard by rising prices. This situation contrasted with the average inflation rate of 6 to 8 per cent since the mid-1960s.

The economy also began to suffer a shortage of labour from the construction and service sectors to white-collar positions. This resulted in a flood of foreign workers with Western Europeans and Americans constituting the largest group. This created fertile ground for resentment. These foreign workers, receiving higher salaries than their Iranian counterparts doing the same type of work, preferred to live in the chic parts of the cities, particularly in Tehran, and were prepared to pay high rents. This development helped drive up housing prices to the point that many middle-class Iranians were forced to give up aspirations to live in these areas. Adding to this tension were cultural clashes as many of the workers from Western countries tended to ignore societal and public norms while instances of car crashes caused by drunk Westerners that resulted in Iranian fatalities were diligently reported. Certainly, all of these problems existed by the end of the 1960s, but they increased rapidly in the 1970s. Concomitantly, public perceptions grew that those Iranians enjoying links to the state's upper levels were taking full advantage of this rise in state income to line their own pockets, either through outright theft or the imposition of commission fees to facilitate all forms of imports or business start-ups.

Recognizing the potential political danger of these developments a loud campaign against corruption was launched. With the Party's establishment the shah proclaimed a new struggle 'against corruption, lying, hoarding, bribery, [and] administrative corruption'. His announcement corresponded with the party's proclaimed duty to recognize openly problems and criticize government action.⁴⁴ The Party immediately initiated a crusade to eradicate corruption: 'One thing that cannot be tolerated in the kingdom is administrative corruption. We must completely uproot it with all our strength'.⁴⁵ The shah gave the Imperial Inspectorate, originally a body charged with oversight of the country's intelligence services, the responsibility for dealing with corruption at the state's highest levels. Although it reported directly to the shah the Party announced that its cadres too would investigate such corruption and turn over all findings to it. The government was put on notice.

At the same time, the shah and Party announced a war against profiteers who were blamed for inflation. In the literature on the Rastakhiz Party great attention has been paid to its anti-profiteering campaign in which thousands of energetic and young party members participated and how it damaged the shah's and Party's credibility. The literature has placed attention on the shah's economic and political motives for this move. Rastakhiz publications, however, emphasized this issue's cultural side. [46]

Rastakhiz considered the spread of corruption, one of whose major forms was profiteering, the consequence of Occidentosis and the presence of its carriers, Western companies and business people in the country.[47] The Party proclaimed: 'A huge amount of corruption in society has been imported'.[48] The Committee for Political Education, acting on the shah's statements and its own research, proclaimed that the answer to corruption was 'a spiritual resurgence' that rejected Western materialism and consumerism.[49] This committee and Rastakhiz publications paid particular attention to the shah's statement made on the occasion of 1975 *aid-e fetr*: 'In this speech the shahanshah linked problems such as profiteering with cultural and moral problems. A distance exists between true Iranian values and culture and Western materialism and consumerism' that had bred this corruption and profiteering. Rastakhiz proclaimed that 'solving the issues of corruption and profiteering requires a return to authenticity' and the curing of Occidentosis.[50]

The ideological approach to this issue was summarized in a lead article, 'Profiteering and Cultural Breakdown'. Denying that rising inflation was solely an economic issue, it argued: 'Profiteering is a sign of the weakening and debasing of Iranian society's moral and spiritual infrastructure ... a reflection of unfortunate changes in Iranian spiritual values ... [and] the result of the importation of the West's consumerist society.' With modernization plans implemented by the Pahlavi state 'came changes in social values that are the consequence of any economic development but were far from the minds and plans of modernizers'. This was an attempt to weaken perceptions that the state had been a wilful spreader of Occidentosis and to say that the Pahlavi elite had good intentions for the people when they initiated Westernization. Their only sin was lack of foresight and ignorance in regard to the possible spread of Occidentosis. Due to economic prosperity

> the majority of Iranians have put aside their spiritual values. ... The first result of this cultural rupture is chaos in economic dealings and societal relationships. The generation that had imagined the West's materialistic culture, in other words the obtainment of money by any path possible, has brought into existence broken ways and methods that cannot continue and grow roots.

The threat was that the main goal of 'this present immature culture and conditions' was 'the exploitation of society ... [since] the overall goal is more and more money'. Occidentosis-ridden Iranians were the cause for this inflation as they sought increasing amounts of money and material goods. Therefore, 'We must strengthen Iranian society's spiritual values and traditional morality.' Their Occidentalized culture stood in sharp contrast to 'Iranian society's ancient and traditional values that for hundreds of years were based on generosity and self-reliance. These characteristics Zoroaster founded in ancient Iran while Islam strengthened our society's moral infrastructure.' Thus, the goal of the profiteering campaign was to combat 'the emergence of the influence of the

West's materialist, superficial and raw culture … on Iran's spiritual values … [and to ensure] that the superficial characteristics of Western culture' were avoided.⁵¹

Another article, 'Family Structure and Consumerist Society', expanded these themes stressing that the Party was concerned about the future of social and familial relationships in the face of Occidentosis.

> Profiteering is a sign of the weakening and debasing of the moral and spiritual infrastructure of Iranian society. … It is not only an economic issue but also a reflection of the unfortunate changes in Iranian spiritual values … resulting from the importation of the Western consumerist society. In the West's consumerist societies every effort is made to increase consumerism. Today's level of consumerism in the West is such that it even destroys the attachments and links between family members.⁵²

Thus, if Western materialism and consumerism can destroy familial relationships by instrumentalizing them they can easily tear a society apart as people engage in the continual struggle for increasing amounts of money to satisfy conspicuous consumerism.

These sentiments were expressed not only by Rastakhiz journalists and publicists. Top party leaders used their platforms to push this Party line. Baheri's speech to a chapter of the Party's Woman's Society provides a good example of this tone. Condemning the impact of technology on familial and social relationships and echoing the sentiments of the shah and Naraqi, he warned about people becoming enslaved to technology, a condition that created a Frankenstein unable to maintain true human relationships. The Western use of technology, now being imposed on Iran, had to be rejected. Flowing from this were condemnations of atomistic individualism, the result of Occidentosis that placed hedonism, conspicuous consumerism and materialism at the centre of one's existence. In such conditions relationships were instrumentalized as individuals sought only personal material fulfilment. Arguing that this consumerist imperialism was waging an existential struggle against Iranian authenticity, he asked: Were the Iranian people 'prepared to give up spirituality?' The loss of spirituality and morality would bring other manifestations of Occidentosis, specifically, 'the following of fashion (*modparasti*) that destroyed individual creativity and identity, licentiousness that would lead to the end of Iranian morality, and the love of luxury goods that placed acquisition of material goods above all else, transforming it into a goal of life'.⁵³

The spread of Occidentosis was also due to the actions and culture of Western companies and their employees. The Party provided frequent updates on the work of its commission investigating corruption in foreign companies operating in Iran. Headlines in *Rastakhiz*, such as 'The Great Levels of the Corruption of Foreign Companies in Iran is Revealed' set the overall tone. *Rastakhiz* and *The Youth of Rastakhiz* reported in detail any corruption scandal involving Western companies as this commission pursued its own investigations. As the following examples show, the reporting and analysis of these corruption scandals were integrated into the discourses of anti-West Occidentalism.

Siemens, General Telephone, Northrop Electronics and Nippon Electric became embroiled in a scandal, at the heart of which was a scheme, according to *Rastakhiz*, to overcharge purposefully for services and goods 'at the expense of the Iranian government and people'.[54] These companies had obtained in 1970 a contract to construct an integrated national telecommunication network. As the project entered its final phases, the scandal broke. The initial *Rastakhiz* headline 'The People of Iran and Foreign Companies' and its accompanying leader initiated the party attack: 'Once again foreign companies in their financial transactions with Iran have proven to public opinion that they are dishonest. They are condemned by public opinion' for their corruption. That a retired US army general, Harvey Jablonsky, was implicated in giving pay-offs on behalf of Northrop to Iranian officials to facilitate the tender only added to the fury about the role of Western culture and Westerners in spreading corruption.

According to Rastakhiz publications this 'thankfully discovered' scheme to overcharge was only the latest example of Western companies engaged in profiteering in most sectors of the economy. Their most common practices in this regard were, it was claimed, raising prices despite provisions in contracts and ignoring market prices. Consequently, inflation rose and the Iranian people suffered. In reality, *Rastakhiz* argued, Western companies with their 'irresponsible and unfettered corruption' were the main agents in 'the plundering of the people' and the infringing of 'the people's rights'. The shah, commenting on the activities of Western companies and the state's economic and financial problems by the end of 1976, grumbled: 'We shall not allow the same vultures to gather from everywhere and tell us to do this or that with our money'.[55]

One of the main targets of the party crusade against Occidentosis was the opinion held by Occidentosis-ridden Iranians that Iranians were inherently dishonest and crooked while Westerners and Western companies were inherently honest, upfront and reliable. Detailing the cases of corruption that involved Westerners and Western companies, *Rastakhiz* charged: 'These foreign companies are particularly competent in the creation of corruption and in the obfuscation and denial of their activities.' The attempts by these companies to project an image of their inherent probity and Eastern inherent dishonesty and corruption were just as 'hypocritical' as the West's claims to superiority in humanism, democratic and economic systems and human rights. Unfortunately, these Western companies were helped by Occidentosis-ridden Iranians in propagating these views. These people had to be exposed.

The infamous 'sugar scandal' too occupied much space in Rastakhiz publications. It involved, on the one hand, two high-ranking Iranian officials, Hossein Alizadeh, director of procurement of sugar, teas and grain and Mohammad Ali Seirafi, director of the imports department, and, on the other hand, the British company, Tate and Lyle.[56] The scheme, as reported at the time, involved 'importing sugar into Iran at prices above those on the world market'.[57] Three elements of the scandal were emphasized. First, the inflated price of sugar had added to every Iranian's cost of living. Second, it was the epitome of the influence of Occidentosis. These Occidentosis-ridden Iranians, overtaken with consumerism and materialism, became susceptible to the offer of personal gain provided by this foreign company. Third, this scandal was additional proof of the baleful influence of the presence of Western companies in Iran. After conducting an investigation the Imperial Inspectorate decried foreign corruption and claimed that the scandal had cost the Iranian government $45 million. Additional calls for greater regulation of the activities of foreign companies in Iran were made. The two Iranian officials were relieved of their duties and the minister of trade and commerce, Fereydoun Mahdavi, who was already increasingly unpopular due to his handling of the war against profiteering, was also removed. However, Hoveyda appointed him an official advisor to the prime minister since the scandal's public side had seemingly started as a result of a factional struggle over roles in the lucrative import of sugar.[58]

The third scandal to which Rastakhiz provided detailed and ongoing coverage involved US companies and the sale of military equipment, namely F-14s. At its centre was the payment of commissions and so-called agents' fees by Grumman Corporation. The shah had paid $2.2 billion for the purchase of eighty F-14s. It soon came to light that Grumman had paid such agents $20 million to clinch the deal despite the shah's banning of such practices. When the scandal first broke General Hassan Tufanian, in charge of military procurement, announced that he had told Grumman executives as early as 1973 that 'Iran had prohibited the use of agents in arranging military sales'. He also claimed that he 'forced the US Defense Department to add to its regulations a rule against employing such agents in government-to-government military sales'.[59] Rastakhiz decried the fact that this $20 million ended up being included in the purchase price and therefore the Iranian government and people suffered financially from this encouragement of corruption by Westerners. To add fuel to the fire, it also came out that US defence secretary, James Schlesinger, increased Iran's financial responsibility in 'the research and development costs involved in F-14 production' given his anger over the shah's role in the increase in the price of oil. *Rastakhiz* concluded: 'The Americans milked an extra $28 million from Iran'.[60] Concomitantly, attacks on the perceptions of the probity and honesty of Westerners were renewed. Tufanian led the charge, whose quote dominated *Rastakhiz*'s front-page news: 'I once considered Americans honest in their dealings. Now I have understood that they are sworn liars!'[61] Tufanian, cognizant of this form of corruption, preferred to work directly through the Pentagon in arranging arms sales.[62] The shah eventually recouped $2.2 million from Northrop and $20 million from Grumman.

This party line was not just instrumentalized propaganda. It was a reflection of the opinion held at the top of the Pahlavi state. Hoveyda in March 1976 told high-ranking Western visitors, including David Rockefeller, chairman of Chase Manhattan Bank and Peter Peterson, chairman of Lehman Brothers and a former US commerce secretary:

> When we opened our doors to the international business community to meet our growing development (al) needs, we seemed to have obtained more than we bargained for. For in some instances, along with goods and services, it appears we have imported a business morality – or more accurately, lack of morality – as well. … Now I am not claiming that Iranians are all angels, but, at least, in two cases that we investigated, it seems that certain operatives of these companies pocketed the money themselves and told their shareholders that they had been paid out to Iranians as bribes. Some crumbs may have been distributed to Iranians, but the meat went back overseas.[63]

The cycles of brown outs that struck Tehran in 1977 have been frequently mentioned in the literature on the Revolution as a sign of the malaise affecting the Pahlavi state and a catalyst for growing popular discontent.[64] Rastakhiz publications, recognizing the popular anger and frustration over this issue, integrated it into its discourses of anti-West Occidentalism. Blame for the shortage of electricity was placed squarely on the French company Alstom which had built power stations and the US contracting firm, Harza International, which was immediately blacklisted by the government. 'The power station at Reza Shah Kabir Dam should have had turbines capable of 250,000 watts p/hour, but had only 100,00 watts p/hour. The French company charged high prices for their construction but provided substandard services and equipment.' After a claimed investigation *Rastakhiz* ran a headline: 'Alstom is responsible for the large-scale black out on Friday.' Worse, as the article pointed out, was that 'Alstom is even now still unprepared and unable to undertake repairs of one power plant'. The Rastakhiz campaign as well as official anger over these issues forced the French company, which feared blacklisting, to attempt to assuage the growing outrage through promises to tend to these deficiencies.

Nonetheless, the rhetorical offensive in this regard continued. Another editorial, while condemning Western technology, argued that the cost to the Iranian people included not only this direct fleecing of the government by this company but also the economic damage rendered by its actions. 'Did Alstom even think of the kind of disaster its faulty, weak technology and irresponsible specialists would bring on our economy? Or how many Iranian factories are suffering because of it?'[65] Looking into the company's previous work, Rastakhiz claimed that several years before it had sold Iran other defective power stations while fiddling with billing in order to milk Iranians. The outrage stemming from these ongoing scandals, whipped up by Rastakhiz publications in the face of growing public criticism, led to the conclusion that foreign companies 'only think of their own interests at the expense of Iran's interests'. Rastakhiz promised it would ensure that the Imperial Commission would deal with this plundering. At the same time, the Party and the government, finding itself on the defensive, called on non-Western countries to prepare a blacklist of Western companies that had failed to live up to their contractual obligations, performed shoddy work and/or were guilty of profiteering. In this way, the East, under the leadership of the Iran, would lead the crusade against the attempt of Western imperialism to exploit non-Western countries.

The conclusion could have been made that these infringements by Western companies and the cases of corruption were uncoordinated and the result of only dirty and dodgy but traditional ways of doing big business. Rastakhiz discourses took aim at this possibility, arguing that such infringements were part of a large plot by Western imperialism to retard Iran's development and destabilize the country's political and economic situation. These companies were agents of imperialism.

> Invasion means not only territorial invasion, the crossing of borders by an enemy or enemies and advancement into the heart of the country. Invasion is also a part of the new imperialism that has changed the color and form [of old imperialism] without changing its essence. The technological invasion, the imposition of economic inflation and plots and conspiracies aimed at the cheap purchase of

raw materials and selling technology and equipment built with these same raw materials at prices ten times their real value and price, the attack on our language and literature, the attack on the culture of Iran constitutes this new imperialism and invasion. ... Iran has a cultural essence that is thousands of years old [that must be protected].[66]

In party discourses another element of this new imperialism was the large number of Western specialists and their families in Iran. The Party from the time of its establishment took aim at them, claiming it was reacting to public opinion and resentment. Khosrow Panhai, a member of the political and executive committees, in an article 'Imported Technology and Third World Countries' helped set the tone of the party approach. 'The West's technology is a form of imperialism and exploitation of the non-Western world' by the West. It condemned the West's wilful 'destruction of indigenous traditional and modern technologies' that led to a growing technological dependence on the West, and the practice 'to force the hiring of Western specialists with very high salaries' in order to ensure its hegemony. The result was 'the inflation of foreign specialists' in various economic sectors that decreased opportunities for educated Iranians and increased costs to the Iranian exchequer. Such a presence had serious cultural implications: 'The activities of foreign specialists in Iran from various aspects and specifically from the cultural point of view must be reviewed.' It concluded with a call for more concerted action to fight these elements of imperialism and cultural Occidentosis.[67]

Sensing correctly public opinion on this issue, the Party launched a campaign of pressure on the government with the declaration: 'The use of foreign specialists has become a chronic disease of our institutions'.[68] The consequences of this excessive use of foreign specialists were clear. It was a boom for the West's economies which were dealing with the problem of high unemployment at Iran's expense. When the government issued its first findings about the number of Western specialists living and working in Iran, the Party, citing public outrage, demanded action to be taken and promised, as the headlines read, that 'Iranian specialists will take the place of foreign specialists'.[69] *Rastakhiz* then reported on party research that showed that Westerners were paid 'exorbitant salaries' and on the consequent growing public fury at both these salaries and government inaction. Condemning the fact that 'no criteria for determining the [exorbitant] salaries of these foreign specialist exists', Rastakhiz promised action and results.[70] At the same time, other pieces stressed that 'the West is the cause of the problems in the Iranian job market. ... The job market is empty, empty that is for Iranians. ... But we import doctors, drivers, technicians from the West. ... This helps the enemy'.[71]

The first mention of the negative economic, cultural and social consequences of this presence came when Hoveyda was still prime minister and party head. Responding to growing popular resentment and party pressure, he announced plans to reduce the number of Western specialists and the founding of a party committee dedicated to the investigation of the cultural and economic consequences of their presence. Moreover, the government promised to establish mechanisms to reduce their numbers and limit future importation of foreign labour, in particular Western white-collar workers and professionals.[72] Rastakhiz publications announced that this committee would also place the government under pressure if it did not back up this rhetoric with action. Within a relatively short period of time, to great fanfare, the Party claimed credit for other victories in the struggle against imperialism and Occidentosis. The government announced 'new policies and regulations requiring equal salaries for everyone', Iranian as well as Western. A short time later, the government established a unified agency that would vet all visa applications of Western specialists and introduced measures severely limiting the ability of Western companies to hire non-Iranian workers and specialists. It also unveiled plans to entice educated Iranians living abroad to return and replace Western professionals.

Discourses of Pahlavi anti-West Occidentalism reached new heights at the Third Extraordinary Party Congress, held on 4 January 1978, that was dedicated to 'the party program for battling imperialism' (Figure 15).[73] This conference was announced at the end of November 1977 by Baheri at the suggestion of the head of the shah's political department at a meeting of the Political Office.[74] The immediate catalyst was anti-Iranian propaganda in the West, signs of growing discontent in Iran and the disaster surrounding the imperial couple's state visit to Washington DC in mid-November 1977.[75] *The Youth of Rastakhiz* outlined the Party's position in the run-up to this conference and the Festival of Culture and Art

> No clever mind can remain impartial to the progress and the technical and scientific movement of different peoples and deny that it is possible to benefit from their experience. But the loss of culture, the forgetting of the self, the abandonment of all the appearances and symbols of one's ethnic group and devotion to the technology and the imported culture of peoples of the West will never be acceptable to us. ... The shah has made every attempt ... to raise public awareness of national and local culture and, vitally, to revive and cultivate the symbols of the precious attributes of ancient [pre-Islamic] Iran ... the true symbols of our ancient culture. ... When

Figure 15 Opening ceremony of III Party Congress dedicated to the struggle against imperialism, January 1978. *Javanan-e Rastakhiz*, author's collection.

we look across the world at the various '–isms' that through varies ruses and tricks deceive people and separate them from their own culture and ethnic group we understand the necessity of seeing and reviewing the past, of the revival of the moral elegance of the Aryan race.[76]

Baheri gave indications of the upcoming conference's themes:

Our Party, over the last month and a half, according to the wishes of various quarters of Iranian society, has held huge demonstrations across the country against the anti-Iranian provocations of the new imperialism as well as reactionary forces. Until now these rallies have been local and regional. For this reason many Iranian citizens want a national response to the imperialists and reactionary forces, in other words a response from the highest Party level – the Party Congress. … The Congress must be the supreme expression of the Rastakhiz Party's position, especially in regard to the anti-Iranian conspiracies of foreigners. … The Party's position is an unwavering anti-imperialist stance against imperialism.

In a televised programme he declared that 'anti-Iranian conspiracies of foreigners' use 'imperialist methods to exploit Iran' and 'destroy any progress made'. These conspiracies hatched by Western imperialism had one primary goal: Iran's submission to its hegemony. Western imperialism 'does not want the voice of Iran to be heard in the world'. Party and people had to mobilize. In this vein, 'Rastakhiz … considers protecting cultural authenticity one of the most important and effective policies, the key, to fighting imperialism. This is why imperialism targets culture and the formation of the Great Civilization'.[77] The Party warned the people that the country's cultural borders were increasingly under direct threat:

The Rastakhiz Party gives great importance to the country's cultural and educational institutions and considers their protection to be one of its greatest duties. For this reason, imperialism is extremely worried about the Party's position and activities. … In response it has intensified conspiracies, plots and provocations that target these institutions and culture. The West's imperialists are worried because our development and progress is a school for others while the high path toward the Great Civilization is the working place, the laboratory, and library.[78]

The Congress' slogan, splashed across party publications, was clear: 'This Extraordinary Congress of the Party must raise the voice of the Iranian people against the conspiracies and provocations of imperialism!'

At this Congress, Amuzegar replaced Baheri as party general secretary; factional and personal struggles continued despite the growing sense that a malaise was overtaking the system. Amuzegar, in his key-note speech, reiterated the themes set by Baheri, but was more direct about the countries behind these conspiracies.

Who suffers from the fact that we daily march forward? Who is upset that Iranian women have become free and, should-to-shoulder with men, are working and striving for the country's development? In reality who is tormented by this? The answer is clear. Those whose hands that once interfered in our internal affairs and no longer can do this thanks to Iran's military power. Those whose hegemony over our national resources and economy was considered the path for the development and growth of their own economies. ... [This imperialism must understand that] we are no longer that country in which on the basis of some excuse it was possible to incite protests and riots [to achieve its exploitative goals].

Imperialism is worried that with the spread of social welfare, increases in the people's income, and strengthening of national unity it will lose its outposts among the people and thus the ability to propagate its deceitfully attractive ideologies. Imperialism is worried by the fact that Iran can become the example for all other peoples struggling to free themselves from, on the one hand, the yoke of the imperialism of Red and Black, and on the other hand, from the yoke of both the old and new imperialisms. Imperialism's provocations against our country began when our shah grabbed OPEC's war banner in the struggle to obtain for all member countries a fair and just price for their oil ... [and] raised oil prices against imperialism's wishes. [Thanks to the shah's leadership] ... for the first time in world history hundreds of millions of dollars from the imperialists' exchequers poured into and overflowed the exchequers of oil-producing countries. ... Naturally the imperialists will not peacefully rest until they have retaliated and obtained some form of satisfaction for this great blow they endured.

One point from his speech needs some elaboration. At the time, the shah and Pahlavi elite were aware of Saudi Arabia's role, supported by the United States, in bringing about within OPEC a decrease in oil prices in 1976–7. Already in 1976 oil income had dropped by $3 billion while another $3 billion in capital had fled the country.[79] This drop exercised a negative influence on national income at a time of growing economic problems and discontent resulting from the pouring of the income derived from the dramatic rise in oil prices into the economy and subsequent attempts to lower inflation through reductions in state spending and credit. The shah was blunt about this new reality:

> Until this point in time we have not asked the people for sacrifices. Instead we kept them wrapped in cotton. Things are going to change now. Everyone must work harder and be ready for sacrifices in the national interest. The Party has the task of inculcating this new state of mind.[80]

A couple of months later, at the beginning of 1977, he admitted that Saudi policy would indeed have a negative impact.[81] The Pahlavi state, having failed to create a reserve stabilization fund that would cushion the damage done to state income by a decrease in oil prices, was forced again to borrow money on international markets and reduce greatly state expenditures in order to meet the new conditions of lower state income. The result was a dramatic decrease in economic growth that, after more than a decade of such growth, felt like a recession.

Amuzegar's use of the term imperialism of the Red and Black targeted the clergy and socialist-communist inspired Islamist groups, as well as secular leftist groups, that took inspiration from either Marxism-Leninism or Maoism. At the same time, the term old and new imperialisms fingered the West's imperialism, including the United States, and its new methods to establish its hegemony and exploitative methods.

Amuzegar continued:

> But the question is why would the young allow themselves to be fooled and duped by the deceitfully attractive provocations of these imperialists? ... The Rastakhiz movement condemns any attempt by this imperialism to provoke our youth and undertake conspiratorial moves ... in order to create disorder and chaos in the country ... [These attempts were the consequence of the fact that] between our national interests and those of imperialism and domestic reactionary forces clear contradictions exist. The Rastakhiz movement condemns all and any provocations by foreigners to dupe our youth. Today's imperialism has chosen the universities to implement their evil intentions because our economic and social development is dependent on the youth's knowledge and consciousness and if this imperialism can by whatever means prevent our youth from continuing their education they would have become closer to their goal. ... However, no foreigner has the ability or strength to violate and transgress Iran's rights.[82]

At the same time the shah, infuriated by Khomeini's denunciation of the Pahlavi government during Carter's New Year's stopover in Tehran as illegal and illegitimate, ordered an article attacking the exiled cleric to be published. Hoveyda, charged with fulfilling this order, called Homayoun at the Congress and told him to expect its delivery. It was to be published in the newspaper *Ettela'at*. On 7 January 1978, two days after this Congress that focused on attacking the West's imperialism, this article attacking Ayatollah Khomeini was published. Two days later demonstrations rocked Qom and Mashad.

Other leading party members echoed these sentiments at the Congress. In a special insert for *The Youth of Rastakhiz* a lead article 'The role of academics ... and Party challenges' provides additional insight into the party's tone:

> The reality of Europe's and America's civilization and so-called freedom must be explained and described for the youth [so that they appreciate what they have]. We must deal with the West's influence on the youth and teenagers. These false perceptions of Europe and America have created the problems and challenges we face today. Only those who have lived there for years and decades understand that the problems they have there are several times more than the ones we have here. In the West freedom of expression exists, but no one listens to what you say. If they did listen then one could say that the freedom of expression exists.[83]

These false sentiments and impressions propagated by the West's imperialism were the reason for 'the spread of Occidentosis'.[84] Other leading party figures and, in particular, the wings' leaders contributed their views. Ansari proclaimed:

> Iran will not surrender to imperialism. ... The Iranian people condemn any form of influence exercised by imperialism in the Persian Gulf or the Indian Ocean. ...

Every foreigner, every imperialist, and every puppet of foreigners and exploitative imperialists must understand that our people are prepared to fight to prevent going back to the past' and thus falling into the clutches of this imperialism.[85]

Ameli-Tehrani warned: 'The West's imperialist forces take advantage of the lack of youth organizations. ... The youth must be aware of the West's imperialist plots. ... Imperialism is using various ways to penetrate [the thought] of our youth and destabilize the country'.[86] Baheri echoed these sentiments:

> We will immunize the youth from the poisonous influences of Iran's enemies. The Party must educate the people and make them aware of the character of the imperialist conspiracies against the country. ... Party members, and especially the youth, must be vigilant in facing the enemy's provocations and the anti-Iran plots hatched by the West.[87]

After all, 'imperialism does not want Iran to be an example for others in the region. ... They don't want Iran to become powerful'.[88] In short, Iran was a besieged fortress that was 'under attack by the foreign agents of destruction' who were targeting 'national culture'.[89]

After the Congress but before the disturbances in Qom Rastakhiz's discursive onslaught continued.

> We know that Iran's enemies, in other words, imperialist forces, in accordance with time and place change their appearances. They don't want, and never did want, the Iranian people to use their talents and abilities to achieve greatness. Historically, we have seen national movements and popular fronts dedicated to the liberation from the shackles they [the imperialist forces] had created for us; these movements and fronts have always come face to face with these imperialist forces which we now face. ... [But] Iranian society is under the wise leadership of the Leader of the Revolution and the protective umbrella of the Rastakhiz Party.[90]

Again it was claimed that the root cause for this discontent was Occidentosis: 'Iranian culture must come out from being under the cultural influence of Westerners. ... Unfortunately authentic Iranian culture and values continue to be damaged and weakened by the culture of foreigners'.[91]

Jafarian, party deputy head, in a speech at a local party meeting outlined the party's understanding of the opposition. Three groups existed: (1) Imperialists and the imperialist powers who 'consider Iran an enemy-they fear a strong independent Iran. They are in opposition with Iran's existence and the imperial system'; (2) Opponents of the Party who 'are not against in principle the imperial system, but oppose the current government and fear that the success of the Rastakhiz Party will mean the success of the government'; and (3) 'Those people who became rooted in the values system of the West's political cultures. They formed and evolved within that system and [thus] only have Western examples and patterns in their mind and nothing else. Then there are the Marxists who also belong to the first group'.[92]

During the revolution's initial stages, in other words, until the beginning of the summer 1978, Rastakhiz publications continued to intensify these discourses of anti-West Occidentalism and specifically the conspiracies and methods of Western imperialism and its Occidentosis-ridden Iranian agents. However, from July until the dissolution of the Party in late September 1978 by Amuzegar's successor, Jafar Sharif-Emami, the focus shifted to reporting on the rising extent of discontent and methods to deal with it.

The Amuzegar call to arms

Amuzegar, again party head, in a major speech to party cadres in the wake of the Congress set the tone for his second tenure: 'Iran and Iranians for eternity will never exchange their cultural richness for any material bounty. This government has taken firm steps to enact the shah's and the empress's wishes in protecting cultural authenticity and richness. ... This cultural richness will remain [despite the threat of Occidentosis]'.[93] This theme was not new. Amuzegar included it in speeches during his first tenure as party head.[94] One of his first practical steps was a large increase in funding in the Sixth Development Plan (1977–82) for policies in the defence of the authenticity of culture and national identity. The Party praised this move since it 'recognized that more official attention needs to be given to cultural issues and the protection of authenticity given changes in society'.[95] A month later Amuzegar sent a letter to the Party and *The Youth of Rastakhiz* calling for an increase in action in protecting authenticity.

> *The Youth of Rastakhiz* must be the expression and carrier of the sacred responsibility of which the Rastakhiz Party is the standard bearer. ... The construction of the new generation with the energy of Iran's rich authentic culture and providing it with a full understanding of the rich heritage of Iran's past as well as of today's technology and science is a necessity. ... When we already have a complete and rich cultural, literary, social heritage ... we must not become the expression of Western culture. ... If today's youth in *The Youth of Rastakhiz* do not become acquainted with the life of Saadi and Hafez and great thinkers such as Moulavi and great patriots such as Ferdowsi then in what publication can this goal be attained? ... [The danger is that] the youth will unconsciously become enchanted with the external forms of Western civilization given the development and spread of Western technology. Additionally, given their lack of meaningful understanding of the deep ocean of our national heritage, language, literature, and culture they become enthralled with Western culture and customs.[96]

Party publications welcomed this new momentum: 'Now we are recognizing the pains and problems of being infected with Occidentosis'.[97]

Amuzegar's call to arms intensified the discourses of anti-West Occidentalism on the heels of the Third Congress. As part of this process *The Youth of Rastakhiz* published in greater quantities than in the past weekly analytical pieces by both state and non-state intellectuals detailing the areas infected by Occidentosis, the role of Western imperialism in its spread and paths to eliminating it. This series of articles continued until the middle of summer of 1978. Presented below is a small sampling of such articles that give a sense of the direction and degree of this intensification.

Ali Akbar Kesmai was a well-known film writer and journalist whose work in the dubbing of foreign films brought him fame. In a series of articles he subjected NIRT to severe criticism for its emphasis on broadcasting foreign television programmes that 'inculcate amongst the people the Western way of life. ... We in the mass media and in official and unofficial organizations and institutions in our actions and behavior show that we suffer from Occidentosis and thus spread the culture of the Occident.' He saved his heaviest attack for the Occidentosis-ridden 'principleless' technocrats who 'have American gestures and accents and serve as conduits of Western society' in Iran. These Occidentosis-ridden technocrats and others similar to them with a sense of superiority made 'a bad impression on the youth' and society.

He argued that the impression made by these Occidentosis-ridden Iranians occupying public positions had two contradictory consequences. 'One group in society, similar to a parrot imitates, them' and tries 'to outdo American and English dandies'. Yet, worse than these Occidentosis-ridden Iranians who blindly mimicked Western appearances and gestures were the Occidentosis-ridden

> pseudo-philosophers with their goatees and pipes who gather on the world stage ... comparing negatively the East with Western civilization, singing the West's praises while proclaiming that they, from head to toe, are Western and that [such a condition] is inevitable and inescapable for all. They are proud that Western philosophy's greatest achievement is the denial of God. We must not accept Western thought or the denial of God. ... We are infected not only with technological Occidentosis. Our philosophy, thought, and literature also suffer from it. This situation is the biggest threat to our youth.

Compare this view published in an official party publication to Shariati's words.

> Many times I have seen that particular group of educated Iranians and intellectuals, especially those who have lived or are living abroad, sit together and criticize [our culture] and tell tales by citing humiliating examples of the weakness, baseness, corruption, and ignorance and stupidity [of our people and culture]. They compare us with others and from the bottom of their being laugh at us. ... They then bring in proper examples of Westerners. ... This is a form of recreation and fun-making [for them].[98]

Kesmai, however, in accordance with Rastakhiz ideology, was not advocating a rigid traditionalism. He accepted the need for economic and technological development. Therefore, he saw another baneful consequence of the behaviour and attitude of Occidentosis-ridden Iranians. They had played a key role in the creation of another group that was 'becoming disgusted with technology and change because of its connection with the West'. The natural knee-jerk reaction to the vainglorious sense of superiority of the Occidentosis-ridden Iranians, the hubris of Westerners and the West's denial of God was transforming increasing numbers of Iranians into opponents of change and technology. Ultimately, 'both groups are detrimental to the country'. In order to struggle against Occidentosis he stressed that 'in our publications and mass media, and in official and unofficial organizations we must not exhibit behavior or gestures that could be taken as manifestations of Occidentosis'. He supported an intensification of the party campaign for the preservation of authenticity and argued for the correct adaptation of technology and economic change according to Iranian values and norms. An Iranian modernity, social imaginary, situated between these Occidentosis-ridden groups and reactionary nativist forces was needed.[99]

Despite the rhetoric arguing for a middle path, the details of which were not provided, the overall tone remained one of anti-West Occidentalism. 'We took from Western culture that which should not and could not be taken.' Outraged and appalled by the urban Occidentosis-ridden Iranians, Kesmai, similar to official party historiography and Slavophiles in Russia, found authenticity in the countryside: 'An Iranian villager living in a distant place in today's Iran is more Iranian than Tehranis who are confused and corrupted by the West'.[100]

Sattar Laqai was a writer and a well-known journalist, who began his career at the magazine *Tehran-e Mosavvar* and eventually became the head of the editorial staff at *The Youth of Rastakhiz*. He was in charge of its interviews and special editions, such as the one on the Third Party Congress. Reflecting party fundamentals he declared: 'Freedom in imperialism's lexicon is shrill and painful to the ear' since 'the goal of the West's imperialism is the struggle against freedom in the name of the defense of freedom. ... In reality, freedom's definition in the imperialist's lexicon is the creation of riots and chaos.' This struggle was against the freedom of non-Western countries, such as Iran, to protect their cultural and geopolitical borders. 'Freedom [in the geopolitical arena] was in reality only for the West.'

The people and in particular the youth had to be alert and not fall for deceitfully attractive Western ideologies and their derivatives since 'the imperialists search for cheap mercenaries' as they sought to expand and maintain Western hegemony. 'Through these deceitfully attractive slogans the imperialist strives to reduce to below zero those social peoples whom it intends to exploit.' Additionally, the belief that becoming infected with Occidentosis would lead to acceptance by the West and respect for the country's sovereignty was baseless. The West denied even societies and countries infected with Occidentosis the freedom that it already enjoys. In any case, this Western 'unlimited and unidentifiable freedom' did not offer civilization since it 'leaves no place for the growth of human virtues' and in fact destroys them. Therefore, the Iranian people had to focus on the creation of an authentically Iranian modernity.[101]

Hadi Seif, a researcher in traditional Iranian music, argued that the warning signs of 'the catastrophe of forgetting traditions and values in the East emerged when the West with the full force of its industrial might launched a destructive and relentless attack on the East's cultural and spiritual values'. Imperialism's plan was to establish and maintain hegemony over the countries of the East, and specifically Iran by 'establishing its imprint on the East's lands with the intention of spreading its materialistic culture ... [that] gradually imposed itself on the spiritual culture of Eastern peoples. [Consequently] ... today's youth, faced with a whirlpool of change in values, is in need of protection of identity'. The reason Western imperialism targeted Iran was clear – it was becoming strong, independent and free. Therefore, using the crisis of identity brought about by Occidentosis to which some Iranian youth had become susceptible, the imperialists claimed to be a defender and promoter of freedom in order to weaken the imperial system. It was a chimera. The West launched a struggle against the shah because he defended Iranian national interests.[102]

Barhan ibn-e Yussof was a well-known writer on Iranian culture, a member of the NIRT Council of Writers and a manager of programming for the working class. In 1976 he established the cultural foundation Mehr-e Iran that was devoted to the protection of cultural authenticity. He welcomed Amuzegar's renewed attention to the preservation of authenticity in the face of 'the cultural invasion of the West'. Stressing that 'Western culture is now replacing national culture', Yussof directed his ire onto the educational system, that familiar target of Rastakhiz discourses. He criticized the curricula of primary, secondary and higher education for their role in this 'deviation' from this authenticity and inculcating 'love of Western culture'.[103]

> The new young generation unwittingly became enchanted with the exterior forms of Western civilization given Western technological development and its spread while not having a deep understanding and knowledge of the heritage of national language, literature and culture. This led to their enchantment with Western culture, literature, and poetry. ... This alienation from national culture begins in kindergarten.

An Occidentosis-ridden youth was an existential danger to the country's future since 'the young generation should and must be the protector and guardian of native culture and its accomplishments'. Statistics also showed the influence of Occidentosis on Iranian studies in Iran. 'Only 1122 students in Iran are studying the language and customs of Pars' while 'in Iran we have only a couple of universities and faculties dealing with the culture of Iran'.[104]

These concerns were expressed in another series of articles by Ibrahim Zalzadeh, a staff writer of *The Youth of Rastakhiz*. He directly condemned the government for failing to adhere to the shah's wishes and 'address its mission to protect authentic culture and customs' in the face of the West's cultural invasion. Dangerously, native solutions to native problems were not being sought. Rather, 'in regard to recognition of problems and bottlenecks we are Occidentosis-ridden'.

He echoed Naraqi's belief that the educational system and in particular the universities were staffed with Occidentosis-ridden instructors who disseminated the idea of the superiority of Western civilization and a national sense of shame: 'For example, a Western-educated law professor with his knowledge of the challenges and problems faced by the West opens for us legal problems and issues existing there and expects that we learn them'. The result of this teaching method is 'cynicism in regard to my own country' given the imposed sense that the West is superior while Iran was so far behind that no one had expectations for a positive future. Moreover, as a result of this

Occidentosis, 'Our youth are more aware of foreign countries than their own'.[105] They would therefore implicitly and unwittingly serve the interests of Western imperialism.

Saboktakin Salur was a well-known writer of historical novels set in Iran's pre-Islamic imperial period and publicist. He too expressed deep concern with the spread of Occidentosis in education curricula.

> For years now in our country 'they' have sought to ensure that the people not pay attention to the symbols and elements of their nationality. 'They' know, as you and I do, that a nation is nothing without history [and] culture. If we destroy national culture and history the people's link with the past will be cut. In such a situation the people will lose their authentic national identity.

In addition to his attack on the discourses of pro-West Occidentalism of the Reza Shah period, he criticized the Pahlavi form of technical Westernization. Addressing Amuzegar he asked:

> All of these strivings for development of the kingdom's economy, industrialization, the creation of universities-in the end what are they for? So that people have no spiritual and emotional link with each other? So that people separate themselves from each other? So that people laugh at the poetry of Saadi? ... This inattention to [Iranian authenticity], this severing of links with the past is the result and fruit of the work of a group who, striving for so-called enlightened renewal wittingly or unwittingly presented being modern as knowledge and adaption of Western civilization and thought, Western ways and methods, anything but Iranian [could be civilized and modern].

These Occidentosis-ridden Iranians

> loudly proclaim and indoctrinate in schools and universities that in the past we had nothing, that our culture is a dead culture of dervishes based on laziness and weakness. This group everyday prospered and developed, they have unity and succeeded-you see it in the situation we now face. We became the imitators of Western culture.

The situation has become so dire that 'families attempt to bring up their children with this fake culture, with this nonsense, with this meaninglessness'.[106]

What this representative sample shows is that as a result of Amuzegar's call to arms the newspaper *Rastakhiz* and *The Youth of Rastakhiz* intensified the discursive and rhetorical crusade against Occidentosis and for the protection of authenticity. Rastakhiz also took this crusade to a new level at which fundamentals of Pahlavi pro-West Occidentalism that were propagated since the time of Reza Shah were attacked and delegitimized. This discursive and rhetorical campaign graphically illustrates the ideological and theoretical tensions and challenges associated with attempts to implement Occidentalism. The Pahlavi state, having been the leading agent of Westernization and propagator of pro-West Occidentalism, by launching the discourses of anti-West Occidentalism risked delegitimizing itself while strengthening opposition forces and intensifying unease at the changes wrought by the process of Westernization. The risk was rooted in not only the long-held view of the Pahlavi state as an agent of Occidentosis but also in Rastakhiz's consistent condemnations of the spread of Occidentosis and, importantly, government inaction in dealing with its manifestations.

Pahlavi modernity

As the Rastakhiz Party trumpeted the myriad crises facing Western civilization and the death of the West's '–isms' that had failed to secure the future, the shah proposed the alternative, his millenarian project, the Great Civilization.[107] Drawn in the cultural, moral and political colours of Aryanism, the imagery of the Great Civilization led the crusade against cultural and moral Occidentosis, the newest weapon in the hands of the West's imperialism. It promised a modernity superior to those offered by the West and preservation of Iranian authenticity, an ancient historical legacy passed on from generation to generation, that would ensure Iran's avoidance of the moral and cultural decline and sense of helplessness now overtaking the West. In an interview, and not in a prepared speech, the shah stated:

> I believe that by seizing only the path and methods of Aryanism is saving mankind from the misfortunes of war, corruption, and decay possible. ... When I read about events in Vietnam or when I see the losers of Western civilization, such as the hippy men and women and those other types of [Western] people who have turned their backs on morality and spirituality, a feeling takes over me that before the end of this century all those [Western] ideologies will drag our civilization into corruption and force humankind into a cave-like existence. ... We must introduce to the world the Aryan path of salvation. ... We are experiencing an Aryan renaissance.[108]

He confidently predicted: 'The Great Civilization will be the complete version of tomorrow's Iran and culture – it is the most perfect expression of the illustrious Aryan civilization'.[109] Following the shah's lead the Party propagated the idea that 'the return to the Aryan path alone can save humankind from drifting toward war, chaos, and catastrophe'.[110]

Farhang Mehr summarized in *Rastakhiz* the Party's thinking and duties in this national endeavour and the contours of its social imaginary. It provides a succinct outline of the themes covered in previous chapters. He rejected both aspects of the West, liberal capitalism and communism, seeing in them threats to Iran's cultural and ideological independence: 'We do not accept the Western belief in historical economic determinism ... [or] the claim of universal linear trajectory of history.' It was the West's emphasis on materialism that brought about 'all the misfortunes that have overtaken the Western world and all its social disorders from racism, crime, corruption, [and] hippy culture to complete hedonism and terrorism'. Praising the monarchy's ideologization, he stressed the splendor of Aryan civilization that stood in contrast to the West: 'These [misfortunes] will not come to us thanks to Aryan culture'.[111] Therefore, in this 'new era of our national resurgence … one of the most vital issues is the recognition and protection of our national heritage and authenticity'.[112] Previous chapters showed that the Great Civilization promised an authentically Iranian modernity based on this Aryanism that included a spiritual Islam that, it was claimed, was significantly derivative of Iranian Zoroastrianism. Simultaneously, it offered economic and technological development, social welfare and geopolitical independence while protecting these authentically Iranian elements in the face of Occidentosis. The ancient imperial system, the source and defender of this authenticity, would guide the people in the creation of the *homo Pahlavicus* and the Great Civilization.

Iran never reached the gates of the Great Civilization. Iranians rejected it. On 25 September 1978 the Rastakhiz Party was dissolved by a government seeking ways to stem the growing revolutionary wave on whose crest sat Ayatollah Khomeini. In a last desperate bid to save his crumbling rule the shah on 4 January 1979 appointed Shapour Bakhtiar as prime minister, a well-known critic and nationalist who had engaged in active opposition to the shah that landed him in prison on several occasions. Twelve days later a tearful shah and the empress boarded a plane, claiming they were going a short vacation while the new prime minister sought to calm the situation. In reality they were flying into exile. Less than one month later on 11 February 1979 the Pahlavi dynasty collapsed.

Epilogue

Pahlavi Iran and Romanov Russia

This study's primary focus on the evolution of the place of the West in Pahlavi state discourses on the authenticity of culture and national identity is complemented by two limited comparative focuses, one looking backward to the example of Romanov Russia and the other looking forward to the IRI. Some of the points emerging from these focuses are outlined here.

Geopolitical Darwinism and cultural Darwinism describe the dynamics behind the adoption of the two forms of Occidentalism by the Romanov and Pahlavi states. The West's system of competitive states and imperialism represented an existential threat to countries such as Iran and Russia, although Iran in the nineteenth and twentieth centuries faced a more formidable West than imperial Russia did when it launched its initial cycles of Westernization. 'The survival of the fittest', Herbert Spencer's famous formulation that reflected the philosophy of social Darwinism and the reality of geopolitics since ancient times, captures the sense of threat and fear generated by the West's strengthening and expanding power.

Pro-West Occidentalism argued that a fundamental cause for the West's development and the consequent intensification of geopolitical Darwinism was culture. Victory in the geopolitical 'survival of the fittest' was a consequence of victory in the cultural 'survival of the fittest'. Therefore countries, such as Russia and Iran, that found themselves lagging behind and vulnerable to the great powers of the West were forced to adopt Western ways. Otherwise, military defeat and political submission at the hands of these powers would be their fate. In this context the discourses of pro-West Occidentalism sought to reformulate understandings of authenticity of culture and national identity in order to justify historically the state's implementation of Westernization by portraying it as a return to cultural authenticity. The goals were the creation of a new person able to produce domestically Western forms of power and the transfer of the masses' primal loyalty from local and religious identities to the monarchical state and its form of nationalism. These discourses propagated a historical and cultural identity that while timeless and eternal had been lost due to historical contingencies and remained so due to self-interested and reactionary domestic social groups. While this identity was sacralized and securitized by its source and defender, the Crown, some of its dimensions were dehistoricized and mythologized. This securitization of authenticity of culture and national identity, which protected an ideologically and politically driven interpretation of history and events that gave meaning and purpose to people now on the path to recovering greatness and grandeur, was justified by the idea of cultural Darwinism. Without taking these steps Iran and Russia would find themselves on the wrong side of the geopolitical survival of the fittest. This conception of the 'survival of the fittest' had within it the binaries of weak and strong, developed and undeveloped, and civilized and barbaric that drew the lines between official conceptions of in-groups and out-groups. Pro-West Occidentalism determined that Occidentalized Russians and Iranians constituted the in-group and the masses that still had not accepted this new identity and non-Western states and peoples who lacked any unique racial–cultural link with the West made up the out-group.

The main targeted domestic out-group was the clerical class and the masses who remained under the influence of its culture and superstitions. Pro-West Occidentalism, justifying state anticlericalism, argued that the continued dominance of this culture would ensure defeat in the world of geopolitical and cultural Darwinism. Before Iran and Russia were forced to react to the challenge of the West, the dynastic state and clergy, and monarchy and religion played mutually legitimating roles despite periods of political tension. The Iranian and Russian monarchies were primarily liturgical in theory and static in practice and focused on defending the realm and its religion and the rendering of justice. When these monarchies sensed the threat to its geopolitical borders posed by the West's development and power they launched pro-West Occidentalism and the practical process of Westernization. This required, it was believed, state centralization and supremacy of state interests over those of self-interested social groups, and particularly the clergy. These monarchies, thus, became statist and anticlerical in nature and transformative in action while their legitimating principles changed. Promises of return to lost authenticity, progress and great power status filled the ideological vacuum created by state anticlericalism. In this way, the discourses of Pahlavi and Romanov pro-West Occidentalism, while justifying the practical process of Westernization, provided the political and ideological means to end the long-standing power tension between the church and the state and to establish monarchical state supremacy over clerical institutions and ultimately in determination of the parameters of high culture and national identity.

The central element behind the discourses that Westernizing reforms represented a return to native authenticity was the claim of a unique racial–cultural link with the West. While conceptions of race in eighteenth- and early-nineteenth-century Europe and Russia were primitive relative to such conceptions from the middle of the nineteenth and twentieth centuries, Romanov pro-West Occidentalism was based on the idea of a fluid conception of whiteness and Christianity, backed up by Russia's geographical position. Romanov state discourses flirted with Aryanism in the overall framework of 'whiteness', but the Pahlavi state placed it at the centre of its claims to racial–cultural links with the West. As textbooks of the Reza Shah period taught, Iranians were Aryans while the future of human civilization belonged to the white race of which Aryans were one of the oldest and most important.

These discourses sought to convince Iranians and Russians that they were indeed Western and that cultural changes and the overall process of Westernization represented a return to a form of lost authenticity rather than the imposition of a foreign culture. Importantly, neither of these discourses rejected the idea of relative

Russian and Iranian distinctiveness. This distinctiveness, however, was situated under a larger civilizational umbrella of Europe/the West and alongside the idea that given these claimed racial–cultural links, there was more that united Russia and Iran with Europe/the West than divided them from it.

These racial–cultural claims of pro-West Occidentalism also sought to strengthen national self-confidence damaged by two realities. The older of the two was the West's practice of Orientalism, which predated the Ages of Enlightenment and Imperialism. It essentialized Russians and Iranians as archetypical Easterners, uncivilized, barbaric, untamed and ultimately untamable. The racial–cultural claims of pro-West Occidentalism sought to rescue Iranians and Russians from this Orientalism. The other reality was the realization of native backwardness relative to the West's growing economic, technological and geopolitical power that seemed to confirm the West's Orientalized view of Russians and Iranians.

The Western practice of Orientalizing Iranians and Russians and the imagery it produced were used by the Pahlavi and Romanov states to their benefit, domestically and internationally. Pro-West Occidentalism integrated this Orientalized view of the Iranian and Russian masses into its discourses in order to strengthen the justification for Westernization. It then held up that view as a relic of a humiliating period ended by the monarchy through its creation of the *homo Romanovicus* and *homo Pahlavicus* and proclaimed a great victory for the monarchy in overturning the West's Orientalized view of Russians and Iranians. Prokopovich in 1715 expressed the sentiments behind this trend that characterized both Romanov and Pahlavi approaches.

> Be it not remembered for shame, because it is true, the opinion we elicited from, the value we were assigned by foreign peoples formerly: by the political people we were considered barbarians, by the proud and the majestic the despised ones, by the learned the ignorant, by the predatory a desirable catch, by all shiftless, insulted from all sides.

But as a result of Peter's reforms

> Those who abhorred us as rude assiduously seek our fraternity; those who dishonored us glorify us; those who threatened us are afraid and tremble; those who despised us are not ashamed to serve us; many European crowned heads are not only willing to ally with Peter, our monarch, but do not consider it dishonorable to give him precedence; they have repealed their opinion, they have repealed their narratives about us, they have erased their antiquated little stories, they have begun both to speak and to write about us differently. Russia has raised her head, bright, beautiful, strong, loved by friends, feared by enemies.[1]

Mohammad Reza Shah frequently expressed similar sentiments. Alam noted in his diary (1973):

> Amongst the backlog of work, I had to report a request from the English royal family. Prince Philip wishes to be elected to the governing committee of the

Iranian Imperial Equestrian Society. His Imperial Majesty was amused by this, commenting, 'In days gone by, an Iranian politician would have considered it a catastrophe if he'd been missed off the guest list to a British embassy cocktail party. Now it appears the boot is on the other foot; a request from the British royal family is filed away amongst insignificant trivia'.[2]

Moreover, as the Romanov and Pahlavi states propagated the claims of unique racial-cultural relations with the West and sought liberation from the West's Orientalization of them, they used these claims in a similar process of Orientalization of particular peoples and polities which, it was stressed, did not enjoy such links. The goal was to use these claims to place Iranians and Russians in a global civilizational position superior to those societies lacking such links with the West. Dostoevsky's statement, quoted in the first chapter, perfectly expresses this dynamic in both Pahlavi and Romanov discourses: 'In Europe we are hangers-on and slaves, but in Asia we are masters. In Europe we are Tatars, but in Asia we too are Europeans'.[3]

The other target audience of pro-West Occidentalism were Westerners themselves and specifically Western intellectual and political opinion. Of the myriad issues that impeded the attempts of pro-West Occidentalism, underpinned by the process of Westernization, to convince Europe/the West that Russia and Iran were indeed a member of the West's club, two are particularly important here. One was the need of the West to have the Orientalized, backward, barbaric and of course exotic other against which it constructed and sustained its own identity as a superior and powerful civilization. In regard to power Iran and Russia differed from each other. No matter how disdainfully Western polities and opinion looked down at Russia, they had to reckon with it. Iran did not occupy a similar position in international politics. The other issue was the nature of monarchical rule and power structure in Iran and Russia that contrasted negatively, in the West's views, with its superior exclusive political civilization.

In this respect the Russian and Iranian experience somewhat differ given temporal differences. When links between Russia and the states to the west of it began to expand in the sixteenth and seventeenth centuries, west-European visitors keenly felt that they were no longer in Europe given the autocracy, the lack of legal protection for land and civil rights for the upper classes, and the absence of a distinct educated professional and business middle class. In their opinion, pre-Petrine Russia, despite the whiteness of its race and following of Christianity, had more in common with Safavid Iran than with Bourbon France, the Hapsburg Court or England. This dominant understanding of Russia was succinctly expressed by Montesquieu at the beginning of the eighteenth century, who characterized Russia as 'a land of absences' dating from even before the Enlightenment that placed it outside the west-European world.[4]

Even before Montesquieu, Peter and his chief propagandists such as Prokopovich and Shafirov, and then his successors, most notably Catherine II, sought to change this impression through the discourses of pro-West Occidentalism and the process of Westernization. The idea of enlightened absolutism according to which an enlightened monarchical state implemented reforms for the state's and the people's welfare without changing the fundamentals of the political system dominated eighteenth-century

Europe. Therefore, Russian monarchs of that century could argue that their country was broadly in sync with this political trend in the West given their implementation of pro-West Occidentalism. Prokopovich was the early propagator of this interpretation. Nonetheless, while Enlightenment-era thinkers, such as Voltaire, had praised Peter's and Catherine's efforts, autocracy, these 'absences' and serfdom did not allow for Western acceptance of Russia as a member of its club.

With the advent of the French Revolution and the idea of secular nationalism and republicanism, the gradual transition to constitutionalism and liberalism, and then, by the middle of the nineteenth century, the growing strength of socialism, the Russian autocracy found itself ever more distant from political and cultural understandings of this increasingly exclusive Western civilization. At the same time, it was progressively confronted by strong ideological and intellectual threats emanating from this West. The Pahlavi dynasty, in contrast, faced simultaneously these ideological threats from the time it was founded and at a time when ideas of monarchical enlightened absolutism seemed to be an anachronism and the challenge and power of mass politics rapidly expanded.

As the idea of an exclusive Western political civilization gained momentum in the nineteenth and early twentieth centuries, the West itself offered a path for possible Iranian redemption from Orientalization that was similar to the path offered by the concept of whiteness in Romanov Occidentalism. In Europe during the nineteenth century, when race became increasingly considered a cause of its rise, the Aryan race or Indo-European hypothesis became popular. Aryanism fulfilled two functions – it explained the rise of Europe in the international arena and traced European origins to the great civilizations of the Ancient East, specifically ancient Iran and India, and distinguished Europeans from Semitic peoples. The premise was that the Aryan race, to which Iranians belonged, was superior to the Semitic peoples. Aryanism and its designation of Persian as an Indo-European language provided the basis for separating Iranians and Iranian civilization from antiquity onward from Mesopotamian, Egyptian, Arab and other regional civilizations. Thus, according to Westerners Iranians were capable of once again obtaining civilization, of course as determined by the West.[5]

Ernest Renan (1823–92), whose works were read by nineteenth-century Iranian intellectuals, played an important role in this regard. He argued that 'the Arabs had enjoyed civilizational success because they had absorbed Persian culture' which was the heritage of the Iranian Sasanian Empire, where 'art and industry flourished', and was 'one of the most brilliant civilizations the Orient had ever known'.[6] Then came the Arab Muslim invasion that spread to the Near East, Africa and parts of Western Asia and beyond. The result for these conquered peoples was the loss of their cultural authenticity and civilizational decline.

> Anyone who has a little idea of our times sees clearly the real inferiority of Muslim countries, the decadence of the states governed by Islam and the intellectual vacuum of the races who take from it their culture and education ... the Berber, Sudanese, Circassian, the Malaysian, [and] the Egyptian ... having become Muslims are no longer Berbers, Sudanese, etc.

But, 'the only exception here is Persia. It was able to protect its genius'.[7] Although being Muslim and chaffing under elements of Arab 'culture', the Persians retained their intellectualism and therefore the right to return at one point to the pantheon of civilization, in other words, to the West. The view also exercised an impact on Russians' perceptions of their own identity and the relationship of that identity to the West. For example, the nineteenth-century Russian thinker Agafangel Krimskii stressed that 'the Persians will become our brothers' since unlike other Muslim peoples 'they have Aryan blood'.[8] In other words, Russians and Iranians were racially united by Aryanism, which also united them to the peoples of the West.

Before Renan, Hegel offered Russians and Iranians a possible path to salvation. Having proclaimed that the history of Western Europe was the history of civilization, freedom and progress, he made Russian and Iranian redemption, from the Western point of view, more difficult. In the eyes of Westerners Russia and Iran, lacking the Western historical and political trajectory, remained barbaric and Asiatic, although not to the same extent to which other countries were, such as India and China. Hegel condemned these polities, claiming they were 'unhistorical' and would remain at the lowest level of self-consciousness, despotism and morality. Having cut the East from history, Hegel was ambiguous in relation to both Russia and Iran. He suspected that although Iran was in the East, it could make the first step towards history, namely west-European civilization, since it belonged to the 'Caucasian, meaning European, race' although he bemoaned that this eastern branch of the European race had sunk into 'effeminacy' and its Aryan men had become 'the slaves of a weak sensuality'.[9] In regard to Russia he claimed 'this entire mass of people [the Slavs] remains excluded from our consideration', because they had not played 'a positive role in the world of reason and progress'. Yet, 'Russia possibly ... carries within its depths great possibilities for the development of its nature'.[10] In sum, while this racial argument strengthened those claims of Pahlavi and Romanov Occidentalism of a racial link, the importance of the character of the political system did not diminish.

Romanov and Pahlavi pro-West Occidentalism eventually gave way to anti-West Occidentalism whose emergence had several roots. The biggest difference between our case studies in this regard is temporal. In Russia the evolution of anti-West Occidentalism came in two major stages. During Nicholas I's reign anti-West Occidentalism, whose parameters and content were expressed by Uvarov's triad, was an immediate reaction to the Decembrist Revolt and an ideological discursive response to the triad of 1789 – *liberté, égalité, fraternité* – and the liberal ideas behind it. To be sure, the tsarist regime and Russia's elite shared a common European elite reaction of horror to the French Revolution. Nonetheless, the Decembrist Revolt was an elite-level insurrection against the monarchy's autocratic power. It was not a mass or large-scale urban rebellion expressing demands for political change or concerns about Occidentosis and the loss of cultural authenticity. Importantly, intellectual movements such as Slavophilism and subsequent derivative movements such as Pan-Slavism deepened and enriched this triad.

After Alexander II's interregnum the state again resorted to anti-West Occidentalism but broadened its appeal to the masses, specifically the peasants and rural migrants. During Nicholas I's reign these discourses targeted ideas of Western constitutionalism and forms of governance, portraying them as alien to the authenticity of Russian culture and national identity. During the reigns of the last two Russian emperors, anti-West Occidentalism, while still targeting the threat of liberal Western-style constitutionalism, also sought to manage the threat of the other modernity offered by the West, socialism and its Russian derivatives. In Iran the transformation to anti-West Occidentalism, caused by similar ideological challenges, occurred in one stage during the reign of Mohammad Reza Shah. Briefly put, everything had become more compressed. Similar to Nicholas II, but unlike Nicholas I, the shah lived in the twentieth-century world of mass politics and a wide range of competing ideologies while confronting the need to implement Westernization.

Anti-West Occidentalism reformulated state conceptions of the constitutive elements of authenticity of native culture and national identity as it proclaimed a struggle against manifestations of political and cultural Occidentosis. The Crown, once the propagator of pro-West Occidentalism and Westernization, now declared it was the source and defender of a sacralized and securitized native culture and national identity that was now positively contrasted with that of the West. Anti-West Occidentalism proclaimed that Iranian and Russian civilizations had a unique essence and authenticity, unchanging and eternal, threatened by an internal Occidentosis that carried an external geopolitical threat. In other words, cultural Darwinism remained but its ideological and discursive content was fundamentally changed. The domestic out-groups were those Iranians and Russians suffering from forms of Occidentosis, and the external out-group was the collective known as the West. Finally, anti-West Occidentalism proclaimed that criticism of the monarchy and its power and advocacy of the ideologies and modernities of the West were traitorous moves against the essence and authenticity of native culture and identity passed down through the generations.

The discourses of anti-West Occidentalism represented a transvaluation of values according to which the West's economic, material and technological advances, the criteria by which Iranians and Russians had determined their backwardness and admitted the West's superiority, were no longer portrayed as the sole criteria of overall civilizational and cultural success and superiority. For example, Rastakhiz publications stressed that collectivism, austere morality, spirituality and genuine social and familial relationships now constituted vital criteria of such superiority. These characteristics, portrayed as primordial elements of Iranian authenticity, would be defended by the Crown in the face of manifestations of Occidentosis—conspicuous consumption, materialism, hedonism and licentiousness, atomistic individualism and rabid commercialization. In short, it would prevent the emergence of Iranian Frankensteins, that civilizational monster created by the West. This bifurcation need not confirm to one's understandings of Western or Eastern civilizations in order to accept its political and ideological importance and significance.

However, anti-West Occidentalism had particular nuances that condition its 'anti-West' character. These nuances played a discursive game with the historical and contemporaneous definitions of the West that aimed to maintain the claims of a unique Russian and Iranian link to the West/Europe. The racial claims, whiteness in the Russian case and Aryanism in the Iranian one, remained, but understandings and views of the cultural West changed. The discourses of Nicholas I's reign portrayed Russia as the defender of the true cultural and political authenticity of Europe that had been infected with a phenomenon called Occidentosis with roots in the radical and liberal Enlightenment which burst onto Europe's political and international arenas in 1789. This position was revived during the reigns of Alexander III and Nicholas II. In this respect Nicholas II's comment that he loved Peter I less than his other ancestors given Peter's 'passion for Western culture and his trampling of pure Russian customs and mores' is indicative of the boundaries between official ideas of Europe, the West and Russia in the closing decades of the nineteenth century. Nicholas rejected the West's claims to represent true European political and cultural authenticity and its future.

It is worth underlining that the internal discourses of anti-West Occidentalism did not exercise a determinative influence on foreign policy. Russia aligned with Republican France and then Britain to counter the growing power of imperial Germany with which it shared, along with Berlin's ally, the Austro-Hungarian Empire, a long border while Pahlavi Iran remained in the West's geopolitical camp during the Cold War out of fear of the USSR that bordered it. The harmonization of domestic discourses of this Occidentalism with foreign policy would be implemented by the revolutionary regimes that succeeded these monarchical states. These Romanov and Pahlavi discourses also did not exercise a determinative influence on the policy of economic development in the context of global capitalism or even the basic thrust of educational policy.

Pahlavi anti-West Occidentalism declared that Iran by preserving the spiritual, moral and collectivist elements of Aryan authenticity offered the now crisis-ridden West a path to its salvation via a return to these true Aryan beliefs it had lost. The shah when speaking of cultural, political and moral crises afflicting the West called for an 'Aryan renaissance' that would return the West to its true self and put an end to its domestic decline and its wars. To be sure, this interpretation of Aryan authenticity and the cultural and moral decline of the West initially emerged in Pahlavi discourses in the late 1930s as relations between Iran and Nazi Germany expanded.

The argument that attributes solely or primarily power considerations to the emergence of anti-West Occidentalism tends to simplify the dynamics at play, reducing the problems facing these polities to a great struggle between authoritarianism and constitutionalism and democracy in the framework of the ineluctable march of all countries towards Western conceptions of the end of history. Obviously, protection of monarchical power was a permanent and constant goal. However, it entailed propagation of discourses that reflected and also shaped particular intellectual and societal trends and tendencies to the state's benefit. Suffice to say only briefly that two main trajectories in the immediate post-revolutionary periods of these two countries show the validity of the view that other elements and trends, existing next to and feeding off each other, were also important in the emergence of discourses within Pahlavi and Romanov anti-West Occidentalism that sought, however haphazardly, a unique Russian and Iranian modernity based on native social imaginaries and on the recognition of the need for change. First, bloody battles and political instability in the immediate years after the implosion of the Pahlavi and Romanov monarchies brought into relief the deep political and social divisions over issues such as authenticity of culture and national identity and proper paths of political and economic development. Second, the popularity of creating an authentically native modernity superior to those on offer by the West, defined as the liberal capitalist West in the USSR and liberal capitalism and socialism/communism in the IRI, underlined the intellectual and societal trends that eventually fed into discourses of anti-West Occidentalism.

In 1991 the USSR collapsed. The Cold War and the clash of the two major forms of modernity to emerge from the Enlightenment came to an end. Francis Fukuyama, reflecting the intellectual and public hubris in the West, proclaimed the end of history which meant 'the endpoint of mankind's ideological evolution and the universalization of Western liberal democracy as the final form of human government'.[11] To use the language of this study, political and cultural Occidentosis would now spread across the globe since other ideologies, including those based around national and religious identities, would be overshadowed and even relegated to the political periphery by Western liberal democracy, ideas of so-called cosmopolitan democracy with some roots in Kant's thinking and the international institutions claiming to represent such values.[12]

Soon after the publication of Fukuyama's book, Samuel Huntington published his controversial work *The Clash of Civilizations* that offered a fundamentally different interpretation not only of history but of the direction of international politics in the post-Cold War era. Looking at the immediate post-Cold War period Huntington saw other trends that threw into great doubt Fukuyama's conclusion that was derivative of Enlightenment thought.

> Peoples and nations are attempting to answer the most basic question humans can face: Who are we? And they're answering that question in the traditional way human beings have answered it, by reference to the things that mean the most to them. People define themselves in terms of ancestry, religion, language, history, values, customs and institutions.[13]

In other words, conceptions of authenticity of culture, national identity and civilization would characterize international and domestic politics. Most liberals, Western as well as non-Western, reacted negatively to a book that questioned the premises of the Enlightenment idea of the end of history and insisted that 'we all share a need to express our identity and have it recognized and respected' and 'that civilizations don't always coexist in harmony with each other, or that they often clash'.[14] Certainly, one need not accept some of Huntington's conclusions about 'the clash of civilizations', but the issues he raised go to the heart of not only Romanov and Pahlavi Occidentalisms but also ideas of identity that reach back to the imperial polities of antiquity.

The Pahlavi and Romanov states sought within the framework of both forms of Occidentalism to answer Huntington's questions while trying to respond to the power of the West through implementation of the process of Westernization. These questions also provide a key to understanding two concomitant developments behind the rise of anti-West Occidentalism. The first development was intellectual and even psychological. As the Pahlavi and Romanov polities pursed cultural Occidentalism intellectuals and society increasingly asked 'Who are we?' A backlash progressively grew against the discourses of pro-West Occidentalism that claimed a return to a temporarily lost authenticity. This process emerged and gained momentum in Russia from the reigns of Catherine II and Nicholas I and in Iran from the beginning of the 1960s. The intelligentsia and educated classes, exhibiting increasingly a crisis of identity, debated the constitutive elements of authenticity of culture and identity as cultural Occidentosis and the consequences of Westernization spread. While these non-state intellectual debates about these elements raged, broad agreement nonetheless existed about the type of threat faced, Occidentosis and its distortion of native paths of development.

These debates were politically dangerous for the Romanov and Pahlavi states for they undermined the discourses of pro-West Occidentalism and these states' claims to be the source and defender of authenticity of native culture and identity. The undermining of such claims brought the undermining of the monarchy's legitimacy. Nicholas I's comment to the arrested Samarin about the dangers of Slavophile thought and the banning by the Pahlavi state of al-e Ahmad's *Occidentosis* show that Pahlavi and Romanov monarchs understood the potential threats in these debates.

These concerns about the loss of native authenticity, however defined, are historically common, dating from before the issues of Westernization and Occidentosis, and powerfully emotive. The degree and extent of the West's power greatly intensified and politicized these concerns. Amin Maalouf, the Christian Lebanese author who lives in France and writes in French, in his work, *Deadly Identities* (*Les identités meurtrières*), summarized the matrix of these sentiments: 'At every turn they [non-Westerners] meet with disappointment, disillusion or humiliation. ... How can they not feel that their identities are threatened? That they are living in a world which belongs to others and obeys the rules made by others, a world where they are orphans, strangers, intruders or pariahs?'[15] Pro-West Occidentalism sought to deal and assuage these sentiments but eventually gave way to anti-West Occidentalism. Some of the elements of pro-West Occidentalism were not politically or even psychologically tenable for a substantial period of time.

The claims of Iranian racial–cultural primordial links with the West and of ancient Iranian cultural contributions to Western civilization were a logical and relatively coherent attempt to strengthen national self-confidence, pride and self-respect given the reality of the West's level of development and power, and to justify the transformations unleashed by the Pahlavi state. Yet, underpinning these claims of pro-West Occidentalism was official recognition of Iranian backwardness vis-à-vis the West and acceptance of the West's position as mentor to an Iran that sought to catch up with its racial cousins. In other words, an implicit and inherent foundation of these discourses was national shame.

The Russian experience in this regard differs somewhat from that of Iran. Karamzin's thinking noted earlier succinctly captured the emergence of this sense of collective shame that became a foundation of the discourses of anti-West Occidentalism. Yet, at times a hubristic sense of Russian power combined with this sense of shame, for example during Nicholas I's reign in light of the victories of 1812 and 1814 or during Alexander III's reign. This sense, however, dissipated and evolved into greater shame after major military defeats, such as the Crimean and Russo-Japanese Wars. In sum, in Iran and Russia the recognition of the West's superiority and position as a teacher to Russians and Iranians underpinned by claims of return to this lost racial–cultural authenticity gradually created shame. Shame is a difficult feeling to endure for any significant period of time.

This sense of shame that fed into state discourses of anti-West Occidentalism played a vital role in the revolutionary ideologies of both countries which proclaimed the construction of a modernity superior to the West's. Stalin in 1917 in the wake of the Bolshevik Revolution already stressed that this new progressive dynamic of Russia made her politically superior to the West: 'It is necessary to reject the exhausted perception that only Europe can show us the correct path'.[16] Anatoly Lunacharskii, the first minister enlightenment of the Russian Soviet Socialist Republic (1917–29) in a major article in *Izvestiia* titled 'The New Russian Person' proclaimed that the revolution proved that the West's stereotypes of Russians as barbarians, alcoholics, lazy and unworthy of modernization and industrialization were completely wrong. In fact, Russians had shown themselves to be superior.[17] The following section examines this issue in regard to the IRI.

The second reality that helped create the conditions for the emergence of anti-West Occidentalism was the sociocultural and economic changes of the practical process of Westernization. Certainly change can be perceived as positive or negative. However for a growing number of people these changes were perceived as alien, disruptive, disturbing, disorienting, elitist-imposed and otherwise objectionable and were attributed to Occidentosis, particularly in Iran where the rate of such change was faster than in Russia. Occidentosis was also held responsible for the fracturing, to extents not seen previously, of old forms of social relations and unity that only increased economic anxiety, a personal sense of loss and cultural disorientation. This fracturing, disorientation and anxiety had several causes: (a) heightened rural–urban migration; (b) the emergence and expansion of the working class and the spread of wage labour in the context of cyclical fluctuations and recessions characteristic of capitalism; (c) the expansion of new professional and industrial capitalist classes that exacerbated socio-economic and cultural cleavages; (d) the increased awareness of socio-economic inequality by the urban poor and rural migrants who in their villages and small towns did not realize the scale and growing levels of inequality and did not experience daily reminders of the living standards of the ostentatious *nouveau riche*; (e) a belief in moral and cultural decline mirroring trends in the West; and (f) the cultural bifurcation between the Occidentosis-ridden groups and those groups that regarded them as alien, elitist and pretentious.

Lurking behind these issues was also a growing sense of nostalgia. A consequence of these rapid and disorientating sociocultural and economic changes, nostalgia was based on the belief that what was once good was lost or would soon be lost and replaced by something alien and thus bad that separated a people not only from their authenticity of culture and identity, however conceived, but also from their familial heritage passed from one generation to another. Nostalgia is a natural feeling that increases in intensity as one grows older. However, in the face of rapid socio-economic and cultural changes feelings of nostalgia correspondingly rise, expressing individual and societal disorientation and anxiety. The attractiveness of nostalgia is the perceived stability, sense of belonging and thus superior and comfortable form of life it offers in the face of disruptive and disorientating changes. These feelings of nostalgia in turn evolve into a powerful political force that threatens the legitimacy of a state and elite perceived as responsible for these perceived negative and disorientating changes, the undermining of conceptions of authenticity and the attempts to separate an individual from one's heritage. Comparatively speaking these feelings held by Iranians and Russians during these periods and their expression in politics are integral to the human experience.

The varied discourses of Pahlavi and Romanov anti-West Occidentalism sought to address these trends and assuage these feelings as the state continued to implement Westernization, the catalyst of these feelings and trends. The discourses of anti-West Occidentalism proclaimed that authenticity of culture and national identity were now under existential threat from Occidentosis and, according to Rastakhiz ideology, a weapon in the arsenal of the West's imperialism. These discourses stressing this existential threat were to paper over class cultural and socio-economic antagonisms, reverse the sensed fracturing of social unity and create mass mobilization for defence of authenticity while pushing into the periphery those Iranians and Russians suffering from political Occidentosis which threatened the political and social order. This defence was led by the source and guardian of this authenticity, the Crown.

Discourses also responded to the growing sense of nostalgia. Rastakhiz attacks on claimed manifestations of Occidentosis in music, cinema, culinary habits, language, education, personal behaviour and morality, and architecture were all reflections of official recognition of nostalgia. To temper it and the belief that the state was responsible for the disorientation and anxiety that led to it, the Crown was portrayed as the leader in struggle against all disorientating forces attributed to Occidentosis and thus a sanctuary from them. It promised continuity and stability in people's lives and a sense of belonging, an encompassing collective while it worked to ensure that in the future these manifestations of Occidentosis would no longer exercise such an influence on society and the individual. In other words, the state was sending a message promising Western forms of economic and technological development and social welfare without disorientating change that fractured social unity and created a heightened sense of nostalgia while preserving moral and cultural authenticity and, of course, the monarchy. In Iran this amalgam of old and new was named the Great Civilization.

During Nicholas II's reign these attempts focused on propagation of the imagery of the *tsar-batushka*, the father and protector of real Russians, and the imagined tranquillity of pre-Petrine Russia. Given differences in historical time and circumstances the Romanov state never attempted the ideologization of the monarchy undertaken by the shah that eventually led to the Pahlavi millenarian project, although ideologization was slowly and haphazardly being taken by Nicholas II after the 1905 Revolution. After all, the challenge of mass politics was much greater for the shah in the second half of the twentieth century than for Nicholas II at the end of the nineteenth and beginning of the twentieth centuries. The *tsar-batushka* within this framework was to transcend class interests and demands and socio-economic and cultural rivalries among self-interested social groups while assuring an encompassing collective that was based on continuity and links to the past and authenticity that provided a sense of security and stability and a suitable path to the future. In other words, the goal for both systems was a national sense of wholeness and unity that would provide comfort in the face of the growing rate of social and economic changes society and individuals were facing as a result of Westernization.

Exogenous circumstances too played an important role in the trajectory of Occidentalism. The influence of Germany on trends in Russia and Iran has already been covered. Another element is the influence of major developments in the leading powers of the West on the shift towards anti-West Occidentalism. In other words, any explanation of the pivot towards anti-West Occidentalism needs to pay attention to how the imagery of a negative West emerged and eventually overshadowed the initial positive imagery of the West in intellectual and political discourses.

In the opinion of Russia's rulers and elite the French Revolution, the revolutionary terror and subsequent political instability that resulted in the rise and fall of Napoleon, the Revolution of 1830 and overthrow of Charles X, the Revolutions of 1848 that ended Louis-Phillipe's rule and spread revolutionary contagion to Prussia and the Austrian Empire, the overthrow of Napoleon III and the horror of the Paris Commune were clear manifestations of the dangers of the West's ideologies and their influence on the masses. Moreover, the siding of Britain and France with the Ottoman Empire against Russia in the Crimean War and Austria's refusal to support St. Petersburg turned public opinion against the imagined West and strengthened the appeal of Pan-Slavism and other nationalist groups. After all, as Danilevsky pointed out, these geopolitical decisions by the Western powers had shown that they did not consider Russia part of their club.

Adding to this tendency were increasing horror and disappointment of many Russian intellectuals with the trajectory of socio-economic and political development within the leading countries of the West. The wretchedness of French and British agricultural labourers and working class as these two countries underwent capitalist industrialization and experienced its cyclical fluctuations and recessions and the West's materialism and consumerism convinced many of the need to find a unique Russian path of development that corresponded with its authenticity and avoided these horrors. The influential Alexander Herzen provides perhaps the best example of this tendency. He initially was a Westernizer with socialist leanings. His experience in Britain and France, however, convinced him that the West and its modernities were not superior and appropriate for all societies. Living in Paris during the 1848 Revolution Herzen was horrified when popularly elected officials in the National Assembly applauded the killing of the wretched, rebellious poor by General Louis-Eugène Cavaignac. He concluded that these events showed that Western liberalism and capitalism were only a mechanism for the elite to protect their property and means for exploitation. The West could not be a model for the future: 'The past of Western Europe serves only as a lesson and only that. We do not consider ourselves the executers of your historical testament … your faith does not inspire us. We also do not think that the fate of humankind belongs to Western Europe'.[18] He thus made a philosophical return to Russia: 'When my last hope disappeared … as a result of the consequences of the horrific events [in Europe], instead of despair, in my chest returned a new belief … belief in Russia saved me at the edge of moral death'.[19] Herzen, and Russian intellectuals in general, held belief not in contemporaneous Russia, but in an imagined future Russia that, while holding true to the best elements of its cultural and moral authenticity, developed and created a modernity superior to those of the West.

Previous chapters showed how the emergence and evolution of intellectual and then state anti-West Occidentalism in Iran were a reflection of serious crises in the West that dissuaded Westerners and many non-Westerners that the West was not a universal civilization to be praised and followed. However, this projection of the negative West in competition with initial images of the positive West evolved more quickly in Iran than in Russia. Whereas during the nineteenth century only those who had travelled to and lived in the West could provide an understanding of its conditions, in Iran from the 1960s advances in media and print technology, along with expanded travel links, brought the negative West, almost on a daily basis, to an increasing domestic audience. This negative West was defined not only by conditions within Western countries but also the West's international politics. The war in Vietnam, French atrocities in Algeria, Western support for Israel against the Palestinians, US intervention in South America, graphically symbolized by its role in the overthrow of Salvador Allende in Chile and strong support of the military dictatorship of General Augusto Pinochet, and British policies in Northern Ireland are some of the major examples of this imperialism Iranians viewed through the prism of the US and UK role in the overthrow of Mossadegh.

The importance of the psychology and view of Iranian and Russian monarchs in regard to their countries' development cannot be underestimated. Shame at the base of pro-West Occidentalism gave way to expressions of confidence about strength and the continued upward trajectory of development. This rising confidence, again, need not correspond with reality in prospect or retrospect in order to accept its political influence. With the defeat of Napoleon Russia became the most powerful military force in continental Europe and the pillar of the Holy Alliance. Nicholas I's role in crushing revolutionary contagion in Austria and Prussia and protecting Russia from such political chaos only strengthened Russians' self-confidence in their country's power. In this context Count Benckendorff proclaimed that 'Russia's past is admirable. Her present is more than splendid. Her future is beyond the grasp of the most daring imagination' while Nicholas I implemented anti-West Occidentalism.

Despite defeats in the Crimean War and the Russo-Japanese War, Alexander III and Nicholas II retained great confidence about Russian power as they implemented discourses of anti-West Occidentalism. This sense comes out in the following incident. One day while Alexander III was fishing, his minister of foreign affairs asked if he would be willing to see the French ambassador. He retorted: 'When the Russian tsar is fishing, Europe can wait.' By the late 1960s the shah's confidence began noticeably to increase, as discussed earlier. In 1974 when the Ford administration was putting pressure on Iran not to support rises in oil prices, the shah during official visits to India and Australia retorted that 'nobody could wag a finger at us because we could wag back. ... Nobody can dictate to us'.[20]

With this context in mind we return to the question of the motives of Iranian and Russian monarchs for the shift to discourses of anti-West Occidentalism. One approach would be based on the belief that 'to study ideology is to study the ways in which meaning (or signification) serves to sustain relations of domination'. Thus, the monarchs' sole or primary motivating factor in propagating these discourses was protection of their power and a particular social and political order in the face of growing pressure from below to open the political system and give society civil and political rights. In other words, they sought power for power's sake. Without doubt power considerations played a vital role. However, does this mean that, for example, Mohammad Reza Shah and Nicholas II were not influenced by the psychological elements and contextual intellectual issues described above and therefore did believe in the discourses of anti-West Occidentalism? Or that Reza Shah or Catherine II did not really believe in enlightened absolutism and the discourses of pro-West Occidentalism given the socio-economic and cultural conditions of their countries? Any answer, positive or negative, is highly debatable. Taking this argument a step further it is necessary to consider that 'if values and beliefs are *not* bound up with power, then the term ideology threatens to vanishing point'.[21] The point is that values and beliefs are bound up with considerations of power and collectively they are inherent elements of any ideology.

By singularly focusing on considerations of power, we lose sight of the complexity of the circumstances that gave birth to the shift towards anti-West Occidentalism. Naturally, if the starting point of analysis is the belief in the thesis of the end of history in which liberal democracy and constitutionalism are the inevitable destinations of historical development, and thus since the period of the Enlightenment history is fundamentally the story of the struggle between the forces of political progress and its enemies the discourses of anti-West Occidentalism were just mechanisms used by decrepit monarchical systems and social orders in a last-ditch effort to preserve themselves in the face of progressive history on whose crest sat the masses. But, to deny the monarchs who propagated anti-West Occidentalism a sense of national pride that conditioned the desire to determine and/or protect authentically Iranian and Russian characteristics, of course as they defined them, in order to distinguish themselves and their polities from the West and prove their superiority to it is perhaps too cynical and goes against human psychology. After all, human psychology on various levels thrives on forms of tribalism and the mentality of 'us versus them', which also are fundamental elements of national identity and nationalism.

To deny the shah, the empress or Nicholas II, as well as their elites, the right to be critical and even horrified about sociocultural and moral conditions in the West and apprehensive about cultural and moral Occidentosis is difficult even while agreeing that they were very sceptical in regard to mass politics and sought to preserve the monarchy and its powers. After all, many of the grievances and criticisms targeting conditions in the West that appeared in discourses of anti-West Occidentalism, for example in Rastakhiz publications, were expressed in Western societies. Additionally, Mohammad Reza Shah and Nicholas II expressed in private their reservations about Western civilization, fears of Occidentosis and desire to determine and protect nativist authenticity as determined by them. In the end, giving due attention to the roles of considerations of power and self-interested social groups in the emergence and evolution of these two forms of Occidentalism should not deflect attention from the importance of the role of the imagery of the positive and negative West in these processes and from attempts, however haphazard, of the Romanov and Pahlavi states to achieve development while preserving authenticity of culture and identity and construct a nativist modernity.

Pahlavi and IRI Occidentalisms

The victory of the 1979 Revolution replaced Mohammad Reza Pahlavi's Great Civilization with Khomeini's Islamist utopia, and *homo Pahlavicus* with *homo Islamicus*. The sources and historiography with which the state constructed its conceptions of authenticity fundamentally changed. Aryanism and pre-Islamic Iranian Empire were succeeded by Islam and concepts of Islamic government. The defender and source of Iranian authenticity became Khomeini's concept of Islamic government, the rule of Islamic jurisconsult, and its pillar the *vali faqi* or, more commonly, the Great Leader of the Revolution (*rahbar-e moazam-e enqelab*). The clergy were portrayed as vigilant defenders of the rights of the people in the face of monarchical despotism since at least the Safavids and as the historical defenders of Iran's cultural and geopolitical borders in the face of the West's imperialism and Occidentosis.

Alongside these differences in late Pahlavi and IRI conceptions of the sources and historiographies of their respective conceptions of authenticity, strong similarities existed in the form and rhetoric these systems used to define the broad contours of that authenticity relative to the West. In other words, the 1979 Revolution did represent a fundamental break in understandings of the sources and accompanying historiography of state conceptions of authenticity of culture and identity but did not constitute a fundamental break in discourses depicting the Occident and the threat posed by Occidentosis to Iranian authenticity. Of course, the IRI intensified and took to new heights the discursive elements of the Pahlavi crusade against Occidentosis. Moreover, the IRI realized these elements in practical measures in domestic and foreign policy to an extent not yet contemplated by the Pahlavi state when it was overthrown. The IRI saw (a) a political Occidentosis; (b) a cultural and moral Occidentosis; (c) an Occidentosis as a weapon of the West's imperialism that sought to establish first cultural and then economic and political hegemony; and (d) the barbarization of people through their enslavement to Western technology and materialism.

Khomeini and his successor have argued that the Occidentosis-ridden person was one who took inspiration from the '–isms' of the West and rejected the authentically Iranian Islamic form of governance and clerical rule.[22] The Great Leader of the Revolution enjoys wide-ranging powers that are rationalized and justified by the threat posed by Occidentosis to the construction of *homo Islamicus* and an Islamist utopian modernity in this world in order to prepare for the coming of the Hidden Imam. According to Khomeini, 'It is the duty of this Leader to promulgate religion and instruct the people in the creed, ordinances, and institution of Islam' in order to achieve the Islamic millenarian project.[23] He stressed that Islam, the fount and framework for this modernity superior to anything on offer from the West, was complete.

> Islam has provided government for some 1,500 years. Islam has a political agenda and provides for the administration of the country. It is a religious-political faith.

Its worship contains politics and its political affairs contain worship. Islam has everything. The Koran has everything. It has politics, it has *fegh*, it has philosophy, it has everything. ... The one thing that is good for you, good for all of us is Islam and the rights of Islam. Islam is complete for many reasons, it will fix the world, it will fix your end and make all of us happy and prosperous.[24]

Shi'i religious narratives, symbolism and revolutionary action drove the struggle to 'fix the world' and create a utopia on this earth for the Hidden Imam, whose re-appearance would symbolize the 'end of history'. Ayatollah Montazeri, his heir apparent until 1988, proclaimed:

Islam takes into account the ideological and spiritual nature of humans as well as economic and political ones because life encompasses economic, political and family issues. Islam is complete. It thus deals with the time a person is born into this world until he/she leaves it.[25]

The path to creating the new peoples propagated by the imperial and IRI systems was long and necessitated elite leadership in light of negative tendencies and elements in mass culture. This sentiment was expressed by the shah when he said that he would act like the king of Sweden when Iranians acted like Swedes. Khomeini proclaimed: 'People are deficient. They need to be perfected and the Islamic government will lead the people towards this perfection' and create the conditions for the emergence of the *homo Islamicus* whom he called 'the perfect, complete person' (*ensan-e kamel*), and 'the exemplary humans' (*ensanha-ye nemune*) who were the bases of the ideal Islamic society. One of the most popular revolutionary songs was called 'The religion that constructs humans' (*din-e ensaansaaz*). This *din-e ensaansaaz* had 'to create a new Islamic person' without which there would be 'no hope that an Islamic Republic shall ever take shape in this country'. *Homo Islamicus* was superior to *homo Occidenticus* because 'the West and the culture of the West destroy human beings'.[26] Thus, Khomeini proclaimed that 'our revolution is a revolution in values'. This revolution would be led by the clergy on the basis of Islamic jurisprudence that 'is a real and complete theory for the governing of people and society from cradle to grave'. This responsibility fell to the clergy who 'not only must guide the nation, but also be involved in ruling because in the Islamic Republic it is the clergy that is entrusted with the duty of ensuring that the regime and society remains Islamic at all times'.[27]

The determination to construct from above a new person on the basis of state conceptions of authenticity of culture and national identity and the powers given to the pillar of the Pahlavi and IRI systems faced the threat of competing ideologies originating in the West and their derivative forms. Addressing this threat and justifying the state's wide-ranging powers, one system, calling itself democracy of the imperial system (*demokrasi-ye nezam-e shahanshahi*) and the other religious democracy (*mardomsaalaari-ye dini*), claimed that their respective political systems were manifestations of authentically Iranian forms of governance. Both claimed they established uniquely Iranian forms of democracy and constitutionalism that were superior to Western forms of governance. They were superior because they ensured political and social unity as the country under the leadership of the Crown and/or Turban built a modernity better than those offered by the West, a modernity the promised economic development and social welfare and the preservation of authenticity of culture and national identity that would protect Iran from the cultural and moral decline that afflicted the West.

Essential to this overall process in the IRI was the struggle against cultural and moral Occidentosis whose elements as recognized by the IRI mirrored to a significant degree those of the Rastakhiz period. One of the IRI's first steps was the launching of a cultural revolution that would combat signs of Occidentosis and create the *homo Islamicus*. Khomeini argued that an Occidentosis-ridden people failed 'to rely on their own potential and actual capabilities' and consequently they 'depend on Westerners for development and progress'. He had no doubt that the Occidentosis-ridden person was devoid of spirituality and imagined that the solutions to one's problems and challenges in this world could be found within Western civilization. Such people, having turned their backs on issues of morality and spirituality, recognized only materialism and hedonism whose pursuance was the goal of one's existence in this world.[28] Targeting such people, this revolution focused on the educational system, the factory producing this new Iranian.

IRI criticisms thrown at the Pahlavi educational system from primary school through university level were similar to Rastakhiz discourses and the conferences of the Revolution in Education. The IRI, acting on Khomeini's stress that 'we will uproot all Western cultural influences', established the Council of the Cultural Revolution and the Ministry of Enlightenment and Islamic Guidance that worked with the Ministry of Education. These institutions, among others, became responsible for the creation and coordination of the policies aimed at the creation of *homo Islamicus*. The goal is 'the expansion and promotion of the influence of Islamic culture and consolidation of the cultural revolution [and] the purification of academic and cultural establishments from materialistic ideas and the country's cultural environment from manifestations of Western influence'. The IRI, according to Khomeini,

> should transform our educational and judicial systems, as well as the ministries and government offices that are now run on Western lines or in a slavish imitation of Western models and make them compatible to Islam. Thus, we will demonstrate to the world true social justice and genuine cultural, economic and political independence.

In the wake of the 1979 Revolution universities were closed in order to implement this cultural revolution. He thundered: 'They are imperialist universities; and those they educate and train are infatuated with the West. ... [They] lack Islamic morality and fail to impart an Islamic education.' The universities during the Pahlavi period were 'propaganda arenas' that 'serve to impede the progress of Iranians' and 'are now effectively serving the West by brainwashing and miseducating our youth. ... They want us to remain in a state of perpetual dependence on the West.' A complete cultural revolution was needed so that 'education reflects the independent nature of Islamic thought' by 'cleansing itself of all Western values and influences'.[29] The issue of morality was quickly addressed with the imposition of gender separation across the educational system from primary to higher education.

But the nativization and Islamization of educational curriculum however required time. History was quickly rewritten to reflect the characteristics of the 'new person' and the historically positive role played by clerics. At all levels of education courses on Islamic history, thought and morality were mandatory as was Arabic, the language of the Prophet and Quran. The IRI under Khomeini's successor, Ayatollah Ali Khamenei, pushed for the Islamization of academic fields such as political science and the social sciences, especially after the 2009–10 demonstrations and the emergence of the Green Movement. In the wake of sporadic demonstrations at the beginning of 2018, he ordered an end to the teaching of English in primary and middle schools.[30]

The IRI called also for a return to Islamic Iranian authenticity in the world of art and culture.

> The only acceptable form of art is that of pure Mohammadian Islam, the Islam of the poor and the disinherited, the Islam of people who have suffered. ... Art is beautiful when it hammers modern capitalism and blood-sucking communism and annihilates the Islam of comfort, luxury and the painless wealthy ... in one word, the US form of Islam. ... The only kind of art [that is permissible] is the one that inculcates confrontation with the blood-sucking world-eaters headed by the USA and the USSR.[31]

Islamic Republic of Iran Broadcasting (IRIB), the successor of NIRT, was assigned to play the role of 'the public university' that would 'cultivate people able to struggle' against Occidentosis and the West's imperialism. It would save the authenticity of culture 'from Occidentosis and imperialism'.[32] *Filmfarsi* was banned while IRIB rejected those Western television programmes and series which the Party had condemned during the 1970s. The bans on nudity, pornography and 'sexual details' in films issued by the Pahlavi Ministry of Culture but, according to the Rastakhiz Party, were poorly enforced, were fully implemented by the IRI. Gone were Iranian and Western films with such images and any forms of even partial nudity, including bare-chested men and the wearing of shorts. Actresses and female newsreaders and reporters had to be clothed in proper Islamic fashion while actors and actresses were not allowed to touch members of the opposite sex in any way. Cinema and television were to serve either a didactic Islamic function or provide clean entertainment value but within a cultural framework corresponding to the criteria for the *homo Islamicus*. Vendors caught selling pirated DVDs of Western films are subject to short imprisonment and confiscation of their goods. If a vendor is caught with pornographic films, the ultimate manifestation of moral Occidentosis, the punishment can be death.

Pop music, the bane of *The Youth of Rastakhiz* and some social groups in Pahlavi society, was banned, as were public singing performances by females. In many cases the wealth and property of such pop singers were confiscated and many fled the country, including Dariush and Hayedeh, while those who remained, such as Delkash and Gugush, found themselves banned from performing. Traditional Iranian music, national as well as regional, were patronized by the state as part of the return to authenticity. Cabarets were closed as well as dancing clubs. However, from the time of the Khatami presidency (1997-2005) some of these restrictions were either eliminated or sporadically not implemented, depending on the political atmosphere and location in the country.

Without a doubt the IRI took the struggle against cultural and moral Occidentosis to heights, into the private sphere of Iranians, not contemplated by the Pahlavi state. Only during the reign of Reza Shah when Western forms of dress were imposed on men and women were forced to unveil did the Pahlavi state intensely involve itself in the people's private non-political sphere. The IRI entertained no qualms. Its ideology underpins a system that does not hold that most aspects of the private sphere exist outside the concern of the state.

> The moral goals of the Islamic Revolution include the creation of an appropriate environment for the development of moral virtues on the basis of belief and piety; the struggle with manifestations of corruption and moral perversion; and the creation of brotherly morality and conscience.

The moral norms stipulated by the Quran and religious traditions provided the base for this cultural revolution. Khomeini stressed that 'Islam and divine governments' had a direct interest in the personal behaviour of people. 'These governments have commandments for everybody, at any place, in any condition. If a person commits an immoral act next to his house, Islamic governments have issue with him'.[33]

Alcohol, prostitution and pre-marital sex were banned. Tehran's red-light district, *shahr-e nou*, was burned to the grown with some prostitutes suffering a similar fate. The revolutionary authorities rounded up prostitutes and executed a great number of them. The veiling of women became the greatest symbol of the return to Islamic authenticity and austere morality and the key victory in the struggle against moral Occidentosis and the construction of *homo Islamicus*. At issue is imposition not only of forms of veils covering a woman's hair but also forms of Islamic clothing that hides from public view the female figure. Institutions such as *Basij*, *Harasat* and then 'Enlightenment Patrols' (*gasht-e ershad*) whose personnel, usually several in number travelling around in specially marked vans, positioned themselves at various points in city streets and squares to reprimand or even arrest women not Islamically dressed, were to ensure adherence to the characteristics of *homo Islamicus* in the face of the threat of cultural and moral Occidentosis. Lastly, claiming that the Pahlavi legal system and specifically its approach to female rights were Occidentosis-ridden the IRI rolled back many of the steps taken by it. For example, a wife's rights in regard to divorce were severely reduced while a man's right to take additional wives was expanded.

In the initial decades after the 1979 Revolution men were banned from wearing shorts in public and short-sleeve shirts in public; the ban on shorts remains. Three-piece suits were maintained but ties, the claimed symbol of Occidentosis, are not part of official IRI fashion. Bureaucrats, newsreaders and reporters, ministers, teachers and professors and other professionals working for the government are not to wear it. Other elements of the struggle against moral and cultural Occidentosis included gender separation on public transportation and the use of law enforcement forces to break up parties and gatherings at which women were not veiled, dancing and music were present, and/or alcohol was being served. Moreover, patrols have the right to ask couples what their status is, although this has significantly declined since the Khatami years. Bans were on playing cards and dice since they were considered vital elements in the spread of gambling.

Important as these differences in policy are, in many ways fundamental elements of *homo Pahlavicus*, as conceived in opposition to negatively essentialized conceptions of the West, were and are shared by many elements of the IRI's *homo Islamicus*. Authentically Iranian, according to state discourses, both looked to the past for their fundamental characteristics of spirituality and morality. This spirituality, morality and consequent dominance of collectivist feelings in familial and social relationships placed them above the imagined *homo Occidenticus* – vain, selfish, materialistic, suffering from conspicuous consumerism, hedonism and atomized individualism. Concomitantly, *homo Islamicus*, as well as *homo Pahlavicus*, looked to the future, taking in those economic and technological elements from the West needed to defend the country's geopolitical and cultural borders in the face of the existential threat of the West. Just as the shah's emphasis on Islamic morality and spirituality propagated as derivative of Zoroastrianism, and his claims as a defender of the authenticity of Iranian culture in the face of the threat of Occidentosis are frequently regulated to the periphery in understandings of his reign, Khomeini's and the IRI's position in regard to Western technology and economic development are at times understated. In many ways the IRI's position in regard to the adoption and use of Western technology and 'machines' is significantly similar to the discourses of the shah and the Rastakhiz Party.

Khomeini did not reject the use of Western technology in the process of modernization or in people's everyday lives; this technology would be harnessed to these projects of construction of the new modernity. He stressed: 'We Muslims are unfortunately in need of Western science and technology'. But he set a framework for its adoption and use.

> We are not opposed to cinema, to radio, or to television; what we oppose is the vice and the use of the media to keep our young people in a state of backwardness and dissipate their energies. We have never opposed these features of modernity in themselves, but ... unfortunately [in Iran] they were used not in order to advance civilization, but in order to drag us into barbarism. ... What we oppose is licentiousness and vice.[34]

The shah had voiced the same sentiments: 'The taking of modern technology ... does not mean adopting its [the West's] moral characteristics, customs, and rituals'.[35]

An essential part of the revolutionary ideology was achievement of social justice and emphasis on Islam's capacity to 'solve the problems of poverty' and 'to understand that first the problems of the poor must be dealt with'.[36] Khomeini stressed before and after the Revolution that it is 'your Islamic duty to take from the rich and give to the poor'.[37] The Revolution was to serve the interests of the underprivileged. The shah, detaching Islam as a religion from the interests of the clerical class, argued that his White Revolution, despite clerical opposition, was fulfilling one of the main elements of Islam, the achievement of social justice that would strengthen personal spirituality and morality. Poverty and social justice not surprisingly have been highly sensitive political issues for the Pahlavi and IRI states.

Khomeini argued that the Revolution he was leading was primarily a revolution in values set in opposition to Occidentosis and on preparing one for the next world. Despite the stress on social justice and criticism of the Western capitalist and Soviet economic models, Khomeini maintained his stress on spiritual issues, seeing in them the true goals of the revolution. He famously remarked that the Revolution was fought not 'over the price of watermelons'. However, in 1989 his successor, Ayatollah Khamenei, underlined a shift that placed greater emphasis on economic development and raising living standards.

> Islam has plans for both this world and the afterlife. ... If we imagine that a utopian society does not deal with material problems and the people's well-being, we are saying that religion, morality, and spiritualism do not concern themselves with the people's lives. This is against the explicit calling of Islam and the constitution. Moves toward the resolution of people's problems and the paving of the way to a healthy and prosperous life in which the population enjoys abundance, access to goods at cheap prices, and [social] facilities, is an Islamic duty on the shoulders of all the country's officials. This is possible and without doubt a part of the ideals of Islam and our dear Imam [Khomeini].[38]

The evolution of Pahlavi and IRI discourses reached the same destination via slightly different paths. A decade after launching his White Revolution that emphasized 'the material problems and well-being of the people' the shah announced:

> I am giving much attention to the issue that our future cannot be based on materialism and technology, but rather on strong spiritual principles that will prevent society from falling into consumerism and materialism ... material progress of society must be accompanied by humanistic and spiritual aspects.[39]

IRI discourses initially focused primarily on these 'humanistic and spiritual aspects' only to evolve and equally emphasize these issues a decade after the Revolution's victory.

The struggle against the imperialism of the West was a motto integral to discourses of both the Rastakhiz period and the IRI, a consequence of the history of imperialism in the country since the first quarter of the nineteenth century. Both propagated the idea that the West's new imperialism targeted the country's cultural borders with Occidentosis as the first step in dividing the people from their authentically Iranian political systems in order to establish economic and geopolitical hegemony. While the shah urged people not to become ridden with Occidentosis, the empress warned of a foreign cultural invasion and Rastakhiz publications spoke of a cultural attack (*hojum*) of the West, the IRI strove to mobilize the people against the West's cultural invasion, (*tahajom-e farhangi*) 'Global [Western] Arrogance' and 'Global hegemony'.[40] Both systems frequently proclaimed that the West was determined to retard and oppose Iranian development. To achieve this goal the West had to weaken the imperial system and the IRI and drive a wedge between the people and the system. Similar to the Pahlavi state, Khomeini and the IRI believed that the imperialism of the West used Occidentosis to attract to itself the youth and the intellectual class.[41] Khomeini warned that the West sought 'to abuse sacred principles such as progress, democracy, civilization, and freedom' in order to achieve its goal of hegemony.[42] The people had to be vigilant:

> Don't think that relations with the USA or ... USSR, will somehow benefit us. This [situation] is similar to the relationship between the sheep and wolf. This type of relationship does not benefit the sheep. They [Westerners] want to cheat and swindle us. They do not want to provide us with anything good and beneficial.[43] The one thing I will repeat here is that we must not blindly emulate the West and its political system. Why should we do this? After all, what has the West ever done for thus that we should emulate it? Is the current revolution an imitation [of the West]? Was it not implemented by authentic Iranian thought?[44]

Certainly, IRI discourses on the West and in particular on the United States and the United Kingdom were more intense, sustained and harsh than those of the Rastakhiz period. The United States became the Great Satan, and the old imperial power, Britain, became the Small Satan.[45] These anti-West discourses were expressed in IRI foreign policy to an extent never contemplated by the shah.

One reason for this is the difference in the revolutionary characters of the late Pahlavi and IRI states. The IRI, despite its power structure, has accepted the idea of mass politics. While feeding off the imagery of mass politics, the IRI manages it through ideology, institutional power, such as that exercised by the Leadership Office and Revolutionary Guards, and regular elections to institutions such as the Majles and presidency whose candidates must be vetted by the Guardians' Council. The shah, also faced with the challenge of mass politics, tried to achieve a similar confluence of state power and imagery and management of mass politics with the establishment of the Rastakhiz Party. An important element in this confluence was the IRI's mass politicization of foreign policy and use of the imagery of external enemies to mobilize the masses to its benefit. Previous chapters showed that the late Pahlavi state had made significant moves in this direction, particularly in the Rastakhiz period.

In conclusion, Pahlavi discourses of anti-West Occidentalism were not haphazard and occasional, blurted out by political figures, state intellectuals and publicists in response to a particular event or mood. Rather, they were at the centre of a systematic and organized fundamental change in the state approach to the place of the West in its conceptions of the authenticity of Iranian culture and national identity. The Pahlavi state not only was cognizant of and responsive to particular intellectual and popular developments, but became concerned, belatedly some could argue, with 'the very complex process dealing with the accommodation of social change in the context of the Iranian cultural and historical experience'. Given this, the axioms of Westernized and blindly Westernizing shah and reactionary and blindly anti-Occident Ayatollah and of a fundamental break made by the Revolution in state discourses on the West and

Occidentosis need to be revised. This revision can play a role in the normalization of the study of the Pahlavi period. It also could lead to a greater focus on issues that transcend the 1979 Revolution, such as state and societal responses to the challenges associated with responding to the power of the West, concerns about authenticity of culture and national identity in the face of social, cultural and economic transformations brought about by changes implemented to respond to this power and their influence on and consequences for politics and development.

Notes

Preface

1. Montesquieu, édition de Jean Starobinski, *Lettres Persanes* (Paris, 2017), Letter XXX, pp. 102–3.
2. Ibid., Letter LIX, p. 151.

Chapter 1

1. *Bayan*, 17/18, (1368/1989).
2. Behrooz Ghamari-Tabrizi, *Foucault in Iran* (Minneapolis, 2016), pp. 60–2.
3. Mohammad Reza Pahlavi, *Mission for My Country* (London, 1961), p. 132.
4. 'Introduction', Françoise Barrès-Kotobi and Mortéza Kotobi, trans., in Djalal Al-e Ahmad, *L'Occidentalite* (Paris, 1988), p. 12.
5. Cyrus Schayegh, 'Seeing Like a State: An Essay on the Historiography of Modern Iran', *International Journal of Middle East Studies* 42 (2010).
6. Ibid., p. 37.
7. Ali Mirsepassi, *Intellectual Discourse and the Politics of Modernization* (Cambridge, 2000), p. 73.
8. See Ali-Reza Isfahani, *Farhang va siasat-e Iran dar asr-e tajaddod* (Tehran, 1386/1997), Abbas-Ali Zanjani, *Enqelab-e islami va risheha-ye an* (Tehran, 1386/1997) and Daftar-e Rahbari, *Engelab-e Islami* (Tehran, 1388/2009).
9. See Mehrzad Boroujerdi, *Iranian Intellectuals and the West* (Syracuse, 1996) and Hamid Dabashi, *Theology of Discontent: The Ideological Foundation of the Islamic Revolution in Iran* (New York, 2005).
10. Zhand Shakibi, 'Pahlavism: The Ideologization of Monarchy in Iran', *Journal of Politics, Religion, & Ideology*, 14 (2013).
11. Jack Hayward, *Fragmented France: Two Centuries of Disputed Identity* (Oxford, 2007).
12. Zhand Shakibi, *Rusie va qarbangari* (Tehran, 1397/2018).
13. François Furet, Elborg Forster, trans., *Interpreting the French Revolution* (Cambridge, 1981), p. 1.
14. See Gholam Reza Afkhami, *The Life and Times of the Shah* (Berkeley, 2009); Ervand Abrahamian, *A History of Modern Iran* (Cambridge, 2008).
15. Furet, *Interpreting...*, p. 15.
16. Leon Trotsky, *Literature and Revolution* (Ann Arbor, 1960), p. 94.
17. See Richard Pipes, *Russia Under the Old Regime* (New York, 1974); Galina P. Naumova, *Istorigrafiia Istorii Rossii* (Moscow, 2008); Alexander Yanov, *Drama Patriotizma v Rossii, 1855-1921* (Moscow, 2009); Peter Duncan, *Russian Messianism* (London, 2000).
18. Martin Malia, *Russia under Western Eyes* (Cambridge, MA, 1999), p. 5.

19   Dominic Lieven, *Empire* (New Haven, 2000), p. 219.
20   See Fakhreddin Azimi, *The Quest for Democracy in Iran* (Cambridge, MA, 2008) and Ali Gheissari and Vali Nasr, *Democracy in Iran: History and the Quest for Liberty* (Oxford, 2009).
21   Ali Rahnema, *Superstition as Ideology in Iranian Politics* (Cambridge, 2011).
22   Christopher Coker, *The Rise of the Civilizational State* (London, 2019), pp. 72–3.
23   Andrew Scott Cooper, *The Fall of Heaven* (New York, 2016), p. 9.
24   Jahangir Amuzegar, *The Dynamics of the Iranian Revolution* (Albany, 1991), p. 39.
25   Nikki Keddie, *The Roots of Revolution* (New Haven, 1981), p. 177.
26   Dariush Ashuri, *Ma va moderniat* (Tehran, 2004), p. 311.
27   *OHFIS*, Pahlbod, Vol. 2, pp. 43–4.
28   Liah Greenfeld, *Nationalism: Five Roads to Modernity* (Cambridge, MA, 1992), pp. 15–18.
29   Manuchir Honarmand, *Pahlavism: Maktab-e nou* (Tehran, 1345/1966); *Shahanshahi-ye Mashruteh va Dohezar va Pansad Saleh-ye Iran:Jeld-e Dovum-e Pahlavism* (Tehran, 1346/1967); *Dilektik-e Nemudha-ye Melli dar Tarikh-e Farsi: Jeld-e Sevvum-e Pahlavism* (Tehran, 1346/1967); *Avalin va Akharin-e Hokumat-e Jahani: Ketab-e Chaharom az Falsafeh-ye Pahlavism* (Tehran, n/a).
30   See Ali Ansari, *Modern Iran* (London, 2010) and *The Politics of Nationalism in Modern Iran* (Cambridge, 2012); Dabashi, *Theology...*; Abrahamian, *A History...*; Nikki Keddie, *Modern Iran* (New Haven, 2003).
31   Dabashi, *Theology...*, p. 10.
32   *Rastakhiz*, (1), 21 April 1975.
33   Borujerdi, *Iranian Intellectuals...*, p. 14.
34   Quoted in W. Bruce Lincoln, *Nicholas I* (Bloomington, 1978), p. 153.
35   Vasilii Kluchevskii, *Russkaia Istoriia* (Moscow, 2012), pp. 652–3.
36   Ian Buruma and Avishai Margalit, *Occidentalism: The West in the Eyes of Its Enemies* (New York, 2004), pp. 10–11.
37   For reviews see Akeel Bilgrami, 'Occidentalism, the Very Idea: An Essay on Enlightenment and Enchantment', *Critical Theory* 32, 3 (2006); Bruce Robbins, 'Not without Reason: A Response to Akeel Bilgrami', *Critical Theory* 33, 3 (2007); Leen Boer, 'Struggling with –isms: Occidentalism, Liberalism, Eurocentrism, Islamism', *Third World Quarterly* 25, 8 (2004).
38   Coker, *The Rise...*, p. 203.
39   Xiaomei Cheng, *Occidentalism: A Theory of Counter Discourse in Post-Mao China* (Oxford, 1995), pp. 4–6.
40   Walter Mignolo, *Local Histories/Global Designs* (Princeton, 2000), pp. 29–30 and *The Darker Side of the Renaissance* (Princeton, 1995).
41   Feodor Dostoevskii, *Dnevik Pisatelia* (St. Petersburg, 1996), Vol. 4, pp. 351–2.
42   Meltem Ahiska, *Occidentalism in Turkey: Questions of Modernity and National Identity in Turkish Radio Broadcasting* (London, 2010), pp. 5–6.
43   See Theodore Von Laue, *The World Revolution of Westernization* (Oxford, 1987); Nils Gilman, *Mandarins of the Future: Modernization Theory in Cold War America* (Baltimore, 2007) and Charles Taylor, *Modern Social Imaginaries* (Durham, 2004). Before the term 'Westernization', the terms 'achievement of progress' and 'Europeanization' were used. By the mid-twentieth century the term 'modernization' came to replace Westernization. Towards the end of the twentieth century, the seemingly neutral term 'globalization' came to describe the same processes.
44   Pahlavi, *Mission...*, p. 135.

45 David Brandenburger, *National Bolshevism: Stalinist Culture and the Formation of Modern Russian Identity, 1931-1956* (Cambridge, MA, 2002). See also Anthony Smith, *National Identity* (London, 1994).
46 Eric Davis, *Memories of State: Politics, History, and Collective Identity in Modern Iraq* (Berkeley, 2005), pp. 4-5. See also Aleksei Millar and Mikhail Lipman, eds., *Istoricheskaia Politika v XXI veke* (Moscow, 2012).
47 Zachary Lockman, *Contending Visions of the Middle East: The History and Politics of Orientalism* (Cambridge, 2010), p. 12.
48 Andrei Nikitin, *Osnovaniia Russkoi Istorii* (Moscow, 2001).
49 Nikolai Shilder, *Imperator Nikolai Pervyi* (St. Petersburg, 1908), pp. 700-2.
50 Mohammad Reza Pahlavi, *Beh sui-ye Tammadon-e Bozorg* (Tehran, 1356/1977), pp. 252-3.
51 Larry Woolf, *The Inventing of Eastern Europe: The Map of Civilization on the Mind of the Enlightenment* (Stanford, 1994).
52 Coker, *The Rise...*, p. 62.
53 Daniel Woolf, *A Global History of History* (Cambridge, 2011).
54 Woolf, *A Global History of History*, p.46.
55 Gleb Musikhin, *Rossiia v nemetskom zerkale* (St. Petersburg, 2002), p. 231.
56 See Stephen Kern, *The Culture of Time and Space, 1880-1918* (Cambridge, Mass, 2003); Joachim Radkau, *Das Zeitalter der Nervosität. Deutschland zwischen Bismarck und Hitler* (Munich, 2000).
57 Michael Burleigh, *Moral Combat: A History of World War 2* (London, 2010), p. 76.
58 Aleksei Liberman, ed., *Moskovia i Evropa* (Moscow, 2000) and Mikhail Sukhman, ed., *Inostrantsi o Drevnei Moskve. Moskva XV-XVII vekov* (Moscow, 1991).
59 See Esther Kingston-Mann, *In Search of the True West* (Princeton, 1998).
60 Saree Makdisi, *Making England Western: Occidentalism, Race, and Imperial Culture* (Chicago, 2014), p. 10.
61 Makdisi, *Making England Western: Occidentalism, Race, and Imperial Culture*, p. 12.
62 Eugen Weber, *Peasants into Frenchmen: The Modernization of Rural France, 1870-1914* (Stanford, 1976).
63 David Bell, *The Cult of the Nation in France: Inventing Nationalism, 1680-1800* (Cambridge, MA, 2003), p. 208.
64 Cemil Aydin, *The Politics of Anti-Westernism in Asia: Visions of World Order in Pan-Islamic and Pan-Asian Thought* (New York, 2007), p. 7.
65 Jennifer Pitts, *A Turn to Empire: The Rise of Imperial Liberalism in Britain and France* (Princeton, 2005).
66 Aydin, *The Politics...*, p. 8.
67 Kluchevskii, *Russkaia Istoriia*, pp. 482-4.
68 Anthony Smith, *The Ethnic Origins of Nations* (London, 1986), p. 2.
69 Smith, *The Ethnic Origins of Nations*, p. 3.
70 Darrin M. McMahon, *Enemies of the Enlightenment: The French Counter-Enlightenment and the Making of Modernity* (Oxford, 2001), p. 22.
71 McMahon, *Enemies of the Enlightenment: The French Counter-Enlightenment and the Making of Modernity*, p. 26.
72 Ibid., p. 32.
73 Suetonius, *On National Costume* quoted in Hadrill, *Rome's Cultural...*, p. 37.
74 Michael Grant, 'Introduction', in Cicero, *On the Good Life* (London, 1971), p. 16.
75 Cicero, C. D. Yonge, trans., *Treatise De Finibus and Tusculan Disputations* (London, 1875), pp. 54-5.

76 Cicero, H. Rackham, trans., *On Ends* (London, 1931), pp. 11-13.
77 Jalal Khaliqi Matlaq, *Sohanha-ye dirine* (Tehran, 1386/2007), pp. 247-50. Ali Panhai, *Sorudekhane vahdat-e melli va hamase-ye melli-ye Iran* (Tehran, 1379/2000).
78 Abolqasem Ferdowsi, Dick Davis, trans., *Shahnameh* (New York, 2007), p. xxxiii.
79 *Farmaeshate alihezrat homayun Shahanshah aryamehr* (Tehran, 1354/1975), p. 201.
80 Kluchevskii, *Russkaia Istoriia*, p. 251.
81 Mohammad Tarsusi, Hossein Esmaili, ed., *Abu Moslemname* (Tehran, 1381/2002).
82 Kathryn Babayan, *Mystics, Monarchs, and Messiahs: Cultural Landscapes of Early Modern Iran* (Cambridge, MA, 2002), p. xxxiv. See also Mohammad Aram, *Andisheh-ye tarikhnegari-ye asr-e safavi* (Tehran, 1386/2007).
83 Kluchevskii, *Russkaia Istoriia*, pp. 710-19.
84 Malkom Khan, Hejatollah Asil, ed., *Resalih-haiye Mirza Malkom Khan* (Tehran, 1381/2002), pp. 371-401.
85 Quoted in Feredyoun Adamiat, *Fekr-e Azadi* (Tehran, 1345/1966), pp. 110-19.
86 Khan, Prince Malcom, 'Persian Civilisation', *Contemporary Review* 59 (1891), p. 243.
87 Abdolreza Hushangmahdavi, ed., *Engelab-e Iran be ravayet-e BBC* (Tehran, 1372/1993), p. 139.
88 Charles Taylor, *Social Imaginaries* (Durham, 2004), pp. 1-2, 23-8.

Chapter 2

1 Sergei Soloviev, *Istoriia Rossii s drevneishikh vremen* (Moscow, 1991), Vol. 13, pp. 18-23.
2 Marshall Poe, *A People Born in Slavery: Russia in Early Modern European Ethnography, 1476-1748* (Ithaca, 2001), pp. 20-2.
3 Igor Shaskolskii, *Borba Rusi protiv krestonosnoi agressii na beregakh Baltiki v XII-XIII vv.* (Leningrad, 1978).
4 Wil Van Den Brecken, *Holy Russia and Christian Europe* (London, 1999), p. 125.
5 Dmitrii Trenin, *Integratsiia i Identichnost: Rossiia kak 'novii Zapad'* (Moscow, 2006), p. 172. See also Fritof Shenk, *Aleksandr Nevskii v russkoi kulturnoi pamaiti* (Moscow, 2007); Aleksandr Lure, *Aleksandr Nevskii* (Moscow, 1939).
6 Sergei Lavrov, 'Istoricheskaia perspektiva vheshnei politiki Rossii', *Rossiia v globalnoi politike* 2 (2016).
7 N. N. Kostomarov, *Russkaiia istoriia v zhizneopisaniakh ee glavneishikh deiietelei* (Moscow, 2016), p. 216.
8 Some disagreement exists concerning the authorship of the conception of the Third Rome. Some consider Filofei to be its original author, while others believe it was Metropolitan Zosima.
9 Naumova, *Istorigrafiia...*, pp. 32-43.
10 R. G. Skrinnikov, *Tretii Rim* (St. Petersburg, 1994), p. 87.
11 Ya Lure, ed., *Perepiska Ivana Groznogo s Andereem Kurbskim* (Moscow, 1993), pp. 229-30.
12 *Pamiatniki literaturi drevnei rusi: XII vek* (Moscow, 1980), pp. 615-19.
13 A. S. Demin, 'Puteshestvie dushi po zagrobnomy miru', *Rossiiskii literaturovedcheskii zhurnal*, Vol. 5-6 (1994).
14 A. V. Borodon, *Inozemtsy - ratnye lyudi na sluzhbe v moskovskom gosudarstve* (Petrograd, 1916), p. 7.

15 Kluchevskii, *Russkaia Istoriia*, pp. 412–13.
16 Sergei Lobachev, *Patriarkh Nikon* (St. Petersburg, 1998), p. 201.
17 Petr Romanov, *Rossiia i Zapad* (Moscow, 2015), p. 299.
18 6 August 1675, *Polnoe sobranie zakonov*, Vol. 1 (St. Petersburg, 1830), p. 967.
19 Ibid., p. 709. See also Galina Talina, *Vibor Puti* (Moscow, 2010).
20 Lindsey Hughes, *The Romanovs: Ruling Russia 1613-1917* (London, 2009), p. 39.
21 Alexander Bordanov, *Letopits i istoriki kontsa XVIII veka* (Moscow, 1994), pp. 92–7.
22 See Paul Bushkovitch, 'The Formation of a National Consciousness in Early Modern Russia', *Harvard Ukrainian Studies* 10, 3/4 (1986) and Lee Trepanier, *Political Symbols in Russian History: Church, State, and the Quest for Order and Justice* (Lanham, MD, 2010).
23 Alexander Pavlov, *Istorichiskii Sekulyarizatsii Tserkovnoi Zemlii v Rossii 1503-1508* (Moscow, 1978).
24 Serhii Plokhy, *Lost Kingdom* (New York, 2017), p. 76.
25 Lobachev, *Patriarkh Nikon*, p. 200.
26 V. F. Ikonomov, *Nakaun Reform Petra Velikago* (Moscow, 1903), p. 132.
27 N. F. Kapterev, *Patriarkh Nikon i Tsar Aleksei Mikhailovich* (St.Petersburg, 1912), Vol. 2, p. 181.
28 Igor Andreev, *Aleksei Mikhailovich* (Moscow, 2003), p. 371.
29 Ikonomov, *Nakaun...*, p. 150.
30 Andreev, *Aleksei Mikhailovich...*, p. 368; SGGD, Vol. 4, No. 28.
31 Ikonomov, *Nakaun...*, p. 153.
32 Talina, *Vibor Puti*, pp. 343–82.
33 Robert Crummey, *The Old Believers and the World of the Antichrist* (London, 1971), p. 16.
34 Plokhy, *Lost...*, p. 94.
35 Ikonomov, *Nakaun...*, p. 161.
36 Nicholas Molchanov, *Diplomatiia Petra Pervogo* (Moscow, 1986), p. 428.
37 *Petr Veliki v ego izrecheniakh* (Moscow, 1991), p. 88. L. N. Maikov, ed., *Raskazi Nartova o Petre* (St. Petersburg, 1891), p. 154.
38 March 1690. Quoted in: Nikolai Pogodin, 'Peter Pervii: pervie godi edimoderyavia, 1689-1694', *Russkii Archiv*, 1 (1879), 11.
39 See Sergei Resyanskii, *Tserkovno-gosudarstvennaia reforma Petra I* (Moscow, 2009).
40 *Petr Veliki v ego izrecheniakh*, p. 97.
41 Feofan Prokopovich, *Slova i rechi* (St. Petersburg, 1760), Vol. 1, pp. 7–8.
42 Viktor Smirnov, *Feofan Prokopovich* (Moscow, 1994), p. 79.
43 Maikov, *Raskazi...*, p. 57.
44 Gregorii Esipov, *Raskolnichnii Dela XVIII Stoletiia* (St. Petersburg, 1861), pp. 72–8.
45 Solovev, *Istoriia Rossii*, Vol. 8, pp. 573–5.
46 Quoted in Pavel Verkhovskoi, *Dukhovnii Kollegiia i Dukhovnii Reglament* (Rostov-na-Donu, 1916), pp. 18–24.
47 LOI, f.270, d.106, l.409.
48 Verkhovoskoi, *Dukhovnii...*, p. 48.
49 'Zapiski Vebera o Petre Vilikom i ego preobrazovaniakh', *Russkii Arkhiv* (1872), 1074–5.
50 Hughes, *Russia in the Age...*, p. 322.
51 'Ucheniia zapiski imperatorskogo kazanskago universiteta' (Kazan, 1873), p. 552.
52 S. P. Luppov, *Kniga v Rossii v pervoi chetverti XVIII veka* (Leningrad, 1973), p. 55.

53 A. Alferov and A. Gruzenskii, *Russkaia Literatura XVIII Veka: Khrestomatiia* (Moscow, 1907), pp. 39–50.
54 The complete text is included in G. H. Moiseevoi, *Russkie Povesti Pervoi-Treti XVIII Veka* (Leningrad, 1965), pp. 191–210.
55 Feofon Prokopovich, *Sochineniia*, I. P. Eremin, ed. (Leningrad-Moscow, 1961), pp. 38–48.
56 Richard Wortman, *Scenarios of Power: Myth and Ceremony in Russian Monarchy* (Princeton, 1995), Vol. 1, pp. 44–7.
57 Dmitry Likhachev, 'Religion: Russian Orthodoxy', in Nicholas Rzhevsky, ed., *The Cambridge Companion to Modern Russian Culture* (Cambridge, 1998), p. 50.
58 Lord Frederic Hamilton, *The Vanished Pomps of Yesterday* (London, 1919), p. 98.
59 Evgenii Anisimov, *Afrodita vo vlasti. Tsarstvovanie Elizaveti Petrovoni* (Moscow, 2010), p. 151.
60 Wortman, *Scenarios*..., p. 86.
61 Catherine II, *O Velichii Rossii* (Moscow, 2003), p. 72.
62 See also Alain Besançon, 'Voyage en Sibérie', *Cahiers du monde russe et soviétique*, 5, 2 (1964).
63 Catherine II, *Sohineniia Imperatritsii Ekaterini*, Vol. 7 (St. Petersburg, 1901).
64 Vera Proskurina, *Mifi imperii: Literatura i vlast' v epokhi Ekaterini II* (Moscow, 2006), p. 176.
65 L. V. Domanovskii, ed., *Istoricheskie pesni XIX veka* (Leningrad, 1973), pp. 28–31, 164–91.
66 Andrei Zorin, *Kormia dvuglavnogo orla* (Moscow, 2004). See also Marlène Laruelle, *Mythe aryen et rêve impérial dans la Russie du XIXe siècle* (Paris, 2005).
67 Vera Proskurina, *Imperiia pera Ekaterini II* (Mosow, 2017), pp. 163–4.
68 Janet Hartley, *Alexander I* (London, 1994), p. 155.
69 Adam Olearii, *Opisanie puteshestviia v Moskoviyu* (Moscow, 2001), p. 130.
70 Ikonomov, *Nakaun*..., pp. 154–7, 237, 276.
71 Maikov, *Raskazi*..., p. 22.
72 Hamilton, *Vanished*..., pp. 89–90.
73 Esipov, *Raskolnichnii*..., pp. 72–8.
74 'Manifest o vyzove inostranstev v Rossii', *Pis'ma i bumagi Imperatora Petra Velikogo* (St. Petersburg, 1889), Vol. 2, no. 421 (16 April 1702).
75 Ikonomov, *Nakaun*..., pp. 152–4.
76 Pytor Shapirov, *Pazsuzhenie* (St. Petersburg, 1700), p. 2. These remarks were part of the work's dedication written for Peter's son and heir, Pytor Petrovich.
77 Maikov, *Raskazi*..., p. 28
78 V. S. Ikonnikov, *Znachenie tsarstvovaniia Ekaterini II* (Kiev, 1897), pp. 26–9.
79 Ivan Boltin, *Premechaniia na istorii drevnii i nineshnei Rossii* (St. Petersburg, 1788), p. 41.
80 E. R. Dashkova, *Vospominaniia kniagini E. R. Dashkova* (Leipzig, 1859), pp. 200–1.
81 Dashkova, *Vospominaniia kniagini E. R. Dashkova*, p. 199.
82 Catherine II to Voltaire, 3 July 1769.
83 For additional examples, see Sigismund Herberstein, A. I. Malein, trans., *Zapiski o Moskovii* (Moscow, 1988); Harry Morely, ed., *The Discovery of Muscovy: From the Collections of Richard Fletcher* (London, 1889) and Giles Fletcher, Charles du Bo
84 I. N. Boltin, *Primichaniia na istoriyu drevnoi i ninishnoi Rossii G. Leklerka*, 2 vols. (St. Petersburg 1788).
85 Denis I. Fonvizin, *Izbrannoe* (Mosow, 1983), pp. 289–90.

86 Alferov, *Russkaia literaturaia...*, pp. 313–15.
87 *Time*, 19 December 2007.
88 Maria Maiofis, *Vozzvanie k Evrope* (Moscow, 2008).
89 *Istoriia filosofhii Rossii* (Moscow, 1995), p. 185.
90 Konstantin Aksakov, *Ob osnovnikh nachalakh russkoi istorii* (Moscow, 1860).
91 Aksakov, *Ob osnovnikh nachalakh russkoi istorii, Sochinennia istoricheskie* (Moscow, 1861), pp. 291–2.
92 Fydor Dostoevskii, *Sobranie sochinenii* (Petersburg, 1997), Vol. 3, p. 201.
93 Dostoevskii, *Sobranie sochinenii*, Vol. 6, pp. 123–4.
94 Ibid., Vol. 4, p. 98.
95 Aleksandr Nikitenko, H. L. Brodskii, ed., *Dnevnik* (Moscow, 1955), Vol.1, pp. 328–9.
96 Vissarion Belinksii, *Polnoe sobranie sochinenie* (Moscow, 1949), Vol. 6, pp. 175–6, Vol. 10, pp. 214–16.
97 Belinksii, *Polnoe sobranie sochinenie*, Vol. 5, pp. 192–3.
98 Ibid., Vol. 7, 45; Vol. 10, pp. 29–31.
99 Nikolai Shilder, *Imperator Nikolai Pervyi* (St. Petersburg, 1908), pp. 700–2.
100 Quoted in Mikhail Zhizhka, *Radishchev* (Moscow, 1934), pp. 97–8.
101 Quoted in Isabel de Madariaga, *Catherine the Great* (New Haven, 1990), pp. 200–1.
102 Quoted in Marie-Pierre Rey, *Alexandre Ier* (Paris, 2013), pp. 75, 113.
103 Nikolai K.Shilder, *Imperator Aleksandr Pervyi* (St. Petersburg, 1898), Vol. 4, pp. 90–2; A. Fateev, *Le Problème de l'individu et de l'homme d'état dans la personalité historique d'Alexandre Ier* (Prague, 1939), p. 26.
104 Quoted in S. Solovev, *Imperator Aleksandr Pervii* (St. Petersburg, 1877), p. 457.
105 Sergei Mironenko, *Aleksandr I Dekabristi* (Moscow, 2017).
106 Quoted in Marc Raeff, *The Decembrist Movement* (Englewood Cliffs, NJ, 1961), p. 50.
107 Quoted in Anatole Mazour, *The First Russian Revolution, 1825* (Stanford, 1961), p. 91.
108 Quoted in V. I. Semevskii, *Politicheskie i obshchestvenniye idei dekabristov* (St. Petersburg, 1909), p. 207.
109 Ibid., pp. 453–4.
110 Shilder, *Imperator Nikolai*, p. 518.
111 'Zapsiki Benkendorfa', *Krasnii Arkhiv*, XXXVIII (1930), p. 132.
112 Modest A. Korf, *Vosshestvie na prestole imperatora Nikolaia I* (Moscow, 2015), pp. 312–13.
113 *Severnaiia Pchela*, 85 (17 July 1826), p. 91.
114 Ibid., p.407.
115 Nikolai Karamzin, *Zapiska o drevnei i novoi Rossii* (Moscow, 2013), p. 148.
116 Sergei S. Uvarov, 'O nekotorikh obshchikh nachalakh, mogushchikh sluzhit rukovodstvom pri upravlenii Ministertsvom Narodnogo Prosveshcheniia', 1833 g.
117 See Yanov, *Zagadka*....
118 Quoted in Romanov, *Rossiia...*, p. 504.
119 Vladimir Odoevskii, *Sochineniia* (Moscow, 1981), Vol. 2, pp. 200–1.
120 Mikhail Pogodin, *Istoriko-kritichekie otrivki* (Moscow, 1846), pp. 344–8.
121 Yanov, *Zagadka...*, pp. 376–81.
122 Petr Chaadaev, *Izbranniie sochineniia i pisma* (Moscow, 1991), pp. 144–7.
123 Zaionchkovskii, *Vostochnaia...* Vol. 1, pp. 703–4.
124 See Shakibi, *Rusie va...* and Vyacheslav Morozov, *Rossiia i Drugie* (Moscow, 2009).
125 Orlando Figes, *The Crimean War* (New York, 2010), p. 81.

Chapter 3

1. 'Manifesto of the Emperor of Russia', *The Times*, 25 October 1853; *Moskovskie Vedomosti*, 18 June 1853.
2. *The Times*, 19 July 1853.
3. Eugène Veuillot, *L'Église, la France, et le schisme en Orient* (Paris, 1875), p. 196; *The Times*, 29 March 1854.
4. *The Times*, 29 March 1854.
5. In 1849–50 Paris sent troops to Rome to overthrow the anticlerical Roman Republic and restore Pope Pius IX to his place and throne in the city. The troops remained until 1870 in order to protect the pontiff.
6. The famous Opium War (1839–42).
7. The Don Pacifico affair (1850).
8. Andrei Zaionchkovskii, ed., *Vostochnaia Voina* (St. Petersburg, 2002), Vol. 1, pp. 702–3.
9. Anna Tiutcheva, *Pri dvore dvukh imperatorov* (Moscow, 1998), p. 124.
10. Nikolai Danilevsky, *Rossiia i Evropa* (St. Petersburg, 1871), p. 297.
11. Andrzej Walicki, Hilda Andrews-Rusiecka, trans., *A History of Russian Thought: From the Enlightenment to Marxism* (Stanford, 1979), p. 291. Also Olga Maiorova, *From the Shadow of Empire: Defining the Russian Nation through Cultural Mythology, 1855-1870* (Madison, 2010).
12. Dominic Lieven, *The End of Tsarist Russia* (London, 2015), p. 28.
13. Quoted in Dominic Lieven, *Nicholas II: Emperor of all the Russias* (New York, 1993), p. 6.
14. Petr Dolgorukov, *Peterburgskie ocherki* (Moscow, 1992), p. 16.
15. Alexander Nikitenko, *Zapiski i dnevnik* (Moscow: Zakharov, 2005), Vol. 1, p. 410.
16. Wortman, *Scenarios...*, p. 417.
17. Leonid Lyashenko, *Alexander II* (Moscow, 2002), p. 156.
18. Ibid., p. 182.
19. P. Annenkov, 'Idealisti tridtsatikh godov', *Vestnik Evropi*, IV, 1883, p. 525.
20. Lyashenko, *Alexander II*, p. 159.
21. Anatole Leroy-Beaulieu, *L'Empire des Tsars et les Russes* (Paris, 1893), Vol. 2, p. 610.
22. Loris-Melikov-Alexander III, 28 January 1881.
23. Quoted in Richard Pipes, *Russian Conservatism and its Critics* (New Haven, 2005), p. 141.
24. A. S. Suvorin, *Dnevnik A.S. Suvorina* (Moscow-Leningrad, 1923), p. 186.
25. Pipes, *Russian Conservatism...*, p. 141.
26. Quoted in Michael Florinsky, *Russia: A History and an Interpretation* (New York, 1968), Vol. 2, p. 115.
27. Pobedonostsev, *Moskovskii....*
28. *Pisma Pobedonostseva k Aleksandru III* (Moscow, 1925), Vol. 1, pp. 315–16.
29. Pobedonostev-Alexander III, 11 November 1881.
30. Vladimir Chicherin, *Vospominaniia* (Moscow, 1934), p. 231.
31. Lieven, *The End...*, p. 23.
32. Irina Ribachonek, *Zakat velikoi derzhavi:vneshnaiia politika Rossii na rubezhe XIX-XX vv* (Moscow, 2012).

33 Quoted in David MacDonald, *United Government and Foreign Policy in Russia, 1900-1914* (London, 1992), p. 55.
34 *Krasnii Archiv*, 2, p. 80.
35 *Byloe*, 4 (1917), pp. 206–7.
36 Petr Stolypin, *Rechi Stolipina* (Moscow, 1993), p. 173.
37 Quoted in Viktor Kuznetsov, *Sudba Tsarya* (Moscow, 2010), pp. 55–6.
38 Sergei Grigorev, *Pridvornaia Tsenzura i Obraz Verkhovnoi Vlasti 1831-1917* (St. Petersburg, 2007), p. 256.
39 Nicholas II to Marie Fedorovna, State Archive of Russian Federation, F.642, Op.1., D.2325., I.24.
40 Muarice Paleologue, *Imperatorskaia Rossiia v Epokhe Velinkoi Voine* (Berlin, 1923), Vol. 2, pp. 142–3.
41 Princess Palei, *Moi Vospominaniia o russkoi revolyutsii* (Leningrad, 1925), p. 339.
42 Princess A. Svytopolk-Mirksaia, 'Dnevnik', *Istoricheckie zapiski* 77 (1965), 34.
43 Robert Massie, *Nicholas and Alexandra* (New York, 2000), pp. 75–6.
44 Quoted in D. A. Kotsyubinskii, *Russkii nationalizm v nachale XX stoletiia* (Moscow, 2001), pp. 80, 93.
45 Ibid., p. 93.
46 Ibid., pp. 117–18.
47 Certainly, differences existed between an elite group, such as the United Nobility, and mass proto-fascist parties even if they agreed on these issues. For example, the United Nobility was committed to the preservation of property and the values of the most Europeanized groups in Russian society – the aristocracy and the gentry. The Union of the Russian People, on the other hand, favoured the expropriation of big estates -or at least at its grass roots level.
48 Sergei Stepanov, *Chernaia sotnia v Rossii:1905-1914 gg* (Moscow, 1992); Iu. I. Kirianov, *Pravye partii v Rossii, 1911-1917* (Moscow, 2001); M. N. Lukyanov, *Rossiiskii konservatizm i reforma, 1907-1914* (Perm, 2001); Iu. B. Solovev, *Samoderzhavie i dvorianstvo v 1907-1914* (Leningrad, 1981); Hans Rogger, 'The Formation of the Russian Right, 1900-1906', *California Slavic Studies* 3 (1964) and 'Was there a Russian Fascism? The Union of Russian People', *Journal of Modern History* 36 (1964).
49 Jacob Langer, *Corruption and the Counterrevolution: The Rise and Fall of the Black Hundred*, PhD dissertation, Duke University, 2007, pp. 42–4.
50 Vladimir Kokovstov, *Iz moego proshlogo: Vospominaniia 1903-1919gg* (Paris, 1933), Vol. 2, pp. 282–3.
51 Kokovstov, *Iz moego proshlogo: Vospominaniia 1903-1919gg*, p. 109.
52 Documentary film, Leonid Parfonev, *Rossiiskaia Imperia: Nikolai II*, Part 2.
53 Marjorie Hilton, *Selling to the Masses: Retailing in Russia, 1880-1930* (Pittsburgh, 2011), pp. 26–7.
54 Lieven, *Nicholas II*, p. 167.
55 Nicholas II to Dowager Empress Marie Aleksandrova, 27 October 1905.
56 Olga Alexandrovna, *25 Chapters of My Life: The Memoirs of Grand Duchess Olga Alexandrovna* (London, 2010), p.182.
57 Quoted in Robert Massie, *Nicholas and Alexandra* (New York, 1974), p. 198.
58 Ibid., p. 227.
59 Kokovstov, *Iz moego…* Vol. 2, p. 107.
60 Quoted in Thomas Riha, ed., *Readings in Russian Civilization* (Chicago, 1969), Vol. 2, pp. 475–6.

Chapter 4

1. *Shafaq-e sorkh*, 3 (1924).
2. Matin-Asghari, *Both Eastern*..., p. 12.
3. Quoted in Kaveh Bayat, 'Andishe-ye bamarafat', *Bokhara*, 108, p. 471.
4. Pahlavi, *Mission*..., p. 12. Hushangmahdavi, ed., *Engelab*..., p. 55.
5. Pahlavi, *Mission*..., p. 59.
6. Hossein Maki, *Tarikh-e bistsale-ye Iran: aqaz-e saltanati-ye diktaturi-ye Pahlavi* (Tehran, 1361/1982), Vol. 4, p. 38.
7. See Afshin Marashi, *Nationalizing Iran: Culture, Power, & the State, 1870-1940* (Seattle, 2008); Mohammad Ali Akbari, *Tabarshenasi-ye hoviat-e jadid-e Irani* (Tehran, 1384/2005).
8. Abbas Amanat, *Pivot of the Universe, Nasir al-Din Shah Qajar and the Iranian Monarchy, 1831-1896* (New Haven, 1997), p. 232.
9. Fath-Ali Shah (r. 1791–1834). He blamed the clergy for pressuring Fath-Ali Shah to start the second Russo-Iranian War that led to the loss of Iranian territory in the Caucasus. Amin Al-Dowleh, *Khaterat-e siasi-ye Mirza Zaeli Khan Amin Al-Dowleh* (Tehran, 1360/1981), pp. 41–2.
10. Maki, *Tarikh-e*..., Vol. 4, pp. 36–40.
11. Hushangmahdavi, *Enqelab*..., pp. 36–7.
12. *Ettelaat- Havades-e yek rob-e qarn* (Tehran, 1329/1950), p. 156.
13. Hushangmahdavi, *Enqelab-e Iran*..., p. 36.
14. Amir Taheri, *The Unknown Life of the Shah* (London, 1991), p. 29.
15. Pahlavi, *Mission*..., p. 166.
16. See Stefan Arvidsoson, Sonia Wichmann, trans.; *Aryan Idols: Indo-European Mythology as Ideology and Science* (Chicago, 2006); Alastair Bonnett, *The Idea of the West* (London, 2004); Tony Ballantyne, *Orientalism and Race: Aryanism in the British Empire* (London, 2002) and Viktor Shirelman, *Arisksii Mif v Sovremennom Mire* (Moscow, 2015).
17. Mohammad Delfani, ed., *Farhangsetizi dar doureh-ye Reza Shah. Asnad-e montarshe nashodeh sazman-e parvaresh-e afkar, 1318-1320* (Tehran, 1375/1996), p. 75.
18. *Tarikh-e sal-e sevvom-e dabirestan* (Tehran, 1319/1940), p. 2. Also *Tarikh-e ommumi va Iran bae daneshpah-ye yekkom-e dabiristanha* (Tehran, 1316/1937); *Ketab-e sevvom-e ebtedai* (Tehran, 1318/1939), p. 163.
19. *Maqalat-e Forughi* (Tehran, 1353/1974), Vol. 2, p. 231. Also quoted in Maki, *Tarikh-e*..., Vol. 6, pp. 39–44.
20. *Yadegar-e jashn-e arus-ye valahazrat homayoun velayatahed* (Tehran, 1318/1939), p. 2. See also Hushang Purkarim, *Elasht, zadegan-e alihezrat Reza Shah Kabir* (Tehran, 1348/1970).
21. Marat succeeded Hekmat as minister of culture (1939–41).
22. Ali Hekmat, *Si Khatereh-e asr-e Farkhund-e Pahlavi* (Tehran, 2535/1976), pp. 138–41.
23. *Ettela'at*, 23 Mehr 1307/1928.
24. Mohammad Hejazi, 'Iran: Old Land, New Country', *Iran-e emruz* (1) Mordad-Sharivar 1318/1939, pp. 5–6, 39.
25. Hekmat, *Si Khatereh*, p. 130.
26. Ibid., p. 138.
27. Fath-Ali Akhundzade, *Maktubat*, M. Sobhad, ed. (N/A., 1364/1985), pp. 15–16.
28. Haji Zinal'abedin Maraqei, *Siahatname-ye Ibrahim-e Beig* (Tehran, 1385/2006).

29 Issa Sadeq, *Yadegar-e omr* (Tehran, 1355/1976), pp. 49, 75.
30 Wilhelm von Blücher, *Zeitwende in Iran* (Berlin, 1949), p. 331.
31 Darya Balieva, *Sovetsko-iranskie kulturnie svyazi, 1921-1960* (Tashkent, 1965), p. 41.
32 Aleksandr Orishev, *Iranskii uzel: Skhvatka razvedok, 1936-1945 gg* (Moscow, 2009), pp. 53-4.
33 Orishev, *Iranskii uzel: Skhvatka razvedok, 1936-1945 gg*, p. 62.
34 *Ettela'at*, 1 Mordad 1315/23 July 1936; 22 Azar 1315.
35 Orishev, *Iranskii...*, p. 50.
36 Ibid., pp. 63-5.
37 Ahmad Daftari, Baqer Alqili, ed., *Khaterat-e yek nokhost vazir* (Tehran, 1370/1991), p. 164.
38 *Iran-e Emruz*, 2 3, Khordad, 1319/1940.
39 Delfani, ed., *Farhangsetizi...*, pp. 4-5, 35-6.
40 [93] Ibid., pp. 73-4.
41 Ibid., pp. 60-3.
42 See Voltaire, Jean Pierre Jackson, eds., *Textes sur l'Orient: L'Empire Ottoman & le Monde Arabe* (Paris, 2005).
43 The bulk of this discussion comes from the works of Pierre Briant. See *Alexandre des lumières: Fragments d'histoire européenne* (Paris, 2012); *Histoire de l'empire perse: De Cyrus à Alexandre* (Paris, 1996); and *Darius dans l'ombre d'Alexandre* (Paris, 2003).
44 Briant, *Histoire de l'Empire perse*, pp. 50-8.
45 *Ettela'at*, p. 52.
46 *Yadegar-e jashn*, pp. 10-12.
47 Delfani, ed., *Farhangsetizi...*, p. 74.
48 Arthurs, *Excavating...*, p. 131.
49 Ibid., pp. 131, 129.
50 Silvana Patriarca, *Italian Vices: Nation and Character from the Risorgimento to the Republic* (Cambridge, 2010), p. 137.
51 Patriarca, *Italian Vices: Nation and Character from the Risorgimento to the Republic*, p. 136.
52 Oriana Fallaci, *Interview with History* (New York, 1979), pp. 143-4.
53 *Ettela'at*, 15 Bahman 1320 (1941).
54 *Ettela'at*, 15 Shahrivar 1315(1936).
55 Pahlavi, *Mission...*, p. 59.
56 Hedayat, *Khaterat...*, p. 520.
57 Sadeq, *Yadgar-e omr*, pp. 306-7; Maki, *Tarikh-e...*, Vol. 6, pp. 201-2.
58 Suetonius, *On National Costume* quoted in Hadrill, *Rome's Cultural...*, p. 37.
59 Said Nafisi, *Tarikh-e moaser-e Iran* (Tehran, 1345/1966), p. 84.
60 Akbari, *Tabarshenasi-ye hoviat...*, p. 242.
61 Mohammad Girami, *Tarikh-e eqtesadi, siasi, ejtemai-ye doran-e Reza Shah* (Tehran, 1355/1977), p. 150.
62 Hekmat, *Si Khatereh*, p. 368.
63 Nafisi, *Tarikh-e moaser-e...*, pp. 82-3.
64 Hekmat, *Si Khatereh*, p. 132.
65 Houshang Chehabi, 'The Banning of the Veil and Its Consequences', in Stephanie Cronin, ed., *The Making of Modern Iran: State and Society under Riza Shah, 1921-1941* (London, 2003), p. 198.
66 *Ettela'at*, 29 Mordad 1306 (1927).

67 H. Mohammadi, *Tarikh-e moaser-e Iran be nazar-e Imam Khomeini* (Tehran, 1375), pp. 131–2.
68 Chehabi, 202. See also in the same volume Shireen Mahdavi, 'Reza Shah Pahlavi and Women: A Re-evaluation'.
69 Maki, *Tarikh-e...*, Vol. 5, pp. 16–28.
70 E. N. Aidin, 'Recent Changes in the Outlook of Women in the Near and Middle East', *Journal of the Central Asian Society* 28 (1931), 525.
71 Sadeq, *Yadegar-e omr*, pp. 304–5.
72 Hekmat, *Si Khatereh*, pp. 88–9.
73 Maki, *Tarikh-e...*, Vol. 6, pp. 253–7.
74 Sadeq, *Yadegar-e omr*, p. 252.
75 Assadollah Alam, Alinaqi Alikhani, ed., *Yaddashtha-ye Alam* (Tehran, 1393/2014), Vol. 4, p. 298.
76 Alam, Alikhani, ed., *Yaddashtha-ye Alam*, p. 247.
77 Nafisi, *Tarikh-e moaser...*, p. 84.
78 Delfani, ed., *Farhangsetizi...*, pp. 103–4.
79 Ibid., pp. 81–8, 97–8.
80 Rashid Yasem, 'Tajadod', *Iran-e Emruz*, 1, 1 (1939).

Chapter 5

1 Pahlavi, *Mission...*, pp. 74–5.
2 Ibid., p. 130.
3 E. A. Bayne, *Persian Kingship in Transition* (New York, 1968), p. 66.
4 William Lewis and Michael Ledeen, *Debacle: The American Failure in Iran* (New York, 1982), p. 11.
5 Those assassinated were Ahmad Kasravi, Abdul-Hussein Hizhir, minister of court, Abdolhamid Zanganeh, minister of education and two prime ministers, Ali Razmara and Hassan Ali Mansur.
6 Abrahamian, *A History of...*, pp. 108–9.
7 Abrahamian, *Iran between Two Revolutions* (Princeton, 1980).
8 See Mark J. Gasiorowski, 'The Qarani Affair and Iranian Politics', *International Journal of Middle East Studies*, 25 (1993).
9 Ali Kani, *Sazman-e farhangi-ye Iran* (Tehran, 1336 /1958), pp. 99–105.
10 'Special National Intelligence Estimate, August 26, 1958', in US State Department, Foreign Relations of the United States (Washington DC, 1958–60), Vol. 12, p. 586. See also Mark J. Gasiorowski, 'The Qarani Affair and Iranian Politics', *International Journal of Middle East Studies* (November 1993).
11 Pahlavi, *Mission...*, pp. 88–9. See also 'Joint Statement on US-Iranian Relations-Need for Iran's Economic Development Seen', *Department of State Bulletin*, 9 January 1950, pp. 54–5.
12 James Bill, *The Eagle and the Lion: The Tragedy of American-Iranian Relations* (New Haven, 1988), p. 132.
13 Erfan Qaneei, *Dar damgeh-ye havades: goftegui ba Parviz-e Sabeti* (Los Angeles, 2012), pp. 87–8, 100.
14 Fereydoun Hoveyda, Roger Liddell, trans., *The Fall of the Shah* (New York, 1980), p. 135.

15 Walter Bagehot, *The English Constitution*, Miles Taylor, ed. (Oxford, 2001), p. 54.
16 Dabashi, *Theology...*, p. 14.
17 See Boroujerdi, *Iranian Intellectuals...*; Dabashi and Houchang Chehabi, *Iranian Politics and Religious Modernism* (London, 1990).
18 Bazm Ahriman, ed., *Jashnaha-ye 2500 sale-ye Shahanshahi be ravaet-e asnad-e SAVAK va darbar* (Tehran, 1378), Vol. 2, pp. 306–7.
19 Ahriman, ed., *Jashnaha-ye 2500 sale-ye Shahanshahi be ravaet-e asnad-e SAVAK va darbar*, Vol. 1, pp. 67–8.
20 Honarmand, *Pahlavism*, Vol. 1, pp. 49–50. In this four-volume set the terms 'socialism' and 'communism' are used interchangeably, although the term 'socialism' is used more frequently.
21 Honarmand, *Pahlavism*, Vol. 1, p. 45.
22 Ibid., pp. 39–40.
23 Ibid., p. 2.
24 [21] Ibid., Vol. 2, pp. 34–5.
25 Ibid., Vol. 1, pp. 7–8.
26 This interpretation of events, on which both Darius and Herodotus broadly agree, is open to controversy. For the most recent evaluation of this issue, see Briant, *Histoire...*, pp. 109–21.
27 Herodotus, Robin Waterfield, trans., *The Histories* (Oxford, 1998), pp. 80–3.
28 Bayne, *Persian Kingship...*, p. 65.
29 Honarmand, *Pahlavism*, Vol. 1, pp. 50–2.
30 Ibid., pp. 6–7.
31 Ibid., Vol. 2, p. 12.
32 Ibid., Vol. 1, pp. 8–9.
33 Ibid., pp. 20–5.
34 Ibid., pp. 52–5.
35 Ibid., Vol. 2, pp. 53–4.
36 Ibid., Vol. 3, p. 44.
37 Ibid.,Vol. 1, p. 7.
38 Ibid., p. 54.
39 Ibid., p. 56.
40 Ibid., Vol. 2, p. 38.
41 Ruhani, *Baresi va talili...*, pp. 263–5.
42 Ibid., p. 309.
43 Ibid., p. 264.
44 Qaneei, *Dar damgeh...*, p. 173.
45 Honarmand, *Pahlavism*, Vol. 1, pp. 22–4.
46 See M. R. Pahlavi, Said Mohammad Baqirnajafi, ed., *Shahanshahi va Dindari* (Tehran, 2535/1976).
47 Honarmand, *Pahlavism*, Vol. 1, pp. 13–14.
48 Ibid., p. 15.
49 Ibid., Vol. 1, pp. 18–20 and Vol. 2, pp. 101–4.
50 Ibid., Vol. 1, pp. 22–4.
51 Ibid., Vol. 1, p. 29 and Vol. 2, pp. 18–19.
52 Ibid., Vol. 1, p. 26.
53 *JR* (Special New Year's edition), 16 March 1978.
54 Honarmand, *Pahlavism*, Vol. 1, p. 10.
55 Ibid., Vol. 1, pp. 88–97.

56 Ibid., Vol. 2, pp. 107, 110.
57 Ibid., Vol. 3, pp. 23–4.
58 Ibid., Vol. 1, pp. 59–60.
59 *Negin*, 121, 21 June 1974.
60 Honarmand, *Pahlavism*, Vol. 1, pp. 51–3.
61 *Negin*, 134, 22 July1976.
62 Honarmand, *Pahlavism*, Vol. 1, p. 62.
63 Ibid., p. 61.
64 Ibid., Vol. 2, p. 73.
65 Ibid., Vol. 4, pp. 26–32.
66 Ibid., Vol. 2, p. 23.
67 Pahlavi, *Mission...*, p. 130.
68 Ibid., p. 253.
69 Mohammad Reza Pahlavi, *Engelab-e sefid* (Tehran, N/A), pp. 23–4, 193.
70 Honarmand, *Pahlavism*, Vol. 1, p. 1.
71 Bayne, *Persian Kingship...*, p. 101.

Chapter 6

1 Wilhelm, paternal uncle of Bill de Blasio, mayor of New York City (2013–), was a US academic who also worked as a US government advisor in various parts of Asia. He was a Cold War warrior whose academic work focused on promoting the superiority of the West to the communist East. See https://www.wnyc.org/story/between-wwii-and-his-suicide-de-blasios-father-cold-warrior.
2 Pahlavi, *Mission...*, pp. 28, 132. *Mamuriat bara-ye vatanam* (Tehran, 1340/1962), pp. 15–16. The book was originally published in English in the United States and the United Kingdom. Months later, a Persian-language edition was published in Iran. Here quotes are taken from the English version. When a difference in meaning exists between the two versions, the Persian text is also mentioned since it was aimed at Iranian readers.
3 Pahlavi, *Mission...*, p. 212.
4 Ibid., p. 160. In the book's Persian version this chapter's title is 'The challenges of adapting the new civilization'. However, in its text the shah states that this new civilization is the West.
5 Ibid., p. 172.
6 Ibid., p. 172.
7 Ibid., p. 160. *Mamuriat...*, pp. 33–4.
8 During the Brezhnev period the shah, while maintaining his fear and suspicion of Soviet communism, followed a realist foreign policy, establishing cordial political and economic relations with the USSR and countries of the Eastern Bloc.
9 Negin Nabavi, *Intellectuals and the State in Iran* (Gainesville, 2003), pp. 90–5. See also Boroujerdi, *Iranian Intellectuals...*; Dabashi, *Theology...* and Mirsepassi, *Intellectual...*.
10 Nabavi, *Intellectuals...*, pp. 90–1.
11 Jalal Al-e Ahmad, *Qarbzadegi* (Tehran, 1386/2007); R. Campbell, trans. Hamid Algar, introduction and annotations, *Occidentosis: A Plague from the West* (Berkeley, 1984); Ehsan Naraqi, *Qorbat-e Qarb*, 2nd edition (Tehran, 1354/1974).
12 Matin-Asgari, p. 32.

13 Quoted in Dabashi, *Theology...*, p. 75.
14 Ibid., pp. 74–5.
15 Ahmad, *Occidentosis*, pp. 27–30.
16 Ibid., p.78.
17 Ibid., pp. 73,81.
18 Ibid., pp. 91–3.
19 Ibid., p. 95.
20 Ibid., p. 104.
21 Ibid., p. 105.
22 Ibid., pp. 127–32.
23 SAVAK, 23 September 1974. *Matbuat-e asr-e Pahlavi be ravayet-e asnad-e SAVAK: Majalle-ye Ferdowsi* (Tehran, 1384), p. 400.
24 Afshin, *Qarbzadegi ya Arabzadegi*, (787), 22 September 1966.
25 A mid-ranking SAVAK official took issue with its argument that the best example of the characteristics of Arabtoxification was 'the silence of the clergy in the face of Mongol invasions and destruction'. Therefore, the clergy were responsible for Iran's backwardness in relation to the West. 'This article to a great extent is inflammatory and will make a bad impression on the clergy. Clearly this magazine intends in future issues to propagate this thesis. ... Permission is requested that a notification be given to those responsible for *Ferdowsi* to abstain from writing such pieces.' Permission was not given. SAVAK, 9 Aban 1345/31 October 1966. *Matbuat-e...*, p. 262.
26 Naraqi, *Qorbat...*, p. 9.
27 Algar, Introduction in Ahmad, *Occidentosis*, p. 10.
28 Dabashi, *Theology...*, p. 77.
29 Algar, *Occidentosis*, p. 18.
30 SAVAK, No.2, 20 February 1970. *Matbuat-e...*, pp. 297–304.
31 SAVAK, unnumbered, 7 March 1966; SAVAK, M-2, 30 December 1968. *Matbuat-e...*, pp. 250–3.
32 SAVAK, 5/M/20/17519, 23 October 1966. It reported on a private conversation the managing editor Abbas Pahlavan had in which 'he frankly said that *Ferdowsi* is the only anti-American magazine and therefore has become so popular and well-known'. M/7/20/836, 21 April 1967. See also: SAVAK, P-324, 22 May 1967. *Matbuat-e...*, pp. 333–5.
33 SAVAK, 19 June 1970; No.1377, 22 June 1967; 23 July 1974. *Matbuat-e...*, pp. 362, 320–1, 413–15.
34 SAVAK, 2H/9649, 20 February 1971. *Matbuat-e...*, pp. 362–3.
35 *Majlis-e Shura-ye Melli* (Tehran, 1343/1965), Vol. 20, p. 1057. Rastakhiz gave much coverage to this ministry. 'For what is the ministry of culture and art responsible?' *JR*, (32), 21 January 1976.
36 *Majlis-e Shura-ye Melli*, Vol. 20, p. 1065.
37 Mohammad Reza Pahlavi, *Talifat, nuqtha, paymanha-ye Alihezrat Homayoun Mohammad Reza Pahlavi*, 11 vols. (Tehran, 2535-7, (1976-78/9)), Vol. 8, pp. 4237–41, 6696.
38 Ibid., Vol. 10, pp. 8732–3. See also pp. 8547–50.
39 Jimmy Carter, *Keep Faith: Memoirs of a President*, p. 444.
40 Pahlavi, *Talifat...*, Vol. 5, pp. 4253–8.
41 Ibid., Vol. 9, p. 7327.
42 'Shahanshah: Strong spiritual principles...' and 'The role of spirituality and religious beliefs', *Rastakhiz*, (605), 21 April 1977.

43 Pahlavi, *Talifat...*, Vol. 10, pp. 9028–9.
44 'Shahanshah and national culture', *Rastakhiz*, (143), 6 October 1976; See also: Pahlavi, *Talifat...*, Vol. 10, p. 8606; 'Human rights is applicable to all', (559), *Rastakhiz*, 5 March 1977; and Vadiei, 'The West's two different and contradictory faces', (561), 17 March 1977.
45 Pahlavi, *Talifat...*, Vol. 10, p. 8470.
46 Mohammad Reza Pahlavi, *Farmaishat-e...*, p. 43. See also Pahlavi, *Talifat...*, Vol. 9, p. 4876; 'The clergy must correctly separate materialism from the following of God', *Rastakhiz*, (605), 4 May1977.
47 Pahlavi, *Beh Sui...*, pp. 249–50.
48 Pahlavi, *Mission...*, p. 132.
49 Aydin, *The Politics...*, p. 7.
50 *Rastakhiz*, (138), 14 October 1975; Pahlavi, *Talifat...*, Vol. 10, p. 6143.
51 'Shahanshah: A strong Iran...', *Rastakhiz*, (325), 27 May 1976.
52 Pahlavi, *Talifat...*, Vol. 5, p. 569.
53 'Empress', *JR*, (38), 15 June 1975.
54 'The empress: welfare and spirituality', *Rastakhiz*, (336), 9 June 1976.
55 Ibid. (210), 8 January 1976. See also: 'Empress: the party is the base of National Unity', (303), 2 May 1976; Editorial: 'Technology and moral values', (334), 6 June 1976.
56 *Rastakhiz*, (269), 21 March 1976.
57 Habib Niksirati, 'The Revolutionary era's cultural and literary foundations', *JR*, (32), 21 January 1976.
58 In 1974 the council's membership was enlarged to include the ministers of village affairs and higher education, the OPB deputy head and the head of NIRT.
59 'Shahanshah: the council...', *JR*, (146), 22 May 1977.
60 Pahlavi, *Talifat...*, Vol. 5, pp. 4468–4644.
61 OHPFIS, Pahlbod, Vol. 1, p. 45.
62 See *Hezb-e Iran-e Novin: Masubat-Nokhostin kongre-ye hezb-e Iran-e Novin* (1346/1968); *Gozaresh-e nakhost vazir va dovvom-e kongreh-ye hezb* (1350/1972), especially pp. 61–9.
63 Alam, *Yaddashta...*, Vol. 7, p. 418.
64 Ibid., Vol. 7, pp. 597–8.
65 Jamshid Behnam, *Nowsazi-ye shetabzadeh* (Tehran, 1350/1972), pp. 135–6.
66 OHPFIS, Jamshid Behnam, Vol. 1, p. 22.
67 Masoud Behnud, 'Cultural Heritage', *Ferdowsi*, (917), 22 June 1969, (918), 29 June 1969.
68 *Farhang va Zendegi*, (1), December–January 1969–70.
69 Ibid., p. 3.
70 Ibid., p. 1.
71 Jamshid Behnam, 'West, What West?' Ibid., (1).
72 'Historical trajectory and today's life', Ibid., (4–5), April 1971. See also: Jamshid Behnam, 'On family and culture in Iran', (16) Autumn, 1974.
73 'Anonymous' was coined by Emile Durkheim to describe a society undergoing a crisis-ridden transitional period that emerges after some form of political turmoil or when rapid changes in values take place. As he put it, 'The old gods are aging or are already dead, and others were not yet born.'
74 Editorial, *Zendegi va Farhang*, (17) Spring, 1975.
75 Ehsan Naraqi, 'There must be a different culture...' Ibid., (12) Autumn, 1973.
76 Dariush Homayoun, 'Several questions about the East's culture', Ibid., (7), 1971.

77 *OHPFIS*, Jamshid Behnam, Vol. 1, p. 22.
78 Dehbashi, *Hekmat…*, p. 242.
79 *OHPFIS*, Pahlbod, Vol. 1, p. 9.
80 Hossein Dehbashi, ed., *Hekmat va siasat: goftegu ba doktor Sayyed Hossein Nasr* (Tehran, 1394/2015), p. 240.
81 *OHPFIS*, Ovanessian, p. 22.
82 *OHPFIS*, Pahlbod, Vol. 1, p. 46.
83 Mozaffar Shahedi, *SAVAK, 1335-1357* (Tehran, 1386/2007), pp. 473–4.
84 *Ferdowsi*, (29) 13 Tir 1340/22 June 1961.
85 SAVAK , 10 July 1961. *Matbuat-e…*, p. 180.
86 SAVAK, No. 335/17863, 12 July 1961. *Matbuat-e…*, p. 181.
87 Yahihi Maruseti, *Ferdowsi*, (112), 21 March 1963.
88 SAVAK, unnumbered, March 1963. *Matbuat-e…*, pp. 231–3.
89 Lead article, *Ferdowsi*, (825), 22 August 1967.
90 Hamid Cherazi, *Ferdowsi*, (843), 22 December 1967.
91 Ibid., Ismail Nuri 'allah'.
92 Ibid., Jamshid Arjmand.
93 SAVAK, No.5H20/33248, 1967, *Matbuat-e…*, p. 296. See also Sayyed Abbas Fatemi, *Zendegi va marg-e jahanpahlavan-e Takhti dar aine-ye asnad* (Tehran, 1377/1998).
94 *Ferdowsi*, (899), 21 January 1969.
95 Hossein Mehri, 'The problem of fairy children', (1109), 21 April 1973. Also Kabiri, 'Warning: the moral dead-ends in freedom without limits'.
96 *Ferdowsi*, (1114), 22 May 1973.
97 Fereydoun Razmjuyan, 'Scandal and the scandal of disgrace', *Ferdowsi*, (1115), 2 June 1973.
98 *Ferdowsi*, (1121), 22 June 1973.
99 Mehrangiz Kar, *Ferdowsi*, (1116), 22 May 1973.
100 *Ferdowsi*, (1120), 22 June 1973; see also: (1131), 23 August 1973.
101 Hossein Mehri, *Ferdowsi*, (1172), 22 June 1974.
102 Ibid., *Ferdowsi* , (1128), 23 August 1973.
103 *Ferdowsi*, (1132), 13 September 1973.
104 *Ferdowsi*, (1124), 23 July 1973.
105 *Ferdowsi*, (1125), 30 July 1973. See also SAVAK, 21 March 1972.
106 *Ferdowsi*, (961), 21 April 1970. See (1101), 20 February 1970.
107 Majid Rahnama, *Ferdowsi*, 23 July 1967. *Ferdowsi* also focused on US activities in Latin America, 'Washington's spread of US-style capitalism and interference in domestic political affairs', (880), 23 September1967.
108 Lead article, *Ferdowsi*, (780), 22 May 1966.
109 Lead article, *Ferdowsi*, (790), 23 August 1966.
110 *Ferdowsi*, (780), 22 May 1966.
111 'After persepolis', *The Economist*, 23 October 1971; 'Iran: the show of shows', *TIME*, 25 October 1971.

Chapter 7

1 Alam, *Yaddashtha…*, Vol. 3, p. 217.
2 Ibid., pp. 522–3.

3 *Keyhan*, 20 February 1976.
4 In reality, this style was first used in a special two-note series issued in 1971–2 to commemorate the 2,500th anniversary of the monarchy.
5 Habib Lajaverdi, ed., *Khaterat-e Abdolmajid Majidi*, Harvard Iranian Oral History Series (Cambridge, MA, 1998), pp. 62–3.
6 Afkhami, *The Life...*, pp. 432–3.
7 Pahlavi, *Mission...*, pp. 77, 162, 173.
8 Milani, *The Shah*, pp. 379–81. See also Dehbashi, *Ayandegan...*, pp. 125–6.
9 SAVAK, 24020/47967, 8 November 1971, *Matbuat-e...*, p. 364.
10 Milani, *The Shah*, pp. 322–3.
11 Ibid., p. 380.
12 Bayne, *Persian Kingship...*, p. 61.
13 Alam, *The Shah and I*, p. 552.
14 Gordon Craig, 'The mann nobody knew', *New York Review of Books*, 29 February 1996, p. 38.
15 Coker, *The Rise...*, p. 74.
16 He had been minister of development and housing (1964–1), head of Pahlavi University (1968–71) and then minister of science and higher education (1978).
17 Alam, *Yaddashtha...*, Vol. 1, pp. 54–5.
18 See Pahlavi, *Talifat...*, Vol. 9, pp. 8053–4.
19 Ibid., Vol. 10, pp. 8528–9. In the final months of the Party's existence in summer 1978 talk circulated of Nahavandi and this group becoming the Party's third wing.
20 Bill, *The Eagle...*, p. 191.
21 Qaneei, *Dar damgeh...*, pp. 347–50.
22 Afkhami, *The Life...*, p. 433.
23 Ibid., p. 434.
24 OHPFIS, Ahmad Qoreishi, Vol. 1, p. 29.
25 Pahlavi, *Talifat,...*, Vol. 10, pp. 8482–4. See also Vol. 9, pp. 8245–6.
26 Alam, *Yaddashtha...*, Vol. 2, p. 873. See also Vol. 4, pp. 114–16.
27 Ibid., Vol. 4, p. 394.
28 Ibid., Vol. 4, pp. 408–9.
29 Dehbashi, *Ayandegan...*, p. 137. The US Embassy in Tehran had come to similar conclusions. See *Asnad-e lanah-ye jasus-e Amrika* (Tehran, 1980), Vol. 17, pp. 100–8.
30 OHPFIS, Qoreishi, Vol. 1, p. 7.
31 *Hezb-e Rastakhiz, Jenah-e Pishrow*, Bulletin 1, pp. 16–17. See also Alam, *Yaddashtha...*, Vol. 3, pp. 530–1.
32 Pahlavi, *Talifat...*, Vol. 9, p. 8246. See also interview on Danish television, Vol. 10, pp. 8556–7.
33 Mehdi Mozaffari, *Nizamha-ye Takhezbi va Rastakhiz-e Mellat-e Iran* (Tehran, 1354/1975), p. 128. A second edition was published the following year.
34 Dehbashi, *Ayandegan...*, pp. 120–6.
35 Qaneei, *Dar damgeh...*, pp. 223–5.
36 Ibid., p. 225.
37 'One way to broaden the base', *The Economist*, 21 October 1972.
38 Alam, *Yaddashtha...*, Vol. 4, pp. 235–6.
39 Ibid., Vol. 3, p. 295.
40 Quoted in Mozzafar Shahedi, *Hezb-e Rastakhiz: eshtebah-ye bozorg* (Tehran, 1383), Vol. 1, p. 216.
41 Dehbashi, *Ayandegan...*, p. 127.

42 Pahlavi, *Mamuriat...*, pp. 223-4.
43 Claire Sterling, 'Can Dr. Amini Save Iran?', *The Reporter*, 30 (17 August 1961).
44 'Alam's announcements', *Rastakhiz*, (131), 7 October 1975.
45 Hasemi Haeri, 'Revolutionary education', *Rastakhiz*, (666), 22 June 1977. Also 'What is to be done before democracy?', *Rastakhiz*, (660), 16 June 1977.
46 'The Rastakhiz Party', *Rastakhiz*, (30), 5 June 1975; 'Democracy and the Party', (34), 10 June 1975.
47 *Si porsesh va pasokh piramun-e osulei bonyadi-ye an va hizb-e Rastakhiz-e mellat-e Iran* (Tehran, N/A).
48 Bayne, *Persian Kingship*, pp. 76-7.
49 *Rastakhiz*, (5), 22 May 1975.
50 *Kongreh-ye Buzurg*, p. 19.
51 'The new revolutionary principle: society's spiritual development', JR, New Year special edition, 1355/1977.
52 Pahlavi, *Talifat...*, Vol. 8, p. 7356.
53 Ibid., Vol. 10, pp. 8737-40.
54 Ibid., Vol. 10, pp. 9111-12.
55 'The obligatory guidance...', (95), 22 May 1977 and (96), 28 May 1977; See also (98), 22 June 1977 and 'The Legion...', (97), 23 June 1977.
56 'Shahanshah: Iran's democracy is not synonymous with chaos and licentiousness', (384), 23 July 1977.
57 *Ayandigan*, 8 (2266), 22 June 1975.
58 *HIOHP*, Mohammad Baheri, (25), 1.
59 Pahlavi, *Talifat...*, Vol. 10, pp. 7860-1.
60 Dehbashi, *Ayandegan...*, pp. 131-2.
61 Hushangmahdavi, *Engelab...*, pp. 263-4.
62 'Mahdavi: Party committees...', *Rastakhiz*, (96), 24 August 1975.
63 'Party committee and institutional issues', JR, (1), 22 May 1975.
64 *Arshiv-e moassese-ye motaleat va pozhuheshha-yi siasi*, 417630, (442).
65 *Rastakhiz*, (19), 23 October 1975.
66 SAVAK, 417611, p. 132.
67 Alam, *Yaddashtha...*, Vol. 3, p. 469.
68 Ibid., Vol. 3, p. 779.
69 Ibid., Vol. 4, p. 403.
70 SAVAK, 417611, quoted in Shahedi, *Hezb-e Rasatakhiz...*, p. 133. See also Dehbashi, *Ayandegan...*, pp. 135-6.
71 Jamshd Amuzegar, *Be raviet-e asnad-e Savak* (Tehran, 1382/2003), pp. 14-15.
72 Alam, *Yaddashtha...*, Vol. 4, pp. 10-11, 74-6.
73 Qaneei, *Dar damgeh...*, p. 610.
74 Hoveyda, *The Fall...*, p. 83.
75 Alam, *Yaddashtha...*, Vol. 4, pp. 583, 610-11.
76 Qaneei, *Dar damgeh...*, pp. 624-7.
77 Parvizi and Baheri, along with others, formed a group called *Azadegan-e Fars* that participated in the 1946 Majles elections. When members of the group failed to win election, they made claims of fraud. Parvizi was condemned to internal exile. Having ended his membership in the Tudeh Party he initially dedicated himself to writing, primarily short-stories that enjoyed popularity in the 1950s and 1960s. It was this popularity that brought him to the attention of Alam. When Alam founded the Mardom party Parvizi became a member of its Executive Committee. Thanks to this

link he served in the 21-3 Majles and eventually entered the imperial senate. He was also deputy in Alam's cabinet. Moreover, he served as managing director of Iranian branch of the United Nations Volunteer programme the shah had proposed during his 1967 visit to the United States. His reputation as a writer and his political position provided him with a platform that he used to propagate discourses of anti-West Occidentalism, especially during the Rastakhiz period. *JR* gave wide coverage to his views. The shah also regarded him as an effective regime publicist. For example, in a discussion with Alam over a *Newsweek* article that criticized SAVAK activities, he ordered him write a strong response and 'to attack'. Alam, *Yaddashtha-ye...*, Vol. 4, p. 256.

78 Ibid., Vol. 3, p. 194.
79 Ibid., Vol. 3, p. 406.
80 *HIOHP*, Baheri, (22), pp. 18–19.
81 Ibid., (25), p. 17.
82 Ibid., (22), p. 17; (24), pp. 1–2, 12; (25), p. 3.
83 Ibid., (25), p. 3.
84 Ibid., (59).
85 Ibid., (25), p. 1.
86 Ibid., (25), p. 1.
87 Qaneei, *Dar damgeh...*, p. 610.
88 *HIOHP*, Baheri, (25), p. 3.
89 *OHPFIS*, Qoresihi, p. 9.
90 *HIOP*, Baheri, (26), p. 2.
91 *OHPFIS*, Qoreishi, p. 10.
92 Ibid., (26), p. 13.
93 Ibid., (27), pp. 1–5.
94 Its membership included Nahavandi, Semsar, Zerangar, Mahmoud Jafarian, Amir Taheri, Rasul Parvizi, Ameli-Tehrani, the top party official for Tehran and Central Province, Hushang Vaziri, editor of *Ayandigan*, Enayatollah Reza, Mohammad Taqi Irvani, director of factories of National Shoe Company, and Firuz Fuladi, the head of the writing board of *Tamasha*, NIRT's publication.
95 *JR*, (114), 27 October 1977.
96 23 August 1976, interview with *Keyhan*.
97 Record of the 24th Majles, (32), 20 February 1976.
98 *HIOHP*, Baheri, (24), p. 12.
99 Record of 24th Majles, session 61, 23 October 1976.
100 *Rastakhiz*, (245), 22 December 1976.
101 Savak 418611 quoted in Shahedi, *Hezb-e Rastakhiz...*, pp. 232–3.
102 Dariush Humayoun, *Andishehha-ye Rastakhiz*, 1, (3), January 1977.
103 *Rastakhiz-e Kargaran*, (35), 23 October 1977. *JR*, (116), 10 November 1977.
104 *HIOHP*, Baheri, (24), pp. 16–17, (26), pp. 9–10.
105 Ibid., (26), p. 10.
106 SAVAK, 217611, 23 October 1976.
107 Gholam Salehyar, *Chehre-ye matbu'at-e moasser* (Tehran, 1351/1973), pp. 95–6.
108 *Rastakhiz*, (1), 3 May 1975.
109 *OHPFIS*, Hossein Sarfaraz, Vol. 1, p. 62.
110 Dehbashi, *Ayandegan...*, p. 161.
111 Shahedi, *Hezb-e Rastakhiz*, p. 386.

112 Until March 1977 it was called *Javanan-e Rastakhiz* (*JK*). After a three-week hiatus it was renamed *Rastakhiz-e Javan* (*RJ*). Some changes were made in its editorial board as well as writers. The title reverted to *Javanan-e Rastakhiz* in August 1977 with the arrival of Baheri as party head and the appointment of Sarfaraz as editor.
113 Salehyar, *Chehre-ye…*, p. 71.
114 Ibid., p. 59.
115 Ibid., p. 94.
116 Zerangar, 'Rastakhiz publications…', *Rastakhiz*, (254), 2 March 1976.
117 Hossein Sarfaraz, Vol. 1, pp. 22–3. Another publication, *Hava-ye Rastakhiz* targeted Iranians living abroad.
118 'The Party's characteristics', *JR*, (96), 23 August 1975.

Chapter 8

1 *Rastakhiz*, Leader, 'The mission', (868), 20 February 1978.
2 'Party Councils pave the way toward the Great Civilization', *Rastakhiz*, (660), 6 May 1977; Also Ehsan Naraqi, 'Every country must find its own path', (569), 17 March 1976; 'Authenticity and the Great Civilization', (329), 1 June 1976.
3 'Interview with Masoud Naini', *Rastakhiz*, (814), 22 December 1977. See also: *Rastakhiz*, (405), 23 August 1976.
4 Mahmoud Jafarian, 'Iran's revolution has made a new value system…', (128), 21 January 1978. See also: 'We must revive our proper and good traditions', Interview with Aligholi Loqmanadham, (239), 12 February 1976; 'Characteristics of the Rastakhiz Party', (70), 22 June 1975.
5 'A revolutionary society must enjoy spirituality above all else', *RJ*, (89), 20 April 1976.
6 For example see Rear Admiral Ibrahim Shahosseini, *Shenakt-e Tamaddon-e Iran va Chehreha-ye Melli* (Tehran, 2535/1976).
7 Both wings of the party actively propagated this issue. See *Hezb-e Rastakhizei mellat-e Iran, Jenah-e pishru, Ketabche avval*, (2536/1977). *Fazaye siasi-ye Iran az didgah-ye jenah-e sazande*, (2536/1977).
8 Hamid Enayat, 'Ahamiat-e shenakht-e enteqadi-ye arzeshha-ye farhangira nadide gerefteim', *Farhang va Zendegi* (9), September 1973.
9 See *Rastakhiz*, 'Attention to moral values', (133), 23 September 1975 and 'Hoveyda…', (164), 23 October 1975.
10 'Shahanshah: Strong spiritual principles will prevent society from falling into the grips of consumerism and imperialism', *Rastakhiz*, (605), 21 April 1977. See also 'A unique Iranian style of management', *Rastakhiz*, (648), 22 June 1977; 'The necessity of a cultural revolution: Interview with Manuchehr Azmun', *JR*, (9), 23 July 1975. Solution to the issue of morality in the age of the machine', *Rastakhiz*, (159), 23 October 1976.
11 *Rastakhiz*, (560), 20 February 1978.
12 *Rastakhiz*, (66), 26 Tir 1354. These remarks were also extensively covered by *JR*, (5), 26 June 1975. He repeated these views weeks later in an interview with *The NYT*, *Keyhan*, 23 September 1975. See also: Pahlavi, *Talifat*… Vol. 9, 8264–9. 'I want to preserve forever the authenticity of Iranian identity, philosophy, and spirit. We do not want to resemble a machine'. This quote was also included in Mozaffari's book and published by Rastakhiz publications after it appeared in *Keyhan*. 'Technology and moral values', *Rastakhiz*, (334), 7 June 1976; 'The spread of the machine threatens

our youth', *Rastakhiz*, (259), 8 March 1976; 'We must revive our venerated traditions', *Rastakhiz*, (238), 11 February 1976.
13. 'The youth must become mobilized...', interview with the Shah. *JR*, (5), 22 June 1975.
14. *Rastakhiz*, (138), 14 October 1975.
15. Farah Pahlavi, *Alihezrat Farah Pahlavi Shabanou-ye Iran az 2517 ta 2535* (Tehran, 2535), p. 321.
16. *JR*, (144), 3 June 1978.
17. *Rastakhiz*, (38), 20 February 1976. See also 'Advice and guidance...', *RJ*, (51), 22 May 1976.
18. *Rastakhiz*, 'The Party is the base of national unity', (303), 21 April 1977. See also, 'The identity crisis', (496), 22 November 1977.
19. *JR*, (126), 22 December 1977.
20. 'The hopes for tomorrow in the Empress' opinion', *JR*, (4), 22 June 1975. See also 'Empress: Universities must be the guardians of Iran's eternal cultural values', *Rastakhiz*, (269), 23 March 1976; 'Empress: We must protect our culture's roots', *JR*, (139), 21 April 1978.
21. 'Party news', *JR*, (45), 6 May 1976.
22. *Rastakhiz*, 'Toward a better understanding of Iran and Iranians', (305), 4 May 1976. See also 'The Shah's Guidelines for political education', (731), 23 September 1977; 'Demonstrations illustrative of Iranians' anti-imperialist will', (819), 22 December 1977; Vadiei 'False consumerism and its antidote', *Rastakhiz*, (512 and 513), 22–23 December 1975.
23. 'The Revolution and Spirituality', *RJ*, (65), 23 September 1977. See also 'The obligatory guidance...', *RJ*, (99), 22 June 1977; 'Interview with the Shahanshah', *Rastakhiz* (450), 23 October 1976; 'People are moving in the direction of superficiality' *Rastakhiz*, (690), 23 July 1977; 'Consumer society and the sickness of inflation of the personality', *Rastakhiz*, (694), 26 July 1977.
24. Hasemi Hairi, 'The attractiveness of the Occident and Iran's teenagers', *Rastakhiz*, (711), 23 August 1977.
25. Pahlavi, *Beh Sui...*, pp. 252–3. See also: Pahlavi, *Talifat...* Vol. 10, p. 8470.
26. 'Iran needs scientific and technical independence', *Rastakhiz*, (679), 11 August 1977.
27. Mozaffari, *Nizamha-ye*....
28. 'The new national identity', *Rastakhiz*, (280), 21 March 1976.
29. Mozaffari, *Nizamha-ye...*, p. 165.
30. Ibid., p. 173.
31. Ibid., p. 140.
32. The Parthian Empire (247 BC–AD 224) was the successor to the Seleucid Empire (312 to 63 BC).
33. 'The threat to the youth', *RJ*, (74), 22 November 1977. See also 'The Shah's advice and guidance to the motherland's young generation', *RJ*, (6), 23 July 1975; 'The Leader's advice: The Party and the young', *JR*, (51), 17 June 1975. Ibrahim Kuhestani, 'The Party's policies for the youth', *JR*, (40), 1 April 1976. 'The youth in the opinion of the Revolution's Leader', *JR*, (39), 1355 (1976), New Year Special Edition.
34. Mozaffari, *Nizamha-ye...*, p. 144.
35. *HIOHP*, Baheri, (25), p. 3.
36. Pahlavi, *Talifat,...*, Vol. 9, pp. 8332–3. See also 'On the order of the Shah...', *JR*, (25), 22 November 1975.
37. *OHPFIS*, Hossein Sarfaraz, Vol. 1, pp. 43–4.

38 See Hamid Shukat, *Negahi az darun be jonbesh-e chap: goftigu ba Kuroush Lashai* (Tehran, 1386/2007).
39 Ibid., pp. 268–70.
40 *HIOHP,* Baheri, (25), p. 2.
41 Alam, Vol. 6, p. 269. See also *Si porsesh va pasokh piramunei osul-e bonyadi-ye an va hizb-e Rastakhiz-e mellat-e Iran.*
42 *HIOHP*, Baheri, (25), pp. 6–8.
43 Dehbashi, ed., *Hekmat...*, p. 418.
44 Alam, *Yaddashtha...*, Vol. 6, pp. 285–6. See also pp. 269, 292.
45 Akhami, *The Shah...*, p. 455.
46 Dabashi, *The Theology...*, p. 110.
47 Honarmand, *Pahlavism*, Vol. 1, pp. 50–2.
48 Dabashi, *The Theology...*, pp. 113–14.
49 *JR*, (120), 17 Azar 2536.
50 Afkhami, *The Shah*, p. 435.
51 *HIOHP,* Baheri, (25), p. 8.
52 Shukat, *Neghai...*, pp. 271–2.
53 Ibid., p. 272.
54 Ibid., pp. 272–4.
55 Dehbashi, *Hekmat...*, p. 417.
56 Shukat, *Negahi...*, p. 274.
57 Alam, *Yaddashtha...*, Vol. 6, pp. 338–42.
58 Ibid., pp. 885–6.
59 Houshangmahdavi, *Engelab-e....*, pp. 263–4.
60 'Crystallization of Rastakhiz's victory' and 'Publication of the philosophy...', *JR*, (70), 23 October 1976. 'The reaction to the philosophy...', *JR*, (99), 5 July 1977; 'The philosophy...', *JR* (88), 24 Farvardin 2536/13 April 1977; Vadiei, 'Everyone needs political education', *JR*, (115), 3 November 1977. 'The revolution's philosophy must be...'
61 *Falsafeh-ye Enqelab-e Iran* (Tehran, 2535/1976).
62 'The philosophy of Iran's revolution', *RJ,* (88), 13 April 1977; See also (89), 20 April 1977; 'Philosophy of Iran's revolution', (90), 5 May 1977; 'The obligatory guidance...', (91), 12 May 1977.
63 *Falsafeh-ye Enqelab...*, p. 11.
64 Ibid., pp. 8–10.
65 *JR*, (90), 5 May 1977.
66 'Mostanad-e zendegi va marg-e Abbas-e Hoveyda', Part 3, *Documentary Channel-Sedao Sima-ye IRI.*
67 Pahlavi, *Be sui-ye...*, p. 7.
68 Ibid., p. 8.
69 Ibid., p. 227.
70 Ibid., pp. 230–1.
71 Ibid., p. 88.
72 Ibid., pp. 126–30.
73 Ibid., p. 235.
74 Ibid., p. 32.
75 Ibid., p. 218.
76 Ibid., p. 227.
77 Pahlavi, *Be sui-ye...*, p. 235.

78 Ibid., p. 80.
79 Ibid., p. 243.
80 Ibid., pp. 243–4.
81 Ibid., pp. 241–2.
82 Alam, *The Shah and I*, p. 171.
83 Alam, *Yaddashtha…* Vol. 2, p. 333.
84 Pahlavi, *Be sui-ye…*, pp. 238–9.
85 Ibid., p. 244.
86 Ibid., p. 78.
87 Ibid., p. 66.
88 Ibid., p. 78.
89 Ibid., pp. 246–7.
90 Ibid., p. 291.
91 Ibid., p. 292.
92 Ibid., p. 294.
93 Ibid., pp. 218–19.
94 Ibid., p. 88.
95 Ibid., pp. 87–8.

Chapter 9

1 *Rastakhiz*, (381), 2 August 1976. See also Muhammad Nadoushan, 'What is culture?' *Rastakhiz*, (482), 1 December 1976.
2 *Rastakhiz*, (328), 22 May 1976. See also Manuchehr Ajman, 'The Party's main goal is to defend authenticity and defeat foreign cultural invasions', (303), 21 April 1976.
3 'Spiritual Rastakhiz', and 'Hoveyda: The Party is mobilized for a spiritual resurgence', *Rastakhiz*, (73), 26 July 1975. See also 'To be alienated from the self', (119), 20 September 1975. 'The Revolution's new principle: societal spiritual development', *JR*, (39), 1355/1976.
4 *Rastakhiz*, (327), 30 May 1976. See also 'Rastakhiz's path', (328), 1 June 1976; Sadeq Homyauni, 'Iran's cultural identity and the new phenomena', (342), 16 June 1976.
5 'Spirituality and Welfare' and Muhammad Orfinezhad, 'The consumerist society is avarious', *Rastakhiz*, (336), 9 June 1976.
6 'Hoveyda: Iran's revolution will destroy the imperialism of consumerism', *Rastakhiz*, (139), 14 August 1975. See also 'Empress: Spending on luxurious unnecessary things must be avoided', *Rastakhiz*, (548), 20 February 1977.
7 'A fateful conference', *Rastakhiz*, (409), 5 September 1977; See also *Rastakhiz*, (668), 22 June 1977; 'The Revolution and the birth of the new Iranian person', *JR*, (127), 26 January 1978.
8 Hushayar Pirayesh, 'The one-dimensional individuals', *Rastakhiz*, (210), 8 January 1976.
9 'Savak sees a ghost', *The Economist*, 2 January 1971.
10 'Narcissism and the intellectual values of Iranian society', *Rastakhiz*, (512), 8 January 1977.
11 *JR*, 'The Youth of the Rastakhiz Era…', Naser Shadman, (56), 22 July 1976.
12 Ehsan Naraqi, 'Our intellectuals view problems on the basis of materialism', *Rastakhiz*, (307), 6 May 1976. 'Iranian villages built the country's spiritual and material thought

and civilization', *Rastakhiz*, (797). 'The invaluable role of the rustic young in the spread of culture...', *JR*, (67), 14 October 1976.
13 *RJ*, (66), 21 October 1976. It ran throughout 1976–7 a column entitled 'Question: What is Iranian youth?' (68), 6 Aban 2536.
14 Hamid Naficy, *A Social History of Iranian Cinema: The Industrializing Years, 1941-1978* (Durham, 2011), pp. 233–7.
15 Hossein Baniahmad, 'The closest path for the elimination of corruption', *Rastakhiz*, (245), 19 February 1976.
16 *Rastakhiz*, (502), 26 December 1977.
17 'Conversation with Keyvan Khosrovani', *JR*, (149), July 1978.
18 'The position of culture and art in the Rastakhiz-era society', *JR*, (20), 30 October 1975.
19 *Ferdowsi*, (144), 29 June 1954; (152), 24 August 1954.
20 Christine Ammer, *Fruitcakes & Couch Potatoes* (Bookbaby, 1995).
21 Naficy, *A Social...*, p. 150.
22 Gaffari, Vol. 1, pp. 27–8. See also Jamal Omid, *Tarikh-e sinemay-ye Iran, 1279-1375* (Tehran, 1374/1995), pp. 886–7.
23 Quoted in Omid, *Tarikh-e...*, p. 886.
24 Ibnid., p. 219.
25 Quoted in Ali Qolipour, *Parvaresh-e zoq-e 'ame dar 'asr-e Pahlavi* (Tehranm 2018), p. 214.
26 Omid, *Tarikh-e...*, pp. 885–6.
27 Ibid., p. 432.
28 Naficy, *A Social...*, p. 150.
29 Basir Nasibi, 'Interview with Hushang Kavusi', *Negin*, (39), August 1968.
30 Naficy, *A Social...*, p. 195.
31 Ibid., p. 422.
32 Naser Shadman, 'The youth of the Rastakhiz Era...', *JR*, (56), 31 Tir 2535/22 July 1976.
33 Hossein Yazdanian, *Dokan be esm-e cinema* (Tehran, 1968), pp. 3, 111. See also pp. 124–8.
34 Kamran Talattof, *Modernity, Sexuality, and Ideology in Iran: The Life and Legacy of a Popular Female Artist* (Syracuse, 2011), p. 52.
35 Mostafa Najafabadi, *Tamasha-ye manfiha* (Tabriz, 1353/1974). After the 1979 Revolution he has made a successful career within the IRI.
36 'The forty-nine sexy ones' *In hafte*, New Years Edition, 1350/1971.
37 '*Eivallah* has gone sexy!' (13), April 1971.
38 'The market for sex is hot!' Ibid.
39 Parviz Khatibi, *Khaterat-e Honarmandan* (Tehran, 1387), p. 134.
40 Ali Assali, *Farhang va Zandegi*, (13–14) Winter 1973–4.
41 Alviri, Morteza, *Khaterat-e Morteza Alviri* (Tehran, 1375), pp. 119–20.
42 During the short period of the publication of *This Week* SAVAK frequently issued warnings to its about content and censored and even banned many issues. The intelligence service, increasingly concerned about the growing clerical and public outcry over this journal amid charges that the Pahlavi state allowed the spread of corrupt Western morality and pornography, was particularly sensitive to the extent of nudity of pictures on the magazine's cover.
43 *JR*, (112), 10 October 1977.
44 Jamal Omid, *Farhang-e filmha-ye cinema-ye Iran*, 2 vols. (Tehran, 1372/1993), Vol. 2, p. 411.

45 'Prostitution in *filmfarsi*', *Ferdowsi*, (1099), 22 January 1972.
46 Naficy, *A Social...*, p. 424.
47 *Keyhan*, 12 December 2007.
48 Hossein Najafian, 'A chunk of Iranian filmmakers, actors, actresses is sick'. Interview with Senator Darya Rasai', *JR*, (31), 15 January 1976.
49 '*Filmfarsi* is in reality cheap trickery', *JR*, (34), 5 February 1976.
50 *Sepide va Siah*, (915), 1 February 1972.
51 'Discussion about discussions on *filmfarsi*', *JR*, (104), 18 August 1977.
52 Mohammad Mamjed, *JR*, (108), 15 September 1977.
53 'A short talk about Persian-language television series and films', *JR*, (30), 8 January 1976.
54 Iraj Homayounmanesh, '*Filmfarsi* plays the leading role in the creation of personality cult...', *JR* (112), 13 October 1977; 'The corruption of *filmfarsi*', *JR*, (34), 5 February 1976. Mohammad Tahaminezhad, 'Morality and cinema in Iran', *JR*, (88), 13 April 1977. See also Bijan Mahjer, 'Commercialization is damaging national cinema's authentic identity', *JR*, (60), 26 August 1976. 'Our cinema is really only a copy of cabaret entertainment', Interview with Karim Rezai', *JR*, (76), 16 December 1976.
55 *Rastakhiz*, (34), 5 February 1976; *JR*, (13), 11 September 1975. See also 'The opponents of art and the cinema Mafia', *JR*, (38), 23 February 1976; See also (112), 13 October 1977.
56 Mohammad Momjed, 'Iranian cinema-without identity, without duty', *JR*, (132), 1 February 1978. 'Today's Iranian filmmaker knows nothing of national arts: Interview with Manuchehr Teyab', *JR*, (76), 22 November 1976.
57 Interview with Haritash, *JR*, (112), 13 October 1977; (110), 30 September 1977.
58 'Defense of *filmfarsi* is a betrayal of Iranian cinema: Interview with Haritash, *JR*, (109), 22 September 1977; See also 'The scandal we condemn', (110), 29 September 1977; 'Those who instead of caviar offer us Pangas' and 'Interview with Haritash, (111), 6 October 1977; 'The scandal we condemn', (131), 20 February 1978; '*Filmfarsi*: the continuation of a cultureless movement', (141), 13 May 1978; 'The scandal we condemn', (37), 27 February 1976; 'The Results of *JR*'s Investigation into Iranian cinema' and 'People are not to blame, it is the fault of government officials...', (39) New Year Edition, 1355/1976.
59 *JR*, (126), 19 January 1978.
60 Yazdian, *Dokan...*, p. 200.
61 Qolipour, *Parvaresh...*, pp. 217–18.
62 *Rastakhiz*, (34), 5 February 1976.
63 'Scandal we condemn', *JR*, (142), 10 May 1978.
64 'Attempts by foreign powers to exercise influence will be prevented', *Rastakhiz*, (30), 6 July 1975. See also (474), 22 November 1976; Masoud Foruzan, '*Filmfarsi*: continuation of an anti-cultural movement', *JR*, (141), 13 May 1978.
65 *Rastakhiz*, (37), 26 February 1976 and *JR*, (45), 6 May 1976. See also (74), 2 December 1977; (28), 5 June 1975; (24), 29 May 1975; (156), 23 July 1978. Similar to *JR*, *Rastakhiz* blamed the influence of Western culture and commercialization: 'Iranian theater has become non-Iranian'. 'We no longer have Iranian theater'. See Ali Nassirian, 'The West's theater culture must pass through the sieve of the Iranian youth's mind-and not use it as a storage room', (290), 17 April 1976. See also 'About the causes of the decline of Iran's cinema', *Rastakhiz*, (220), 21 January 1976; 'Attack on *Filmfarsi*', (246), 21 February 1976; 'Alienation from culture and the youth's lack of

identity', (606), 5 May 1977; 'Iranian cinema: The big lie that grew', (814), 11 January 1978.
66 Mohammad Eraqinezhad, interview with Barbod Taheri, 'Support the prestige of Iranian cinema', *JR*, (60), 26 August 1976.
67 Iraq Homayounmanesh, '*Filmfarsi*: lack of standards and full of corruption', *JR*, (145), 10 June 1978. Another article in the series 'We are condemning scandal and corruption'. This article focused on the 'false and fake actors and actresses'. 'Most of the actors and actresses in Film Farsi come from among assistant drivers, mason apprentices, and street people'. See also 'Dressing as women for laughs', (146), 17 June 1978.
68 Sush Square is located in the central-southern part of Tehran.
69 'The scandal we condemn', *JR*, (142), 10 May 1978.
70 *JR*, (122), 22 December 1977. Interview with Farrokh Qafari. See also its second part (131), 20 February 1978 and interview with Hushang Kavusi, (127), 26 January 1978.
71 *JR*, (98), 30 June 1977.
72 'A great national duty', *Rastakhiz*, (35), 12 February 1976.
73 *OHPFIB*, Pahlbod, Vol. 1, p. 66.
74 *OHPFIB*, Pahlbod, Vol. 2, p. 32.
75 Ibrahim Zalzadeh, 'Television production: a mission against culture', *JR*, (126), 19 January 1977.
76 Iraq Homayounmanesh, 'Series serving no purpose outside of Occidentosis', *JR*, (114), 27 October 1977.
77 This is the story of the seven ordeals of the national hero of *Shahnameh* based on the traditional theme of truth vanquishing evil.
78 'Conversations with Rasul', Ibid., (114), 27 October 1977.
79 One programme targeted was *Aqaye Marbutih*, described as 'cheap, worthless, garbage, and of low culture'.
80 *JR*, (123), 29 December 1978. See also 'Today an Iranian filmmaker knows nothing of national native art...', 7 October 1977, (76), 16 December 1976; Mohammad Tahaminezhad, 'Morality and cinema in Iran', (88), 13 April 1977; 'Seductive and glamorous: the mirage of Iranian cinema', (129), 9 February 1978.
81 'Party news', *JR* (118), 24 November 1977.
82 *Rastakhiz*, (640), 6 October 1977. See Yousef Mohammadinezhad, 'National duty: Protection of Iranian culture in face of the West's cultural invasion', *JR*, (145), 11 June 1978 and Mahmoud Jafarian, 'Iran's revolution...' and 'Interview with Yousef Mohammadinezhad', (128), 2 February 1978.
83 The positive aspects of Western technology, such as recording equipment, were not part of these discourses.
84 Rastakhiz reporting on this scandal differs from some others, in particular the physical nature of their relationship before and after the divorce. The veracity of these varying narratives is not important to this study. How Rastakhiz used a particular narrative of these events to expand the offensive against Occidentosis and Occidentosis-ridden Iranians is examined here.
85 Iraj Homayounmanesh, 'How and where does moral decline begin?', *JR*, (107), 8 September 1977.
86 'The anatomy of a scandal: The adventure of "Dariush" and 'Maryam', *JR*, (108), 15 September 1977.

87 'The Disseminators of Cultural Obscenity and Culturelessness', *JR*, (109), 23 September 1977. In the same issue was an article on the continuing story of Dariush and the acid spraying. Several pages were dedicated to readers' responses. Dariush was called '*motrebak*' in several letters.
88 *JR*, (109), 23 September 1977. See also 'The agents of chaos and the collapse of songwriting', (115), 3 November 1977.
89 They were two other singers who, in the eyes of Rastakhiz writers and social conservatives, including clerics, led corrupted Occidentosis-ridden lives that served as bad examples for the youth and spread Occidentosis. Susan was a particular target since she had once been a prostitute and was functionally illiterate while Aqassi was a singer in second-rate nightclubs in Lalehzar Street in central Tehran.
90 Abbas Milani, *Eminent Persians: The Men and Women Who Made Modern Iran, 1941-1979* (Syracuse, 2008), p. 993.
91 *JR*, 'A phenomena, an excuse', (21), 6 November 1975.
92 'The opium of society' and Manuchehr Jahanbeglu, 'Western music is an imported and unathentic art', *JR* (144), 3 June 1977 and 'Iranian jazz: the blind mimicking of licentious and corrosive Westerners', (146), 17 June 1978. Firuz Barzin, 'The catastrophe these "Jazz Misters" imposed on Iranian music', *JR*, (111), 6 October 1977.
93 *JR*, (74), 2 December 1976.
94 For examples of Rastakhiz attacks on sensationalist and yellow journalism, see *JR*, (114 and 115), 27 October and 3 November 1977.
95 'The scandal we condemn', *JR*, (110), 29 September 1977; See also 'The scandal we condemn', (121), 15 December 1977. 'Heroes are the epitome of ideals, wishes and goals', *Rastakhiz*, (63), 14 July 1975.
96 'The cultural didactic role of poetry and songs', *JR*, (25), 4 December 1975.
97 'The scandal we condemn', *JR*, (114), 27 October 1977.
98 Iraj Homayounmanesh, 'With the publication and spread of scandal do not posion society' and *JR*, (113), 20 October 1977. See also: 'The scandal we condemn', (122), 22 December 1977; 'The scandal we condemn', (132), 2 March 1978; Pari Nadimi, 'Our songwriters of today are musically illiterate. Interview with Morteza Hanane', *JR*, (76), 2 December 1976.
99 'The corruption and scandal that must be condemned', *JR*, (118), 24 November 1977. See also Barzin, 'The corruption and scandal that must be condemned', *JR*, (120), 9 December 1977; 'The *Abgushti* songs-the death knoll for real art', *JR*, (134), 16 March 1978 and (135), 1 April 1978.
100 *JR*, (72), 18 November 1976.
101 'The sudden birth of triteness and banality', *JR*, (147), 24 June 1978.
102 See also Iraj Homayuonmanesh, '*Filmfarsi*: lack of standards and full of corruption', *JR*, (145), 10 June 1977 and Masoud Foruzan, '*Filmfarsi*: the continuation of a cultureless movement', (141), 13 May 1978.
103 Shahrokh Dasturtabar, 'Today's songs in the movement toward triteness and banality. Interview with Ali Reza Khajenuri', *RJ*, (67), 14 October 1976; 'The scandal we condemn', *JR*, (110), 28 September 1977; Firuz Barzin, 'The drums of cultural corruption...', *JR*, (113), 20 October 1977. 'When songwriters are illiterate', (114), 27 October 1977; 'The agents of the chaos and collapse of songwriting, 7-8', *JR*, (115/116), 3 and 10 November 1977. Firuz Barzin, 'Review of the agents of the collapse of songwriting', and Ibrahim Zalzadeh, 'National culture faces an attack of agents of destruction', (125), 13 January 1978.

104 Ansari, *Man va...*, pp. 51–3.
105 Mehdi Amani, 'Cultural continuation...', (90), 16 August 1975; Rahmat Mostafavi, 'They want to destroy the Persian language', *Rastakhiz*, (98), 25 August 1975; 'The Persian language must put aside all signs of triteness and banality', *Rastakhiz*, (238) 'For projects we still don't have sources in Persian', *JR*, (32), 22 January 1976. 'Advertising bombards the city', *JR*, (93), 26 May 1977; Iraj Homanyounmanesh, 'What will happen to our ancient culture and language?', *JR*, (122), 22 December 1977.
106 *Rastakhiz*, (685), 7 August 1977.
107 Ibid., (690), 13 August 1977; See also 'Studios and filmmaking in Tehran over the last twenty-three years: A "Persian" review of *filmfarsi*', *JR*, (99), 10 July 1977.
108 'Interview with Vartan Hovanessian', *JR*, (60), 26 August 1976.
109 *JR*, (120), 8 December 1977.
110 'The problem of cultural identity in urban architecture', *JR* (99), 7 July 1977. 'Abdolhamid Eshraq, 'Iranian architecture and the danger of apartment complexes', *Rastakhiz*, (123), 25 September 1975.
111 Hassan Nekouei, 'The cultural authenticity of the East's architecture has been destroyed', *Rastakhiz*, (48), 5 Tir 1354/26 June 1975. See also Abdulhamid Eshraq, 'National architecture and industrial architecture', (90), 23 July 1975; 'The private sector and the problems of architecture and residential housing', (436), 23 September 1976.
112 Useff Khanali, 'Iran's authentic architecture...', *Rastakhiz*, (27), 2 June 1975 and Abdolhamid Eshraq, 'Modern architecture and national identity', (61), 12 July 1975.
113 Azita Naser-Azari, 'A talk with Keyvan Khosrovani', *JR*, (149), 8 July 1978.
114 'In memory of the Iranian home', *Rastakhiz*, (340), 14 June 1976. Also 'Where have Tehran's yards and gardens gone?', *JR*, (92), 10 May 1977; 'Empress: the construction of spiritless and identiless cities must be prevented', *Rastakhiz*, (789), 12 December 1977.
115 *JR*, (139), 29 April 1978.
116 'Party committee resolution', *Rastakhiz*, (666), 14 July 1977.
117 Azadeh Mashayekhi, 'The 1968 Tehran master plan and the politics of development in Iran (1945-1979)', *Planning Perspectives,* (2018), p.24.
118 'Authentic Iranian architecture', *Rastakhiz*, (344), 19 June 1976. 'More attention must be paid to national architecture', *Rastakhiz*, (808), 4 January 1978.
119 Naficy, *A Social...*, p. 124.
120 Ibid., *Rastakhiz*, (340), 14 June 1976 and (138), 5 October 1975.
121 'Native culture the only refuge of the lonely person', *JR*, (73), 25 November 1976.
122 Mahmoud Bakhtiari, 'To be cut off from Iranian culture means decline and collapse', *JR*, (107), 8 September 1977.
123 'The Iranian home and neighborhood', *JR*, (139), 29 April 1978.
124 'Interview with Khosrow Khajenuri and Ali Giahi', *JR*, (126), 19 January 1978.

Chapter 10

1 Afkhami, *The Shah*, p. 404.
2 Sheherazade Afshar Ghorbi, ed., 'Shiraz-Persepolis Festival of Arts (1967-1977): Detailed Catalogue of Events', January 2018. For a contemporaneous catalogue of the festival, see Iraq Gorgin, ed., *Ketab-e Jashn-e Honar* (Tehran, 1354/1975).

3. *Jashn-e Honar-e Shiraz be ravaet-e asnad-e SAVAK* (Tehran, 1381), No.5/14455, 51/6/25/, p. 212.
4. Qolipour, *Parvaresh...*, pp. 166–7.
5. *OHPFIS*, Pahlbod, Vol. 2, p. 74.
6. Alam, *Yaddashtha...*, Vol. 1, p. 361. 17–19 Shahrivar 1347.
7. *Ettela'at*, 14 Shahrivar 1351. See also the post-revolution remarks of another festival official, Bijan Saffari. *OHPFIS,* Saffari, Vol. 1, p. 3.
8. 'The necessity for emphasis on national culture', *Rastakhiz*, (147), 23 October 1975. In same issue, see: Sha'ale Nazarian, 'Art Festivals and cultural changes of Iran'.
9. Masoud Foruzan, 'Artistic and literary imitation and copying', *JR*, (105), 3 Shahrivar 2536.
10. 'Party news', *JR* (110), 29 September 1977.
11. *OHPOFIS*, Arby Ovanessian, Vol. 1, p. 11.
12. Ibid., p. 12.
13. *Ettela'at*, 7 Shahrivar 1349.
14. *Keyhan*, (10247), 22 August 1977.
15. *Keyhan*, (10249), 24 August 1977.
16. *Keyhan*, (10247), 22 August 1977.
17. *Keyhan*, (10248), 23 August 1977.
18. 'Monsieur Ovanessian ... lover of foreign ways...' *Keyhan*, 23 August 1977.
19. *Keyhan*, (10246), 21 August 1977.
20. 'Pig, Child, Fire! and Ovanessian', *Ettela'at*, (15395), 23 August 1977.
21. *Rastakhiz*, (700), 24 August 1977.
22. *Rastakhiz*, (714), 11 September 1977.
23. Mohammad Orfinezhad, 'Everything in Shiraz was chic', *JR*, (106), 1 September 1977.
24. SAVAK reports on the Festival come from *Jashn-e honar-e Shriaz be ravaet-e asnad-e SAVAK* (Tehran, 1381), pp. 383–407.
25. Ibid., p. 383.
26. Ibid., 385–6.
27. Yuseff Khanali, *JR*, (105), 25 August 1977.
28. Charles Harrision and Paul Wood, eds., *Art in Theory 1805-1900: An Anthology of Changing Ideas* (Oxford, 1998), p. 40.
29. Nadeije Laneyrie-Dagen, *Histoire de l'art pour tous* (Paris, 2011), p. 458.
30. Eksteins, *Rites...*, p. 31.
31. *Pravda*, 28 January 1936.
32. *Pravda*, 13 February 1936.
33. Modris Eksteins, *Rites of Spring: The Great War and the Birth of the Modern Age* (New York, 1989), p. 27.
34. Tom Service, 'The Rite of Spring: "The work of a madmad"', *Guardian*, 12 February 2013.
35. Eksteins, *Rites...*, p. 10.
36. Laneyrie-Dagen, *Histoire...*, p. 462.
37. Eksteins, *Rites...*, pp. 47–8.
38. Ibid., p. 48.
39. Lucien Romier, *Qui sera le maître? Europe ou Amérique?* (Paris, 1927), p. 239.
40. Georges Duhamel, *America: The Menace-scenes from the life of the future* (New York, 1931), pp. 8–9.
41. Romy Golan, *Modernity & Nostalgia: Art and Politics in France between the Wars* (New Haven, 1995), p. 83.

42 For an overview on this topic, see Philippe Roger, *L'Ennemi améicain, Généalogie de l'antiaméricanisme français* (Paris, 2002).
43 Ibid., p. 7.
44 Ibid., p. x.
45 Paul Léon, *La Renaissance des ruines* (Paris, 1918), p. 39. Quoted in Golan, *Modernity...*, p. 23.

Chapter 11

1   Meeting Record, 1 February 1968, *FRUS 1964-1968*, XXI, pp. 131-2.
2   Roham Alvandi, *Nixon, Kissinger, and the Shah: The United States and Iran in the Cold War* (Oxford, 2014), p. 3.
3   Alvandi, *Nixon, Kissinger, and the Shah: The United States and Iran in the Cold War*, Chapter 3.
4   Ibid., Chapter 1.
5   For example see William J. Butler and Georges Levasseur, *Human Rights and the Legal System in Iran* (Geneva: International Commission of Jurists, March 1976). 'Iran Accused at Meeting here of Torture and Repression; Speakers Urge "Tyranny" End', *New York Times (NYT)*, 29 February 1976; Reza Baraheni, 'Torture in Iran: "It is a Hell Made by One Man for Another Man"', *NYT*, 21 April 1976; 'Iran and the Arms Trade', *Washington Post*, 5 August 1976; Tom Wicker, 'President and Shah', *NYT*, 6 July 1976. US Senate, Committee on Foreign Relations, Subcommittee on Foreign Assistance, *U.S. Military Sales to Iran* (Washington, DC, 1976). Leslie Gelb, 'Study Finds Iran Dependent on U.S. in Using Weapons', *NYT*, 2 August 1976.
6   Alvandi, *Nixon...*, p. 128.
7   'Another beginning', *Rastakhiz*, (414), 11 September 1976; See also Koroush Lashai, 'Imperialism recognized Iran and its rulers as their own possessions', *Rastakhiz*, (563-5), 4-6 March 1977.
8   Andrei A. Zhdanov, *Za bol'shevistskuyu ideinost'* (Riga, 1951), pp. 92-5.
9   David Caute, *The Dancer Defects* (Oxford, 2005); K. V. Solokov, *Khudozhestvennaya Kultura i Vlast v Poststalinskoi Rossii: Soyuz i Borba, 1953-1985* (St. Petersburg, 2007).
10 *Rastakhiz*, (414), 11 September 1976. See also: Mozaffari, 'The new imperialism', *JR*, (60), 26 August 1976; (59), 18 August 1976; and 'New imperialism's tactics', *Rastakhiz*, (799), 25 December 1977.
11 Naficy, *A Social...*, pp. 51-5.
12 Pahlavi, *Mission...*, pp. 82-131.
13 *JR*, (59), 19 August 1976.
14 'Yesterday's imperialism and economic development', *Rastakhiz*, (8), 11 May 1975. 'The friendship between Third World countries must expand', *Rastakhiz*, (70), 22 July 1975.
15 Alam, *Yaddashtha...*, Vol. 2, pp. 10-11. See Pahlavi, *Talifat...*, Vol. 6, pp. 5520-3.
16 Edwin Bacon, ed., *Brezhnev Reconsidered* (New York, 2002); Leonid Mlechin, *Brezhnev: Razocharovanie Rossii* (St. Petersburg, 2007); and T. V. Paul, Deborah Larson, William Wohlworth, eds., *Status in World Politics* (Cambridge, 2014).
17 'The philosophy of Iran's revolution', *Rastakhiz*, (225), 21 January 1976.
18 'Iran's revolution and the imperialism of red and black', *JR*, (41), 8 April 1976.

19 'Foreign interventionists don't like authentic national culture', *Rastakhiz*, (783), 29 November 1977; See also 'Attempts by foreign powers to exercise influence will be prevented', *Rastakhiz*, (30), 22 May 1975.
20 'Anti-American demonstrations in Tehran', *Rastakhiz*, (785), 7 December 1977 and (787), 10 December 1977.
21 *Rastakhiz*, (141), 18 October 1975.
22 Mozaffari, *Nezamha-ye...*, p. 143. *Rastakhiz*, (789), 13 December 1977.
23 'Communism: new imperialism's instrument', *Rastakhiz*, (18), 16 October 1975.
24 'Party news', *JR*, (142), 20 May 1978.
25 *Rastakhiz*, (675), 1 August 1977. *JR*, (69), 28 October 1977.
26 *Rastakhiz*, (790), 13 December 1977; Deputy Party head, 'Western models in all areas are not appropriate to Iran's social structure and system', *Rastakhiz*, (685), 7 August 1977.
27 'Shahanshah: Iran's democracy is not synonymous with chaos and licentiousness', (384), 5 August 1977. 'Iranian democracy', *Rastakhiz*, (665), 13 July 1977.
28 Alam, *Yaddashtha...*, Vol. 6, p. 885.
29 *Rahnamud-e Amuzish-e siasi: barnameh-ye ejarii*. Approved by the Party's Executive Committee on October 1977. See also, *JR*, (142–3) and *Seminar-e barresi-ye masael-e hezbi, bashgah-e nakhost vaziri, 16-17 Azar 2537*.
30 For example see: *Enqelab-e Sefid-e Iran: Rahi be sui-ye tamaddon-e bozorg* (Jendipour, 1351).
31 *Keyhan*, (575), 5 October 1975. The Great Civilization's humanistic and spiritual aspects', *Rastakhiz*, (460), 6 November 1976.
32 *Rastakhiz*, (88), 10 April 1977.
33 Mozaffari, *Nezamha-ye...*, p. 143.
34 *Rastakhiz*, (130), 7 October 1975.
35 'Baheri', *Rastakhiz*, (788), 11 December 1977.

Chapter 12

1 Masoud Behnud, 'Cultural heritage', *Ferdowsi* (917), 30 June 1969, (918), 7 July 1969.
2 'Review of conferences', *JR*, (12), 4 September 1975.
3 Ehsan Naraqi, 'The levels of education and cultural identity', *Rastakhiz*, (485), 6 December 1976.
4 Nafisi, *Tarikh-e Moaser-e...*, pp. 81–2.
5 'The damaging preconditions of cultural terrorism', *Rastakhiz*, (308), 21 April 1976. Naraqi, 'Levels of education and cultural identity', *Rastakhiz*, (485), 1 December 1976. 'Nationalism in the front ranks of the Iranian youth's education', *JR*, (98), 30 June 1977.
6 Naraqi, 'The Third World in the face of the West's science and technology', *Rastakhiz* (37), 14 June 1975.
7 *Rastakhiz*, (151), 16 July 1975.
8 *Rastakhiz*, (150), 17 July 1975.
9 'The revolution in education', *JR*, (13), 11 September 1975.
10 'Rastakhiz in the revolution in education', *JR*, (12), 4 September 1975; 'The revolution in education and bottlenecks in higher education', *JR*, (32), 22 January 1976; Bahman Razani, 'The bottlenecks and goal of our education?' *JR*, (108), 15 September 1977.

11 Ibid., and 'Rastakhiz will fulfill the great goal of societal popular participation', *Rastakhiz*, (30), 7 June 1975; 'Hoveyda: The revolution in education', (101), 30 August 1975. See also interview with Ahmad Shaifi, Education Minister, (205), 3 January 1976; 'Problems of studying abroad', (203), 31 December 1975 and (337), 10 June 1976.
12 *JR*, (18), 8 December 1975.
13 *Rastakhiz*, (436), 19 October 1976. 'School education and imported culture', *Rastakhiz*, (414), 11 September 1976. 'The Third World's youth: Education's duty is recognition of national identity: Interview with Mohammad Hejabi', *JR*, (5), 17 July 1975; 'The ninth conference on the results of the revolution in education', *Rastakhiz*, (408); 'Education is the guardian of national values', (408). 'A fateful conference', (409, 411, 412). 'New reports at the conference of the revolution in education', (413), 23 August 1976. 'Shahanshah: Implementation of educational policies needs a public crusade', *JR*, (103), 21 August 1977.
14 'A great national duty', *Rastakhiz*, (35), 12 February 1976.
15 Ministry of Education, Publication No. 18, *Barrisi kutahi dar piramun-e se asl-e rastakhiz-e mellat-e Iran*.
16 'A fateful conference', *Rastakhiz*, (409), 5 September 1976. See also (408), 4 September 1976; 'The conference', (411), 7 September 1976; 'The revolution in education', (412), 8 September 1976; 'New reports at the conference of the education in revolution', (413), 9 September 1976.
17 Ibid., (409), 5 September 1976; 'Rastakhiz in the revolution of education', *JR*, (12), 4 September 1976.
18 *Rastakhiz*, (414), 11 September 1976 See also (415), 12 September 1976; (513), 9 January 1977. Calls were made that those teaching history and literature had to be native (*bumi*) in form and thought. See also *Rastakhiz*, (659), 6 July 1977. 'National education must be endowed with unique Iranian cultural characteristics. ... Education's goal is the renovation and rebuilding of authentic thought'.
19 For structural changes brought about by this conference see *Amuzesh-e ali dar Iran* (Tehran, 2535/1976).
20 'Sadeq Homayouni, 'Socio-cultural movements and the perspectives of today's Persian literature', *Rastakhiz*, (735), 26 September 1976.
21 'Report on education', *JR*, (79), 6 January 1977. See also 'The importation of teaching technology pollutes our culture', *JR*, (151), 22 July 1978.
22 'Report on the fiftieth meeting of the imperial commission', (714), 11 September 1977.
23 Ibrahim Zalzadeh, 'Today culture and customs are caught in a whirlpool of materialism and consumerism', *JR*, (147), 24 June 1978. See also: (143), 27 May 1978.
24 *RJ*, (79), 6 January 1978.
25 'The conference on education', (406), 1 September 1976.
26 *Rastakhiz*, (406), 1 September 1976. *JR*, (57), 29 July 1976.
27 *JR*, (151), 22 July 1978.
28 *JR*, (104), 18 August 1977.
29 Shahpour Rasekh, 'Today's generation is distancing itself from the old one-why?', *JR*, (104), 18 August 1977.
30 'FulFul Jun for an education in sex and debauchery goes to the West', Ibid.
31 *RJ*, (75), 9 December 1977. See also 'Identity crisis, the youth must know their culture, history, spirituality', (103), 11 August 1977; 'Need for preservation of cultural authenticity and national identity, (107), 8 September 1977.
32 Interview with Parvizi, (113), 20 October 1977. See also: Youseff, 'Alienation from national authentic culture begins in childhood', (146), 17 June 1978, and 'National

duty: protection of Iranian culture in the face of the West's cultural invasion', (145), 10 June 1978.
33 The first literary example of this phenomenon is the well-known play of Hassan Moqqadam, *Jafar Khan Has Returned from the West* written at the end of the Qajar period.
34 'A conversation with Rasul', *JR*, (114), 27 October 1977. See also Sadiq Homayouni, 'Authenticity', (115), 3 November 1977.
35 'The Party creates the conditions and leads the people toward the Great Civilization', *JR*, (118), 24 November 1977.
36 'Interview with Ameli-Tehrani', *JR*, (133), 9 March 1978.
37 He was another repentant ex-member of Tudeh Party who had been imprisoned for two years in the 1950s for anti-regime activities.
38 Mahmud Jafarian, 'Iranian culture...', *JR*, (42), 15 April 1976.
39 M. Jafarian, 'The forms of usefulness...', *Rastakhiz*, (296), 24 April 1976; Jafarian, '(National) Radio and television must speak the truth', (302), 1 May 1976; 'Rastakhiz's path', (328), 31 May 1976; Naraqi, 'The levels of education and cultural identity', (485), 6 December 1976; 'Iranian ideals', (662), 7 July 1977.
40 M. Jafarian, 'Iranian...', *JR*, (42), 21 March 1976. See also 'The necessity of a cultural revolution...', *Rastakhiz*, (9), 14 August 1975; 'Party issues', (55), 15 July 1976 and 'Toward the Great Civilization', (129), 9 February 1978.
41 Hossein Sarfaraz, 'To be alienated from the self', *Rastakhiz*, (121), 22 September 1975.
42 Abualqasem Rahmani, *Engelab-e sefid dar sima-ye mihan: rahnama-ye sepahian-e enqelab* (Tehran, 1347/1969).
43 'The new plan of the organization of the Guardians of the Revolution', *JR*, (32), 22 January 1976; 'The University of the Guardians of the Revolutions has accepted 2500 students', *Rastakhiz*, (28), 18 January 1976; 'For the Party the use of the Guardians of the Revolution is of the utmost importance', *Rastakhiz*, (559), 5 March 1977. 'The Guardians-the revolution's avant-garde', *JR*, (32), 22 January 1976.
44 Ameli, 'Classes of political education...', *Rastakhiz*, (254), 2 March 1976.
45 'Native and political education for pupils is necessary' *JR*, (114), 26 October 1977. 'Political education or national education?', *JR*, (115), 3 November 1977; Hashemi Hariri, 'Revolutionary education's characteristics', *Rastakhiz*, (667), 16 July 1977 ; 'The Shah's guidelines for political education', *Rastakhiz*, (731), 2 October 1977; 'Political education must be accompanied by national education', *Rastakhiz*, (731). 'Guidelines for political education...', *JR*, (117), 17 November 1977. 'Implementation of political education', *JR*, (119), 22 November 1977.
46 *HIOHP*, Baheri, (26), p. 12.
47 *JR*, (121), 15 December 1977.
48 CIA, Secret Special Memorandum #9-68, 'The Shah's Increasing Assurance', 1968/05/07, NSA, no. 663.
49 *RJ*, (60), 1 September 1976; (61), 2 September 1976; (81), 20 January 1978.
50 Speech by Ameli-Tehrani, *JR*, (132), 13 October 1977.
51 Abdollahzade Patruazm, *Rastakhiz*, (2), 4 May 1975.
52 Sayyid Hasan Taqizadeh (1878–1970), politician and thinker of the late Qajar and Pahlavi periods: 'The only path open to Iran and Iranians for their salvation is the unconditional acceptance and promotion of European civilisation and complete submission to Europe and adoption of its customs, habits, mores, form of upbringing, science, industry, life and the complete framework of Europe without exception – except language – and the putting aside of any form of egoism and meaningless protest

which emerges from a misplaced sense of patriotism'. *Kaveh*, 26 August 1912. Over time he distanced from this pro-West Occidentalism.
53 For example, see *Rastakhiz*, 'Attention to moral values', (133), 23 September 1975 and 'Hoveyda', (254), 23 October 1975.
54 'Interview of the Empress with Canadian television', (558), 3 March 1978. See Rastakhiz editorials: 'Mechinization and machines threaten our youth', *Rastakhiz*, (259), 7 March 1976; 'One must not be ignorant of the damages rendered by materialism', *Rastakhiz*, (595), 9 June 1976.
55 Hossein Mehri, 'The creation of superfluous needs', *JR*, (109), 22 September 1977.
56 The work of Charles Frankel was also propagated but due to a translation mistake. His book, *The Case for the Modern Man* was translated as *The Crisis of the Modern Man* and thus portrayed as an American critique of modern civilization. See *JR*, (42), 19 June 1976.
57 Qaneei, *Dar damgah…*, p. 350.
58 'The Renewed Rise of Spiritual Insight and Iranian Culture', *Rastakhiz*, (274), 29 March 1977.
59 Sadeq Homayouni, 'Authenticity', *JR*, (115), 3 November 1977.
60 *Rastakhiz*, (89), 14 August 1975.
61 See *L'Utopie ou la Mort* (Paris, 1973).
62 *JR*, (109), 22 September 1977. Similar themes were addressed in a series called, 'The West and the Fall of Moral Values'; 'Mohammad Orfinezhad, 'The consumerist society is avarious', *Rastakhiz*, (336), 9 June 1976.
63 See *L'agressivité détournée* (Paris, 1970); *Éloge de la fuite* (Paris, 1976).
64 *JR*, (109), 19 September 1977.
65 Hossein Mehri, *JR*, (116), 10 November 1977.
66 *Rastakhiz*, (711), 25 December 1977; See also: Mehri, 'Mankind's problems', *JR*, (100), 14 July 1977.
67 H. Mehri, 'Mankind's problems', *JR*, (112), 13 October 1977.
68 Hushang Nasirzadeh, *JR*, (117), 17 November 1977.
69 See also *L'Occident et ailleurs* (Paris, 1973).
70 *JR*, (112), 13 October 1977.
71 H. Mehri, 'The new cultural, social and personal changes in the West', *JR*, (125), 12 January 1978. In this regard the works of Roger Garaundy (1913–2012) were propagated. He had been a French resistance fighter who also strongly sympathized with communist thought. He converted to Islam in 1982. His views on Western civilization, imperialism and the Israel–Palestine issue found official recognition in Pahlavi and IRI publications. See *Pour un dialogue des civilisations* (Paris, 1977).
72 H. Mehri, 'The Civilization of the West: Unsuccessful and Corrosive', *JR*, (107), 8 September 1977.
73 H. Mehri, 'The West's civilization: Is it moving in the direction of destruction?' *JR*, (110), 29 September 1977. See also 'Conversations with Rasul', (115), 3 November 1977; Shahram Hedayat, 'War against the machine', (108), 24 15 September 1977.
74 'Party news', (141), 13 May 1978.
75 Dehbashi, ed., *Ayandegan …*, p. 217 and *Hikmat…*, p. 129.
76 *Rastakhiz*, (306), 5 May 1976. 'Economic development and national culture'. Naraqi, Ibid., (308), 8 May 1976.
77 *Rashtakhiz*, (306), 5 May 1976. See also (408), 2 September 1976; (421), 20 September 1976; *JR*, (59), 19 August 1976.
78 Jacques Attali, *La Parole et l'ouetil* (Paris, 1975).

79 *Rastakhiz*, (38), 15 June 1975.
80 *Rastakhiz*, (72), 24 July 1975.
81 See Bahram Firivishi, 'The industrialized person and the violence of the machine civilization', *Rastakhiz*, (126), 27 September 1975.
82 Mohammad Habibi, 'With Nasr in the crossword of Islamic values and Iran', *Rastskhiz*, (19), 23 October 1975 and (20), 24 October 1975.
83 'Interview with Nasr', *Rastakhiz*, (458), 20 February 1977.
84 'Nasr: Between Islamic Philosophy and Western philosophy no internal links exist', *Rastakhiz*, (282), 7 April 1976.
85 *Rastakhiz*, (547), 20 February 1978.
86 'Moral decline of the West', (127) *JR*, 26, January 1978. Bahman Gholami, 'The West and the collapse of moral values', *Rastakhiz*, (799), 25 December 1977 and 'The Western person and the base of Eastern civilization, '*Rastakhiz*, (800), 26 December 1977.
87 'American police worried by rise in male prostitution', *Rastakhiz*, (377), 28 July 1976. Coverage of this issue was not only the result of independent reporting by Rastakhiz journalists. There were also summaries of and commentaries on reports published in the West, and specifically the *NYT*. See *NYT*, 3 March 1973, George Vecsey, 'A Police Crackdown Impedes Homosexuals' Search for "Chickens"'; 9 June 1974; 22 February 1976, 'East Side Pornography in Upwardly Mobile Areas'; 31 May 1976, Frank Prial, Jr., 'At Night, Block Belongs to the Male Prostitutes'; 14 February 1977, '"Chicken-Hawk" Trade Found Attracting More Young Boys to Times Square Area'; 23 May 1977, Seth S. King, 'Chicago Jury to Probe Pornography and Prostitution Involving Boys'.
88 Hedayatollah Hakim-e Elahi, *Ba man be shahr-e nou biaid* (Tehran, 1327/1949), p. 11. He wrote several other books that, using a similar approach, examined many aspects of Iranian society, from insane asylums and schools to service in the military and the judicial system and called for dramatic and rapid reform.
89 For an official report on this issue, probably the best of the period, see Setareh Farmanfarmanian, *Piramun-e Roospigari dar shahr-e Tehran* (Tehran, 1349/1971).
90 'Report on the Collapse of Morals and Tradition in the West', *JR*, (123), 29 December 1977.
91 'French fifteen-year olds: Free sexual relations' and 'The disaster America faces: Twelve-year olds', *JR*, (123), 28 December 1977. See also translation of *TIME* article, ' "The Other Face of the West's Youth" and "The young prostituting themselves" The issue shocking America', Iraq Jamshidi, trans., *JR*, (127), 26 January 1978.
92 'Baheri: We must not for one moment be unaware of the conspiracies of all Iran's enemies', *Rastakhiz*, (763), 7 January 1978. 'The West's youth perishing on the ominous trails of loneliness and atomization', *JR*, (106), 1 September 1977.
93 *JR*, (70), 4 November 1976. See also: *Rastakhiz*, (138), 22 April 1978}; (100), 14 July 1977.
94 'Drug addiction, licentiousness, and poverty are killing the West's youth', (108) *JR*, 15 September 1977. *JR*, (101), 21 July 1977; (107), 9 September 1977; See also *Rastakhiz*, (153), 5 August 1978. These elements were already visible in Rastakhiz publications in their first year: 'America: The supermarket of drugs', and 'Alcohol and drugs are destroying America's teenagers', *JR*, (26), 23 November 1975. 'The West's hippies are destroying Dervishes' monasteries', *JR*, (109), 23 September 1977; 'Europe in the face of the invasion of heroin', *JR*, (90), 5 May 1977.

95 Martin Evans, 'Harold Macmillan's "never had it so good" speech...', *The Daily Telegraph*, 19 November 2010.
96 'The industrialized nations have fallen to their knees...', *Rastakhiz*, (123), 25 September 1975. Hossein Banahmad, 'Victory over the industrialized nations of the West', *Rastakhiz*, (146), 23 October 1975.
97 *JR*, (10), 21 August 1976. See also *JR*, (2), 23 May 1975; 'Western Europe and the nightmare of recession and decline', *Rastakhiz*, (70), 22 July 1975.
98 'The West's cultural economic problems', *Rastakhiz*, (559), 20 February 1978. See also 'Shahanshah: interview', *JR*, (16), 26 September 1975; 'Shahanshah: European societies are not well administered because their governments and leaders are not good', *Rastakhiz*, (521), 22 December 1976.
99 Alam, *Yaddashtha...*, Vol. 6, pp. 368–9.
100 *JR*, (84), 2 March 1978. Also (155), 19 August 1977.
101 *Rastakhiz*, (547), 20 February 1978.
102 H. Mehri, 'In the West's great cities', *JR*, (106), 1 September 1977. 'The catastrophe of the industrial century: millions suffering from psychological illness', *JR*, (17), 9 October 1975.
103 Rahim Tazri, 'The city of learning for an American is the city of crime', *JR*, (29), 1 January 1976 and (13), 11 September 1975. 'New York – the filthiest city in the world', (84), 20 February 1977; 'New York: on the brink of bankruptcy and complete destruction', *Rastakhiz*, (812), 9 January 1978.

Chapter 13

1 *Amnesty International Briefing: Iran*, November 1976, p. 1.
2 He, along with his friends Al-e Ahmad and Gholamhossein Saedi, founded the Writers Association of Iran, in 1966. His activities led to his eventual imprisonment in 1973. He was held for little more than three months.
3 Amir-Hussein Radjy, 'Rewriting the Iranian Revolution', *New Republic*, 6 July 2017.
4 *Rastakhiz*, (520), 17 January 1977.
5 *JR*, (85), 9 March 1977.
6 Ibid., 'Shahanshah', (83), 25 February 1978.
7 'Amnesty International is a puppet of international politics', *Rastakhiz*, (521), 18 January 1977.
8 'The worldwide anti-Iran struggle', *JR*, (81), 27 January 1977. Also (82), 4 February 1976.
9 'The issue of human rights is applicable to all', *Rastakhiz*, (559), 5 March 1977. Two weeks prior the shah had mentioned to *Newsweek* this issue of the Cambodians when he condemned US double standards in regard to human rights: 'If you Americans are going to be so moral, you must apply a single standard to the whole world'.
10 Sir Anthony Parsons interview for television program *BBC Reputations: The Last Shah*, (1996).
11 24 February 1977, US Embassy cable to Secretary of State, 'Shah Comments on Human Rights and Student Dissidents', NLC-21-44-4-15-0.
12 Alam, *Yaddashtha...*, Vol. 4, p. 535.
13 Ibid., p. 321.

14 'Amuzegar: 'The West must cease its struggle to keep oil prices down', 14 July 1977. See Alam,*Yaddashtha...*, Vol. 4, pp. 79–80.
15 *Rastakhiz*, (558), 3 March 1977.
16 *JR*, 23 February 1977 (85) and *Rastakhiz*, (559), 1 March 1977. From early on, themes of racism were common in Rastakhiz publications. For the first feature article on this issue, see 'The Blacks of America, Why are they rebelling?' *JR*, (27), 30 November 1975. The last in this series came in the party's final months, see 'America, America: Black poverty, Black violence ... and Human Rights!' *JR*, (155), 19 August 1978.
17 Zohak is a figure of evil from Ferdowsi's *Shahnameh*. A tyrannical Arab monarch, he had two snakes protruding from his shoulders that ate only the brains of young Iranian males.
18 Vadiei, 'The West's two different and contradictory faces', *Rastakhiz*, (561), 7 March 1977.
19 Rahmat, 'History's voice', (122), 23 September 1975. See also 'Culture's place', *Rastakhiz*, (123), 24 September 1975.
20 *Rastakhiz*, (788), 11 December 1977. Also 'National committees condemn the foreign anti-Iranian conspiracies', (791), 14 December 1977.
21 'Empress: attention to individual rights has deep roots in Iran', *Rastakhiz*, (657), 3 July 1977. Also Interview with the empress, (663), 11 July 1977.
22 Qaneei, *Dar damgah-ye...*, pp. 390–3.
23 Parviz Radji, *In the Service of the Peacock Throne* (London, 1984), p. 81.
24 Ibid., p. 89.
25 Qaneei, *Dar damgah-ye...*, pp. 421–2.
26 Ibid., pp. 389–91.
27 William Sullivan, *Mission to Iran* (New York, 1981), p. 115.
28 'Shahanshah: we will obtain peaceful nuclear power', *Rastakhiz*, (70). 'Iran is moving in the direction of nuclear technology', *JR*, (118), 24 November 1977. 'Plans for the development of nuclear research centers', *Rastakhiz*, (28), 3 June 1975. 'The Atomic Agency of Iran is hiring new specialists', *Rastakhiz*, (65), 16 July 1975. 'The atom in the service of the individual, and not the other way around', *Rastakhiz*, (660), 7 July 1977. 'Baheri: we are on the path to the use of nuclear energy', *JR*, (67), 22 Mehr 2535/14 October 1975.
29 For example, see US Embassy Tehran cable 5389 to State Department, 1 July 1974.
30 Tehran Embassy cable 5939 to State Department, 'Multinational Nuclear Centers: Assessment of Iranian Attitudes toward Plutonium Reprocessing'. July 17, 1975.
31 Office of Assistant Secretary of Defense for International Security Affairs to Secretary of Defense, 'Nuclear Energy Cooperation with Iran', June 1974.
32 'Iran's warning against a form of the new imperialism', *Rastakhiz*, (430), 2 October 1977.
33 'Shahanshah: Iran gives priority to the wide use of nuclear energy', *Rastakhiz*, (585), 11 April 1978.
34 Akbar Etemad, 'The bottlenecks in the use of nuclear energy in Iran', *Rastakhiz*, (440), 13 October 1977.
35 'Is not the monopoly of nuclear energy a form of imperialism?', *Rastakhiz*, (587), 13 April 1978. See also Ahmad Sharafi, 'Nuclear power and the Third World', (595), 23 April 1978.
36 *JR*, (81), 27 January 1977; 'Tehrani: united front against all imperialists', *Rastakhiz*, (791), 14 December 1977; 'Imperialism is attacking our national existence's foundations' and 'Ameli: the Party's Congress will determine Iran's response to imperialism', (801), 25 December 1977}.

37 See 'The backwardness imposed by West', *JR*, (83), 26 February 1978.
38 *JR*, (88), 10 April 1977.
39 *Rastakhiz*, (47), 25 June 1975.
40 Report from US Embassy in Tehran, 8 July 1976, 'Bolster Iran's Modernizing Monarchy',
Asnad-e lanah-e jasus-e amrika, Vol. 7, p. 171.
41 Hossein Razavi, *The Political Environment of Economic Planning in Iran, 1971-1983: From Monarchy to Islamic Republic* (Boulder, CO, 1984), p. 74.
42 Robert Graham, *Iran: The Illusion of Power* (London, 1980), p. 80.
43 Alam, *Yaddashtha...*, Vol. 4, p. 176.
44 'Democracy and the Party', (34), *Rastakhiz*, 5 February 1976; 'The strengthening of moral principles...' and Mehdi Amani, 'The struggle against corruption...', (232), 4 February 1976; 'The spread of the machine threatens our youth', (259), 3 March 1976; 'Technology and moral values', *Rastakhiz*, (334), 7 June 1975; 'The spread of the machine and self-alienation', *JR*, (40), 31 March 1976. Shahram Hedayat, 'War against the machine', *JR*, (108), 15 September 1977.
45 'A great national duty', *Ratakhiz*, (35), 12 February 1976. See also (275), 30 March 1976; 'Iran's cultural values', (282), 7 April 1976; 'The Rastakhiz Party negates and rejects class warfare', (281), 6 April 1976.
46 *Rastakhiz*, (8), 7 August 1975; Iraj Alumi 'The Crusade against profiteering', *Rastakhiz*, (62–6), 13–17 July 1975; 'The Party's mobilization for the struggle against inflation', *Rastakhiz*, (73), 25 July 1975 ; 'The Rastakhiz Party and the Profiteers', *Rastakhiz*, (90), 11 August 1975; 'The youth and the large wave of the struggle against profiteering', *JR*, (7), 31 July 1975.
47 Mohammad Fakhrdai, 'The family system and the consumerist society', *Rastakhiz*, (231), 5 February 1976.
48 Hashemi Hariri, 'The struggle with corruption and the moral revolution', *Rastakhiz*, (249), 24 February 1976. See also *Rastakhiz*, (232), 7 February 1976 and (238), 1 February 1976.
49 'Toward a better idea of Iran and Iranians', *Rastakhiz*, (305), 21 April 1976.
50 Mehdi Amani, 'The struggle against corruption', *Rastakhiz*, (232), 4 February 1976. Also Hariri, (249), 23 February 1976.
51 Ahmad Shiknia, 'Profiteering and inflation: the result of being cut-off from authentic culture', *Rastakhiz*, (86), 23 July 1975.
52 Amir Fakhrdai, *Rastakhiz*, (232), 21 January 1976. Also 'The cultural relations of Asia's peoples must be changed', (249), 20 February 1976. 'Attention to moral values-leader', *Rastakhiz*, (133), 31 August 1975. 'The second phase of the struggle against inflation and profiteering', (159), 27 September 1975.
53 *JR*, (110), 23 September 1977. 'Interview with Shahpour Rasekh', *JR*, (108), 23 August 1977.
54 Ibid., (146), 23 October 1977.
55 'Iran rebuilds its confidence', *Business Week*, 31 January 1977.
56 'The struggle against corruption', *Rastakhiz*, (238), 21 January 1976.
57 '2 Britons Accused of Role in Iranian Sugar Scandal', *NYT*, 11 February 1976. While Rastakhiz publications enjoyed using this scandal, the imperial inspectorate eventually found Alizadeh innocent. For a short historical record of this scandal, see Milani, 'Fereydun Mahdavi' in *Eminent Persians...* Vol. 1, pp. 210-11. That Mahdavi was a close associate of Hoveyda probably also played a role in Rastakhiz coverage of this issue.

58 Ahmad Ali Masoud Ansari, *Man va Khandan-e Pahlavi* (Tehran, 1384/2005), pp. 20–1.
59 *NYT*, 23 February 1976. The scandal followed another one involving Northrop Corporation which eventually issued a $2 million rebate to the Iranian government 'to atone for ethically questionable payments to third parties' paid in the sale of F-5A and F-5Es to Iran.
60 In January 1979 the US SEC charged Grumman for paying $24 million 'in secret commissions to sales agents' who had claimed to be working on the deal with the shah. See Seymour Hersh, *NYT*, 11 September 1976. John F. Berry, 'Iran payoff is charged to Grumman', *Washington Post*, January 5, 1979.
61 *Rastakhiz*, (241), 15 February 1976; (245), 19 February 1976. Also 'New charges made on Gruman moves in F-14 Sales to Iran', *NYT*, 11 January 1978 and Toufanian, (17), pp. 8–10.
62 Afkhami, *The Shah*, p. 312.
63 Eric Pace, 'Iranian Prime Minister Assails Unethical Foreign Companies', *NYT*, 4 March 1976.
64 Qaneei, *Dar damgah…*, pp. 396–7.
65 'What kind of technology has the West sold us?' and 'The French are guilty', (692), 22 July 1977; 'Party demand: the loss rendered to Iranian factories will be compensated', *Rastakhiz*, (669), 18 July 1977. 'From today the blackouts are one hour shorter in length', *Rastakhiz*, (679), 28 July 1977. Also Marvine Howe, 'Iran fights power shortage, threat to development', *NYT*, 11 July 1977.
66 Ibid., (666–7), 16 July 1977; (794), 23 July 1977.
67 'The Iranian people and Western companies', *Rastakhiz*, (238), 21 January 1976.
68 'Ensuring the human resources needed by the country', *Rastakhiz*, (156), 4 November 1975. Also 'The need for a solution for the bottlenecks in the 'shortage' of skilled labor', *Rastakhiz*, (65), 23 July 1975.
69 'Iranian workers and specialists will replace Western ones', *Rastakhiz*, (124), 25 September 1975.
70 Naraqi, 'Today's and tomorrow's difficulties of industrialized Iran', Ibid., (615), 21 April 1977.
71 *Rastakhiz*, (785), 7 December 1977. *JR*, (137), 23 September 1975. See also 'Empress: dependence on Western technology is not good', *Rastakhiz*, (549), 21 February 1978; Hashmi Hariri, 'Iran is in need of scientific and technological independence', *Rastakhiz*, (679), 23 July 1977.
72 *Rastakhiz*, (114), 23 September 1975.
73 On the eve of this congress the anti-West/anti-imperialist rhetoric in *Rastakhiz* increased. See *Rastakhiz*, (800–7), 24 December 1977 to 3 January 1978.
74 *JR*, (122), 22 December 1977. 'The extraordinary congress', *JR*, (123), 29 December 1977.
75 Baheri, (27), p. 5.
76 *JR*, (117) 26 Aban.
77 *JR: Vizhehnameh-mavaz'-e zed-e est'mari-ye Rastakhiz*, January, 1978. Also *Rastakhiz*, (800), 22 December 1977 and 'Ameli: The extraordinary congress…', *Rastakhiz*, (801), 23 December 1977; 'Baheri: imperialism with great resentment is targeting our cultural centers', *Rastakhiz*, (805), 26 December 1977. 'Report of Dr. Baheri to the congress' and 'Iranian culture and its values', *Rastakhiz*, (809), 5 January 1978.
78 *JR*, (121), 15 December 1977.
79 *Business Week*, 31 January 1977.

80 *Keyhan*, 30 October 1976.
81 See 'Tough talk on oil, arms, and investments-Interview with Shah Mohammad Reza Pahlavi', *Business Week,* 24 January 1977.
82 'The Iranian people must and will rise against imperialism', *Rastakhiz*, (809), 5 January 1978. *JR,* (125), 12 January 1978.
83 'Foreigners given our development see their interests in danger', (121), 22 November 1977. Also: Vadiei 'There are a number who know…'; Lashai, 'Political education is an eternal project ; 'Party General Secretary: the intellectuals' role of in the struggle against the provocations of Iran's enemies', *Rastakhiz,* (789), 22 November 1977.
84 Ardeshir Larudi, 'The popularity of Westoxification', *JR,* (152), 23 July 1978. 'Alienation from culture and the lack of identity amongst the youth', *Rastakhiz,* (814), 22 December 1977.
85 *JR,* (126), 19 January 1978.
86 *JR,* (132), 2 March 1978. Also: *Rastakhiz,* (148), 26 October 1975; (155), 4 November 1975; (65), 16 July 1975.
87 'The imperialists' conspiracies', (120), 22 November 1977.
88 'The Shah's goals', *Rastakhiz,* (811), 8 January 1978.
89 *JR,* (125), 12 January 1978. See also 'Political and national unity' *Rastakhiz,* (119), 20 September 1975; Hoveyda: we have no need for propaganda', *JR,* (140), 6 May 1977; *Rastakhiz,* (799), 25 December 1977. See also: *JR,* (88) 'The philosophy of Iran's revolution', 15 July 1977; (110), 6 October 1977; (111), 13 October 1977.
90 'Workers united against new imperialism's conspiracies', *Rastakhiz,* (794), 22 December 1977.
91 'Iranian culture must emerge from under Westerners' influence', (590), 21 March 1978. Also (594), 21 April 1978.
92 'Iran's enemies are opposed to political organizations of the Iranian people', *JR,* (147), 22 June 1978.
93 Ibid., (131), 23 February 1978.
94 *Rastakhiz,* (547), 20 February 1977.
95 *Rastakhiz,* (814), 22 December 1977.
96 *JR,* (140), 6 May 1978.
97 *JR,* Ibrahim Zalzadeh, 'The work of culture and customs has been pawned off to materialism and consumerism', (147), 24 June 1978. See also Jahanbeglu, 'Our music must be representative of society's identity', (150), 15 July 1978 and Sattar Laqai, 'Imperialism's goal: the struggle against freedom in the name of the defence of freedom', (143), 27 May 1978; (141), 13 May 1978.
98 Ali Shariati, *Bazshenas-e hoviat-e Irani-Islami* (Tehran, 1381), pp. 213–25.
99 *JR,* (141), 21 April 1978. 'Technology in the name of imperialism', (159), 16 September 1978. See also (142), 10 May 1978.
100 Ibid., (158), 23 August 1978.
101 'The Shah's goal is the construction of Iranian authority and power', *Rastakhiz,* (811), 22 December 1977; 'The imperialists' conspiracies', *JR,* (120), 22 November 1977. Baheri also propagated these discourses on television.
102 *JR,* (143), 27 May 1978.
103 Ibid., (145), 10 June 1978.
104 Ibid., (146), 17 June 1978.
105 Ibid., (147), 24 June 1978.
106 Ibid., (148), 1 July 1978.
107 Pahlavi, *Beh Sui,* pp. 82–7.

108 Pahlavi, *Talifat...*, Vol. 8, pp. 6088–92. See also: *Rastakhiz*, (243), 18 June 1976 and (616), 17 May 1977.
109 Pahlavi, *Beh Sui*, p. 255.
110 *Rastakhiz*, (617), 18 May 1977.
111 *Rastakhiz*, (239), 12 February 1976.
112 Ibid., (660), 6 May 1977. See also (569), 17 March 1976; (329), 1 June 1976.

Epilogue

1 Quoted in Riasanovsky, *The Image of Peter...*, p. 12. For original see: Prokopovich, *Sochineniia*, p. 56.
2 Alam, *The Shah and I*, pp. 294–5.
3 Dostoevskii, *Dnevik Pisatelia...*, pp. 351–2.
4 Montesquieu, *The Spirit of Laws*, Vol. 1, p. 393.
5 Others include W. Barthold, R. Ghirshman and A. Olmstead, among others.
6 Ernest Renan, *Discours et conferences*, 10th ed. (Paris, 1938), pp. 375–409.
7 Renan, *Discours et conferences*, pp. 380–1.
8 A. Krimskii, *Musul'manstvo i ego budushchnost'* (St. Petersburg, 1899), p. 114.
9 Hegel, *Werke in zwanzig Bänden, XII: Verlesungen über die Philosophie der Geschichte* (Frankfurt, 1979), pp. 136–8, 215, 233–4.
10 Ibid., p. 44., D. I.Chizhevskii, *Gegel' v Rossii* (Paris, 1939), p. 13.
11 Francis Fukuyama, 1989, p. 4. This was written when the Berlin Wall collapsed.
12 For example see Daniele Archibugi & David Held, eds., *Cosmopolitan Democracy: An Agenda for a New World Order* (Cambridge, 1995).
13 Samuel Huntington, *The Clash of Civilizations* (New York, 1996), p. 21.
14 Coker, *The Rise...*, p. 3.
15 Amin Maalouf, Barbara Bray, trans., *In the Name of Identity, Violence and the Need to Belong* (New York, 2000), p. 74.
16 *Protokoli* (Moscow, 1958), pp. 250–1.
17 *Izvestiia*, 9 March 1923.
18 Alexander Herzen, *Biloe i Dumi* (Moscow, 1958), Ibid., Vol. VII, p. 143.
19 Herzen, *Biloe i Dumi*, Vol. IV, p. 120.
20 *New York Times*, 9 October 1974.
21 Terry Eagleton, *Ideology* (London, 1991), p. 5.
22 Ruhullah Khomeini, *Sahifih-ye Nur*, 22 vols. (Tehran, 1365/1986), Vol. 7, p. 71.
23 Ruhollah Khomeini, Hamd Algar, trans., *Islam and Revolution* (Washington, 1981), p. 127.
24 Khomeini and Algar, trans., *Islam and Revolution*, p. 114; Khomeini, *Sahifih...*, Vol. 5, p. 138.
25 M. Ranjbar, *Hoquq va azadiha-ye fardi az didgah-ye Emam Khomeini* (Tehran, 1382/2003), p. 135.
26 Khomeini, *Sahifih-ye...*, Vol. 7, pp. 53–4.
27 *Resalat*, 1 May 1992.
28 'Imam va Qarbzadegi', *Farhang-e Kosar* (41), May 2010.
29 Khomeini, *Sahifih-ye*, Vol. 2, pp. 295–9.
30 *Sharq*, 8 January 2018.
31 Khomeini, *Sahifih-ye.*, Vol. 3, pp. 295–6.

32 Ibid., Vol. 9, pp. 185–6.
33 Khomeini, *Sahifih-ye...*, Vol. 1, pp. 234–5.
34 Ibid., Vol. 3, p. 278.
35 *Rastakhiz* (138), 14 October 1975.
36 Ruhollah Khomeini, *Tarikh-e Iran az didgah-ye Imam Khomeini* (Tehran, 1378/1999), p. 268.
37 Algar,trans., *Islam and Revolution,* p. 74.
38 *Keyhan,* 31 August 1989.
39 For example, see *Rastakhiz,* 'Attention to moral values', (133), 23 September 1975 and 'Hoveyda', (254), 23 October 1975.
40 Ayatollah Ali Khamenei, *Farhang va tahajum-e farhangi* (Tehran, 1385/2006).
41 Khomeini, *Sahifih-ye...*, Vol. 7, p. 23.
42 Ibid.,Vol. 3, pp. 156–7.
43 Ibid.,Vol. 10, p. 55.
44 *Ettelaat,* 14 May 197.
45 Algar, trans., *Islam and Revolution,* p. 215. See also *Bayan* (4) 1990, p. 8.

Select bibliography

Periodicals

Party publications
Andisheha-ye Rastakhiz
Javan-e Rastakhiz
Mabna-ye Rastakhiz
Rastakhiz
Rastakhiz-e Havaii
Rastakhiz-e Javanan
Rastakhiz-e Kargar
Rastakhiz-e Rustai
Talash

Non-party publications
Ayande
Ayandegan
Ettellaat
Farhang va Zendegi
Farman
Ferdowsi
In Hafte
Iran-e Emruz
Iranshahr
Jame-ye Novin
Jashn-e Shahanshai-ye Iran (Official newspaper 1970-1971).
Kaveh
Keyhan
Sepide va Siah

Primary sources

Alam, Assadollah, A. Alikhani, ed. *Yaddashtha-ye Alam*, 7 vols. (Tehran, 1393/2014).
Al-Dowleh, Amin, *Khaterat-e siasi-ye Mirza Zaeli Khan Amin Al-Dowleh* (Tehran, 1360/1982).
Amir-e Abbas-e Hoveyda be ravayet-e asnad-e SAVAK (Tehran, 1383, 2004), 2 Vols.
Antovskii, Mikhail, ed., *Perepiska Rossiiskoi Imperatritsi Ekaterini Vtoroi s Voltairom* (St. Petersburg, 1802).

Ardeshir-e Zahedi be ravayet-e asnad-e SAVAK (Tehran, 1378/1997).
Asnad-e lanah-ye jasus-e Amrika (Tehran, 1980).
Baheri, Mohammad, *Iranian Oral History Project* (H. Ladjeverdi, Editor) Harvard University, 1982.
Behzadi, Ali, *Shabe-ye Khaterat* (Tehran, 1375).
Bing, Edward. ed., *Letters of Tsar Nicholas II and the Empress Marie* (London, 1937).
Blücher, Wilhelm von *Zeitwende in Iran* (Berlin, 1949).
Boltin, Ivan, *Premechaniia na istorii drevnii i nineshnei Rossii* (St. Petersburg, 1788).
Borozdin, A. K., ed., *Iz Pisem i nokazanii Dekabristov* (St. Petersburg, 1906).
Catherine II, *Zapiski Imperatritsi Ekaterini II* (London, 1859).
Chap dar Iran: Be ravayet-e asnad-e SAVAK, ravabet-e Iran va shuravi (Tehran, 1381/2002).
Chicherin, Vladimir, *Vospominaniia Zemstvo* (Moscow, 1934).
Ministry of Culture and Art, Dabirkhane-ye shura-ye ali-ye farhang va honar, *Gozaresh-e f'aliatha-ye farhangi-ye Iran*, 1349–56.
Daftari, Ahmad, *Khaterat-e yek nokhost vazir*, B. Alqeli, eds. (Tehran, 1370/1992).
Daftar-e Rahbari (Leadearship Office) *Engelab-e Islami*, Fourth Edition (Tehran, 1388/2009).
Danilevskii, Nikolai, *Rossiia i Evropi* (Moscow, 1871).
Dashkova, Princess Elena, *Vospominaniia kniagini E.R.Dashkova, pisanniye eyo samoi* (Leipzig, 1859).
Dastmalchi, Mahin, *Fehrest-e gozideh-ye maqalat-e ruznameha-ye Iran* (Tehran, 2536/1977).
Davani, Ali, *Nehzat-e domah-ye rohaniat-e Iran be manzur-e defa az osul-e moqdas-e Islam* (Qom, 1341/1963).
Dehbashi, Hamid, ed., *Ayandegan va ravandegan: Khaterat-e Dariush Homayoun* (Tehran, 1393/2014).
Dehbashi, Hamid, ed., *Hekmat va siasat: goftegu ba doktor Sayyed Hossein Nasr* (Tehran, 1393/2014).
Dehgan, Naser et al., *Dastavardha-ye engelab* (Tehran, 2535/1976).
Delfani, Mohammad, ed., *Farhangsetizi dar doureh-ye Reza Shah. Asnad-e montarshe nashodeh sazman-e parvaresh-e afkar, 1318–1320* (Tehran, 1375/1996).
Emami, Karim, ed., *Dahomin-e jashn-e honar* (Tehran, 2535/1976).
Ettelaat: Havades-e yek rob-e qarn (Tehran, 1329/1947).
Fallaci, Oriana, *Interview with History* (New York, 1979).
Fonvizin, Denis, *Izbrannoe* (Mosow, 1983).
Gertsin, Alexander, *Biloe i Dumi* (Moscow, 1993).
Gorgin, Iraj, *Ketab-e Jashn-e Honar*, 46–52 (Tehran, 1352/1973).
Gurko, Vladimir, *Features and Figures of the Past* (Stanford, 1939).
Hamilton, L. F., *Vanished Pomps of Yesterday* (London, 1919).
Hedayat, M. A., *Khaterat va Khatarat* (Tehran, 1355/1976).
Hekmat, Ali-Asqar, *Si Khatereh* (Tehran, 2535/1976).
Herberstein, Sigismund, A. I. Malein, trans., *Zapiski o Moskovii* (Moscow, 1988).
Hezb-e Iran-e Novin va Engelab-e Iran, 5 Vols. (Tehran, N\A).
Hezb-e Rastakhiz-e mellat-e Iran be ravayet-e asnad (Tehran, 1885/2006), 2 Vols.
Honarmand, Manuchehr, *Pahlavism: Maktab-e nou* (Tehran, 1345/1966).
Honarmand, Manuchehr, *Dialetik-e nemudha-ye melli dar tarikh-e Farsi: jeld-e sevvum-e Pahlavism* (Tehran, 1346/1967).

Honarmand, Manuchehr, *Shahanshahi-ye mashruteh va dohezar va pansad saleh-ye Iran: jeld-e dovvum-e Pahlavism* (Tehran, 1346/1967).
Honarmand, Manuchehr, *Avalin v akharin hokumat-e jahani: ketab-e chahrom az falsafeh-ye Pahlavism* (Tehran, N/A).
Hoshangmahdavi, Abdolreza, *Engelab-e Iran be ravayet-e BBC* (Tehran,1372/1994).
Hoveyda, Fereydoun, Roger Liddell, trans., *The Fall of the Shah* (New York, 1980).
Hushang-e Nahavandi be ravayet-e asnad-e SAVAK (Tehran, 1384/2005).
Iranshahr, Kazemzadeh, *Ta'lifat-e Iranshahr* (Tehran, 1353/1974).
Ivan IV, Ya. S. Lure and Yu. D. Rikov, eds., *Perepiska Ivana Groznogo s Andreem Kurbskim* (Leningrad, 1979).
Jamshid-e Amuzegar be ravayet-e asnad-e SAVAK (Tehran, 1382/2003).
Jashn-e honar-e Shiraz be ravayet-e asnad-e SAVAK (Tehran, 1381/2002).
Jebhe-ye Melli be ravayet-e asnad-e SAVAK (Tehran, 1379/2001).
Katkov, Mikhail, D. Vorlov, ed., Ideologiia *okhranitelstva* (Moscow, 2009).
Kavusi, Fereydoun, *Kargar-e Irani dar Iran-e emruz* (Tehran, 2535, 1976).
Khomyakov, Dmitrii, *Samoderzhavie, pravoslavie i narodnost* (Moscow, 2011).
Ketab-e sevvom-e ebtedai, (Tehran, 1318/1939).
Khan, Malkom, *Resalehha-ye Mirza Malkom Khan Nezam Al-Dowleh* (Tehran, 1381/2003).
Khatami, Mohammad, *Reza Khan dar matbuat-e diruz* (Tehran, 1377).
Kokovstov, Vladimir, *Iz moego proshlogo* (Paris, 1933), 3 Vols.
Ladjevardi, Habib, ed., *Hushang Nahavandi*. Harvard *Oral History Project* (Cambridge, MA, 1985).
Lajaverdi, Habib, ed., *Khaterat-e Abdolmajid Majidi*. Harvard Oral History (Cambridge, MA, 1998).
Lamsdorff, Vladimir, *Dnevnik V.N.Lamsdorffa* (Paris, 1929).
Liberman, A., ed., *Moskovia i Evropa* (Moscow, 2000).
Lord Frederic Hamilton, *Vanished Pomps of Yesterday* (London, 1919).
Lure, Ya, ed., *Perepiska Ivana Groznogo s* Andereem *Kurbskim* (Moscow, 1993).
Maikov, L. H., *Rasskazi Nartova o Petre Velikom* (St. Petersburg 1891).
Manuchehr-e Azmun be ravayet-e asnad-e SAVAK (Tehran, 1381/2002).
Matbuat-e asr-e Pahlavi: Ketab-e hastom, majale-ye Ferdowsi (Tehran, 1384).
Matbuat-e asr-e Pahlavi: Ketab-e nohom, ruzname-ye Farman (Tehran, 1384).
Matbuat-e asr-e Pahlavi: Sepide va Siah (Tehran, 1381/2002).
Masoudi, Ali, *Ketab-e Pahlavi* (Tehram, 1345/1967).
Miliukov, Pavel, *Vospominaniia* (New York, 1955).
Ministry of Education, *Sokhani kutah dar piraman-e mafahim va barkhi vizhagiha-ye engelab-e shah va Mellat, nashri-ye 14*.
Ministry of Education, *Sarmayedari va Sosialism*, Nashri-ye 20.
Ministry of Education, *Marksism va Islam*.
Ministry of Education, *Marksism Islami-yeknirang-e taze-ye estemar*.
Ministry of Education, *Dar rah-ye shenakht-e bonyadha-ye fekri va ideuluzhik-e engelab-e 'shah va mellat'*.
Ministry of Education, *Barresi-ye kutahi dar piramun-e se asl-e Rastakhiz-e Mellat-e Iran*.
Mohammad-e Baheri be ravayet-e asnad-e SAVAK (Tehran, 1388/2009).
Mosolov, Aleksandr, *Pri dvore imperatora* (Riga, 1939).
Mozaffari, Mehdi, *Nezamha-ye takhezbi va Rastakhiz-e mellat-e Iran* (Tehran, 1354/1976).
Nahavandi, Hushang, *Iranian Oral History Project*, H. Ladjeverdi, Editor (Harvard University Press, 1985).

Nikitenko, Alexander, *Dnevnik* (Moscow, 1955), 3 Vols.
Nikolai II, *Polnoe sobranie rechei Imperatora Nikolaia II, 1894–1906* (St. Petersburg, 1906).
Nosrat-e Moinian be ravayet-e asnad-e SAVAK (Tehran, 1384/2005).
Odoevskii, V., *Sochineniia* (Moscow, 1981).
Olearii, Adam, *Opisanie puteshestviia v Moskoviyu* (Moscow, 2001).
Pahlavi, Ashraf, *Faces in a Mirror* (Englewood Cliffs, 1980).
Pahlavi, M. R., *Mamuriat baraye vatanam* (Tehran, 1340/1962).
Pahlavi, M. R., *Farmaeshat-e alihezrat homayun Shahanshah aryamehr* (Tehran, 1354/1975).
Pahlavi, M. R., *Mission for My Country* (London, 1960).
Pahlavi, M. R., *Shahanshahi va dindari*, M. Baqernajafi, ed. (Tehran, 2535/1976).
Pahlavi, M. R., *Talifat, nughtha, paymanha-ye alihezrat homayoun Mohammad Reza Shah*. 11vols. (Tehran, 2535–7/1976–1978).
Pahlavi, M. R., *Be su-ye tamaddon-e bozorg* (Tehran, 2536/1978).
Pahlavi, M. R., *Engelab-e Sefid* (Tehran, N/A).
Pahlavi, Reza, *Safarname-ye Mazandaran* (Tehran, 1976).
Pahlavi, Reza, *Yaddashtha-ye serri-ye Reza Shah* (Tehran, 1327/1949).
Pobedonostsev, Konstantin, *Pima Pobedonostseva k Aleksandru III* (Moscow, 1925).
Prokopovich, Feofan, I. P.Eremin, ed., *Sochineniia* (Leninigrad-Moscow, 1961).
Qaneei, Erfan, *Dar damgeh-ye havades: goftegui ba Parviz-e Sabeti* (Los Angeles, 2012).
Radji, Parviz, *In the Service to the Peacock Throne* (London, 1984).
Rahmani, A., ed., *Enqelab-e sefid dar sima-ye mihan: rahnama-ye sepahian-e enqelab* (Tehran, 1353/1972).
Rastakhiz Party, *Falsafeh-ye Enqelab-e Iran va Hezb-e Rastakhiz* (Tehran, 2535/1976).
Rastakhiz Party, *Si porsesh va pasokh piramun-e Iran, osul-e bonyadi-ye an va hezb-e Rastakhiz-e Iran*.
Rastakhiz Party, *Rahnemud-e amuzesh-e siasi-barname-ye ejraii*.
Rastakhiz Party, *Seminar-e barresi-ye masael-e hezbi, 16–17 Azar* 2536.
Rastakhiz Party, *Faza-ye Siasi-ye Iran az didgah-ye Jenah-e Sazande* (Tehran, 2536/1977).
Sadeq, Issa, *Yadegar-e omr* (Tehran, 1355/1976).
Safai, Ibrahim, ed., *Reza Shah Kabir dar aine-ye khaterat* (Tehran, 2535/1976).
Salehyar, G. H., *Chehre-ye matbuat-e moasser* (Tehran, 1351/1972).
Samii, M. M. (1985). *Iranian Oral History Project* (H. Ladjevardi, Editor) Harvard University.
Shahhosseini, Ibrahim Rear Admiral, *Shenakht-e Tammadon-e Iran va chehre-haye melli* (Tehran, 2535).
Shapirov, Pytor, *Pazsuzhenie* (St. Petersburg, 1700).
Shariati, Ali, *Baz Gasht* (Tehran, 1382/2003).
Shukat, Hamid, *Negahi az darun be jonbesh-e chap-e Iran: Goftegu ba Kuroush-e Lashai* (Tehran, 1381).
Stolypin, Pytor, *Rechi Stolipina* (Moscow, 1993).
Taghir-e lebas va kashf-e hejab be ravayet-e asnad (Tehran, 1378/1997).
Tarikh-e sal-e sevvom-e dabirestan (Tehran, 1319/1940).
Toufanian, H., H. Ladjeverdi, ed., *Harvard Iranian Oral History Project* (Cambridge, 1985).
Vyroubova, Anna, *Memoirs of the Russian Court* (New York, 1923).
Yadegar-e jashn-e arusi-ye valahazrat homayoun velayatahd (Tehran, 1318/1939).
Zaionchkovskii, Andrei, ed., *Vostochnaia Voina* (St. Petersburg, 2002).

Secondary sources

Abrahamian, Ervand, *A History of Modern Iran* (Cambridge, 2008).
Abrahamian, Ervand, *Iran Between Two Revolutions* (Princeton, 1982).
Abramov, Mikhai, ed., *Opit russkogo liberalizma: Antologia* (Moscow, 1997).
Adamiat, Fereydoun, *Amir Kabir va Iran* (Tehran, 1375/1997).
Adamiat, Fereydoun, *Andisheha-ye taraqi va hokumat-e qanun* (Tehran, 1351/1973).
Adamiat, Fereydoun, *Nehzat-e mashrutiat-e Iran* (Tehran, 1354/1975).
Afkhami, Gholam Reza, *The Life and Times of the Shah* (Berkeley, 2009).
Ahiska, Meltem, *Occidentalism in Turkey: Questions of Modernity and National Identity in Turkish Radio Broadcasting* (London, 2010).
Ahmad, Jalal Al-e, *Qarbzadegi* (Tehran, 1385/2006).
Ahmad, Jalal Al-e. *Occidentosis: A Plague from the West*, R. Campbell, trans. (Berkeley, 1984).
Ahmadi, Mohammad Ali, *Gofteman chap dar Iran* (Tehran, 1396/2017).
Aidin, E. N., 'Recent Changes in the Outlook of Women in the Near and Middle East'. *Journal of the Central Asian Society* 28 (1931).
Akbari, M. A., *Tabarshenasi-ye hoviat-e jadid-e Iran* (Tehran, 1384/2006).
Aksakov, Konstantin, *Ob osnovnikh nachalakh russkoi istorii* (Moscow, 1860).
Aksakov, Ivan, 'V chem nedostatochnost russkogo patriotizma', *Den*, 17 October 1864.
Alvandi, Roham, *Nixon, Kissinger and the Shah: The United States and Iran in the Cold War* (Oxford, 2014).
Amanat, Abbas, *Pivot of the Universe: Nasir al-Din Shah Qajar and the Iranian Monarchy, 1831–1896* (New Haven, 1997).
Amanat, Abbas and Farzin Vejdani, eds., *Iran Facing Others: Identity Boundaries in a Historical Perspective* (New York, 2012).
Amnesty International, *Amnesty International Briefing: Iran* (1976).
Amuzegar, Jahangir, *The Dynamics of the Iranian Revolution: Triumph and Tragedy of the Pahlavis* (Albany, 1991).
Ansari, Ali, *Modern Iran* (London, 2010).
Ansari, Ali, *The Politics of Nationalism in Modern Iran* (Cambridge, 2012).
Anisimov, Evgenii, *Afrodita vo vlasti*. Tsarstvovanie Elizaveti Petrovoni (Moscow, 2010).
App, Urr, *The Birth of Orientalism* (Philadelphia, 2010).
Aram, M. B., *Andisheh-ye tarikhnegari-ye asr-e Safavi* (Tehran, 1386/2007).
Arjomand, Said, *The Turban for the Crown: The Islamic Revolution in Iran* (Oxford, 1988).
Arthurs, Joshua, *Excavating Modernity: The Roman Past in Fascist Italy* (Ithaca, 2012).
Arvidsoson, Stefan, trans., Sonia Wichmann, *Aryan Idols: Indo-European Mythology as Ideology and Science* (Chicago, 2006)
Ashuri, Dariush, *Ma va moderniat* (Tehan, 2004).
Asimov, Evgenii, *Afrodita u vlasti*. Tsarstvovanie Elizaveti Petrovoni (Moscow, 2010).
Atabaki, Touraj, ed., *Iran in the 20th Century: Historiography and Political Culture* (London, 2009).
Avrekh, Aron, *Raspad treteiunskii sistemi* (Moscow, 1985).
Avrekh, Aron, *Tsarizm nakanune sverzheniia* (Moscow, 1989).
Aydin, Cemil, *The Politics of Anti-Westernism in Asia: Visions of World Order in Pan-Islamic and Pan-Asian Thought* (New York, 2007).
Azimi, Fakhreddin, *The Quest for Democracy in Iran: A Century of Struggle against Authoritarian Rule* (Cambridge, MA, 2009).

Babayan, Kathryn, *Mystics, Monarchs, and Messiahs: Cultural Landscapes of Early Modern Iran*. (Cambridge, MA, 2002).
Bagehot, Walter, *The English Constitution*, M. Taylor, ed. (Oxford, 2001).
Ballantyne, Tony, *Orientalism and Race: Aryanism in the British Empire* (New York, 2002).
Bayat, Mangol, *Iran's First Revolution* (Oxford, 1991).
Bayne, E. A., *Persian Kingship in Transition* (New York, 1968).
Bazhenov, Ivan, *Yubileinii Sbornik Kostromskogo tserkovno-istoricheckogo obshchestva v pamyat 300-letiia tsartsvovaniia Doma Romanovikh* (Kostroma, 1913).
Beales, Derek, *Enlightenment and Reform in Eighteenth-Century Europe* (London, 2005).
Behnam, Jamshid, *Nowsazi-ye shetabzadeh* (Tehran, 1350/1972).
Belinskii, Vissarion, *Polnoe sobranie sochinenie* (Moscow, 1949).
Bell, David, *The Cult of the Nation in France: Inventing Nationalism, 1680–1800* (Cambridge, MA, 2001).
Bilgrami, Akeel, 'Occidentalism, the Very Idea: An Essay on Enlightenment and Enchantment'. *Critical Theory* 3, 32 (2006).
Bill, James, *The Eagle and the Lion: The Tragedy of American-Iranian Relations* (New Haven, 1998).
Blanning, T. C. W., *The Culture of Power and the Power of Culture: Old Regime Europe 1660–1789* (Oxford, 2002).
Bluche, François, *Le despotisme éclairé* (Paris, 1969).
Boer, Leon, 'Struggling with -isms: Occidentalism, Liberalism, Eurocentrism, Islamism'. *Third World Quarterly* 8, 25 (2006).
Bokhanov, A. N., *Aleksandr III* (Moscow, 1998).
Bokhanov, A. N., *Nikolai II* (Moscow, 1997).
Bokhanov, A. N. ed., et al., *Rossiia i mirovaiia tsivilizatsiia* (Moscow, 2000).
Bokhanov, A. N., *Russkaiia Ideia* (Moscow, 2005).
Boltin, Ivan, *Premechaniia na istorii drevnii i nineshnei Rossii* (St. Petersburg, 1778).
Bonnett, Alan, *The Idea of the West* (New York, 2004).
Bordanov, Aleksandr, *Letopis i istoriki kontsa XVIII veka* (Moscow, 1994).
Borodon, A.V., *Inozemtsy-ratnye lyudi na cluzhbe v moskovskom gosudarstve* (Petrograd, 1916).
Boroujerdi, Mehrzad, *Iranian Intellectuals and the West: The Tormented Triumph of Nativism*. (Syracuse, 1996).
Borzakovskii, Pavel, *300-letie Tsarstvuyushchago Doma Romanovikh* (Odessa, 1913).
Bosworth, R. J. B, *Mussolini's Italy* (New York, 2007).
Boutsov, Mikhail, *Sprednevekovaiia Evropa: Vostok i Zapad* (Moscow, 2015).
Brandenburger, David, *National Bolshevism: Stalinist Culture and the Formation of Modern Russian Identity, 1931–1956* (Cambridge, MA, 2002).
Brecken, W. V., *Holy Russia and Christian Europe* (London, 1999).
Briant, Pierre. *Alexandre des lumieres: fragments d'histoire europenne* (Paris, 2012).
Briant, Pierre. *Darius dans l'ombre d'Alexandre* (Paris, 2003).
Briant, Pierre. *Histoire de l'empire perse: De Cyrus a Alexandre* (Paris, 1996).
Bushkovitch, P. 'The Formation of a National Consciousness in Early Modern Russia'. *Harvard Ukrainian Studies* 10, 3/4 (1986).
Bushkovitch, Paul, *Peter the Great: The Struggle for Power* (Cambridge, 2001).
Bushkovitch, Paul, *Religion and Society in Russia, The Sixteenth and Seventeenth Centuries* (Oxford, 1992).
Bushuev, S. V. and G. E. Mironov, eds., *Istoriia gosudarstva rossiiskogo* (Moscow, 1991).
Carrier, James, ed., *Occidentalism: Images of the West* (Oxford, 1995).

Chaadaev, Petr, *Filosoficheskie pisma* (Moscow, 2006).
Chechulin, Nikolai, ed., *Gosudari iz Doma Romanovovikh, 1613–1913* (Moscow, 1913).
Chehabi, Houchang, *Iranian Politics and Religious Modernism* (London, 1990).
Chehabi, Houchang, 'Staging the Emperor's New Clothes: Dress Codes and Nation-Building under Reza Shah'. *Iranian Studies* 26, 3/4 (1993).
Cheng, Xiaomei, *Occidentalism: A Theory of Counter Discourse in Post-Mao China* (Oxford, 1995).
Chernyaev, Nicholas, *Neobkhodimost samoderzhavie dlya Rossii* (Kharkov, 1901).
Chistovig, N., *Feofan Prokopovich i ero vremya* (Moscow, 1868).
Cooper, A. S., *The Fall of Heaven: The Pahlavis and the Final Days of Imperial Iran* (New York, 2016).
Cracraft, James, *The Church Reforms of Peter the Great* (Stanford, 1971).
Cracraft, James, *The Petrine Revolution in Russian Culture* (Cambridge, MA, 2004).
Cracraft, James, *The Revolution of Peter the Great* (Cambridge, MA, 2006).
Crummey, Robert, *The Formation of Muscovy 1304–1613* (London, 1987).
Crummey, Robert, *The Old Believers and the World of the Antichrist* (London, 1971).
Cruz, C., 'Identity and Persuasion: How Nations Remember Their Pasts and Makes Their Futures'. *World Politics* 52, 3 (2000).
D'Encausse, Hélène Carrère, *Catherine II: Un âge d'or pour la Russie* (Paris, 2002).
Dabashi, Hamid, *Theology of Discontent: The Ideological Foundation of the Islamic Republic* (New York, 2005).
Dezfuli, F *Tarikh-e andishe-ye jadid-e Irani* (Tehran, 1390/2011).
Dmitriev, R., *Skazanie o Kniazakh Vladimirskikh* (Moscow-Leningrad, 1955).
Dolgorukov, Petr, *Peterburgskie ocherki* (Moscow, 1992).
Domanovskii, L.V., eds., *Istoricheckie pesni XIX veka* (Leningrad, 1973).
Donskis, Leonidas, *Troubled Identity and the Modern World* (New York, 2009).
Dostoevskii, Feodor, *Dnevnik Pisateliia* (St. Petersburg, 1996).
Dukes, Paul, *Catherine the Great and the Russian Nobility* (Cambridge, 1967).
Duncan, Peter. J., *Russian Messianism: Third Rome, Revolution, Communism, and After* (London, 2000).
Eagleton, Terry, *Culture* (New Haven, 2016).
Egereva, Tatyana, *Russkie Konservatori kontsa XVIII-pervoi chetverti XIX vv.* (Moscow, 2014).
Eksteins, Modris, *Rites of Spring: The Great War and the Birth of the Modern Age* (New York, 1989).
Esipov, Georgii, *Raskolnichnie dela XVIII stoletiia* (St. Petersburg, 1861).
Fateev, Alex, *Le Probleme de l'individu et de l'homme d'etat dans la personalite historique d'Alexandre Ier, empereur de toutes les Russies* (Prague, 1939).
Ferdowsi, *Shahnameh*, D. Davis, trans. (New York, 2007).
Figes, Orlando, *The Crimean War* (New York, 2010).
Flamm, Michael, *Law and Order: Street Crime, Civil Unrest, and the Crisis of Liberalism in the 1960s* (New York, 2005).
Francois Furet, trans., Elborg Foster, *Interpreting the French Revolution*. (Cambridge, 1981).
Funks, V., *Tsarstvovanie Romanovikh* (Moscow, 1913).
Gane, Mike, Auguste Comte (London, 2006).
Gasiorowski, Mark. J., *U.S. Foreign Policy and the Shah: Building a Client State in Iran* (Ithaca, 1991).

Gasiorowski, Mark J., 'The Qarani Affair and Iranian Politics'. *International Journal of Middle East Studies* 25, 4 (1993).
Ganim, John, *Medievalism and Orientalism* (New York, 2005).
Gentile, Emilio, *The Sacralization of Politics in Fascist Italy* (Cambridge, 1996).
Ghamari-Tabrizi, Behrooz, *Foucault in Iran* (Minneapolis, 2016).
Ghani, Cyrus, Iran *and the Rise of Reza Shah* (London, 1998).
Gheissari, Ali, *Iranian Intellectuals in the Twentieth Century* (Austin, 1998).
Gielgud, Adam, ed., *Memoirs of Prince Adam Czartoryski and his correspondance with Alexander I* (London, 1888).
Gilman, Niles, *Mandarins of the Future: Modernization Theory in Cold War America* (Baltimore, 2007).
Girami, Mohammad, *Tarikh-e Eqtesadi, siasi, ejtemai-ye doran-e Reza Shah* (Tehran, 1355/1976).
Gogolevskii, Aleksandr, *Ocherki istorii russkogo liberalizma XIX-nachala XX veka* (St. Petersburg, 1996).
Golan, Romy, *Modernity & Nostalgia: Art and Politics in France Between the Wars* (New Haven, 1995).
Golovachev, A. A., *Desyat let reformi, 1861–1871* (St. Petersburg, 1872).
Goody, Jack, *The East in the West* (Cambridge, 1996).
Gordin, Yakov, *Nikolai I: bez retushi* (Moscow, 2013).
Graham, Robert, *The Illusion of Power* (London, 1980).
Greenfield, Liah, *Nationalism: Five Roads to Modernity* (Cambridge, MA, 1992).
Grigorev, Sergei, *Pridvornaia tsenzura i obraz verkhovnoi vlasti 1831–1917* (St. Petersburg, 2007).
Gruzenskii, Anton, *Russkaia Literatura XVIII veka: Khrestomatiia* (Moscow, 1907).
Hamedi, Zahra, *Mabna-ye idiuluzh-ye hakemiat va tasir-e an bar matun va mavad-e darsi dar asr-e Pahlavi aval* (Tehran, 1394/2016).
Hamid, Hamid, *Iran dar asr-e Aryamehr* (Tehran, 2535).
Hartley, Janet, *Alexander I* (London, 1994).
Hayward, Jack, *Fragmented France: Two Centuries of Disputed Identity* (Oxford, 2007).
Heretz, Leonid, *Russia on the Eve of Modernity: Popular religion and Tradition Culture under the Last Tsars* (Cambridge, 2008).
Herodotus, *The Histories*, R. Waterfield, trans. (Oxford, 1998).
Hoffman, David, *Stalinist Values* (Ithaca, 2003).
Hosking, Geoffrey, *The Russian Constitutional Experiment: Government and Duma* (London, 1973).
Hosking, Geoffrey, *Russia: People and Empire 1552–1917* (Cambridge, MA, 1998).
Hughes, Lindsey, *Russia in the Age of Peter the Great* (New Haven, 1998).
Ikonnikov, Vladimir, *Znachenie tsarstvovaniia Ekateriny II* (Kiev, 1897).
Ikonomov, Vassili, *Nakaun reform Petra Velikogo* (Moscow, 1903).
Isfahani, A. R., *Farhang va siasat-e Iran dar asr-e ajaddod* (Tehran, 1386/2007).
Isfahani, Reza Mokhtari, *Hekayat-e Hekmat: zendegi va zamane-ye Ali Asghar Hekmat Shirazi* (Tehran, 1396/2017).
Isoaho, Mari, *The Image of Alexander Nevskiy in Medieval Russia* (Boston, 2006).
Israel, Jonathan, *A Revolution of the Mind: Radical Enlightenment and the Intellectual Origins of Modern* Democracy (Princeton, 2011).
Jackson, M. H. ed., *Civilizational Identity: The Production and Reproduction "Civilizations" in International Relations* (New York, 2007).
Jafarian, Rasul, *Siasat va farhang-e ruzegar-e Safavi* (Tehran, 1388/2009).

Kani, Ali, *Sazman-e farhangi-ye Iran* (Tehran, 1336/1958).
Kantor, Viktor, *Sankt-Petersburg: Rossiiskaia Imperiia protiv Rossiiskogo Khaosa* (Moscow, 2009).
Kapterev, Nicholas, *Patriarkh Nikon i Tsar Aleksei Mikhailovich* (St.Petersburg, 1912)
Kara-Murza, Aleksandr, ed., *Rossiiskii Liberalism: idei i lyudi* (Moscow, 2014).
Kashani-Sabet, Firoozeh, *Frontier Fictions: Shaping the Nation, 1804–1946* (Princeton, 1999).
Kashtanov, Sergei, *Moskovskoe Tsarstvo i Zapad* (Moscow, 2015).
Keddie, Nikki, *The Roots of Revolution* (New Haven, 1981).
Khomyakov, Aleksei, *Uchenie o tserkvi* (St. Petersburg, 2010).
Kirianov, Iu., *Pravye partii v Rossii, 1911–1917* (Moscow, 2001).
Kluchevskii, V *Russkaia Istoriya* (Moscow, 2002).
Kochetkova, N. D., *Fovinzin v Peterburge* (Leningrad, 1984).
Korf, Modest, *Vosshestvie na prestol imperatora Nikolaia I* (Moscow, 2015).
Kostomarov, N. N., *Russkaia istoriia v zhizneopisaniakh ee glavnesishikh deiatelei* (Moscow, 2016).
Kotilaine, Jarmo and Marshall Poe, eds., *Modernizing Muscovy: Reform and Social Change in Seventeenth-280.* Kotov, A., *"Tsarskii put" Mikhaila Katkova* (St. Petersburg, 2016).
Kotsyubinskii, D. A., *Russkii Nationalizm v nachale XX stoletiia* (Moscow, 2001).
Kylakova, L. I., *Denis Ivanovich Fonvisin* (Moscow/Leningrad, 1966).
Laneyrie-Dagen, Nadeije, *Histoire de l'art pour tous* (Paris, 2011).
Laruelle, Marlène, *Mythe aryen et rêve impérial dans la Russie du XIXe siècle* (Paris, 2005).
Laue, Theodore V., *The World Revolution of Westernization* (Oxford, 1987).
Lebedev, A. P., *Tserkovnaiia Istoriografiia v glavnikh eia predstaviteliakh* (St. Petersburg, 1903).
Lebow, Ricahrd N., *A Cultural Theory of International Relations* (Cambridge, 2008).
Ledeen, W. L., *Debacle: The American Failure in Iran.* (New York, 1982).
LeDonne, John P., *The Grand Strategy of the Russian Empire, 1650–1831* (Oxford, 2004).
Leroy-Beaulieu, Anatole, *L'Empire des Tsars et l.es Russes* (Paris, 1893).
Lieven, Dominic, *Empire: The Russian Empire and Its Rivals.* (London, 2000).
Lieven, Dominic, *The End of Tsarist Russia* (New York, 2015).
Lieven, Dominic, *Nicholas II: Emperor of all the Russias* (New York, 1993).
Lincoln, W. Bruce, *In the Vanguard of Reform: Russia's Enlightened Bureaucrats 1825–1861* (DeKalb, IL, 1982).
Lincoln, W. Bruce, *Nicholas I: Emperor and Autocrat of all the Russias* (Dekalb, IL, 1989).
Lipman, A. M., ed., *Istoricheskaia Politika v XXI veke* (Moscow, 2012).
Lobachev, Sergei, *Patriarkh Nikon* (St. Petersburg, 1998).
Lockman, Zachary, *Contending Visions of the Middle East: The History and Politics of Orientalism* (Cambridge, 2010).
Longworth, Philip, *Alexis: Tsar of All the Russias* (London, 1984).
Lotman, Urii, *Istoriia i tipologiia russkoi kulturi* (St. Petersburg, 2002).
Lotman, Urii, *Karamzin* (Moscow, 1998).
Lukyanov, M. N., *Rossiiskii konservatizm i reforma, 1907–1914* (Perm, 2001).
Luppov, S. P., *Kniga v Rossii v pervoi chetverti XVIII veka* (Leningrad, 1973).
Lure, A., *Aleksandr Nevskii* (Moscow, 1939).
Lyuks, Leonid, *Tretii Rim? Tretii Reich? Tretii put? Istoricheckie ocherki o Rossii, Germanii, i Zapade* (Moscow, 2002).
Lyalikov, F., *Pravoslavie, samoderzhaviia i narodnost: tri neziblemiia osnovi russkogo tsarstva* (Odessa, 1851).

Lyashenko, Leonid, *Aleksandr II* (Moscow, 2002).
Macfie, A. L., *Orientalism* (London, 2002).
Madariaga de, Isabel, *Catherine the Great* (New Haven, 1990).
Madariage de, Isabel, *Russia in the Age of Catherine the Great* (London, 1981).
Madariaga de, Isabel, *Politics and Culture in Eighteenth Century* (London, 1998).
Mahdavi, Mozaffar al-Din, *Ozah-e Ejtamai-ye nim qarn-e akhir* (Tehran, 1348/1970).
Maiofis, Mariia, *Vozzvanie k Evrope* (Moscow, 2008).
Maiorova, Olga, *From the Shadow of Empire: Defining the Russian Nation through Cultural Mythology, 1855–1870* (Madison, 2010).
Makdisi, Saree, *Making England Western: Occidentalism, Race, and Imperial Culture* (Chicago, 2014).
Maki, Hossein, *Tarikh-e bistsale-ye Iran* (Tehran, 1361/1983).
Malia, Martin, *Russia under Western Eyes: From the Bronze Horseman to the Lenin Mausoleum* (Cambridge, MA, 1999).
Manning, Roberta, *The Crisis of the Old Order in Russia* (Princeton, 1982).
Marashi, Afshin, *Nationalizing Iran: Culture, Power, & the State, 1870–1940* (Seattle, 2008).
Marreze, Michelle Lamarche, *Babe tsarstvo: Dvoryanki i vladenine imushchestvom v Rossii, 1700-1861* (Moscow, 2009).
Margalit, Avishai and Buruma, Ian, *Occidentalism: The West in the Eyes of its Enemies* (New York, 2004).
Matin-Asgari, Afshin, *Both Eastern and Western: An Intellectual History of Iranian Modernity* (Cambridge, 2018).
Mashayakhi, Mohammad, *Nazariat-e salahi-ye darbare-ye farhang-e Iran* (Tehran, 1332).
Massie, Robert, *Nicholas and Alexandra* (New York, 1974).
Matlaq, J. K. *Sohanha-ye dirine* (Tehran, 1386/2007).
Mazlish, Bruce, *Civilization and Its Contents* (Standford, 2004).
Mazour, Anatole, *The First Russian Revolution, 1825* (Stanford, 1961).
McMahon, Darrin, *Enemies of the Enlightenment: The French Counter-Enlightenment and the Making of Modernity* (Oxford, 2001).
Mehrabi, Masoud, *Tarikh-e cinema-ye Iran* (Tehran, 1395/2017).
Mignolo, Walter, *The Darker Side of the Renaissance: Literacy, Territoriality, and Colonization* (Princeton, 1995).
Mikhailova, Nichik, *Feofan Prokopovich* (Moscow, 1977).
Milani, Abbas, *The Persian Sphinx: Amir Abbas Hoveyda and the Riddle of the Iranian Revolution* (Washington, DC, 2000).
Milani, Abbas, *Eminent Persians: The Men and Women Who Made Modern Iran, 1941–1979*. (Syracuse, 2008).
Milani, Abbas, *The Shah* (New York, 2008).
Miller, Aleksei, *The Romanov Empire and Nationalism* (New York, 2008).
Mirsepassi, Ali, *Intellectual Discourse and the Politics of Modernization* (Cambridge, 2000).
Mironenko, Sergei, *Aleksandr I i Dekabristi: Rossiia v pervoi chetberti XIX veka* (Moscow, 2017)
Mitchell, Colin, *The Practice of Politics in Safavid Iran: Power, Religion, and Rhetoric* (London, 2009).
Motazed, Khosrow, *Chakme va qalam: Reza Shah va ruznamenegari* (Tehran, 1390/2011), 2 Vols.
Moiseevoi, G., *Russkie povesti pervoi treti XVIII veka* (Leningrad, 1965).
Mosolov, Aleksandr, *Pri dvore poslednogo imperatora* (St. Petersburg, 1992).
Mosse, William, *Alexander II and the Modernization of Russia* (New York, 1962).

Multatuli, P. *Vheshnaia politika Imperatora Nikolaia II (1894–1917)* (Moscow, 2013).
Musikhin, Gleb, *Rossiia v nemetskom zerkale* (St. Petersburg, 2002).
Nabavi, Negin, *Intellectuals and the State in Iran* (Gainesville, 2003).
Naficy, Hamid, *A Social History of Iranian Cinema: The Industrializing Years, 1941–1978* (Durham, 2011).
Nafisi, Said, *Sakhanrani-haye Aqa-ye Said Nafisi: Mozuh-pishhraftha-ye Iran dar asr-e Pahlavi* (Tehran, N/A).
Nafisi, Said, *Tarikh-e farhang-e Iran* (Tehran, 1336/1958).
Nafisi, Said, *Tarikh-e shahryari-ye shahanshah Reza Shah Pahlavi* (Tehran, 1344/1966).
Nafisi, Said, *Tarikh-e moaser-e Iran* (Tehran, 1345/1967).
Najafabadi, Mostafa, *Tamasha-ye manfiha* (Tabriz, 1353/1974).
Naraqi, Ehsan, *Anche khod dasht* (Tehran, 2535/1976).
Naraqi, Ehsan, *Qorbat-e Qarb*, 2nd ed. (Tehran, 1354/1975).
Naraqi, Ehsan, *Tam' Kham* (Tehran, 2536, 1977).
Nasr, Vali & Ali Gheissari, *Democracy in Iran: History and the Quest for Liberty* (Cambridge, 2001).
Nemo, P., *Qu'est-ce que l'Occident?* (Paris, 2005).
Nikitin, A., *Osnovaniia Russkoi Istorii* (Moscow, 2001).
Nuriollah, Qeisari, *Nokhbegan va tahvot-e farhang-e siasi dar Iran-e dore-ye Qajar* (Tehran, 1388/2009).
Ogden, C.K., ed., *The History of Civilization: The Aryans* (London, 1926).
O'Hagan, Jacinata, *Conceptualizing the West in International Relations: From Spengler to Said.* (New York, 2002).
Omid, Jamshid, *Tarikh-e sinemay-ye Iran, 1279–1375* (Tehran, 1995).
Orishev, Aleksandr, *Iranskii Uzel: Ckhvatka razvedok, 1936–1945 rr* (Moscow, 2009).
Orlovsky, Daniel, *The Limits of Reform: The Ministry of Internal Affairs in Imperial Russia, 1802–1881* (London, 1981).
Osipov, Igor, *Filosofiia russkogo liberalizma XIX-nachalo XX v.* (St. Petersburg, 1996).
Painter, Borden Jr., *Mussolini's Rome: Rebuilding the Eternal City* (New York, 2005).
Panhai, A., *Sorudekhane-ye vahdat-e melli va hamase-ye melli-ye Iran* (Tehran, 1379/2001).
Patriarca, Sheila, *Italian Vices: Nation and Character from the Risorgimento to the Republic* (Cambridge, 2010).
Pavlov, A., *Istoricheskii sekulyarizatsii tserkovnoi zemlii v Rossii, 1503–1508* (Moscow, 1978).
Perrie, Maureen, 'The Time of Troubles (1603–1613)', in Perrie, Maureen, ed., *The Cambridge History of Russia*, Vol. 1 (Cambridge, 2015).
Pipes, Richard, *Russia Under the Old Regime* (New York, 1974).
Pipes, Richard, *Russian Conservatism and Its Critics: A Study in Political Culture* (New Haven, 2005).
Plokhy, Sergei, *Lost Kingdom* (New York, 2017).
Pobedonostsev, Konstantin, *Istoricheskaiia Izsledovaniia i stati* (St. Petersburg, 1876).
Poe, Marshall, *A People Born in Slavery* (Ithaca, 2001).
Pogodin, Mikhail, *Istoriko-kritichekie otrivki* (Moscow, 1846).
Poliakov, Leon, *The Aryan Myth* (New York, 1974).
Pozhkov, V., *Treskovnie voprosi v gosudarsbennoi dume* (Moscow, 2004).
Proskurina, Vera, *Mifi imperii: Literatura i vlast v epokhi Ekaterini II* (Moscow, 2006).
Proskurina, Vera, *Imperiii pera Ekaterini II: Literatura kak politika* (Moscow, 2017).
Qolipour, Ali, *Parvaresh-e zogh-e aame dar asr-e Pahlavi* (Tehran, 1397).
Radjy, A.-H., 'Rewriting the Iranian Revolution', *New Republic*, 6 July 2017.

Raeff, Marc, *The Decembrist Movement* (Englewoods, 1961).
Raeff, Marc, *Politique et culture en Russie 18e-20e siècles* (Paris, 1996).
Rahnema, Ali, *An Islamic Utopian: A Political Biography of Ali Shariati* (London, 2000).
Rahnema, Ali, *Superstition as Ideology in Iranian Politics* (Cambridge, 2013).
Rasmussen, K, 'Catherine II and the Image of Peter I', *Slavic Review* 37, 1 (1978).
Rawson, Don, *Russian Rightists and the Revolution of 1905* (Cambridge, 1995).
Razavi, Hamid, *The Political Environment of Economic Planning in Iran, 1971–1983: From monarchy to Islamic Republic* (Boulder, 1984).
Resyanskii, Sergei, *Tserkovno-gosudarstvennia reforma Petra I* (Moscow, 2009).
Rey, M.-P., *Alexander Ier, le tsar qui vainquit Napoleon* (Paris, 2013).
Riasanovsky, Nicholas, *The Image of Peter the Great in Russian History and Thought* (Oxford, 1985).
Riasanovsky, Nicholas, *Nicholas I and Official Nationality in Russia, 1825–1855* (London, 1959).
Ribachonek, Irinia, *Zakat velikoi derzhavi: vneshnaiia politika Rossii na rubezhe XIX-XX vv* (Moscow, 2012).
Rohani, Hamid, *Baresi va tahlili az nehzat-e Imam Khomeini* (Tehran, 1979).
Romanov, Petr, *Rossiia i Zapad* (Moscow, 2015).
Rosenthal, Bernice Glatzer and Martha Bohachevsky-Chomiak, eds., Marian Schwartz, trans., *A Revolution of the Spirit: Crisis of Values in Russia, 1890–1924* (New York, 1990).
Sadovnikov, D. ed., *Zagadki Russkago Naroda* (St. Petersburg, 1901).
Schayegh, Cyrus, 'Seeing Like a State: An Essay in the Historiography of Modern Iran'. *International Journal of Middle East Studies* 42 (2010).
Schimmelpenninck, David van der Oye, *Russian Orientalism* (New Haven, 2010).
Shaskolskii, Igor, *Borba Rusi prtotiv shvedskoi ekspansii v Karelii konets XIII-nachalo XIV v.* (Kapeliia, 1987).
Shahedi, Mozaffar, *Hezb-e Rastakhiz: eshtebah-ye bozorg, khodkhamegi dar Iran-e asr-e Pahlavi* (Tehran, 1383/2004).
Shahedi, Mozaffar, *SAVeAK, 1335–1357* (Tehran, 1386/2007).
Shahedi, Mozaffar, *Se hezb: hezb-e melliyun, hezb-e mardom, hezb-e Iran-e novin* (Tehran, 1378/1999).
Shahid, Jafar, *Panjahe-ye Pahlavi: saddeha-ye melligerai* (Tehran, 2535/1976).
Shakibi, Zhand, 'Pahlavism: The Ideologization of Monarchy in Iran'. *Journal of Politics, Religion, & Ideology* 14 (2013).
Shakibi, Zhand, 'The Rastakhiz Party and Pahlavism: the beginnings of state anti-Westernism in Iran'. *British Journal of Middle Eastern Studies* 45, 2 (Autumn 2016).
Shakibi, Zhand, *Rusie va qarbengari* (Tehran, 2018).
Shaskovskii, Igor, *Borba Rusi protiv krestonosnoi agressii na beregakh Baltiki v XII-XIII vv.* (Leningrad, 1978).
Sheybani, Ali, *Tarah-e coudetat* (Tehran, 2535).
Shenk, F., *Aleksandr Nevskii v russkoi kulturnoi pamaiti* (Moscow, 2007).
Shilder, N., *Imperator Aleksandr Pervyi: ego zhizn i tsarstvovanie* (St. Petersburg, 1898).
Shilder, N., *Imperator Nikolai Pervii* (St. Petersburg, 1908).
Shirazi, Asqar, *Iraniat, meliat, qomiat* (Tehran, 1395/2018).
Shirelman, V., *Ariiskii Mif v Sovremennon Mire* (Moscow, 2015).
Sikka, Sonia, *Herder on Humanity and Cultural Difference: Enlightened Relativism* (Cambridge, 2011).
Skrinnikov, Ruslan, *Ivan Groznii* (Moscow, 1983).

Skrinnikov, Ruslan, *Smutnoe Vremya*, Krushenie Tsarstva (Moscow, 2007).
Smirnov, Victor, *Feofan Prokopovich* (Moscow, 1994)
Smith, Anthony, *The Ethnic Origins of Nations* (London, 1986).
Smith, Anthony, *National Identity* (London, 1994).
Solovev, Iu. V., *Samoderzhavie i dvorianstvo v 1907–1914* (Leningrad, 1981).
Solovev, Vladimir, *Istoriia Rossii s drevneishikh vremen* (Vol. 13) (Moscow, 1991).
Soloviev, Vladimir, *L'idée russe* (Paris, 1886).
Sorokin, Pitirim, *Social and Cultural Dynamics* (New York, 1970).
Steiner, George, *Nostalgia for the Absolute* (Chicago, 1977).
Stepanov, Sergei, *Chernaia sotnia v Rossii:1905-1914 gg.* (Moscow, 1992).
Stites, Richard, *Serfdom, Society, and the Arts in Imperial Russia* (New Haven, 2005).
Struve, Pyotor, *Obshchestvennoe dvizhenie pri Aleksandre II* (Paris, 1905).
Sukhman, M., ed., *Inostrantsi o Drevnei Moskve* (Moscow, 1991).
Sullivan, William, *Mission to Iran* (New York, 1981).
Suny, Ronald, 'Constructing Primordialism: Old Histories for New Nations'. *The Journal of Modern History* 73, 4 (2001).
Suvorin, A., *Dnevnik A.S. Suvorina* (Moscow-Leningrad, 1923).
Tabrizi, Masoud, *Mohajerat-e rustaian be shahrha va tasirat-e eqtesadi, siasi-ye an dar duran-e Pahlavi dovvom* (Tehran, 1383).
Tahamaseb, A.ed., *Tarikh-e shahanshahi-ye alihezrat-e Reza Shah Kabir* (Tehran, 2535/1976).
Taheri, Amir, *The Unknown Life of the Shah* (London, 1991).
Talina, Galina, *Vibor Puti: Russkoe samoderzhavie vtoroi polovini XVII-pervoi chetverti XVIII veka* (Moscow, 2010).
Talattof, Kamran, *Modernity, Sexuality, and Ideology in Iran* (Syracuse, 2011).
Tarafdari, Ali Mohammad, *Melligerai, tarikhangari, va sheklgiri-ye hoviat-e melli-ye novin-e Iran* (Tehran, 1397/2018).
Tarle, E., *Krimskaiia voina* (Moscow, 2011).
Tavakoli-Targhi, Mohammad, *Refashioning Iran: Orientalism, Occidentalism and Historiography* (London, 2001).
Theiss-Morse, J. S.-H., 'National Identity and Self-Esteem'. *Perspectives on Politics* 1, 3 (2003).
Trenin, Dmitry, *Integratsiia i identichnost: Rossii kak novii Zapad* (Moscow, 2006).
Trepanier, Lee, *Political Symbols in Russian History: Church, State, and the Quest for Order and Justice* (Lanham, MD, 2010).
Trigos, Ludmilla, *The Decembrist Myth in Russian Culture* (New York, 2009).
Turner, Bryan, *Orientalism, postmodernism, and globalism* (London, 1994).
Tvardovskaia, Valentina, *Ideologiia poreformennogo samoderzhaviia* (Moscow, 1978).
Utkin, A, *Vizov Zapada i Otvet Rossii* (Moscow, 2005).
Vejdani, Farzin., ed., *Iran Facing Others: Identity Boundaries in a Historical Perspective* (New York, 2012).
Vejdani, Farzin, *Making History in Iran: Education, Nationalism, and Print Culture* (Stanford, 2015).
Venn, C., *Occidentalism: Modernity and Subjectivity* (London, 2000).
Verkhovoskii, P., *Uchrezhenie dukhovnoi kollegi i dukhovnii reglament* (St. Petersburg, 1916).
Verner, Andrew, *The Crisis of Russian Autocracy: Nicholas II and the 1905 Revolution* (London, 1990).
Villiers, Gerard de, *L'irresistible ascension de Mohamamd Reza, Shah d'Iran* (Paris, 1975).

Vladimirskii-Budanov, M., *Gosudarstvo i narodnoe obrazovanie XVIII-oro veka* (Yaroslavl, 1874).
Volkov, Solomon, *Istoriia rysskoi kulturi XX veka* (Moscow, 2008).
Wade, Ira, *Intellectual Origins of the French Enlightenment* (Cambridge, 1971).
Waldron, Peter, *Between two revolutions: Stolypin and the politics of renewal in Russia* (London, 1996).
Weber, Eugen, *Peasants into Frenchmen: The Modernization of Rural France, 1870–1917* (Stanford, 1976).
Whittaker, C. H., 'The Idea of Autocracy among eighteenth-century Russian Historians'. *The Russian Review* 55, 2 (1996).
Widdis, S. F. ed., *National Identity in Russian Culture* (Cambridge, 2004).
Woolf, David, *A Global History of History* (Cambridge, 2011).
Woolf, Larry, *The Inventing of Eastern Europe: The Map of Civilization on the Mind of the Enlightenment* (Stanford, 1994).
Wortman, Ricahrd, *Scenarios of Power: Myth and Ceremony in Russian Monarchy* (Princeton, 1995).
Yanov, Aleksandr, *Drama Patriotizma v Rossii, 1855–1921* (Moscow, 2009).
Yanov, Aleksandr, *Zagadka Nikolaeivskoi Rossii, 1825–1855* (Moscow, 2007).
Yazdanian, Hossein, *Dokan be esm-e cinema* (Tehran, 1968).
Zakharova, Larisa, *Samoderzhavie i otmena krepostnogo prava v Rossii, 1856–1861* (Moscow, 1984).
Zanjani, A. A., *Engelab-e islami va risheha-ye an* (Tehran, 1386/2007).
Zapiski Vebera o Petre Vikilom i ego preobrazovaniakh.' (1872). *Russkii Arkhiv*, 1074–1075.
Zerangar, Kazem, *Sarnevesht-e farda-ye dehat va shahrha-ye ma* (Tehran, 1337).
Zerbakht, Morteza. *Khaterati az Sazman-e Afsaran-e Hezb-e tudeh-ey Iran* (Tehran, 1394).
Zhirkov, G. V., *Istoriia tsenzuri v Rossii XIX-XX vv.* (Moscow, 2001).
Zhizhka, Mikahil, *Radishchev* (Moscow, 1934).
Zorin, A., *Kormia dvuglavnogo orla* (Moscow, 2004).
Zuckerman, Frederic, *The Tsarist Secret Police in Russian Society, 1880–1917* (New York, 1996).

Index

Achaemenid Empire 108–9, 115–17, 139–42
Afarin, Noush 259, 261
Afkhami, Gholam Reza 194
Afshar, Toghrol 249–50
al-e Ahmad, Jalal 156–61, 163–4, 176–7, 226, 299
Akhundzadeh, Mirza Fath-Ali 110–11
Aksakov, Ivan 62
Aksakov, Konstantin 62–3
Alam, Assadollah 193, 195–6, 243
   cultural policy 170, 242
   establishment of Rastakhiz Party 189
   party system 198–9
   Philosophy of the Revolution 231–2, 234, 236–7
   queen mother 123
   Rastakhiz Party 209–13, 309
   Shiraz Arts Festival 283–4
Aleksei I 41–5
Alexander I 51–4, 66–7
Alexander II 36, 79–83
Alexander III 83–5
Alexandrova, Grand Duchess Olga 98
Allamirdolu, Javad 255
All-Russian Peoples Union 95–6
Alviri, Mortaza 257–8
Ameli-Tehrani, Mohammad Reza 229–30, 234, 308, 320, 356
Ameri, Naser 198–9
Amnesty International 335–7, 341
Amuzegar, Jamshid 230, 294, 321
   cultural policy 360–1
   party leadership 210–11, 213, 215–17
   views of the West 338–9, 353–5
Ansari, Hushang 204, 213, 217, 312, 337, 365
Aron, Robert 299
Aryanism 21, 151
   Iran 108–13, 117, 124
   Mohammad Reza Shah 153, 168–9, 241–2, 362

Pahlavism 137–8, 140, 151–3
Rastakhiz Party 220, 241–2, 338, 354–5, 362–3, 366–7
Russia 53–4, 370
Ashrafizadeh, Hesam al-Din 218, 292
Ashuri, Dariush 9, 173
Attali, Jacques 328
Azmun, Manuchehr 234–6

Bafghi, Ayatollah Mohammad 122–3
Baheri, Mohammad 309, 313, 321, 341, 347, 352–3
   Philosophy of the Revolution 230–7
   Shiraz Arts Festival 290, 292, 293
Behnam, Jamshid 171–2, 175, 177, 194
Behnud, Masoud 172–3
Beklemishev, Ivan Nikitich 33–4
Belinskii, Vissarion 64–5
Benckendorff, Alexander von 68, 378
Berlin Circle 103–4
Blanqui, Adolphe 27
Blücher, Wilhelm von 111–12
Boltin, Ivan 58–9
Bushehri, Javad 135
Byzantine Empire 5–6, 40–1, 46, 53

Carter, James E. 116, 341–2
Catherine II
   anticlericalism 48–9
   French Revolution 65–7
   historiography and the West 52–4, 58–60
   Pugachev rebellion 63
Chaadaev, Peter 62, 72
Churchill, Winston 25
Cicero 32
Cold War 5–6, 18–19, 151–2, 304–8, 309–10, 373–5
Comte, August 23, 67
Crimean War 75–8, 377–8
Cyrus the Great, cult of 115–18, 150, 241, 339–41

Daftari, Ahmad Matin   113–14, 119
Danilevsky, Nikolai   77–8
Dariush, Hezhir   173, 264
Darwinism, cultural   7, 365–6, 371
Dashkova, Princess Ekaterina   58–60
Dashti, Ali   103
Dastgheib, Ayatollah Abdolhossein
   290–1
d'Auteroche, Chappe, abbé   52–3, 59
Davar, Ali Akbar   103, 107
Decembrist Revolt   22, 57, 65–9,
   370
de Custine, Marquis, Astolphe Louis
   Lenor   74
Delkash (Esmat Baboli)   273, 276, 383
de Tocqueville, Alexis   5
Dostoevsky, Fyodor   16, 63–4, 368
Duhamel, Georges   298–9
Dumont, René   326
Durnovo, Peter   99–100

Enayat, Hamid   223, 226
Enlightenment, the   22–7, 62–3, 91–2,
   371–5
Eurasianism   6

Fardid, Ahmad   156, 230, 269
Ferdowsi   164, 172–3, 246, 326
   arabtosis   161
   filmfarsi   250, 259–60
   and the West   179–86
Ferdowsi, Abdolqasim Tusi   32–3, 117,
   140
Fonvisin, Denis   60–1
Ford, Gerald   302–3, 332, 337, 342–3,
   378
Foruqi, Mohammad Ali   109
France
   anti-Americanism   298–300
   counter Enlightenment   30–1
   Crimean War   75–7
   Franco-Prussian War   23
   Revolution of 1789   4, 23, 31, 73, 83,
      370–2
   Revolution of 1848   72, 77, 91, 377
   Vichy period   298, 300
Fromm, Erich   325
Fukuyama, Francis   373
Furet, François   4

Ganji, Manuchehr   194–5
Germany
   imperial period   23–5
   Nazi period   111–13, 191
   Romanticism   31–2, 63
Ghaffari, Farrokh   266, 283–6, 293
Gladstone, William   24
Golpayegani, Akbar   273
Gowharshad Rebellion   123
Gugush (Faeqeh Atashin)   264, 271–7,
   290, 383

Hakim-Elahi, Hedayat   329–30
Hamilton, Lord Frederic   51, 55–6
Haritash, Khosrow   259–60, 263, 280
Haxthausen, August von   63
Hekmat, Ali Asghar   109, 112, 114, 121
Herodotus   115, 138–9
Herzen, Alexander   82, 377
Holy Alliance   23, 54, 73, 378
Homayoun, Dariush   327, 365
   cultural policy   176–7, 266
   Rastakhiz Party   196–7, 205, 211,
      215–16, 321
Honarmand, Manuchehr   134–5, 146
Hovanessian, Vartan   279
Hoveyda, Amir Abbas   137, 344, 349–51,
   355
   cultural policy   170–1, 177, 223, 225,
      245, 253, 314
   Philosophy of the Revolution   230–1,
      233–6
   Rastakhiz Party   191, 193, 194–6,
      198–9, 203, 209–15
Huntington, Samuel   373–4

Italy, and the West   117–18
Ivan IV, tsar of Russia   39–41, 43

Jafarian, Masoud   320, 356
Jaulin, Robert   326
Jenabi, Fereshte   259
Johnson administration   301–2

Kani, Alinaqi   198–9
Karamzin, Nicholas   61–2, 69, 90–1
Kavusi, Hushang   250–3, 264
Kennedy administration   130–1, 155
Kermani, Mozaffar Baghai   135

Kesmai, Ali Akbar 358–9
Khamenei, Ayatollah Ali 381–6
Kharazmi, Maryam 285–9, 296
Khatibi, Parviz 255
Khermand, Hashem 266–7
Khomeini, Ayatollah Ruhollah 1–2, 107, 121
   ideology 380–7
Khomyakov, Aleksei 62
Khosrovani, Keyvan 248, 279, 282
Khrushchev, Nikita 131, 148
Kipling, Rudyard 16
Kireevsky, Ivan 62–3
Kluchevskii, Vasilii 14, 28, 390
Kokovstov, Vladimir 96–8
Krimskii, Agafangel 370
Krizhanich, Urii 34–5

Labroit, Henri 325
Laqai, Sattar 359
Lashai, Kuroush 231, 234–6
Lavrov, Sergei 40, 59–60
Likhachev, Dmitrii 51
Lippmann, Walter 131
Loris-Melikov, Count Mikhail 81–4
Louis XVI 66, 83

Maalouf, Amin 374
Macmillan, Harold 331
Majidi, Abdolmajid 190, 204, 251, 266
Maleki, Khalil 135
Malkom Khan 35–7, 323
Mann, Thomas 192
Mansur, Ali 164–5, 171, 210
Mardom Party 129, 137, 197–8, 211, 214, 218, 335, 381
Marxism-Leninism 6, 113, 232, 235–8
Mathieu, George 326
Maxim Grek 33–4
Mehr, Farhang 219–20, 362
Mehri, Hossein 326–7
Meybodi, Ali Reza 266–7
Mikhail I 42–3
Ministry of Culture and Art 177, 180, 223, 319
   censorship of film 251–3, 260–1, 264–8
   establishment of 164–5

Mohammad Reza Shah
   approach to political parties 197–9
   attacks on imperialism 150–1, 305–6, 310, 332, 336–7, 348, 353–4
   clergy, approach to 142–3, 167, 223–5, 355
   Constitutional Revolution 190–1, 195, 200–3
   cultural policy 164–5, 170, 177, 241, 357
   the Great Civilization 240–4, 344–5
   hippieism 242–3, 362
   Pahlavism, origins of 134–5
   promotion of spirituality 166–7, 174, 223–4, 310, 323–4
   propagation of Aryanism 153–5, 362–3, 372–3
   Revolution in Education 311–15
   views on democracy 153–5, 165–6, 190–1, 194–5, 200–5
   warnings against Occidentosis 165–9, 223–4, 226, 241, 323–4, 345–6
   White Revolution 142–3, 147–9, 189
Mohammad Reza Shah, foreign policy 150–1
   military purchases 349–50
   nuclear power 342–3
   Saudi Arabia 301–2, 338, 354
   USA 128–9, 302–3, 306, 338–42
   USSR 127–8, 131, 301, 306, 338–42
Mohammad Reza Shah, Rastakhiz Party
   conditions of party leadership 214–17
   party role 188–9, 202–5, 208–9
   Philosophy of the Revolution 230–9
   Political Education 319–20
   reasons for establishment 189–97, 199
Moinian, Nosrat 193, 216, 283
Montazeri, Ayatollah Hossein Ali 381
Mosolov, Alexander 91
Mossadegh, Mohammad 128–9, 132, 135, 142, 145, 155–7
Mostafavi, Rahmat 341
Mozaffari, Mehdi 227–8
Munich pact 113

Nafisi, Said 114, 120, 312
Nahavandi, Hushang 193–5, 201, 227, 230–1

Naraqi, Ehsan
  Atomization and Loneliness in the West 156, 161–4, 322
  clergy 106
  cultural terrorism 312–13
  Philosophy of the Revolution 230, 234
  Westernization 269, 312, 315, 328
Naser al-Din Qajar 105–6
Nasr, Seyyed Hossein 193–4, 240
  cultural policy 221, 279, 327–8
  nativism, definition of 13
  Philosophy of the Revolution 230, 236
  Supreme Council of Culture and Art 177
Nevskii, Prince Alexander 40
New Iran Party 137, 170–1, 191, 194–7, 208–10
Nicholas I
  Crimean War 75–9
  and the West 68–74
Nicholas II 6, 85–7, 95–9
  tsar-batushka 98–9, 376
  West, view of 89–92
Nikitenko, Alexander 78–9
Nikkhah, Parviz 213
Nikon, patriarch of Moscow and all the Russias 43–5
Nixon, Richard 302–3, 307, 322, 332, 337

Occidentalism, definition of 15–19
Odoevskii, Prince Vladimir 71
Olearius, Adam 54–5
Organization of Public Enlightenment 111–19, 124–5
Ottoman Empire 34, 36, 40–1, 53, 75–8, 377
Ovanessian, Arby 279, 285–90

Pahlavi, Farah
  cultural policy 168–9, 225, 248, 279, 323
  revolution in education 311, 336, 341
  Shiraz Arts Festival 283–5, 290–4
  Supreme Council of Culture and Arts 172, 177–8
Pahlavi, Shahnaz 242–3

Pahlavism
  anticlericalism 141–3
  historiography 137–41
  international relations 150–2
  universal superiority 147–50
Pahlbod, Mehrdad 9, 177–8, 268, 284
Panin, Nikita 60, 65
Pan-Slavism 77–8, 95, 370, 377
Parsons, Sir Anthony 337–8
Parvizi, Rasul 211, 269, 318–19
Paul I 65–6
Pecherskii, Feodisi 41
Peter I
  anticlericalism 46–9
  cultural revolution 54–7
  historiography, reform of 49–54
  and *The Story of the Russian Sailor Vasilii* 50–1
Peter III 57, 63
Petrov, Vasilii Petrovich 53
Pig, Child, Fire! 285–93
Pobedonostsev, Konstantin 84–5
Pogodin, Mikhail 71–3, 76
Possivino, Antonio 41
Pourshariati, Hushang 218
Prokopovich, Feofan archbishop 47–8, 51, 367–9
Putin, Vladimir 3–4, 31, 40, 62

Qoreishi, Ahmad 194–6, 207, 213
Qotbi, Reza 177, 193, 232, 268, 283, 287

Radishchev, Alexander 65–6
Radji, Parviz 341
Rastakhiz Party
  campaign against corruption 345–50
  campaign against foreign workers 351–2
  Constitutional Revolution 219–20
  cosmopolitanism 309–10
  crisis of identity 223–7
  decline of the West 321–33
  filmfarsi 261–9
  Great Civilization 240–4
  Guardians of the Revolution 212–13, 320–1
  historiography 227–30
  ideology 199–205
  institutions 205–8, 213–14

music 269–77
party wings 203–5
Philosophy of the Revolution 230–9
Political Education 319–21
publications 217–19
Revolution in Education 314–19
White Revolution 219–23, 231–4
Renan, Ernest 369–70
ressentiment 9–10, 58, 61, 72, 77
Revolutions of 1848 18, 72, 77, 82, 91, 377
Reza, Enayatollah 230, 234, 324
Reza Shah
  anticlericalism 104–8
  cultural revolution 119–25
  historiography, reform of 108–18
  Nazi Germany, relations with 111–14
Romain, Jules 243
Romier, Lucien 298–9

Sabeti, Parviz 131, 178, 193–4, 335, 341–2
  clergy 143
  cultural policy 268
  party system 198
  Rastakhiz Party 210–11, 213
Sadeq, Issa 109–10, 114
Safavid dynasty 34, 117, 229
Sahrudi, Hakim Aliqadr 163
Saint-Simon, Claude 294–5
Saleh, Seyyed Ebrahim 251, 254
Salur, Saboktakin 361
Samarin, Urii 62, 64, 374
Samii, Mehdi 191–3, 199
Samii, Mohammad Ali 252
Sarfaraz, Hossein 218, 292, 320
Sasanian Empire 108–9, 117, 139–42, 369
SAVAK 173, 223, 234, 251, 259, 335
  censorship 178–86
  Ferdowsi analysis of 161, 164
  Manuchehr Honarmand 134–5
  Occidentosis 157
  party system, analysis of 191, 194, 199
  Rastakhiz Party 208–10, 217
  Shiraz Arts Festival 284, 290–2

Schirach, Baldur von 112
Schlesinger, James 303, 349
Seif, Hadi 359
Semsar, Mehdi 217, 230
Sepahr, Lasan 115–16
Shafirov, Peter 50, 56, 368
Shariati, Ali 8, 232–3, 238, 358
Shostakovich, Dmitrii 295–6
Slavophilism 62–5, 199, 370
Solovyov, Sergei 39
Spanish civil war 113
Splenger, Oswald 298
Stalin, Josef 127–8, 295, 304, 375
Stolypin, Peter 88, 90, 94, 96
Stravinsky, Igor 296–7
Suetonius 32
Sullivan, William 342
Supreme Council of Culture and Art 165, 170–8, 180, 223, 268, 311
  Culture and Life 173–6, 223, 255–6

Taheri, Amir 230, 287
Taj ol-Moluk, queen mother 123
Takhti, Gholam Reza 182–3, 246
Taqizadeh, Hassan 103–4, 322
Teymourtash, Abdolhassan 117, 122
Third Rome, the 41–3, 51–4, 73
Tiutchev, Fyodor 77
Tiutcheva, Anna 77
Travels of Ibrahim Beig 110–11
Trotsky, Leon 5
Tudeh Party 128–9, 134–5, 156, 211, 230, 236
Tufanian, Hassan 349

Union of Russian People 95–6
Uvarov, Count Sergei 69–71

Vadiei, Kazem 184, 214, 246–7, 314–15, 339–40
Valuev, Peter 81

Weber, Frederick 49–50
White Revolution 132–7, 142–3, 147–9, 164–5, 189–201
Wilhelm Jr., Donald 153
Witte, Sergei 85–6

Yasemi, Gholam Reza 114, 124, 125
Yazdanian, Hossein 284
Yeganeh, Naser 230, 234
Yussof, Barhan 360–1

Zandanian, Shahpour 230
Zerangar, Mohammad Ali 218
Zhdanov, Andrei 304–5
Zimmerman, Apollon 13

www.ingramcontent.com/pod-product-compliance
Lightning Source LLC
Chambersburg PA
CBHW050322020526
44117CB00031B/1443